# INCLUSION

## Effective Practices for All Students
## Second Edition

**James McLeskey**
University of Florida

**Michael S. Rosenberg**
Johns Hopkins University

**David L. Westling**
Western Carolina University

Boston   Columbus   Indianapolis   New York   San Francisco   Upper Saddle River
Amsterdam   Cape Town   Dubai   London   Madrid   Milan   Munich   Paris   Montreal   Toronto
Delhi   Mexico City   São Paulo   Sydney   Hong Kong   Seoul   Singapore   Taipei   Tokyo

Vice President and Editorial Director:
　Jeffery W. Johnston
Executive Editor: Ann Castel Davis
Editorial Assistant: Penny Burleson
Executive Development Editor: Hope Madden
Vice President, Director of Marketing: Margaret Waples
Marketing Manager: Joanna Sabella
Senior Managing Editor: Pamela D. Bennett
Senior Project Manager: Sheryl Glicker Langner
Senior Operations Supervisor: Matthew Ottenweller

Senior Art Director: Diane C. Lorenzo
Cover Designer: Wanda Espana
Cover Image: Corbis
Media Producer: Autumn Benson
Media Project Manager: Rebecca Norsic
Full-Service Project Management: Element LLC
Composition: Element LLC
Printer/Binder: Quebecor/Versailles
Cover Printer: Lehigh/Phoenix Color
Text Font: Berkeley

Credits and acknowledgments for material borrowed from other sources and reproduced, with permission, in this textbook appear on appropriate page within text.

Every effort has been made to provide accurate and current Internet information in this book. However, the Internet and information posted on it are constantly changing, so it is inevitable that some of the Internet addresses listed in this textbook will change.

Photo Credits: photo credits are on page 485

---

**Library of Congress Cataloging-in-Publication Data**

McLeskey, James, 1949-
　Inclusion : effective practice for all students / James McLeskey,
Michael S. Rosenberg, David L. Westling.—2nd ed.
　　p. cm.
　Includes bibliographical references and index.
　ISBN 0-13-265820-8 (alk. paper)
1. Inclusive education—United States. 2. Special Education—United
States. 3. Children with disabilities—Education—United States. 4.
Mainstreaming in education—United States. I. Rosenberg, Michael S.
II. Westling, David L. III. Title.
　LC1201.M385 2013
　371.9'046--dc23
　　　　　　　　2012000901

10 9 8 7 6 5 4 3 2 1

ISBN 10: 0-13-265820-8
ISBN 13: 978-0-13-265820-1

To Nancy, for the personal and professional paths we've traveled together.
JM

To Irene and Dan—So much! Again and Always
MSR

To Wendy, for more than 35 years of love and support,
DLW

# Preface

## OUR VISION

Students with special needs continue to be included in our nation's schools in increasing numbers, providing learning and social opportunities that did not exist in the past. Although much progress has been made, inclusion continues to be a source of controversy. Even though the vast majority of educators are committed to providing an inclusive education for their students, the reality of how to effectively address the academic and behavioral needs that students with disabilities bring to a classroom continues to be a challenge. Clearly, many questions remain regarding how to best design, deliver, support, and evaluate effective, inclusive educational programs. It is our view that the responses to these questions are best presented to current and future educators in a practical and straightforward fashion, using a format that integrates evidence-based practices with applications and examples that reflect school settings and working conditions.

This text is built on a pragmatic, "real-world" approach to inclusion. That is, we assume that all general education classrooms should be designed to accommodate the needs of a diverse range of students, and all students with disabilities should be included to the maximum extent appropriate. Moreover, we take the perspective that many students (including those with and without disabilities) will at times need intensive, small-group instruction that may be provided in either a general education classroom or in a separate setting.

In this book, we anchor content to three key themes: (1) **Values** underlying inclusion, (2) the importance of **Professional Educators**, and (3) **Effective Applications** (evidence-based practices). To provide a complete picture of inclusion, and to emphasize how it relates to our three key themes, we have organized the text into three parts: Foundations of Successful Inclusion, Meeting the Needs of All Students, and Effective Practices for All Students. This three-part format allows us to address the needs of the diverse range of teacher-preparation students typically enrolled in inclusion coursework: traditional special education students, traditional general education students, and the growing number of alternative certification students.

## NEW TO THIS EDITION

- **A View From . . .** appears in every chapter and shares the voices of students and educators involved in inclusion.
- **Tips from Effective Teachers** in Part II share recommendations from the classrooms of the featured inclusive schools highlighted in the text.
- **Strategy Fact Sheets** in Part III describe highly effective, evidence-based practices that may be used in inclusive classrooms to improve academic and behavioral outcomes of students with disabilities and others who struggle to succeed.
- **Completely refocused chapters** on *Effective Practices for Students from Diverse Backgrounds* (Chapter 12) and *Effective Instruction in Core Academic Areas: Teaching Reading, Writing, and Mathematics* (Chapter 13) take a fresh, classroom-oriented approach to these topics.
- **Response to Intervention** coverage has been reconsidered and integrated in appropriate chapters to provide a framework as well as implementation ideas.

# Values Underlying Inclusion

The values theme emphasizes the perspective that students with disabilities should be active participants in the academic and social activities (or communities) of their classrooms and schools. This means that from the beginning, the curriculum and instructional practices of all classrooms should be designed to accommodate and support the academic and social needs of a broad range of students, including those with disabilities. When this occurs, some (perhaps many) students with disabilities should be included as a natural part of the general education classroom, with no need for special accommodations or adaptations.

## FOUNDATIONS OF SUCCESSFUL INCLUSION

The two chapters in Part I provide readers with background/foundational information regarding inclusion, address the values that underlie this movement, and introduce the three highly successful inclusive schools that will be used throughout the text.

We use a number of pedagogical features to provide examples of the themes throughout the text. Many of these features use examples taken from professional educators in highly effective inclusive schools and classrooms. This ensures that the examples we use are grounded in the real-world experiences of teachers, and address both the strengths and challenges of developing inclusive classrooms.

## THREE INCLUSIVE SCHOOLS

A significant amount of content within the text is situated in three highly successful inclusive schools at the elementary, middle, and high school levels. These schools have diverse student bodies, and are located in a variety of settings. We provide a lengthy description of the schools in Chapter 1, and teachers, parents, administrators, and students from the three schools are used in features and as examples throughout the text. These schools provide a foundation for the pragmatic approach we take to inclusion, ensuring that the information we provide is situated in real-world settings and across all grade levels.

# Professional Educators

The second theme emphasizes the importance of highly effective professional educators in meeting the needs of all students. Highly effective professional educators are those who have the knowledge, skills, and dispositions to effectively meet the needs of a broad range of students. These professionals use evidence-based practices, have in-depth knowledge of the content they teach, and continue to learn and grow as they seek to better meet the needs of all students who enter their classrooms and schools.

## MEETING THE NEEDS OF ALL STUDENTS

Chapters 3 through 9 are relatively brief. They provide descriptive information regarding disability categories and address general principles and issues regarding the application of effective practices with these students. All categorical chapters use the same general outline to facilitate reader comprehension and consistency. Each chapter is written in a clear, succinct, practical, and approachable style and has the same pedagogical elements and themes throughout.

## A VIEW FROM . . .

This feature begins all chapters in the text and a second View feature is included in Chapters 1 through 9. This feature provides the perspective of teachers, parents, students, and administrators from the three schools (elementary, middle, and high schools) described in Chapter 1. These real-life scenarios address the themes of the text and provide readers with an understanding of

- Teacher, parent, student, and administrator views regarding inclusion
- Benefits of inclusion and the value of inclusive practices/classrooms/schools

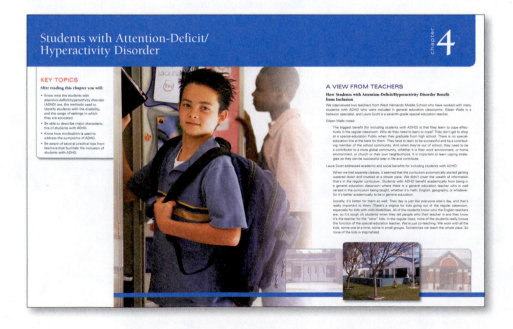

# PAUSE & REFLECT MARGIN NOTES

In every chapter of the text, Pause & Reflect margin notes focus on specific concepts addressed in the text and ask readers to examine their own perspectives and beliefs on these topics. These notes also are connected to our three themes in the text.

**Pause & Reflect**

Some believe that the requirements of NCLB are admirable but in some cases unattainable. What do you think? Can all teachers be highly qualified? Is it possible that all students will meet state-mandated standards of proficiency?

| Just the Facts | Students with ADHD |
| --- | --- |
| Who are the students? | Children with ADHD manifest "a persistent pattern of inattention and/or hyperactivity-impulsivity that is more frequently displayed and more severe than is typically observed in individuals at a comparable level of development" (APA, 2000, p. 85). To be identified in a school, these behaviors must significantly impede the student's educational performance. |
| What are typical characteristics? | • Impulsivity—Responding without thinking.<br>• Hyperactivity—Much more active than other students of the same age.<br>• Inattention—Inability to focus, selectively attend, or maintain attention for sustained periods of time.<br>• Coexisting conduct problems—About 30 to 50% of students with ADHD have significant conduct problems.<br>• Coexisting academic problems—About 80% of these students have some level of academic problem, and about 25% are identified with a learning disability. |
| What are the demographics? | • Estimates vary regarding how many school-aged students have ADHD. Recent research indicates that parents report that about 7% (or about 4.1 million) of children ages 4 to 17 are currently identified with ADHD.<br>• About 1.25% of the school-aged population are identified under IDEA as "other health impaired," the category that includes ADHD. About 1% of students are identified as ADHD under Section 504 of the Rehabilitation Act.<br>• The use of prescription medication varies across states and communities. Overall, about 5% of school-aged students receive some form of medication (mostly stimulant medications) for ADHD.<br>• About 3 of every 4 students with ADHD are male.<br>• Students who live in high poverty settings are substantially more likely to be identified with ADHD when compared to students from middle- and high-income settings. |
| Where are students with ADHD educated? | • Most general education classes have from 1 to 3 students with ADHD for much or all of the school day. |
| How are students identified? | • Criteria from *DSM-IV-TR* (APA, 2000) are widely used to identify students with ADHD. (See Figure 4.1 for more information regarding these criteria.)<br>• Information from parents and teachers regarding the student's behavior is the most critical information used to identify students with ADHD. This information is collected using interviews, observations in multiple settings, and rating scales. |
| What causes ADHD? | • The cause of ADHD is often unknown.<br>• Professionals speculate that ADHD most often seems to result from the complex interaction of many factors. Contributing factors may include:<br>  • *Brain injury.* Many students who have had documented brain injury exhibit one or more of the symptoms of ADHD. This includes about 5 to 10% of all students with ADHD.<br>  • *Brain abnormalities.* Research has shown that students with ADHD often have different brain chemistry when compared to children who do not have ADHD (DuPaul, Barkley, & Connor, 1998). For example, many of these students have deficiencies in neurotransmitters or chemicals in the brain that influence the transmission of signals between nerve cells.<br>  • *Hereditary influences.* If a parent or sibling has ADHD, the probability that another sibling will have ADHD increases significantly.<br>  • *Family influences.* Poor parenting does not cause ADHD as some have suggested, but poor parent behavior management skills can make the symptoms of ADHD worse. Furthermore, extreme stress in a family can temporarily result in the manifestation of symptoms related to ADHD. |
| What are the outcomes? | • About 1 in 3 students with ADHD has no symptoms of ADHD in adulthood.<br>• About 1 in 4 students with ADHD has conduct disorders in adulthood.<br>• About 1 in 4 students with ADHD develops major depression in adulthood. |

# JUST THE FACTS

Because Chapters 3 through 9 are brief, a Just the Facts feature addresses definition, identification, assessment, prevalence, and service delivery practices (least restrictive environment statistics). This feature will help readers identify the key components on the basic categorical issues covered in each of these chapters.

Well-organized, carefully structured instruction often works well for students with ADHD and others who struggle to learn.

In comparing the outcomes of medication with other treatments (e.g., behavioral interventions), medications have proven to be the most effective treatment for the symptoms of ADHD (MTA Cooperative Group, 2004). However, it is important to recognize that although medication often may be used to control many of the symptoms of ADHD, other interventions are needed if students' academic and social needs are to be effectively addressed. Indeed, after medication controls negative student behavior, teachers find behavioral interventions to be most helpful in addressing academic needs and social adjustment of students with ADHD (Fabiano, Pelham, Coles, et al., 2009).

## Teaching Students with ADHD in Inclusive Classrooms: Tips from Teachers

We were provided tips for teaching students with ADHD in inclusive classrooms by Laura Scott, a seventh-grade special education teacher from West Hernando Middle School who has extensive experience working with students with ADHD. As Ms. Scott noted in the "View from Teachers" feature at the beginning of this chapter, the challenges for addressing the needs of students with ADHD vary, depending on the type and severity of the student's symptoms. She also suggested that teachers keep in mind that some of the behavior issues presented by students with ADHD may be a front to escape from having to do work that they know they can't do. "My job is to make sure there's a lot of academic support, making them sure they *can* do the work." Laura recommends the following:

• **No two students with ADHD are exactly alike.** One of the keys to being successful in teaching these students is to know the particular student well. "The teacher has to be very proactive and stay on top of things." For example, if a student is having a difficult time paying attention or blurts out inappropriate things or loses control quickly, the teacher needs to be able to see the signs that something is coming. This requires knowing the child so well that the signs become obvious, and the teacher recognizes that the child is getting frustrated or aggravated. At times, it may be another student who sets him off, or he may have missed breakfast that morning, or maybe he had a fight with his brother. The teacher has to make every attempt to catch the behavior before it gets started, and redirect the behavior toward something more appropriate and acceptable.

# TIPS FROM TEACHERS

This feature, included in Chapters 3 through 9, provides tips from teachers regarding inclusion of students with different disabilities. These tips provide real-world examples from the three schools featured in this text, as teachers provide their perspectives on key issues for including students who exhibit a range of different academic and behavior challenges in an inclusive classroom.

# Effective Applications

Finally, the third theme of effective applications emphasizes evidence-based practices that meet the needs of students with disabilities and others who struggle to learn or adjust socially. These practices may be applied with all students in a general education classroom (e.g., class-wide peer tutoring), or implemented with small groups of students either in the general education classroom or in a separate setting (e.g., intensive reading instruction). Evidence-based practices ensure that all students learn the academic and social skills needed to be successful in school and in life beyond school.

## PART III CHAPTERS

Chapters 10 through 16 address key topical issues for the inclusive classroom and effective practices that can be used with all students. The first half of each chapter discusses the theory and background of each issue (e.g., collaboration, classroom management, technology) and the second half of each chapter provides in-depth, step-by-step strategies (up to 10 strategies per chapter topic) related to these issues.

## PUTTING IT ALL TOGETHER AND STRATEGY FACT SHEETS

To connect the theory of the first half of Chapters 10 through 16 with the strategies covered in the second half of these chapters, we provide a list of key points regarding the topic of the chapter, followed by a Strategy Fact Sheet that includesd a brief description of each strategy. These organizers contain the following helpful information:

- The name of each effective practice
- A brief narrative description of the strategy
- Special considerations regarding the use of the strategy in an inclusive classroom

### EFFECTIVE INSTRUCTION IN CORE ACADEMIC AREAS

#### Putting It All Together

Delivering effective instruction in core academic areas involves not just knowledge of practices but also much additional information related to collaboration, planning, classroom management, and the use of technology, among other things. With this in mind, we offer several suggestions for your consideration.

1. **Effective instruction depends on collaboration.** In an inclusive setting, a general education teacher often brings a deep knowledge of the content, whereas a special education teacher brings a toolbox of strategies to ensure that all students learn the material. When teachers combine these areas of expertise, they learn valuable new skills and provide more effective instruction. Thus, all students learn more. Collaboration is often essential to provide support for effective instruction in inclusive classrooms.

2. **Effective instruction is well organized.** Vicki Eng, a teacher from West Hernando Middle School, made this point well: "When you walk into a class with kids with LD or students who struggle, you need to be well organized; you can't wing it, or you lose control of your class. You need to have guidelines, rules posted early, so issues don't become problems you can't control." The information we presented previously on effective instruction clearly demonstrates that instruction for students who struggle should be explicit, intensive, and systematic. Furthermore, this information should be presented in a classroom where instruction is predictable, and disruptions to instruction are kept to a minimum.

3. **Effective teachers have a toolbox of strategies that work.** No effective practice works every time for every student. Effective teachers monitor the effectiveness of instructional approaches and have alternatives available when a strategy does not work with a student. These strategies are obtained from many places, including from other teachers, online resources, textbooks, professional development activities, and so forth. Teachers improve their practice by adding effective instructional strategies to their toolbox that can be used to meet the needs of all their students.

4. **Effective teachers are lifelong learners.** The best teachers are those who continue to improve and are constantly adding new strategies to help their students who struggle. These are teachers who reflect on their practice, use progress-monitoring data to determine if students are making sufficient progress, and change instructional strategies as necessary to improve outcomes for students. Teachers who continue to learn new practices observe effective practices in other teachers' classes whenever possible. They also welcome observation in their own classrooms, as well as coaching support from peers when they are learning new practices (McLeskey, 2011).

#### Strategy Fact Sheet

In the remainder of this chapter, we describe eight effective strategies, which we referred to previously in the chapter, to help you plan effectively to meet the needs of all students.

| STRATEGY | DESCRIPTION | SPECIAL CONSIDERATIONS |
|---|---|---|
| Strategy 13.1: Principles of Research-Based Instruction in Core Content Areas | Most states and local school districts emphasize the use of instructional practices that have been demonstrated effective. Here, we describe general principles of instruction that have been proven effective for students who struggle with learning academic content. | Principles of research-based instruction provide a general framework for delivering high-quality core instruction in the general education classroom. |

*(Continued)*

| STRATEGY | DESCRIPTION | SPECIAL CONSIDERATIONS |
|---|---|---|
| Strategy 13.2: Direct Instruction of Core Academic Skills | As students learn basic academic skills, a direct, systematic approach to instruction is needed, especially for those who struggle. Direct instruction provides such an approach, which has been demonstrated effective in teaching core academic skills. | A direct instruction approach is used to teach facts, rules, and action sequences that are building blocks for later learning. The more time students spend actively being taught, reviewing, and practicing these skills, the more information they will retain. |
| Strategy 13.3: Cooperative Learning | A grouping strategy that uses mixed-ability groups for instruction. The goal is to ensure that all students learn assigned content, which may range from basic academic skills to complex group projects. | Formal cooperative learning approaches may be used for an extended period of time. However, more informal approaches to cooperative learning may be used to work on specific tasks for brief periods of time. |
| Strategy 13.4: Reading Recovery | A tutoring approach for beginning readers that employs effective instructional strategies to reduce the number of students who have difficulty learning to read. | Reading Recovery requires special, extensive training for tutors, and it can be expensive to implement. Students can be taught in pairs to reduce costs. Reading Recovery may be used as a Tier-3 approach to instruction. |
| Strategy 13.5: Peer-Assisted Learning Strategies | Peer tutoring that offers an efficient, cost-effective method for providing students with independent practice on the skills they need in order to develop in-depth knowledge of content. | Peer-tutoring programs such as PALS can be used in any subject area, and they are flexible, easy to implement, cost-effective, and time efficient. These qualities likely account for the acceptance and use of these interventions by many teachers in elementary and secondary classrooms. |
| Strategy 13.6: Beginning Reading: Tiers of Instruction & RTI | Assumes that a student should be identified with a disability only after high-quality instruction has been provided, and the student has continued to struggle to learn. | In an RTI model, high-quality, effective instruction includes core instruction in the general education classroom (Tier 1), instruction in small groups (Tier 2), and intensive, individualized instruction focusing on specific student needs (Tier 3). |
| Strategy 13.7: Self-Regulated Strategy Development and Writing Instruction | An approach used to support students in using writing strategies effectively and independently. Teachers provide explicit instruction as students learn the strategy and how it can be applied. | Many elementary students with disabilities have difficulty planning and regulating writing strategies. SRSD may be used to improve student planning and self-regulation as they learn to write. |

# STEP-BY-STEP STRATEGIES

Up to 10 effective strategies are included in Chapters 10 through 16. Each strategy is presented in a step-by-step manner. You will notice that the pages in this text are perforated and hole punched—this enables students to remove these evidence-based strategies and put them into a binder for future use as they enter their own classroom.

Each strategy includes the following information:

- Rationale that gives background information regarding the strategy—when and how it should be used
- Step-by-step instruction on how to use the strategy with students or in the classroom
- Applications and Examples of the strategy in a real-world context
- A Keep in Mind section that helps readers address specific "speed bumps" they may encounter when applying the strategy
- Key references that provide citations for further information regarding the topic

## Strategy 14.3    MNEMONIC STRATEGIES

### Rationale

Remembering subject-area information and having ways of applying what one has learned are essential for success in school. *Mnemonic strategies* are procedures that enhance memory by forming associations that do not exist naturally in the content. Mnemonic techniques form associations by building meaningful connections to seemingly unconnected concepts by recoding, transforming, and elaborating on existing material (Hughes, 1996; Mastropieri, Sweda, & Scruggs, 2000). To readily retrieve the content, students need to be explicitly taught effective ways to input (or encode) information. Mnemonic instruction and materials have produced significant gains in content-area instruction for students with and without disabilities (e.g., Marshak, Mastropieri, & Scruggs, 2011). Mnemonics are versatile techniques, easily implemented in secondary-content classes, and applicable to a wide range of subject-area curricula. They are not, however, a specific curricular approach, educational philosophy, or even a method of improving comprehension. Mnemonics are embedded in instructional sequences and simply help students remember things.

### Step-by-Step

**1** *Help students develop an understanding of mnemonics* by demonstrating how first-letter strategies help organize and retrieve information through the acronyms FIRST and LISTS (Hughes, 1996).

- FIRST is used to help design the mnemonic by:
  - **F**—Form a word.
  - **I**—Insert a letter.
  - **R**—Rearrange the letters.
  - **S**—Shape a sentence.
  - **T**—Try combinations.
  - *Sample:* HOMES = First letters of the Great Lakes (Huron, Ontario, Michigan, Erie, Superior)

- LISTS for making and designing lists:
  - **L**—Look for clues.
  - **I**—Investigate the items.
  - **S**—Select a mnemonic using FIRST.
  - **T**—Transfer information to a card.
  - **S**—Self-test.

**2** *Demonstrate how keyword mnemonics enhance associations, making information to be learned meaningful.*

- Transform an unfamiliar concept to a word or phrase (keyword) that the student knows. For example, the keyword for barrister would be *bear*, represented in a picture of a bear acting as a lawyer (Mastropieri & Scruggs, 1998).
- Provide a strategy for and practice retrieval of the concept. When asked to define *barrister*, students should think of the picture of the keywords. This facilitates the association and assists in the retrieval of the definition.

**3** *Promote generalization across subject areas* by embedding mnemonics in various instructional situations (e.g., peer tutoring) and teaching students to generate their own keywords using a specific strategy such as IT–FITS (King-Sears, Mercer, & Sindelar, 1992; Marshak et al., 2011).

- **I**—Identify the term.
- **T**—Tell the definition of the term.
- **F**—Find a keyword.
- **I**—Imagine the term doing something with the keyword.
- **T**—Think about the term doing something with the keyword.
- **S**—Study what you imagine and think until you know the definition.

**4** *Actively teach independent mn[...]*

- Alert students as to the purpose [...] gies and how practice will impr[...] mance.
- Model mnemonic use, and reinf[...] tions.
- Be explicit in your thinking p[...] ing and using the mnemonics; h[...] their own thinking when using [...]
- Provide adequate opportuni[...] across topics and subject areas.

### Applications and Examples

Teachers have used keyword mnemonic instruction to help students with disabilities to learn SAT vocabulary words (Terrill, Scruggs, & Mastropieri, 2004). At the conclusion of a 6-week instructional period, students with learning disabilities learned 92% of the words taught with the mnemonic, compared to only 49% of the words taught traditionally. Note how Terrill and colleagues (2004) connected vocabulary to keywords:

| WORD | KEYWORD | MEANING | ILLUSTRATION |
|------|---------|---------|--------------|
| Abhor | Horrible | Regard with horror; hate deeply | A monster regarded with horror |
| Extant | Ant | Still existing | Ants continue to come to picnics over the years |
| Turbulent | Turtle | Violent, stormy | A turtle swimming through a violent storm |

### Keep in Mind

Like all instructional techniques, the effectiveness of mnemonic use should be monitored regularly. Specifically, mnemonics can be a time-consuming activity and the relative cost-effectiveness of the technique needs to be considered in terms of student outcomes. In some cases, the addition of keywords to an already burgeoning curriculum can frustrate students and actually detract from lessons and units. Also, several research efforts (e.g., King-Sears et al., 1992; Marshak et al., 2011) indicate that teacher-provided keywords and pictures are more effective than requiring students to generate their own. With limited instructional time, decisions as to when to use mnemonics must be made judiciously, considering student characteristics and actual measures of performance.

**Key References**

Hughes, C. A. (1996). Memory and test taking skills. In D. D. Deshler, E. S. Ellis, & B. K. Lenz (Eds.), *Teaching adolescents with learning disabilities* (pp. 209–266). Denver: Love.

Marshak, L., Mastropieri, M. A., & Scruggs, T. E. (2011). Curriculum enhancements in inclusive secondary classrooms. *Exceptionality, 19*, 61–74.

Mastropieri, M. A., & Scruggs, T. E. (1998). Enhancing school success with mnemonic strategies. *Intervention in School and Clinic, 33*(4), 201–208.

Mastropieri, M. A., Sweda, J., & Scruggs, T. E. (2000). Putting mnemonic strategies to work in an inclusive classroom. *Learning Disabilities Research & Practice, 15*(2), 69–74.

Sabornie, E. J., & deBettencourt, L. (2009). *Teaching students with mild and high-incidence disabilities at the secondary level.* Upper Saddle River, NJ: Merrill/Pearson Education.

# Supplements for Students and Instructors

The student and instructor support package for *Inclusion: Effective Practices for All Students* includes **MyEducationLab**, an Online Instructor's Manual with Test Items, Online TestGen assessment software, and Online PowerPoint Presentations.

## MyEducationLab

Proven to **engage students**, provide **trusted content**, and **improve results**, Pearson MyLabs have helped over 8 million registered students reach true understanding in their courses. **MyEducationLab** engages students with real-life teaching situations through dynamic videos, case studies, and student artifacts. Student progress is assessed, and a personalized study plan is created based on the student's unique results. Automatic grading and reporting keeps educators informed to quickly address gaps and improve student performance. All of the activities and exercises in MyEducationLab are built around essential learning outcomes for teachers and are mapped to professional teaching standards.

In *Preparing Teachers for a Changing World*, Linda Darling-Hammond and her colleagues point out that grounding teacher education in real classrooms—among real teachers and students and among actual examples of students' and teachers' work—is an important, and perhaps even an essential, part of training teachers for the complexities of teaching in today's classrooms.

In the MyEducationLab for this course you will find the following features and resources.

### STUDY PLAN SPECIFIC TO YOUR TEXT

MyEducationLab gives students the opportunity to test themselves on key concepts and skills, track their own progress through the course, and access personalized Study Plan activities. The customized Study Plan—with enriching activities—is generated based on students' results of a pretest. Study Plans tag incorrect questions from the pretest to the appropriate textbook learning outcome, helping students focus on the topics with which they need help. Personalized Study Plan activities may include e-book reading assignments, and review, practice, and enrichment activities.

After students complete the enrichment activities, they take a posttest to discover the concepts they've mastered or the areas where they may need extra help. MyEducationLab then reports the Study Plan results to the instructor. Based on these reports, the instructor can adapt course material to suit the needs of individual students or the entire class.

### CONNECTION TO NATIONAL STANDARDS

Today it is easier than ever to see how coursework is connected to national standards. Each topic, activity, and exercise on MyEducationLab lists intended learning outcomes connected to CEC Standards and INTASC Standards.

### ASSIGNMENTS AND ACTIVITIES

Designed to enhance your understanding of concepts covered in class, these assignable exercises show concepts in action (through videos, cases, and/or student and teacher artifacts). They help you deepen content knowledge and synthesize and apply concepts and strategies you read about in the book. (Correct answers for these assignments are available to the instructor only.)

## BUILDING TEACHING SKILLS AND DISPOSITIONS

These unique learning units help users practice and strengthen skills that are essential to effective teaching. After presenting the steps involved in a core teaching process, you are given an opportunity to practice applying this skill via videos, student and teacher artifacts, and/or case studies of authentic classrooms. Providing multiple opportunities to practice a single teaching concept, each activity encourages a deeper understanding and application of concepts, as well as the use of critical thinking skills. After practice, students take a quiz that is reported to the instructor gradebook.

## LESSON PLAN BUILDER

The **Lesson Plan Builder** is an effective and easy-to-use tool that you can employ to create, update, and share quality lesson plans. The software also makes it easy to integrate state content standards into any lesson plan.

## IRIS CENTER RESOURCES

The IRIS Center at Vanderbilt University (http://iris.peabody.vanderbilt.edu), funded by the U.S. Department of Education's Office of Special Education Programs (OSEP), develops training enhancement materials for preservice and practicing teachers. The Center works with experts from across the country to create challenge-based interactive modules, case study units, and podcasts that provide research-validated information about working with students in inclusive settings. In your MyEducationLab course we have integrated this content where appropriate.

## COURSE RESOURCES

The Course Resources section of MyEducationLab is designed to help you put together an effective lesson plan, prepare for and begin your career, navigate your first year of teaching, and understand key educational standards, policies, and laws. It includes the following:

**Beginning Your Career** offers tips, advice, and other valuable information on:
- *Resume Writing and Interviewing:* Includes expert advice on how to write impressive resumes and prepare for job interviews.
- *Your First Year of Teaching:* Provides practical tips to set up a first classroom, manage student behavior, and more easily organize for instruction and assessment.
- *Law and Public Policies:* Details specific directives and requirements you need to understand under the No Child Left Behind Act and the Individuals with Disabilities Education Improvement Act of 2004.

**The Certification and Licensure** section is designed to help you pass your licensure exam by giving you access to state test requirements, overviews of what tests cover, and sample test items. The Certification and Licensure section includes the following:

- **State Certification Test Requirements:** Here, you can click on a state and will then be taken to a list of state certification tests.
- You can click on the **Licensure Exams** you need to take to find:
  - Basic information about each test
  - Descriptions of what is covered on each test
  - Sample test questions with explanations of correct answers
- **National Evaluation Series™** by Pearson: Here, students can see the tests in the NES, learn what is covered on each exam, and access sample test items with descriptions and rationales of correct answers. You can also purchase interactive online tutorials developed by Pearson Evaluation Systems and the Pearson Teacher Education and Development group.
- **ETS Online Praxis Tutorials:** Here, you can purchase interactive online tutorials developed by ETS and by the Pearson Teacher Education and Development group. Tutorials are available for the Praxis I exams and for select Praxis II exams.

Visit **www.myeducationlab.com** for a demonstration of this exciting new online teaching resource.

# INSTRUCTOR'S RESOURCE CENTER

The Instructor Resource Center at www.pearsonhighered.com has a variety of print and media resources available in downloadable, digital format—all in one location. As a registered faculty member, you can access and download pass code–protected resource files, course-management content, and other premium online content directly to your computer.

Digital resources available for *Inclusion: Effective Practices for All Students*, second edition, include the following:

- A test bank of multiple-choice and essay tests
- PowerPoint presentations specifically designed for each chapter
- An Online Instructor's Manual with numerous recommendations for presenting and extending text content. It is organized by chapter and contains chapter objectives, chapter summaries, key terms, presentation outlines, discussion questions, and application. The test item bank contains multiple-choice, short-answer, and essay questions that can be used to assess students' recognition, recall, and synthesis of factual content and conceptual issues from each chapter.

To access these items online, go to www.pearsonhighered.com and click on the Instructor option. You'll find an Instructor Resource Center option in the top navigation bar. There, you will be able to log in or complete a one-time registration for a user name and password. If you have any questions regarding this process or the materials available online, please contact your local Pearson sales representative.

# Acknowledgments

To make an inclusive classroom function well, professionals must work together, sharing expertise and providing support as it is needed. We have witnessed this firsthand on numerous occasions in schools, as teachers and administrators work collaboratively to provide extraordinary educational opportunities for all students. The same is true when writing a textbook. Although three of us are listed as authors of this text, we had a broad range of support in completing this project. As the second edition moved toward completion, the level of support, creativity, and knowledge that colleagues provided was extraordinary, and we are extremely privileged and grateful to have had this support.

First, we gratefully acknowledge the superlative effort of the professionals at Pearson Education for their unparalleled support. Our Executive Editor Ann Davis provided the momentum to get this project started, then used her extensive knowledge of special education textbooks and marketing to provide us with a unique direction for our inclusion text. Throughout the many months we spent writing and now revising this text, she continually kept us on-message and encouraged us to produce a unique text with features that were a good fit for the real world of teaching and inclusive classrooms.

Our many requests for support and information at the Pearson Education offices were cheerfully and quickly addressed in editorial by Penny Burleson and Joanna Sabella in marketing. Finally, we are grateful for the creative coordination of Senior Production Editor Sheryl Langner, who was always there to make sure that the pieces of this project fit together and resulted in a product that was both logical and attractive.

We provide a special thanks to our main contact and support person at Pearson Education, Executive Development Editor Hope Madden. Hope's matter-of-fact style and willingness to dive into complex and at times sensitive issues have helped us question and improve many parts of this text. Although at times we dreaded opening e-mails from Hope—which often had suggestions for more changes, deadlines, or other tasks—her suggestions were consistently on the mark and significantly improved the quality of this text. In particular, she pushed us to get away from our professorial roles, and write in a way that is accessible and user friendly.

For their fine work on an earlier draft of Chapter 13, we thank Dorene Ross and Margaret Kamman from the University of Florida, Vivian Correa from the University of North Carolina–Charlotte, and Jennifer Huber from Arizona State University. Many of the ideas that these colleagues included in the original version of this chapter remain in Chapter 13, and we thank them for sharing their expertise and many experiences working with students from diverse backgrounds.

A highlight for each of us as we wrote this book was having the opportunity to interview and observe a group of extraordinarily dedicated teachers and administrators in our three feature schools, Gilpin Manor Elementary School, West Hernando Middle School, and Heritage High School. We are very appreciative to these professionals for allowing us to enter their schools, and for their willingness to share their expertise, ideas, and creativity. We are especially appreciative of the following teachers, administrators, and school staff at the three schools.

Much assistance was provided by the administration in Cecil County Public Schools in Maryland and especially by the administration, faculty, and staff at Gilpin Manor Elementary School. We especially appreciate assistance provided by Associate Superintendent Dr. Carolyn

Teigland, and by Principal Jennifer Hammer of Gilpin Manor Elementary School. We also thank the teachers and related services professionals at GMES whom we interviewed, including Alice O'Mullane, Alison McMahon, Alison Meyer, Jeannie Huskins, Kim Miller, Malee Taylor, Megan Law, Melissa Pratt, Shellee Decker, Stephanie Walsh, and Susan Huff. Finally, we thank the parents and students who were willing to talk to us about their experiences at GMES.

At West Hernando Middle School, we appreciate the support of Principal Rick Markford; Counselor Susan Dean; teachers Jan Patterson, Maureen Finelli, Sue Atkins, Susan Davis, Michelle Duclos, Vicki Eng, Lisa Grover, Lisa Hallal, Laura Scott, Eileen Walls; and two students who shared their thoughts about the peer-support program. We also appreciate the assistance and support from the Hernando County Exceptional Student Education office, including Special Education Director Cathy Dofka, and district specialists Susan Gemmati and Alison O'Reilly.

At Heritage High School, we are grateful for the support and cooperation of Principal Margaret Huckabee, Special Education Supervisor Toni DeLuca-Strauss, Assistant Principal Kim Turner, and the always energetic Dean of Special Education Susan Hill. For several years, these dedicated administrators went above and beyond to make us feel part of their academic community. We are indebted to the master teachers at Heritage, including Debbie Buttery, Melanie Buckley, Denise Pohill, Gina Craun, Anthony Long, Tracey Ludwig, Casey Van Harssel, Steve Kennedy, Jon Preuss, Steve Williams, Kristen Tham, Kim Turner, Megan Wagner, Mike Wagner, and Shana Watson. Finally, we are extremely appreciative of the candid conversations with the students and parents of Heritage. Thanks for sharing your expertise, insightful opinions, and suggestions for improving teacher preparation.

The staff at all three of our universities assisted us on a range of tasks, and covered for us when we were hidden away writing chapters. We are most appreciative for this support. Staff at the University of Florida included Shaira Rivas-Otero, Vicki Tucker, Linda Parsons, and Michell York. At Johns Hopkins, support was provided by Sharon Lampkin and Kristen Lohman. At Western Carolina, support was provided by staff members, including Susan Buchanan and Michael Beasley, and by colleagues, including Karena Cooper-Duffy, Kelly Kelley, and Glenda Hyer.

For the first edition, we sent out many drafts of each chapter for review, and received valuable feedback from a range of colleagues. We appreciate the time these colleagues provided, as well as their willingness to share expertise on topics from each chapter in this text, which helped us ensure accuracy and improve the quality of this project. In particular, we would like to thank Tammy Abernathy, University of Nevada; Christopher Bloh, Kutztown University; Alice C. Giacobbe, Oklahoma State University; Ann Gilles, University of South Florida; and Bianca Prather-Jones, Northern Kentucky University.

Finally, completing this extensive revision required frequent absences from our homes. In spite of this, it is our great fortune that we continue to have the love and support of our families, and for this we are eternally grateful. This includes our wives, Nancy, Irene, and Wendy; children Gaby, Robby, Matthew, Zeke, Daniel, Jennifer, Jessica, and Meredith; and grandchildren Dylan, Ethan, Hayden, Riley, and Nicholas.

JM
MSR
DLW

# Brief Contents

**PART I**   Foundations of Successful Inclusion

Chapter **1**   What Is Inclusion, and Why Is It Important?   2

Chapter **2**   Inclusion: Historical Trends, Current Practices, and Tomorrow's Challenges   28

**PART II**   Meeting the Needs of All Students

Chapter **3**   Students with Learning Disabilities   52

Chapter **4**   Students with Attention-Deficit/Hyperactivity Disorder   66

Chapter **5**   Students with Intellectual Disabilities   82

Chapter **6**   Students with Emotional and Behavioral Disabilities   96

Chapter **7**   Students with Autism Spectrum Disorders   110

Chapter **8**   Students with Communication Disorders and Students with Sensory Impairments   124

Chapter **9**   Students with Physical Disabilities, Health Impairments, and Multiple Disabilities   140

**PART III**   Effective Practices

Chapter **10**   Collaboration and Teaming   154

Chapter **11**   Formal Plans and Planning for Differentiated Instruction   198

Chapter **12**   Effective Practices for Students from Diverse Backgrounds   240

Chapter **13**   Effective Instruction in Core Academic Areas: Teaching Reading, Writing, and Mathematics   278

Chapter **14**   Teaching Students in Secondary Content Areas   320

Chapter **15**   Effective Practices for All Students: Classroom Management   358

Chapter **16**   Using Technology to Support Inclusion   400

Glossary   442

References   450

Name Index   473

Subject Index   477

Photo Credits   485

# Contents

**PART I**    Foundations of Successful Inclusion

**Chapter 1**    What Is Inclusion, and Why Is It Important? 2

A VIEW FROM PARENTS 3
Is Inclusion Good for Grace?

Introduction 4

Inclusion Is for All Students 5

DESCRIPTIONS OF THREE HIGHLY EFFECTIVE, INCLUSIVE SCHOOLS 5
Students with Disabilities and Special Education 8
Other Students Who May Need Support in the General Education Classroom 10

Concepts That Support Inclusive Practices 11
Normalization 12
Least Restrictive Environment 13

What Are Effective Inclusive Programs? 15

A VIEW FROM HER PARENTS AND TEACHER 15
Inclusive Programs: Research on Effectiveness 17

Teaching in an Inclusive School 19
Your Role as a Teacher 19
Teacher Attitudes toward Inclusion 21

Being a Good Teacher of All Students 23
Appropriate Dispositions 23
Positive Teacher Qualities 23
Summary 25

Addressing Professional Standards 27

**Chapter 2**    Inclusion: Historical Trends, Current Practices, and Tomorrow's Challenges 28

A VIEW FROM A PARENT 29
Sarita Celebrates Inclusion

Introduction 30

The Evolution of Inclusive Special Education Services 31
From Segregation to Inclusion 31
Civil Rights and Parent Advocacy 33
Current Status of Inclusive Practices 34

A VIEW FROM THE PRINCIPAL 36

Legal Foundations of Special Education and Inclusion 37

Individuals with Disabilities Education Improvement Act (IDEA 2004) 37
Elements of IDEA 2004 38
No Child Left Behind (NCLB) 42
Elements of NCLB 42
Section 504 of the Rehabilitation Act of 1973 (PL 93-112) and the
Americans with Disabilities Act 44

**Inclusion Today: Multi-tiered Response to Intervention (RTI)
Frameworks** 45
Response to Intervention (RTI) 45
Elements of an RTI Framework 46
RTI Efficacy 47

**Tomorrow's Challenges** 48
AYP and Students with Disabilities 48
Highly Qualified Professionals 49
Summary 50

Addressing Professional Standards 51

**PART II**   **Meeting the Needs of All Students**

**Chapter 3**   Students with Learning Disabilities 52

A VIEW FROM TEACHERS 53
How Students with Learning Disabilities Benefit from Inclusion

**Introduction** 54

**Who Are the Students with Learning Disabilities?** 54
Definition 54
Identification of Students with Learning Disabilities 56
Prevalence 58
Service Delivery 59

**Major Characteristics of Students with Learning Disabilities** 60
Academic Characteristics 60

A VIEW FROM A TEACHER 61
Cognitive Characteristics 62
Social and Motivational Characteristics 62

**Teaching Students with Learning Disabilities in Inclusive
Classrooms: Tips from Teachers** 63
Summary 64

Addressing Professional Standards 65

**Chapter 4**   Students with Attention-Deficit/Hyperactivity Disorder 66

A VIEW FROM TEACHERS 67
How Students with Attention-Deficit/Hyperactivity Disorder Benefit from Inclusion

**Introduction** 68

**Who Are Students with Attention-Deficit/Hyperactivity Disorder?** 69
Definition 69
Identification of Students with ADHD 71
Prevalence 73
Service Delivery 73

**Major Characteristics of Students with ADHD** 74

Inattentive, Hyperactive, and Impulsive Behaviors 74

A VIEW FROM A TEACHER 75
Executive Functions and Working Memory 76
Social and Behavior Difficulties 76
Academic Difficulties 77

The Use of Medication to Address the Symptoms of ADHD 77
Teaching Students with ADHD in Inclusive Classrooms: Tips from Teachers 79
Summary 80

Addressing Professional Standards 81

Chapter 5 Students with Intellectual Disabilities 82

A VIEW FROM THE TEACHER 83
How Susan Huff Includes Students with Disabilities

Introduction 84

Who Are Students with Intellectual Disabilities? 84
Definition 84
Identification of Students with Intellectual Disabilities 86
Prevalence 87
Service Delivery 88

A VIEW FROM A STUDENT 88

Major Characteristics of Students with Intellectual Disabilities 89
Academic Characteristics 89
Cognitive Characteristics 90
Social and Behavioral Characteristics 91

A VIEW FROM PEERS 92

Keys to Successful Inclusion: Tips from Effective Teachers 92
Summary 93

Addressing Professional Standards 94

Chapter 6 Students with Emotional and Behavioral Disabilities 96

A VIEW FROM THE TEACHER 97
Behavioral Support Program Coordinator Steve Williams on Including Students with Challenging Behavior

Introduction 98

Who Are Students with Emotional and Behavioral Disabilities? 99
Definition 99
Identification of Students with Emotional and Behavioral Disabilities 100
Prevalence 101
Service Delivery 102

Major Characteristics of Students with Emotional and Behavioral Disabilities 103
Externalizing Behavior Problems 103
Internalizing Behavior Problems 103

A VIEW FROM A STUDENT 104
Intelligence and Academic Characteristics 105
Social Behavior 105

**Teaching Students with Emotional and Behavioral Disorders in Inclusive Classrooms: Tips from Teachers** 106
Summary 108

Addressing Professional Standards 109

**Chapter 7**    Students with Autism Spectrum Disorders 110

A VIEW FROM A BEHAVIOR SPECIALIST 111
Eileen Walls Describes the Benefits of Including Students with ASD

**Introduction** 112

**Who Are Students with Autism Spectrum Disorders?** 113
    Definition 113
    Identification of Students with Autism Spectrum Disorders 114
    Prevalence 115
    Service Delivery 115

A VIEW FROM A STUDENT 116

**Characteristics of Students with Autism Spectrum Disorders** 117
    Primary Characteristics 117
    Secondary Characteristics 119

**Teaching Students with ASD in Inclusive Classrooms: Tips from Teachers** 120
Summary 122

Addressing Professional Standards 123

**Chapter 8**    Students with Communication Disorders and Students with Sensory Impairments 124

A VIEW FROM A SPEECH/LANGUAGE PATHOLOGIST 125
Malee Taylor's Thoughts on Inclusion and Communication

**Introduction** 126

**Who Are Students with Communication Disorders?** 127
    Definitions 127
    Identification of Students with Communication Disorders 128
    Prevalence 129
    Service Delivery 130

**Major Characteristics of Students with Communication Disorders** 130
    Academic Characteristics 130
    Social and Behavioral Characteristics 131

**Who Are Students with Sensory Impairments?** 131
    Definitions 131
    Identification of Students with Sensory Impairments 134
    Prevalence 134
    Service Delivery 134

**Major Characteristics of Students with Sensory Impairments** 135
    Academic Characteristics 135

A VIEW FROM A PARENT 136
    Social and Behavioral Characteristics 137

**Keys to Successful Inclusion: Tips from Effective Teachers** 137
Summary 138

Addressing Professional Standards 139

**Chapter 9**   Students with Physical Disabilities, Health Impairments, and Multiple Disabilities  140

A VIEW FROM PROFESSIONALS  141
How a Pre-K Team Includes a Child with Multiple Disabilities

Introduction  142

Who Are Students with Physical Disabilities, Health Impairments, and Multiple Disabilities?  143
Definitions  144
Identification of Students with Physical Disabilities, Health Impairments, and Multiple Disabilities  146
Prevalence  147
Service Delivery  147

Major Characteristics of Students with Physical Disabilities, Health Impairments, and Multiple Disabilities  147

A VIEW FROM A PEER  148
Academic Characteristics  148
Social and Behavioral Characteristics  149

Keys to Successful Inclusion: Tips from Effective Teachers  150
Summary  151

Addressing Professional Standards  153

## PART III   Effective Practices for All Students

**Chapter 10**   Collaboration and Teaming  154

A VIEW FROM TEACHERS  155
Why Is Collaboration an Absolute Necessity to Support Inclusion?

Introduction  156

Collaboration: What to Expect  157
What Is Collaboration?  157

Dispositions and Skills Needed for Successful Collaboration  159
Dispositions Needed for Successful Collaboration  159
Skills Needed for Successful Collaboration  162

Collaborative Roles in Inclusive Schools  162
Collaborative Teams  163
Co-Teaching  163
Collaborative Consultation  166

Students as Collaborators: Peer Assistance in Inclusive Classrooms and Schools  168

The Peer Buddy Program  169

A VIEW FROM STUDENTS  169
Summary  170

Addressing Professional Standards  171

**EFFECTIVE STRATEGIES FOR COLLABORATION AND TEAMING** 173

Putting It All Together 173

STRATEGY FACT SHEET 173

Strategy 10.1 **Key Components of Effective Collaboration** 175

Strategy 10.2 **Communication Skills and Successful Collaboration** 177

Strategy 10.3 **Teacher Assistance Teams (TATS)** 179

Strategy 10.4 **Planning for Co-Teaching** 183

Strategy 10.5 **Working with Paraeducators** 187

Strategy 10.6 **Working with Families: Home–School Collaboration** 191

Strategy 10.7 **Peer Buddy Programs** 195

**Chapter 11**   Formal Plans and Planning for Differentiated Instruction 198

A VIEW FROM FACULTY AND ADMINISTRATORS 199
Planning for Inclusion at Gilpin Manor Elementary School

**Introduction** 200

**Response-to-Intervention Plans** 200

**Individualized Education Programs** 201

**Section 504 Plans** 203

**Behavior Intervention Plans** 203

**Planning for Differentiated Instruction** 205

Getting to Know Your Students and Their Strengths 206

Level-1 Planning: Identifying Students' Learning Needs 207

Level-2 Planning: Preparing for Daily Instruction 208

Level-3 Planning: Interactive Planning During Instruction 211

Monitoring Student Progress 212

Grading Students with Disabilities 213

Arranging the Classroom for Inclusion 213

Summary 215

Addressing Professional Standards 216

**EFFECTIVE PRACTICES** 217

Putting It All Together 217

STRATEGY FACT SHEET 217

Strategy 11.1 **Contributing to Individualized Education Programs** 219

Strategy 11.2 **Procedures for Developing a 504 Plan** 221

Strategy 11.3 **Planning for Differentiated Instruction** 223

Strategy 11.4 **Identifying Instructional Needs** 225

Strategy 11.5 **Using Person-Centered Plans to Support Inclusion** 227

Strategy 11.6 **Planning for Basic Skills Instruction in an Inclusive Classroom** 229

Strategy 11.7 **Planning for Academic Content Instruction Using UDL Principles** 231

Strategy 11.8 **Using CBM to Measure Student Academic Progress** 233

Strategy 11.9 **Developing a Personalized Grading Plan** 237

**Chapter 12** Effective Practices for Students from Diverse Backgrounds 240

A VIEW FROM THE TEACHER 241
Navigating Cultural Responsiveness at Heritage High School

Introduction 242

Students from Diverse Backgrounds: What to Expect 243
What to Expect Regarding Student Diversity 243
What to Expect Regarding Diversity in Special Education 243
What You Need to Know about Student Diversity and Academic Achievement 245

Principles and Practices to Support Effective Instruction 246
How Teachers Establish Connections across the Demographic Divide 246
What Is Culture and Why Is It So Important? 247
Becoming a Culturally Responsive Teacher 249
Demonstrating Care 250

A VIEW FROM A TEACHER 251
High Expectations: What Does "No Excuses" Really Mean? 253
Using a Diverse Curriculum 254

Summary 255

Addressing Professional Standards 256

EFFECTIVE PRACTICES FOR STUDENTS FROM DIVERSE BACKGROUNDS 257
Putting It All Together 257

STRATEGY FACT SHEET 257
Strategy 12.1 Culturally Responsive Teaching 259
Strategy 12.2 Teaching Reading to Students Who Are English-Language Learners (ELLs) 263
Strategy 12.3 Highly Effective Instructional Practices for Students from CLD Backgrounds 265
Strategy 12.4 Culturally Responsive Classroom Management 269
Strategy 12.5 Double-Check: A Culturally Responsive Approach to Classroom Management 273

**Chapter 13** Effective Instruction in Core Academic Areas: Teaching Reading, Writing, and Mathematics 278

A VIEW FROM TEACHERS 279
What Is Effective Instruction?

Introduction 280

Effective Instruction in an Inclusive Classroom: What to Expect 281

Principles and Practices to Support Effective Instruction 282
Effective Instruction: Teacher Behaviors in Delivering Instruction 282
Grouping Students to Support the Delivery of Effective Instruction 284
Individual Tutoring 285
Peer Tutoring 286

Effective Instruction in Reading, Writing, and Mathematics 287
Reading Instruction 287
Writing Instruction 290

Mathematics Instruction 293

Summary 295

Addressing Professional Standards 296

**EFFECTIVE INSTRUCTION IN CORE ACADEMIC AREAS** 297

Putting It All Together 297

STRATEGY FACT SHEET 297

Strategy 13.1 **Principles of Research-Based Instruction in Core Content Areas** 299

Strategy 13.2 **Direct Instruction of Core Academic Skills** 303

Strategy 13.3 **Cooperative Learning** 307

Strategy 13.4 **Reading Recovery** 309

Strategy 13.5 **Peer-Assisted Learning Strategies** 311

Strategy 13.6 **Beginning Reading: Tiers of Instruction and Response to Intervention** 313

Strategy 13.7 **Self-Regulated Strategy Development and Writing Instruction** 315

Strategy 13.8 **Cognitive Strategy Instruction For Teaching Mathematics Problem Solving** 317

**Chapter 14** Teaching Students in Secondary Content Areas 320

A VIEW FROM A TEACHER-LEADER 321

Susan Hill Addresses the Challenges of Teaching Secondary Content to Students with Disabilities

Introduction 322

Content Learning Differences: What to Expect 323

Understanding Curriculum 324

Working Collaboratively 324

Models and Approaches for Inclusive Content-Area Instruction 325

Universal Design for Learning 325

Direct Instruction 325

Guided Discovery Learning 326

Cooperative Learning 326

Learning Strategies 327

Content Enhancements 327

Content Survival Strategies 329

Content-Area Instruction for Students with Severe Disabilities 331

Summary 333

Addressing Professional Standards 334

**EFFECTIVE STRATEGIES FOR TEACHING SECONDARY CONTENT AREAS** 335

Putting It All Together 335

STRATEGY FACT SHEET 335

Strategy 14.1 **Content Enhancements: Unit and Lesson Organizers** 337

Strategy 14.2 **Improving Expository Writing Across Content-Area Classes** 341

Strategy 14.3 **Mnemonic Strategies** 345

Strategy 14.4 **Content-Area Reading** 347

Strategy 14.5 **Developing and Supporting Note Taking** 349

Strategy 14.6 **Developing Effective Test Taking** 353

Strategy 14.7 **Problem-Centered Learning (PCL)** 355

**Chapter 15** Effective Practices for All Students: Classroom Management 358

A VIEW FROM A TEACHER 359
Eileen Walls Describes the Success of West Hernando Middle School's Tiered Classroom Management System

Introduction 360

Student Behavior: What to Expect 361

Behavior Management Readiness and Tiered Management Strategies 362
Classroom Organization 362
Effective Instruction 363
A Climate of Care and Respect 364
Tiered Management 365
Universal Inclusive Practices and Supports 365
Targeted Interventions 368
Functional Behavioral Assessment 368
Behavior Intervention Plans 371
Wraparound Supports 374

Summary 375

Addressing Professional Standards 375

EFFECTIVE PRACTICES FOR CLASSROOM MANAGEMENT 377
Putting It All Together 377

STRATEGY FACT SHEET 377
Strategy 15.1 **Developing and Maintaining Rules and Procedures** 379
Strategy 15.2 **Surface Management Techniques** 383
Strategy 15.3 **Developing Consequences and Delivering Them with Consistency** 385
Strategy 15.4 **Defusing Confrontations and Responding to Dangerous Behavior** 387
Strategy 15.5 **Check-In, Connect, and Check-Out Systems** 389
Strategy 15.6 **Behavioral Contracts** 391
Strategy 15.7 **Function-Based Thinking, Functional Behavior Assessments, and Behavior Intervention Plans** 393
Strategy 15.8 **Direct Teaching of Social Skills: Social Stories** 397

**Chapter 16** Using Technology to Support Inclusion 400

A VIEW FROM AN ASSISTIVE TECHNOLOGY SPECIALIST 401
Allison McMahon Explains How AT Facilitates Inclusion

Introduction 402

Educational Technology and Assistive Technology 402
Types of Educational Technology 403
Types of Assistive Technology Devices 404

Principles and Practices for Effectively Using Educational Technology and Assistive Technology 412
Use of Educational Technology to Facilitate Inclusion 412
Teaching Students to Use Educational Technology 413
Use of Assistive Technology to Facilitate Inclusion 414
Teaching Students to Use Assistive Technology 414

Universal Design for Learning 415

Principles and Guidelines of UDL 415
Applying Principles and Guidelines of UDL 416
Example of the Effectiveness of UDL Applications 416
Summary 417

Addressing Professional Standards 419

**EFFECTIVE STRATEGIES FOR USING TECHNOLOGY TO SUPPORT INCLUSION** 420
Putting It All Together 420

STRATEGY FACT SHEET 420
Strategy 16.1 **Teaching Students to Use Educational Technology Programs** 423
Strategy 16.2 **Using the Smart Board to Teach in an Inclusive Classroom** 425
Strategy 16.3 **Using Read 180 in the Classroom** 427
Strategy 16.4 **Using the Computer Game Plato® Achieve now on PSP® (Mathematics) to Improve Students' Homework Performance** 429
Strategy 16.5 Evaluating Educational Technology 431
Strategy 16.6 A Decision-Making Process for Selecting Assistive Technology Devices 433
Strategy 16.7 Using Word Processing and Related Software to Support Student Writing 435
Strategy 16.8 Teaching Students with Disabilities To Use Calculators 437
Strategy 16.9 Supporting Students who Use Augmentative/Alternative Communication Devices 439
Strategy 16.10 **Supporting Students who Use Motorized Wheelchairs** 441

Glossary 443
References 450
Name Index 473
Subject Index 477
Photo Credits 485

# What Is Inclusion, and Why Is It Important?

## KEY TOPICS

**After reading this chapter you will:**

- Understand why inclusion is for all students.
- Know the concepts that support inclusive practices.
- Be aware of the characteristics of effective, inclusive programs.
- Describe the role of the teacher and other professionals in an inclusive school.
- Know the importance of being a good teacher for all students.

# chapter 1

## A VIEW FROM PARENTS

### Is Inclusion Good for Grace?

In June 2007, Annette and Larry Jeffrey (pseudonyms are used for Grace and her parents) had their third child, Grace, a bubbly, active girl. Like the other two children, Grace was typical in every way, and for the first year of her life, she developed just as her siblings had. However, shortly after her first birthday, Grace contracted transverse myelitis (TM), a neurological disorder caused by inflammation on both sides of her spinal cord (for more information on transverse myelitis, see NIH, 2011). About one in three people who contract TM fully recover, but Grace was not so fortunate. Her lower body remains weak. She has very limited mobility from the waist down, and uses a wheel-chair to get around. Her parents report that difficulty exploring her environment has also contributed to somewhat delayed language development.

Annette and Larry both work outside the home and had to make a difficult decision about where to place Grace in day care. There was considerable pressure from some of their relatives who felt strongly that Grace should be placed with other students with disabilities because they felt that she needed to be protected from what might happen in a setting with typical children and "because the professionals in those settings know what to do with those children." Putting Grace in such a setting didn't feel right to Annette and Larry, however, and so they decided to place her in a day-care setting with students without disabilities, while she continued to receive services from specialists to support her physical and language development.

When they placed Grace in day care, Annette and Larry readily admitted, "We were pretty apprehensive. Are they paying enough attention to Grace?" They found that Grace enjoyed being around the other children in the day care and was able to play with them, but they were surprised to find that the teachers seemed to pay *too much attention* to her. "They weren't sure or confident whether it was going to be safe for her, so she was often secluded. When they would go outside to play, one of the day-care teachers would take Grace and sit on the mat while the other kids played on the slides and all that stuff." Annette and Larry didn't know how to react to this, as they, too, were apprehensive about Grace's safety. However, they knew that by overprotecting Grace, "they were restricting her; they weren't letting her grow."

Overall, Annette and Larry found that the day-care setting was good for Grace. She made many friends, and her language development began to accelerate. But as Grace's third birthday approached in June 2010, they had another decision to make regarding whether to try to find a local, inclusive school, or to accept a placement in a separate class with other students with disabilities. As Annette said, "We were apprehensive about putting her in school at a young age.

She's only three, and I thought, 'Hmmm, my baby in school!?'" Grace's parents also realized that many schools did not offer inclusive programs for preschool children with disabilities.

Fortunately for Annette and Larry, their decision would be made easier because they lived near a model inclusive school—Gilpin Manor Elementary—that had an excellent preschool teacher who valued inclusion for all students. In the fall of 2010, Grace began school at Gilpin Manor in Allison Meyer's inclusive preschool class for 3- and 4-year-old children. Annette and Larry had decided that inclusion was good for Grace, but what would the school year bring? Would the teachers provide too much protection for Grace, or would they treat her much like other students and encourage her to grow and flourish? You can read more about Gilpin Manor Elementary in the descriptions of our model schools, and we'll provide more information about Grace Jeffrey's first year at Gilpin Manor later in this chapter.

# Introduction

What does being included in a community mean to you? For most people, being part of a community means that others care for and respect them for who they are, regardless of their particular strengths and shortcomings. It also means that people have a sense of belonging that brings satisfaction and comfort, and knowing that they can depend on others for support when it is needed. Many go to great lengths to achieve this sense of belonging by moving to certain neighborhoods, joining clubs, and participating in productive and meaningful group activities.

For those of us who work in education with students with disabilities, being part of the school community is often referred to as *inclusion*. In this text, we take the perspective that inclusion is not a place or a classroom setting but is a philosophy of education. *We define* **inclusion** *quite simply as including students with disabilities as valued members of the school community.* This suggests that students with disabilities *belong* to the school community and are accepted by others; that they actively *participate* in the academic and social community of the school; and that they are given supports that offer them the *opportunity* to succeed. In short, they participate in the school community in ways that we all want to participate in a community.

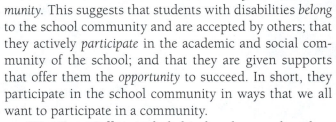

## Pause & Reflect

What does it mean to you to be *included* as part of a community? Perhaps reflecting on instances of when you have been excluded will provide insight into why being included is so important.

Was Grace Jeffrey included in her day care based on this definition of inclusion? Although she seemed to be valued, she certainly didn't actively participate in all aspects of the day-care community, nor did she always receive the necessary supports to have an opportunity to succeed. Is it reasonable for Grace's parents to expect that Grace be valued and supported in the day-care setting? Were these expectations different from what other parents would want for their children?

We agree with Grace's parents that an inclusive setting is best for her, and that placing her in such a setting is well worth the effort and apprehension that may occur. Although most teachers want to provide an inclusive education for all students, we recognize that providing such programs can be challenging, time-consuming, and frustrating. In fact, the reality of how to address effectively the academic and behavioral challenges associated with students with special needs is often daunting to school personnel. Many questions remain regarding how to develop effective, inclusive programs, and provide support for teachers as these programs are implemented (McLeskey & Waldron, 2011a).

In this text, we present evidence-based practices with examples from real-world schools and classrooms. We do this because it is our view that information regarding effective, inclusive programs and practices

Students with disabilities are included in most general education classrooms.

is best presented in a practical and straightforward fashion. Consequently, throughout this book, you will notice that we explain a significant amount of content within the context of three effective, inclusive schools: Gilpin Manor Elementary School, West Hernando Middle School, and Heritage High School. These schools serve students of different age and grade levels and have diverse student bodies.

It is important to note that we do not present these schools as examples of ideal inclusive practices. Indeed, the work of developing an inclusive school is never done (McLeskey & Waldron, 2000), as school professionals must adapt to the ever-changing needs of students as each school year progresses. These three schools are no exception, as they continue to actively strive to meet the needs of all their students. You will hear from the teachers, administrators, parents, and students from these schools throughout this text, as they provide a real-world perspective on their continuing quest to provide effective, inclusive programs. We introduce you to these schools in the accompanying box, "Descriptions of Three Highly Effective, Inclusive Schools."

## Inclusion Is for All Students

If you reflect on your experiences in K–12 general education classrooms, you'll readily recognize that many students have difficulty making academic and social progress in these settings or do not fit in well and need supports or accommodations to succeed. We say this because inclusion is not just about students with disabilities. Although much of our focus in this text is on students with disabilities, many of the interventions we describe are useful for a wide range of students who need support in general education classrooms.

## Descriptions of Three Highly Effective, Inclusive Schools

### Gilpin Manor Elementary School

Elkton, Maryland (population 14,842), is a small town located off of I-95, midway between Baltimore and Philadelphia, just north of the Chesapeake Bay. Many of the people who live in Elkton work in Baltimore or Philadelphia and choose to live in this rural community because of its more laid-back lifestyle. About six years ago, the schools in the Cecil County School District (in which Elkton is the county seat) adopted the philosophy and practice of inclusion for students with disabilities. Gilpin Manor Elementary School (GMES) was one these schools.

Built in 1952, Gilpin Manor was originally a "side-by-side" school. On one side was the "regular" elementary school for children without disabilities in grades K–5. On the other side (actually a back wing) was the "special school," in which students with disabilities spent their days separated from the other children by two heavy double doors that were always closed. According to Mrs. Jennifer Hammer, the current principal and former assistant principal at Gilpin Manor, the two groups of children lived completely separate lives during the school day.

Mrs. Hammer played a significant role in ending the separation and guiding Gilpin Manor toward becoming an inclusive school. Dr. Carolyn Teigland, Associate Superintendent in Cecil County, said, "Mrs. Hammer is an advocate for inclusion for *all* students. She has been at Gilpin throughout the change process and has provided her staff with the vision, training, and support necessary to transform the school into one that educates students with disabilities within inclusive settings along with their peers who are age appropriate."

Mrs. Hammer explained how Gilpin Manor moved from separate schools within a school to become a fully inclusive school. "Approximately seven years ago, I was assigned to Gilpin Manor as an assistant principal. I remember our associate superintendent meeting with my principal and me to discuss our plan to fully include all students in our school.

"We first established an Inclusive Practices Committee. This committee was supported with a representative from Maryland Inclusive Practices Coalition. The committee had several stakeholders, including regular education and special education teachers, paraprofessionals, parents, and community members. The committee first established a vision. One of our first tasks was to help our community understand the legal implications of least

*(Continued)*

restrictive environment (LRE). We scheduled meetings and began to identify our plan for including students in the regular setting.

"We began by integrating the Level 4 students (students with milder disabilities) into the regular classroom. We had to conduct individualized education program meetings to change the definition of *least restrictive environment* and deploy staff to provide support to the students. All Level 4 classrooms were fully integrated in the first year. Over the next three years, we integrated the students who were in the remaining Level 5 classrooms (students with more significant disabilities). At the same time, we stopped the 'pipeline' that brought students with special needs to GMES. After students completed their preschool experience, they transitioned to their home schools.

"The journey was not without tension, stress, and challenges. At the very beginning, we asked our county's attorney to make a presentation explaining LRE to our staff. Many members of our staff were resistant to this change and feared for their students' futures. They challenged our county vision and questioned the need for a continuum of services. However, in the end, all students successfully integrated into their home schools with appropriate support, including Gilpin Manor."

Today, Gilpin Manor is a school where a very diverse group of children learn together in inclusive classrooms throughout the day. Its mission statement says that its goal is to "support the academic, social, and behavioral development of every child" and it does so with a great deal of pride and success. It serves about 450 children, from preschool to fifth grade, from various backgrounds: 1% of the students are American Indian or Alaska Native, 1% are Asian Pacific Islanders, 31% are African American, and 62% are European American. Among these students, 25% are identified as students with special needs, 1% are English-language learners (ELLs), 2% are homeless, and 67% participate in the free or reduced lunch program.

How can a school like Gilpin Manor be successful with so many students with so many diverse needs and characteristics? Here is what Mrs. Hammer said: "I believe that our greatest strength is that everything that we do is based on what is best for children.… The culture in this building is positive and child centered. You can almost feel the warmth when you enter the building. Teachers support one another and are eager to fill their tool boxes with the strategies and techniques that will meet their students' needs."

Tucked away in the small town of Elkton, Gilpin Manor Elementary School offers an inclusive learning environment for students with a range of abilities. As you will see throughout this book, you can learn a lot about the real-world practices used in Gilpin Manor and the impact that these practices have on its students. Knowing about these practices will make educators more successful at including all students and creating effective, inclusive schools.

## West Hernando Middle School

West Hernando Middle School (WHMS) is located outside the small town of Brooksville, FL, in rapidly growing Hernando County, a suburban area 50 miles north of Tampa. West Hernando enrolls approximately 1,050 students in grades 6–8, and is the county's cluster school for students with disabilities. About 75% of students in WHMS are Caucasian, and the remaining 25% are Hispanic, African American, American Indian/Alaska Native, multiethnic, or Asian. Over 19% of the students in WHMS have disabilities, and 76% qualify for free or reduced lunch.

Rick Markford has been the principal of West Hernando for the past two years. Prior to that time, he was an assistant principal at a high school and a K–8 school. It is noteworthy that most of his prior administrative experience has been in an inclusive high school that is next door to West Hernando. It was at this school that he learned firsthand about inclusion and the importance of a peer-support program for students with more substantial disabilities.

An inclusive philosophy pervades the West Hernando school community in all activities, and is reflected in the following belief statement that guides the work of the school improvement team and all school staff.

WHMS students soar with WINGS (W—Wise choices, I—Innovative learning, N—new challenges, G—Good citizenship, S—Strong positive attitudes). WHMS faculty and staff work to create an environment where all community stakeholders embrace innovative learning strategies and new challenges. We intend to accomplish this by encouraging strong positive attitudes, practicing good citizenship, and recognizing students' wise choices. We are dedicated to providing a rigorous curriculum delivered through research-based programs and practices with differentiated instruction to ensure that all student can and will learn.

The school community at West Hernando is close-knit and supportive of all students. This philosophy is obvious to a visitor when entering the school, as a quote by Booker T. Washington is prominently displayed on the building opposite the entry: "If you want to lift yourself up, lift up someone else." It is also obvious from observing students walking in halls, congregating in the large courtyard that the school building surrounds, or interacting in classrooms. Teachers and students at WHMS are a community of learners who support one another in a range of ways, formal and informal, large and small.

Mr. Markford discusses this emphasis on building relationships and supporting all students as part of West Hernando's culture. "At West Hernando, success is the only option, and the foundation of that success is relationship building. My mantra from my teaching days has always been 'discipline without relationships leads to rebellion.' If you don't have that relationship first, everything else will be impossible or at least a struggle." Mr. Markford goes on to note that at West Hernando, relationships are established with all students early in the school year to provide a foundation for behavioral and academic success.

We'll discuss many of the instructional approaches used at WHMS to support students with disabilities in general education classrooms and as part of the school community throughout the chapters that follow. These activities include co-teaching, peer buddies, differentiated instruction, grouping practices, collaborative teaming, and a range of other effective practices. However, the most powerful aspect of the education students receive at West Hernando Middle School is the dedication of the school staff and students to build a community that supports and includes all students, and the pride that staff and students feel in being part of this special community.

Mr. Markford also emphasizes the importance of teacher collaboration at West Hernando Middle School to support all students. This collaborative work ethic has been especially important as a response-to-intervention (RTI) model has been developed at West Hernando to identify students and provide them with high-quality, tiered instructional support in their classrooms. "Collaboration is one of the key components of RTI at West Hernando as we emphasize working together as a team to develop a system of student support," Mr. Markford states. He also emphasizes the importance of collaboration as part of the many co-taught classrooms at West Hernando. In these classrooms, general and special education teachers work as partners to differentiate instruction for all students. As Mr. Markford notes, "The basis of the inclusion model at West Hernando is the collaboration between co-teachers to develop lesson plans and deliver differentiated instruction."

The success of WHMS can be measured in several ways, including the awards the school has received (an "A" school in Florida for each of the last 5 years, and receiving an award from the Governor of Florida as one of the Top 50 Combination Schools for Making Progress in the state), the rates at which students with a range of disabilities are included in general education classrooms (well above the state average), or by student academic progress, as measured by several state and local tests. By any of these measures, WHMS excels. It also excels as an extraordinary middle school, where all students belong to a school community that provides academic and social support, and where teachers work collaboratively to ensure that success is the only option for every student.

## Heritage High School

Heritage High School, a modern comprehensive high school of approximately 1,340 students, is located in Leesburg, Virginia. Leesburg, the county seat of Loudoun County, is a historic area, having once, during the War of 1812, been the temporary location for the U.S. government and its archives. The areas surrounding the town center are also known for their Civil War battlefields (e.g., Antietam). Located at the far end of the densely populated Washington, DC, and the northern Virginia corridor, Leesburg has experienced tremendous growth in population, particularly among Hispanic and Asian immigrant groups. Reflecting the influx of families from these cultures, Heritage High School is considerably diverse, with 17.8% of its students of Hispanic origin, 12.1% African American, 4.6% multiracial, and 10.2% of Asian descent. The remaining 55.1% are European American. Among all students enrolled, approximately 18% are eligible for free or reduced lunch, and 12.6% have identified disabilities.

Margaret Huckaby, the founding principal of Heritage, had the rare and challenging opportunity of developing the school's administrative structure, climate, and culture from the ground up. With an energetic, positive, and creative interactive style, she garnered considerable input from all the school's stakeholders—from cafeteria workers to psychologists—to develop student-centered approaches and procedures to provide sustained success for all students.

Visitors to Heritage can readily see the results of these efforts: Collaboration and empowerment pervade the school's administrative, instructional, and extracurricular policies and activities. Teams of administrators, teachers, and professional staff work together, ensuring that all students have opportunities to receive supportive instruction and caring related services. This teaming is not left to chance: Margaret and her administrative staff

*(Continued)*

are sensitive to interpersonal dynamics and form teams that build on how teachers' strengths can be combined to improve student outcomes.

Heritage High's efforts at collaborative teaming have resulted in a number of impressive outcomes. The school routinely scores well above the state average on Virginia State Report Card measures, resulting in the all-important designation of meeting adequate yearly progress (AYP). Numerous Advanced Placement courses are offered, and approximately one third of graduating students receive an Advanced Studies Diploma with the coveted Governor's Seal.

Perhaps the most notable element of teaming at Heritage is the day-to-day operation of its inclusive education philosophy. Monitored and nurtured by Dean Susan Hill, special education services are delivered in a variety of ways, depending on the unique needs of the student. Most students with disabilities at Heritage receive services within general education content classrooms. Depending on the instructional and behavioral profile of the student, special education teachers either consult or co-teach with general education content-area specialists. Teachers often use universally designed instructional techniques (adaptations and accommodations that are useful for students with and without disabilities) or curricular supports in lessons and unit plans. In many other cases, classes are actively co-taught by both highly qualified general and special education teachers. Because co-teaching has been a mainstay of the Heritage instructional delivery system since the school opened, it is not viewed as strange or unusual. It is just the way things are done at Heritage.

Some students at Heritage require supplemental supports in addition to what is provided in their general education classrooms. For these students, small-group sessions are arranged and delivered in a private area of the school (i.e., the library) or another classroom. Students with significant disabilities are included in general education classrooms for social, behavioral, and general knowledge exposure and also may spend time receiving direct instruction in separate class settings. Peer Teams are employed to support these students in their classrooms and during extracurricular activities. Based on the success of their programs, Heritage is embracing several new challenges. Students with challenging behaviors who had been placed in segregated day school placements have been returned to Heritage, their neighborhood school, and essential supports and accommodations are being provided. Not surprisingly, these students are achieving academically and socially at heretofore unseen levels of success. The school has also stepped up its efforts in the area of transition to the world of work. In particular, The SWEET (Student Work Experience Enabling Transition) Shop, staffed by students and job coaches, offers valuable job skills training to students while providing time-saving clerical services (e.g., copying, laminating) to teachers and staff.

As in any school, things are not perfect at Heritage. Situations arise that require swift action, creative problem solving, and sometimes difficult decision making. However, with a solid foundation of administrative support, substantive parent involvement, and collaborative teaming, staff feel empowered and supported in their attempts to address the many issues typical of teaching and managing large numbers of developing adolescents.

We provide information that illustrates the diversity of the general education classroom in the following sections. In addition to students with disabilities, students in general education classes who contribute to this diversity and may need **accommodations** include students who are at risk for difficulty in school, students from diverse cultural and linguistic backgrounds, and students identified as gifted and talented.

## Students with Disabilities and Special Education

Special education consists primarily of services and supports that teachers provide to meet the needs of students who are identified with disabilities. Although the categories used to define disabilities vary across states, most use some variation of the federal definitions of disability categories. Table 1.1 includes brief descriptions of the disability categories used by the federal government in the Individuals with Disabilities Education Improvement Act, or PL 108-446 (IDEA, 2004).

As you will note, these disability categories include a broad range of students with abilities and disabilities related to cognitive, social, physical, and sensory skills. To simplify disability categories, some states use more general categories such as *mild-to-moderate*

**Table 1.1**    Disability Categories and Definitions adapted from PL 108-446, IDEA 2004

| Disability Category | Brief Definition |
| --- | --- |
| **Learning disability** (called *specific learning disability* in IDEA, 2004) | Includes students who have difficulty making adequate academic progress in school, especially in basic skill areas such as reading, writing, and/or mathematics. |
| **Speech or language impairment** | Includes students with communication disorders (e.g., difficulty articulating certain speech sounds or difficulty using or understanding words) that affect educational performance. |
| **Other health impairments** | Includes a range of health impairments (e.g., epilepsy, diabetes) that adversely affect a student's educational performance. Attention-deficit/hyperactivity disorder (ADHD) is included as part of this category. |
| **Intellectual disabilities** (called *mental retardation* in IDEA, 2004) | Includes a broad range of students, from those with mild to significant impairments in intellectual and adaptive skills. |
| **Emotional disturbance** | Includes a broad range of students, including those who exhibit aggressive behavior as well as students who have more internalized emotional disorders (e.g., pervasive unhappiness or depression). |
| **Autism** (often referred to as *autism spectrum disorders*) | Includes students who exhibit a developmental disability that significantly affects verbal and nonverbal communication and social interaction. |
| **Multiple disabilities** | Includes students who have disabilities in more than one area (e.g., intellectual disability and blindness, intellectual disability and orthopedic impairment) that often result in substantial impairments and significant educational needs. |
| **Developmental delay** | Includes students who experience delays in physical, cognitive, communication, emotional, or adaptive development. This category is used at the discretion of states, and can be used for students ages 3 through 9. |
| **Hearing impairments and deafness** | Students with hearing impairments have some residual hearing that may be used to understand oral speech. In contrast, children who are deaf lack such residual hearing. |
| **Orthopedic impairments** | Includes students who have physical limitations and may use a wheelchair. These students have a full range of intellectual abilities but may have difficulty demonstrating this ability without specialized supports. |
| **Visual impairments including blindness** | Includes students who are blind and those with significant visual impairments. |
| **Traumatic brain injury** | Includes students who have an acquired injury to the brain caused by an external physical force, resulting in a disability that adversely affects educational performance. This is the only category limited to students who acquire a disability after birth. |
| **Deaf-blindness** | This is the smallest disability category, and includes only individuals with significant educational needs. |

*disabilities* and *significant disabilities*. The mild-to-moderate category includes most students who are identified with learning disabilities and speech or language impairment and some students from other categories (e.g., autism, other health impairments, intellectual disabilities). About 90% of students with disabilities are included in the mild-to-moderate category. The significant disability category includes about 10% of all students, and most students who are identified with multiple disabilities and deaf-blindness fall into this category. In addition, some students in several other categories may be identified with significant disabilities (e.g., autism and intellectual disabilities).

About 11.2% of school-aged students in the United States are identified with disabilities (U.S. Department of Education, 2011). Special education services and supports are specially designed to meet the needs of these students. Several factors make special education "special," including the following (Kauffman & Hallahan, 2005):

- **Intensity.** Special education instruction may involve adjusting the intensity of instruction provided to a student. More time for **direct instruction** and practice are critical elements of more intensive instruction. This may involve a lower teacher–pupil ratio, using strategies such as class-wide **peer tutoring**, **cooperative learning**, or **co-teaching**.
- **Structure.** Students with disabilities are provided with learning conditions that are more organized, explicit, and predictable.
- **Curriculum.** Almost all students with disabilities learn based on the general education curriculum (i.e., the same curriculum as all other students), but many of these students require specialized supports and accommodations to access this material. Some students with significant disabilities require an alternative curriculum for some part of the school day that addresses basic life skills, alternative communication skills, or social skills.
- **Collaboration.** For a successful educational experience, professionals from general and special education must combine their expertise to address the needs of students with disabilities.
- **Monitoring/Assessment.** Teachers monitor the student's progress in an academic area, and adjust instructional methods based on this information. Thus, teachers may use a variety of approaches if a student with a disability has difficulty learning critical elements of the curriculum.

## Other Students Who May Need Support in the General Education Classroom

Many teachers and other school professionals have noted that the effective practices used in inclusive classrooms are beneficial for many students who do not have disabilities but struggle academically or socially. As Cathy Dofka, Director of Special Education in Hernando County Florida (and for West Hernando Middle School), notes, "Inclusion benefits all students academically and socially. Effective teaching methods are good for all students who struggle, not just those with disabilities." Students who benefit from these practices may include students who are at risk for difficulty in school, students from diverse cultural and linguistic backgrounds, and students identified as gifted and talented.

### Students at Risk for Difficulties in School

Students who grow up in poverty are at greater risk than other students for having academic or social difficulty in school. But as you will recognize, many students who have risk factors in their backgrounds do quite well in school; for others, however, these factors may

Many students with and without disabilities need supports to be successful in general education classrooms.

contribute to academic or social difficulties. At least five factors related to growing up in poverty influence student performance in school (Kauchak & Eggen, 2012):

1. Fulfillment of basic needs, including sufficient nutrition and medical care

2. Family stability, including marital stability, and parent frustration related to economic struggle

3. School-related experiences, including exposure to educational experiences (e.g., visits to museums, libraries) or educational activities (e.g., computer classes, dance lessons) outside of school

4. Interaction patterns in the home, including the use of less elaborate language, and the tendency to "tell" rather than to "explain"

5. Parental attitudes and values, including the value placed on getting a good education and reading in the home

Students who are at risk in school are placed in general education classrooms and are the responsibility of general education teachers. Effective practices that are designed to address the needs of all students in inclusive classrooms will often work with these students as well. For example, these practices may improve academic achievement levels, and ensure that many of these students achieve at levels that are similar to classroom peers (Torgesen, 2009).

### Students from Diverse Cultural and Linguistic Backgrounds

Another major component of diversity in general education classrooms relates to students from culturally and linguistically diverse backgrounds. These students often come from backgrounds that are different from that of their teachers, who most often are European American. In 2008–2009 (National Center for Education Statistics, 2009), approximately 45% of all school-aged students in public schools in the United States were from non-European American backgrounds. This includes 21.5% of students who are of Hispanic or Latino origin, and 17.0% who are African American. Further adding to the diversity in classrooms across the United States is the range of languages that are spoken. The U.S. Census Bureau (2008) reported that in 2007, a language other than English was spoken in 20.5% of all homes.

Key considerations for teachers (Ross, Kamman, & Coady, 2011) in meeting the needs of individuals from diverse language and cultural backgrounds include (1) understanding the students' cultural and linguistic backgrounds and (2) learning to adapt teaching based on this information to ensure positive student outcomes.

### Students Who Are Gifted and Talented

Children who are identified as gifted or talented are those who learn academic content in one or more areas much more rapidly than most other students, or have high levels of performance ability in visual or performing arts, creativity, or leadership. In some states, students who are identified as gifted or talented must meet a cutoff for IQ and/or achievement (e.g., an IQ cutoff of 130 or higher) that is significantly higher than average performance by peers (Rosenberg, Westling, & McLeskey, 2011).

Gifted and talented is not a category of disability, and thus is not addressed in IDEA 2004. Identification criteria and funding for programs for these students are typically addressed in state law. The level of support for gifted and talented programs across the United States varies widely. Many general education classrooms have students who achieve at a level that is much higher than most other peers in the class. Some of these students are assigned to separate classes (e.g., advanced mathematics) for part of the school day. Further, many schools have teachers who provide support for gifted and talented students in general education classrooms.

## Concepts That Support Inclusive Practices

Two critical concepts provide the foundation on which inclusive practices are built. These concepts are *normalization* and the *least restrictive environment*.

Biklen (1985) describes one of Bengt Nirje's favorite illustrations of the principle of normalization. While Nirje was president of the Swedish Association for Retarded Children, he asked a group of adults with intellectual disabilities what requests they would make to change national policies that affect their lives. These individuals did not ask to be given special privileges (e.g., preference for housing during housing shortages that all Swedes faced at the time). Presumably, they already received enough treatment that they viewed as "special." Rather, they said that they wanted to go on outings (e.g., shopping) in groups of two or three rather than in large groups. Further, they did not want to go to camps for persons with intellectual disabilities, but rather wanted to vacation like everyone else, in vacation resorts in Europe. In short, persons with intellectual disabilities wanted to be treated like everyone else, and have the same opportunities as others, and did not want to receive special activities or privileges because of their disability. This is the crux of the principle of normalization.

## Normalization

The concept of **normalization** originated in Scandinavia and was initially used to address individuals with intellectual disabilities. This concept has since been applied to all people with disabilities. Bengt Nirje defined *normalization* as making available to all persons with intellectual disabilities "patterns of life and conditions of everyday living, which are as close as possible to the regular circumstances and ways of life of society" (p. 6, cited in Biklen, 1985). This suggests that persons with disabilities should have the opportunity to live their lives as independently as possible, making their own life decisions regarding work, leisure, housing, and so forth. See Figure 1.1 for an example of this principle.

This concept sharply contrasts perspectives on people with disabilities that were previously held by many educators, and continue to be held by much of the general public. For example, people with intellectual disabilities were long held to be "eternal children" who needed to be protected and could not live independently or make their own life decisions. In contrast, the concept of normalization suggests that people with disabilities should be **self-determined**, making their own life decisions, and accorded the dignity of risk, rather than protection, in making decisions about their lives as they grow older, similar to other individuals. Furthermore, a goal of schooling for people with disabilities should be to provide them with the knowledge and skills needed to lead as typical a life as possible and to live as independently as possible, with a job, a place to live in the community, and leisure activities that result in a full, enjoyable, productive life. In short, persons with disabilities should be provided opportunities similar to those that are desired by everyone—to be treated with respect, to be independent, and to be given the opportunity to make their own decisions.

Cathy Dofka, Director of Special Education in Hernando County, Florida, emphasizes the importance of this perspective, when she states, "Students with disabilities have been too isolated in separate classes, where they only see other students with disabilities. They don't learn to get along with other people in these settings. You don't have (a special education) Wal-Mart or Publix. Students with disabilities need to learn to get along in a community with everyone else."

The wide acceptance of the concept of normalization has led to increased expectations for life outcomes and increased value for the lives of people with disabilities. Coupled with these changes, disability rights advocates

Inclusion is intended to provide students with disabilities a school experience that is as typical as possible.

| Figure 1.2 | People-First Language |
| --- | --- |

People-first language emphasizes that persons with disabilities are just that: people who happen to have an intellectual, sensory, physical, or emotional disability. Language should be used that is respectful of people with disabilities. For example, language should not be used to express pity for persons with disabilities, nor should words that are used to describe people with disabilities be used in negative ways. For example, "He's a *retard*." Some terms have taken on such a negative connotation that they are no longer used to describe people with disabilities (e.g., retarded or handicapped, suggesting a person begging with "cap in hand"). A law that was passed in 2010 by the U.S. Congress that eliminates the use of the term *mental retardation* in federal laws, and replaces this term with *intellectual disability* illustrates this. Language describing a disability should be used only when it is necessary to communicate clearly with others. It often isn't necessary to point out that a person has a disability. Suggestions for using respectful, people-first language include:

| People-First Language | Inappropriate Language |
| --- | --- |
| Disability | Handicap |
| Intellectual disability | Retarded or mental retardation |
| John has an intellectual disability. | John is retarded. |
| Nancy uses a wheelchair. | Nancy is wheel-chair bound. |
| | (*Or:* Nancy is confined to a wheel-chair.) |
| Dane has cerebral palsy. | Dane suffers from cerebral palsy. |
| Karson has Down syndrome. | She's Down's. |
| The boy with a learning disability | The learning disabled boy |

*Source:* For more information on people-first language, see www.disabilityisnatural.com and www.r-word.org

have demanded the use of more respectful language when discussing persons with disabilities, including the use of **people-first language**. (For more information regarding people-first language, see Figure 1.2.) Inclusive practices in schools are built on the assumption that the principle of normalization should be applied in school settings; that is, students with disabilities should have school experiences that are as typical as possible, and student differences should be accommodated in as typical a manner as possible. Further, it is assumed that this type of school experience is more effective in preparing a person with a disability to live an independent, self-determined life as an adult.

## Least Restrictive Environment

A second concept that provides support for inclusion in federal law is the **least restrictive environment (LRE)** mandate. This mandate was included in the Individuals with Disabilities Education Improvement Act when the U.S. Congress initially passed this law in 1975 (the law was then called the Education for All Handicapped Children Act). The LRE mandate states, "To the maximum extent appropriate, children with disabilities . . . are educated with children who are non-disabled; and special classes, separate schooling, or other removal of children with disabilities from the regular educational environment occurs only if the nature or severity of the disability is such that education in regular classes with the use of supplementary aids and services cannot be achieved satisfactorily" (PL 108-446, IDEA, 2004, Regulations Part 300, Sec. 300.114).

Although the term *inclusion* is not included in federal law, the LRE mandate creates a presumption in favor of educating students with disabilities in the general education classroom (McLeskey, Landers, Williamson, & Hoppey, 2011). The law is interpreted to mean that every student with a disability has a right to be educated in a classroom with peers without disabilities, if they can succeed in that setting with appropriate supports. Thus, students with

### Pause & Reflect

Is people-first language important, or is it an overreaction to a minor concern? What language have you heard being used in schools to describe people with disabilities? In social settings outside of school? What does this language say about our attitudes toward people with disabilities?

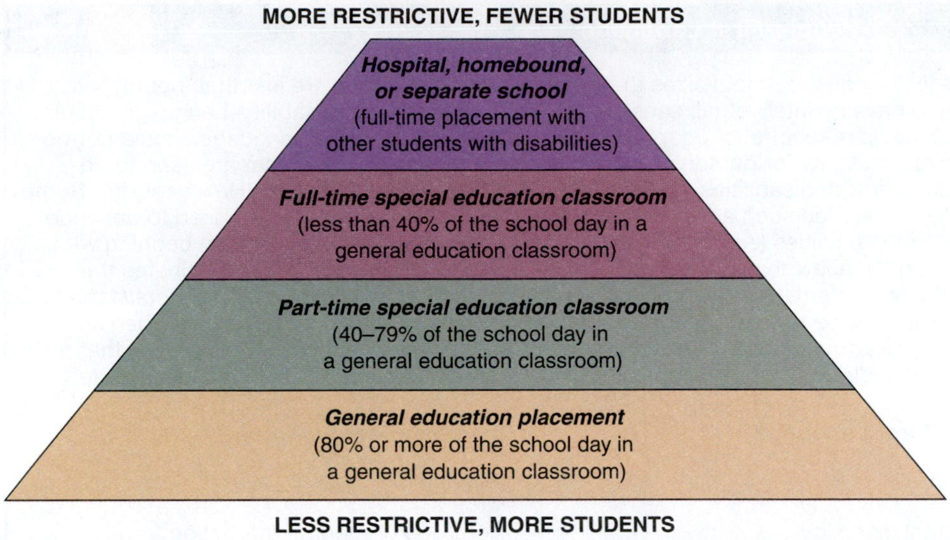

Figure 1.3

Continuum of
Educational Services
for Students with
Disabilities

**MORE RESTRICTIVE, FEWER STUDENTS**

*Hospital, homebound,
or separate school*
(full-time placement with
other students with disabilities)

*Full-time special education classroom*
(less than 40% of the school day in a
general education classroom)

*Part-time special education classroom*
(40–79% of the school day in
a general education classroom)

*General education placement*
(80% or more of the school day in
a general education classroom)

**LESS RESTRICTIVE, MORE STUDENTS**

disabilities should be placed in more restrictive settings (i.e., a separate, special education class, or separate school) only if they do not succeed in the general education classroom with supports and if the separate class can lead to more success than the general education placement.

To ensure that the needs of all students with disabilities are met, IDEA 2004 requires provision of a continuum of services for students with disabilities. Figure 1.3 provides a description of the continuum of services as it exists in most school systems. As you will note in this figure, placement options differ based on the time students with disabilities spend in the general education classroom with peers without disabilities.

### General Education Classroom

Approximately 62% of students with disabilities are provided services in a general education classroom for most of the school day (U.S. Department of Education, 2011). If separate special education services are provided, the student is in a separate classroom for no more than 20% of the school day. This placement includes students who are in a general education classroom full time, with only consultation services from a special education teacher; students who are served in a general education classroom that is co-taught by a general and a special education teacher; and students who are provided short-term, intensive instruction in particular content areas (e.g., reading, learning strategies) or instructional support in specific content areas (e.g., science, social studies) in separate, special education settings.

### Part-Time Special Education Classroom

These settings are often referred to as *resource classes*. In these classes, a small number (e.g., three to eight) of students with disabilities are provided instruction for short periods of time in basic skills (i.e., reading, writing, mathematics), tutorial support in specific subjects, or instruction in the use of learning strategies. Students with disabilities who are in part-time special education classes spend from 40 to 79% of the school day in general education classrooms, and the remainder of the day in a special education classroom. A special education teacher and/or a paraeducator, under the supervision of a special education teacher, provide services in these part-time classes. Approximately 21% of all students with disabilities are served in these settings (U.S. Department of Education, 2011).

### Full-Time Special Education Classroom

Approximately 16% of all students with disabilities are served in full-time special education classrooms on local school campuses (U.S. Department of Education, 2011). These students with disabilities spend most of the school day (60% or more) in a classroom with other students with similar disabilities. These classrooms typically include a small number of students (5 to 10 or more, depending on the severity of the disabilities and the number of professionals in the classroom), a special education teacher, and one or more paraeducators. Students most often served in these settings include those with intellectual disabilities, emotional disturbance, multiple disabilities, deaf-blindness, and autism.

### Hospital, Homebound, Separate Residential Schools, and Separate Day Schools

Students who are educated in these settings attend school full time in a placement other than their neighborhood schools. These schools may be separate settings in the local school system, or residential schools in another city where students live full time during the school year. Separate schools are designed to provide highly specialized instruction and supports for students with disabilities and often include students from a single disability category (e.g., deaf or hearing impaired, blind or visually impaired, significant intellectual disabilities, serious emotional disturbance), or a limited number of disability categories. Approximately 1.5% of all students with disabilities are served in these settings (U.S. Department of Education, 2011).

## What Are Effective Inclusive Programs?

You will note that none of the service-delivery settings we described are called "inclusive." This is because inclusion is not a place or a setting. As we noted previously, inclusion is a philosophy of education, and we define *inclusion* quite simply as including students with disabilities as valued members of the school community. This suggests that students with disabilities *belong* to the school community and are accepted by others; that they actively *participate* in the academic and social community of the school; and that they are given supports that offer them the *opportunity to succeed*. In short, they participate in the school community in ways that are much the same as other students. You will remember that this is just what Annette and Larry Jeffrey wanted for their daughter Grace in her day-care setting, and what most parents want for their children with disabilities. For more about Grace's first year in an inclusive preschool classroom at Gilpin Manor Elementary, see "A View from Her Parents and Teacher: Has Inclusion Been Good for Grace?"

## A View from Her Parents and Teacher

### Has Inclusion Been Good for Grace?

As you will recollect from the vignette that opened this chapter, during the summer of 2010, Grace Jeffrey's parents, Annette and Larry, had a difficult decision to make. Grace became eligible to attend a preschool class in a local elementary school. However, Annette and Larry remained apprehensive. For one thing, they were fearful "that not all children are as respectful as some, and she might be picked on." They also found it difficult to watch when their daughter was with other students who could walk around, given her inability to actively participate. As they pondered these feelings, they realized that they were having difficulty making a decision because they were overprotecting Grace, and that they had to overcome these feelings if she was going to be successful in school. After putting off the decision for several months, they decided to place Grace in Allison Meyer's inclusive preschool class at Gilpin Manor Elementary in the fall of 2010.

Allison Meyer collaborates with a co-teacher and paraeducator to provide inclusive services for students in her preschool classroom of 3- and 4-year-old children. She also works closely with an occupational therapist and a physical therapist to provide push-in services (i.e., professionals come into the general education classroom) for Grace and any other students who need support in the general education classroom, while occasionally pulling students out of the class for specialized services. Grace also receives occasional services from a speech–language pathologist.

*(Continued)*

The approach the teachers take in Grace's inclusive preschool differs dramatically from her experience in day care. The teachers expect Grace to participate in all class activities, and they treat her like every other student whenever possible. Her parents have appreciated this respectful and challenging perspective. "I really appreciate that they don't seclude her when activities occur and her disability comes into play. When children are playing on the playground, they always find a way to include her. They're there to help her participate."

Allison Meyer reports that Grace has flourished during her first year in an inclusive preschool program. "She wants to be mobile . . . she wants to do what the other children are doing. She can keep up with them in conversation and play, so it motivates her to be more independent, to do more on her own like her peers are." During the school day, Grace spends about half an hour in her wheelchair. For the remainder of the day "she's either on the floor crawling or sitting in a chair with the group during whole-group sessions. There are times when she just tells us no (she doesn't want help), and she wants to get herself across the room (by herself)." And she does that successfully.

According to Ms. Meyer, Grace has developed "fabulous social skills. It was difficult at the beginning of the year with her physical restrictions, because it's painful, the therapy she goes through. She gets very shaky." She went on to note that as the year progressed, Grace has gotten more comfortable and has made several friends. "The other kids love her. She had a couple that wanted to 'mommy' her at first, treating her like a baby. But now she's their buddy." Her parents concur that Grace has made many friends who have been "a big motivation for her. I've seen her try things that she wouldn't have tried before. Being with these other children has really just sparked her interest. It's given her that kind of attitude where she says 'I can do this!' She wants to do what the other kids are doing. She tries harder."

After one year in an inclusive preschool class, Annette and Larry Jeffrey feel that Grace has made significant progress in speech and language. "Her speech has come a long way. She did have speech therapy frequently, but now she doesn't need it much. She's been around the other kids and her communication has improved tremendously—and her awareness. Since she's been here I've noticed a lot more questions and interest in different things." They go on to say, "She loves to interact with the other kids. She really enjoys school!"

Perhaps the most important change in Grace that her parents have noticed is her level of motivation and confidence. Being in an inclusive classroom "is a huge motivational factor. She wants to do everything that everybody else is doing. It's almost like, at times, she doesn't realize that she has any limitations. She has those moments when she will get frustrated. But my biggest fear was her loss of confidence. (That hasn't happened as) she fully thinks that she can do everything the other children can do." Grace's parents believe that "if she was with other children (with disabilities) she would just accept her limitations." But in her inclusive classroom, she is "motivated to overcome her limitations" and continues to grow.

As Annette and Larry Jeffrey look to the future, they want to continue to have Grace attend Gilpin Manor and participate in inclusive settings. As their comments suggest, they want her to be a valued member and active participant in the school community, and they want her to receive supports that give her an opportunity to succeed. Such a setting will "give her the confidence to face her disability down the road." Just like any other parents, Annette and Larry want Grace to have as typical a childhood as possible, participating in T-ball and swimming alongside her peers. Annette notes that the children in her class will be her friends and peers in the future as she grows up. She then concludes, "I never saw inclusion when I was growing up, I never went to school with a child with a disability. That was why we were initially apprehensive about it. This is a change in society, and I think it's a good change. I think it will benefit children in the long run. Those with disabilities and those without will learn to understand and respect each other."

Not all educators define *inclusion* in the same way. It is important to seek clarification when discussing inclusion to ensure a clear understanding of the intended meaning of the term. For example, much controversy has surrounded the use of the term **full inclusion**, and the perspective taken by some that all students with disabilities should be included in general education classes for the entire school day (Fuchs & Fuchs, 1994; McLeskey, 2007; McLeskey & Waldron, 2011b). We find that this approach to inclusion is less likely to occur in today's schools, as most parents, teachers, and administrators emphasize that schools be both inclusive and effective in meeting student needs, and this may require occasional separate class instruction that is highly specialized for students with disabilities (McLeskey & Waldron, 2011a). However, there remain instances of inclusion that could be characterized as ineffective or irresponsible. To be successful, inclusion takes careful planning involving teachers, administrators, and parents. Irresponsible and ineffective inclusion occurs when students with disabilities are moved (often quickly)

## Pause & Reflect

Does it surprise you that Annette and Larry Jeffrey want the same things from school for Grace that all parents want? Do you think that persons with disabilities want the same things from life that everyone else wants? What does this say about the importance of inclusive programs in schools?

into general education classrooms with limited planning and little support for general education teachers (e.g., Dymond & Russell, 2004). This results in poor outcomes for many students with and without disabilities, and much frustration on the part of their teachers.

When we discuss inclusive programs or classrooms in this text, we refer to well-designed, effective inclusive programs. We thus make the following assumptions regarding these programs:

1. All students with disabilities are part of the academic and social community of the school. They are valued members of the school, and participate in the school community in much the same way as all other students.

2. Most students with disabilities are educated for most of the school day in general education classrooms, but specialized, highly effective instruction is provided in separate settings as needed to improve student outcomes.

3. Student academic and social progress is monitored to ensure the effectiveness of instruction and improved student outcomes. Educational materials, instruction, and/or placement are changed as needed to improve student outcomes.

4. Resources, including both personnel and materials, are available to provide appropriate supports for students in general education classrooms or separate settings.

5. Time is available to allow general and special education teachers and other professionals to collaboratively plan the delivery of services and their instructional roles. This time is available to plan the inclusive program before it begins, as well as to conduct ongoing planning once the program is implemented.

6. Teachers are provided high-quality professional development to learn new skills needed to provide students with appropriate services.

7. Teachers adapt the general education curriculum to meet the needs of all students. This may include providing supports to ensure access to the general education curriculum or providing alternative curriculum for some students with highly specialized needs.

8. Teachers plan instruction so that most student needs are met as a natural part of the school day.

9. Teachers provide classroom supports in a manner that is natural and unobtrusive. These supports are used with a range of students, not just those with disabilities, and serve to make student differences a natural part of the school day.

10. The rhythm of the school day for students with disabilities is similar to the rhythm of the day for all students. The schedules of students with disabilities are similar to those of other students, and their school day is not readily identifiable because they have a disability.

## Inclusive Programs: Research on Effectiveness

Much controversy has surrounded research on the effectiveness of inclusive programs (Fuchs & Fuchs, 1994; Kavale & Forness, 2000; McLeskey, 2007; McLeskey & Waldron, 2011b). This controversy largely relates to how *effectiveness* is defined. Some have argued that researchers, educators, and policy makers have placed too much emphasis on providing students with disabilities access to general education classrooms in neighborhood schools and too little emphasis on improving student outcomes (McLeskey & Waldron, 2011a). These criticisms have taken on added importance with the passage of the No Child Left Behind (NCLB) Act (2001), which mandates that schools must be held accountable for educational outcomes for all students, including those with disabilities.

Most of the needs of students with disabilities should be met as a natural part of the school day.

With the passage of the NCLB Act, local schools must provide access to the general education classroom for students with disabilities and also ensure improved student outcomes. As we're sure you would speculate based on the previous information in this chapter, as well as any previous experience you've had with inclusion, it is not a simple task to develop an effective, inclusive program. However, research evidence supports the effectiveness of well-designed inclusive programs (e.g., Cole, Waldron, & Madj, 2004; Salend & Garrick Duhaney, 2007). These programs allow students with disabilities to benefit from access to the general education curriculum, as well as to have intensive, focused instruction in critical skill areas (i.e., reading, writing, mathematics) as needed. They also provide a context for developing social skills, making friends, and so forth, that serve to prepare all students, including those with disabilities, for a successful, independent life beyond their school years. Key findings from research regarding the academic and social benefits of inclusive programs are included in Figure 1.4.

As Figure 1.4 reveals, many students with disabilities benefit from well-designed inclusive programs in a range of ways. However, three caveats should be noted regarding this research. First, several studies have revealed that students with disabilities do not make improved academic progress when inclusive programs are not well designed (e.g., Pivik, McComas, & Laflamme, 2002). In fact, these investigations reveal that poorly designed (or irresponsible) inclusive programs may have negative effects on academic outcomes for students with disabilities as well as their peers without disabilities.

A second caveat relates to the fact that no matter how well an inclusive program is designed, most research has revealed that some students with disabilities do not make as much academic progress as we'd like them to make (Lindsay, 2007; McLeskey & Waldron, 2011b). To improve outcomes of inclusive programs, some researchers have studied the use of well-designed, intensive, small-group instruction to support inclusive program placements (Fuchs, Fuchs, Craddock, et al., 2008; Rashotte, MacPhee, & Torgesen, 2001; Torgesen, 2009; Vellutino, Scanlon, Small, & Fanuele, 2006). Several of these programs

| **Figure 1.4** | Research on Academic and Social Outcomes for Students in Inclusive Placements |
|---|---|

- Students with disabilities do at least as well, and often better, on academics in inclusive programs than when they are educated in resource or self-contained classrooms (Cole, Waldron, & Madj, 2004; Freeman & Alkin, 2000; Rea, McLaughlin, & Walther-Thomas, 2002; Ryndak, Morrison & Sommerstein, 1999; Salend & Garrick Duhaney, 2007; Waldron & McLeskey, 1998; Waldron, McLeskey, & Pacchiano, 1999).
- Students with disabilities in inclusive programs benefit from improved work habits, increased self-confidence, increased willingness to take risks, and more on-task or attentive behavior (Dore, Dion, Wagner, & Brunet, 2002; Foreman, Arthur-Kelly, Pascoe, & King, 2004; Waldron, McLeskey, & Pacchiano, 1999).
- Students without disabilities do at least as well, and often better, academically when educated in a well-designed inclusive classroom (Cole, Waldron, & Madj, 2004; Salend & Garrick Duhaney, 2007).
- Given appropriate supports, inclusive placements have been shown to improve self-esteem, increase interactions with other students, improve social competence, develop richer and more long-lasting friendships, and improve social status of students with disabilities (Boutot & Bryant, 2005; Freeman & Alkin, 2000; Salend & Garrick Duhaney, 1999; 2007).
- Students without disabilities benefit socially from inclusion through increased personal growth, appreciation and acceptance of other children, feelings of accomplishment as they provide assistance to others, development of friendships with students with mild and significant disabilities, and improved understanding of disability-related issues (Boutot & Bryant, 2005; Burstein, Sears, Wilcoxen, Cabello, & Spagna, 2004; Carter & Hughes, 2006; Gun Han & Chadsey, 2004; Idol, 2006; Lee, Yoo, & Bak, 2003; Peck, Staub, Galucci, & Schwartz, 2004; Salend & Duhaney, 1999).

have resulted in improved student achievement outcomes. This instruction occurs for brief periods of time, includes small groups of students (e.g., two to five students) who have similar academic needs, focuses on the development of certain academic skills (e.g., **phonemic awareness**), and includes frequent assessment of student progress to ensure the effectiveness of the intervention (McLeskey & Waldron, 2011a).

Finally, research has revealed that simply placing students with disabilities in general education classrooms does not improve their social skills or social status (Carter, Sisco, Brown, Brickham, Al-Khabbaz, & MacLean, 2008). It is often necessary for teachers in inclusive classrooms to provide instruction and support to ensure that social interactions for these students are successful and beneficial. If this does not occur, placement of some students with disabilities in general education classrooms can result in limited social interactions (Rotheram-Fuller, Kasari, Chamberlain, & Locke, 2010) and may produce negative outcomes such as social isolation and negative interactions with peers that are characterized by teasing, negative comments, staring, and isolation (Meadan & Monda-Amaya, 2008; Pivik, McComas, & Laflamme, 2002).

> ## Pause & Reflect
>
> Why do you think students with disabilities often do better academically in general education classrooms? What is it about general education classes that often lead to higher achievement levels?

## Teaching in an Inclusive School

### Your Role as a Teacher

Similar to Allison Meyer at Gilpin Manor Elementary, if you work as a general education teacher in a well-developed inclusive school, you will very likely teach in an inclusive classroom with a range of students with disabilities and other students from diverse backgrounds (e.g., different language and cultural backgrounds) for much or all of the school day. Moreover, in any school, you will likely spend at least part of the day teaching in an inclusive setting. Let's look at the data for a moment to put this in perspective. In an average school with 1,000 students, about 112 students will be identified with disabilities (U.S. Department of Education, 2011). About 101 of these students will have mild disabilities (e.g., learning disabilities, speech and language impairments, and other health impairments such as ADHD), and about 11 will have significant disabilities (e.g., significant intellectual disability, multiple disability).

These data suggest that if you are a general education teacher, it is very likely that you will have one or more students with mild disabilities in your classroom each year. In addition, over a number of years, you will likely have a student with a significant disability in your class. Successfully meeting the needs of students with disabilities presents a range of challenges and requires that school professionals work collaboratively to meet these needs. In the following section, we look at different professionals within schools and see how they can contribute to successful inclusion as they work collaboratively with other professionals.

### General Education Teachers

Whether an elementary or secondary educator, the general education teacher is expected to have knowledge of the curriculum content students are to learn and to design instruction with an expectation that all students will be successful learners. The practice of including students with disabilities in general education classrooms and having them participate in the general curriculum places the general education teacher in a critical role. To ensure that all students succeed, the general education teacher often works closely with the special education teacher and other professionals to develop accommodations and supports for students with special needs.

Although the special education teacher continues to play a central role as students with disabilities are included in general education classrooms, the general education teacher *shares* responsibility for providing instruction to these students. An important ingredient for the general education teacher to succeed in this role is an open mind and a willingness to collaborate. The general education teacher not only needs to help students with disabilities feel that they belong in an inclusive classroom but he also needs to be a catalyst for acceptance of these students among their classmates.

### Special Education Teachers

When working with students with special needs in general education classrooms, special educators may provide direct support to students by working with the general education teacher as a co-teacher. When working as co-teachers, the general and special education teachers plan instruction collaboratively, and their roles in the classroom are often indistinguishable to students because both teach all of the students at different times.

Special education teachers may also provide indirect support by observing in the classroom and working with the general education teacher as a consultant to plan instruction and related supports for students with special needs. This may include collaborative supervision with a general educator of a paraeducator who works in the general education classroom to support students with special needs.

### Related Services Professionals

Related services are special supports required by federal law for students in special education that are necessary to help the students benefit from other school services. For example, if a student needs **physical therapy** to participate in learning activities, then physical therapy must be provided. The result of this legal requirement is that public schools employ many professionals besides general education or special education teachers to serve students with special needs.

According to data from the U.S. Department of Education (2011), U.S. public schools employ approximately 30,800 school psychologists, over 18,000 social workers, about 60,600 speech–language pathologists, more than 7,900 physical therapists, and over 18,000 occupational therapists to work with students with disabilities. Additionally, educational administrators, counselors, rehabilitation specialists, and school psychologists play significant roles in the education of students with special needs. We can't fully describe all of these professionals, but Table 1.2 lists and briefly describes the roles of some who often work with students with special needs.

In many schools where students with special needs are included in general education classrooms, related services professionals work closely with general education teachers to support these students. They do this in several ways. For example, a speech–language pathologist might help the student work on communication skills that allow more participation in class activities; a physical therapist might help design the layout of a classroom so it will be accessible to students with physical disabilities. Similarly, a school psychologist might provide collaborative support to develop a behavior intervention plan to improve a student's challenging behavior.

Paraeducators often provide support to students with disabilities in general education classrooms.

### Paraeducators

Teacher assistants, often referred to as *paraeducators*, *paraprofessionals, educational assistants,* or *teacher aides,* also play a major role in the education of students with special needs in general education classrooms (Giangreco, Suter, & Doyle, 2010). Paraeducators perform a range of instructional and noninstructional activities under the supervision of the special and general education teachers. These activities may include tutoring a student after a teacher provides primary instruction, preparing instructional materials and games, reading a story to students, and a range of other activities (Correa, Jones, Thomas, & Morsink, 2005). When paraeducators are assigned to work with students with disabilities included in general education classrooms, they are in a position

**Table 1.2**  Other Professionals Who Work with Students with Disabilities

| Professional | Role |
|---|---|
| School psychologists | The primary roles of the school psychologist are to conduct assessments used to identify students with disabilities, and work with teachers and other professionals to plan academic and behavioral interventions. |
| Physical and occupational therapists (PTs and OTs) | The PT evaluates, plans, and develops interventions to improve posture and balance; to prevent bodily misformations; and to improve walking ability and other gross-motor skills. The PT works primarily with students who have significant disabilities. The OT has knowledge and skills similar to the PT, but has an orientation toward purposeful activities or tasks such as the use of fine-motor skills related to daily living activities. |
| Speech–language pathologists (SLPs) | The SLP evaluates a student's speech and language skills and develops appropriate goals in this area if necessary. SLPs also may work with students with more significant disabilities to develop alternate or augmentative communication systems. |
| Social workers | Social workers address many issues that occur outside of the school related to families. They often make home visits to help resolve conflicts or improve parent–child interactions, and also may arrange for support from community service agencies. |
| School guidance counselors | Guidance counselors provide support for students in the areas of academic achievement, personal/social adjustment, and career development. |
| Art, music, and recreational therapists | These professionals use their particular specialties to help improve students' functioning in several areas, such as communication or social skills. |

to have a very positive influence, as they help students to learn successfully and adapt to an inclusive setting.

## Teacher Attitudes toward Inclusion

One of the most important issues in determining whether an inclusive program will be effective and sustained over time is support for the program by teachers who are involved in implementing inclusive practices in their classrooms. Working in an inclusive setting can be challenging for a teacher, but many teachers find this work very rewarding.

Consider the perspective of Vicki Eng, a seventh-grade special education teacher at West Hernando Middle School.

Teaching in an inclusive classroom can be frustrating at times, but it's not what's best for me, it's what's best for the child. I can make a difference in their lives during the 7 1/2 hours a day they're in school. And that's what I tell myself; that's what keeps me going. And you know what, we make progress, and it's exciting to make progress, and to know that you've helped somebody by including them and helping them learn. And inclusion is more like real life. You're going to meet people with all types of abilities and disabilities, no matter where you are. That's what we're preparing them for. We're not just teaching them academics; we're preparing them for life.

| Figure 1.5 | Questions Teachers Ask Regarding Inclusive Programs |
|---|---|

1. Do students with disabilities benefit from inclusion?
2. Do students without disabilities benefit from inclusion?
3. Do students with disabilities have a negative effect on the classroom environment, especially related to disruptive behavior?
4. Do teachers have enough time to effectively teach all students?
5. Do teachers have sufficient knowledge and skills to address the needs of all students?
6. Is sufficient professional development available to ensure teachers are well prepared for inclusive classrooms?
7. Do teachers have sufficient instructional materials?
8. Do teachers have sufficient personnel support in the classroom?
9. Do teachers have consultative support for highly specialized student needs from a team of professionals?
10. Do teachers have sufficient time to collaborate with other professionals?

*Sources:* Carter & Hughes, 2006; McLeskey, Waldron, So, Swanson, & Loveland, 2001; Scruggs & Mastropieri, 1996; Waldron, 2007; Werts, Wolery, Snyder, & Caldwell, 1996.

In the well-developed inclusive schools that we described previously, most teachers are strongly supportive of inclusive programs. But how did they get to this point? What were their concerns as they began discussing the development of inclusive programs? When such major changes occur, teachers are often anxious about these changes, and have many questions that need to be answered. This area has been extensively researched, providing insight into the nature of teacher attitudes toward inclusion and factors that influence these attitudes.

Although some have contended that teachers are not supportive of inclusion, most research has not supported this perspective, instead indicating that most teachers support the concept of inclusion and find it a desirable practice (Scruggs & Mastropieri, 1996; Waldron, 2007). However, although most teachers tend to support the concept of inclusion, many have concerns regarding how these programs are implemented. These concerns do not relate to social prejudice or negative attitudes toward students with disabilities, but rather are related to whether general education teachers could make inclusion work in their classrooms and to concerns regarding the substantial changes necessary to make these efforts succeed (Waldron, 2007). These concerns must be addressed if inclusive programs are to succeed and be sustainable. The primary questions teachers express regarding inclusive programs are included in Figure 1.5.

As you can see from reviewing the questions teachers have regarding inclusion, all of the concerns that are raised are justified and reflect teacher concerns regarding whether they will be effective in an inclusive classroom. Indeed, these are questions any responsible teacher should ask when major changes are occurring in classroom practices (Waldron, 2007). For example, teacher concerns regarding whether they are well prepared for teaching students with disabilities and have the resources and support to ensure that the inclusive program succeeds are basic questions that must be addressed when any change occurs in classroom practice. Similarly, when teachers express concern regarding the need for support in addressing highly specialized student needs, it is reasonable to assume that professionals with this knowledge will be available to provide support to the teacher. Indeed, given the diversity of the needs of students with disabilities, it is not possible for any single teacher to have all the knowledge and skills that are needed to meet every student's needs.

As this research suggests, teachers' attitudes toward inclusion provide insight into issues that arise when inclusive programs are developed. When inclusive programs are poorly designed, as has been the case in some settings (e.g., Fox & Ysseldyke, 1997), teachers express justifiable concerns regarding these programs, and raise questions

## Pause & Reflect

Are you surprised that teachers are generally supportive of the concept of inclusion? As you review the questions teachers ask about inclusion in Figure 1.5, do these questions seem reasonable and appropriate? What other questions do you think teachers may ask about inclusion?

about whether students benefit from such programs. However, when these programs are well developed, teachers tend to be very supportive of having students with disabilities in general education classrooms.

# Being a Good Teacher of All Students

There is no doubt that the success of inclusion for students with special needs rests largely on the collaborative efforts of general education and special education teachers. We can state it no more simply than to say that without teachers of high quality who are committed to teaching *all* students, inclusion will not succeed.

So what does it take to be a good teacher for all students? What personal qualities are important? What areas of knowledge and sets of skills must teachers learn? The following attributes and characteristics are necessary for teachers who wish to be effective for *all* their students.

## Appropriate Dispositions

The most effective teachers have a **disposition** that values human differences and recognizes the importance of being a good teacher for *all* students. Teacher dispositions are just as important as having appropriate content knowledge and pedagogical skills. If you plan to be a professional educator, it is critically important that you accept the responsibility to teach all students regardless of their different challenges or special needs.

Having an appropriate disposition means having an outlook that maintains that all students are important and should be valued as members of the learning community. Without such a disposition, the quality of a teacher is likely to be diminished. Effective, inclusive schools, such as those we described at the beginning of this chapter, have a philosophy that supports teachers who have these types of dispositions.

## Positive Teacher Qualities

It is important that teachers reflect on their own qualities to see how those qualities might influence their teaching. Here we examine some critical characteristics that are necessary for an effective teacher. These qualities are important for teaching all students, but are especially important for teaching students with disabilities in inclusive settings.

Caring, fairness, and respect are not just good qualities for teachers to have; they are essential. A teacher who cares about her students is more likely to have a positive impact because most students will be more responsive to a caring teacher (Gay, 2010). Fairness and respect are also important qualities for teachers. Fairness means that teachers provide, without bias, the instruction and support that individual students need. This doesn't mean providing every student the same instruction; rather, it means providing each student with the instruction that particular child needs. Respect means that a teacher interacts with students in ways that acknowledge their humanity and strengths. Stronge (2002) reports that students feel most strongly about the following:

- They expect teachers to treat them as people.
- They view effective teachers as those who do not ridicule students or allow them to be embarrassed in front of their peers.
- They believe effective teachers are fair with regard to gender and ethnicity.
- They see teachers who are consistent and allow students to have input into the classroom as fair and respectful.
- They believe effective teachers offer all students opportunities to participate and to succeed.

Students' interest in what is being taught is affected by the teacher's interest. Teachers who are excited about what they are doing tend to increase the excitement and interest of their students (Stronge, 2002). If you are enthusiastic about teaching, you will likely also be motivated to be an effective teacher. Your enthusiasm and motivation can sustain you through challenging times and improve your students' motivation and interest in what is being taught.

Effective teachers are highly interested and invested in their students' learning as well as their own learning. They constantly search for better ways to teach and more effective ways to support the learning of their students. They collaborate with other professionals, share and receive ideas, and improve their practice by actively seeking and participating in opportunities to learn new teaching strategies. Effective teachers also continue to increase their expectations for student success, and provide students with high-quality instruction to meet these expectations.

Finally, a critically important quality of effective teachers is "personal teaching efficacy," or how teachers view their potential for success. This quality suggests that a teacher can have a positive impact on students, *regardless* of the nature or degree of the students' needs. Teachers with high levels of personal teaching efficacy believe that they can positively influence student achievement and motivation. These beliefs correlate positively with student achievement and with a teacher's willingness to learn to use innovative strategies to be a more effective teacher (Bruce, Esmonde, Ross, Dookie, & Beatty, 2010; Carlson, Lee, & Schroll, 2004). Think for a moment about the importance of these qualities when a teacher searches for ways to successfully include Grace Jeffrey on the school playground, especially when "her disability comes into play" and her wheelchair can become a hindrance to participation.

## Using Evidence-Based Teaching Approaches

Although we cannot underestimate the importance of appropriate dispositions and positive qualities for teachers, this is not enough to be a highly effective teacher. Successful teachers use the most effective teaching strategies. This is especially true when students have learning difficulties or special needs.

To be highly effective, teachers must seek and use strategies that have been proven effective, including evidence-based instructional approaches, whenever possible. **Evidence-based practices** are those that are supported by scientific research and have been shown to demonstrate a high degree of success in terms of student learning outcomes. It is important to note that although some strategies are much more effective than others, no strategy works for *all* students *all* the time. Thus, coupled with the use of effective, evidence-based instructional practices, highly effective teachers monitor the progress their students are making, to make sure that instructional strategies are effective and meet the needs of each student. In short, to be a successful teacher, it is important to learn about the most effective ways to teach your students, while monitoring student learning to ensure that instructional strategies are effective.

## Differentiated Instruction: Making Instruction Work for All Students

Inclusive schools and classrooms work because teachers create instructional settings in which the needs of all students can be met. A term that is widely used and that provides a perspective on assuring that this occurs is **differentiated instruction**, which has been defined as "shaking up what goes on in the classroom so that students have multiple options for taking in information, making sense of ideas, and expressing what they learn" (Tomlinson, 2001, p. 1). In a general sense, all of the methods we discuss in this text relate to differentiated instruction. These are methods that result in significant benefits for all students, but especially those with special needs. For a perspective on how students with disabilities (and others) benefit from these supports as they are educated in inclusive settings, see the following comments from teachers at West Hernando Middle School.

### How Students Benefit from Being Taught in Inclusive Settings

We interviewed several teachers and staff at West Hernando Middle School regarding how students benefit from inclusion. Here's what they had to say.

The school counselor, Susan Dean, said, "All students benefit from inclusion. Students who have difficulty with academics have the opportunity to work with their same-age peers, and they are challenged more to be the best that they can be." Vicki Eng, a seventh-grade special education teacher, added, "Inclusion teaches all students tolerance and sensitivity. They learn that everybody has something they're good at, and some things they're not so good at. Everybody has strengths and weaknesses. And we try to help them recognize what their strengths and weaknesses are." Susan Dean continued by stating, "Including students with more significant disabilities benefits all students even more. The general education students who volunteer in our peer program, for example, gain by learning about these students, knowing these students, understanding these students. They gain as much as the students with disabilities."

Several teachers noted benefits of placement in general education classrooms that would not occur if students with disabilities were educated in a separate setting. For example, a sixth-grade teacher, Lisa Grover, stated that inclusion helps "kids realize that everyone is different. When they are all in general education classrooms, they tend not to make fun of one another. Kids can be very cruel to one another. When the kids with disabilities are separated, that's when the kids tend to pick on them. When they're included in their classrooms, you see those kids trying to help them out a lot."

Several teachers noted that the quality of the instruction in the general education classroom is often better. For example, behavior specialist Eileen Walls stated, "Even the best special education teacher can never reproduce the richness of what happens in [the general education] classroom in terms of class discussion and student interaction, the stuff that naturally occurs. You have more teachable moments that occur in a class discussion in a regular class, when the kid finally gets it."

Finally, everyone we talked with mentioned the importance of being in a class with models for good academic and social behavior. For example, many teachers at West Hernando Middle School noted the importance of providing students with the opportunity to model appropriate strategies to gain knowledge and improve outcomes. Eileen Walls eloquently illustrated this point, as she said,

> When you take a group of kids and put them with others with similar types of problems, they think that's what normal is. Kids with disabilities in separate settings learn from other kids in that setting. Take a kid who's not a desk thrower and put him in a class with desk throwers, he's going to become a desk thrower. When that's the only thing you know in the separate environment, you don't have a chance to practice more appropriate behaviors to behave or learn, or know more appropriate behaviors. You develop a self-fulfilling prophecy that is so destructive in preventing kids from reaching their potential. That's a very strong casualty of separate classes, and an argument for more inclusion.

## Summary

This chapter addressed the following topics:

### Inclusion is for all students

- Inclusion is for all students with disabilities, including those in all 13 categories of disability in IDEA 2004, ranging from mild-to-moderate disabilities, such as learning disabilities and speech and language impairments, to significant disabilities, such as deaf-blindness and multiple disabilities. Some categories include students with disabilities that range from mild-to-moderate to significant disabilities, including intellectual disabilities and autism.

- Other students may need accommodations or supports in a general education classroom, including students who are at risk for difficulties in school related to growing up in high poverty backgrounds, and students from culturally and linguistically diverse backgrounds.
- Students who are gifted or talented may achieve at a level that is much higher than most of their peers and may need accommodations in the general education classroom.

### Concepts that support inclusive practices

- The key concept underlying inclusion in federal law is the least restrictive environment (LRE), which requires that all students be educated with typical peers to the maximum extent appropriate.
- *Normalization* is a concept that has influenced inclusion. This concept suggests that all persons with disabilities should have the opportunity to live their lives in as typical a manner as possible.

### What are effective inclusive programs?

- Not all educators define *inclusion* the same way. Some educators have developed programs that were called "inclusive" that did not meet student needs.
- Effective inclusive programs are designed to ensure that all students with disabilities are part of the academic and social community of the school.
- Effective inclusive schools are designed to ensure that teachers receive needed support and all students benefit.
- Research reveals that the academic outcomes for students with disabilities are at least as good, and sometimes better, in well-designed, effective, inclusive settings.
- Simply placing a student in an inclusive setting does not improve social outcomes. Teacher instruction and support are needed to improve social outcomes.
- Students without disabilities often benefit socially from inclusive placements, and do at least as well, and often better, academically in well-designed inclusive classrooms.

### Teaching in an inclusive school

- Most general education teachers will have one or more students with disabilities included in their classes.
- General education teachers share responsibility with special education teachers for educating students with disabilities in their classes.
- Special education teachers are responsible for providing intensive, specialized instruction to students with disabilities to improve performance in basic skill areas.
- Related services professionals (e.g., school psychologists, speech–language pathologists, physical therapists) are available to provide support to students with disabilities who are educated in inclusive settings.
- Paraeducators often work with students with disabilities and general education teachers in inclusive settings.
- Most general education teachers support the concept of inclusion but have concerns regarding how these programs are implemented.
- Concerns of general education teachers relate to the need for appropriate levels of support to meet student needs and to ensure that all students benefit from inclusion.

### Being a good teacher of all students

- Good teachers' classroom practice reflects qualities such as caring, fairness, respect, enthusiasm, motivation, and dedication.
- Good teachers have high expectations regarding their ability to teach all students.
- Good teachers use effective, evidence-based teaching approaches.

## Addressing Professional Standards

At the end of each chapter we will include professional standards that are addressed in that chapter. These standards are used to design teacher education programs, and are widely viewed as necessary for effective teaching. Standards are taken from the Council for Exceptional Children (CEC), the largest organization for special education teachers and other professionals in the United States.

Standards addressed in Chapter 1 include:

**CEC Standards:** (1) foundations, (2) development and characteristics of learners, (3) individual learning differences.

---

### MyEducationLab

Go to the topic Inclusive Practices in the **MyEducationLab** (www.myeducationlab. com) for *Inclusion*, where you can:

- Find learning outcomes for Inclusive Practices, along with the national standards that connect to these outcomes.
- Complete Assignments and Activities that can help you more deeply understand the chapter content.
- Apply and practice your understanding of the core teaching skills identified in the chapter with the Building Teaching Skills and Dispositions learning units.
- Examine challenging situations and cases presented in the IRIS Center Resources.
- Check your comprehension on the content covered in the chapter with the Study Plan. Here you will be able to take a chapter quiz, receive feedback on your answers, and then access Review, Practice, and Enrichment activities to enhance your understanding of chapter content.

# Inclusion: Historical Trends, Current Practices, and Tomorrow's Challenges

## KEY TOPICS

**After reading this chapter you will:**

- Know how the evolution of inclusive education has been shaped by social history, civil rights, and parent advocacy.

- Understand how four major legislative acts—the Individuals with Disabilities Education Improvement Act (IDEA 2004), No Child Left Behind (NCLB), Section 504 of the Rehabilitation Act, and the Americans with Disabilities Act (ADA)—serve as the legal foundation for special education and inclusion.

- Know the elements of multi-tiered response-to-intervention frameworks and understand how they contribute to growth and improvement of today's inclusive education efforts.

- Be able to identify two issues that challenge educators and policy makers seeking to improve inclusive educational programs: adequate yearly progress (AYP) for students with disabilities and the need for a highly qualified workforce.

# chapter 2

## A VIEW FROM A PARENT

### Sarita Celebrates Inclusion

Sarita could hardly believe her ears. At the family dinner table, her daughter Krista, then a tenth grader at Heritage High School, mentioned that for the first time in her life she was enjoying school. What were the reasons for Krista's positive feelings? She had a group of friends and was participating in extracurricular activities. Most important, she didn't feel strange when she needed help in her classes. Many of the subject-area classes were co-taught by two teachers, and students had easy access to support and assistance within the usual procedures of the classroom. Sarita had suspected that things were going well. Krista seemed less depressed and was no longer making excuses to avoid going to school. Morning discussion now centered on what Krista wanted to wear rather than on why it was essential that she attend school.

What accounted for Krista's change in attitude and behavior? Sarita believes it is the inclusive education program at Heritage High School. Krista was referred for special education services when she was a second grader due to reading and attention problems. She was identified as having a learning disability and was placed in segregated pullout programs for significant portions of the school day. Although Krista was "mainstreamed" for many of the nonacademic parts of the school day, she didn't feel part of the school community. She always felt sick and had few friends and limited opportunities to participate in the school's social activities.

This changed when Krista entered Heritage. Both Krista and Sarita were impressed with the faculty and staff's commitment to providing support in subject-area classes. In some classes (e.g., math, biology), support was provided through co-teaching. In others, peer-tutoring structures were developed, leading to relationships that benefited Krista academically and socially. Sarita was especially impressed with the level of support provided by the administration: A case manager monitored Krista's progress in all her classes and, when necessary, study halls were provided to supply intensive one-to-one instruction. The administration was also receptive to new ideas and welcomed Sarita's observations of Krista's progress and attitude toward school.

Sarita noticed that inclusion at Heritage provided Krista with a comprehensive and caring system of supports. Seeing the difference in her daughter's behaviors and attitude toward school has made her a believer in this method of special-education service delivery. "Inclusion is the best program for a student with learning difficulties to achieve academically, develop a social life, and build self-esteem. A well-developed inclusive model shows that people really care and that you are really part of the community."

**MyEducationLab**

Visit the MyEducationLab for *Inclusion* to enhance your understanding of chapter concepts with a personalized Study Plan. You'll also have the opportunity to hone your teaching skills through video and case-based Assignments and Activities, building Teaching Skills and Disposition lessons, and IRIS Case Studies.

# Introduction

The U.S. society's desire for knowledgeable and responsible citizens is reflected in the numerous laws and public policies that promote education for the nation's children and youth. For example, as early as 1918, every state in the union passed compulsory school attendance laws providing, and requiring, a free public education for all children (Yell, Rogers, & Rogers, 1998). Ironically, these *universal* attendance laws did not apply to all students. Those with disabilities could be, and often were, denied the opportunity to receive their free public *compulsory* education. Until the 1970s, access to school could be withheld if a school district claimed it was unable to accommodate a student with special needs—an exclusionary practice that was usually upheld in the courts.

Two cases illustrate the extreme insensitivity of these exclusionary practices (Yell et al., 1998). In 1919, the Wisconsin Supreme Court allowed the exclusion of a fifth-grade student who had a disability that caused speech problems, facial contortions, and drooling. The reasons for the exclusion: The school district claimed that the student's presence *nauseated* teachers and students and impacted discipline and academic progress negatively. Although the student was not hearing impaired, the school district recommended that the student attend a special day school for students who were deaf. In 1958, the Supreme Court of Illinois held that the state's compulsory attendance laws did not apply to those whose limited intelligence precluded the ability to benefit from a good education. This included students who were considered "feeble-minded" and "mentally deficient." The message was clear: Those with intellectual disabilities would not benefit from education, so why provide one to them.

Fortunately, several significant legislative acts, including the landmark PL 94-142, the Education for All Handicapped Children Act of 1975 (EAHCA), provide access to a free and appropriate public education (FAPE) for all children regardless of their disability status. No longer are students denied an education because of their special needs and behavioral characteristics. The *total* exclusion of students with disabilities from educational settings was stopped by the historic litigation and federal legislation of the 1970s.

However, access to schooling alone does not automatically result in an appropriate education. Even though students with disabilities are provided full access to schools, practices in some schools actually limit full participation in appropriate academic and social activities. Some students with disabilities are *functionally excluded,* meaning that they occupy the same locations as their peers without disabilities, but they do not truly participate in the academic and social activities of the school. Moreover, they are not given supports that offer an opportunity to thrive and succeed in general education settings (Turnbull, 1993). The students with disabilities appear superficially to be part of the general education environment but are never fully integrated into the academic and social fabric of the school community. Unfortunately, many of these practices are so institutionalized and subtle that well-intentioned educators fail to notice when they occur. Consider how the following examples of placement in the general education environment do not allow for truly inclusive educational opportunities:

- Placing students with behavioral challenges in segregated classrooms with few opportunities to interact with normally achieving peers
- Assigning secondary students with disabilities to large subject area, general education classes with no organizational supports, peer assistance, or curricular accommodations
- Relegating students with disabilities to segregated lunch, physical education, and recess periods and locations that are removed from their age-appropriate peers
- Placing elementary students with disabilities in general education classrooms and having a special-education teacher provide them with instruction in separate groups away from their classmates

Although today we have clearly moved beyond the total exclusion of students with disabilities, more work

**Pause & Reflect**

Think of an instance when you were part of an activity or event but felt that you were *functionally excluded* from full participation. Describe the elements of the situation that made you feel uncomfortable or uneasy. Could you have been made to feel truly part of the activity? How?

needs to be done to minimize instances of functional exclusion. As noted by Sarita, the parent in our opening vignette, her daughter Krista believed she was truly part of her subject-area classes when she was provided with naturally occurring **peer tutoring**. Clearly, access to inclusive environments is not enough to ensure belonging and academic success. We believe that the first steps in facilitating true involvement—the *functional inclusion* of all students—are an understanding of the evolution of special-education service delivery, the legal foundations of inclusive special education, and an awareness of emerging issues and controversies that impact typical school and classroom practices.

# The Evolution of Inclusive Special Education Services

The current delivery of inclusive education has been shaped by special education's rich social history, landmark litigation and legislation, significant political events, and the courageous advocacy of parents. An awareness of the evolution of inclusive education will enable you to understand why practices such as appropriate dispositions, collaboration, and positive behavioral supports (discussed in later chapters) are essential to successful student outcomes.

## From Segregation to Inclusion

Until the 1960s, most students with disabilities were educated in settings that were segregated from peers without disabilities for most or all of the school day. Those educated on regular school campuses were typically isolated from other students in separate wings or in basements of the main school building. Others were educated in separate schools that served only students with disabilities (McLeskey, 2007). Many criticized these segregated settings as ineffective, stigmatizing, and resulting in low expectations for those students (Deno, 1970; Dunn, 1968; Johnson, 1962). Furthermore, a disproportionate number of students who were identified with mild disabilities and educated in these settings were poor children from diverse backgrounds. Such findings led to a call to mainstream students with mild disabilities into general education classrooms for at least part of the school day (Dunn, 1968).

As educators were mainstreaming students with disabilities, they made several assumptions regarding these students and their education (see Figure 2.1). Mainstreaming addressed only students with mild disabilities, not those with severe disabilities. Moreover, students with disabilities were assumed to belong to special education and were simply visiting the general education classroom, primarily to improve their social skills or improve academic skills if they could work at grade level. The responsibility for student outcomes remained with special education.

At the same time, policies of **normalization** and **deinstitutionalization** were being implemented (Nirje, 1972; Wolfensberger, 1972). Normalization required agencies to provide persons with disabilities with living and learning experiences that were as "normal" as possible. Skills to be taught were those that would allow greater independence and life patterns that were parallel to those of people without disabilities. And the instructional procedures for teaching these skills were to be as close to

Placing students with disabilities in general education classes without organizational supports, peer assistance, or curricular accommodations is not effective inclusion.

Figure 2.1

Comparisons of Assumptions Under-lying Mainstreaming and Inclusion

> **Mainstreaming** addresses the needs of students with mild disabilities.
>
> **Inclusion** addresses the needs of all students with disabilities who benefit from inclusive placements.
>
> **Mainstreaming** is provided to students as a privilege.
>
> **Inclusion** is a student's basic right.
>
> General education teachers volunteer to teach students with disabilities who are **mainstreamed.**
>
> All general education teachers are expected to teach students with disabilities who are **included.**
>
> To be **mainstreamed,** students are expected to fit into the general education classroom.
>
> The general education classroom is changed to support students who are **included.**
>
> Special education is responsible and accountable for students who are **mainstreamed.**
>
> When students are **included,** general and special education share responsibility and accountability.

"normal" as possible. The policy of deinstitutionalization resulted in a decline in the number of persons living in large residential institutions and an increase in the number living with their families and in smaller community-based residences. Community facilities were intended to be homelike and included foster homes, group homes, intermediate-care facilities, and sheltered apartments. In these smaller facilities located in neighborhood communities, individuals were to receive services traditionally provided only in the institutions (Westling & Fox, 2009).

By the 1980s, advocates and researchers were concerned about the effectiveness of mainstreaming (Reynolds, Wang, & Walberg, 1987; Stainback & Stainback, 1984). Even with efforts such as the **regular education initiative (REI)**—a largely special-education effort to have general and special-education teachers share the responsibilities of educating students with disabilities in mainstream settings (Will, 1986)—concerns regarding mainstreaming continued, as a result of the following:

- Students with disabilities were not making adequate academic progress.
- Only the needs of students with mild disabilities were addressed; thus, many students with more severe disabilities did not have access to the general education classroom and curriculum.
- Few changes were occurring in general education classrooms to accommodate for the needs of students with disabilities.
- Additional collaboration was needed between general and special education to provide more support for students with disabilities in general education classrooms.

In response to these concerns, the inclusion movement began in the mid-1980s, resulting in major changes (see Figure 2.1). You will note that the assumptions underlying *inclusion* differ significantly from those underlying *mainstreaming.* For example, advocates of inclusion consider the education of students with disabilities in general education classrooms to be a fundamental right for all students with disabilities and the instruction of these students to be the responsibility of every general education teacher. Furthermore, proponents of inclusion assume that general and special educators will share the responsibility and accountability for educating students with disabilities and that students with disabilities will be as much a part of the educational community of the school as are other students who do not have disabilities. Finally, the collaboration between general and special educators is expected to ensure that students with disabilities receive appropriate supports, ensuring adequate progress academically and socially.

Increasing numbers of students with disabilities have been included in general education classrooms since the mid-1980s (McLeskey, Landers, Williamson, & Hoppey, 2011; Williamson, McLeskey, Hoppey, & Rentz, 2006), but controversy continues to surround the movement. The major concern relates to positions taken by some advocates regarding **full inclusion** (Fuchs & Fuchs, 1994; Kauffman, 1993; McLeskey, 2007). Full inclusion suggests that all students with disabilities be educated for the entire school day in general education classrooms. In recent years, however, educators have placed less emphasis on full inclusion and more on including all students with disabilities as members of the school's academic and social community. Furthermore, policy makers and administrators have increasingly emphasized student outcomes as a key element of inclusive efforts.

## Civil Rights and Parent Advocacy

The **civil rights movement** of the mid-20th century had a monumental effect on the lives of many members of disenfranchised groups, including individuals with disabilities. Until the mid-1970s, no guarantee existed that a child with a disability would receive a free and appropriate public education. Schools educated only one in five children with disabilities, and many states had laws that explicitly excluded students with certain types of disabilities. Mirroring the earlier efforts of civil rights workers for African American schoolchildren, advocates for people with disabilities used the schools as a prominent battleground in efforts to achieve equal rights and due process of law. In fact, many of the original decisions rectifying the exclusion and segregation of students based on race were expanded to include students with disabilities (Murdick, Gartin, & Crabtree, 2002).

In the courtroom, as well as in the court of public opinion, parents and civil rights advocates took on state governments and school districts to ensure that students with disabilities had access to a FAPE (Weintraub & Abeson, 1976). Using the precedent of *Brown v. Board of Education* of Topeka, Kansas (1954)—in which the U.S. Supreme Court ruled that African American students attending segregated schools were not receiving an equal education—disability rights advocates made the case that access to an appropriate education was being denied because of the students' disabilities. The *Brown* plaintiffs and those advocating for children with disabilities were very similar. Both groups (1) challenged segregation in education, (2) proved they were denied equal educational opportunities, and (3) advanced an enduring public policy that views the function of school as meaningfully educating *all* students (Turnbull, Stowe, & Huerta, 2007).

One constant in the enduring legal processes of gaining access to education for students with disabilities has been active parent advocacy. Although many parents would have preferred to invest this time into their own quality-of-life efforts (Soodak et al., 2002), significant legislative gains such as the original passage of EAHCA (PL 94-142) would not have been possible without these efforts. Today, it is likely that you will encounter many parents of students with disabilities actively advocating for the inclusion of their children. The majority of parents of students with disabilities support inclusion and believe it contributes positively to

Active parent advocacy has been a major factor in securing inclusive programming for students with disabilities.

social, emotional, and academic development (Duhaney & Salend, 2000). With greater access to appropriate role models and friendships, parents like Sarita at Heritage High School see inclusion contributing positively to their children's socialization, self-image, happiness, and confidence.

You will also find that parents have several realistic concerns about inclusion. Among the more prominent issues are the availability of qualified personnel and the ability of teachers in general education settings to provide needed supports. Many parents, particularly those of children with severe disabilities, fear that too many educators do not have the necessary skills and resources to implement inclusion effectively and that there is no long-term plan or vision connected to the delivery of services. Consequently, many parents believe they must be extremely vigilant, ensuring that their children are not mistreated or isolated, or just not receiving the services to which they are entitled when placed in general education settings (Duhaney & Salend, 2000; Erwin & Soodak, 2000; Meaden, Sheldon, Appel, & DeGrazia, 2010).

## Current Status of Inclusive Practices

Today, most students with disabilities are educated in their neighborhood schools and in general education classrooms. Table 2.1 represents the extent to which students who are

**Table 2.1** Percentage of School-Aged Students with Disabilities, Ages 6–21, Served in Different Placement Settings in the 2008–2009 School Year

| | Percentage of Time Spent Inside of General Education Classroom | | | |
|---|---|---|---|---|
| **Disability** | **Most of the School Day (80% or more)** | **Some of the School Day (40%–79%)** | **Limited Amount of the School Day (less than 40%)** | **Separate School/ Residential or Correctional Facility/Private School/ Home-Hospital Setting** |
| Speech–language | 86.5 | 5.7 | 4.7 | 3.1 |
| Developmental delay | 61.8 | 20.1 | 16.2 | 1.9 |
| Visual impairment | 62.2 | 13.7 | 12.7 | 11.4 |
| Other health impairments | 60.4 | 24.4 | 11.2 | 4.0 |
| Learning disabilities | 61.6 | 27.9 | 8.4 | 2.1 |
| Orthopedic impairment | 51.5 | 16.5 | 24.7 | 7.3 |
| Hearing impairment | 53.7 | 17.1 | 15.7 | 13.5 |
| Traumatic brain injury | 45.0 | 23.1 | 23.0 | 8.9 |
| Emotional disorders | 39.3 | 19.3 | 23.1 | 18.3 |
| Autism | 36.3 | 18.2 | 35.7 | 9.8 |
| Deaf-blindness | 31.2 | 16.3 | 28.5 | 24.0 |
| Intellectual disabilities | 17.3 | 27.0 | 48.2 | 7.5 |
| Multiple disabilities | 13.7 | 16.4 | 45.9 | 24.0 |
| **All disabilities** | **58.5** | **21.4** | **14.9** | **5.2** |

*Source:* U.S. Department of Education (2011).

identified with different disabilities are served in inclusive or in more restrictive settings. These data reveal that students with mild disabilities (i.e., speech–language impairments, developmental delays, visual impairments, other health impairments, and learning disabilities) are educated in general education classrooms for most or all of the school day. Students who are placed in the more restrictive settings include those who are identified with multiple disabilities, intellectual disabilities, deaf-blindness, autism, and emotional disturbance.

On average, across the United States, about four of every five students with disabilities spend a substantial portion of the school day (40% or more) in a general education classroom; the remaining one in five

Most students with disabilities—about 80%—spend a sizable portion of their school day in general education settings.

students spends very little time in a general education classroom (U.S. Department of Education, 2011). Wide variation, however, exists among states, local school districts, and even across schools within districts in the percentage of students with disabilities who are educated in inclusive settings. For example, up to 87% of all students with intellectual disabilities are educated in general education settings for most of the school day in one state, but in other states, very few of these students are educated in these settings (Williamson et al., 2006). The rate of inclusion appears to depend on the extent to which inclusion is a priority in the individual schools and districts.

Clearly, more and more students are being educated in neighborhood schools and general education classrooms. Nonetheless, as many parents of students with disabilities know, access—and the official numbers used to index integration into the inclusive environment—is not enough. As mentioned earlier, access to general education settings must not functionally exclude students from successful participation but must truly result in significant involvement in the school community. To meet this goal, inclusion cannot be viewed strictly as a disability issue. Efforts to improve services and include students with disabilities require initiatives that benefit all children and schools (Bricker, 2000; Lee, Soukup, Little, & Wehmeyer, 2009).

Dianne Ferguson, a special education scholar and parent of a child with a disability, related how her thinking of inclusion changed as a result of her family's efforts to secure a more "normalized" school experience for her son Ian (Ferguson, 1995). With severe and multiple disabilities, Ian was in self-contained classrooms with few opportunities for contact with nondisabled peers. Through her research and advocacy, Ferguson found that typical efforts to mainstream or integrate students with disabilities did little to fully facilitate full participation in the learning community. Inclusion efforts merely relocated the special education but did little to change the perception that the students were "irregular," even when they were in "regular" classrooms. The challenge was to find out how to create an environment where a person with a disability is truly part of the community (an experience Ian had when in a drama class).

Ferguson realized that if inclusion were to really work, tactics would need to change. Rather than merely "adding on" to the existing systems to accommodate a few students,

## Pause & Reflect

How would you convince others that inclusion is not only a disability "problem" that requires solving? What strategies would you employ to ensure that inclusion is viewed as a core value applied to all students and integrated in schools?

inclusion had to be viewed as a core value that applied to all students, regardless of disability status. For inclusion to really work, it must be viewed as

> a process of meshing general and special education reform initiatives and strategies in order to achieve a unified system of public education that incorporates all children and youth as active, fully participating members of the school community; that views diversity as the norm; and that ensures a high quality education for each student by providing meaningful curriculum, effective teaching, and necessary supports for each student. (Ferguson, 1995, p. 285)

## A View from the Principal

### Margaret Huckaby Embraces Inclusion

Ask Margaret Huckaby, principal of Heritage High School, about her inclusive educational philosophy and she will tell you in no uncertain terms that every student is worth *a best effort*. Where did this strong conviction come from? A former vocal music teacher, Margaret taught students with and without disabilities, and found that the presence of a disability did not prevent a student from enjoying and benefiting from choral activities. In fact, she found that with the right mix of accommodations, encouragement, and peer support, her students regularly assisted one another in order to improve the overall quality of the group's performance. As with the adolescents on the popular television program *Glee*, Margaret's students were able to look beyond their differences and work together toward a common goal. By focusing on student strengths, modeling cooperative problem-solving strategies, and being sensitive to interpersonal dynamics, Margaret found that her *best effort* was paying off. Among the many positive outcomes: Students with disabilities, many of whom had experienced problems making friends, were becoming more socially active in and out of school, were behaving more appropriately, and were actually enjoying school.

As she moved on to administrative positions, Margaret found that several of the team-building strategies she applied as a vocal music teacher with students were useful in advocating her inclusive education philosophy with sometimes reluctant faculty and staff. For example, when faced with the rare and daunting opportunity of opening the newly constructed Heritage High School (HHS), Margaret encouraged her new teaching staff to (1) infuse essential notions of equity and opportunity into an inclusive mission statement for the school and (2) develop explicit processes that ensured that all students would have opportunities to receive a quality education—their *best effort*. To complete these challenging activities, she emphasized the importance of administrators, teachers, and professional staff being able to work together in a climate of trust and mutual respect. To promote these values, a number of staff retreat activities—from bowling tournaments to scavenger hunts—were scheduled. These activities provided faculty and staff with opportunities to experience the value of working together toward a common goal. Over time, the faculty and staff began to trust one another, and realized that they could address a wide range of academic and behavioral challenges in the general education environment. Confidence and trust were also promoted by Margaret's insistence on frequent open communication about the "nuts and bolts" necessary for successful inclusive programming implementation.

How did all of this turn out? Nine years after the opening of HHS, inclusion is no longer a novelty for teachers or an embarrassing stigma for students. Like drivers' education, advanced placement classes, and spring football practice, the full range of inclusive programming techniques—co-teaching, consultation, behavioral support, and universal design for learning—are essential components of the fabric of the HHS experience. For Margaret Huckaby, there are a number of sources of satisfaction. Hearing from parents, such as Sarita, that the school's emphasis on supportive inclusion has led to meaningful improvements in their family's life is very gratifying. Still, Margaret's greatest source of satisfaction comes each June, during commencement ceremonies, when she has the opportunity to confer full academic diplomas to students with disabilities. Margaret knows that these are students who would be in a far different place if they were not seen as worth *a best effort*.

# Legal Foundations of Special Education and Inclusion

Four major legislative acts influence how schools structure, and how individual teachers deliver, special education services in inclusive schools:

- The Individuals with Disabilities Education Improvement Act of 2004 (IDEA 2004)
- The No Child Left Behind (NCLB) Act of 2001
- Section 504 of the Rehabilitation Act
- The Americans with Disabilities Act (ADA)

In our discussions of each of these acts, we describe the major components of the legislation and consider how these laws impact the delivery of inclusive education programs.

## Individuals with Disabilities Education Improvement Act (IDEA 2004)

Generally, IDEA 2004 is regarded as the most significant piece of legislation supporting the education of children and youth with disabilities. Because of IDEA, most children and youth with disabilities are educated in their neighborhood schools in general education classrooms with their nondisabled peers. Moreover, postschool employment rates for people with disabilities, although not where they should be, are twice those of older adults with similar profiles who did not have the rights and protections of the law. Even more heartening are the numbers of students with disabilities who attend college; compared to 1978, the number of first-year college students with disabilities has more than tripled (U.S. Department of Education, n.d.).

IDEA 2004 updates and amends earlier legislation that served as the legal basis for the education of those with disabilities: EAHCA of 1975; the 1983 and 1986 EAHCA amendments; and the Individuals with Disabilities Education Act (IDEA) of 1990, 1992, and 1997. Reauthorizations of the law have sought to improve the law by strengthening the role of parents, encouraging nonadversarial resolution of disputes, and requiring participation in the general education curriculum and state- and district-wide assessments. "Just the Facts: IDEA 2004" provides an overview of the major components of the current IDEA. "Just the Facts: Evolution of 1975 Legislation" illustrates how the original 1975 legislation evolved into the current statute.

In addition to evolving legislation, litigation (legal cases in which a judge or a jury interprets the law in situational disputes) influenced the initial passage and prompted improvements in the provisions of IDEA 2004. Six legal principles have had significant influence in the advancement of special education law:

1. **Due process.** Fair and specific procedures related to assessment, identification, and placement must be followed for all students (Turnbull, Stowe, & Huerta, 2007).

2. **Equal protection.** Consistent with the equal protection clause of the 14th Amendment, states are required to provide the same rights and benefits to students with disabilities as to those without disabilities.

3. **Zero reject.** Regardless of severity of disability, no child can be excluded from school.

4. **Free and appropriate public education.** Individual students must be provided with an individualized educational program that has a full range of appropriate direct and related educational services at no cost to their families.

5. **Least restrictive environment (LRE).** Students with disabilities should be educated, to the maximum extent appropriate, with students who do not have disabilities, and they should be removed from a general education classroom only when the curriculum and instruction cannot be adapted to achieve satisfactory results.

## Just the Facts — IDEA 2004 Components

| | |
|---|---|
| Free and appropriate public education | • All children, regardless of severity of disability, can learn and are entitled to a FAPE.<br>• Special education and related services are provided at public expense in conformity to an IEP. |
| Nondiscriminatory assessment | • All testing and evaluation used to identify and assess students with disabilities are not racially or culturally discriminatory.<br>• Evaluations requiring tests are in the child's native language or appropriate mode of communication, validated, and administered by trained personnel. |
| Least restrictive environment | • Preferred placement for students with disabilities is the general education classroom.<br>• When success in the general education classroom cannot be achieved, even with significant alterations, alternatives on the continuum of placements are considered. |
| Individualized education program | • An IEP is developed for each student with a disability and includes (1) current levels of performance, (2) annual goals, (3) extent of participation in general education programs, (4) beginning dates and anticipated duration of service, and (5) evaluation methods.<br>• Participants in IEP planning include at least one special and general educator, a local education agency (LEA) representative, an evaluation specialist, related service specialists, and parents. |
| Parent participation | • Written permission from parents is needed for all testing, evaluation, and changes in services.<br>• Parents are entitled to active participation in IEP development and annual reviews. |
| Procedural safeguards | • Adequate notice must be provided to parents for meetings.<br>• Allow for the settling of disagreements through mediation and due process hearings. |

6. **Nondiscriminatory assessment.** Biased evaluation instruments and/or procedures constitute a denial of equal access to education. Students can be harmed by assessments that wrongly label them and mistakenly place them in environments that deprive them of opportunities for advancement.

## Elements of IDEA 2004

The major elements of IDEA reflect what all teachers and service providers should know and be able to do when teaching students with disabilities (Rosenberg, O'Shea, & O'Shea, 2006).

### Nondiscriminatory Identification, Assessment, and Evaluation

The Individuals with Disabilities Education Improvement Act requires schools and community agencies to locate and evaluate students who may have disabilities. The goal is to determine if there is evidence of a disability and, if so, to identify the full spectrum of educational services needed for the student to succeed in school settings. When conducting such evaluations, the law requires that a multidisciplinary team (1) use testing materials and procedures in the student's primary language or mode of communication; (2) use more than one method to determine disability or placement status; (3) provide a full-scale evaluation in all areas of functioning (e.g., intelligence, achievement, social skills, language, motor skills, and adaptive behavior) related to the suspected disability; (4) ensure qualified personnel use validated assessments; (5) employ tests and procedures that are not racially, culturally, or ideologically biased or discriminatory; (6) secure written consent and input from parents and guardians for both initial evaluation and reevaluations; and (7) summarize data into a format that is readily accessed and understood.

## Just the Facts

### Evolution of 1975 Legislation into IDEA 2004

| | |
|---|---|
| PL 94-142, Education for All Handicapped Children Act (EAHCA; 1975) | The precursor to IDEA 2004, EAHCA is often referred to as the Bill of Rights for students with disabilities. This law guaranteed the availability of a free and appropriate public education, due process, and IEPs to all students with disabilities. |
| PL 98-199, Parent Training and Information Centers (1983) | Provided for training and provision of information to parents and volunteers. |
| PL 99-457, Education of the Handicapped Students Act Amendments (1986) | Extended the mandate from PL 94-142 to include special education and related services beginning at age 3 and created a discretionary early intervention program to serve students from birth through age 2. |
| PL 101-476, Individuals with Disabilities Education Act (IDEA; 1990) | Further amended the provisions of PL 94-142 and PL 99-457, renamed the act IDEA, and mandated that the IEP include a statement of transition services. |
| PL 101-336, Americans with Disabilities Act (ADA; 1990) | Prohibited discrimination based on disabilities in the areas of employment, public services, transportation, public accommodations, and telecommunications. |
| PL 101-392, Carl D. Perkins Vocational and Technology Education Act (1990) | Provided resources for improving educational skills needed in a technologically advanced society, guaranteeing full vocational educational opportunities for all special populations. |
| PL 103-239, School-to-Work Opportunities Act (1994) | Encouraged partnership models between school-based and employment-based sites at the local level by encouraging schools and employment site personnel to plan, implement, and evaluate integrated school-based and work-based learning. It encouraged interagency agreements, technical assistance, and services to employers, educators, case managers, and others. |
| PL 102-476, Individuals with Disabilities Education Act (IDEA) | Passed in 1990 and amended in 1997. It established a number of new provisions designed to improve outcomes for students with disabilities. Provisions inherent in the reauthorized law, IDEA '97, include requirements that students with disabilities must be included in state- and district-wide assessments, that students' IEPs address the issue of students' access to general education curricula, and that states establish performance goals and indicators for students with disabilities. |

### Least Restrictive Environment

Would it surprise you to learn that IDEA does not use the terms *mainstream, include, segregate,* or *integrate*? The language used in the law requires that the education of students with disabilities occur in the LRE, which means that placement is determined at least annually and is based on an individual student's educational needs. Placement is not viewed as permanent, and teachers work to move students to less restrictive—and in our view, functionally inclusive—levels of service. To the greatest degree possible, students with disabilities are educated with nondisabled peers, and have access to the general education curriculum and extracurricular activities. Finally, removal from the general education environment occurs only when the nature and the severity of the disability preclude the satisfactory delivery of educational services with appropriate supplemental aids and services (Murdick et al., 2002).

### Individualized Education Programs

IDEA 2004 requires that each student identified as having a disability receive an **individualized education program (IEP)**, a document that informs and guides the delivery of instruction and related services. Requirements for the development of an IEP are quite specific in terms of information included and the individuals who develop the plan. The IEP requires six categories of information: (1) the student's current levels of academic and functional performance; (2) measurable annual goals related to meeting the student's needs resulting from the disability and enabling progress in the general education curriculum; (3) a description of how the student's progress toward meeting annual goals is measured and reported; (4) a statement of special education and related services and supplementary aids and services provided for or on behalf of the student; (5) the extent, if any, to which the student will not participate with nondisabled students in the general education environment; and (6) the projected date for the beginning of services and the anticipated frequency, location, and duration of those services and modifications.

The IEP team also addresses postsecondary transition issues for students turning age 16 (or younger, if deemed necessary by the team). Consequently, the IEP must include measurable goals and corresponding services based on appropriate transition assessments. Finally, as the student approaches the state's legal age, the IEP must include a statement that the student has been informed of his or her rights in regard to IDEA 2004.

Successful development and implementation of IEPs require input from a team of informed stakeholders. Consequently, IDEA 2004 requires that the IEP process involve

- At least one general education teacher of the student (if the student is participating, or is planning to participate, in general education activities)
- At least one special educator of the student
- A school district representative who is knowledgeable about available service-delivery options and programs as well as the general education curriculum and related-service availability
- An evaluation specialist who can interpret the instructional implications of assessments
- Other specialists who can provide important information, such as related-service providers, transportation specialists, physicians, lawyers, and advocates
- Parents, guardians, surrogate parents, and, when appropriate, the student

Individual team members can be excused from attending if their area is not being discussed or if there is agreement that written input is acceptable.

IDEA 2004 requires that development and implementation of IEPs be based on input from a team of informed stakeholders, including, whenever appropriate, the student with a disability.

## Procedural Safeguards

One of the requirements of IDEA 2004 is that schools must ensure that parents, guardians, or surrogates have the opportunity to participate in every decision related to the identification, assessment, and placement of their child. In addition to providing adequate notice for meetings and scheduling them at a mutually agreed-on time and place, schools are to notify parents when considering changes in educational programming or related services.

If parents believe that their rights have been violated or if they disagree with educators regarding the development of their child's IEP, they can appeal specific decisions. One voluntary step is mediation, a process in which a qualified, impartial facilitator works with the parties to come to resolution. If mediation does not satisfy the parties, IDEA 2004 mandates the convening of a due process hearing. These hearings allow dissenting parties to question decisions and actions. Parties also have the right to appeal due process hearing decisions in federal court if they remain unsatisfied. To reduce the need for protracted and costly legal activities associated with due process hearings and appeals, IDEA 2004 urges states to strengthen their mediation procedures.

## Suspensions and Expulsions

For those inappropriate behaviors deemed not a manifestation (i.e., caused by or substantially related to the disability or a failure to implement IEP procedures) of the student's special needs, schools can apply disciplinary actions in the same manner as they do for students without disabilities (so long as special education services continue). However, schools cannot remove a student with a disability from his or her current placement for more than 10 days if it is determined that the problem behaviors are a function of the disability. Nonetheless, for violations such as (1) bringing a dangerous weapon to school, (2) selling or possessing illegal drugs, or (3) inflicting serious bodily injury on another person while at school or at a school function, IDEA 2004 provides schools with the authority to consider unique circumstances on a case-by-case basis. In such cases, the school district may unilaterally place a student in an interim alternative placement for up to 45 school days.

## Confidentiality and Access to Information

IDEA 2004 requires that one official in each school district assume responsibility for ensuring confidentiality of school records and ensuring that those who have contact with student records are trained in records-management procedures. By law, parents have the right to inspect and review all information on their child, and it is not unusual for them to request an explanation regarding the information in the records.

## Services to Infants, Toddlers, and Preschoolers

It was not until 1986, and an early reauthorization of IDEA, that preschool special education services were mandated for children ages 3 to 5, and incentives were provided to states encouraging the development of programs for infants, toddlers, and their families. Preschoolers are afforded the same services and protections available to school-aged children. Because infants and toddlers with disabilities often require medical, psychological, and human service interventions, as do members of the entire family, the federal government has encouraged the development of statewide, multidisciplinary, interagency programs by offering increased grant support.

## Funding for Early Intervention Services

IDEA 2004 allows school districts to use up to 15% of federal special education funds for students who have not been identified as having a disability, but who do need enhanced academic and behavioral support in their general education classes. This change in policy aligns IDEA with NCLB's emphasis on using evidence-based practices and ongoing data-based decision making to improve the educational outcomes of all students (see next section). Although not explicitly in IDEA 2004, the law promotes the use of multi-tiered service delivery models, such as response to intervention (RTI), which focuses on how students respond to differing levels and intensities of instruction.

## No Child Left Behind (NCLB)

The NCLB Act of 2001 is a comprehensive federal initiative designed to improve the educational performance of *all* students. A reauthorization of earlier Elementary and Secondary Education Acts (ESEA), NCLB explicitly mandates compliance to high standards and sanctions states and schools that fail to meet set criteria (Hardman & Mulder, 2004; Yell & Drasgow, 2005). In enacting NCLB, the federal government asserted that states were not doing enough to ensure that all students were performing adequately in school. The act requires states to reduce the disparity in performance between those groups of students who typically achieve and those students who have had difficulties meeting standards, often due to economic disadvantage, linguistic differences, or disability status. Figure 2.2 offers a brief introduction to NCLB.

## Elements of NCLB

Five core principles form the foundation of NCLB: (1) strong accountability for results; (2) expanded flexibility and local control of schools; (3) an emphasis on teaching methods based on scientific research; (4) expanded options for parents, particularly those whose children attend low-performing schools; and (5) highly qualified teachers.

### Strong Accountability for Results

No Child Left Behind requires states to develop clearly defined goals, or proficiency standards, and then assess whether individual students and schools meet these targets. Comparing student performance data to the standards allows parents to know how their child is doing at

---

| Figure 2.2 | The No Child Left Behind Act of 2001 |
| --- | --- |

**Accountability for Results**

- States create assessments to measure what children know and learn.
- Annual report cards on school performance allow parents to know of the quality of the children's schools, the qualifications of teachers, and progress in key subjects.
- Statewide performance reports are disaggregated according to race, gender, and other relevant criteria to assess closing of achievement gap.

**Expanded Options for Parents**

- Parents with children in failing schools are allowed to transfer their children to a better-performing public school, including charter schools.
- Parents can request schools to use Title I funds to provide supplemental educational programs (e.g., tutoring, after-school services, summer school) for children in failing schools.
- Federal support for charter schools is expanded.

**Strengthening Teacher Quality**

- A highly qualified teacher will be in every public school classroom.

**Teaching Methods Based on Scientific Research**

- Requires use of programs that have demonstrated effectiveness.

**Flexibility and Local Control**

- Demonstrates greater sensitivity to the needs of local schools by allowing flexibility in the use of federal funds without prior government approval.

school. Aggregating the data from groups of students, policy makers, government officials, and school leaders can assess how individual schools and school districts are performing in relation to state standards. States are also required to analyze data for specific groups of students, including those who are economically disadvantaged, members of varying culturally and linguistically diverse groups, and students with disabilities. The goal is to make **adequate yearly progress (AYP)**—the minimum standard, or benchmark, expected of every student and school. Schools that meet their goals receive positive public acknowledgment of effort. Those that do not meet their goals may be designated "in need of improvement." Historically, students with disabilities were excluded, both formally and informally, from school and district assessments, perpetuating low expectations throughout their educational careers. Now they are included in assessments. Although many have welcomed this inclusion in accountability policies, questions remain regarding the appropriateness of including students with cognitive disabilities in overall determinations of school effectiveness. (We address several of these questions later in this chapter in the "Tomorrow's Challenges" section.)

### Expanded Flexibility and Local Control

Local school personnel have greater sensitivity to the needs of neighborhood schools than do federal administrators. Consequently, NCLB provides the freedom for school districts to transfer up to 50% of federal funds among a number of programs without the need to obtain prior government approval. The act also allows school districts to consolidate funds from several programs and to enter into flexible state–local partnerships.

### Teaching Methods Based on Scientific Research

Rather than consulting recent educational research, some teachers adopt programs and instructional methods based on fads, anecdotes, and personal whims, usually with dismal results (Kauffman, 1981; Yell & Drasgow, 2005). With NCLB, federal support is targeted to only those programs that have a proven track record, demonstrating effectiveness through rigorous scientific research.

### Expanded Options for Parents

What would happen if a parent had a ninth-grade child who attended a low-performing school that continually experienced significant discipline issues? Under NCLB, the parent would have options. First, if the school did not meet state goals for two consecutive years, the parent could choose to transfer his child to a better-performing school in the district, with transportation provided. Second, if the school failed to meet goals for three consecutive years, the child would be eligible for a range of supplemental activities, including free tutoring and after-school instruction.

### Highly Qualified Teachers

According to NCLB, all teachers must be highly qualified. This means being appropriately licensed and having the requisite qualifications in core academic subject areas. For content-area teachers, this requirement is fairly straightforward. In order to teach, one must (1) have a college degree; (2) have full state certification or licensure; and (3) demonstrate competency in the areas she teaches by passing subject-specific, state-administered tests. Being highly qualified is not so clear-cut for special educators. In

> ## Pause & Reflect
>
> Some believe that the requirements of NCLB are admirable but in some cases unattainable. What do you think? Can all teachers be highly qualified? Is it possible that all students will meet state-mandated standards of proficiency?

addition to developing their special education skills, those who teach at the elementary level must pass a test of subject knowledge and teaching skill in the standard elementary curriculum (e.g., reading, writing, mathematics). Special education teachers at the middle and high school levels must be highly qualified in special education as well as in each of the core subject areas they teach. Not surprisingly, these requirements can be overwhelming and burdensome for many individuals who are thinking of a special education teaching career.

# Section 504 of the Rehabilitation Act of 1973 (PL 93-112) and the Americans with Disabilities Act

Section 504 is a component of the Rehabilitation Act that authorizes federal support for the rehabilitation and training of individuals with physical and mental disabilities. More a civil rights law than an education act, Section 504 is significant for students with special needs because it provides protections for those whose disabilities do not match the definitions under the IDEA statute. In addition to using a categorical approach to disability, Section 504 protects students with (1) communicable diseases; (2) temporary disabilities arising from accidents; and (3) allergies, asthma, or environmental illnesses. Under Section 504, a student has a disability if he or she functions as though having a disability (Murdick et al., 2002), and the law provides these students with equal opportunities to obtain the same results as those without disabilities. Section 504 also extends protections against discrimination beyond education settings to employment and social and health services.

The major differences between Section 504 and IDEA are in the flexibility of the procedures and the reduced procedural criteria required of school personnel. Schools typically offer less assistance and monitoring with Section 504 because fewer federal regulations address compliance. Indeed, no IEP is required for students. Still, Section 504 levels the playing field by eliminating barriers that exclude those with disabilities from full participation in activities (Rosenfeld, 2005). These barriers can be physical (e.g., architectural impediments that stop a person with a physical or sensory disability from accessing a building), or they can be programmatic (e.g., not giving a student with attention-deficit/hyperactivity disorder [ADHD] supports and accommodations so that he can benefit from instruction).

Section 504 ensures that appropriate educational services are delivered to children with disabilities. Appropriate services are educational activities designed to meet the needs of those with disabilities to the same extent that the needs of those without disabilities are met. Eligibility for Section 504 services is based on a team's determination of whether there is a substantial limitation to major life activities resulting from a physical or mental impairment. Once a determination is made, an individual accommodation plan is developed. The accommodation plan is not as extensive as an IEP, but it should include clear information on how school personnel can implement accommodations to meet individual student needs.

Examples of situations that may require a Section 504 Plan include:

- Providing an **acoustical amplification system** and distraction-free seating for a student with ADHD who has difficulty attending to instruction
- Developing a management plan that trains school personnel to meet the needs of a student with diabetes, including specialized snacks, lavatory access, and exercise opportunities
- Providing appropriate training to those who work with a student with bipolar disorder, and providing the student opportunities for **time-out** when unpredictable mood swings occur
- Creating a health-care plan for management of acute and chronic phases of student illnesses such as cystic fibrosis and epilepsy, or hypersensitive allergic reactions to certain foods (e.g., peanuts) or environmental events (odors, noise, etc.)

Similar to Section 504, the Americans with Disabilities Act (ADA; PL 101-336) is civil rights legislation for those with disabilities. Passed in 1990, the ADA requires nondiscriminatory protections such as equal opportunity to participate fully in community life, equal opportunity to live independently, and accessibility of all buildings and physical facilities to individuals with disabilities. The ADA applies to all segments of society—employment, education, and recreation services—with the exception of private schools and religious organizations. Similar to Section 504, the ADA uses a functional definition of *disability*. Rather than listing all possible conditions, a person with a disability is defined as someone with a physical or mental impairment that limits participation in major life activities (Moses, 1990).

Viewed by many as the Emancipation Proclamation for individuals with disabilities, the ADA prohibits discrimination in employment, governmental entities, and public accommodations (Smith, 2001). Consider the frustration experienced by a student with a physical disability unable to play with peers because of an architectural barrier precluding entry to the gymnasium or playground. The ADA requires removal of existing physical barriers or the provision of alternative means of service implementation.

Many of the ADA requirements for schools were already addressed by Section 504. However, the ADA did clarify certain lingering issues. For example, the ADA ensures that students with contagious diseases, such as HIV/AIDS, are protected from discrimination as long as they do not threaten the health and safety of others (Murdick et al., 2002). Also, protections are extended to those who are associated with a person with a disability. Specifically, a child whose parent or sibling has a communicable disease cannot be prevented from attending school.

Section 504 plans allow for acoustical amplification systems for students with ADHD who have difficulties attending to lessons.

## Inclusion Today: Multi-tiered Response to Intervention (RTI) Frameworks

In this chapter, we have described the history of service delivery to students with disabilities by tracing the evolution of inclusive services and then describing the laws that guide current educational programming. As a result of the tireless efforts of disability advocates and landmark legislative efforts such as IDEA and NCLB, considerable progress has been made in the inclusive education of students with disabilities. How successful have these efforts been? Consider these findings from a study commissioned by the National Council on Disability (2008) assessing the impact of IDEA and NCLB on special education outcomes. Since the laws were (re)authorized, students with disabilities are doing better academically, with fewer scoring in the "below-basic" proficiency level and with more attaining "proficient" or higher levels, than were in previous years. Moreover, students with disabilities are graduating with diplomas and certificates at higher rates than in the past. Equally important, attitudes and expectations of key stakeholders—policy makers, teachers, parents, and students—have been changing in a positive direction. Students with disabilities have increased access to higher-level curricula, and a culture of high expectations for these students has taken root. Arguably, much of this increased access and enhanced support can be attributed to the evolution and increased use of multi-tiered service delivery systems, often referred to as **response to intervention (RTI)** frameworks.

### Response to Intervention (RTI)

Response to intervention is rooted historically in two key elements of IDEA 2004: (1) allowing a portion of federal special education funds to benefit students without disabilities who need additional supports to succeed in general education classes and (2) considering an alternative to the traditional IQ-achievement discrepancy approach for identifying students with learning disabilities. In each element, student progress is monitored regularly, serving as the foundation for instructional decision making. Movement toward more intensive services, including eligibility for special education services, is based on student responsiveness to evidence-based instructional practices.

Since its modest beginnings in 2004, RTI has expanded considerably and, arguably, is the most prominent service delivery framework for addressing the needs of students with academic, social, and behavioral challenges. The growth and popularity of RTI is likely a function of common sense, simplicity, and its inherent coordinated organizational structure.

Effective instruction is delivered to prevent problems from occurring and effective interventions are applied to address problems that do arise (Baker, Fien, & Baker, 2010). Therefore, if a student does not respond positively to the best intervention available in the general education classroom, he or she is eligible for additional and specialized assistance. Such thinking may be new to education, but other fields, such as medicine, have used tiered approaches to guide treatment for a number of generations (Gresham, 2007). Consider how physicians typically monitor critical health indicators such as weight, blood pressure, and cholesterol levels during routine physical examinations. If any one of these measures indicates a problem with a patient's well-being, a course of action based on scientifically based practices is prescribed. If subsequent data indicate that the patient is not responding adequately to the initial treatment plan, either the intervention is strengthened or other, more intensive treatment options are applied.

## Elements of an RTI Framework

There is no single type of RTI framework. Most approaches contain prevention and intervention tiers; evidence-based practices; screening, identification, and progress monitoring; distinctive intervention delivery methods; and some are beginning to integrate elements of universal design for learning (UDL).

### Prevention and Intervention Tiers

The central element of RTI is a series of increasingly intensive tiers of support, available to all students—those with and without disabilities—based on an assessment of individual needs. Most RTI frameworks use three tiers. Typically, the first tier is a high-quality, universal general education program that employs evidence-based instructional practices. Tier-2 instruction supplements Tier-1 instruction with focused, targeted interventions for those students who do not meet expected patterns of growth and achievement. These interventions—typically increased instructional time, repeated practice, differentiated instruction, and/or flexible grouping—are usually implemented by the general education teacher. Tier-3 instruction is highly intensive intervention and is designed for students who do not respond to Tier-2 efforts. Most often, Tier-3 instruction is provided by special education teachers.

A major advantage in using tiers is that struggling students will receive assistance immediately. Rather than waiting for teacher referrals and accompanying psychometric tests typically required to justify additional resources, students receive needed assistance exactly at the times they experience their difficulties (Baker et al., 2010; Council for Exceptional Children, 2007; Fletcher & Vaughn, 2009; Gresham, 2007; Hoover & Patton, 2008; Martinez, Nellis, & Prendergast, 2006).

### Evidence-Based Practices

A core component of the RTI framework is the application of evidence-based practices in daily instructional routines. A practice, be it a curriculum or a specific intervention protocol, is considered evidence-based if it has been proven to be effective through peer-reviewed scientific research. Unfortunately, far too many instructional practices are based on anecdote and convenience, making it difficult to determine if students' academic and/or behavioral problems are in need of more intensive intervention options or the result of inadequate instruction. When students receive evidence-based instruction, lack of adequate instruction as the reason for poor performance can be ruled out. A number of useful sources (e.g., The What Works Clearinghouse, www.w-w-c.org; The Best Evidence Encyclopedia, www.bestevidence.org) are available to help educators identify and select evidence-based instructional practices.

### Screening, Identification, and Progress Monitoring

Integrated screening, identification, and progress monitoring systems allow teachers to (1) determine which students are in need of additional intervention and (2) assess how students respond to the instruction they receive. In some RTI frameworks, all students are screened on brief measures of academic and behavioral performance, and those who fall below a specific normative cutoff point are provided with more intensive interventions. In other systems, universal screening is provided to identify those who are potentially at risk for poor outcomes. Additional performance monitoring is conducted for approximately 5 weeks to validate the results of the initial screening. In general, systems that identify students based on a one-time screening tend to identify large numbers of students who do not need higher tiered services. Consequently, it is recommended that RTI systems incorporate short-term academic and behavioral progress monitoring prior to identifying students for more intensive interventions. After students are identified, data need to be collected on a frequent basis to (1) establish what constitutes an adequate response to an intervention and (2) ensure that the intervention is truly addressing the identified problems (Burns, Deno, & Jimerson, 2007; Fuchs & Fuchs, 2007).

### Intervention Delivery Methods

There are two approaches to delivering interventions within an RTI framework. With the *problem-solving approach,* teams of educators develop individualized intervention plans tailored to students' unique needs. For each student, the presenting academic or behavioral problem is defined in measurable terms, the gap between current and expected performance is determined, an intervention plan is designed, and the efficacy of the intervention is evaluated. In contrast, the *standard protocol approach* makes use of specific instructional and behavioral programs that are linked to the various tiers or intensities of instruction. Procedures are standardized, meaning that students who respond inadequately to instruction and behavioral expectations during general class instruction would receive preselected prescribed interventions (Division for Learning Disabilities, 2007; Gresham, 2007; Little, 2009). Typically, standardized protocols are used to address academic difficulties. However, the idiosyncratic nature of behavior problems often requires individualized interventions based on a problem-solving approach.

### Universal Design for Learning

There are indications that application of universal design for learning (UDL) principles may enhance the delivery of evidence-based practices, particularly during Tier-1 instruction (Basham, Israel, Graden, Poth, & Winston, 2010; Edyburn, 2009). Universal design for learning is best thought of as a series of proactive curriculum design structures that accommodate a wide range of student abilities and learning preferences. To minimize barriers to learning, students are provided teaching methods and materials that contain multiple means of presentation, expression, and engagement. To accommodate the widest variety of learners in general education settings, the design of instruction and materials should allow for flexibility in use, equitable use, tolerance for error, low physical effort, and simplicity in responding (Edyburn, 2010; King-Sears, 2009; Rose & Meyer, 2002).

Technology often plays a major role in the application of UDL. For example, consider how digital versions of textbooks can allow a student with reading problems to succeed in general education settings. Digital textbooks integrate multiple modes of presenting content, supplementing text material with images and video, and transforming text to speech. Moreover, with minimal disruption, the technology allows for modification in how content is presented, allowing students to repeat passages or alter the size, shape, or color of the text or image (Hitchcock, Meyer, Rose, & Jackson, 2002). Still, UDL does not have to involve technology. Concrete manipulatives or tangible visual representations of shapes and corresponding formulas can provide students with the necessary supports and accommodations to understand challenging math content (King-Sears, 2009).

## RTI Efficacy

Response to intervention has been successful in addressing the academic and behavioral needs of students in inclusive general education settings. Specifically, a number of studies (e.g., Dexter, Hughes, & Farmer, 2008; Torgesen, 2009; Vaughn, Wanzek, Linan-Thompson, & Murray, 2007) have found that tiered intervention systems can increase the reading and math performance of at-risk elementary students, and reduce the number of students who are referred for special education. In some cases, these results have been impressive. For example, in a major investigation of an RTI model using the Reading First program with students in grades K–3, the percentage of students with reading difficulties was reduced by 30% and the rate of students identified as having a learning disability dropped by 81% (Torgesen, 2009). At the secondary school level, RTI is less established and initial findings suggest that additional work is needed in modifying the framework to address the lengthy history of academic problems typical of older students (Fuchs, Fuchs, & Compton, 2010; Vaughn et al., 2010). Research efforts that have applied RTI to the social behavior of students are encouraging (Cheney, Flower, & Templeton, 2008; Fairbanks, Sugai, Guardino, & Lathrop, 2007; Hawken, Vincent, & Schumann, 2008). As with the academic outcomes, a significant number of students respond to the intensive Tier-2 interventions and fewer students are identified for special education services.

Although RTI has been successful, a number of logistical issues require increased attention. For example, how will the roles and responsibilities of teachers change as an increased number of students receive instruction within a multi-tiered framework? Currently, this remains unclear. General educators likely will be responsible for delivering evidence-based Tier-1 instruction, necessitating that all teachers remain current on what constitutes effective practices for a range of learners in a variety of skill and subject areas (Mastropieri & Scruggs, 2005). Special educators would likely support students at risk and with disabilities in all three of the tiers. According to Hoover and Patton (2008), this would require that special education teachers assume a multitude of roles, including (1) modeling data-driven decision making, (2) being a resource for evidence-based practices, (3) providing differentiated instruction and behavioral supports, and (4) being a model of collaborative practice.

## Pause & Reflect

Special education has evolved from a segregated to a more inclusive multi-tiered mode of service delivery. How have the roles and responsibilities of general and special educators changed as a result of this evolution?

# Tomorrow's Challenges

As students with disabilities gain greater access to challenging academic environments, several issues continue to pose challenges to teachers and policy makers. Two of the more prominent issues are (1) how best to assess AYP of students with disabilities and (2) building and sustaining a highly qualified workforce.

## AYP and Students with Disabilities

In our earlier discussion of No Child Left Behind, we noted that states determine adequate yearly progress by adopting or designing content-specific standardized tests and setting proficiency score benchmarks that students are required to attain. Although there has been movement among policy makers to allow circumstantial waivers, NCLB requires 100% proficiency by 2014. A factor contributing to the discussion of waivers has been the observation that some students with disabilities are unable to meet the same standards and time frame as their peers without disabilities. Currently, schools are allowed to have 1% of their students (typically, students with serious cognitive disabilities) take **alternate assessments**. Alternate achievement standards are based on performance expectations that differ in complexity from grade-level achievement standards. An additional 2% of students with disabilities—from any category under IDEA—are eligible for assessments that are based on modified achievement standards. These standards are aligned with typical grade-level standards but with reduced depth and breadth of content coverage. It is presumed that alternate and modified assessments are technically sound and reflect grade-level content (Yell, Shriner, & Katsiyannis, 2006).

In addition to the challenges involved in designing alternative assessments for students under the "1% and 2% options," some professionals believe these exemptions from traditional AYP requirements to be inadequate. Large numbers of students receiving special education services have disabilities that interfere with their learning. These students typically perform at much lower levels on state tests, making it far more likely that schools with a large special education subgroup will fail to make AYP (Olson, 2005). Although special education advocates welcome being part of inclusive assessments, some fear that failures to make AYP, due to the limited performance of students with disabilities, could increase the "already existing anti-special education bias" (Allbritten, Mainzer, & Ziegler, 2004, p. 157). Not surprisingly, a number of teacher groups (e.g., American Federation of Teachers, 2006) are advocating that the number of students with disabilities assessed under alternative and modified standards not be limited by arbitrary federal percentages. Rather, knowledgeable IEP teams should determine how students participate in required assessments.

## Highly Qualified Professionals

The quality and skill of a student's teacher are critical factors in the development of academic proficiency, and, as required by NCLB, a well-prepared, highly qualified teacher is needed in every classroom. Unfortunately, in several areas such as math, science, and special education, a severe and chronic shortage of fully credentialed teachers continues to plague our nation's schools. Consider some of the special education numbers: Of the entire nation's school districts, 98% report shortages of special education teachers, and approximately 11.4% of those teaching students with disabilities lack special education certification. Moreover, in spite of this serious shortage, the number of people interested in pursuing a career in special education has gradually declined (Cook & Boe, 2007; McLeskey, Tyler, & Flippin, 2004).

Among the many unfortunate effects associated with the shortage of highly qualified and certified teachers is a lack of skill in providing collaborative and supportive inclusive programming. As you will note throughout this text, successful inclusive practices require that teachers possess general and specialized skills in both instructional and interpersonal domains. In the chapter-opening vignette interview, for example, Sarita (the parent) noticed a positive difference in the education of her daughter when she entered Heritage High School, which is adequately staffed with highly qualified professionals. Lacking sufficient numbers of personnel who possess the needed skills to implement inclusive programs can ultimately derail successful efforts of educating students in high-demand general education environments.

As you can imagine, addressing teacher quality in a time of persistent shortages is complex. For example, although few argue with the need to increase the number of highly qualified special-education teachers who, in the words of Margaret Huckaby, give their "best effort," many educators and policy makers are concerned that additional requirements can exacerbate current shortages. At the same time, there is apprehension that exempting special education teachers from some of the highly qualified standards could widen the achievement gap between students with and without disabilities and promote separate systems of teacher qualifications and accountability (Rosenberg, Sindelar, & Hardman, 2004). Moreover, policy makers remain unsure of how the current economic downturn and reduced budgets for education will influence the demand for special education teachers (Boe, deBettencourt, Dewey, Rosenberg, Sindelar, & Leko, 2011).

The dilemma of enhancing quality at a time of teacher shortages has led policy makers to consider **alternative routes to certification** and streamlined teacher preparation programs (Rosenberg, Boyer, Sindelar, & Misra, 2007). These nontraditional teacher preparation efforts vary in terms of breadth of coverage and level of support. Although these programs remain controversial, most people agree that the programs need to be evaluated in terms of long-term retention rates, measures of teacher quality, and impact on student learning.

# Summary

Providing an inclusive education for all students requires an understanding of the evolution of special education service delivery, the legal foundations of special education, and an awareness of emerging issues. We presented the following major points in this chapter.

### The evolution of inclusive service delivery

- Until the 1960s, the majority of students with disabilities were educated in segregated settings for most or all of the school day.
- Mainstreaming was a policy of integrating students with mild disabilities into general education settings, although those students still "belonged" to special education.
- The inclusion movement, founded on the assumption that general and special educators share responsibility and accountability in educating students with disabilities, gathered strength in the mid-1980s.
- Parents and civil rights advocates used the precedent of *Brown v. Board of Education* (1954) to achieve access to education and due process of law.
- Parents of students with disabilities tend to support inclusion but remain concerned that too many educators lack the skills to implement such programming effectively.
- Today, most students with disabilities are educated in their neighborhood schools and in general education classes.

### The major legislative acts that are the legal foundation for special education and inclusion

- The Individuals with Disabilities Education Improvement Act (IDEA 2004), the most recent iteration of the landmark Education for All Handicapped Children Act (EAHCA) of 1975, is the most significant legislative effort supporting the education of students with disabilities.
- IDEA, a confluence of significant legal decisions and principles, ensures that all students, regardless of their disability, receive a free and appropriate public education (FAPE) in the least restrictive environment (LRE).
- As part of IDEA, an individualized education program (IEP) containing current students' levels of functioning, annual goals, special education and related services, projected dates of services, and the extent of participation in the general education environment guides instructional efforts.
- Under IDEA, students and their families have procedural due process protections and are ensured of receiving a nondiscriminatory assessment of strengths and weaknesses.
- No Child Left Behind (NCLB), a comprehensive federal initiative designed to improve the educational performance of *all* students, mandates compliance to high standards and sanctions states and schools that fail to meet set criteria.
- The major components of NCLB are strong accountability for results, expanded flexibility and local control, scientifically based teaching methods, expanded options for parents, and highly qualified teacher requirements. These components are having a substantial impact on how all students are being educated.
- Section 504 and the Americans with Disabilities Act (ADA) are significant pieces of legislation that provide protections for students with disabilities who do not match the definitions provided under the IDEA statutes.
- Section 504 considers a child with a disability to be one who functions as having a disability.
- The Americans with Disabilities Act expands protections to prohibit discrimination in employment and public accommodations.

### Inclusion today: Multi-tiered RTI frameworks

- Much of the increased access and enhanced support observed in inclusive schools can be attributed to the increased use of multi-tiered RTI service delivery systems.

- Although there is no one type of RTI framework, most systems consist of prevention and intervention tiers; evidence-based practices; screening, identification, and progress monitoring; and intervention delivery methods—and some are beginning to integrate UDL.
- The implementation of RTI has been successful in addressing the academic and behavioral needs of elementary students in inclusive general education classes, yet it is likely that these systems will require changes in the roles and responsibilities for both general and special educators.

### Tomorrow's challenges

- Although it is generally accepted that some students with disabilities are unable to meet the same standards as their peers, educators and policy makers continue to struggle with determining how best to set high standards and assess academic progress.
- A severe and chronic shortage of highly qualified and fully certified special education teachers may derail efforts to deliver collaborative and supportive inclusive programming.

## Addressing Professional Standards

Standards addressed in Chapter 2 include:
**CEC Standards:** (1) foundations, (8) assessment, (9) professional and ethical practice

---

### MyEducationLab

Go to the topics Law and Response to Intervention in the **MyEducationLab** (www .myeducationlab.com) for *Inclusion,* where you can:
- Find learning outcomes for the topic Law and the topic Response to Intervention, along with the national standards that connect to these outcomes.
- Complete Assignments and Activities that can help you more deeply understand the chapter content.
- Apply and practice your understanding of the core teaching skills identified in the chapter with the Building Teaching Skills and Dispositions learning units.
- Examine challenging situations and cases presented in the IRIS Center Resources.
- Check your comprehension on the content covered in the chapter with the Study Plan. Here you will be able to take a chapter quiz, receive feedback on your answers, and then access on Review, Practice, and Enrichment activities to enhance your understanding of chapter content.

# Students with Learning Disabilities

## KEY TOPICS

**After reading this chapter you will:**

- Know who students with learning disabilities are, methods used to identify students with learning disabilities, and the range of settings in which they are educated.

- Be able to describe major characteristics of students with learning disabilities.

- Be aware of several practical tips from teachers that facilitate the inclusion of students with learning disabilities.

# chapter 3

# A VIEW FROM TEACHERS

## How Students with Learning Disabilities Benefit from Inclusion

We interviewed teachers from Gilpin Manor Elementary School and West Hernando Middle School about how students with learning disabilities (LD) benefit from inclusion. The teachers were Melissa Pratt (pre-K special education teacher), Jeannie Huskins (second-grade teacher), Susan Huff (fifth-grade teacher), and Vicki Eng (seventh-grade special education teacher). Here's what they had to say.

Jeannie Huskins, who taught for several years in a separate, special education class at Gilpin Manor Elementary, noted the benefits of inclusion by stating, "When they're included, they're in the classroom with their age-appropriate peers. They have, for the most part, good role models. It helps to build their self-esteem when they're not away from everybody else . . . when they're included. They are also presented the same curriculum that all other students are getting. They miss out on that when they're in a separate class."

Vicki Eng, who also taught for several years in a separate class, commented that placing students with LD in an inclusive class "causes me to set my expectations a little higher. When you're in a pull-out program, you might think, 'Oh, well, I don't know if that student can do this right now—let's not even attempt it.' In a regular class, you're expecting everybody else to do it, so you set the bar higher, and you often find out that [students with LD] can meet it and they feel better about themselves, and you take a step back and say, 'Hey, they can do anything that everybody else can do.'"

Melissa Pratt reflected on the long-term benefits of placement in an inclusive classroom. "If kids are included from the time they're in pre-K, they can learn great things from the other kids. It's important that [students with LD] see that coping mechanisms are so important for them. I have kids that come back to me that are in high school. When I ask how they're doing, 9 times out of 10 they're doing OK, give or take a few bumps in the road. But it's coping mechanisms that help them make it and survive. It's really knowing how to figure out your place in the classroom and how you cannot rely on the teacher all the time. I think that's a big issue and something they learn."

Vicki Eng addressed the importance of placement in an inclusive setting so that students with LD can learn to self-advocate. "Many students with LD don't understand their disability or why they are provided accommodations. I try to help them understand their disabilities, and also talk with them about appropriate ways to approach the teacher for support. Being in an inclusive class helps them understand their disability better, and gives them an opportunity to learn to advocate with teachers and others for accommodations and other supports they need. They learn to advocate in a way that is appropriate and doesn't bring negative attention to them."

Finally, Susan Huff summed up the benefits of inclusion for students with learning disabilities by stating, "I think it presents an opportunity for them to learn without being judged. It's a nonstigmatizing environment for them. Everyone sees them as students, and not based on their labels. They get that chance to be normal, and that's an esteem builder for them, when their disability is not an excuse."

**MyEducationLab**

Visit the MyEducationLab for *Inclusion* to enhance your understanding of chapter concepts with a personalized Study Plan. You'll also have the opportunity to hone your teaching skills through video and case-based Assignments and Activities, Building Teaching Skills and Disposition lessons, and IRIS Case Studies.

# Introduction

About 43% of all students with disabilities have a learning disability (U.S. Department of Education, 2011). As you might expect, more students with learning disabilities are included in general education classrooms than any other students with disabilities. At least one student with a learning disability is included in most general education classes, and many have more than one such student.

Students with learning disabilities are often perplexing to teachers and parents. Perhaps the major reason this occurs relates to the fact that most students with learning disabilities do not have an obvious disability. Many teachers and parents assume that these students should be able to learn the academic content of the classroom with little difficulty. Additionally, students with learning disabilities often have difficulty in a specific academic area (most often reading or math) and perform much better in other areas. If you know a person with a learning disability, you readily recognize how puzzling and sometimes frustrating this disability can be.

In general education classrooms, students with learning disabilities struggle to learn academic content, in spite of high-quality instruction, and often need assistance or support to succeed. As Susan Huff, a fifth-grade teacher from Gilpin Manor Elementary School noted, students with learning disabilities benefit from being in a well-designed inclusive classroom that incorporates the necessary supports to ensure student success. Benefits include greater access to the general education curriculum, higher expectations, and improved self-esteem. In this chapter, we address how students with learning disabilities are identified, as well as the characteristics of these students that need to be understood and addressed to ensure that they succeed in an inclusive classroom.

# Who Are the Students with Learning Disabilities?
## Definition

A quick review of the learning disabilities category is provided in the accompanying box, "Just the Facts." The most widely used definition of *learning disability* is included in IDEA (2004), which states:

Many general education classrooms include students with learning disabilities.

A) In general—The term "specific learning disability" means a disorder in one or more of the basic psychological processes involved in understanding or in using language, spoken or written, which disorder may manifest itself in the imperfect ability to listen, think, speak, read, write, spell, or do mathematical calculations.

B) Disorders included—Such term includes such conditions as perceptual disabilities, brain injury, minimal brain dysfunction, **dyslexia**, and **developmental aphasia**.

C) Disorders not included—Such term does not include a learning problem that is primarily the result of visual, hearing, or motor disabilities; of mental retardation; of emotional disturbance; or of environmental, cultural, or economic disadvantage. (PL 108-466, Sec. 602[30])

## Just the Facts   Students with Learning Disabilities

| | |
|---|---|
| Who are the students? | Students with learning disabilities have an uneven pattern of academic development, including unexpected underachievement in one or more academic areas. This underachievement is not explained by another disability or by environmental, cultural, or economic disadvantage. To be identified, the student must need special education services, and the academic problem cannot be overcome in general education without these services. |
| What are typical characteristics? | • Academic achievement in one or more academic areas is significantly below grade level.<br>• Cognitive skill deficits related to memory, attention, impulsivity, and/or meta-cognition.<br>• About one in four students with a learning disability is also identified with attention-deficit/hyperactivity disorder (ADHD).<br>• About one in three students with a learning disability also has problems related to social skill deficits and difficulty getting along with others.<br>• Motivational problems, especially among adolescents, often result from long-term academic difficulty and can result in passive learning or learned helplessness. |
| What are the demographics? | • Approximately 4.8% of school-aged students (ages 6 to 17) are identified with learning disabilities.<br>• About 43% of all school-aged students who have a disability have a learning disability.<br>• About three of four students with learning disabilities are male. |
| Where are students educated? | • Almost 9 of 10 students with learning disabilities are educated for some or most of the school day in a general education classroom.<br>• About 1 of 10 students with a learning disability is educated in separate settings for most or all of the school day. |
| How are students identified? | • Unexpected underachievement in one or more academic areas is the primary criterion for identifying students with learning disabilities.<br>• A severe discrepancy between expected achievement level (as determined by a standardized test of intelligence) and actual achievement level (as determined by a standardized achievement test) has traditionally been used to identify unexpected underachievement.<br>• After unexpected achievement is documented, the exclusion clause is applied to student identification. This ensures that another disability or environmental, cultural, or economic disadvantage did not cause the underachievement.<br>• IDEA 2004 has mandated that a student's response to a scientific, research-based intervention may be used to identify unexpected underachievement for students with learning disabilities. This response-to-intervention approach is being increasingly used in states for student identification. |
| What causes learning disabilities? | • The cause of a learning disability in most instances is unknown.<br>• Researchers assume that some type of abnormal brain function causes learning disabilities.<br>• Hereditary factors contribute to learning disabilities, as these difficulties often tend to run in families.<br>• Research using highly effective, research-based practices has demonstrated that some learning disabilities are caused by the lack of high-quality instruction. |
| What are the outcomes? | • Reading disabilities tend to cause students to have difficulty with other academic areas (e.g., mathematics, social studies, science) as they move through school and content becomes more complex and requires more advanced reading skills.<br>• About 6 of 10 students with learning disabilities graduate with a standard diploma, and about 3 of 10 drop out of school.<br>• Most learning disabilities persist into adulthood, although many learn to at least partially compensate for the disability.<br>• Many adults with learning disabilities have difficulty finding good employment and achieving satisfaction in life. |

As you review this definition, you will see that the most important consideration in defining a learning disability is low achievement in one or more academic areas such as reading or mathematics. It is assumed that some type of underlying **psychological processing** disorder causes this difficulty. For example, a student may have difficulty learning to read because of a problem with language, or a student may have difficulty using sound–symbol relationships to sound out words, often referred to as a **phonological processing** problem (Ritchey, 2011).

The federal definition of *learning disability* includes several terms that have been used in the past or are currently used by some (e.g., dyslexia, perceptual disabilities) and are included as part of this category. A final aspect of the definition is the so-called **exclusion clause**, which educators use to make sure that the primary reason the student struggles academically is a learning disability. Other possible causes of the underachievement are excluded, such as another type of disability (e.g., visual impairment) or environmental conditions such as poor teaching.

**Pause & Reflect**

Have you known a person with a learning disability? Discuss this person's learning characteristics with a peer in class. Did the person perform well in some areas and not in others? Was the disability perplexing? Frustrating (especially to the person with a disability)?

Federal law does not require that states use this definition. Nonetheless, more than 80% of states use the federal definition of learning disability as written in law or with slight alterations. The remaining states use sections of the federal definition or definitions from other sources, but these alternative definitions tend to include underachievement and the exclusion clause as key components (Reschly & Hosp, 2004).

## Identification of Students with Learning Disabilities

From the 1970s until recently, the primary approach that educators have used to identify students with learning disabilities has included the determination of *unexpected underachievement* (also called a *severe discrepancy*). Educators determine this underachievement by examining the discrepancy between a student's actual and expected achievement levels and then using the exclusion clause to make sure the discrepancy is not caused by other factors (e.g., environmental factors, poor teaching, or another disability).

### Identification Using a Severe Discrepancy Approach

When educators use the **severe discrepancy** approach to identify students with learning disabilities, the primary criterion relates to unexpected underachievement. This is determined based on a severe discrepancy between the student's expected achievement level and actual achievement level. To illustrate how educators determine a severe discrepancy, consider a student with an average score of 100 on a standardized test of intelligence, who would be expected to achieve at an average level or on grade level. If this student is a fifth grader and achieves on a second-grade level in reading on a standardized reading test, the difference between his

Many students with learning disabilities have difficulty in some academic areas, but do well in others.

expected achievement level (fifth grade) and actual achievement level (second grade) in reading would be evidence of a severe discrepancy or unexpected underachievement.

Based on this approach, the presence of a severe discrepancy is the primary criterion used for identification of students with learning disabilities. However, after determining that a student has a severe discrepancy, other factors must be excluded as possible causes of the unexpected underachievement. This exclusion clause criterion is used to ensure that the severe discrepancy is not the result of another disability or environmental factors such as the student's cultural background, language used in the home, economic disadvantage, or poor teaching. The primary cause of the underachievement must be the learning disability, and not other, related factors.

In addition to these criteria, a student who is identified with a learning disability must demonstrate a need for special education and related services to an extent that the academic underachievement cannot be overcome in the general education classroom without these services. This requirement relates to the exclusion clause, in that students may not be identified with a learning disability if they have not had the opportunity to learn due to factors such as school absences or poor teaching.

Educators have criticized the severe discrepancy approach to student identification for three primary reasons. First, this method requires that a student fall significantly behind grade level academically before a severe discrepancy exists. Thus, it is difficult for children in the early elementary grades to meet this criterion, when they are learning basic academic skills and can only be one or two years behind grade level. Furthermore, a student will often fail academic subjects and perhaps be retained in grade before the discrepancy is large enough to be identified with a learning disability. Many professionals have expressed a strong preference for using preventive approaches to addressing student needs rather than this type of "wait-to-fail" approach (Fletcher, Denton, & Francis, 2005).

A second criticism of this approach is that many professionals have found that the methods that are used to determine a severe discrepancy are not reliable or valid (Fletcher, Lyon, Fuchs, & Barnes, 2007; Gresham & Vellutino, 2010). This has resulted in the use of a range of alternatives for determining a severe discrepancy across states that have been called "confusing, unfair, and logically inconsistent" (Gresham, 2002, p. 467). This use of differing methods has contributed to a wide variation in the identification rates for school-aged students (ages 6 to 17) with learning disabilities across states, which range from 1.9% to 7.3% (McLeskey, Landers, Hoppey, & Williamson, 2011).

A final criticism of this severe discrepancy approach to identification is that professionals have lacked a systematic method for determining whether a student's academic difficulty is due to a lack of good teaching or a persistent learning disability. This shortcoming presents a serious problem with regard to student identification. Some students may be struggling with academic content areas because they have not been provided with evidence-based, highly effective instructional strategies, while others have a learning disability and struggle academically in spite of receiving high-quality instruction. Do these criticisms seem extreme enough to change the approach used to identify students with learning disabilities? Educational professionals continue to debate what method should be used to identify students with learning disabilities (Fletcher & Vaughn, 2009; Hale, Alfonso, Berninger, et al., 2010).

As a result of criticisms regarding the severe discrepancy approach to the identification of students with learning disabilities, IDEA 2004 included a stipulation that states must permit the use of a method to identify these students that emphasizes the student's response to scien-

## Pause & Reflect

Does the severe discrepancy approach to identifying students with learning disabilities seem logical to you? Is the criticism that this approach requires a student to "wait to fail" before identification an important criticism? Why or why not?

tific, research-based interventions (IDEA, 2004, PL 108-466, Sec. 614 (b)). IDEA 2004 also included a stipulation that states cannot require local schools to use a severe discrepancy to identify students with learning disabilities (PL 108-466, Sec. 614 [b] [6] [A-B]. Educators have developed an alternative approach to student identification, **response to intervention (RTI)**, in reply to these changes (Mellard, McKnight, & Jordan, 2010; Fletcher & Vaughn, 2009).

### Identification Using a Response-to-Intervention Approach

The RTI approach to identifying students with learning disabilities continues to emphasize the use of unexpected underachievement as the primary criterion for student identification. However, this approach is conceptualized differently than when a severe discrepancy is used. Response to intervention typically includes the following steps (Reschly, 2005):

1. Students receive high-quality instruction in the general education classroom in core content areas (i.e., reading and mathematics). This is often called Tier 1, or primary prevention.

2. Educators use screening measures to determine which students are struggling academically, in spite of high-quality instruction in the general education classroom. For students who struggle academically, teachers provide secondary prevention, or Tier-2 instruction, in the general education classroom. This instruction may include systematic, structured teaching, small-group instruction (three to six students), peer tutoring, and so forth.

3. Teachers monitor student progress during Tier-2 instruction. For those who continue to struggle, Tier-3 instruction is provided, which includes intensive, individualized interventions using highly effective instruction and frequent monitoring of student progress.

For more information on the use of RTI, see Chapter 13.

For students who do not respond to this high-quality instruction, poor teaching has been eliminated as a possible cause of the students' low achievement. These students are then referred to a multidisciplinary team for possible identification with a disability. Although several states have adopted an RTI approach to the identification of students with learning disabilities (Zirkel & Thomas, 2010), IDEA 2004 allows states to continue to use a severe discrepancy approach, or a combination of these methods to identify students with learning disabilities.

## Prevalence

Learning disability is the largest disability category and includes about 43% of all students with disabilities (U.S. Department of Education, 2011). Approximately 4.8% of all school-aged students (ages 6 to 17) in the United States are identified with learning disabilities. To put this information into perspective, in a typical classroom of 25 students, it would be expected that most often 1, but occasionally 2, students would be identified with a learning disability. This number may vary based on a variety of factors, including differing identification rates across states and local school districts and clustering of students with learning disabilities in certain schools or classrooms within schools.

It is noteworthy that identification rates for students with learning disabilities vary considerably both across and within states (U.S. Department of Education, 2011). For example, identification rates in states range from a low of 1.9% in Kentucky to a high of 7.3% in Iowa. Delaware, Pennsylvania, and Oklahoma identify more than 6% of students with learning disabilities. In contrast, 11 states identify fewer than 4% of students with learning disabilities, including Arkansas, Colorado, Connecticut, Georgia, Idaho, Kentucky, Louisiana, Maryland, Minnesota,

Many students are identified with learning disabilities based on how they respond to high-quality instruction in a general education classroom.

Mississippi, and Missouri (McLeskey, Landers, Hoppey, & Williamson, 2011). Similar differences exist across school districts within states, likely as a result of differing approaches used to identify students and demographic factors (e.g., poverty rate).

The number of students with learning disabilities grew rapidly from the 1970s through the 1990s, and peaked at 5.75% of the school-aged population in 2000 (McLeskey, Landers, Hoppey, & Williamson, 2011). This growth likely reflected the newness of the category (the term *learning disability* and a related definition initially appeared in federal law as part of the Learning Disabilities Act of 1969 [Part G, Title VI, PL 91-230]) and a subsequent federal law (i.e., PL 94-142, the Education for All Handicapped Children Act, later renamed IDEA, passed in 1975) mandating that all students with disabilities be identified and provided services. Since the 2000–2001 school year, the identification rate for students with LD has declined significantly, to approximately 4.8% for the 2008–2009 school year (McLeskey et al., 2011).

## Service Delivery

During the 1970s and 1980s, many students with learning disabilities were educated in separate settings for much of the school day (McLeskey, Henry, & Axelrod, 1999; McLeskey & Pacchiano, 1994). More recently, the number of students with learning disabilities who are included in general education classrooms for most or all of the school day has increased significantly (McLeskey et al., 2011). These increases have been influenced by two primary factors: (1) research demonstrating that most students with learning disabilities benefit from spending most of the school day in general education classrooms (McLeskey & Waldron, 2011a, 2011b; Salend & Garrick Duhaney, 2007); and (2) federal and state initiatives emphasizing that students with disabilities should be educated in less restrictive settings (e.g., Will, 1986).

The changes in the number of students with learning disabilities who are included in general education classrooms are illustrated in Table 3.1. For example, in the early 1990s, 22% of students with learning disabilities spent most or all of the school day (i.e., 80% or more) in a general education classroom. By 2008–2009, this number had increased significantly, as 62% of students with learning disabilities spent most of the school day in a general education setting.

Another important change that is illustrated in Table 3.1 is the decrease in the number of students with learning disabilities who spend very little of the school day in general education classrooms (i.e., less than 40%

### Pause & Reflect

The rapid growth of inclusive programs in schools has caused some problems with developing high-quality programs for students and has produced some teacher opposition to inclusion. Why do you think this occurred? Is it important that schools overcome this opposition? How might this be done?

**Table 3.1**    Percentage of School-Aged Students with Learning Disabilities, Ages 6–21, Taught in Different Placement Settings, 1990–1991 and 2008–2009

| | Placement Settings | | |
| --- | --- | --- | --- |
| **School Year** | **Most of the School Day (80% or more)** | **Some of the School Day (40% to 79%)** | **Limited Amount of the School Day (less than 40%) or Separate School[a]** |
| 1990–1991 | 22% | 53% | 25% |
| 2008–2009 | 62% | 28% | 10% |

[a]This setting is made up of several placement settings that are reported by the U.S. Department of Education, including a public separate facility, private separate facility, public residential facility, private residential facility, and home/hospital environment.

*Source:* Data from U.S. Department of Education (2011). Individuals with Disabilities Education Act Data. Retrieved May 31, 2011, from https://www.ideadata.org/index.html

of the school day or in a separate school). In 1990, about 1 in 4 students with learning disabilities were educated in one of these highly restrictive settings. This number declined substantially by 2008–2009, as only 1 in 10 students with learning disabilities are now educated in these settings.

The data in Table 3.1 illustrate that schools have rapidly moved toward educating increasing numbers of students with learning disabilities in general education classrooms for most of the school day. Much of this growth in general education placements has occurred since the 2000–2001 school year (McLeskey et al., 2011), and we anticipate that this trend toward educating increasing numbers of students with learning disabilities in general education classrooms will continue in the coming years.

## Major Characteristics of Students with Learning Disabilities

The major characteristic of the learning disability category is its heterogeneity (Mercer & Pullen, 2009). This diversity has resulted in what some researchers have characterized as different subtypes of learning disabilities (Fletcher, Lyon, Fuchs, & Barnes, 2007). Given the heterogeneity of the learning disability category, it is important to keep in mind that the characteristics we discuss in the following sections apply to *some but not all* students with learning disabilities. A second point to keep in mind as you review this information is emphasized by Vicki Eng, seventh-grade teacher at West Hernando Middle School: "It's amazing that other students who are not labeled have many of the same characteristics as students with learning disabilities." Many students who are not identified with a learning disability exhibit some of these characteristics at some level, although often not to the extremes exhibited by students with learning disabilities.

### Academic Characteristics

As we've noted previously, the main characteristic that educators use to identify students with learning disabilities is underachievement. All of these students share a common characteristic related to academic difficulty in one or more of the following areas: oral expression, listening comprehension, written expression, basic reading skill, reading fluency skills, reading comprehension, mathematics calculation, and mathematics problem solving.

The most common LD is in the area of reading. Approximately 80% of students with learning disabilities have difficulty in learning to read (Feifer, 2011). Evidence suggests that reading difficulties often relate to problems with word recognition and spelling, reading fluency and automaticity, and/or reading comprehension (Fletcher, Lyon, Fuchs, & Barnes, 2007).

As students move through school, reading difficulties can cause problems with all subject areas. For example, in later elementary school, mathematics requires greater levels of reading skill as the curriculum includes word problems and increasingly complex steps for problem solving. Reading difficulties become more and more challenging for adolescents with learning disabilities, as the content-area curriculum in all areas becomes more complex, and the gap between student skills and classroom demands increases

Most students with learning disabilities have difficulty learning to read.

(Lenz & Deshler, 2004). This contributes to the difficulty students with learning disabilities have in passing high-stakes tests and making passing grades; about one in three of these students fail content-area courses (Lerner & Johns, 2009). A close collaborative relationship between a general and special-education teacher is often needed to address the complex needs of a student with LD who struggles with learning to read. See the View from a Teacher feature for more information regarding how to make co-teaching with these students successful.

We provide more information on collaboration and co-teaching in Chapter 10.

Some students with learning disabilities also have difficulty in learning mathematics. These problems may relate to math computations (e.g., learning math facts at a level that allows quick, automatic responses, or difficulty learning strategies to complete math calculations) or math problem solving (e.g., using strategies to complete word problems) (Fletcher et al., 2007; Geary, Hoard, & Bailey, 2011). The number of students with learning disabilities who have difficulty with math increases as these students get older, primarily because other difficulties such as limited reading skills or attentional problems impede the development of math skills.

Finally, some students with learning disabilities have difficulty with written expression. These students tend to produce written products with technical errors (i.e., punctuation, grammar), as well as poor organization and limited development of ideas (Lerner & Johns, 2009). As with reading and math problems, difficulty with written expression tends to cause increasingly more problems for students with learning disabilities as they move through grade levels and as the curriculum becomes more complex.

## A View from a Teacher

### Two Teachers Are Often Needed to Support Students with LD

Kim Miller is a special education teacher who has worked with several co-teachers in grades 3 and 4 at Gilpin Manor Elementary. When working with students with LD, she emphasizes the need to collaborate with her general education co-teachers to meet the needs of all students who are struggling to learn to read. This is especially true when providing intensive tiers of instruction for students with LD, and coordinating this instruction with the curriculum of the general education classroom.

When collaborating with co-teachers, Kim advises them to "get to know your teammates. You have to get to know their strengths, their weaknesses, what they feel comfortable with." She goes on to note that co-teaching "is all about attitudes. You can tell right away. . . . You really have to have a teacher who is willing to work with these students and understands their disabilities. It's all about teachers' relationships with each other."

Kim's favorite co-teachers are those who have some background in special education, especially a teacher who is dual certified in general and special education, as she is. These are teachers who have both deep knowledge of the content taught in the classroom, as well as methods for adapting instruction to ensure that all students learn this content. "I enjoy having a general education teacher that is on board with inclusion, and she [or he] is basically a special education teacher as well. That makes a big difference. They are more understanding, nurturing, and tolerant of students with disabilities, and can meet the students' needs when I'm not in the classroom."

Kim concludes by noting "you have to have a great teammate. You have to be flexible and have good communication with your co-teaching partner. Scheduling is a big thing. You have to respect [your partner's] schedule, and [she or he has] to respect yours. The other thing is being prepared. You have to know ahead of time what's going on. There are always times when you adapt a test on the run, we have to do that. But being prepared whenever you can is important. [My co-teacher will] shoot me an e-mail and say tomorrow in math we're going to be doing this lesson; I want you to work with these kids. Then I know what lesson, what the kids' needs are, then I can develop a lesson or pull whatever I have."

We provide additional information regarding instructional strategies for teaching students who struggle learning core content in reading, mathematics, and writing in Chapter 13.

# Cognitive Characteristics

Students with learning disabilities have a range of cognitive deficits that contribute to their learning problems. As with academic problems, none of these deficits is common to all students with learning disabilities. We discuss the most common deficits next.

### Memory Problems

Memory problems may be manifested in learning relatively simple material such as sight vocabulary or math facts, or may reflect a lack of effective strategies for learning more complex material. Students with learning disabilities also frequently have difficulty with **working memory**, which is the memory that is needed to perform a particular task (Feifer, 2011). Problems with working memory impact the ability to see something, think about it, and then act on this information (Siegel, 2003).

### Attentional Problems

Approximately 25% of students with learning disabilities also have ADHD (DuPaul, 2007), and many more have some difficulty with attention or impulsive behavior. These students have difficulty selectively attending to information and sustaining attention over time. They also have problems related to impulsivity (i.e., responding without thinking) when presented with oral and written problems or questions in class. Finally, these students might have difficulty sitting still in class and may be easily distracted.

### Metacognitive Deficits

Many students with learning disabilities have problems with monitoring their thinking processes (Mercer & Pullen, 2009). These difficulties with **metacognition** often prevent students from using a series of steps in solving a complex math problem or monitoring their attention to information to ensure that they comprehend written material. Strategies for addressing metacognitive problems have been used effectively with students with learning disabilities. These include the use of **advance organizers** before presenting material, and providing students with strategies for planning and organizing material as they study academic content.

# Social and Motivational Characteristics

Many students with learning disabilities have social and motivational difficulties that influence school performance. Social problems relate to how well these students get along with others; motivational difficulties may influence academic progress. This might result in what Susan Davis, an eighth-grade teacher at West Hernando Middle School, describes as an "I can't do it attitude" for many students with learning disabilities. Descriptions of the more common social and motivational problems manifested by students with learning disabilities are subsequently provided.

## Pause & Reflect

Discuss with a peer in class an activity that is important to you but in which you do not perform well (e.g., music, sports, science, mathematics). How does your poor performance affect your motivation to engage in this task? How does your experience relate to motivational problems exhibited by persons with learning disabilities who repeatedly fail when attempting to learn to read or learn mathematics skills?

### Social Problems

Social skills are a strength for many students with learning disabilities, but researchers estimate that approximately one third of these students have social-skills deficits (Lerner & Johns, 2009). These difficulties relate to how well students get along with teachers and peers, and may relate to:

- Lack of skills needed to build social relationships
- Exhibiting aggressive actions or negative verbal behaviors
- More attention-seeking or disruptive behaviors
- Displaying more insensitive and less tactful or cooperative behaviors when interacting with others (Bryan, Burstein, & Ergul, 2004)

These social-skills difficulties may lead to social isolation of students with learning disabilities and problems getting along with peers and teachers. They may also result in students with learning disabilities being the target of bullies (Weiner, 2004). It is important to note that the low social status of some students with LD may relate to the students' low achievement (e.g., placement in a separate class with other students who are low achieving). Thus, when students with learning disabilities are included in general education classes, it is important that teachers recognize and address these social issues, to ensure that they do not increase the students' adjustment problems and contribute to underachievement.

### Motivational Problems

Repeated difficulty in learning academic content often leads students to avoid the content, deny that a problem exists, and give up quickly when presented with new information related to the content. In short, the student's motivation is influenced by continued difficulty in mastering content.

As students with learning disabilities move into middle and high school, motivational problems often become more extreme. For some of these students, repeated failure may cause them to become passive learners and develop an attitude toward learning that has been characterized as *learned helplessness* (Lerner & Johns, 2009). These students react passively to tasks, do not actively engage in learning, and often wait for the teacher to tell them what to do rather than actively try to solve a problem.

When students with learning disabilities are pulled out of general education classrooms, they should be provided high-quality, intensive, small-group instruction.

The most important factors in maintaining a high motivation level for students with learning disabilities involve recognizing when these issues arise and addressing them by providing effective instruction that is appropriate to the students' needs. Teachers may also address these problems by teaching students learning strategies that they can use to actively engage in learning and by directly teaching social skills.

> We provide information on effective instructional strategies for teaching students in secondary content areas in Chapter 14.

## Teaching Students with Learning Disabilities in Inclusive Classrooms: Tips from Teachers

Although students with learning disabilities are often characterized as having mild difficulties, including them in general education classrooms can become very complex and demanding, even for skilled teachers. We interviewed four teachers who co-teach in inclusive classrooms at Gilpin Manor Elementary School and West Hernando Middle School, including Melissa Pratt (preschool special education teacher), Susan Huff (fifth-grade teacher), Susan Davis and Lisa Hallal (eighth-grade special education teachers). They offered the following tips to support the successful inclusion of students with learning disabilities in elementary and secondary classrooms.

- **Differentiate instruction by using technology.** Melissa Pratt addressed the importance of differentiating instruction for all students, even though this task is difficult and time consuming. Melissa emphasized the importance of using technology to ensure that all student needs are met. She went on to note that students with disabilities need models, and that a multisensory approach works best for them. She feels that technology is going to provide a "gateway" to support teachers as they differentiate instruction. Melissa provides an example from her class using a Smartboard to make instruction multisensory and interactive. "I did the story of *The Three Bears* and we actually got to see Goldilocks eat the different things, break the chairs, and run away when the bears came home." The teacher goes on to note that if her students had simply read the text of the book, they would have seen the pictures, and some might have been able to provide some of the information from the book. "But we read it, they saw the pictures, they saw the animation, they were engaged, and they can answer questions about the story." Melissa concludes that the use of this type of multi-sensory teaching using technology improves learning outcomes for all students, and makes learning more enjoyable.

- **Provide students extra help when they don't learn something during a class period.** Lisa Hallal noted that there are times when students don't understand the content during a class period, and she doesn't have time to help them. "Some students need more than we can give them during class, or they just don't get it during some lessons. It doesn't take much time to help them get it in small groups or one on one. We need to give them time and patience and help them walk through the work with guided practice."

  When this occurs, teachers at West Hernando do not pull students out of academic subjects. Rather, they find other times to help the students that do not take time away from other instructional time. This is done during an after-school program that gives students the extra help they need. Thus, if some students do not get the math lesson during class, they receive tutoring after school addressing the content they do not understand. As Lisa Hallal noted, "Our help takes a little frustration away from them. Knowing they have the support they need helps them get through things. They don't resist because they know we really want to help them. They learn that it's not easy, but if I put an effort into it, the extra work does pay off."

- **Keep expectations high for students with learning disabilities.** Susan Davis believes that this is one of the major challenges teachers face when students with LD are included in general education classrooms. She noted that when students with learning disabilities move from a separate class to an inclusive general education classroom, expectations for their academic achievement and behavior increases substantially, and the students are usually able to fulfill the expectations. However, it is not easy. Some students with LD in an inclusive classroom "see the high expectations and often come in at first with a 'can't do it' attitude." She went on to note that teachers "need to give them support to make sure they do get it. You may do some guided practice, and they get it. Or provide them with scaffolding until they get the information. It takes them a while to learn that you'll give them the support they need and they can do it."

- **Continuously grow as a teacher.** Susan Huff talked about the complexity of teaching a broad range of students in an inclusive classroom, and the need to continuously grow as a teacher to meet this challenge. "I think that I am continually growing. . . . I don't know if I would say that I am successful just yet. I know I've learned a lot. I know I've changed—made modifications in my style of teaching—and it's just a continual growing process. I'm not where I would want to be just yet, but I'm getting there." Susan went on to note that she uses many approaches to continue to grow as a teacher. One approach she uses is to "work with special educators, having them help me with my planning, having them use their background knowledge to help me." She commented that she also learns by taking advantage of good professional development that fits her needs, and learns from her own experiences in the classroom.

## Summary

This chapter addressed the following topics:

### Who are students with learning disabilities?

- The primary criterion used to identify students with learning disabilities is unexpectedly low achievement. This criterion is defined by either a severe discrepancy between expected and actual achievement levels, or a procedure that examines the student's response to research-based interventions (i.e., response to intervention).

- About 43% of all students with disabilities, or 5% of the school-aged population, are identified with learning disabilities.

- The number of students with learning disabilities grew rapidly across the United States until the mid-1990s. Since that time, the number of students in this category has decreased significantly.

- We do not know what causes most learning disabilities, although it is assumed that these disabilities are somehow related to abnormal brain function. Learning disabilities seem to run in families, and they may be caused by poor teaching.
- Most students identified with learning disabilities are educated for most of the school day in general education classrooms.

### Major characteristics of students with learning disabilities

- Students with learning disabilities are characterized by unexpectedly low achievement. About 80% of students with learning disabilities have low achievement in reading. Other common areas of underachievement include mathematics and written expression.
- The learning disability category is very heterogeneous. Significant subgroups of these students, however, are characterized by:
  - Cognitive skills deficits related to memory, attention, and/or metacognition
  - Social problems that result in difficulty getting along with others
  - Motivational problems that often result from prolonged failure in one or more academic content areas

### Teaching students with LD in inclusive classrooms: Tips from teachers

- Technology should be used to support differentiation of instruction for all students, including those with LD.
- Expectations for students with learning disabilities should be kept high when they are taught in inclusive classrooms.
- Students with LD should be provided with additional instruction when they do not master content in the general education classroom.
- Teachers should continue to learn and grow professionally to meet the challenge of teaching students with LD in inclusive classrooms.

## Addressing Professional Standards

Standards addressed in Chapter 3 include:

**CEC Standards:** (1) foundations, (2) development and characteristics of learners, (3) individual learning differences, (4) instructional strategies.

### MyEducationLab

Go to the topic Learning Disabilities/ADHD in the **MyEducationLab** (www .myeducationlab.com) for *Inclusion*, where you can:

- Find learning outcomes for Learning Disabilities/ADHD, along with the national standards that connect to these outcomes.
- Complete Assignments and Activities that can help you more deeply understand the chapter content.
- Apply and practice your understanding of the core teaching skills identified in the chapter with the Building Teaching Skills and Dispositions learning units.
- Examine challenging situations and cases presented in the IRIS Center Resources.
- Check your comprehension on the content covered in the chapter with the Study Plan. Here you will be able to take a chapter quiz, receive feedback on your answers, and then access Review, Practice, and Enrichment activities to enhance your understanding of chapter content.

# Students with Attention-Deficit/ Hyperactivity Disorder

## KEY TOPICS

**After reading this chapter you will:**

- Know who the students with attention-deficit/hyperactivity disorder (ADHD) are, the methods used to identify students with the disability, and the range of settings in which they are educated.

- Be able to describe major characteristics of students with ADHD.

- Know how medication is used to address the symptoms of ADHD.

- Be aware of several practical tips from teachers that facilitate the inclusion of students with ADHD.

# chapter 4

## A VIEW FROM TEACHERS

**How Students with Attention-Deficit/Hyperactivity Disorder Benefit from Inclusion**

We interviewed two teachers from West Hernando Middle School who have worked with many students with ADHD who were included in general education classrooms. Eileen Walls is a behavior specialist, and Laura Scott is a seventh-grade special education teacher.

Eileen Walls noted:

> The biggest benefit [for including students with ADHD] is that they learn to cope effectively in the regular classroom. Why do they need to learn to cope? They don't get to shop at a special-education Publix when they graduate from high school. There is no special-education line at the bank for them. They have to learn to be successful and be a contributing member of the school community. And when they're out of school, they need to be a contributor to a more global community, whether it is their work environment, or home environment, or church or their own neighborhood. It is important to learn coping strategies so they can be successful later in life and contribute.

Laura Scott addressed academic and social benefits for including students with ADHD:

> When we had separate classes, it seemed that the curriculum automatically started getting watered down and covered at a slower pace. We didn't cover the wealth of information that's in the regular curriculum. Students with ADHD benefit academically from being in a general education classroom where there is a general education teacher who is well versed in the curriculum being taught, whether it's math, English, geography, or whatever. So it's better academically to be in general education.

> Socially, it's better for them as well. Their day is just like everyone else's day, and that's really important to them. There's a stigma for kids going out of the regular classroom, especially for kids with mild disabilities. All of the students know who the English teachers are, so it's tough on students when they tell people who their teacher is and they know it's the teacher for the "slow" kids. In the regular class, none of the students really knows the function of the special-education teacher. We're just co-teaching. We work with all the kids, some one at a time, some in small groups. Sometimes we teach the whole class. So none of the kids is stigmatized.

Laura Scott also discussed two key issues when teaching students with ADHD in inclusive classrooms. One key is to get to know the student well:

> The challenges for these students are different, depending on the severity of the ADHD. Some kids are pretty easy to handle; others need more help. The key is really knowing the child, and what that child can handle. What are the warning signs that they are going to have a bad day? You can put the label of "ADHD" on lots of kids, but the label doesn't look the same on every child.

A second key is to recognize that academics and the student's ADHD-type behaviors are closely related:

> I always keep in mind that much of their behavior is a front or escape from having to do the work that they know they can't do. My job is to make sure there's a lot of academic support, making them sure they can do the work. Reassuring them that I will help them, I'm not going to leave them out there hanging on their own. If they think they're going to get help and support, they're much more likely to tackle the work and alleviate some of that behavior that comes from wanting to escape the work.

**MyEducationLab**

Visit the MyEducation-Lab for Inclusion to enhance your understanding of chapter concepts with a personalized Study Plan. You'll also have the opportunity to hone your teaching skills through video and case-based Assignments and Activities, Building Teaching Skills and Disposition lessons, and IRIS Case Studies.

# Introduction

What do you think of when someone says a child is "hyperactive," or "He's ADHD"? Most of us have many preconceived notions about **attention-deficit/hyperactivity disorder (ADHD)**. You've probably heard friends mention this term, and you may have seen stories on television, in the print media, or on the Web addressing ADHD. This widespread media coverage likely occurs, at least in part, because the primary characteristics of this category—inattention, impulsivity, and high levels of activity—are so common. Almost all young children exhibit these behaviors at some level, and so do many adults. As you may have noticed, circumstances may increase the occurrence of these behaviors for any of us. (Think of a young child left unsupervised in a grocery store, or a college student who sits through a boring 50-minute lecture.) Circumstances may also decrease the occurrence of these behaviors. (Remember that highly stimulating college class, when time passed so quickly, or a child watching a movie that he finds very interesting.)

It seems that ADHD is so interesting to many people because persons who are given this label are so much like the rest of us. As a special educator once noted, "Students with ADHD are just like everybody else, only more so." This perhaps is the essence of the ADHD category. These are students who bring many strengths into the classroom; however, certain aspects of their behavior (inattention, impulsivity, and/or activity level) are so extreme that they interfere with everyday life activities such as school.

Eileen Walls and Laura Scott, teachers at West Hernando Middle School in the chapter-opening "View from Teachers" feature, noted that students with ADHD benefit in many ways when they are included in general education classrooms. These benefits may relate to improved academic skills or social adjustment as well as preparation for coping with life beyond school. In this chapter, we address how students with ADHD are identified, and the characteristics of these students that need to be understood and addressed to ensure that they succeed in an inclusive classroom. We also discuss the use of medication to control the symptoms of ADHD, and conclude the chapter with a description of several tips from teachers regarding how to successfully include these students in general education classrooms.

Many students in general education classrooms have some of the characteristics of ADHD (inattentive, impulsive, highly active).

# Who Are Students with Attention-Deficit/ Hyperactivity Disorder?

## Definition

For a quick overview of the ADHD category, refer to "Just the Facts: Students with ADHD" on the next page. The definition that is most widely used to identify students with ADHD was developed by the American Psychiatric Association (APA, 2000) and defines ADHD as "a persistent pattern of inattention and/or hyperactivity-impulsivity that is more frequently displayed and more severe than is typically observed in individuals at a comparable level of development" (p. 85). This definition also includes symptoms that are used for student identification that are shown in Figure 4.1. This definition and related criteria have been thoroughly researched and revised on several occasions.

As you review the behavioral symptoms used to identify ADHD in Figure 4.1, you should attend to several key issues that are intended to improve the reliability of student identification:

> ### Pause & Reflect
>
> Do you know someone who exhibits one of the primary characteristics of ADHD with some frequency (i.e., inattentive, impulsive, or highly active)? Do certain circumstances (e.g., a boring college lecture) influence the occurrence of these behaviors? Why does this occur? What does this say about inclusive classrooms that might be better (or worse) for educating students with ADHD?

- Students must exhibit six of nine explicit behaviors related to either inattention or hyperactivity-impulsivity.
- These behaviors must be exhibited frequently (e.g., much more often than observed in peers) over a 6-month period.

| Figure 4.1 | Symptoms for Identifying ADHD—Inattentive, Hyperactive, and Impulsive Behavior from DSM-IV-TR |
|---|---|

**(1) Inattentive Behavior**
- (a) Often fails to give close attention to details or makes careless mistakes in schoolwork, work, or other activities
- (b) Often has difficulty sustaining attention in tasks or play activities
- (c) Often does not seem to listen when spoken to directly
- (d) Often does not follow through on instructions and fails to finish schoolwork, chores, or duties in the workplace (not due to oppositional behavior or failure to understand instructions)
- (e) Often has difficulty organizing activities
- (f) Often avoids, dislikes, or is reluctant to engage in tasks that require sustained mental effort (such as schoolwork or homework)
- (g) Often loses things necessary for tasks or activities (e.g., toys, school assignments, pencils, books, or tools)
- (h) Is often easily distracted by extraneous stimuli
- (i) Is often forgetful in daily activities

**(2) Hyperactive Behavior**
- (a) Often fidgets with hands or feet or squirms in seat
- (b) Often leaves seat in classroom or in other situations in which remaining seated is expected
- (c) Often runs about or climbs excessively in situations in which it is inappropriate (in adolescents or adults, may be limited to subjective feelings of restlessness)
- (d) Often has difficulty playing or engaging in leisure activities quietly
- (e) Is often "on the go" or often acts as if "driven by a motor"
- (f) Often talks excessively

**(3) Impulsive Behavior**
- (a) Often blurts out answers before questions have been completed
- (b) Often has difficulty awaiting turn
- (c) Often interrupts or intrudes on others (e.g., butts into conversations or games)

*Source:* Adapted from the *Diagnostic and Statistical Manual of Mental Disorders*, Fourth Edition, Text Revision, Copyright 2000. American Psychiatric Association.

## Just the Facts
### Students with ADHD

| | |
|---|---|
| Who are the students? | Children with ADHD manifest "a persistent pattern of inattention and/or hyperactivity-impulsivity that is more frequently displayed and more severe than is typically observed in individuals at a comparable level of development" (APA, 2000, p. 85). To be identified in a school, these behaviors must significantly impede the student's educational performance. |
| What are typical characteristics? | • Impulsivity—Responding without thinking.<br>• Hyperactivity—Much more active than other students of the same age.<br>• Inattention—Inability to focus, selectively attend, or maintain attention for sustained periods of time.<br>• Coexisting conduct problems—About 30 to 50% of students with ADHD have significant conduct problems.<br>• Coexisting academic problems—About 80% of these students have some level of academic problem, and about 25% are identified with a learning disability. |
| What are the demographics? | • Estimates vary regarding how many school-aged students have ADHD. Recent research indicates that parents report that about 7% (or about 4.1 million) of children ages 4 to 17 are currently identified with ADHD.<br>• About 1.25% of the school-aged population are identified under IDEA as "other health impaired," the category that includes ADHD. About 1% of students are identified as ADHD under Section 504 of the Rehabilitation Act.<br>• The use of prescription medication varies across states and communities. Overall, about 5% of school-aged students receive some form of medication (mostly stimulant medications) for ADHD.<br>• About 3 of every 4 students with ADHD are male.<br>• Students who live in high poverty settings are substantially more likely to be identified with ADHD when compared to students from middle- and high-income settings. |
| Where are students with ADHD educated? | • Most general education classes have from 1 to 3 students with ADHD for much or all of the school day. |
| How are students identified? | • Criteria from *DSM-IV-TR* (APA, 2000) are widely used to identify students with ADHD. (See Figure 4.1 for more information regarding these criteria.)<br>• Information from parents and teachers regarding the student's behavior is the most critical information used to identify students with ADHD. This information is collected using interviews, observations in multiple settings, and rating scales. |
| What causes ADHD? | • The cause of ADHD is often unknown.<br>• Professionals speculate that ADHD most often seems to result from the complex interaction of many factors. Contributing factors may include:<br>  • *Brain injury*. Many students who have had documented brain injury exhibit one or more of the symptoms of ADHD. This includes about 5 to 10% of all students with ADHD.<br>  • *Brain abnormalities*. Research has shown that students with ADHD often have different brain chemistry when compared to children who do not have ADHD (DuPaul, Barkley, & Connor, 1998). For example, many of these students have deficiencies in neurotransmitters or chemicals in the brain that influence the transmission of signals between nerve cells.<br>  • *Hereditary influences*. If a parent or sibling has ADHD, the probability that another sibling will have ADHD increases significantly.<br>  • *Family influences*. Poor parenting does not cause ADHD as some have suggested, but poor parent behavior management skills can make the symptoms of ADHD worse. Furthermore, extreme stress in a family can temporarily result in the manifestation of symptoms related to ADHD. |
| What are the outcomes? | • About 1 in 3 students with ADHD has no symptoms of ADHD in adulthood.<br>• About 1 in 4 students with ADHD has conduct disorders in adulthood.<br>• About 1 in 4 students with ADHD develops major depression in adulthood. |

- The behaviors must be evident across two or more settings (i.e., school and home).
- The impulsive and inattentive behavior must be exhibited before the age of 7.
- Students may be identified as having one of three types of ADHD:

> ADHD, predominantly inattentive type (ADHD-PI);
> ADHD, predominantly hyperactive-impulsive type (ADHD-PHI); or
> ADHD combined, or those who exhibit inattentive *and* hyperactive-impulsive behaviors (ADHD-C).

Another consideration regarding the definition of ADHD is the fact that students exhibit these symptoms in different ways and at different levels as they age. For example, if you observe a group of preschool students in a setting where they are expected to sit and listen to someone read, you will see many examples of all the behaviors that are used to identify ADHD. As children mature, many learn to monitor and control these behaviors (e.g., inattentive behavior lessens with age for all students) and channel them in more positive directions (e.g., high levels of activity are delayed until time for recess). Furthermore, as West Hernando Middle School teacher Laura Scott noted in the "View from Teachers" at the beginning of this chapter, every student with ADHD is different, and each of these students exhibits a different pattern of impulsive, inattentive, and hyperactive behaviors.

Given these considerations, how can a definition be developed that can be reliably used to identify students with ADHD? This is the source of much controversy about this category, as professional judgment must be used to determine if behaviors that appear often are manifested frequently enough, at a level that is so extreme when compared to peers, that a student should be identified with ADHD.

## Identification of Students with ADHD

As we begin a discussion of the identification of students with ADHD, you should note that this category is unique and somewhat confusing when it comes to identification. This occurs in large part because ADHD is not a separate special education category but is included as part of the other health impairments (OHI) category in IDEA.

*Other health impairments* are defined in IDEA as follows:

> Other health impairment means having limited strength, vitality or alertness, including a heightened alertness to environmental stimuli, that results in limited alertness with respect to the educational environment, that—
>
> (i) Is due to chronic or acute health problems such as asthma, attention deficit disorder or attention deficit hyperactivity disorder, diabetes, epilepsy, a heart condition, hemophilia, lead poisoning, leukemia, nephritis, rheumatic fever, sickle cell anemia, and Tourette syndrome; and
> (ii) Adversely affects a child's educational performance. (PL 108-446 Regulations, Sec. 300.8(c)(9)(i))

You will note that two terms are used in this definition for students with ADHD: attention-deficit disorder (ADD) and attention-deficit/hyperactivity disorder (ADHD). ADD was formerly used for children with predominantly inattentive behaviors (ADHD-PI) and continues to be used by some to identify these students. Neither of these terms is defined in IDEA. This is also true of the other conditions that are included in the OHI category (i.e., diabetes, epilepsy, etc.). It is thus assumed that these conditions are medically defined and that a physician will make a determination regarding whether the conditions exist.

A physician typically identifies students with ADHD, using information provided by parents, teachers, school psychologists, and others. The American Academy of Pediatrics (Reiff, 2004) has developed guidelines that pediatricians use to identify students with ADHD. The six-step process includes the following:

1. If a child from ages 6 to 12 is described as unusually inattentive, hyperactive, impulsive; underachieving in school; or exhibiting behavior problems, the child should be evaluated for ADHD.

2. To identify a student with ADHD, the *DSM-IV TR* criteria (APA, 2000) should be used.

3. Evidence collected should include information from parents or caregivers regarding the symptoms of ADHD (i.e., impulsivity, inattention, hyperactivity) across settings; the age at which the behaviors were initially noticed; how long the child has exhibited the behaviors; and the degree to which the behaviors interfere with the child's ability to function (i.e., learn in school, get along with peers).

4. The pediatrician should obtain information from the child's teacher or other school professional regarding the symptoms of ADHD that the child exhibits in the classroom, how long the symptoms have been manifested, the degree to which the symptoms interfere with the child's ability to function; and whether any other conditions (e.g., learning disability, emotional/behavior disorder) are suspected.

5. An evaluation of any **co-existing conditions** (e.g., learning disability, emotional and behavioral disability) should be conducted.

6. Other diagnostic tests (e.g., blood tests, brain scans) or psychological tests are not routinely necessary to identify students with ADHD.

After a student is identified with ADHD, the school-based multidisciplinary team addresses Section (ii) of the OHI definition. This team must determine whether the student's ADHD adversely affects her educational performance. If the multidisciplinary team determines that the child's educational performance is affected (e.g., the child is significantly underachieving in reading or mathematics) and that the child needs special education services, she is then determined eligible as OHI for these services as part of IDEA.

It is noteworthy that eligibility for special education services is not based on the identification of a disability, but rather depends on whether the disability adversely affects the child's educational performance and whether special education services are required to address this need. With respect to students with ADHD, it is possible that the symptoms of this disability may be very mild, and educational performance is not adversely affected. Parents report that about half of all students with ADHD have mild symptoms (Centers for Disease Control [CDC], 2010). In still other instances, the symptoms of ADHD may be controlled sufficiently by medication, so that the student does not need special education services. (We will provide more information regarding the use of medication as an intervention for students identified with ADHD later in this chapter.)

If a student is identified as ADHD but is not eligible for special education services, the student still may be eligible for accommodations in the general education classroom as part of **Section 504 of the Rehabilitation Act** of 1973. This law is a civil rights act, designed to ensure that persons with disabilities receive reasonable accommodations and are not discriminated against as a result of their disability (Zirkel, 2009). These accommodations may include modification of tests used in a general education classroom to ensure student attention to relevant information, or moving the student to a location in the room where distractions will be minimized.

We offer one final cautionary note regarding the identification of students with ADHD and the use of medication to control the symptoms associated with this disability. Much information regarding this disability has appeared in the popular media, resulting in much discussion by parents and teachers. Given this widespread discussion of ADHD, you should keep in mind that a teacher should not recommend to a parent that a child should be referred to a physician to be evaluated for ADHD or suggest that the student could benefit from medication. A school's multidisciplinary team should provide information to parents regarding the nature of

A physician typically determines if a student has ADHD, using information from teachers, parents, school psychologists, and others.

a child's difficulty in school and whether these difficulties merit an evaluation by a physician who will make a decision regarding possible use of medication to address the child's behavior.

## Prevalence

For other categories of disability that are part of IDEA, data are collected by the U.S. Department of Education regarding the number of students who are identified and other related information (e.g., the setting in which the student is educated). These data are not collected for students with ADHD, which is not a stand-alone category of disability under IDEA. Although researchers agree that ADHD is the most common behavior problem among school-aged students (CDC, 2010; Ryan, Katsiyannis, & Hughes, 2011), specific estimates of the prevalence of students with ADHD vary widely.

The APA (2000) estimates that from 3 to 7% of students are identified with ADHD. Data from studies across settings have supported this estimate (Barkley, 2006b), although the prevalence rate seems to decline as children move through school (Costello et al., 2003). Recent interviews with parents from across the country (CDC, 2010) suggest that the prevalence of students with ADHD may fall within the high end of the 3 to 7% range, as parents revealed that about 7% of their children were identified with ADHD.

The range of prevalence rates suggests that the percentage of students identified with ADHD varies across settings (e.g., schools, school districts, states). However, no matter the setting, a substantial number of students are identified with ADHD (CDC, 2010). For example, at least 3 of 100 students are identified as ADHD in most school districts, and from 2 to 4.5 million students are so identified in the United States (Holler & Zirkel, 2008; U.S. Department of Education, 2011). This means that most general educators will have one to three students with ADHD in their classroom each school year.

Far more boys are identified with ADHD than girls. Early in the school years, approximately twice as many boys are identified as having ADHD. This ratio increases to approximately three or more boys to every girl later in the school years (CDC, 2010; Smith, Barkley, & Shapiro, 2006). Some evidence also indicates that ADHD is more common among children from low socioeconomic backgrounds; however, it is unclear whether differences exist across different racial groups (CDC, 2010).

Another factor that complicates the determination of how many students are identified with ADHD is that more than 50% of these students are also identified with another disability (Reiff, 2004). For example, the percentage of students who also have ADHD is approximately 25% of students identified with learning disabilities, 25 to 40% of students with intellectual disabilities, 50 to 60% of students with emotional and behavioral disabilities, and 25% of students with autism spectrum disorder (DuPaul, 2007; Reiff, 2004).

Perhaps the most important point we can make is this: Although prevalence rates vary significantly across the United States, every general education classroom includes students who exhibit many of the symptoms that are characteristic of these students. As Laura Scott notes in the "View from Teachers" feature that opens this chapter, the behaviors exhibited by students with ADHD vary significantly. This includes some students whose behavior does not seem to be significantly different from other students, to those with more extreme behaviors that can place significant demands on the classroom teacher and require substantial support from special education.

## Service Delivery

Most students with ADHD spend the majority of the school day in general education classrooms. Those students who are identified with ADHD and receive accommodations as part of Section 504 are typically educated full time in general education classrooms and have accommodations made in those settings. These are students who have mild symptoms of ADHD, and the symptoms have a limited impact on the students' educational performance

### Pause & Reflect

Students with ADHD who are often off task or respond impulsively in a general education classroom can be very frustrating for teachers. How can you ensure that these student behaviors do not negatively influence how you as a teacher interact with students with ADHD? In other words, how can you ensure that you model appropriate reactions to inappropriate student behaviors?

and social interactions. Students identified under Section 504 with ADHD include only about 1% of the school-aged population (Holler & Zirkel, 2008).

Students who are identified under the OHI category as ADHD, and are in need of special education services, can be assumed to have somewhat more extreme symptoms related to ADHD that affect educational performance. A majority of these students are also educated in general education settings for most of the school day. In 2008, 60% of students in the OHI category (most of whom are identified with ADHD) spent most of the school day (80% or more) in general education classrooms, while only 15% of students identified with OHI spent most of the school day in separate settings (U.S. Department of Education, 2011).

A final consideration relates to students with ADHD who are identified in another category of disability. As we noted previously, many students identified with learning disabilities, emotional and behavioral disabilities, intellectual disabilities, and autism spectrum disorders also are identified with ADHD. These are often the students with the most extreme ADHD symptoms that interfere with academic progress and social interactions, and may result in placement in special education settings for more of the school day.

When considering all students identified with ADHD, it is likely that most general education teachers will have from one to three students with ADHD in class for most of the school day. This suggests the need for knowledge regarding the characteristics of these students and how to effectively address their needs in the general education classroom.

## Major Characteristics of Students with ADHD

### Inattentive, Hyperactive, and Impulsive Behaviors

Students who are hyperactive may present challenges to classroom teachers during instructional activities that require seatwork.

As Laura Scott, a seventh-grade special education teacher at West Hernando Middle School, notes at the beginning of this chapter in "A View from Teachers," the behaviors exhibited by students with ADHD vary significantly. The behavior of some of these students isn't significantly different from other students in a typical classroom; others, however, have more extreme behaviors. In any form, teachers may find the impulsive, inattentive, and hyperactive behaviors of these students frustrating and perhaps annoying.

Inattention may take several forms. For example, students with ADHD may have difficulty orienting in an appropriate direction in a classroom (i.e., looking out a window rather than orienting in the direction of the teacher or toward a Smartboard at the front of the class). After orienting in an appropriate direction, these students may have difficulty sustaining attention for an appropriate amount of time, or they may be easily distracted by extraneous activities or noises. Finally, even with an appropriate level of sustained attention, some students with ADHD have difficulty selectively attending, or determining just what they should attend to on a Smartboard (e.g., should the student look at pictures, the words describing the pictures, or both?).

To describe students with ADHD, teachers often use terms such as *inattentive; careless; unable to concentrate; disorganized; easily distracted; unable to follow directions; forgetful;* and *poor at listening, following directions, and completing tasks.* Laura Scott, seventh-grade special education teacher at West Hernando Middle School, described students with ADHD as "having a hard time paying attention, blurting out, saying inappropriate things, or losing control quickly."

Another major characteristic of students with ADHD is **hyperactivity**, or a high level of activity that is inappropriate for a given setting and is not age appropriate. The level of activity varies significantly among students with ADHD. Some activity levels are annoying to teachers and peers but do not adversely affect the student's educational performance. At the other extreme, some students with ADHD have activity levels that are so high that they disrupt class, impede the student's educational progress, and interfere with interactions with teachers and peers.

When teachers describe students who exhibit hyperactive behaviors, they use terms or phrases such as *never slows down, driven by a motor, constantly talks out, cannot sit still*, and *wants to do things now!* Teachers also note that these students have difficulty following rules or listening to directions, and they engage in behaviors that prevent them from getting along well with others, including peers and teachers.

**Impulsivity** is often seen as part of a hyperactive-impulsive type of ADHD. Students who are impulsive often respond quickly before they think. Thus, teachers often describe students who are impulsive as *talking before they put their mind in gear, refusing to wait their turn, unable to follow the rules of a game*, and *intruding on others in social situations*. As you think about these behaviors, we're sure you'll readily recognize many ways that impulsive

## A View from a Teacher

### Learning from a Student's Success

Laura Scott is a seventh-grade special education teacher at West Hernando Middle School. She works as a co-teacher in general education classrooms to support students with disabilities. She is widely respected among her peers, especially for her knowledge and skills related to addressing the needs of students with ADHD. As she noted, "They're seventh graders. They all have ADHD at times! All teenagers have some of the symptoms at times," as they have difficulty paying attention or thinking before responding.

Even with her experience, Ms. Scott was quick to admit that she still makes mistakes at times when working with students with ADHD, and has to continuously examine her practice, monitor student outcomes, and figure out what works because every classroom and student are unique. She described an example of how she misjudged a student with ADHD, and learned from that experience and the student's success.

"We have a young man, Stephen, who is very active, impulsive, and yells out all the time. Usually with the right answer, but he doesn't follow the protocol and often gets off task. A few days ago he was in a language arts class doing centers with several things going on. The co-teacher and I had just finished our centers, and the other kids were finishing up, and this young man went to a table to read a book. Some other students in class were working in a group and doing a cause-and-effect center, and there were some inferences they needed to make. One of them said, 'Ms. Scott, we need your help.' I said, 'Did you ask three before me?' (They're supposed to ask three peers before asking me a question.) They said that they had and none of them were getting it, so I started to go over to their table. But just then Stephen put up his hand and said, 'I've got this, I can help them' and he went over to their table. I must admit that I thought 'Oh no! What's going to happen now!' I didn't have much confidence in Stephen.

"He proceeded to explain to the group how to form the inference, pointed out all the evidence like a teacher would have done, and did this beautifully. Then he left. A hand in the group went up a minute later, and my co-teacher smiled and said, 'Stephen, your class needs you.' He went over again and proceeded to tell them how he processed the information, and resolved the cause-and-effect problem. He did a very good job and he wanted to stay there. Typically he would be off task, but he stayed there and led that group."

Ms. Scott admitted that she had expected too little of Stephen, and learned from this experience. "That showed me I've got to give him more to do. He's a bright young man, and the more he had to do, the more he will do, and the better he will perform. And it's a pleasure to see him do that." Probably the most important reason Ms. Scott is an exceptional teacher after 25 years in the classroom is that she continues to learn from her students, as she reflects on the effectiveness of her practices, and seeks to continually become more effective. That's a big reason why so many students with ADHD, including Stephen, have been so successful in her co-taught inclusive classrooms.

behaviors have the potential to significantly affect a student's academic performance and social interactions in school settings.

Although most students who are impulsive or inattentive are actually not paying attention in class, and these behaviors negatively influence their academic progress, this is not always the case. It is important to keep in mind that the complexity of the characteristics associated with ADHD can lead to students who surprise us at times, as is the case in the following "A View from a Teacher" feature that describes a student's success story, and how Laura Scott learned from this student.

## Executive Functions and Working Memory

Many students with ADHD have difficulty with **executive functions**, including a range of cognitive processes that are used to engage in complex, goal-directed behavior or solve complex problems (Johnson & Reid, 2011). This includes knowledge regarding strategies and how they may be used to solve problems or complete tasks (i.e., metacognitive skills); attention and memory skills; and the ability to plan and self-monitor (Meltzer, 2007). In a classroom, teachers note these behaviors when students with ADHD exhibit poor planning skills, have difficulty developing a strategy to address a task, and do not effectively monitor progress toward completing a task (Johnson & Reid, 2011).

A core skill related to executive functions that is often a problem for students with ADHD is **working memory**. This construct has been described as a person's mental workspace, and has been more formally defined as a very limited capacity for storing and manipulating information that is used for cognitive tasks such as reasoning, learning, or comprehension (Martinussen & Major, 2011). For example, when a student is solving a multistep math problem (e.g., long division), working memory is used to monitor problem solving. As the student completes one step toward solving the problem, this information is held in memory, evaluated ("Is this the correct action? Did I perform the action appropriately and accurately?"), and used to determine when it is time to move to the next step.

Many students with ADHD have difficulty with executive functions and working memory that lead to academic skill deficits, especially when these students are working on complex tasks (e.g., writing, long division) (Johnson & Reid, 2011). Teachers can support students with ADHD who have these difficulties by providing supports to reduce demands on working memory, and by teaching students strategies to promote goal-oriented behavior. This may include scaffolding complex problems by breaking the task into multiple steps; providing explicit instruction regarding strategies that may be used to solve a complex task; and providing external memory aids (e.g., a written guide that includes the steps for a complex task such as long division) (Martinussen & Major, 2011).

## Social and Behavior Difficulties

If you've had the opportunity to interact with someone with ADHD, or who exhibits some of the symptoms we've discussed previously, you can readily understand why these students might have social problems and difficulty getting along in school. Briefly review the symptoms used to identify students with ADHD in Figure 4.1. Do all of these criteria have the potential to create social problems or disrupt classroom activities? Certainly, most do. These are students who have difficulty sustaining attention even during play activities, exhibit behaviors that interfere with the flow of activities during social interactions, have difficulty taking turns, and have problems engaging in a two-way conversation with a peer.

Although many students with ADHD get along well with others in school, some may have difficulty and create disruptions. For example, some students with ADHD are more negative and unskilled when interacting with peers, and when introduced to some students with ADHD, peers

### Pause & Reflect

Have you had an acquaintance with whom you've talked in a group or individually who had some of the symptoms we've discussed related to ADHD? For example, perhaps you knew someone who "talked without thinking." How did you and others react to this person? How would peers react to a person with these symptoms in a general education classroom? How would a teacher react?

may notice and react negatively to the student's behaviors (Wenar & Kerig, 2006).

Students with ADHD may also create disruptions in classrooms because of their inattentive, impulsive, and/or hyperactive behaviors. The previous feature that described Stephen's behavior in a general education classroom is an example of a student who exhibits positive behaviors at times, but Stephen also exhibits behaviors that create disruptions in the classroom. Some of the more extreme difficulties students with ADHD exhibit include problems with stubbornness, defiance or refusal to obey requests, verbal hostility, and temper tantrums (Barkley, 2006a). Students who are identified with ADHD who exhibit the most extreme disruptive behaviors are often identified with emotional and behavioral disabilities. Approximately 50 to 60% of students with emotional and behavioral disabilities are also identified with ADHD (DuPaul, 2007; Reiff, 2004).

Although many students with ADHD get along well with others, some of these students may be socially isolated because of their behavior.

## Academic Difficulties

A quick review of the symptoms used to identify students with ADHD in Figure 4.1 reveals that many of these behaviors also have the potential to have a negative impact on a student's academic performance. For example, academic classwork, homework, and tests require concentration for a sustained period of time, attention to details, listening for information and assignments, careful work, and good organizational skills, among others. When students lack these skills, their academic achievement is bound to suffer.

Some students with ADHD also have characteristics that interfere with learning certain complex academic skills. For example, as we noted previously, students with ADHD who have difficulty with executive functions and working memory will likely have problems learning complex academic skills in mathematics, writing, and other content areas. This results from poor planning skills and difficulty monitoring behavior as complex problems are being addressed.

These behaviors, as well as the previously noted socially inappropriate and disruptive behaviors that many students with ADHD manifest, result in approximately 80% of these students having at least some problems with academic achievement in school (Reiff, 2004; Wenar & Kerig, 2006). Some of these students have severe academic problems, which results in a substantial proportion of students identified with a learning disability (about 25%) who also have ADHD (DuPaul, 2007; Reiff, 2004).

## The Use of Medication to Address the Symptoms of ADHD

Recent data indicate that as many as 2.7 million of all school-aged students (or about 5%) are given medication to manage their symptoms related to ADHD (CDC, 2010). The widespread use of stimulant medications to control the symptoms of children with ADHD has produced much controversy. Most of this controversy has addressed concerns regarding the use of powerful medications to control student behavior as well as related concerns that these medications may be used with too many children (Scheffler, Hinshaw, Modrek, & Levine, 2007). Although issues clearly remain in consistently identifying students with ADHD, and some students are likely misidentified, the appropriate use of identification criteria and recommended procedures result in appropriate identification of most students with ADHD (American Academy of Pediatrics [AAP], 2000; Reiff, 2004).

## Pause & Reflect

You have likely seen information in the media regarding the controversy surrounding the use of medication to control the behavior of students with ADHD. Why do you think some parents react negatively to the use of medication? How would you, as a professional, address a parent's concerns?

Much research has been conducted regarding the use of medications to control the symptoms of ADHD (Someki & Burns, 2009), stimulated in part by the previously noted controversy. This research has revealed that **stimulant medications** such as methylphenidate (Ritalin or Concerta) or **amphetamines** (Dexedrine or Adderall) are highly effective treatments for addressing the symptoms of ADHD for 70 to 80% of these students (Ryan, Katsiyannis, & Hughes, 2011). See Figure 4.2 for a list of medications that are widely prescribed for students with ADHD. For up to 30% of students with ADHD who do not respond to stimulants, alternatives that have been proven effective as second-line options include antihypertensive medications (e.g., Guanfacine). Finally, research has revealed that a nonstimulant medication, atomoxetine (Strattera), may be effective in reducing symptoms for many students with ADHD (Ryan, Katsiyannis, & Hughes, 2011).

The classroom teacher plays an important role in monitoring student behavior and reaction to medication in the classroom. For example, the teacher may be asked by a school psychologist or a physician to monitor the impact of medication on the symptoms of ADHD as the effectiveness of the medication and an appropriate dosage level are being determined. A dosage that is too great may produce unresponsive behavior, or behavior "like a zombie," yet a dosage that is too small may produce negligible effects. It is also important to monitor closely the side effects of the medication, which may include physical symptoms such as skin rash and difficulty breathing, behavioral symptoms such as irritability and anxiety, and other side effects such as insomnia, digestive disorders, dizziness, and headaches (Ryan et al., 2011).

Appropriate levels of medications have been shown to have a significant impact on the negative behaviors of children and adolescents with ADHD (Someski & Burns, 2009). These outcomes include increased vigilance, impulse control, fine motor coordination and reaction time; improved social interactions with peers and adults; and reduced hostile and negative behavior toward peers and adults (Connor, 2006). These improved behaviors also result, as you might expect, in improved reactions of others toward students with ADHD.

| Figure 4.2 | Medications Prescribed for ADHD | |
|---|---|---|
| **Medication Name** | **Dosage Schedule** | **Duration** |
| *Methylphenidate* (generic name) Short-acting: Ritalin, Methylin | 2 times per day | 2–4 hrs. |
| Intermediate-acting: Ritalin SR, Methylin SR | 1 or 2 times per day | 4–8 hrs. |
| Extended-release: Concerta, Daytrana (transdermal patch), Metadate CD, Ritalin LA | 1 time per day | 8–12 hrs. |
| *Amphetamine* (generic name) Short-acting: Dexedrine | 2–3 times per day | 3–6 hrs. |
| Intermediate-acting: Adderall | 1–2 times per day | 5 hrs. |
| Extended-release: Adderall-XR, Dexedrine Spansules | 1 time per day | 6–9 hrs. |

*Sources:* Reiff, 2004; Ryan, Katsiyannis, & Hughes, 2011.

Well-organized, carefully structured instruction often works well for students with ADHD and others who struggle to learn.

In comparing the outcomes of medication with other treatments (e.g., behavioral interventions), medications have proven to be the most effective treatment for the symptoms of ADHD (MTA Cooperative Group, 2004). However, it is important to recognize that although medication often may be used to control many of the symptoms of ADHD, other interventions are needed if students' academic and social needs are to be effectively addressed. Indeed, after medication controls negative student behavior, teachers find behavioral interventions to be most helpful in addressing academic needs and social adjustment of students with ADHD (Fabiano, Pelham, Coles, et al., 2009).

## Teaching Students with ADHD in Inclusive Classrooms: Tips from Teachers

We were provided tips for teaching students with ADHD in inclusive classrooms by Laura Scott, a seventh-grade special education teacher from West Hernando Middle School who has extensive experience working with students with ADHD. As Ms. Scott noted in the "View from Teachers" feature at the beginning of this chapter, the challenges for addressing the needs of students with ADHD vary, depending on the type and severity of the student's symptoms. She also suggested that teachers keep in mind that some of the behavior issues presented by students with ADHD may be a front to escape from having to do work that they know they can't do. "My job is to make sure there's a lot of academic support, making them sure they *can* do the work." Laura recommends the following:

- **No two students with ADHD are exactly alike.** One of the keys to being successful in teaching these students is to know the particular student well. "The teacher has to be very proactive and stay on top of things." For example, if a student is having a difficult time paying attention or blurts out inappropriate things or loses control quickly, the teacher needs to be able to see the signs that something is coming. This requires knowing the child so well that the signs become obvious, and the teacher recognizes that the child is getting frustrated or aggravated. At times, it may be another student who sets him off, or he may have missed breakfast that morning, or maybe he had a fight with his brother. The teacher has to make every attempt to catch the behavior before it gets started, and redirect the behavior toward something more appropriate and acceptable.

- **Provide praise that works for the student.** Ms. Scott states that it is important to praise students with ADHD when they do something well. However, to use praise successfully, it is important to know the students well. She notes that many students in middle school "like to look tough," and may not respond well to verbal praise, or do not want to be praised in front of others. She goes on to say that these students "still like positive comments, notes, praise to make it through the class." However, the teacher may have to save the praise for later, or praise the student quietly or individually and not in front of the whole class. "They want to do well and please their teachers. It's important to praise anything you can, but in a way that works for the child."

- **Have a bag of tricks filled with simple strategies.** Teachers should have a bag of tricks filled with simple strategies to redirect the student, keep the student focused, and help address inattentive, impulsive, and hyperactive behaviors. To do this, Ms. Scott pays close attention to the student to see when she needs to redirect behavior. She does this at times by giving the student a little extra attention. "It doesn't have to be too long, too wordy, or lengthy. Sometimes I walk over and tap on the desk, and say, "you doing OK?" Or I may simply ask the student, "Do you have any questions?" or have the student repeat what's just been said in class to make sure he's paying attention." For other students with ADHD, the challenge may be to get them to stay on task and concentrate on class work. "We use beads in one class. The teacher made rings with beads and told the student to keep the beads in his hand and rub them, fiddle with them, rather than getting out of his seat when he gets anxious." This approach helped the student stay on task for more of the class, and concentrate more on class work.

- **Make small adaptations in lessons to keep students engaged.** This might include writing steps on a paper the students are working on that shows them what to do and in what order. Ms. Scott states, "They might listen to instructions but may not remember them or may lose focus. I put simple, concise instructions on their paper, so if I can't sit with them, I can tap on their desk and say, 'Look, you need to be on step 2.'" She goes on to note that it is important for students with ADHD to know what's coming next in class, so they are not surprised. It also may be useful to break the lesson down and just give them part of it at one time, to prevent them from getting overwhelmed.

- **Nothing works every time for students with ADHD (or any student).** A final tip from Laura Scott suggests that no matter what the strategy is, it will not work every time. This is why it's important that teachers have many tools in their toolboxes. She also says that teachers of students with ADHD should know that they are going to fail sometimes, and these failures should not be taken personally. "It's easy to get annoyed with a child who is constantly tapping, or moving, or talking out. Some things work one day and not the next. For your own peace of mind, don't take any of these things personally; just keep pulling things from your bag of tricks until something works."

## Summary

This chapter addressed the following topics:

### Who are students with ADHD?

- Attention-deficit/hyperactivity disorder is defined as "a persistent pattern of inattention and/or hyperactivity-impulsivity that is more frequently displayed and more severe than is typically observed in individuals at a comparable level of development" (APA, 2000, p. 85).
- Researchers estimate that about 3 to 7% of students have ADHD.
- Most students with ADHD are also identified with another disability, including emotional and behavioral disability, learning disability, intellectual disability, and autism spectrum disorder.

- We do not know what causes ADHD in the vast majority of cases, but factors that likely contribute to the development of this disability for some students include brain abnormalities, hereditary influences, and family issues.
- Most general education classrooms will have from one to three students identified with ADHD for much of the school day.

### Major characteristics of students with ADHD

- The major characteristics of students with ADHD are impulsivity, inattention, and hyperactivity.
- The characteristics of students with ADHD may lead to difficulty in getting along with others, and some of these students develop behavior problems.
- The characteristics of students with ADHD often lead to academic difficulty for as many as 80% of these students, while approximately 25% may develop a learning disability over time.

### The use of medication to address the symptoms of ADHD

- The use of stimulant medication has been shown to be effective in reducing the symptoms of ADHD for 70 to 80% of elementary and secondary students with this disability.
- Although medication is often effective in controlling the symptoms of ADHD, other interventions (e.g., well-structured academic activities, cognitive behavioral strategies) are needed if students' academic and social needs are to be effectively addressed.

### Teaching students with ADHD in inclusive classrooms: Tips from teachers

- No two students with ADHD are exactly alike.
- Provide praise that works for the student.
- Develop a bag of tricks that is filled with simple strategies.
- Make small adaptations in lessons to keep students engaged.
- Nothing works every time for students with ADHD (or any student).

## Addressing Professional Standards

Standards addressed in Chapter 4 include:
**CEC Standards:** (1) foundations, (2) development and characteristics of learners, (3) individual learning differences, (4) instructional strategies.

---

### MyEducationLab

Go to the topic Learning Disabilities/ADHD in the **MyEducationLab** (www.myeducationlab.com) for *Inclusion*, where you can:
- Find learning outcomes for Learning Disabilities/ADHD, along with the national standards that connect to these outcomes.
- Complete Assignments and Activities that can help you more deeply understand the chapter content.
- Apply and practice your understanding of the core teaching skills identified in the chapter with the Building Teaching Skills and Dispositions learning units.
- Examine challenging situations and cases presented in the IRIS Center Resources.

# Students with Intellectual Disabilities

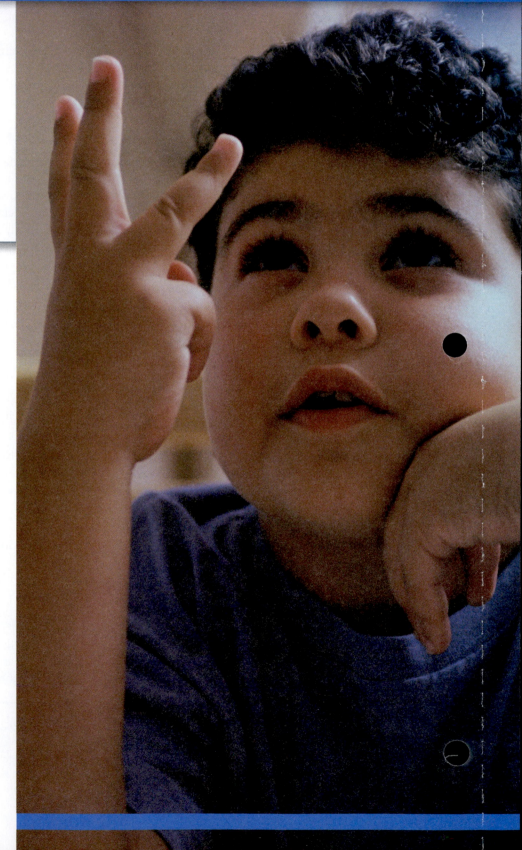

## KEY TOPICS

**After reading this chapter you will:**

- Know the definitions and criteria used to identify students with intellectual disabilities (ID).

- Be able to describe major characteristics of students with ID.

- Be aware of several valuable tips from effective teachers that facilitate the inclusion of students with ID.

## A VIEW FROM THE TEACHER

### How Susan Huff Includes Students with Disabilities

Susan Huff's fifth-grade class at Gilpin Manor is like many you would find in other elementary schools. On a cool fall day, the room is comfortably warm and buzzing as her 21 students work together in their groups to learn about graphing quantities. When Mrs. Huff wants to make a point, she gets her students' attention, and then uses the classroom's Smartboard to present a mini-lesson or let students find the solution to a problem. Mrs. Healy works with Mrs. Huff in her classroom as the special education interventionist who helps support the students with special needs in the classroom.

The students are using pizza to learn how to graph quantities. The graphs show amounts of different toppings that various teachers and students like on their pizzas. There is a lot of talk about who likes what and how much they like it as paper topping pieces are added to the paper pizzas. Graphs are drawn by groups of student to compare how much of which topping which person likes. It's a fun activity and a good learning experience.

It's fun for Zachary, too. Unlike the other students, Zachary has a *moderate intellectual disability*. But despite his disability, he has been included in general education classrooms since kindergarten. His speech is quiet but clear, and his smiling face shows that he is happy to be where he is and doing what he's doing with his friends. Mrs. Huff says that Zachary has had a lot of success and has clearly benefited from his inclusion placement. She reports, "He started last year reading at an unmeasurable level" but by the end of the year he had made significant gains. "To see him go up that much because of different guided reading, (and) small-group interventions—it was huge! But I don't know if I've seen all of the positive impacts just yet."

Zachary will smile and tell you that his school and classroom are "good" and his teacher is "great" because he "learns a lot." But he also knows he has to continue to improve. He admits that sometimes he's a "goofball" and right now is working on keeping his giggling under control. But this doesn't seem to be a major impediment of Zachry's success in Mrs. Huff's classroom.

**MyEducationLab**

Visit the MyEducationLab for *Inclusion* to enhance your understanding of chapter concepts with a personalized Study Plan. You'll also have the opportunity to hone your teaching skills through video and case-based Assignments and Activities, Building Teaching Skills and Disposition lessons, and IRIS Case Studies.

# Introduction

Today, almost everyone has had some experience with a person with **intellectual disabilities (ID)**. Perhaps you have a family member, a relative, or a friend with intellectual disabilities, or maybe you went to school with students who had intellectual disabilities. More than at any time in history, people with intellectual disabilities are becoming increasingly visible in schools, neighborhoods, and communities.

Based on your experience, you might have developed a personal perception of what individuals with intellectual disabilities look like, what they can do, and how they act. However, you should be very cautious about adhering to any stereotyped images. Individuals with intellectual disabilities are very diverse in their characteristics, abilities, and needs. Some, like Zachary, may have mild-to-moderate disabilities and be able to manage most of their personal daily needs, whereas others may have more severe disabilities and will need more support to participate in various life activities.

Over the last several years, we have learned the same thing through research that Gilpin Manor Elementary School teacher Susan Huff learned through personal experience: Inclusion of students with intellectual disabilities in schools and general education classrooms can be very beneficial. Studies have shown that students with intellectual disabilities, even those with more severe disabilities, can benefit from inclusion in general education classrooms. They can become more attentive, develop better social and communication skills, become more socially accepted, and demonstrate academic progress (Fisher & Meyer, 2002; Foreman, Arthur-Kelly, Pascoe, & King, 2004; Ryndak, Morrison, & Sommerstein, 1999; Siperstein, Glick, & Parker, 2009). Primarily for these reasons, it is important for general education teachers to collaborate with special education teachers and make every possible effort to include students with intellectual disabilities in meaningful ways in general education classrooms.

## Pause & Reflect

How common is inclusion of students with intellectual disabilities in the schools with which you are familiar? What have been some of the benefits of their inclusion for these students? Have students without disabilities benefited? What is your personal perspective on this issue?

# Who Are Students with Intellectual Disabilities?

## Definition

According to the American Association on Intellectual and Developmental Disabilities (AAIDD), an intellectual disability is characterized by "significant limitations both in intellectual functioning and in adaptive behavior as expressed in conceptual, social, and practical adaptive skills. This disability originates before age 18" (AAIDD, 2010, p. 1). Similarly, the Individuals with Disabilities Education Improvement Act of 2004 (IDEA) defines the condition in this way: "[Intellectual disability] means significantly subaverage general intellectual functioning, existing concurrently with deficits in adaptive behavior and manifested during the developmental period, that adversely affects a child's educational performance" (20 U.S.C. 1401). According to both definitions, for a person to be considered to have an intellectual disability, a formal assessment of intelligence must result in a significantly low score (usually an IQ at or lower than 70 to 75 points); the individual must demonstrate difficulty carrying out typical daily activities (i.e., the absence of adaptive skills); and the limitations must have originated before the person attained maturity, considered within the definition to be 18 years of age. Additionally, according to IDEA, the condition must result in inadequate educational performance.

A number of years ago, in 1992, the AAIDD stopped using the traditional subcategories of intellectual disabilities with which you may be familiar (e.g., mild, moderate, severe, or profound intellectual disabilities) but instead suggested that an individual who is considered intellectually disabled should be described within a multidimensional context that provides a comprehensive description of the person and necessary supports. The AAIDD theoretical model implies that a person's functioning is not due solely to characteristics of the individual but also to the supportive context in which the person lives and functions. AAIDD therefore looks at intellectual disabilities not as a personal deficiency per se, but in terms of needed supports.

| Just the Facts | Students with Intellectual Disabilities |
|---|---|
| Who are the students? | Individuals with intellectual disabilities are characterized by significant limitations both in intellectual functioning (generally an IQ below 70 to 75) and in adaptive behavior as expressed in conceptual, social, and practical adaptive skills (or skills for day-to-day functioning). This disability originates before age 18. |
| What are typical characteristics? | Individuals with intellectual disabilities will often demonstrate:<br>• Low achievement in all academic areas<br>• General weaknesses in basic learning abilities such as attention, memory, problem solving, and skill generalization<br>• Weak social skills and sometimes challenging behavior<br>• Deficits in daily living skills |
| What are the demographics? | • Prevalence estimates of persons with intellectual disabilities range between 1 and 3%.<br>• About 1.1% of the school-aged population is likely to have intellectual disabilities. Formal classifications may include "mental retardation," "multiple handicaps," or "developmental delay."<br>• Most individuals with intellectual disabilities have "mild" disabilities and are not identified until they begin school.<br>• Persons with more severe degrees of intellectual disabilities can often be identified when they are infants or toddlers. |
| Where are students educated? | • About 17% of students with intellectual disabilities spend most of their school day (80% or more time) in the general education classroom.<br>• Around 76% spend part of the day in the general education classroom (less than 80% of the time) and the rest of the day in a special class.<br>• The remaining 7% of the students with ID are placed in separate schools or residential settings, remain at home, or are in hospitals. |
| How are students identified? | • Individuals with more severe disabilities can often be identified at birth or as infants or toddlers.<br>• Physical features and behavioral characteristics often lead to assessment by physicians and other clinicians, which determine the presence of a significant developmental delay.<br>• Individuals with milder degrees of intellectual disabilities often do not have obvious physical characteristics and may not be identified until they are in school and begin to display academic and/or social behavior problems. |
| What causes intellectual disabilities? | • The causes of more severe intellectual disabilities are often physiologically based, including genetic conditions, chromosomal anomalies, maternal illness during pregnancy, or maternal use of toxic substances such as alcohol during pregnancy.<br>• For most individuals with milder levels of intellectual disabilities, the specific cause cannot always be identified. However, the condition often correlates with mild intellectual disabilities in one or two parents, poverty, and inadequate physical and psychological conditions within the home. |
| What are the outcomes? | Many individuals with intellectual disabilities can enjoy a high quality of life during adulthood. They can work and enjoy leisure activities in the community, and many can live independently or with different levels of support. The outcomes for persons with intellectual disabilities depend largely on the quality of their education as children and adolescents and on the support they receive from key persons in their lives. |

There are many benefits for students with intellectual disabilities in general education classrooms.

Although the AAIDD eliminated subcategories of intellectual disabilities based on levels of measured intelligence, these (or other) categories are still maintained by many state and local education agencies and in the American Psychiatric Association's (APA) official guide (*Diagnostic and Statistical Manual of Mental Disorders, Fourth Edition, Text Revision; DSM-IV-TR*; APA, 2000). Because these subcategories also are often referred to in professional writing and discussions, you should be familiar with these levels and their corresponding approximate IQ ranges: mild (50 to 70), moderate (35 to 50), severe (20 to 35), and profound (below 20 to 25) intellectual disabilities.

Another important change regarding terminology came when President Barack Obama signed a new law called "Rosa's Law" on October 5, 2010, that requires all federal agencies to stop using the term *mental retardation* and *mentally retarded*. Instead, federal agencies must now use the term *intellectual disability*. Rosa's Law was modeled on a law passed in the state of Maryland and was named after Rosa Marcellino, a 9-year-old girl with Down syndrome. The Marcellino family first influenced their state representative to pass the legislation in Maryland and then Senator Barbara Mikulski introduced the proposal in the U.S. Senate. It became law with President Obama's signature and made a signifcant contribution to the nationwide movement to "end the *r* word" (see www.specialolympics.org).

## Identification of Students with Intellectual Disabilities

### Identification in the Early Years

We can identify some children likely to develop intellectual disabilities when they are very young, even when they are infants or toddlers. These children may have distinctive features (such as in the case of children with **Down syndrome**) or physical disabilities (such as when **cerebral palsy** occurs) that suggest the presence of a developmental delay or the possibility that a delay is likely to occur. Usually, parents or pediatricians are the first to observe that children are not achieving key **developmental milestones**. For example, language development or motor skills may be below average for the child's chronological age.

When children are identified as possibly having a disability, agencies can begin to provide services if assessments by physicians and other skilled clinicians show that a child is truly experiencing a delay. The clinicians will conduct their evaluations using medical and developmental assessments to determine how much of a delay is occurring and in what areas of development. States use different criteria in determining a significant delay, but typically they include a substantial delay in one area (e.g., a 25% delay or 2 standard deviations below the mean) or a significant, but less serious, delay in two or more areas (e.g., a 20% delay or 1½ standard deviations below the mean) (Shackelford, 2006).

Children identified at a very young age as having intellectual disabilities usually have the condition because of **genetic inheritance, chromosomal anomalies,** or various **prenatal causes**. Often, professionals refer to very young children as having a "developmental delay"—as opposed to an intellectual disability—because accurate diagnosis of the nature or degree of their disability is difficult.

## Pause & Reflect

Providing early intervention to infants and toddlers with developmental delays can have an important effect on later development. Why do you think it is important to provide services as early in life as possible? What kinds of services or specific intervention might reduce the impact of a disability? What kinds might be helpful to families?

**Identification in the School Years**

The proportion of children who can be identified early in life as having an intellectual or developmental disability is relatively small. Instead, most children in public schools who are classified as having intellectual disabilities are not identified before they begin school; initially they draw attention to themselves in school when they exhibit academic or behavioral challenges. These children usually have a less severe degree of intellectual disability and have traditionally been referred to as having "mild" intellectual disabilities.

Most students with mild intellectual disabilities appear very similar to others in school, except for the fact that they learn academic material much more slowly than most other students and may be less socially mature.

When a school-aged child demonstrates academic or behavioral characteristics that cause concern, the school will first try to find a way to remediate the student in the general education classroom without referring her for special education evaluation. The school will develop and apply a response-to-intervention (RTI) plan and assess whether the child improves academically or behaviorally. If the intervention plan succeeds, then the child will not require formal evaluation. However, if the student continues to have difficulty succeeding, the school will refer her for evaluation by a multidisciplinary team.

If, as a result of formal psychological evaluation, the student scores at or below 70 to 75 points on a standardized test of intelligence and continues to exhibit weaknesses in academic skills and other conceptual, social, and practical adaptive skills, then school administrators will identify the student as having an intellectual disability and will ask parents to formally endorse this decision. It is important for you to understand that it is primarily the low score on the intelligence test that leads to a classification of intellectual disabilities. Without a significantly low score on this assessment, as well as evidence of a deficit in adaptive behavior, school personnel may place the student in another disability category, such as learning disabilities.

## Prevalence

Most authorities have reported the overall prevalence of intellectual disabilities as being somewhere between 1 and 3%, depending on the criteria used to define the condition and the ways in which the numbers are estimated (Beirne-Smith, Patton, & Kim, 2006; Taylor, Richards, & Brady, 2005). According to the U.S. Department of Education (2009), however, slightly less than 1% (0.84%) of public school students between the ages of 6 and 21 years are classified as having intellectual disabilities. This may be a little misleading because students with intellectual disabilities may be included in other disability categories. For example, within the same age group (6 to 21), 0.2% of the student population is classified as having "multiple disabilities," and 0.11% is classified as having "developmental delays." Thus, we might estimate that approximately 1 to 1.1% of the school-aged population has intellectual disabilities.

Across different states, the percent of students classified by the public schools as having intellectual disabilities varies considerably. Some states are quite a bit below the U.S. Department of Education figure of 0.84%, and others are significantly above it. According to the U.S. Department of Education (2009), states that report having fewer students classified as students with intellectual disabilities (0.5% or less) include Alaska (0.42%), California (0.46%), Colorado (0.34%), Connecticut (0.41%), Maine (0.32%), New Hampshire (0.33%), New Jersey (0.33%), New Mexico (0.33%), New York (0.35%), Texas (0.49%), Utah (0.49%), and Washington state (0.40%). In contrast, those reporting have significantly more than the average (1.25% or more) include Arkansas (1.75%), Washington, DC (1.64%), Georgia (1.33%), Indiana (1.52%), Iowa (1.81%), Kentucky (2.0%), Nebraska (1.36%), North Carolina (1.44%), Ohio (1.77%), South Carolina (1.49%), and West Virginia (2.48%). So, the average percent of students with intellectual disabilities really isn't uniform throughout the country.

So where does the larger estimate, the 3% figure, come from? Professionals who study the prevalence of conditions such as intellectual disabilities, referred to as *epidemiologists*, often use different criteria of a condition and different data collection methods to arrive at their

## Pause & Reflect

Looking from states with the lowest prevalence of students with intellectual disabilities to those with the highest, proportionally six to seven times more students with intellectual disabilities are in the highest-prevalence states than in the lowest-prevalence states. What do you think accounts for these great differences?

Most general education teachers will have students with intellectual disabilities for at least a part of the day.

estimates. Thus, if a very broad criterion were used (e.g., counting all persons in society with an IQ of 75 or less, not just those in public school, and without consideration of adaptive behavior), then the larger percentage would be more likely.

## Service Delivery

Based on U.S. Department of Education (2009) data, we know that almost 93% of students classified as intellectually disabled (between 6 and 21 years old) go to regular public schools with other students without disabilities. Therefore, contact with these students by all teachers is very likely. However, *where* in the schools these students spend their day may vary. About 17% of them are in general education classrooms most of the time (i.e., 80% or more of the time) and another 27% are in the general education classroom between 40 and 79% of the time. But 48% are in the general education classroom less than 40% of the time. Also segregated are the relatively small number of students (about 7%) with intellectual disabilities who spend their school days in public or private special schools (schools only for students with disabilities), in public or private residential facilities, or in their homes or a hospital. In sum, these figures mean that although some students with intellectual disabilities, like Zachary, are included in general education classrooms, most spend most of their school day in special classes or in other separate settings.

But the Department of Education data reveal other information as well. Keeping in mind that nationwide about 17% of students with intellectual disabilities are primarily served in general education classrooms, a great deal of variability around this figure occurs in different states, meaning that the amount of inclusion of students with intellectual disabilities varies from state to state. For example, Colorado, Iowa, Kentucky, Nebraska, New Hampshire, North Dakota, Rhode Island, and Vermont report that *more than* 25% of their students with intellectual disabilities spend most of their time in general education classrooms, whereas Nevada, Texas, Utah, and Washington, DC, report that *less than* 5% of their students with intellectual disabilities spend the same amount of time in the general education classroom. Therefore, the amount of inclusion of students with intellectual disabilities that may occur is somewhat based on where the student lives (Smith, 2007).

There are other causes of variability related to including students with intellectual disabilities. We know that more students with intellectual disabilities are included at the elementary level and fewer at the middle school and high school level. Additionally, students with multiple disabilities, who are likely to have more severe intellectual disabilities, are more often placed in separate schools, and students who exhibit challenging behavior are more likely to be placed in separate settings if their behavior does not improve.

## A View from a Student

### What It Means to Be Included

In our earlier visit to Susan Huff's classroom we met Zachary, a fifth grader with moderate intellectual disabilities. Zachary can't tell you anything about why some students who are like him are included and some are not, but he can tell you what it means to him. When you ask Zach about his school, he answers, in a high-pitched, excited voice, "It's good. I like it more than better!" and about his teacher, Mrs. Huff, he says, he likes her "'cause she's great." He says

*(continued)*

the same about Mrs. Healy, the special education interventionist who works in the room with Mrs. Huff to provide support for Zachary and the other students with disabilities who are in the classroom.

It's clear from his smiling and laughing that Zach likes being in Mrs. Huff's room, but he's not there just to socialize. Mrs. Huff emphasizes that the students with disabilities in her classroom are expected to learn like the other students; in fact, she finds their learning a very satisfying aspect of her work. She explains, "I think with children with disabilities you can see a lot of progress. They're sometimes the ones that show you that what you're doing is worth it. There are those little 'a-ha' moments and you say, 'Wow—you get it.'"

Zach takes part in lessons that have been adapted to meet his abilities and needs, and is given assistance by the other students as well as Mrs. Huff and Mrs. Healy. He'll tell you, "I learn a lot," and when you press him, he'll reveal to you what he likes to learn the most: "I'm learning about social studies. Social studies is great." He's most proud of the project he has been working on about Native Americans and smiles broadly as he points to his work when Mrs. Healy prompts him to do so.

When asked, Zachary will also share with you some of the problems about going to school. Recently he had an unpleasant encounter with a boy named Brandon. He explained, very quietly, "Some kids . . . some kids . . . I have a problem with Brandon. He . . . he . . . he says. 'Get out of his face.'"

So now, Zach explains, "I leave him alone." Mrs. Healy explains that Zachary annoyed Brandon on the bus and Brandon told him to leave him alone and the bus driver scolded both of them. And Zach adds, "And Brandon got on to me and Brandon cursed on the bus."

Although to Zach the experience with Brandon was unpleasant, it was also another important learning experience. Despite the fact that most of the students in the fifth grade at Gilpin Manor like Zach, he realizes that not everybody does. And when asked if he is going to stay away from Brandon, he says, "Leave Brandon alone." This is another important lesson learned through inclusion.

# Major Characteristics of Students with Intellectual Disabilities

As with other disabilities, the diverse range of strengths and weaknesses that we see in students with intellectual disabilities makes it almost impossible to make generalizations about their abilities. Although, by definition, they all will find learning challenging, you may also be surprised to discover that many people with intellectual disabilities, like Zach, have personal strengths and assets that add much value to the world around them. Students with mild or moderate intellectual disabilities will often be able to take part in class activities and benefit from the general curriculum, as other students do. Those with more significant intellectual disabilities can also participate and learn if teachers make critical accommodations and adjustments to support them.

## Academic Characteristics

Students who are identified with mild intellectual disabilities lag behind grade-level peers in developing academic skills and are likely to be delayed in learning to read, learning basic math skills, and learning other academic skills that are based on these building blocks. Although students with mild intellectual disabilities will be behind age-level peers in academic achievement throughout their school years, over time, many will develop basic literacy and math skills, often up to about the fourth-grade level. Also, they should be able to achieve skills necessary for relatively independent functioning, such as using money, telling time, and self-management. The greatest challenges to these students will be skills that require reasoning such as reading comprehension, problem solving, and planning ahead (Beirne-Smith et al., 2006; Taylor et al., 2005).

Students with moderate intellectual disabilities, like Zach, will function somewhat lower than students with mild intellectual disabilities but may still learn a number of basic academic and practical skills. They can master a significant list of letter names and sounds, and most can learn sight words and how to tell time and use money. In comparison to individuals without disabilities, their ultimate academic achievement may be up to about a first- or second-grade level. However, they can learn adequate verbal communication, daily living skills, and domestic skills; and they can learn to operate in the community by doing things such as using public transportation, shopping, and eating at restaurants. As adults, most will be able to work in the community in jobs such as performing clerical tasks in offices, or bagging groceries or stocking shelves in stores (Brown, Shiraga, & Kessler, 2006).

Students with more severe intellectual disabilities typically do not possess many academic skills, such as reading or math skills, but they may be able to recognize some words and common signs. They may know that money is of value but may not comprehend the specific value of bills or coins. Communication skills will be very diverse. Many can communicate adequately (with signs, words, or symbols), but some cannot. Some will be able to take care of their personal needs, but others may not. The more severe the disability, the more likely the person is to experience physical or medical conditions in addition to an intellectual disability (Petry & Maes, 2007). Recent advances in assistive technology (AT) have greatly advanced these students' ability to participate in various activities. Assistive technology devices and support services can assist them with communication, daily living skills, and mobility (Westling & Fox, 2009).

## Cognitive Characteristics

Students with intellectual disabilities experience challenges with a range of cognitive abilities. The following are some challenges that you will likely note in these students. Think about Zachary and how his activities and experiences reflected some of these characteristics.

### Language Skills

Individuals with intellectual disabilities will typically have restricted language abilities. Their expressive language limitations may be indicated by problems in articulation, grammar, vocabulary, and general expressive ability. Their receptive language ability, or comprehension, may not be as limited as their expressive ability but will still be problematic. Their difficulties with receptive language may range from having trouble understanding simple verbal directions to being able to engage in a two-part conversation.

### Observational and Incidental Learning

*Observational learning* is learning through watching and imitating another person who is serving as a model. *Incidental learning* is learning something that was not taught directly but that might be learned if attended to. Many students with intellectual disabilities do not profit from these forms of learning as well as students who do not have intellectual disabilities.

### Skill Synthesis

Most individuals who do not have intellectual disabilities learn separate skills such as reading, writing, and arithmetic, and then pull these skills together in an organized, useful way to undertake a particular activity, such as grocery shopping. For students who have intellectual disabilities, however, the ability to synthesize information and skills is very limited. They often fail to see the relation of one bit of information to another.

Students with intellectual disabilities require meaningful learning experiences to develop adaptive behavior skills.

### Generalization

One of the most significant learning weaknesses of students with intellectual disabilities is their diminished ability to generalize acquired skills—to apply what was learned in one situation to another situation. Generalization is usually considered the demonstration of skills with different people, using *different* objects or materials, in *different* settings, and at *different* times. One of the benefits of inclusion is that it provides more opportunities for students to practice generalizing new skills.

## Social and Behavioral Characteristics

Many students with mild-to-moderate intellectual disabilities can function quite well in social situations, exhibit socially appropriate behavior, and enjoy friendships and acquaintances. For some, however, exhibiting socially acceptable behaviors and engaging others in typical, desirable ways can be challenging.

### Social Interactions

Some students with mild or moderate intellectual disabilities may have difficulty interacting socially (remember Zach talking about Brandon?), but with instruction and practice in real-world settings, their social skills can improve. One problem is that restricted cognitive and language development may cause a student with intellectual disability to have difficulty understanding the content of verbal interactions and understanding social-communicative expectations, such as when to listen and when and how to respond during conversations. Similarly, difficulty with attention and memory can affect social interactions. Students with mild or moderate intellectual disabilities may have difficulties reading social cues and interacting in a socially appropriate manner, especially if they lack support. This may lead to a poor self-concept, a lower social status, and withdrawal in social situations (Beirne-Smith et al., 2006). More positively, as you can see next, well-constructed social relationships with peers who do not have disabilities can benefit all students.

## A View from Peers

### Including Students with Intellectual Disabilities

Any fifth-grade teacher would love to have students like Marissa and Anna, and Mrs. Huff most certainly is among them. These two girls are bright, articulate, and motivated to learn, and they're on track to develop into very successful young women. They are great friends with each other, but they are also close buddies with Zachary, having known him since the second grade. Students like Marissa and Anna contribute a lot to Zach's success, and he contributes to their enthusiasm for their school day at Gilpin Manor. They spoke freely about Zach and his place in Mrs. Huff's classroom.

"I think he fits in a lot," Marissa said. "Like everybody knows him and like . . . a lot of other people are good friends with him and like him, and he fits in with everybody else." But should he go to a special school or a special classroom only for students with special needs? "No," Marissa answered. "He should stay 'cause he does the same thing that we do. Um . . . he doesn't look at stuff the same way as other kids or talk the same way, but after you get to know him . . . you know that, like, he can do a lot of stuff. He just needs a little bit extra help. I don't think he needs to go anywhere. And there're a lot of nice teachers that will help him here too." Also, Marissa pointed out, "He's at our table and everybody at our table lends a hand and helps him out."

Anna's comments were similar. "He's just like any other kid but he does different stuff from us and he has different kinds of feelings. Even though he's different from everybody else, he's fun to be around. He makes everybody in the class laugh when they're sad. And he does his work, he's responsible. . . . He likes to talk to the teachers, he likes to cooperate, [and] he likes being part of the class. He doesn't, like, think of himself 'I'm different, I have to be somewhere else, I'm not allowed to be with other people.' He thinks of it like, 'This is going to be a fun day. . . . I can't wait to go see my friends.' He's just full of happiness and he won't let go of that."

How fortunate that when Marissa and Anna become "very successful young women," they will have their friendship with Zach as an important part of their childhood history.

### Behavioral Challenges

Although it is not an issue with Zach, some students with intellectual disabilities will demonstrate uncommon, sometimes challenging behaviors. Such behaviors are probably the greatest impediment to social success for students with more severe intellectual disabilities. Some challenging behaviors that students may exhibit include **stereotyped behaviors** (repetitive behaviors, e.g., hand flapping, also referred to as **stereotypies**), **self-injurious behaviors (SIBs)** (e.g., head banging), aggressive behaviors (e.g., hitting other people), or noncompliance.

Although the cause of these behaviors is often difficult to interpret, behavior specialists have recognized the importance of understanding the context in which inappropriate behavior occurs and possible motivating factors. In some cases, the behavior may occur as a basic form of communication; in others, it may occur in order to escape from a demanding situation, one in which the individual does not want to participate. Other causal factors also exist, leading several experts to strongly recommend evaluating both the individual and conditions in the environment to determine factors that may be causing or maintaining the challenging behavior. This type of assessment, called **functional behavioral assessment (FBA)**, can usually lead to the development of a **behavior intervention plan (BIP)** (Carr et al., 1999, 2002; Hanley, Iwata, & McCord, 2003).

## Keys to Successful Inclusion: Tips from Effective Teachers

Given the characteristics of students with intellectual disabilities, what are some keys to successful inclusion? As we saw earlier in this chapter, inclusion of students with intellectual disabilities is uneven throughout the United States, occurring frequently in some places and not very much in others. What makes a school such as Gilpin Manor successful in including students with intellectual disabilities? Some important lessons can be learned by looking at how Susan Huff and others at Gilpin Manor created an effective school for all students.

- **Understand individual student's strengths and limitations.** To begin, you might want to forget some of the general characteristics discussed previously and focus on each individual student. Learn about them as persons, get to know what they are good at and what their challenges are, develop relationships with them. Make sure you understand your students' educational and social needs. You must know the content that is expected of all students and then work with a special educator to differentiate your instruction for students with intellectual disabilities.

- **Work closely with your colleagues.** Teachers who have students with intellectual disabilities in inclusive settings will tell you that collaborating and planning with other teachers and other professionals is essential to successful inclusion. This doesn't happen incidentally; it requires time for meeting and planning. There is also need for support in the classroom. In the past, many teachers viewed themselves more as solo artists, but for inclusion to work, teamwork is essential.

- **Have confidence in yourself as a teacher.** You may not feel that you are being successful immediately, but you need to have confidence in yourself as a teacher and give yourself time to get to where you want to be. Many teachers do not feel sufficiently prepared to teach students with intellectual disabilities in inclusive classrooms, but they must learn to be patient and trust themselves to become effective with all students.

- **Get students without disabilities involved.** The involvement of students without disabilities can make a great deal of difference in the success of including students with disabilities in the general education classroom. They can provide both academic and social support and will serve as good role models for the students with intellectual disabilities. Students without disabilities will also learn about how people may be different from each other and are likely to develop greater understanding of diverse abilities. Students in the classroom working as part of the team supporting inclusion can play an invaluable role.

- **Learn to enjoy and celebrate small gains.** Anyone who has been there can tell you that teaching is hard work, but it is also good work. As Susan Huff said, "[Teaching is] very time-consuming. It's very stressful. It's emotionally draining. But at the end of the day, I love it. I go home exhausted and some days are better than others. But that's life." And about teaching students like Zach, she added, "They're sometimes the ones who show you that what you're doing is worth it."

## Summary

This chapter addressed the following topics:

**Definition of intellectual disabilities and criteria used for identification**

- Intellectual disabilities are defined by the AAIDD as "significant limitations both in intellectual functioning and in adaptive behavior as expressed in conceptual, social, and practical adaptive skills. This disability originates before age 18."
- Educators will evaluate infants and toddlers who may have intellectual disabilities based on lack of achievement of developmental milestones.

- During the school years, educators will use a significantly low score (less than about 70 to 75 IQ points) on a standardized intelligence test and weakness in adaptive behavior to determine that a student has intellectual disabilities.

### Prevalence of students with intellectual disabilities

- The overall prevalence of intellectual disabilities is often reported as being somewhere between 1 and 3%.
- Slightly less than 1% of public school students between the ages of 6 and 21 years are classified as intellectually disabled.
- Other disability categories including "multiple disabilities" and "developmental delays" may increase the estimate in public schools to a little more than 1%.

### Educational placements for students with intellectual disabilities

- About 51% of students with intellectual disabilities spend more than 60% of their education time outside the general education classroom; only 13% are outside the general education classroom for less than 21% of the school day. This suggests most students are served in full-time or part-time special classrooms.
- About 6.5% of the students with intellectual disabilities are in separate facilities, including public or private special schools, residential facilities, or in homes or a hospital.

### Major characteristics of students with intellectual disabilities

- Students with mild intellectual disabilities will be below grade level in academic skills but may develop basic academic skills up to about the fourth-grade level.
- The greatest challenges will be the use of reasoning skills in areas such as reading comprehension, problem solving, and planning ahead.
- Students with moderate intellectual disabilities may be able to achieve up to about the first- or second-grade level and learn practical skills such as sight words, how to tell time and to use money, as well as verbal communication, self-help, and domestic and community skills.
- Most adults with mild to moderate intellectual disabilities will be able to work in community jobs.
- Students with severe-to-profound intellectual disabilities will have a wide range of abilities in areas such as communication and self-care.
- Many students with intellectual disabilities may have difficulty understanding the content of verbal interactions and social-communicative expectations.
- Students may develop poor self-concepts and withdraw in social situations.
- Students with more severe disabilities may exhibit challenging behaviors such as stereotyped behaviors, self-injurious behaviors, aggressive behaviors, or noncompliance.

### Keys to successful inclusion: Tips from effective teachers

- Understand individual student's strengths and limitations.
- Work closely with your colleagues.
- Have confidence in yourself as a teacher.
- Get your students without disabilities involved.
- Learn to enjoy and celebrate small gains.

## Addressing Professional Standards

Standards addressed in Chapter 5 include:

**CEC Standards:** (1) foundations, (2) development and characteristics of learners, (3) individual learning differences.

## MyEducationLab

Go to the topic Intellectual Disabilities in the **MyEducation Lab** (www.myeducationlab .com) for *Inclusion*, where you can:

- Find learning outcomes for Intellectual Disabilities, along with the national standards that connect to these outcomes.
- Complete Assignments and Activities that can help you more deeply understand the chapter content.
- Apply and practice your understanding of the core teaching skills identified in the chapter with the Building Teaching Skills and Dispositions learning units.
- Examine challenging situations and cases presented in the IRIS Center Resources.
- Check your comprehension on the content covered in the chapter with the Study Plan. Here you will be able to take a chapter quiz, receive feedback on your answers, and then access Review, Practice, and Enrichment activities to enhance our understanding of chapter content.

# Students with Emotional and Behavioral Disabilities

## KEY TOPICS

**After reading this chapter you will:**

- Know who students with emotional and behavioral disabilities (EBD) are, understand the methods used to identify students with the disability, and be aware of the range of settings in which they are educated.

- Be able to describe major characteristics of students with EBD.

- Be aware of several practical tips from teachers that can facilitate the inclusion of students with EBD.

# chapter 6

# A VIEW FROM THE TEACHER

## Behavioral Support Program Coordinator Steve Williams on Including Students with Challenging Behavior

Steve Williams coordinates the school-within-a-school (SWAS) behavioral support program at Heritage High School. This dynamic, comprehensive program seeks to reintroduce and successfully maintain students, most of whom have emotional and behavioral disabilities (EBD), in the general education environment. Many of the students succeed with the assistance of co-taught content-area classes and brief monitoring on an as-needed basis. Even with supports, however, not all students with EBD are ready for instruction in general education classrooms. For those with more intensive needs, Mr. Williams and his staff provide focused instruction in social skills, immediate recovery room services for crisis management, and personalized content-area instruction in their self-contained setting. In Loudoun County, Virginia, this SWAS continuum is recognized as a model approach for teaching appropriate behaviors and supporting students with challenging behaviors in the neighborhood school.

Why does the program work? Mr. Williams is quick to attribute the success of the program to teamwork and a positive philosophy of inclusion that starts at the administrative level and pervades all aspects of the school. School administrators ensure all students are part of the school community and have opportunities to participate in all school activities—required and extracurricular—and that the school provides support to enhance participation. Members of the SWAS clinical team work with individual general educators to make instructional accommodations as well as to develop and maintain behavior intervention plans. Most important is the climate of commitment, respect, and trust among members of the faculty and administration, with everyone doing all they can to help students manage their own behaviors.

Clearly, many challenges are associated with day-to-day administration of the SWAS and the multiple stressors that come with working with students whose behaviors can be volatile and threatening to others. For example, a small group of students with EBD has resisted all efforts to become involved in the program. Trying different creative ways to integrate these students is both energizing and, unfortunately, sometimes frustrating. Outreach efforts are not always successful. Mr. Williams recognizes that he must be both persistent and relentless in his attempts to involve students positively in the culture of the school. He models this behavior by making a special effort to be active in all aspects of the Heritage High School community (Steve Williams is a football coach) and goes to great lengths to maintain communication with his colleagues and assistants.

On those inevitable challenging days, Steve makes every effort to make sure he does not bring the stress of school home. To navigate the tough days, endurance and motivation come largely from the empathy he feels for the students and their families. By recognizing the perspectives of these stakeholders, Mr. Williams humanizes the process of education and inclusion, going beyond the often-distant jargon-filled talk of placements, levels, and hours of service delivery. He reminds himself that these are real kids, with real families and, unfortunately, with behavioral challenges. He also reminds himself that the program and his efforts provide hope and success in a climate of fairness and respect. Steve's advice for those who seek to include students with EBD: Always be prepared, adapt lessons for success, work as a member of the team, and keep the commitment to the students as the number-one priority.

# Introduction

Is it prudent to include students with extremely challenging behaviors in general education classrooms? Won't these students disrupt the flow of instruction and endanger the safety of other students? What should I do if one of these students has a crisis or acts out repeatedly? Isn't it best for students with **emotional and behavioral disabilities (EBD)** to be assigned to classrooms of their own, environments where they can have sustained opportunities to learn socially appropriate behaviors with professionals specially trained to deal with them?

Questions such as these are typical when educators discuss the inclusion of students with EBD. Because of the frequency and intensity of these students' challenging behaviors, many of them are excluded from key elements of the general education experience. A large number of students with EBD require focused and individualized instruction in social and emotional skills—lessons that are best delivered in separate settings. Although focused, segregated instruction may be necessary, it is usually not sufficient. To practice improvements in social and emotional functioning, students with challenging behaviors require inclusion in typical general education settings. Opportunities to attend one's neighborhood school, to interact with appropriate peer role models, and to participate in high-level content learning are essential elements of educational efforts that lead to generalized and sustained changes in behavior.

Steve Williams of Heritage High School (see the "View from the Teacher" feature) recognizes that educating students with EBD requires the availability of a range of specialized supports and accommodations, while simultaneously providing opportunities for students to benefit from general education classes. With the school-within-a-school (SWAS) approach, teachers respond to individual student needs by offering a balance of separate and inclusive programming with varying levels of behavioral support, mentoring, small-group instruction, and monitoring. Teachers in the SWAS environment also recognize the importance of responding to the needs of their general education colleagues, who, like most teachers, are at their best when immediate assistance and consultation are available (Shapiro, Miller, Sawka, Gardil, & Handler, 1999). As we present the defining characteristics and effective practices for this group of students with challenging behaviors, begin thinking of the range of ways that educators can organize schools and classrooms to deliver focused interventions, promote a safe learning environment for all, and maximize the benefits associated with inclusive environments.

Students with EBD respond well to positive behavior supports and mentoring provided by caring adults.

# Who Are Students with Emotional and Behavioral Disabilities?

## Definition

Although frequently faulted for its vague and general terminology, the definition of *emotional and behavioral disabilities* that professionals use today is historic and well-worn. It was originally published by Eli Bower in 1960 and included as *serious emotional disturbance (SED)* in the landmark Education of All Handicapped Children Act (EAHCA) of 1975 and all subsequent reauthorizations (later known as the Individuals with Disabilities Education Improvement Act—IDEA). As you review the following definition, first focus on the positive elements of the definition; then identify the components that are difficult to quantify and/or subject to broad interpretation.

> The term emotional disturbance means a condition exhibiting one or more of the following characteristics over a long period of time and to a marked degree that adversely affects a student's educational performance: (a) An inability to learn which cannot be explained by intellectual, sensory, or health factors; (b) An inability to build or maintain satisfactory interpersonal relationships with peers and teachers; (c) Inappropriate types of behavior or feelings under normal circumstances; (d) A general pervasive mood of unhappiness or depression; (e) A tendency to develop physical symptoms or fears associated with personal or school problems. The term includes children who are schizophrenic. The term does not include children who are socially maladjusted, unless it is determined that they have an emotional disturbance. (U.S. Department of Education, 2005)

Among the positive elements of the definition are the descriptive manifestations of the disability, presented in terms teachers typically use and understand. Most teachers believe they can recognize *satisfactory interpersonal relationships* and *inappropriate behaviors or feelings*. However, like advocates who have been seeking to strengthen the definition (e.g., Forness & Kavale, 2000), you probably have concerns with the lack of precision surrounding the actual measurement of these descriptors as well as what is meant by the initial qualifying terms *to a marked extent* and *over a long period of time*. Vague terms such as these are prone to a wide range of differing interpretations, resulting in students' being

## Just the Facts — Students with Emotional and Behavioral Disabilities

| | |
|---|---|
| Who are they? | Students with EBD have pervasive behavioral and emotional behaviors that differ significantly from appropriate age, cultural, or ethnic norms. These behaviors affect their educational performance adversely. |
| What are typical characteristics? | • Some students with EBD exhibit primarily externalizing behavioral characteristics such as aggression, rule breaking, and noncompliance.<br>• Others present internalizing behavior problems such as social withdrawal, anxiety, and depression.<br>• Secondary characteristics include social skills difficulties and problems attending to instruction. |
| What are the demographics? | • Researchers estimate that 0.78% of the school-aged population (approximately 417,872 students) are identified with EBD.<br>• Approximately 7.1% of all students identified as having a disability are identified as having EBD. Approximately 80% are male, and 50% receive medication. |
| Where are students educated? | • Approximately 80% of students with EBD are educated in neighborhood schools with approximately one-half of these students spending at least 80% of their day in general education classes.<br>• Over 16% of students with EBD are served in separate day-treatment facilities, in residential facilities, or in their homes. |

mistakenly included or excluded from this disability category. Not surprisingly, students identified as having EBD vary in characteristics across and within classrooms, schools, and communities.

Keep in mind, however, that developing a truly objective, fail-safe definition of EBD may be difficult if not impossible. Consider the obstacles: First, no single trusted measure of social or emotional functioning is equivalent to those used for assessing intelligence or achievement. Second, the range of behaviors presented by those with EBD often overlaps with the behaviors of those without disabilities. Finally, the variety of theories that attempt to explain the development and maintenance of EBD—such as the behavioral and the psychodynamic models—often conflict.

## Pause & Reflect

Although they cannot actually measure it, many teachers believe they know EBD when they see it. Do you agree with this belief? What are the advantages and disadvantages of using teacher judgment in the identification of students with EBD?

## Identification of Students with Emotional and Behavioral Disabilities

Educators typically identify and assess students with EBD through a three-step approach that includes screening, identification, and the direct assessment of targeted behaviors. This three-step approach allows for determination of the disability and, more importantly, pinpoints specific behaviors in need of intervention.

Screening is the process of determining if a student has the broad set of behavioral patterns *suggesting* risk for EBD. Most teachers, through their daily instruction, interactions, and observations, informally screen for these patterns on a regular basis. Although these informal activities are practical and straightforward, they can have some negative consequences. Generally, teachers vary greatly in the range and frequency of students they identify. Those teachers with low tolerance levels refer large numbers of students, while those with high tolerance identify fewer students, overlooking a significant proportion of students at risk (Rosenberg et al., 2004). Not surprisingly, teachers tend to identify students who exhibit externalizing and disruptive behaviors, sometimes neglecting those with significant internalizing behavior problems. One way to address these shortcomings is to formalize the screening process. One fairly easy method is to actively rank students on categories of functioning such as appropriate classroom behavior, social interaction, and problem solving. Those at the extreme ends of the classroom distribution are considered for additional, more structured evaluation. Also available are highly structured commercially prepared systems of screening such as the Systematic Screening for Behavior Disorders (SSBD) (Walker & Severson, 1992) and the Early Screening Profile (ESP) (Walker, Severson, & Feil, 1995), which guide teachers through the specific steps of the screening process.

When screening indicates a possible disability, educators refer students for a more in-depth examination. Two types of assessment methods are most often used: behaviorally based rating scales and personality-oriented methods. *Behavior rating scales* are easy to administer, apply readily across settings and sources (teachers, parents, and students), and serve as efficient summaries of different types of behaviors (Elliott & Busse, 2004). The Child Behavior Checklist (CBCL) (Achenbach & Rescorla, 2001, the Behavioral and Emotional Rating Scale (BERS) (Epstein & Sharma, 1998), and the Social Skills Rating System (SSRS) (Gresham & Elliott, 1990) are among the more frequently used scales.

The goal of *personality-oriented methods* is to ascertain how a student thinks and feels across situations and over periods of time. Educators use two types of personality measures, objective and projective, in the identification of EBD (Cullinan, 2004). *Objective instruments,* such as the Piers-Harris Self-Concept Scale (Piers & Harris, 1984), present items in a standard fashion, use a protocol for scoring, and employ normative data to assess differences. *Projective measures,* such as the Rorschach Ink-Blot test (Rorschach, 1932), require that individuals interpret or project meaning onto ambiguous pictures, images, or statements. It is assumed that these responses reveal an individual's innermost thoughts, feelings, needs, and motives.

Arguably, the most important aspect of the identification process is pinpointing specific instructional and behavioral problems, a prerequisite for the selection or generation of appropriate interventions. The most effective and comprehensive method for instructional and behavioral planning is a **functional behavioral assessment (FBA)**. The logic underlying the FBA is that much of an individual's behavior is supported by the environment, occurs within a particular context, and serves a specific purpose. Specifically, all people behave in ways to satisfy needs or achieve desired outcomes. Unfortunately, many students with EBD use extreme, often disturbing methods to reach their goals. These students require guidance in seeking alternative ways, or **replacement behaviors**, to meet their needs. The FBA is a series of tools that help identify events, activities, and situations associated with a student's problem behaviors and, more importantly, help plan environmental adjustments that can alter the frequency and intensity of such behaviors (Gable, Hendrickson, & Van Acker, 2001; Landrum, 2011; Scott & Kamps, 2007).

## Prevalence

The prevalence, or frequency of occurrence, of students with EBD is less than 1% (0.78%) of the school-aged population. This represents approximately 417,872 students, which accounts for 7.1% of all students identified as having a disability (U.S. Department of Education, 2011). More than three fourths are boys, and those identified with the disability are more likely than other students to live in households with several risk factors, including poverty, a single parent, an unemployed parent, and a sibling with a disability (Wagner et al., 2005).

Advocates and teachers alike believe the actual number of students who need services far surpasses the number identified. Nonetheless, although the number of students identified is relatively small, considerable concern exists that certain populations of students are

## Pause & Reflect

Why are certain groups of students disproportionately represented among students identified as having EBD? Why are issues like this difficult to discuss? What can be done to address this issue in a fair and direct manner?

overrepresented. For example, compared to students of European American descent, African Americans are approximately 1.7 times more likely to be identified as having the disability. Still, little consensus exists as to cause of this disproportionality, and unfortunately, many educators are reticent to discuss racial disparity issues directly (Coutinho, Oswald, & Forness, 2002; Skiba, Simmons, Ritter, Kohler, Henderson, & Wu, 2006).

## Service Delivery

With behaviors that can be aggressive, perseverative, and sometimes threatening, students with EBD are educated in restrictive settings more often than any other students with disabilities. Approximately one fourth all students with EBD between the ages of 6 and 21 spend more than 60% of their time outside general education classes in their neighborhood schools, 13% are served in separate day treatment facilities, and 1% are educated in their homes or in hospitals (U.S. Department of Education, 2011). Accordingly, educators continue to debate how best to deliver the variety of special services students with EBD need. As we mentioned at the beginning of the chapter, this debate is a function of tensions among the desire to provide essential services, the need to maintain these students in the least restrictive environment, and the responsibility of maintaining a safe and orderly instructional environment for all students (Oluwole, 2009). Few argue that students with challenging behaviors should garner the benefits of inclusive programming whenever possible. However, many general educators feel unprepared to deal with students with challenging behaviors and believe they can best serve students by collaborating with knowledgeable special educators. Consequently, the consensus among educators is that students with EBD require team-implemented, individually tailored programs that make use of the full continuum of placement and service options.

Heritage High School's school within a school model is an example of a team-based, full-continuum service-delivery program. As presented briefly in the chapter-opening vignette, Steve Williams employs a series of activities to support students with EBD (and their teachers) in inclusive classrooms. Some students benefit from the typical co-teaching of general and special education teachers in content-rich classes such as geometry, physics, and biology. In those classes, the co-teaching team adapts instruction to minimize frustration and provides directed encouragement and reinforcement for students to persevere when the going gets tough. Other students at Heritage require the support of one-to-one support personnel, adult mentors, and peer facilitators, all of whom assist the individual student to manage his behavior in the classroom. In all cases, the program emphasizes success with a number of in-class curricular techniques that teachers use to promote inclusive programming. These techniques include **self-management**, cooperative learning, peer tutoring, and problem-solving training. Teachers monitor data weekly, and students move among levels of support depending on their success. Still, the faculty and

General educators can best serve students with EBD by collaborating with knowledgeable special educators.

staff at Heritage remain aware that students with EBD may be easily frustrated and act out, making readily accessible crisis procedures and protocols for directed social skills instruction necessary.

# Major Characteristics of Students with Emotional and Behavioral Disabilities

The primary characteristics of students with EBD fall into two major categories: externalizing behavior problems and internalizing behavior problems. We describe the specific patterns of behavior that fall into each of these two categories and also describe common academic and social difficulties.

## Externalizing Behavior Problems

**Externalizing behavior problems** are overt instances of defiance and disruption. According to Steve Williams at Heritage High School, these behaviors, most notably *aggression* and *noncompliance,* are the most frequent reasons fellow teachers give for needing support from their SWAS program. These extremely troublesome behaviors begin early in a child's development and are most responsible for disciplinary removals from classrooms and schools across the nation; for referrals for specialized psychological, psychiatric, and juvenile justice services; and for immense difficulties faced by families and local communities (Cullinan & Sabornie, 2004; Loeber & Burke, 2011; Wiley, Siperstein, Forness, & Brigham, 2009).

**Aggression** can be either verbal or physical. *Verbal aggression* includes yelling, teasing, whining, tantrums, and using profanity, as well as orally threatening or humiliating another person. *Physical aggression* includes abusive and violent actions such as hitting, kicking, grabbing, and biting (Patterson, Reid, Jones, & Conger, 1975; Rosenberg et al., 2004). You will observe that some students with EBD use aggression to bully, intimidate, and manipulate others. Unfortunately, you will also notice that others tend to acquiesce to these students' demands in order to avoid confrontations. Unfortunately, these situations can result in other students' learning that aggressive tendencies can result in desired outcomes.

Students with EBD also frustrate their teachers because they simply refuse to do what is requested of them. **Noncompliance** is the term used to describe those instances when students actively choose not to respond to instructions or requests. A history of these refusals disrupts academic and social development, results in fewer educational opportunities, and often leads to serious patterns of antisocial behavior (Austin & Agar, 2005; Walker & Walker, 1991). Consider the long-term effects: An individual who fails to respond to requests would be unable to maintain employment and would have a difficult time developing and maintaining friendships.

## Internalizing Behavior Problems

In sharp contrast to externalizing problem behaviors, teachers tend to under-refer students with suspected **internalizing behavior problems** (Gresham & Kern, 2004). Because internalizing problems involve inwardly directed actions, teachers often have difficulty identifying them in classroom situations. Among students with EBD, the more common internalizing behavior problems are social withdrawal, anxiety disorders, and depression.

Students with **social withdrawal** tend to spend an excessive amount of time in solitary play and have low rates of verbalization and positive social interactions with peers and adults (Schrepferman, Eby, Snyder, & Stropes, 2006). It is important that teachers identify these students as early as possible, because young children learn from interacting with one another and experimenting on how best to get along with others (Kennedy & Shukla, 1995). Also, not developing appropriate peer relationships in childhood is predictive of social adjustment and psychological problems in adolescence and adulthood, most notably for depression and loneliness (Gresham, Lane, MacMillan, & Bocian, 1999).

Students who do not develop appropriate peer relationships are at risk for later psychological challenges such as depression and social adjustment problems.

**Anxiety** is the uncomfortable physical signal for concern, thought, and action regarding our daily life challenges. The majority of child and adolescent anxiety is normative and transitory, rarely interfering with typical development. However, approximately 2 to 5% of children have severe anxiety characterized by persistent worry occurring for a significant amount of time and often requiring clinical intervention (Landrum, 2011). Common forms of anxiety among children and adolescents (and their symptoms) include (1) generalized anxiety (restlessness, fatigue, irritability, muscle tension, sleep disturbances, and difficulty concentrating); (2) separation anxiety (excessive worry about being separated from primary caretakers); (3) obsessive-compulsive disorder (OCD: ritualistic and repetitive hand washing, thoughts, and checking on events and thoughts); and (4) social anxiety (extreme fear of social or performance situations). Approximately 14% of students identified with EBD meet the diagnostic criteria for an anxiety disorder, and students, like Ryan before he received intervention (see the "View from a Student" feature below), underperform academically and are more likely to drop out of school than their nonanxious peers (Schoenfeld & Mathur, 2009).

## A View from a Student

### Ryan and the Benefits of Supported Inclusion at Heritage High School

Ryan is not your average college student. A freshman at a university located in south-central Virginia, he is a straight A student studying computer science and a recent inductee into a national honor society. A gifted writer, one of Ryan's term papers was recently accepted by a scholarly journal. Aware of Ryan's successes, it should come as no surprise that the faculty and staff at Heritage High School, Ryan's alma mater, characterize his accomplishments as amazing and awesome!

Here is what makes Ryan's success at college amazing and awesome: Just a few years earlier, as a student at Heritage High School, Ryan experienced a number of behavioral challenges. Identified as having an emotional and behavioral disability, he was often overwhelmed at school, experiencing what he describes as intense emotional turmoil and an inability to plan for and meet his academic requirements. Reflecting on his high school years, Ryan recognizes that a number of factors contributed to his initial lack of success. Dealing with a form of epilepsy that often led to hundreds of petit mal seizures each day, he was anxious, unable to concentrate, and fearful of other people. Feeling guilty and angry, Ryan fell into a deep depression and required mental health services outside of the school setting.

Ryan attributes his turn-around to the rapid action of the committed administration, faculty, and staff at Heritage High School. Rather than place Ryan in a segregated or residential facility for students with emotional and behavioral disabilities, a team of teachers, coordinated by Dean of Students Susan Hill, worked with Ryan and his parents on a structured plan for supporting Ryan in inclusive classes throughout the school day. Components of the plan Ryan found most useful were (1) the organizational/time management strategies he developed with Mrs. Hill; (2) the opportunity, location, and adult guidance to calm down when he felt overwhelmed; and (3) the school's Check and Connect program that provided him with a mentor and a supportive, structured process for self-monitoring and adjusting his behaviors. Ryan believes the combination of flexibility in scheduling at Heritage High School (early on, he needed a shortened school day), the high level of teacher commitment, and his acquisition of learning strategies for managing his assignments (e.g., not waiting till the last minute on big projects) helped him graduate with solid grades and acceptances to several excellent colleges.

Today, Ryan applies much of what he learned at Heritage High School to his studies at college. For example, he makes frequent use of the strategies for organizing his work that he learned from Mrs. Hill. He minimizes his anxiety by developing a reasonable time line for project completion; breaks down big projects into smaller, more manageable components; and uses detailed outlines to guide his writing. Most important, he monitors his own thinking and knows when it is important to reach out to others who can remind him not to obsess over all of his assignments.

**Depression** is a pervasive and insidious group of symptoms that affect a person's mood, thoughts, and carriage. Symptoms of student depression that teachers may observe include a depressed or irritable mood, decreased interest in activities, diminished academic performance, fatigue, and verbalization of hopelessness and despair (Montague, Enders, Dietz, Dixon, & Cavendish, 2008).

**Pause & Reflect**

Internalizing behaviors are difficult to identify. What indicators should teachers check for among students, and how should teachers conduct these observations?

Although precise incidence rates are unknown, it is estimated that between 2 and 21% of all students experience some symptoms of depression; estimates among students with special education needs range from 14 to 54%. What makes depression particularly frightening is that it often coexists with a range of conduct disorders and is a contributing factor in more than half of all suicides (Maag, 2002; Newcomer, Barenbaum, & Pearson, 1995; Wolff & Ollendick, 2006).

## Intelligence and Academic Characteristics

Students with EBD tend to have IQ scores in the low-average range (Kauffman, 2001; Mattison, 2004). When compared to the academic profiles of typically developing peers, they present moderate-to-severe academic difficulties in multiple areas that tend to improve only slightly over time (Rice & Yen, 2010). Without appropriate academic supports, students with EBD earn lower grades, fail courses, and are retained in grade more often than their general education peers (Lane, Carter, Pierson, & Glaeser, 2006; Wagner et al., 2005). The presence of these academic deficits is not surprising. As a result of their disability, many students with EBD do not attend to relevant aspects of instruction; rather, they disrupt class and respond impulsively with little thought or reflection. Because extreme social and emotional behaviors are the defining characteristics of EBD, it is not surprising that little attention is paid to the academic needs of these students.

Still, it is imperative for students with EBD to receive appropriate and adequate amounts of academic instruction; anything less would exacerbate gaps in basic reading and math acquisition, as well as in high-stakes content area instruction. Dropout rates for students with EBD are a tragic 58.6%, more than three times that of their peers and only 41% of students with the disability actually graduate (Osher, Morrison, & Bailey, 2003; Schifter, 2011; Wagner & Blackorby, 1996). Correspondingly, secondary students with EBD do not always have a successful transition to postschool life. Approximately one half of students with EBD are unemployed 3 to 5 years after leaving school, and only 40% of those with EBD live independently (Corbett, Clark, & Blank, 2002; Wagner, Blackorby, Cameto, Hebbeler, & Newman, 1993). On a more positive note, vocational education and work experience, alone or in combination, are associated with greater instances of positive postschool outcomes (Cheney & Bullis, 2004; Sitlington & Nuebert, 2004).

## Social Behavior

Students with EBD have consistently and significantly lower social skills than peers with and without disabilities (Wagner et al., 2005). Some students simply have skill deficits and have not acquired the knowledge or skills required to perform essential social behaviors. Others have performance deficits; they have acquired the social behaviors but do not have the opportunity to perform the behavior, or have made a decision not to perform the behavior because of particular circumstances (e.g., not motivated to do so, considerable secondary gain in misbehavior, etc.). Still others are not fluent in social behavior because they have not had adequate exposure to models of social skills and/or have had too few opportunities to practice appropriate behavior.

Social skills instruction can be particularly valuable for young students with EBD. Effective instructional sequences are comprehensive and usually include (1) identification of social skills needing improvement, (2) modeling and explaining the identified skills, (3) providing opportunities for practice while being coached, (4) delivering

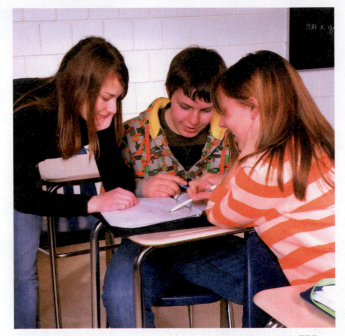

Peer-mediated approaches to instruction help students with EBD develop and strengthen social skills.

feedback and reinforcement during practice, and (5) identifying real situations where the skills can be applied (Kamps, 2010; Kavale, Mathur, & Mostert, 2004). The goal for many older students is to regulate their acquired behaviors and apply academic skills independent of teachers and service providers. Self-control is one technique that has helped students with EBD to assume larger and more independent roles in their own academic and behavior change efforts. Self-control develops by prompting students to focus on three activities: self-assessment, goal setting, and self-determination of reinforcement (Polsgrove & Smith, 2004). In self-assessment, students reflect on their own behavior, and they consider whether the behavior of interest is inadequate or inappropriate. Students then reflect on the required behaviors, set goals, and select strategies that help regulate those behaviors. Finally, through the process of self-determination, the students evaluate their performance and consider the nature and scope of reinforcement that they should receive for performance of the target behavior.

# Teaching Students with Emotional and Behavioral Disorders in Inclusive Classrooms: Tips from Teachers

In addition to the coordination of a number of practices related to effective instruction and behavior management, the inclusion of students with EBD requires that teachers maintain a professional disposition and prepare themselves for high rates of challenging behaviors. The faculty and administration at Heritage High School—including Steve Williams, coordinator of the SWAS program; Dean Susan Hill; special education supervisor Toni DeLuca-Strauss; and special education teacher Debbie Buttery—offer the following suggestions.

### Develop Authentic Relationships with Students

At Heritage High School, it is all about *relationships;* adults actively get to know their students and deliver instruction and accommodations with what is best characterized as *the human touch.* For students with EBD, this human touch involves regularly checking in with designated faculty who monitor the students' mood, behavior, and performance, and, when necessary, helping the students *calm down and get it together.* These structured safety nets are successful (i.e., they minimize classroom disruptions and get students back to their academic tasks quickly), in large part, because students recognize that the teachers are acting in their best interests. Trusting relationships develop when teachers communicate in ways that reflect a genuine concern for students' academic performance and emotional well-being. For example, John, a college-bound senior who had been part of the SWAS program, knows firsthand the importance of having teachers who truly listen to and care for their students. Working through his high school years with Steve Williams and Susan Hill, John recognized that much of the anxiety he experienced in school could be overcome by talking with his teachers and developing ways to organize and restructure certain assignments. John respects how his teachers rarely focused on the negative aspects of his disability, remained flexible in helping him meet course requirements, and conveyed their guidance with tact, subtlety, and humor, and is confident he has the skills to be successful in college.

## Expect Appropriate Behavior

The professionals at Heritage High School have seen how students often live up to and sometimes exceed their teachers' expectations. Unfortunately, the presence of students with EBD can conjure up a number of negative self-fulfilling prophecies that can lead to and maintain inappropriate behavior. To minimize these types of situations, the administrative team at Heritage suggests that teachers communicate positive expectations for behavior in the following ways: First, develop reasonable goals for behavior with student input and review them on a regular basis. Second, communicate these expectations for behavior explicitly in a straightforward fashion by having (1) positively stated classroom rules, (2) a consistent management system in which all students are treated equally, and (3) consequences for compliance and noncompliance that are delivered with consistency. Finally, emphasize that each student's expectations for behavior are based on current instances of behavior rather than prior history or teacher's lounge gossip (Rosenberg et al., 2006).

## Think Community

The often pervasive and multifaceted nature of problems faced by students with EBD and their families requires a highly structured, coordinated, and integrated system of service delivery. The term *wraparound* describes this service coordination at Heritage High School; it reflects that intervention plans are family and child centered and that services provided, as they were for Ryan, go beyond the boundaries of the school building. Wraparound is not a specific program or type of service but a definable planning process that re-

As they are models of behavior for students, teachers should remain poised during stressful and frustrating situations.

sults in a unique set of community services and supports designed to meet the unique needs of children and families (Burns & Goldman, 1998). Teachers at Heritage recognize that they are part of a team of professionals from education, health, and human service backgrounds convened to develop comprehensive interventions. Within the school, administrators, behavior specialists, counselors, social workers, psychologists, and behavior-support teams implement specialized programs of outreach and intervention. Outside the school, educators are involved as students are "wrapped around" by services from physicians, mental health service providers, family preservation personnel, and state protective service officers.

## Maintain a Professional Demeanor

The faculty and staff at Heritage High School recognize that even with the best of plans, programs, and supports, frustrating events will occur. Things will not go as planned, and students with EBD will act out and disrupt school activities. Moreover, colleagues may disagree over a specific course of action to address the disruption and parents may not fully understand an evidence-based approach for dealing with their child's misbehavior. Knowing that these things will happen, the faculty, administration, and staff at Heritage High School take great care to ensure that they respond to all situations and conflicts in a professional manner. For example, Steve Williams knows that he cannot take his students' (or their parents') behaviors personally. He remains poised and recognizes that how he behaves in stressful situations serves as a model of behavior for his students. Although he has been involved in his share of stressful and emotional situations, he looks to settle conflicts in ways that are in the best interest of his students. Like most of his Heritage colleagues, he recognizes that his role is educative and not vindictive.

# Summary

The goal of including students with EBD is to provide specialized supports and accommodations while simultaneously providing all appropriate opportunities to benefit from general education programming. We presented the following major points in this chapter:

**Who are students with EBD?**

- Emotional and behavioral disorders is defined as an inability to learn that cannot be explained by intellectual, sensory, or health factors; an inability to develop satisfactory interpersonal relationships; inappropriate behaviors and feelings; and the tendency to develop physical symptoms or fears under normal circumstances.
- Because several of the defining characteristics of EBD are vague and imprecise, it is unlikely that a truly objective definition can be developed.
- The three-step process used for identifying and assessing EBD includes screening, identification, and direct assessment of targeted behaviors.
- The prevalence of EBD is less than 1% (0.78%) of the school-aged population and is about 7.1% of all students with disabilities.
- Certain groups such as African American males are overrepresented in the EBD disability category.
- Students with EBD are educated in restrictive settings more often than are students with other types of disabilities.
- Approximately one-fourth of students with EBD spend more than 60% of their time outside general education classes.
- Over 13% of students with EBD are served in separate day-treatment facilities, in residential facilities, or in their homes.

**Major characteristics of students with EBD**

- The primary characteristics of students with EBD fall into two categories: externalizing and internalizing behavior problems.
- Externalizing problems are overt manifestations of defiance and disruption and include aggression and noncompliance.
- Internalizing problems are inwardly directed actions and include social withdrawal, anxiety, and depression.
- As a group, students with EBD tend to have IQ scores in the low-average range, lower social skills than their peers, and, without appropriate support, moderate-to-severe academic difficulties.
- Students with EBD do not transition to postschool life successfully; dropout rates approximate 58%, and more that 50% are unemployed 3 to 5 years after leaving school.

**Tips from teachers**

- Develop authentic relationships with students; doing so will promote trust, communication, and successful outcomes.
- Demonstrate appropriate expectations for students with EBD explicitly by having positively stated rules, a consistent management system, and consequences that are delivered with consistency.
- The complex and multifaceted needs of students with EBD and their families require teachers to "think community" and be part of an integrated system of service delivery.
- Respond to conflicts, inappropriate behavior, and frustrating circumstances in a professional manner.

## Addressing Professional Standards

Standards addressed in Chapter 6 include:

**CEC Standards:** (1) foundations, (2) development and characteristics of learners, (3) individual learning differences, (4) instructional strategies.

---

### MyEducationLab

Go to the topic Emotional and Behavioral Disorders in the **MyEducationLab** (www.myeducationlab.com) for Inclusion, where you can:

- Find learning outcomes for Emotional and Behavioral Disorders, along with the national standards that connect to these outcomes.
- Complete Assignments and Activities that can help you more deeply understand the chapter content.
- Apply and practice your understanding of the core teaching skills identified in the chapter with the Building Teaching Skills and Dispositions learning units.
- Check your comprehension on the content covered in the chapter with the Study Plan. Here you will be able to take a chapter quiz, receive feedback on your answers, and then access Review, Practice, and Enrichment activities to enhance your understanding of chapter content.

# Students with Autism Spectrum Disorders

## KEY TOPICS

**After reading this chapter you will:**

- Know who students with autism spectrum disorders (ASD) are, the methods used to identify students with the disability, and the range of settings in which they are educated.

- Be able to describe major characteristics of students with ASD.

- Be aware of several practical tips from teachers that can facilitate the inclusion of students with ASD.

# chapter 7

# A VIEW FROM A BEHAVIOR SPECIALIST

### Eileen Walls Describes the Benefits of Including Students with ASD

Eileen Walls, the behavior specialist at West Hernando Middle School, has heard the questions, *Can students with ASD be included successfully in general education classes? What about their unusual behaviors and their lack of communicative language and socialization? Will there be many disruptions to instruction? Is it fair to the other students? Are there sufficient benefits for the students to justify all the effort?*

Among her many responsibilities, Eileen coordinates evidenced-based responses to the learning needs of students with ASD. She has seen, firsthand, how students with the disability can disrupt lessons and have difficulties interacting with peers and teachers when they are not provided appropriate supports and interventions. Regardless of how they appear on television or in movies, students with ASD are challenging in the classroom. Students with severe ASD often appear in a world of their own. They pay little attention to typical routines and procedures, rarely making eye contact with adults or peers. Indeed, it can be quite frustrating when well-meaning approaches and creative initiatives are virtually ignored or sometimes met with bizarre patterns of behavior.

Regardless of the challenges and frustrations, Eileen (and many of her colleagues) is a strong advocate for including students with ASD, so long as the students are provided appropriate supports. Quite simply, she has seen the benefits that come with integrating these students in general education settings, and, yes, it is worth the effort! She attributes some of the success to her collection ("a huge bag") of specific strategies that work in modifying instruction for the students.

How do students with ASD benefit from inclusive programming at West Hernando? According to Eileen, participation in general education provides students with ASD essential experiences with peers who socialize and communicate appropriately. Consistent exposure to these students allows for an endless supply of direct and indirect opportunities to practice communication and friendship-making skills. Moreover, Eileen has observed that explicit instruction in functional behaviors and coping skills delivered in the general education classroom promotes generalization of the students' behaviors to other normative environments. Specifically, she has seen how explicit instruction in sequenced assignment-completion procedures generalizes to successful ordering of items in a community fast-food restaurant. Such gains contribute to the overall goal of achieving independence. Students with higher-functioning ASD have the additional benefit of acquiring higher-order content as they participate in structured socialization activities.

These benefits do not come easily. Eileen is quick to point out that individualized supports and accommodations require a tremendous amount of planning. Teachers need to identify the essential content of lessons and units and highlight methods for directing students with ASD to that content. In addition to preparing modified unit and lesson plans, Eileen believes that it is critical to make the other students in the class aware of, and sensitive to, the student(s) being included. In the event that the student with ASD engages in self-stimulatory behaviors or makes strange noises during the lesson, students in the class know not to make a big deal of it; that is just the student's way of dealing with things.

Still, Eileen believes that the biggest obstacle in meeting the needs of students with ASD is that many teachers lack sufficient knowledge about the disability. Not only are they unaware of the characteristics typical of ASD, but they also lack experience in how to structure lessons and learning environments. Knowing that an increasing number of students with ASD are being educated in general education classrooms, Eileen recognizes that all teachers need to be trained to address their instructional needs. In her opinion, students with ASD are the most interesting kids to work with. She views their behaviors as "puzzles" that need to solved, and she recognizes that it is up to her (and her colleagues) to make the personal connections that can get through to them.

**MyEducationLab**

Visit the MyEducationLab for *Inclusion* to enhance your understanding of chapter concepts with a personalized Study Plan. You'll also have the opportunity to hone your teaching skills through video and case-based Assignments and Activities, Building Teaching Skills and Disposition lessons, and IRIS Case Studies.

# Introduction

**Autism spectrum disorders (ASD)**, also known as pervasive developmental disabilities (PDDs), are among the most mysterious, puzzling, and diverse disabilities you will encounter. Some students with ASD, like Kevin at Heritage High School (see the vignette titled "A View from a Student," later in this chapter), exhibit rigid and seemingly uncomfortable patterns of communication and socialization, but usually they can complete academic tasks. Other students with ASD, such as those described earlier by Eileen Walls, the behavior specialist at West Hernando Middle School, exhibit more severe manifestations of the disability, seldom communicating, empathizing, or socializing with others. Although frequently featured in the media, a rare few with the disability have unusual savant-like talents, such as rapidly solving complex equations without the benefit of a calculator or re-creating intricate piano concertos with little or no practice.

As you consider the characteristics of students with ASD and consider some of the practical tips for teachers on how to address the needs of these students and their families, be aware of three important points: First, as noted previously, the spectrum of behaviors that characterize ASD is wide and variable. Behaviors exist on a continuum, from so-called higher functioning to lower functioning. For example, most students with **Asperger's disorder**, one type of ASD, do not have extreme delays in language, cognitive development, and acquisition of age-appropriate self-help skills, as do many of those with autistic disorder, another form of ASD. Second, as with other children and youth, students with ASD are ever-changing individuals whose behaviors evolve in unique ways over time. With appropriate supports, accommodations, and encouragement, many students with ASD benefit from instruction in inclusive environments.

Finally, be aware that although teaching students with ASD and providing the necessary supports and accommodations for successful inclusion are rewarding, they can also be time-consuming and challenging. Some students with ASD appear to be in a world of their own, often exhibiting behaviors and facial expressions that separate them from activities, events, and interactions that enrich learning and socialization. Even those who participate in lessons are often hampered by an inability to pick up on the subtle flow of classroom activities, often misunderstanding the communicative intent of lively class discussions. For these reasons, an essential prerequisite for teaching students with ASD successfully is an awareness of the academic and social behaviors encountered in schools and classrooms.

## Pause & Reflect

In the past few years, media portrayals of individuals with ASD have increased considerably. Have these media accounts impacted how students with the disability are welcomed and educated in inclusive school environments? If so, has the impact been predominantly positive or negative? Explain.

# Who Are Students with Autism Spectrum Disorders?

## Definition

*Autism spectrum disorder* refers to five clinical conditions: **autistic disorder**, **Asperger's disorder**, **Rett disorder**, **childhood disintegrative disorder**, and **pervasive developmental disorder—not otherwise specified (PDD-NOS)**. Because autistic and Asperger's disorders are by far the most prevalent, we focus on these two disorders.

| Just the Facts | Students with Autism Spectrum Disorders |
|---|---|
| Who are they? | • *Autism spectrum disorders* refers to five specific conditions, among which autistic disorder and Asperger's disorder are the most prevalent.<br>• Students with ASD tend to have pervasive, lifelong difficulties in social interaction and deficiencies in communication skills as well as rigid interests and behaviors. |
| What are typical characteristics? | • Students with autistic disorder exhibit the following:<br>  • Significant limitations in expressive and receptive language<br>  • Difficulties in social reciprocity, including infrequent eye contact and little apparent pleasure in the company of others<br>  • Repetitive, stereotypical, and ritualistic behaviors<br>• Students with Asperger's disorder have similar problems but with less severity, including:<br>  • Difficulty comprehending and using figurative language<br>  • Reduced ability understanding and using implicit rules of social exchanges |
| What are the demographics? | • Prevalence estimates of ASD range from 0.34 to 0.9%, leading many to believe we are in the midst of an autism epidemic.<br>• Approximately 292,818 children (approximately 4.92% of all students with disabilities) receive special education services under the autism classification in the Individuals with Disabilities Education Improvement Act, a 200% increase in the past 10 years.<br>• Four times as many boys as girls are identified with ASD. |
| Where are students educated? | • Although approximately 36% of students with ASD spend less that 40% of the school day outside general education classrooms, most (54.5%) are taught in inclusive classrooms more than 40% of the school day.<br>• Approximately 8.3% of students with ASD are educated in separate environments for the entire school day. |
| How are students identified? | • Common methods for screening and identification include rating scales, direct observation, and interviews.<br>• Functional behavioral assessments provide information for instructional and behavioral planning. |
| What causes ASD? | • Although the causes of ASD remain uncertain, it likely that they are the product of one or more nature-based factors such as genetic, neurochemical, and neurobiological irregularities. |
| What are the outcomes? | • ASD is an enduring disability and most students, particularly those with autistic disorder, have ongoing problems with social aspects of life, jobs, and independence.<br>• Positive outcomes depend on early intervention, the quality and stability of the network of supports, the person's cognitive ability, and symptom severity.<br>• An increasing number of students with high-functioning ASD are transitioning to postsecondary or higher-education settings. |

### Autistic Disorder

Autistic disorder, routinely referred to simply as *autism,* is a severe developmental disability characterized by an early age of onset, poor social development, impairments in language development, and rigidity in behavior (APA, 2000). In his classic paper "Autistic Disturbances of Affective Content," Kanner (1943) initially detailed descriptions of 11 children "whose condition differs so markedly and uniquely from anything reported so far, that each case merits . . . a detailed consideration of its fascinating peculiarities" (p. 217).

The definition and classification of autism, as it relates to eligibility for special education services, has changed over the years. Earlier iterations of the Individuals with Disabilities Education Act (IDEA) included it with physical and other health impairments (Rosenberg, Wilson, Maheady, & Sindelar, 2004). In more recent reauthorizations, autism received a category of its own and is defined as

> a developmental disability significantly affecting verbal and nonverbal communication and social interaction, generally evident before age 3, that adversely affects a child's educational performance. Other characteristics often associated with autism are engagement in repetitive activities and stereotyped movements, resistance to environmental change or change in daily routines, and unusual responses to sensory experiences. The term does not apply if a child's educational performance is adversely affected primarily because the child has an emotional disturbance. (34 C.F.R., Part 300.7[c] [1][i][1997])

### Asperger's Disorder

Asperger's disorder is characterized by severe and sustained difficulties in social interactions and the development of restricted, repetitive patterns of behavior, interests, and activities (APA, 2000). These descriptors resemble those that define autism, except that students with Asperger's often develop large vocabularies and tend not to have the same intensity of difficulty with language development, cognition, and self-help skills. Some students with Asperger's have superior cognitive skills but still experience problems socializing with others. Hans Asperger, an Austrian pediatrician, documented the disorder based on investigations of more than 400 children. Only in the past decade has Asperger's disorder become widely known, in large part because of its increased prevalence (Ryan, Hughes, Katsiyanis, McDaniel, & Sprinkle, 2011; Smith-Myles & Simpson, 2001).

## Identification of Students with Autism Spectrum Disorders

The identification of students with ASD requires measurement of functioning across disciplines, including pediatrics, neurology, psychiatry, speech–language, and education. These assessments are comprehensive processes, requiring time and collaboration among health care and educational professionals as well as families (Caterino & Mahoney, 2011; Hyman & Towbin, 2007).

Children suspected of having ASD are first screened for the disability. Screening for ASD is critical: Children who are not identified or provided interventions until they are older lose valuable early intervention opportunities (Coonrod & Stone, 2005). There are two approaches for screening: nonspecific and ASD-specific. *Nonspecific approaches* screen for deficits in a wide range of developmental areas, including language, behavior, cognitive skills, and motor skills as well as social and self-help skills. Irregularities in any of these areas can indicate the presence of various disabilities, including ASD. *Autism-specific screening*

The identification of students with ASD requires collaboration among health professionals, educators, and families.

*approaches,* such as the Checklist for Autism in Toddlers (CHAT) (Baird et al., 2000), the Modified Checklist for Autism in Toddlers (M-CHAT) (Robins et al., 2001), and the Screening Tool for Autism in Two-Year-Olds (STAT) (Stone, Coonrod, & Ousley, 2000), specifically target behavioral manifestations of ASD and help determine whether evidence of that specific disability exists.

Children with results suggesting possible ASD are referred for more intensive evaluations. Typically, multidisciplinary child study teams that include a physician with expertise in ASD, a developmental psychologist, a speech–language specialist, a social worker, and an educator conduct the evaluation. The content of the evaluation usually includes a psychological evaluation and a developmental history of the child; tests of hearing, speech, language, and communication; cognitive assessment; medical and neurological exams; and an evaluation of current family functioning (Caterino & Mahoney, 2011; Hyman & Towbin, 2007; Klin, McPartland, & Volkmar, 2005). Evaluators take care to ensure that indicators of performance are assessed over time and in a variety of settings.

## Prevalence

Autism spectrum disorders are found throughout the world, occur across all socioeconomic levels, and affect males four to five times more often than females (Centers for Disease Control and Prevention, 2011; Conroy, Strichter, & Gage, 2011; Grinker, 2008). *The Diagnostic and Statistical Manual of Mental Disorders, Fourth Edition, Text Revision* (American Psychiatric Association, 2000) reports the prevalence of ASD to range from 2 to 20 cases per 10,000 persons. However, recent estimates indicate that the prevalence is much higher than rates reported in the early 1990s, ranging from 0.34% (3.4 per 1,000 children) to almost 0.9% (9 per 1,000) of the total population of children (Autism Information Center, 2008; Centers for Disease Control and Prevention, 2011; Yeargin-Allsopp et al., 2003). There are 292,818 students (0.55% of the school-aged population between the ages of 6 and 21 and 4.92% of all students with disabilities) who are being served under the autism classification for special education services (U.S. Department of Education, 2011). This figure is generally regarded as an understatement of prevalence in schools because many students with ASD receive special education services through other disability designations and many older individuals are not enrolled in school programs. In addition, some higher-functioning students with ASD who are academically strong and do not present behavioral challenges may not need special education services to succeed in the general education classroom (Autism Information Center, 2008; Safran, 2008).

Not surprisingly, many believe we are in the midst of an autism epidemic. Although issues surrounding prevalence rates remain controversial, several factors should be considered when comparing rates of ASD over time. First, recent measures of prevalence include all forms of ASD (e.g., Asperger's disorder), but previous studies employed a more narrow definition of autism. Second, in the past, many students with ASD, because of their low IQ scores, were identified as having intellectual impairments. As a result of improved identification systems and the increased competence of professionals who use them, many of these students are now identified correctly as having ASD (Fombonne, 2003). Finally, as public awareness of ASD increases, parents and clinicians may be looking earlier and more intensively for signs of the disability.

## Service Delivery

Students with ASD should receive educational services in the least restrictive environment. As with other students with disabilities, educators make placement decisions based on individual student's needs. Among students identified as having autism under IDEA, 55% are included in general

### Pause & Reflect

Do you know a person with Asperger's disorder? How does this person behave in social situations? Do you have difficulty communicating with this person? What elements of the person's behavior made socialization and communication challenging?

### Pause & Reflect

Why are more children and youth identified with ASD? Do you think we are in the midst of an autism epidemic? Defend your response.

Positive peer interactions are essential elements in the successful inclusion of students with ASD.

education classrooms for 40% or more of the school day (U.S. Department of Education, 2011). For higher-functioning students, the least restrictive environment is typically the general education classroom with academic and behavioral supports. For those with more intensive instructional and behavior-management needs, programming is usually provided in more restrictive settings with variable amounts of opportunities for inclusion (Handleman, Harris, & Martins, 2005).

Why are opportunities for inclusion important? Regularly scheduled meaningful contact with typically developing peers augments direct instruction in many of the social and behavioral skills that students with ASD require. Peers are essential models of appropriate behavior and can be enlisted to initiate, prompt, and reinforce important social responses of students with ASD. Classmates without disabilities can clarify instructional requirements, correct inappropriate behaviors, minimize displays of certain symptoms, and, as is the case with Kevin at Heritage High School, include the students with ASD in school activities and social events (Ochs, Kremer-Sadlik, Solomon, & Sirota, 2001).

At Heritage High School, students across the ASD continuum have numerous opportunities to apply social, behavioral, and academic skills in inclusive settings. Teachers at Heritage ensure that regularly scheduled opportunities occur for students to attend content-area classes for social, behavioral, and general knowledge exposure. Moreover, through the school's Peer Team, a network of peers support students with ASD (and other disabilities) in class, during lunch breaks, as well as at sports events and extracurricular activities. Many of these opportunities succeed because faculty, students, and staff work in collaboration with the special education staff to ensure that student participation is positive, purposeful, and genuinely interactive.

## A View from a Student

### Kevin Enjoys and Benefits Socially from Inclusion at Heritage High School

Kevin is one busy high school junior! In addition to carrying a full academic load, including advanced placement classes in French and Geometry, Kevin is an active participant in a number of Heritage High School's extracurricular activities, most notably the Chaos Crew, a club that organizes a wide range of support activities for the school's athletic teams. Not surprisingly, Kevin regularly attends HHS football and basketball games and is an avid supporter of his friends who are on the teams. Like most teens, Kevin attends school dances and spends much of his free time on his laptop, communicating with his classmates through Facebook, e-mail, and other social networks. Although this requires a substantial time commitment and the assistance of his parents (i.e., driving to and from afterschool events), Kevin is thrilled to be part of the social scene and is enjoying every minute of it. Moreover, he is having great success in his classes, earning excellent grades.

This had not always been the case. Although he is reluctant to talk about it, Kevin had considerable difficulty developing and maintaining social relationships when he was in elementary and middle school, despite the support he received from school professionals. Kevin and his parents recognized that a number of behaviors related to his autism

*(Continued)*

spectrum disorder put other kids off and made other parents apprehensive about developing friendships and arranging play dates with their children. Kevin was frequently left out of activities and sometimes he was bullied by insensitive peers.

Things are different at Heritage High School. With considerable support and frequent home–school collaboration, Kevin is included in all academic and school-based social activities. Kevin's case manager Debbie Buttery and Dean of Students Susan Hill engage in a number of activities to ensure that Kevin and his classmates have productive and rewarding instructional and social experiences. First, for each of his content classes, Debbie and Susan meet with Kevin's teachers and peers to make them aware of some of Kevin's behavioral characteristics. A significant part of this conversation revolves around a series of specific suggestions for teachers and peers to help Kevin sustain his involvement during small-group work sessions and how to redirect his attention when he begins to feel anxious. Second, Debbie also spends considerable time with Kevin scripting and rehearsing a menu of possible responses to the many social interactions that he will face as a fully participating member of his content-area classrooms. Sometimes, they create a portable *social story* chart that Kevin can consult when in class. (For more information about social story charts, see Strategy 15.8 in Chapter 15.) Finally, both Debbie and Susan stay in frequent touch with Kevin's parents who have learned that many of Kevin's challenges at home are related to events at school, and that the resolution of these flare-ups are best addressed "behind the scenes" with the dedicated Heritage faculty and staff.

Kevin's parents are pleased that Kevin is integrated into both the academic and social fabric of Heritage High School. Sure, they have to transport him to and from school as well as other recreation locations. Sure, they have to nag him to rein in the social networking and get to his homework. Kevin and his parents recognize that all of this takes a lot of time and effort—but it is so much better than the alternative!

# Characteristics of Students with Autism Spectrum Disorders

As a spectrum disability, characteristics of students with ASD vary considerably. We focus first on primary characteristics, those manifestations that are universal and specific to the disability. By universal and specific, we mean that these behaviors are found in nearly all students with ASD and are infrequent among those who do not have the disability (American Psychiatric Association, 2000; Rutter, 1978). We then address secondary correlates, those behaviors that often occur along with the primary characteristics.

## Primary Characteristics

Three categories of characteristics experienced by students with ASD are (1) communication skill difficulties; (2) limitations in social reciprocity; and (3) repetitive, stereotypical, and ritualistic behaviors.

### Communication Skills

Difficulties with communication skills are characteristic of all students with ASD, although levels of severity vary considerably. For those with autistic disorder, impairments in communication skills are pervasive, involving most aspects of expressive and receptive language development. Approximately 50% of these students do not acquire **functional language**, and many are nonverbal or exhibit **echolalia**, which is the immediate repetition of something just heard (American Psychiatric Association, 2000; Heflin & Alaimo, 2007). Those who do speak often use speech in a monotonous tone accompanied by pronoun reversal as well as unusual pitch, rhythm, and syntax. Because these students rarely use speech for social communication, gestures, body movements, eye contact, and instances of sharing of attention with another person are infrequent. Students with autistic disorder also have difficulty understanding spoken language, likely the result of their inability to decipher verbal and nonverbal cues (National Research Council, 2001; Orsak, 2011).

Limitations in communication are not as severe for students with Asperger's disorder. Many have difficulty, however, in comprehending and making use of **figurative language**— idioms, metaphors, slang, and jokes that add vigor and emotion to communication. When

## Pause & Reflect

Describe a memorable performance, event, or meal *without* using metaphors, slang, or idiomatic phrases. Next, enhance your description incorporating elements of figurative language. List how the two descriptions differ in terms of emotion and utility.

students with Asperger's disorder encounter figurative phrases, they often interpret the words literally and have difficulty deciphering the communicative intent of the message. Also, when these students express themselves, they usually enunciate words and phrases in an odd, robotic fashion accompanied by a limited range of gestures, facial expressions, and eye movements (Rosenberg et al., 2004; Safran, 2002).

Language instruction is based on the student's ability to verbalize along with her corresponding intelligence level. Students who are nonverbal may learn to communicate through the use of pictures, symbols, communication boards, sign language, and electronic devices that enable the child to press a button representing a symbol that is produced verbally. For those who are verbal, instruction often focuses on aspects of language production, including pragmatics, syntax, semantics, and articulation. For students with Asperger's disorder, **pragmatics**, the social use of language, is one area that usually requires intensive instruction. Specific instruction focuses on recognizing the purpose of communication, speaking in a conversational manner, being sensitive to the needs of the listener, as well as beginning and ending conversations in a socially appropriate fashion (Paul, 2005).

### Limitations in Social Reciprocity

Social reciprocity is the multifaceted process of interacting with another person. Because of their reduced ability to understand or use the basic implicit rules that govern social exchanges, students with ASD often experience difficulty in social situations (American Psychiatric Association, 2000). They seem oblivious to the feelings and thoughts of others, are challenged by conventional notions of personal space, and can appear rude and tactless (Kelley & Herrick, 2011). Many with autistic disorder do not respond to familiar faces with a warm, social smile and exhibit little pleasure in the presence of others. They appear aloof, avoid eye contact, and do not attain many of the usual developmental benchmarks such as friendships, play, and expressions of empathy (Rutter, 1978). Limitations in socialization for those with Asperger's disorder are less severe yet still problematic. These students engage others socially, but the quality of their interactions tends to be blunt, rigid, one-sided, and filled with contextually inappropriate verbalizations (Linn & Smith-Myles, 2004). Due to these awkward exchanges, students with Asperger's disorder can become targets of ridicule and become even further distanced from positive social interactions with peers. Some students, seeking to avoid social interactions, may even act out in hope of being sent to a disciplinary time-out setting.

Efforts to improve social-behavioral functioning typically focus on age-appropriate behaviors that students must learn to survive and ultimately thrive in the real world. Although based on assessed strengths and needs, instruction for elementary students with autistic disorder typically involves daily living skills, self-care skills, functional communication skills, and those intangible social graces that enable one to participate in the community. It is not unusual for some students with ASD to need explicit instruction in how to play with peers and, as they grow older, how to deal with the emotions and anxiety of being "different." Students with Asperger's disorder need instruction in understanding facial expressions and gestures, comprehending nonliteral figurative language (i.e., idioms and

Due to limitations in communication and social skills, students with ASD are often left out of group activities.

metaphors), discriminating when others' intentions do not match their words, and under-standing the implicit rules of social functioning—*the hidden curriculum* of ways of behaving that are not acquired through direct instruction (Lee, 2011; Smith-Myles & Simpson, 2001).

### Repetitive, Stereotypical, and Ritualistic Behaviors

At Heritage High School, the most obvious and frequently observed behaviors of students with ASD are repetitive, stereotypical, and ritualistic actions. Students with autistic disorder exhibit several of the more extreme high-frequency motor behaviors—rocking, spinning, arm flapping, and finger flicking—and the school addresses these behaviors by providing additional support, sometimes in more self-contained settings. Many students with autistic disorders often cling to certain objects (e.g., pieces of fabric, dolls, etc.), repeatedly spin toys, or spend large amounts of time lining up objects in a carefully designed, elaborate pattern. Others seem to experience unusual reactions to sensory stimuli and are easily upset by certain sights, sounds, odors, and textures in the environment (McCoy, 2011).

Although less extreme, students with Asperger's disorder present their own unusual forms of ritualistic behavior (American Psychiatric Association, 2000). Many have intense interests in weather systems, maps, or the telephone book as well as schedules for trains, airlines, and television shows (Loveland & Tunali-Kotoski, 2005). Teachers report that it is not unusual for these students to be extremely anxious and upset when daily routines are changed due to unforeseen circumstances. For example, Gina Kraun and Denise Pohill, science teachers at Heritage High School, noticed that Leon (not his real name), a student with Asperger's disorder, often became agitated when he knew an answer, raised his hand to respond, and was not called on. Leon would tap on his desk and whisper repeatedly, "I know, I know, I know . . . ." To address this disruptive, repetitive behavior, his teachers developed a peer-response system in which Leon could demonstrate to his partner that he knew the answer. This approach reduced Leon's anxious behavior and increased his levels of appropriate class behavior.

## Secondary Characteristics

### Age of Onset

Many students with autistic disorder can be identified before reaching 3 years of age. Parents generally report concerns when their child reaches between 15 and 22 months of age, usually because of lack of speech and emergence of ritualistic and repetitive behaviors (Chawarska & Volkmar, 2005; Robins, Fein, Barton, & Green, 2001). Most children with the Asperger's disorder do not have significant delays in language acquisition, cognitive development, or self-help skills, and limitations are not apparent until the child is in social situations with peers. Although some parents of children with Asperger's disorder are apprehensive about differences in their child's behaviors as toddlers, the disorder is typically diagnosed at a later age, usually when the student is 11 years old (Foster & King, 2003).

### Intelligence and Academic Characteristics

The measured intelligence of students with ASD ranges from superior to profound intellectual disability (American Psychiatric Association, 2000); however, most students with the disability have scores below 70 (Heflin & Alaimo, 2007). Higher IQ scores do not mean that other challenging characteristics of ASD are not prominent. Increased measured intelligence does not always lead to corresponding gains in adaptive skills and improvements in the social use of language. However, students with higher IQ scores are less likely to exhibit (1) gross deficits in social interaction and emotional expression, (2) inappropriate play, (3) self-injurious behavior, and (4) delays in motor and language development (National Research Council, 2001).

Some students with ASD learn academic skills readily, while others struggle with basic preacademic skills. Regardless of their level of functioning, students with ASD have difficulty remembering and organizing information and need instructional supports to increase attention to critical elements of a task. Higher-functioning students with Asperger's

Students with ASD benefit from instructional supports and accommodations when learning academic content.

disorder also benefit from individualized supports and accommodations, particularly in subjects that require large amounts of oral comprehension encountered in lectures and written assignments. No specific academic curriculum or methodology exists for teaching academics to elementary students with ASD. State standards, the school district curriculum, assessments of students' needs, and, to some degree, common sense dictate the academic programs for students with autistic and Asperger's disorders (Olley, 2005).

### Self-Injurious Behavior

Self-injurious behavior (SIB) is self-directed aggression manifested by severe head banging, punching, scratching, and/or biting, and it is among the most frightening behaviors exhibited by some students with severe disabilities. More common in children with autistic disorder than those with Asperger's disorder, approximately 10 to 20% of those with the disability engage in SIB. Elimination of these behaviors is a high priority. In addition to the obvious health issues, self-injury precludes placement in inclusive settings and limits access to many learning, working, and community opportunities (O'Reilly, Sigafoos, Lancioni, Edrisinha, & Andrews, 2005). One speculation is that SIB serves a neurological function and is related to the child attempting to either enhance or reduce levels of stimuli from the environment. From the behavioral perspective, SIB is believed to be a learned response reinforced by positive and/or negative stimuli. Examples of positive reinforcement include others' attention and sensory gain; **negative reinforcement** takes the form of escape from demands or situations the individual with ASD wishes to avoid. Fortunately, interventions based on functional behavioral assessment can reduce self-injury, and many structured techniques and programs have been developed to do so (Rosenberg et al., 2004).

## Teaching Students with ASD in Inclusive Classrooms: Tips from Teachers

The inclusion of students with ASD requires the coordination of a number of practices related to effective instruction and behavior management as well as a thorough understanding of the characteristics of the disability that can affect classroom performance. At Heritage High School, collaborative interventions across academic and social domains have been considerably successful in meeting the intensive needs of students with ASD. A portion of this success can be attributed to input provided by Toni DeLuca-Strauss, a Loudoun County special education supervisor assigned to the district's middle and high schools. What makes Toni's suggestions especially insightful and useful goes beyond her expertise in special education instructional methods; Toni is also a parent of a child with ASD. To have success in meeting the needs of students with ASD, Toni recommends the following:

### Understand That Student Behaviors Communicate Needs and Feelings

Many of the unusual behaviors exhibited by students with ASD are a means of communicating their needs, feelings, and fears. Therefore, when students with ASD engage in inappropriate behaviors, it is critical that teachers recognize what events in the classroom may be precipitating the behaviors. For example, the science co-teaching team, content specialists Casey Van Harssel and Gina Craun, and special educator Denise Pohill recognize that their students with ASD do not respond well to surprises and can disrupt class activities. However, the students find support and comfort in specific routines and perform best when explicitly prepared for activities. Students in the class are "primed" for lessons by using a series of graphic organizers that visually contextualize objectives and activities into the big picture of an instructional unit. Also, knowing that group activities can result in anxiety and withdrawal, the co-teaching team enlists the help of peers to work with the students during labs, cooperative learning activities, and guided practice activities. The co-teaching team is very careful when selecting peers, ensuring that team members have the social maturity to deal with unusual behaviors. The helping peers also get a "crash course" on the typical characteristics of ASD and how best to respond to both appropriate and inappropriate behaviors when they occur.

Some students with ASD become anxious and upset when daily classroom routines or procedures are changed.

### Give Prompt Attention and Establish Eye Contact with Students

Some students with ASD appear oblivious to class activities and can appear aloof or uncaring to teachers and peers. Rather than accept these avoidance behaviors, Toni DeLuca-Strauss strongly suggests that teachers directly engage the attention of these students. This can be done by moving close to the student and explicitly prompting attention and/or eye contact prior to giving directions and using the power of proximity. For younger students, Toni has seen engagement and attention improve when students with ASD contribute an important or treasured object (e.g., a special toy, picture, book, etc.) to the classroom environment. This provides the student with a tangible connection to the room and is a useful tool for beginning conversations that can lead to extended social interactions or task engagement.

### Be Flexible and Provide Accommodations

As a consultant to many classrooms, Toni has observed that a rigid student paired with a rigid teacher will almost always lead to frustration and failure. Consequently, when working with students with ASD, it is important that teachers remain flexible and recognize that they may need to differentiate their lessons and provide support and accommodations for students to succeed. For example, Casey Van Harssel and Gina Craun, the science specialists at Heritage High school, ensure that the science lessons for students with ASD are differentiated yet still rigorous. They work with Denise Pohill to identify essential components of the curriculum and help integrate them into whatever lesson and assignment accommodations and supports are necessary, such as guided notes and study guides. The teachers have found that the new "high-tech white board" helps cue specific elements of most lessons and, in general, has increased student attention to large-group presentations.

### Understand and Engage Parents

Knowing firsthand the challenges associated with both parenting and teaching a child with ASD, it is little surprise that Toni DeLuca-Strauss is a fierce advocate for tight-knit home–school relationships. Toni urges school personnel to understand that many parents and families of students with ASD are still on their journey to acceptance of the child's disability and rely on school personnel for information, support, and empathy. Often, parents are in need of strategies for addressing their child's needs at home and how best to coordinate efforts with their child's school. Toni views special education teachers as being responsible for disability awareness at the school, and for developing networks of communication (e.g., telephone, e-mail, etc.) that sustain family–school relationships. Correspondingly, family members can be a teacher's greatest resource for meeting the needs of social and behavioral students with ASD. In many cases parents and siblings have developed techniques at home that can be readily incorporated in inclusive classrooms (Caruso & Crawford, 2011).

## Summary

When provided appropriate supports and accommodations, students with ASD benefit from participation in general education settings. We presented the following major points in this chapter:

**Who Are Students with ASD?**

- The two most common forms of ASD are autistic disorder and Asperger's disorder.
- Autistic disorder is a severe developmental disability characterized by an early age of onset, poor social development, impairments in language development, and rigidity in behavior.
- Asperger's disorder is characterized by severe and sustained impairments in social interactions and the development of restricted, repetitive patterns of behavior, interests, and activities.
- The identification of ASD requires measurement of functioning across disciplines. Students are first screened, and those suspected of having the disability are referred to more intensive evaluations.
- Recent estimates indicate that the prevalence of ASD ranges from 3.4 to 9 per 1,000 children—much higher than rates reported in the 1990s.
- Some 292,818 students, 0.55% of the school-aged population between the ages of 6 and 21 and 4.92% of all students with disabilities, are served under the autism classification for special education services.
- ASD occurs worldwide and affects males four to five times more often than females.
- Over half (54.5%) of students with ASD are included in general education classrooms more than 40% of the school day.
- Opportunities for inclusion are important because they allow for meaningful contact with typically developing peers as well as activities that augment instruction in the academic, social, and behavioral skills that students with ASD require.

**Major Characteristics of Students with ASD**

- Three primary characteristics are universal and specific to difficulties experienced by students with ASD: communication skills; social reciprocity; and repetitive, stereotypical, and ritualistic behaviors.
- Children with autism are typically identified before the age of 3; Asperger's disorder is typically diagnosed at approximately 11 years of age.
- The measured intelligence of students with ASD ranges from superior to profound intellectual disability, with the majority having scores below 70.
- Some students with ASD acquire academic skills readily, but others need a variety of instructional supports to succeed on classroom tasks.
- Approximately 10 to 20% of those with ASD engage in some form of self-injurious behavior (SIB).

**Tips for Teachers**

- Recognize that many of the unusual behaviors of students with ASD are a means for communicating needs, feelings, and fears.
- Prompt attention and establish eye contact to engage students with ASD in classroom activities.
- To facilitate student success, remain flexible, differentiate lessons, and provide support and accommodations.
- Understand and engage parents by providing disability awareness and developing networks of communication that sustain family–school relationships.

## Addressing Professional Standards

Standards addressed in Chapter 7 include:

**CEC Standards:** (1) foundations, (2) development and characteristics of learners, (3) individual learning differences, (4) instructional strategies.

---

**MyEducationLab**

Go to the topic Autism Spectrum Disorders in the **MyEducationLab** (www .myeducationlab.com) for *Inclusion,* where you can:

- Find learning outcomes for Autism Spectrum Disorders, along with the national standards that connect to these outcomes.
- Complete Assignments and Activities that can help you more deeply understand the chapter content.
- Apply and practice your understanding of the core teaching skills identified in the chapter with the Building Teaching Skills and Dispositions learning units.
- Examine challenging situations and cases presented in the IRIS Center Resources.
- Check your comprehension on the content covered in the chapter with the Study Plan. Here you will be able to take a chapter quiz, receive feedback on your answers, and then access Review, Practice, and Enrichment activities to enhance your understanding of chapter content.

# Students with Communication Disorders and Students with Sensory Impairments

## KEY TOPICS

**After reading this chapter you will:**

- Know who students with communication disorders and students with sensory impairments are, the methods used to identify these students, and the range of settings in which they are educated.

- Be able to describe major characteristics of students with communication disorders and students who have sensory impairments.

- Be aware of several practical tips from teachers that can facilitate the inclusion of students with communication disorders and students with sensory impairments.

# A VIEW FROM A SPEECH/LANGUAGE PATHOLOGIST

## Malee Taylor's Thoughts on Inclusion and Communication

Inclusion can't be successful without teamwork, and the speech–language pathologist (SLP) is an important team player who helps students with and without disabilities develop more effective communication skills. Malee Taylor, the SLP who works with the pre-kindergartners at Gilpin Manor Elementary School, fits in well with her team, working with young children in and outside the classroom to help them acquire communication skills that will help them live more successfully in an inclusive world. One of the children she works with is a Ryley, a 4-year-old boy with autism. Even though Ryley's disability is more severe than most of the disabilities of other children with whom Malee works, he has been in a preschool classroom with nondisabled peers for nearly 2 years. Ryley receives 1½ hours of direct speech–language service per week spread across five days: 15 minutes Monday, Tuesday, Thursday, and Friday, and 30 minutes on Wednesday. Malee explained, "He was only able to handle 15 minutes up until this year. Now I'm trying to, one time a week, really push him up to 30 minutes." Ryley gets one-on-one therapy, but he gets it in the pre-kindergarten classroom with the other children present. And earlier this year he started working on improving his expressive language. He began by using the **Picture Exchange Communication System (PECS)**, but then moved to using *Proloquo2go* on an iPod.

Malee explains that being among children without disabilities is generally a plus for those children with communication disorders. Speaking about Ryley, she says, "He is sometimes in his own little space, but he does interact with the kids. They'll take his hand and try to play with him [and] he'll sit in circle time for calendar and weather." And she sees this as being beneficial for Ryley. "I think that he sees what kids his age are doing," she says, and this helps him learn. "Last year he had a little friend who would always sit with him, a little girl. And he always wanted the one girl. And he likes [his classmates'] faces and he'll follow them over to the computer to play with them. . . . He does want to interact with them, it's just . . . teaching him how." And what difference might this make for Ryley? "I see him going into regular ed. I think once we can get him to communicate his needs and wants . . . he has it cognitively," Malee said.

The key to effective inclusion from Malee's point of view is working closely with the teachers on her pre-K team. Malee and the teachers will look closely at the lesson plans for each day to see how they can imbed communication instruction into those lessons. For

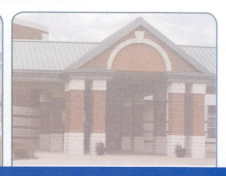

example, talking about one teacher, Malee said, "She was asking me about [a child's] sentences; she wanted sentence strips. We work on different pictures and they were asking 'What kind of pictures should we do?'—that kind of thing." But Malee adds that it takes a while to become effective at teamwork. "I would say it took 5 years of really working and trying to figure out my role in it . . . you have to build those relationships up with the teachers. . . . It's like a work in progress." Although Malee believes her work in inclusive classrooms is important, she sometimes feels frustrated. She explained that sometimes it becomes challenging when a student like Ryley starts learning a communication system and the teachers want things to happen right away. "But it takes time," she says, "and that can be frustrating."

But ultimately, the work is very rewarding. Malee stated, "To me, what's most rewarding is seeing the kids communicate—like when they say their first words. With Ryley, last year we didn't get very many verbalizations, and this year, he's just starting and I know [the words are] in there and they're coming out. He did the 'Hi there' the other day and recently he's been doing 'Bye-bye' at least once a week. I'm hearing more and more words." It's not surprising that when Malee was asked what she thought about her job, she answered quickly, "I love it."

# Introduction

Students with **communication disorders** and students with **sensory disabilities** face unique yet very different kinds of challenges, yet successful placements in inclusive classrooms can be advantageous for both groups.

Some students with communication disorders not only have trouble conveying what they mean but, because of their disability, they can also experience secondary negative effects such as being embarrassed in front of peers. As a result, they might shut down, participate very little, and consequently may not experience learning opportunities other students enjoy.

To improve communication skills and to counter these other outcomes, speech–language pathologists such as Malee Taylor, and the teachers they work with, make every effort to help students overcome their communication disorders. Close collaboration with an SLP is an essential component for effective instruction for students with communication disorders. Although in the past, SLPs worked almost exclusively by pulling students out of the classroom for one-on-one therapy, today much of their work is done in general education classrooms and in other natural settings. Only rarely will these students leave the classroom for brief periods of time to meet with an SLP. And when this does occur, it becomes critical for the teacher and SLP to communicate closely so the work done outside the classroom can be imported for successful application in the more natural setting of the classroom. This is how Malee worked with the teachers on her team.

The other group of students we discuss in this chapter—students with sensory impairments—include those who are blind or have a significant vision loss; those who are deaf or have a significant hearing loss; and those who have both a vision and hearing loss, which could result in a classification of deaf-blindness. Like students with communication disorders, students with sensory disabilities also face serious challenges, although of a different nature. Their limitations involve obtaining adequate information through residual sensory abilities and/or through the use of their other senses. Students with sensory impairments require strategies to help them gain information easily available to other students.

If you have a student in your classroom with sensory disabilities, usually you will have the benefit of collaborating with a special education teacher with expertise in visual disabilities or hearing impairments. This individual will work closely with you to better ensure an appropriate and successful education for the student.

# Who Are Students with Communication Disorders?

## Definitions

The two major types of communication disorders are language disorders and speech disorders. **Language disorders** include problems in formulating and comprehending spoken messages, and **speech disorders** consist of problems related to the verbal transmission of messages. Justice (2010) explained communication disorders in this way:

Sometimes students with communication disorders may avoid participation because of their disability.

> individuals are functional and effective communicators when they are able to successfully formulate, transmit, receive, and comprehend information from other individuals. A communication disorder or impairment is present when a person has significant difficulty in one of more of these aspects of communication when compared with other people sharing the same language, dialect and culture. (pp. 21–22)

Speech disorders interfere significantly with the speaker's ability to say something in a way that can be easily understood. A speech disorder can also call attention to the speaker and sometimes cause personal discomfort or stress. The most common speech disorders include **phonological and articulation disorders, fluency disorders, voice disorders,** and **motor speech disorders** (Justice, 2010). Figure 8.1 describes common speech disorders.

| Figure 8.1 | Common Speech Disorders |
| --- | --- |

- *Phonological and articulation disorders* impair a person's ability to clearly create speech sounds. Instead of producing standard speech sounds, the speaker produces sounds that include distortions, substitutions, omissions, or additions. A distortion occurs when the speaker produces a nonstandard phoneme, like a lisp. A substitution is the replacement of one phoneme with another, such as "shair" for "chair." An omission is the deletion of a phoneme such as saying "chai" for "chair." An addition is the addition of an extra phoneme such as "chuh air" for "chair" (Owens et al., 2003).
- *Fluency disorders* are interruptions in the normal flow of speech. The most common fluency disorder is stuttering. Stuttering is often affected by environmental and circumstantial conditions and can draw a great deal of attention to the speaker and often cause stress. Definitions of stuttering usually note that it consists of producing an abnormally high number of sound and syllable repetitions, prolongations, or blocks (Shapiro, 2011). People who stutter usually have primary stuttering behaviors and secondary behaviors. The primary behaviors are speech characteristics such as repetitions, prolongations, and blocks. The secondary behaviors are reactions to stuttering that occur as a person tries to deal with the verbalizations such as blinking eyes, opening the jaws, pursing lips, substituting easier words for words that are more difficult, or inserting "uh" before a difficult word (Gillam, 2000).
- *Voice disorders* occur when a person's pitch, loudness, or phonatory quality differs significantly from others of the same sex, age, ethnicity, and cultural background. When compared to peers, the person with a voice disorder has an uncommonly high- or low-pitched voice, or a voice that is too soft or too loud or that has unusual phonatory qualities. To be considered a "disorder," the condition of the voice must be different enough to draw attention to the person or to adversely affect performance in school, at home, or in the community. Speech therapists use a variety of terms to describe a person's voice, but the most commonly used are a harsh or strained voice, a breathy voice, and a hoarse voice (Dalston, 2000).
- *Motor speech disorders* are neurological disorders that affect a person's speech. Speaking requires complex, coordinated movements of very small muscles. Because these movements have a neurological origin, neurological insult or trauma may adversely affect one or more of the building blocks of speech (Maas & Robin, 2006).

## Pause & Reflect

Speech disorders that are very obvious, such as stuttering, will draw a great deal of unwanted attention to the speaker. How do you think a young child or an adolescent would react to having such a condition? What are some things you think you could do as a teacher to help mitigate this potential embarrassment?

A language disorder may occur even though a person's speaking ability may be fine. For example, an elementary school student might have a language disorder if he has a difficult time finding and using the right word or combination of words; using words in the right order; or using the correct words, phrases, or sentences at the right time. With a language disorder, the listener's ability to understand a speaker's words may be fine, but the listener may still have a difficult time comprehending what the speaker is trying to say. Experts usually divide language disorders into three major categories: **form disorders**, **content disorders** (or **semantic disorders**), and **usage disorders** (or **pragmatic disorders**) (Justice, 2010; Owens, Metz, & Farinella, 2011; Peña & Davis, 2000). Figure 8.2 provides descriptions of different language disorders.

## Identification of Students with Communication Disorders

Children as young as 12 to 18 months may show signs of delayed or impaired communication development. For some of these children, the delays evolve into disorders that continue into the preschool and school years and perhaps beyond. The communication challenges exhibited by children may range from relatively mild to more severe. Parents, pediatricians, and preschool or elementary school teachers may identify communication problems and refer the child to an SLP for formal evaluation.

Because many different types of communication disorders exist, the SLP must use an assessment procedure that will best identify the type of disorder and relevant conditions related to the disorder. In a comprehensive assessment, the SLP will evaluate language, speech, cognition, voice, fluency, hearing, feeding, and swallowing to determine if specific disorders are present. During the assessment, the SLP will do the following:

- Review existing records to gather relevant historical, medical, educational, and psychological information.
- Interview the student, parents, caregivers, and teachers to acquire information about the student's communication history and current condition.
- Ask different individuals, including the classroom teacher, to fill out questionnaires about the student's communication characteristics.
- Conduct a systematic observation to assess key skills and abilities such as paying attention, understanding abstract concepts, answering questions, seeking help, or explaining complex details.

| **Figure 8.2** | **Language Disorders** |
| --- | --- |

- *Form disorders* are disorders in the formation of sounds used to make words and word parts (phonology); disorders in the rules for constructing words and parts of words so that they have meaning (morphology); and disorders in applying rules for connecting the words together correctly (syntax).
- *Content disorders*, or semantics disorders, occur when an individual does not use the specific words or word combinations as language rules require. For example, if a person consistently uses words or phrases that are not meaningful to other people who use the same language, or uses words or phrases that are not valid for the situation, the person is experiencing a content or semantics problem.
- *Use disorders*, or pragmatics disorders, are characterized by individuals who do not use language appropriate for their current social context. A child who has a problem in pragmatics might have difficulty initiating conversations, taking turns with partners, engaging in extensive dialogues, or engaging in a wide range of other language uses in specific situations (e.g., greetings, making requests, or commenting).

| Just the Facts | Students with Communication Disorders |
|---|---|
| Who are the students? | • Students with communication disorders include those with language disorders, speech disorders, or sometimes a combination of both. |
| What are typical characteristics? | • Language disorders include (1) form disorders (difficulty making correct sounds, constructing words, or connecting the words correctly); (2) content or semantic disorders (lack of word-meaning knowledge); and (3) use or pragmatic disorders (application of language in social contexts).<br>• Speech disorders include (1) phonological/articulation disorders (distortions, substitutions, or omissions of speech sounds); (2) fluency disorders (the most common is stuttering); (3) voice disorders (e.g., speaking with a harsh or raspy voice); and (4) motor speech disorders (difficulty using the physical components of speech, often due to a neuromuscular disorder). |
| What are the demographics? | • About 2.5% of children enrolled in public schools are classified under IDEA as having "speech or language impairments." This does not include other students with speech or language disabilities served under other disability categories.<br>• About 5% of school-aged individuals have speech disorders, and between 7 and 10% have primary language impairments. |
| Where are students educated? | • Most students with speech disorders are served in general education classrooms and receive speech therapy provided by speech–language pathologists (SLPs).<br>• Communication disorders are common among many students with disabilities who may be in special education or general education classrooms. |
| How are students identified? | • Speech and language disorders are often recognized by parents, preschool teachers, or pediatricians.<br>• Identifying the specific nature of the speech or language problem requires formal assessment by an SLP. |
| What causes communication disorders? | • Sometimes the cause of a communication disorder can be tied to a specific physiological etiology, an organic cause; sometimes it cannot, in which case it is referred to as a *functional disorder*.<br>• Organic causes of speech disorders can be congenital (present from the time of birth), or they may be acquired later in life. |
| What are the outcomes? | • Many language and speech disorders improve either without therapy (especially with young children) or with therapy.<br>• Some individuals with these disorders have them throughout life. |

- Conduct a speech- or language-sampling procedure with the student to get a clearer picture of the key communication characteristics.
- Use formal tests to learn more about the student's speech and language characteristics. (Justice, 2010; Owens et al., 2011)

## Prevalence

According to U.S. Department of Education (2011) data, over 1.1 million public school students are classified as having speech–language impairments. About 2.65% of children from 3 to 5 years old and 2.25% of those between 6 to 17 years old receive speech–language services through public schools.

It is important to realize that these numbers and percentages represent students whose *primary* IDEA disability category is "speech or language impairment." In addition, many students classified as having other disabilities have communication disorders, like Ryley, the student with Autism Spectrum Disorders with whom Malee Taylor worked. These students also receive therapy services from the more than 60,000 SLPs employed in public schools (U.S. Department of Education, 2011).

| Figure 8.3 | Range of Responsibilities of Speech–Language Pathologists |
|---|---|

**Prevention:** SLPs are integrally involved in the efforts of schools to prevent academic failure in whatever form those initiatives may take; for example, in response to intervention (RTI). SLPs use evidence-based practice (EBP) in prevention approaches.

**Assessment:** SLPs conduct assessments in collaboration with others that help to identify students with communication disorders as well as to inform instruction and intervention, consistent with EBP.

**Intervention:** SLPs provide intervention that is appropriate to the age and learning needs of each individual student and is selected through an evidence-based decision-making process. Although service delivery models are typically more diverse in the school setting than in other settings, the therapy techniques are clinical in nature when dealing with students with disabilities.

**Program Design:** It is essential that SLPs configure schoolwide programs that employ a continuum of service delivery models in the least restrictive environment for students with disabilities, and that they provide services to other students as appropriate.

**Data Collection and Analysis:** SLPs, like all educators, are accountable for student outcomes. Therefore, data-based decision making, including gathering and interpreting data with individual students, as well as overall program evaluation, are essential responsibilities.

**Compliance:** SLPs are responsible for meeting federal and state mandates as well as local policies in performance of their duties. Activities may include individualized education program (IEP) development, Medicaid billing, report writing, and treatment plan/therapy log development.

*Source:* From American Speech-Language-Hearing Association. (2010). *Roles and Responsibilities of Speech-Language Pathologists in Schools* [Professional Issues Statement]. Available from www.asha.org/policy. Retrieved February 5, 2011, from http://www.asha.org/docs/html/PI2010-00317.html#sec1.2.

## Service Delivery

Most preschool-aged children (3 to 5 years old) who receive services for communication disorders are in early childhood education settings with children without disabilities, although some are also served in early childhood special education programs. During their school years (ages 6 to 21), about 87% of students with communication disorders spend more than 80% of their school day in the general education classroom, suggesting a high rate of inclusion (U.S. Department of Education, 2011). Although students with communication disorders are almost always included in general education settings, SLPs will develop individual therapy plans for each of them. The SLP will interpret the results of the assessment and develop an intervention plan designed to be effective, efficient, and easy for the student to follow (Justice, 2010).

Speech–language pathologists may provide support for students in the general education classroom, or they may work with students in separate therapy settings. For example, Malee Taylor works with her team in the general education setting, but she may also pull students for one-to-one or small-group therapy sessions outside of the classroom. The responsibilities of SLPs in schools, as outlined by the American Speech-Language-Hearing Association (ASHA, 2010), are described in Figure 8.3.

# Major Characteristics of Students with Communication Disorders

Many students with communication disorders will not vary a great deal from their peers except for their specific communication disorder. However, in some cases the student's communication disorder may be related to other characteristics.

## Academic Characteristics

A student can have a speech disorder yet be as capable academically as the student sitting next to him. Although the speech disorder may be of concern, especially from a personal or social point of view, it will not necessarily have an impact on the student's learning ability. Other students may be classified as having a **specific language impairment (SLI)** (Justice, 2010). Although children with SLI have significant variety in their language profiles, Justice reports that you are likely to see the following characteristics:

- Inconsistent skills across language domains (e.g., being strong in phonology but weak in syntax and morphology)
- A history of slow vocabulary development
- Word-finding problems
- Difficulty with grammatical production and comprehension, particularly with the use of verbs
- Problems with social skills, behavior, and attention

Many SLPs can work effectively with students with communication disorders in general education settings.

Many students who exhibit language disorders at the preschool level successfully overcome them because of either intervention or language growth and development. However, about 50% of these children continue to have language disorders during elementary school and even into high school and adulthood. When language disorders continue beyond the preschool years, the students who exhibit them are likely to be ultimately classified as having learning disabilities, intellectual disabilities, or emotional and behavioral disabilities (Owens et al., 2011).

## Social and Behavioral Characteristics

Because communication skills are an essential part of social relations, if an individual lacks adequate speech or language skills, social behavior might be affected in different ways. A student may become withdrawn and avoid others, for example. Others may interact inappropriately or may try to compensate for communication weaknesses by undesirable interactions such as aggression or disruption (Nungesser & Watkins, 2005).

Evidence is not entirely clear that communication disorders can *cause* behavioral or emotional disabilities, but researchers have documented a correlation; communication disorders occur very frequently among students classified as having emotional or behavioral disabilities. In one review of research, 71% of students who were labeled with emotional and behavioral disabilities had language deficits, and 57% of the students identified with language deficits also were classified as having emotional and behavioral disabilities (Benner, Nelson, & Epstein, 2002). Clearly, having a language disorder places a child at greater risk for emotional and behavioral challenges.

### Pause & Reflect

Have you ever experienced a communication problem—even a temporary one—that led to your engagement in some atypical or uncommon behavior? How did others react to your problem? How did you react? Was it emotionally difficult?

## Who Are Students with Sensory Impairments?

### Definitions

There are three classifications of students with sensory impairments: (1) students who are **deaf** or who have **hearing impairments**, (2) students who are **blind** or who have **visual disabilities**, and (3) students who are **deaf-blind**.

## Deafness and Hearing Impairment

*Deafness*, as defined under IDEA, means a loss of hearing that is so severe that the student is "impaired in processing linguistic information through hearing, with or without amplification, that adversely affects a child's educational performance." In comparison, IDEA defines a *hearing impairment* as a loss of hearing, "whether permanent or fluctuating, that adversely affects a child's educational performance *but that is not included under the definition of deafness*" (IDEA, 2004).

Hearing loss can be described in terms of the sound volume required for a person to hear; the greater the volume required, the more severe the hearing impairment. The unit of measure used to report degree of hearing loss is called **decibels (dB)**. Those who have normal hearing can hear sounds from 0 to 15 dB—that is, at a very low volume. As hearing loss becomes more severe, individuals require progressively higher decibel levels, or greater volume, to hear. A slight hearing loss is defined as a 16 to 25 dB loss; a mild hearing loss is 26 to 40 dB; a moderate loss, 41 to 55 dB; a moderately severe loss, 56 to 70 dB; a severe loss, 71 to 90 dB; and a profound loss, 90 dB or greater (American Speech-Language-Hearing Association, 2011).

Hearing loss can also be described according to the *type of hearing loss*, which refers to the location in the auditory system where the loss occurs. The types of hearing loss include a **conductive hearing loss** (in the outer and/or middle ear); a **sensorineural hearing loss** (in the cochlea, inner ear, or eighth cranial nerve); a **mixed hearing loss** (both conductive and sensorineural); and a **central auditory processing disorder**. *Configuration of the hearing loss*, another type of description, describes qualitative aspects of hearing, such as whether both ears are affected or whether different frequencies are differentially affected (American Speech-Language-Hearing Association, 2011).

## Blindness and Visual Disabilities

Degree of vision loss is often described according to a person's **visual acuity**. Visual acuity is reported as a ratio (e.g., 20/20), with the first number stating the distance from an object a person is located, and the second number stating the distance at which a person with normal vision could see the same object or figure that is 20 feet away. For example, on a Snellen chart, acuity is measured using letters aligned in rows, and 20/20 is considered normal because you can see from 20 feet as well as another person with good vision can see at 20 feet. In contrast, 20/40 means that the letters or symbols you can correctly read at 20 feet is one that a person with normal vision can read at 40 feet (that is, you have to be closer to see what others can see at a greater distance). Thus, the larger the bottom number, the worse your visual acuity. A person with 20/200 visual acuity must stand 20 feet from a figure or an object in order to see it as well as a person with normal vision could see it from 200 feet.

Along with visual acuity, one's vision can be reported according to one's **visual field**. That is the area in front of a person that she can see while looking forward and not moving her head, often referred to as *peripheral vision*. Visual field is usually measured by an assessment administered by an optometrist or ophthalmologist.

According to IDEA (2004), "Visual impairment including blindness means an impairment in vision that, even with correction, adversely affects a child's educational performance. The term includes both partially sighted and blindness." *Partially sighted* means a visual impairment has resulted in a need for special education. *Low vision* is often used by vision experts in reference to a severe visual impairment. An individual with low vision has sight but is unable to read the newspaper even with the aid of eyeglasses or contact lenses. *Totally blind* refers to an individual who does not have sufficient sight to learn to read even with magnification and must learn through braille or other nonvisual media (National Dissemination Center for Children with Disabilities [NICHCY], 2004).

Blindness, as defined by IDEA, and legal blindness are not necessarily the same. **Legal blindness** refers to a central acuity of 20/200 or less in the better eye with the best possible correction or a visual field of 20 degrees or less. Being legally blind is used as an eligibility criterion for various benefits such as a reduction in income tax. The definition of *visual impairment including blindness* under IDEA is broader than the definition of legal blindness and includes more individuals. Students with visual difficulties who do not meet the requirements of legal blindness may still be served under IDEA because the IDEA definition is concerned more with the educational impact of the vision loss rather than a clinical measure of loss.

### Deaf-Blindness

According to IDEA (2004), "Deaf-blindness means concomitant hearing and visual impairments, the combination of which causes such severe communication and other developmental and educational needs that they cannot be accommodated in special education programs solely for children with deafness or children with blindness." Most students who are classified as deaf-blind have some residual use of their vision, or hearing, or both. Relatively few individuals are completely without both vision and hearing, which means their ability to function might be better than anticipated.

## Just the Facts | Students with Sensory Impairments

| | |
|---|---|
| **Who are the students?** | • Students with sensory impairments may include those who are blind or visually impaired, deaf or hard of hearing, or deaf-blind. |
| **What are typical characteristics?** | • Students with sensory impairments may have total or partial vision loss, total or partial hearing loss, or a loss of both hearing and vision to a significant degree.<br>• The hearing and/or vision loss must interfere with the student's learning ability in order for the student to qualify for special education. |
| **What are the demographics?** | • According to the U.S. Department of Education (2011), almost 26,000 school-aged students are classified as having a visual impairment as a primary disability (either partially sighted or blind).<br>• About 71,000 students have hearing impairments (either deaf or hard of hearing).<br>• Nearly 1,700 students are deaf-blind (significant loss of both hearing and vision). |
| **Where are students educated?** | • Some students with sensory impairments are served in residential schools.<br>• Others are served in general education classes or in special education classes, often in general education schools.<br>• Some 54% of students with hearing impairments, 62% of students with visual disabilities, and 31% of students with deaf-blindness are in general education classrooms for more than 80% of the day (U.S. Department of Education, 2011).<br>• These students are also served in special classes, special schools, and residential settings. |
| **How are students identified?** | • Individuals are often identified at birth or during infancy through testing by medical personnel. |
| **What causes sensory impairments?** | • Deafness and hearing loss can be caused by heredity, accidents, or illness, but in many cases the cause is unknown.<br>• Major causes of blindness or low vision in children include congenital cataracts, optic atrophy, albinism, retinopathy of prematurity, rod-cone dystrophy, cortical visual impairment, and optic nerve hypoplasia.<br>• Deaf-blindness may result due to a syndrome, prematurity, low birth weight, or a congenital infection. |
| **What are the outcomes?** | • Most persons with visual disabilities will live as adults in integrated society.<br>• Many people who are deaf participate more in the Deaf culture but may also live in an integrated society.<br>• Persons with deaf-blindness will usually require some degree of ongoing support. |

## Identification of Students with Sensory Impairments

Most children with sensory impairments will be identified early in life, usually very soon after birth. Successful early identification means that specialized intervention services can begin earlier in a child's life and thus reduce the impact of the disability.

Any degree of hearing loss can have an adverse effect on language, social, and cognitive development. The earlier the loss is detected, the sooner intervention can begin. In the past, children with hearing loss often were not identified until they were 1 or 2 years old or even older and had missed important experiences during their development. Today, most states use *universal newborn hearing screening programs* that are designed to assess infants' hearing before they leave the hospital (National Center for Hearing Assessment and Management [NCHAM], n.d.). According to NCHAM, the average cost to screen a newborn for hearing impairments is between $10 and $50, depending on the procedure and the technology used. The benefit is that identified children and their families can be referred for early intervention services.

As with deafness and hearing impairments, children who have any degree of vision loss will experience delays in early development. Unless early intervention is provided, they will be impaired in their ability to make visual contact and imitate others, explore their environment, crawl and walk, use fine-motor skills for daily activities such as self-feeding, and experience delayed language development. Pediatricians are most likely to first determine that a child has a visual impairment, and they usually refer children whom they identify to the state's **Child Find services**. These services are designed to identify children with disabilities and help families identify appropriate early intervention or early childhood education services. Most children with sensory impairments will usually begin receiving special services in infant and toddler programs (0 to 2 years) and continue to receive them as preschoolers (3 to 5 years) and also as school-aged students until they are 21 years old.

> ### Pause & Reflect
>
> The ability to hear and see allows people not only to learn and understand academic material but also to learn to operate within complex social structures. How would your personal life with your friends and family be affected if you had no vision, hearing, or both?

### Prevalence

According to the U.S. Department of Education (2011), individuals with sensory impairments eligible for public school special education services (from age 6 to 21 years) are relatively few in number. The data show that within schools in the United States, approximately 71,000 students are deaf or have hearing impairments, 26,000 are blind or have visual disabilities, and only about 1,700 are deaf-blind.

As you look at these numbers, remember that they represent students within their respective primary special education classifications. This means that these students have no other disability and that their disabilities interfere with their ability to learn under normal conditions. Therefore, other data sources report different numbers:

- The Gallaudet Research Institute estimates that anywhere from 9 to 22 of every 1,000 people have a severe hearing impairment or are deaf (Mitchell, 2005).
- The American Foundation for the Blind (AFB, 2005) estimates that 25 million people "have trouble seeing, even when wearing glasses or contact lenses, or that they are blind or unable to see at all."
- The National Consortium on Deaf-Blindness (NCDB, 2010) reported that 10,208 students ages 0 to 21 were classified as deaf-blind.

### Service Delivery

Services for students with sensory impairments may be provided in different types of settings. The U.S. Department of Education (2011) data for children between 3 and 5 years with hearing impairments show that almost 33% of them attend regular early childhood education programs for most of the day (which means 80% or more of the day), 21% are in regular settings for less time, and most of the others are placed in special classes (27%) or in special schools (14%). Preschool children with visual disabilities are served similarly: Data show that 42% are in regular early childhood settings for most of the day and another 17% are in these settings for less time, 24% are in special classes, and 10% are in special schools. The pattern for young children with deaf-blindness is somewhat different: Only 24% are in regular early childhood settings for most of the day and about 22% are there for less time, 31% are served in special classes, and 16% are served in separate special schools.

When students are older (6 to 21 years), they are likely to be taught, at least to some extent, in general education classrooms. According to the U.S. Department of Education (2011), 54% of the students with hearing

Most students with hearing impairments will be taught most of the time in general education classrooms.

impairments are in the general education classroom most of the day and another 33% are in these classrooms for at least part of the school day, about 8% are in special schools, and about 4% are in residential facilities. Among students with visual disabilities, 62% are in general education classrooms for most of the day and another 25% are in these classrooms for at least part of the day, about 6% are in special schools, and 4% are in residential programs. Fewer students with deaf-blindness are included in general education settings. Only 31% of these students are in the general education classroom for most of the day, although another 45% are there for at least part of the day, 15% of students with deaf-blindness are placed in separate schools, and 7% are in residential facilities.

As a group, students with sensory impairments are less frequently included in general education classrooms than many other students with disabilities, and students with deaf-blindness are the least included. Would inclusion be important for these students? In the following "A View from a Parent," read about Jacob Hartshorne and his mother Nancy Hartshorne and see what you think.

# Major Characteristics of Students with Sensory Impairments

The academic abilities and social behavior of students with sensory impairments depend on a number of factors, including the specific nature of their disability, any associated disabilities that may be present, and previous experiences in different settings. Although we do not want to overgeneralize, some characteristics that occur frequently are important to note. As you become aware of these characteristics, it is important that you understand that the impact of sensory impairments on learning is usually more a function of the lack of sensory input and critical experiences at an early age rather than an inability to learn.

## Academic Characteristics

A sensory impairment per se does not necessarily mean that a student has a reduced level of cognitive or academic ability; in fact, many students with sensory impairments are as academically gifted and talented as their peers without disabilities. However, conditions that occur during prenatal development that result in sensory impairments can also affect central nervous system development and thus have a direct impact on cognitive development and learning ability. It is estimated, for example, that about 66% of students who are deaf-blind have intellectual disabilities in addition to their sensory loss (NCDB, 2007).

## A View from a Parent

### Why Inclusion Was Important for Her Child Who Was Deaf-Blind

From ages 3 to 5, Jacob Hartshorne, who had multiple disabilities including deaf-blindness, was educated in a classroom for students with severe multiple impairments, segregated from peers without disabilities. All services (including lunch) were provided in the classroom, and the one-to-one nature of the instructional activities precluded socialization with other children. Furthermore, since physical and language skills were not taught in natural contexts, there were limited opportunities for practicing these skills with peers, and generalization and maintenance were limited.

Because of these shortcomings, Jacob's mother Nancy advocated for changes in Jacob's education. Consequently, beginning in kindergarten, Jacob received his educational program in the natural context of his school and classroom alongside his same-aged peers. By the sixth grade, Jacob was participating in all classroom activities with the assistance of a one-on-one intervener (a paraeducator with particular skills in addressing the needs of a students who is deaf-blind). Related services such as physical therapy and occupational therapy were delivered in natural contexts (e.g., during physical education). Language was taught and practiced naturally throughout the school day, and Jacob was an active participant in extracurricular activities such as school plays, music concerts, and talent shows. Perhaps most important, Jacob developed a strong, active group of friends.

Clearly, school personnel provided extensive supports to Jacob to make his inclusion successful. However, one might ask, "Are all of the creative, high-energy efforts of Jacob's team worth the effort?"

Jacob's mother is convinced that without inclusive programming, Jacob would not have:

- Walked independently and used signs to communicate
- Responded to invitations to birthday parties and had classmates attend his annual birthday bash
- Attended Cub Scout campouts and earned honors for his outstanding participation
- Enjoyed the sincere support of his "Circle of Friends," which included 18 students, many of whom have been friends since first grade

Now, as an adult, Jacob continues to exceed the expectations of others. His mother is convinced that without inclusive programming Jacob would not have:

- Walked in graduation with his same-aged peers and received the loudest applause of any from the student body
- Continued to work within his home community, shredding paper alongside his same-aged peers at the local university, and feeding animals alongside same-aged volunteers at the local animal shelter
- Moved into his own home last summer, with his same-aged peers assisting with remodeling, redecoration, and providing him with 24-hour support.

*Source:* From N. Hartshorne, "It sounds nice, but is inclusion really worth it?" *Deaf-Blind Perspectives, 9*(2) (2001/2002): 12–13. Adapted and expanded with permission.

Therefore, depending on the specific nature of an individual's disabilities, learning ability may be impacted to a greater or lesser degree.

Perhaps the most significantly affected academic area for students with hearing impairments is the acquisition of literacy skills, which are based heavily on language development (Luckner, Sebald, Cooney, Young, & Muir, 2006). Although most students who are deaf or who have hearing impairments have adequate intellectual ability to develop reading and writing skills, their delays in language development will often result in delays in learning to read. Early literacy, which is heavily focused on matching spoken sounds and words to printed letters and words, can be especially difficult. As a result, when compared to hearing students, many students who are deaf or hearing impaired will lag in literacy skills during their school years (Schirmer, 2001a, 2001b; Traxler, 2000).

Students who are blind, especially those who are blind from birth or who lost their vision at a very early age, are particularly challenged in learning concepts that are difficult to comprehend without vision. Even though vision specialists provide instructional strategies and materials that allow students to access information through auditory and tactile input (e.g., braille, large print, assistive and adaptive technology, and audio material), learning many concepts can still be difficult. For example, how do you explain what the sky is like or what water molecules look like? Learning such concepts as these will be challenging for many students with visual disabilities.

## Social and Behavioral Characteristics

The social skills of students with sensory impairments will often be impacted, but this is not usually due to an impairment directly related to social development. Instead, it is more often caused by a lack of experiences resulting from the student's sensory loss.

Students with visual disabilities will learn more through tactual exploration.

For most of us, the development of social skills occurs through incidental learning experiences and social reinforcement. In other words, people learn to behave appropriately for their age and culture based on what they see and hear others do and how others react to what they do. Individuals who have sensory impairments are often deprived of this common opportunity, and so their social skills sometimes are atypical. To overcome this lack of natural experiences, students often need direct instruction in appropriate social behavior.

Another serious drawback of having a sensory impairment is that spontaneous relationships and friendships may not occur as frequently as for others. When you cannot hear casual comments or see facial expressions, when you can't determine if someone is serious or joking, or when you don't know if someone is speaking to you or to someone else, your ability to respond in a socially fitting fashion is hampered.

## Keys to Successful Inclusion: Tips from Effective Teachers

Most students with communication disorders and most with hearing impairments or visual disabilities will be included in general education classrooms for much of the day. There are a few simple strategies that teachers can use to be successful in teaching these students. Here are some things that effective teachers do. You can expect your SLP and special education teachers for students with hearing or visual loss to help you implement these strategies.

### Focus on Building Students' Communication Skills

If you are teaching students with communication disorders, you should communicate regularly with your SLP team member and ask how you can build speech or language exercises for these students into your classroom activities. For example, ask the SLP to look at your lesson plan with you and help find ways for you to focus on communication skills for specific students during different lessons. Make sure you know the specific communication targets the SLP is working on with different students and how you can reinforce them in the classroom. Keep the SLP informed about your students' communicative progress (Hampton et al., 2002; Reed & Spicer, 2003; Santos, 2002).

### Make Sure You Are Communicating Clearly

If you have students with hearing impairments, always look at the students when you are speaking, and let the students sit close so they can see your face and body language. If a student has an interpreter in the classroom, make sure this person can hear and understand what you are saying and allow plenty of time for questions. Use lots of visual aids: charts, posters, pictures, graphic organizers, and maps can all be useful. Try to reduce any distractive noises so that the student can focus more on you or other students during a discussion (Rosenberg, Westling, & McLeskey, 2011).

### Help Students Use Their Intact Sensory Abilities

If someone in your class has a vision loss, you can facilitate that student's learning by presenting materials in ways that allow the use of other senses, mainly hearing and touch. When possible, present real objects or models or other tangible items so the student can touch them, and be sure to provide enough time for a thorough tactual examination. If the student uses computerized systems for magnification or to read braille, check that there is adequate room for the equipment. Give rich verbal descriptions of materials and activities in the classroom, even simple things like when someone comes into or leaves the room. Find out from the vision specialist if you need to adjust lighting for the student and let the student sit where he or she can make the greatest use of any residual vision (Rosenberg et al., 2011).

## Summary

This chapter discussed the following topics:

**Definitions of students with communication disorders and students with sensory impairments**

- Communication disorders include students who have language disorders and speech disorders.
- Speech disorders interfere with verbal expression and include phonological and articulation disorders, fluency disorders, voice disorders, and motor speech disorders.
- Language disorders include disorders of form, content (or semantics), and use (or pragmatics).
- *Deafness* means a loss of hearing that is so severe that the student is "impaired in processing linguistic information through hearing, with or without amplification."
- Hearing impairment is a loss of hearing "that adversely affects a child's educational performance but that is not included under the definition of deafness."
- Visual impairment, including blindness, means an impairment that, even with correction, adversely affects a child's educational performance.
- *Legal blindness* refers to a central acuity of 20/200 or less in the better eye with the best possible correction or a visual field of 20 degrees or less.
- *Deaf-blindness* means "concomitant hearing and visual impairments, the combination of which causes such severe communication and other developmental and educational needs that they cannot be accommodated in special education programs solely for children with deafness or children with blindness."

**Prevalence of students with communication disorders and sensory impairments**

- Over 1.1 million public school students receive speech–language services because of their communication disorders.
- Approximately 71,000 students are deaf or have hearing impairments; 26,000 are blind or have visual disabilities; and only about 1,700 are deaf-blind.

**Educational settings used by students with communication disorders and sensory impairments**

- About 87% of students with communication disorders are served primarily in the regular classroom and are provided individual therapy by a speech–language pathologist (SLP).
- Some 54% of school-aged students with hearing impairments are in the general education classroom 80 to 100% of the day, 33% are in the general education classroom for at least part of the school day, and 12% are served in separate schools or in residential facilities.
- About 62% of students with visual disabilities are in the general education classroom for most of the day, 25% are in the general education classroom for at least part of their school day, and about 10% of students with visual disabilities are in separate schools or residential facilities.
- Some 31% of students with deaf-blindness are in the general education classroom for most of the day, while the remainder spend less time there (45%); 22% are in separate schools or residential facilities.

**Major characteristics of students with communication disorders and of students with sensory impairments**

- Students with speech disorders often have typical academic abilities.
- Students with language disabilities may have their learning affected in different ways and may be classified as having a learning disability. They may have mixed language abilities, slow vocabulary development, word-finding problems, and difficulty with grammatical production and comprehension.
- The social behavior of some students with communication disorders might be adversely affected. A student may be withdrawn, interact inappropriately with others, or try to compensate for communication weaknesses through aggression or disruption.
- Sensory impairments may impact both academic learning and social development. This impact is largely a function of the lack of sensory input and critical experiences at an early age rather than an inability to learn.
- Sensory impairments often have an adverse effect on developing social relationships, which can be especially difficult during adolescence.

**Tips from teachers for including students with communication disorders and students with sensory impairments**

- When teaching students with communication disorders, communicate regularly with your SLP, focus on communication skills for specific students during different lessons, and keep the SLP informed about your students' communicative progress.
- When teaching students who are deaf or have hearing impairments, look at the students when you are speaking, let the students sit close to you, use a variety of visual aids, and try to reduce any distractive noises.
- When teaching students who are blind or have visual disabilities, introduce materials in ways that allow the use of hearing and touch; present real objects, models or other tangibles; give rich verbal descriptions of materials and activities; adjust lighting for the student; and let the student sit where he can make the greatest use of any residual vision.

## Addressing Professional Standards

Standards addressed in Chapter 8 include:
**CEC Standards:** (1) foundations, (2) development and characteristics of learners, (3) individual learning differences.

### MyEducationLab

Go to the topics Communication Disorders and Sensory Impairments in the **MyEducationLab** (www.myeducationlab.com) for *Inclusion*, where you can:
- Find learning outcomes for both the topic Communication Disorders and the topic Sensory Impairments, along with the national standards that connect to these outcomes.
- Complete Assignments and Activities that can help you more deeply understand the chapter content.
- Apply and practice your understanding of the core teaching skills identified in the chapter with the Building Teaching Skills and Dispositions learning units.
- Examine challenging situations and cases presented in the IRIS Center Resources.
- Check your comprehension on the content covered in the chapter with the Study Plan. Here you will be able to take a chapter quiz, receive feedback on your answers, and then access Review, Practice, and Enrichment activities to enhance your understanding of chapter content.

# Students with Physical Disabilities, Health Impairments, and Multiple Disabilities

## KEY TOPICS

**After reading this chapter you will:**

- Know who students with physical disabilities, health impairments, and multiple disabilities are, the methods used to identify students with these disabilities, and the range of settings in which they are educated.

- Be able to describe major characteristics of students with physical disabilities, health impairments, and multiple disabilities.

- Be aware of several practical tips from teachers that can facilitate the inclusion of students with physical disabilities, health impairments, and multiple disabilities.

# chapter 9

## A VIEW FROM PROFESSIONALS

### How a Pre-K Team Includes a Child with Multiple Disabilities

Saranna is a pretty, blonde-haired, 4-year-old girl who is in the pre-K classroom at Gilpin Manor Elementary School. She has a lot going for her, but she is also facing some extraordinary challenges. For example, Saranna is just learning to communicate, walk, and develop several other basic skills because she has "multiple disabilities." Her conditions include cerebral palsy, seizures, chronic lung disease, non-accidental trauma, and developmental delay, all of which developed as a result of her premature birth. Saranna was born at 24 weeks and spent the majority of the first 13 months of her life in the hosipital.

Many years ago, Saranna would have been a prime candidate for institutionalization. And even today, most children with Saranna's characteristics attend separate, special schools. But at Gilpin Manor, Saranna has a team of dedicated professionals who support her and other pre-kindergarten–aged children with and without disabilities so they can achieve a foundation of success for future years. Saranna is taught daily by her teacher, Alison Bryan, and receives additional instruction and support from Melissa Pratt, the pre-K interventionist; Dianna Melrath, the pre-K special education paraeducator; Malee Taylor, the speech–language pathologist on the team; Diana Shaffer, the physical therapist who helps Saranna work on functional mobility skills; and Alice O'Mullane, the occupational therapist who helps Saranna work on daily living skills.

During the past year, Saranna's progress could be described as slow but steady. She is now able stand up when instructed to do so and is able to locate, pull to her, and play with developmentally appropriate toys. Her progress is made possible because of teamwork and the commitment of the professionals on the pre-K team. The team uses photographs to help the child communicate, a lot of hand-over-hand guidance to complete tasks, verbal cuing to enhance her comprehension of directions, and music and movement to encourage motor skills development.

Being in an inclusive school such as Gilpin Manor has helped Saranna grow and develop. She has had the benefit of a sound early education while still having the chance to learn from her peers. The efforts made by the pre-K team working with Saranna have already resulted in some immediate benefits, and it is likely that there will also be many long-term payoffs thanks to her participation in an inclusive classroom.

# Introduction

As we have seen in earlier chapters, many students are classified as having disabilities because of their cognitive, learning, or behavioral characteristics. Others may have communication disorders, hearing impairments, or visual disabilities. All of these conditions can adversely affect a student's performance in school and lead to the need for special educational services. As we will learn in this chapter, many other students have physical disabilities, health impairments, or multiple disabilities that will also require special education services. Their physical and health conditions are often of such a magnitude that they can interfere with their learning. When this is the case, special education services are necessary.

As a professional educator, you will readily recognize that some of your students have physical or medical conditions; yet, other such conditions, for the most part, are invisible. For instance, some students' physical disabilities are easily noticeable. These include students who have cerebral palsy or muscular dystrophy, for example, who are often in wheelchairs or who use orthopedic devices. But others have conditions such as asthma, diabetes, or epilepsy and they may not be as noticeable on a day-to-day basis.

From the perspective of public schools, students with physical disabilities, health impairments, and multiple disabilities fall into one of three categories: requiring (1) no accommodations, (2) some accommodations, or (3) an individualized education program (IEP). For example, a number of these students may attend school without any special services or accommodations. Like a student with poor visual acuity who needs nothing more than to wear corrective lenses, many students with physical or medical conditions simply come to school and manage their own needs.

The second group includes students who require some accommodations, but because their condition does not impair their ability to learn, they do not require special education services. These students will usually have Section 504 Plans that list the ways school personnel can meet their needs so that they can participate like other students.

Finally, the third group includes students whose disabilities adversely affect their learning ability and who are therefore considered eligible for special education under the Individuals with Disabilities Education Act (IDEA). These students will have an IEP.

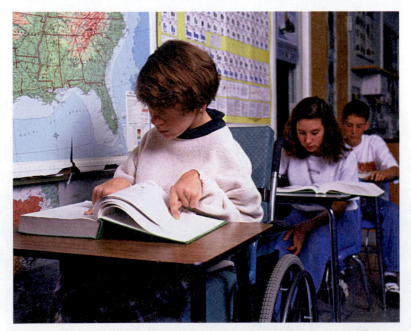

Some students' physical or medical needs will be very apparent; others' will not.

# Who Are Students with Physical Disabilities, Health Impairments, and Multiple Disabilities?

In an inclusive classroom, you are likely to encounter students from each of these categories. The accompanying box, "Just the Facts," provides you with basic information about these students. Please keep in mind that as you look at the information in "Just the Facts," and as you read the rest of this chapter, the medical information that we present on the selected

| Just the Facts | Students with Physical Disabilities, Health Impairments, and Multiple Disabilities |
|---|---|
| Who are the students? | • *Physical disabilities:* Students with conditions such as cerebral palsy, spina bifida, or other conditions that affect their ability to walk or use their arms or legs.<br>• *Health impairments:* Students with chronic health conditions such as asthma, epilepsy, and HIV/AIDS, which may or may not be terminal, that cause weakness or fatigue or in some other way adversely affect school performance.<br>• *Multiple disabilities:* Students with intellectual disabilities and other physical or sensory disabilities. |
| What are typical characteristics? | • The conditions of students with physical disabilities may be relatively mild to more severe.<br>• Different body parts may be affected.<br>• Disabilities may be due to central nervous system damage or muscular or orthopedic impairments.<br>• Students with health impairments may be weak and sometimes in pain. Lack of stamina may often be a debilitating factor. They may miss a lot of school due to their illnesses.<br>• Students with multiple disabilities may have sensory and physical impairments and may exhibit uncommon characteristics such as self-stimulatory or self-injurious behavior. Many will have serious medical conditions. |
| What are the demographics? | Within the school-aged population:<br>• About 0.1% have physical disabilities.<br>• About 0.99% have other health impairments.<br>• About 0.2% have multiple disabilities. |
| Where are students educated? | • The majority of students with physical disabilities and other health impairments are educated in general classes.<br>• Many students with multiple disabilities are placed in special classes. |
| How are students identified? | • Individuals with physical disabilities, health impairments, and multiple disabilities are initially identified by physicians as having special medical needs.<br>• Educational personnel evaluate these students to determine if special education services or other accommodations are necessary. |
| What are the causes? | • Physical disabilities may originate before, during, or after birth. They may be genetically based or occur because of trauma or injury.<br>• Health impairments can also be due to inherited conditions or may occur through transmitted viral infections.<br>• Some conditions have unknown causes.<br>• Multiple disabilities are usually due to prenatal causes such as maternal infections, teratogens, or trauma. |
| What are the outcomes? | • The physical, social, emotional, and health challenges faced by students with physical disabilities, health impairments, and multiple disabilities often continue into their adult years.<br>• Some of these conditions lead to early death. |

conditions is updated regularly. For the most current information on different disabilities and conditions, we suggest you visit the websites at the National Institutes of Health (www .nih.gov/) or the Centers for Disease Control and Prevention (www.cdc.gov/).

## Definitions

### Physical Disabilities

Although most people commonly use the term *physical disabilities;* IDEA (Sec. 300.8) uses the term *orthopedic impairments* and defines it as follows:

> Orthopedic impairment means a severe orthopedic impairment that adversely affects a child's educational performance. The term includes impairments caused by congenital anomaly (e.g., clubfoot, absence of some member, etc.), impairments caused by disease (e.g., poliomyelitis, bone tuberculosis, etc.), and impairments from other causes (e.g., cerebral palsy, amputations, and fractures or burns that cause contractures).

As you are undoubtedly aware, many different types of physical disabilities exist, and we could not possibly discuss all of them here. However, we will describe four conditions that are seen relatively often in inclusive classrooms, notably: cerebral palsy, muscular dystrophy, spina bifida, and orthopedic and musculoskeletal conditions.

Cerebral palsy (CP) is a neurological disorder caused by brain damage before, during, or after birth that impairs a person's posture and movement ability. Cerebral palsy is called a *nonprogressive* disability because the brain damage does not continue to worsen with the passage of time. Treatment is necessary, however, to prevent postural deterioration and to improve movement and independence (Best & Bigge, 2010; Griffin, Fitch, & Griffin, 2002; Pellegrino, 2007).

The four major forms of CP are *spastic CP* (characterized by stiff muscles and exaggerated reflexes), *dyskinetic CP* (characterized by involuntary, nonpurposeful movements), *ataxic CP* (characterized by lack of balance and uncoordinated movements), and *mixed CP,* meaning that more than one form of the condition occurs in the same person. Physicians also describe CP according to the area of the body that is affected: Hemiplegia means that one side of the body is more affected; diplegia means the legs are more affected than the arms; and quadriplegia means that all four limbs are affected as well as the trunk and the muscles that control the neck, mouth, and tongue.

The brain damage that results in cerebral palsy can sometimes lead to other problems as well. These may include intellectual disabilities, visual disabilities, hearing impairments, speech and language disorders, seizures, feeding problems, growth abnormalities, learning disabilities, emotional or behavioral disabilities, and ADHD.

Muscular dystrophy, like CP, is a relatively common physical disability. Unlike CP, however, muscular dystrophy is a progressive disorder that results in ongoing muscle weakness. When children have muscular dystrophy, their muscle tissue gradually degenerates, turning into fatty tissue, and the condition worsens as time passes. Also, unlike CP, the central nervous system is not involved. Duchenne muscular dystrophy is the most common form and is a genetically inherited condition (Best, 2010a).

Muscular dystrophy first appears during early childhood, between about 2 and 6 years of age, when the calves seem to be growing larger, a condition called pseudohypertrophy. Actually, fat tissue is replacing muscle tissue in the legs as the legs become weaker and weaker. Gradually, the muscle weakness moves up the body, from the legs to the trunk and arms. Often, these children lose the ability to walk and must use a wheelchair. As they become weaker, they can no longer power a manual wheelchair and may require an electric wheelchair for mobility control. Even holding the head erect becomes difficult (Escolar, Tosi, Tesi Rocha, & Kennedy, 2007).

## Pause & Reflect

Individuals who have CP can have speech impairments that may be interpreted by some as an intellectual disability. Such an assumption might lead someone to misinterpret the real ability of the person. Do you see any danger in doing this? How might this be avoided?

Spina bifida is a break in the spinal column that can leave a person with a loss of physical ability in the lower part of the body. The extent of loss depends on the location of the break in the spinal column. Different types of the condition exist, but the most severe form, called myelomeningocele, results in a loss of sensation and muscle control in parts of the body below the lesion. Persons with this condition use a wheelchair for mobility and are usually unable to feel touch, temperature, pressure, or pain (Best, 2010a).

Orthopedic and musculoskeletal conditions are a variety of conditions in which bodily structures involving the bones and muscles do not develop normally. Some that you may encounter are curvature of the spine (scoliosis), congenital hip dislocations, juvenile arthritis, osteogenesis imperfecta, and limb deficiencies. Individuals with some of these conditions may require surgery; may be fitted with prosthetic devices, such as artificial hands or legs; and usually must use adapted approaches for accomplishing daily tasks.

## Health Impairments

Like physical disabilities, some chronic health impairments can seriously affect a student's ability to receive an appropriate education. Sometimes these conditions occur in combination with other conditions (e.g., a student with cerebral palsy may also have epilepsy); in other cases, however, the health impairment is the primary disability. According to IDEA (Sec. 300.8), "other health impairment" means

> having limited strength, vitality, or alertness, including a heightened alertness to environmental stimuli, that results in limited alertness with respect to the educational environment, that—(i) Is due to chronic or acute health problems such as asthma, attention deficit disorder or attention deficit hyperactivity disorder, diabetes, epilepsy, a heart condition, hemophilia, lead poisoning, leukemia, nephritis, rheumatic fever, sickle cell anemia, and Tourette syndrome; and (ii) Adversely affects a child's educational performance.

We devoted Chapter 4 to ADHD, which is classified as a health impairment, because it is relatively common. That is why we do not discuss it here.

In this section, we briefly describe five health impairments that you likely will encounter among your students at some time in your career as a teacher.

*Asthma.* Asthma is a chronic lung condition that can result in attacks characterized by difficult breathing, wheezing, coughing, excess mucus, sweating, and chest constriction. Attacks may result from different triggers, which may be allergens such as tiny dust particles, cigarette smoke, and pet dander, or even cold, dry air or physical exertion (Best, 2010b).

*Sickle-Cell Disease.* In sickle-cell disease, a block in normal blood flow results in episodic pain in the arms, legs, chest, and abdomen as well as priapism (painful prolonged erection). Sickle-cell disease also causes damage to most organs, including the spleen, kidneys, and liver. Young children with sickle-cell disease can be easily debilitated by certain bacterial infections. Sickle-cell disease is most common among those with sub-Saharan and West African ancestry (Schonberg & Tifft, 2007).

*Epilepsy.* Epilepsy is a neurological condition that causes seizures. Different types of seizures may occur. The most common type is a tonic-clonic seizure, referred to in the past as a grand mal seizure. During a tonic-clonic seizure, the person loses awareness, ceases to engage in any activity, and loses consciousness. She becomes stiff (tonic), and then jerking (clonic) movements begin. Although the tonic-clonic seizure is the most common type of seizure among persons with severe disabilities who have seizures, other types may also occur. One form that you may encounter is called absence seizures, previously referred to as petit mal seizures. During absence seizures, which are very brief, lasting perhaps 1 to 10 seconds, the person experiences a loss of consciousness, but otherwise remains stable. Observers sometimes assume that a student with absence seizures is simply daydreaming (Weinstein & Gaillard, 2007).

*Type-1 Diabetes.* Type-1 diabetes, also called juvenile diabetes or insulin-dependent diabetes, is an autoimmune disease that destroys the cells in the pancreas that produce insulin.

Chronic health impairments sometimes require special accommodations in schools.

## Pause & Reflect

Have you or anyone in your family had a health impairment that affected learning ability? Can you think of how such conditions could have a detrimental effect on student learning? How would having a health condition affect your own ability to participate in class?

Type-1 diabetes develops most often in children or young adults but can occur at any age. Children with Type-1 diabetes require insulin shots. Without medication, the student may become very thirsty, need to urinate often, lose weight, and become very weak (National Institutes of Health, 2011).

*Cystic Fibrosis.* Cystic fibrosis is a disease that affects major body organs that secrete fluids. The disease primarily affects the lungs, where airway passages become blocked, and the digestive system, where the mucus interferes with the release of digestive enzymes. The secretions of normal fluids are blocked by the mucus, which causes cysts to develop, which become surrounded by scar tissue (Best, 2010b).

### Multiple Disabilities

As defined by IDEA (Sec. 300.8), *multiple disabilities* are "concomitant impairments (e.g., mental retardation–blindness, mental retardation–orthopedic impairment), the combination of which causes such severe educational needs that they cannot be accommodated in special education programs solely for one of the impairments. The term does not include deaf-blindness."

Students with multiple disabilities, like Saranna whom you met at the beginning of the chapter, have a relatively severe intellectual disability and at least one additional disability, often a physical disability. Additionally, students with multiple disabilities usually have various health problems that complicate and worsen their disabilities. They often develop conditions such as high blood pressure, obesity, brittle bones, depression, and general tiredness. Other conditions include cardiovascular (heart) diseases, respiratory diseases, eating disorders, and growth impairments (Heller, 2004; Thuppal & Sobsey, 2004).

## Identification of Students with Physical Disabilities, Health Impairments, and Multiple Disabilities

Parents will often recognize atypical physical or health conditions relatively early in their child's life and will report these conditions to their pediatrician or family doctor, who will then conduct evaluations to establish a diagnosis. Other medical specialists may conduct subsequent evaluations to assess the physical and health status of the child and determine the child's medical needs. As a result of these evaluations, the physicians will prescribe medications or medical interventions, including surgery, to improve the child's physical or health status.

After physicians establish a medical diagnosis, educational personnel must determine through educational assessment whether the condition has a significant negative impact on the student's education. If it does, then the student is evaluated for early intervention or special education services, depending on the child's age. An individualized family service plan (IFSP) or IEP is then developed.

When considering the provision of special education services, school professionals must also consider whether related services are necessary for the student to benefit from education. For students with physical disabilities, health impairments, and multiple disabilities, this means that physical therapists and occupational therapists will conduct evaluations, and, if necessary, create intervention programs to meet a student's needs.

**Table 9.1**  Percent of Time Spent in Public School Settings by School-Aged (6 to 21 Years) Students with Physical Disabilities, Health Impairments, and Multiple Disabilities

| Disability | Percentage of Time Spent Inside of General Education Classroom | | | |
|---|---|---|---|---|
| | Most of the School Day (80% or more) | Some of the School Day (From 40%–79%) | Limited Amount of School Day (Less than 40%) | Separate School/ Residential or Correctional Facility/Private School/ Home-Hospital Setting |
| Other health impairments | 60.4 | 24.4 | 11.2 | 4.0 |
| Orthopedic impairment | 51.5 | 16.5 | 24.7 | 7.3 |
| Multiple disabilities | 13.7 | 16.4 | 45.9 | 24.0 |

*Source:* U.S. Department of Education (2009).

## Prevalence

According to the most recent data from the U.S. Department of Education (2009), students with physical disabilities, health impairments, and multiple disabilities who are served in public schools under IDEA comprise a very small fraction of the population. At the preschool level (3 to 5 years old), the percentage of children with physical disabilities is 0.07%; those with health impairments is 0.11%; and those with multiple disabilities is 0.07%. During the school-aged years (6 to 17 years), the percentages increase somewhat: Physical disabilities increase to 0.1%; health impairments to 0.99%; and multiple disabilities to 0.2%. Nevertheless, all together, the students in these categories make up less than 1% of all students in public schools.

Overall, the number of students identified with these disabilities increases from the preschool to the school years. The greatest increase is in the health impairments category, which increases almost six times. This is likely due at least in part to the fact that students with ADHD, who usually are not identified until the school years, are included in this category.

## Service Delivery

As shown in Table 9.1, most students with physical disabilities and health impairments are included in general education classrooms either for most or part of the school day. In contrast, students with multiple disabilities spend less time in the general education classroom, and more attend separate schools or residential facilities for students with severe disabilities (U.S. Department of Education, 2009).

# Major Characteristics of Students with Physical Disabilities, Health Impairments, and Multiple Disabilities

The range of abilities among students with physical disabilities, health impairments, and multiple disabilities is greater than in the general population. As an educator, you should consider the individual strengths and weaknesses of each of these students. In the following sections, we provide a general description of some of the characteristics that you may observe.

## A View from a Peer

### Why Inclusion Is Important

Saranna, whom you met at the beginning of this chapter, is doing well in her inclusive pre-K classroom. The team that works with her is using effective methods that are helping her to be successful. But Saranna's placement isn't only important for her; it's important for the other kids around her. Melissa Pratt believes that the methods she uses with Saranna and other pre-kindergartners with special needs is not just good for them, but for the children without disabilities as well. "They need models, they need visuals," she says, adding, "And not just for them, all the kids benefit. And that's another benefit, because we're doing this with our special ed kids . . . [but] our regular ed kids benefit from that. You know your teaching practices change based on the needs of the kids."

There are also some personal benefits for the students without disabilities, like Saranna's friend, Olivia. Olivia is 4 years old ("almost five," she says, smiling) and is Saranna's best buddie in her pre-K classroom. They hang out a lot together, and Saranna's limited communication and mobility skills do nothing to detract from their relationship. Malee Taylor, the SLP on the team, says that Olivia is a little like a "mother hen" always hovering around Saranna, helping her from time to time, and just enjoying being close to her. When asked why she likes Saranna, Olivia answered that it's because Saranna "lets me hold her hand" and likes to walk with her. And when asked if she thinks Saranna likes her, Olivia, who used her words sparingly, smiled, nodded her head, and said, "She loves me."

Olivia said it was good that Saranna was in her class. Why? "Well," Olivia said, "She is learning to talk" and she has a lot of friends, like her, and Evan, and others. And is it a problem for Saranna to be in your class with the other children? "Nooo," Olivia said clearly, acting like it was a silly question. In fact, she said that she hopes she is in the same class with Saranna next year.

What does it mean to a 4-year-old (almost five!) like Olivia to have a friend with multiple disabilities like Saranna? Right now it means she has a good friend to hang out with. But we can also ask what it will mean 10 or 20 years from now. Our best guess can only be that it will continue to have a positive impact on some of Olivia's most important attitudes toward others with different abilities.

## Academic Characteristics

Students with physical disabilities have a full range of academic abilities and disabilities: Some are gifted, and others have severe intellectual disabilities. For some students, such as a student with severe cerebral palsy, determining the actual degree of cognitive ability is often difficult. Standardized intelligence tests rely on a person's verbal and motor abilities, and because cerebral palsy, for example, often affects these abilities, attaining a precise determination of intelligence level is difficult (Best & Bigge, 2010; Pellegrino, 2007). Assessment of students with spina bifida faces similar issues: Some of these students may have intellectual disabilities, some may have learning disabilities, and others may have average or above-average intelligence. Even those with higher intellectual abilities may have learning difficulties in the areas of attention, memory, comprehension, organization, and reasoning (Spina Bifida Association, 2008). For many other students with different types of physical disabilities (particularly those with orthopedic or musculoskeletal disorders), their physical condition likely will not affect their intellectual ability. Those students will be able to integrate readily into the general education classroom and the general curriculum, given adequate supports.

An important consideration for the academic success of students with physical disabilities is the provision of assistive technology (AT) devices and services to meet their needs. Numerous AT devices can be quite helpful to students with physical disabilities, and a number of these devices can make a difference in student success. In fact, there is some evidence that interactive computer play facilitates the movement ability of some students with limited motor abilities by improving movement quality, spatial orientation, and mobility (Sandlund, McDonough & Häger-Ross, 2009). Teachers are likely to encounter students with physical disabilities who will manage quite well academically if the school has provided them with appropriate AT devices and services.

Most students with health impairments will have adequate cognitive and learning abilities for participation in the general education curriculum, but some may have learning

We discuss AT devices in Chapter 16.

disabilities associated with their health conditions. With others, their health impairment may have an indirect adverse effect on learning. A common difficulty is that the health condition may cause the student to miss an inordinate number of instructional activities because of pain, discomfort, illness, fatigue, or treatment side effects. For example, think of a student who has asthma. Besides being very dangerous, even potentially life-threatening, asthma can affect a student's progress in school. According to the American Academy of Asthma Allergy and Immunology (2005), in one school year, children with asthma have a total of 10 million absences from school. This obviously translates to a great deal of lost instructional time. Depending on the student, this loss of time can have a significant impact on learning.

Assistive technology can be a key for students with physical disabilities achieving academic success.

A major factor for the academic success of many students with health impairments is how well they can take and respond to prescribed medications. Although most school districts do not allow teachers to administer medications to students, it will sometimes be important for you to be able to monitor students' progress in school and report to parents or the school nurse if the student's participation is declining. This might suggest that the current regimen of medication should be reevaluated.

Students classified as having multiple disabilities will have some degree of intellectual disability in addition to their physical disabilities. This implies that their learning abilities within the general education curriculum will be limited. However, these students *can* participate if the general education curriculum has been adapted in a way that is meaningful to the student yet still reflects the essence of the material (Browder, Spooner, Wakeman, Trela, & Baker, 2006). Special education teachers skilled in working with students with multiple disabilities will provide assistance and support in making these adaptations and ensuring the success of these students in the general education classroom.

## Social and Behavioral Characteristics

The personal thoughts, feelings, and social behavior of students with physical disabilities, health impairments, and multiple disabilities can be negatively impacted by the students' conditions. As a result, they may have poor self-esteem or self-worth, and their social interactions with other students may be adversely affected. Their view of the world and their interactions with others are likely to differ from others without disabilities or health conditions.

In one study of high school students with physical disabilities (Doubt & McColl, 2003), the students reported that to be better accepted, they tried to avoid calling attention to their disability, sometimes made fun of their own condition, and found a special niche among their peers without disabilities, such as serving in a support role on a sports team. Sometimes, they said, they tried to educate their peers about their condition. Still, certain factors tended to isolate them, including their physical limitations as well as their own decisions to exclude themselves. Sometimes they did this because they could not keep up, but in other cases, they excluded themselves because they felt they would not be accepted by others. The study's authors concluded that the students' lack of inclusion resulted from both intrinsic and extrinsic factors. That is, in some cases their own self-views or real physical limitations led to exclusion; and in others, the overt reactions by their peers excluded them. Regardless, the students' physical disabilities meant that they were less socially involved (Doubt & McColl, 2003).

## Pause & Reflect

Think about a specific physical disability or ongoing health condition we have described. If you had this disability or condition, how well would you fit into your social group? How would the disability or condition affect how you fit in? Do you think your relationships would change?

Is there a way to facilitate students' inclusion in spite of their physical limitations? There may well be. In a study of younger children, researchers found that the students without disabilities said involvement of children with physical disabilities would be easier if the activities did not demand a great deal of physical involvement. They were also more likely to be accepting if teachers stressed the importance of equity and fairness. These findings suggest that teachers may play an important role in promoting the social involvement of children with disabilities (Diamond & Hong, 2010).

As with physical disabilities, health impairments can sometimes impact normal social behavior, interactions, and relationships. For example, peers might avoid students who experience frequent asthma attacks, and, at the same time, parents and teachers might limit play and recreational activities to reduce the chance of an attack (Best, 2010b). Similarly, peers might avoid a student with epilepsy who has had a seizure if they are unfamiliar with epilepsy and have not previously witnessed a seizure. Because seizures often first appear during adolescence, this can be very embarrassing for the student, who may be shunned or subjected to taunting and ridicule.

Peers might also react differently to students with chronic health impairments such as cancer or HIV/AIDS. Students with such conditions might miss a great deal of school because of their illness and, when in school, they could be weak or tired. As a result, they have limited opportunities to take part in play activities, adolescent bantering, or other typical social activities. Some peers, not fully understanding the nature of a student's condition, might fear it and thus avoid the student. Others may feel sorry for the student and be uncomfortable with normal age-appropriate interactions. In all of these circumstances, the challenge is the same: The student with the condition will not be likely to interact with other students in common ways.

We discuss positive behavior support in Chapter 15.

Students who have multiple disabilities might be subjected to these same social conditions. Worse for these students, however, is their proneness to engage in various uncommon behaviors that cause them to appear very different and lead others to avoid them or, even worse, fear them. These behaviors might include repetitive movements (called **stereotypies**, such as hand flapping, or **self-injurious behaviors**, such as head banging), or making loud and atypical vocalizations. Many times these behaviors can be improved through the use of positive behavior support principles, but the reaction of other students will usually be problematic.

## Keys to Successful Inclusion: Tips from Effective Teachers

Including students with physical disabilities, health impairments, or multiple disabilities can usually be managed effectively by thinking about the nature or the disability and what you can do to provide the student with more access to the classroom environment or to support the student's unique health needs. Here are a few things effective teachers suggest to create more inclusive environments for these students.

### Arrange Your Classroom to Increase Accessibility

If you have a student with physical disabilities, health impairments, or multiple disabilities in your classroom, you should work closely with your colleagues in physical or occupational therapy, or in health-care services, to learn about specific needs, accommodations, and adaptations for your student. Review the student's Section 504 Plan (if there is one) or the health-care plan, and make sure you understand it. Arrange for a conference in your classroom so that key professionals can give you advice and direction on specific practices and arrangements you should make. Working with your team members, consider how you may need to arrange your classroom to accommodate a student's physical or health needs. Ensure that there is access to all parts of the room, including centers and materials, so that a student in a wheelchair or using orthotic devices can get to everything. Sometimes classroom temperatures may have to be adjusted to accommodate a student's physical or health needs. Make sure that there is access to all parts of the room, including centers and materials so a student in a wheelchair or using orthotic devices can get to everything.

### Make Sure Your Classroom Promotes Good Health

Some students will have health issues that may require you to consider how healthy your classroom is. For example, consider the student with asthma. If the cause of asthma attacks can be identified, teachers can sometimes prevent them from occurring. Taking steps such as using air-cleaning systems, implementing rigorous and frequent room cleaning, and avoiding pet dander can reduce the risk of asthma attacks. Knowing this, teachers can try to reduce any sources of antigens in their classrooms by working with the school custodial staff to ensure that a room is as clean and dust-free as possible.

### Understand How Students Are to Use Their Assistive Technology Devices

Some students with physical disabilities, health impairments, or multiple disabilities will use assistive technology devices to meet their unique needs. These might range from wheelchairs to communication devices to personal computers with accommodating peripheral devices. You do not have to be an expert on these devices, but you should have some basic understanding of how they operate and know a few simple things like how to turn them on and off. You also should be able to monitor how well they are working and whether or not the student is using them effectively. The feedback you provide to the SLP, the PT, or the OT can be very useful in helping the student get the most out of the AT devices and arranging for support services to improve their usage.

### Know What to Look for When Students Are Taking Medications

Many students with physical disabilities, health impairments, or multiple disabilities will be taking one or more medications. You should know when the student takes the medications and what to expect from the effects and side effects of the medications, especially how they might affect the student's attention, learning ability, motivation, and other behavioral characteristics. If you notice a departure from the typical characteristics of the student, you should inform the school's health-care provider or the student's parents.

### Understand the Specific Disabilities or Health Conditions of Your Students and Help Them Be Successful Despite Those Challenges

In this chapter, we introduced you to several conditions that you may see in some of your students, and of course there are others that are less common. The more you can learn about the specific conditions of your students, the more you will know how it affects them and their performance in school. Your knowledge will help you understand why they might lack attention, be tired, miss class, or not turn in their homework. By understanding the nature and impact of the different conditions, you might help a student be more successful.

## Summary

This chapter addressed the following topics:

**Definitions of students with physical disabilities, health impairments, and multiple disabilities**

- "Orthopedic impairment [the term used in IDEA instead of *physical disabilities*] means a severe orthopedic impairment that adversely affects a child's educational performance. The term includes impairments caused by congenital anomaly (e.g., clubfoot, absence of some member, etc.), impairments caused by disease (e.g., poliomyelitis, bone tuberculosis, etc.), and impairments from other causes (e.g., cerebral palsy, amputations, and fractures or burns that cause contractures)."

- Health impairment, according to IDEA, means "having limited strength, vitality or alertness, including a heightened alertness to environmental stimuli, that results in limited alertness with respect to the educational environment, that—(i) Is due to chronic or acute health problems such as asthma, attention deficit disorder or attention deficit hyperactivity disorder, diabetes, epilepsy, a heart condition, hemophilia, lead poisoning, leukemia, nephritis, rheumatic fever, and sickle cell anemia; and (ii) Adversely affects a child's educational performance."
- According to IDEA, multiple disabilities are "concomitant impairments (e.g., mental retardation–blindness, mental retardation–orthopedic impairment), the combination of which causes such severe educational needs that they cannot be accommodated in special education programs solely for one of the impairments. The term does not include deaf-blindness."

### Identification of students with physical disabilities, health impairments, and multiple disabilities

- Students' medical conditions are normally identified early in life by health-care specialists. Educational specialists determine if the student requires special education services.

### Prevalence of students with physical disabilities, health impairments, and multiple disabilities

- During the school year, 0.10% of students will have physical disabilities, 0.99% will have health impairments, and 0.20% will have multiple disabilities.

### Educational placements for students with physical disabilities, health impairments, and multiple disabilities

- The large majority of students with physical disabilities and those with health impairments are in the general education classroom for most or part of the day.
- The majority of students with multiple disabilities are placed in special schools or special classes within regular schools for most of the day.

### Major characteristics of students with physical disabilities, health impairments, and multiple disabilities

- Academic and cognitive performance
  - *Students with physical disabilities:* Most of these students have typical cognitive ability and can do academic work with the use of assistive technology. Some may have other disabilities that may affect their abilities.
  - *Students with health impairments:* Most of these students have adequate cognitive and learning abilities, but some may have learning disabilities. They may also be adversely affected by the amount of school they miss due to their health impairment.
  - *Students with multiple disabilities:* These students have intellectual disabilities that may be in the severe-to-profound range and require an adapted curriculum.
- Behavior performance and social skills
  - *Students with physical disabilities:* These students sometimes have difficulty developing social relations with their peers because of differences in their physical characteristics.
  - *Students with health impairments:* Some of these health impairments may make participation in typical social activities difficult. Sometimes these students may be subjects of discrimination because of their conditions.
  - *Students with multiple disabilities:* These students often lack the opportunity for social interactions.

### Keys to successful inclusion

- Arrange your classroom to increase accessibility.
- Make sure your classroom promotes good health.
- Understand how students are to use their assistive technology devices.
- Know what to look for when students are taking medications.
- Understand the specific disabilities or health conditions of your students and help them be successful despite their challenges.

## Addressing Professional Standards

Standards addressed in Chapter 9 include:

**CEC Standards**: (1) foundations, (2) development and characteristics of learners, (3) individual learning differences.

---

### MyEducationLab

Go to the topic Physical Disabilities and Health Impairments in the **MyEducationLab** (www.myeducationlab.com) for *Inclusion,* where you can:

- Find learning outcomes for Physical Disabilities and Health Impairments, along with the national standards that connect to these outcomes.
- Complete Assignments and Activities that can help you more deeply understand the chapter content.
- Apply and practice your understanding of the core teaching skills identified in the chapter with the Building Teaching Skills and Dispositions learning units.
- Examine challenging situations and cases presented in the IRIS Center Resources.
- Check your comprehension on the content covered in the chapter with the Study Plan. Here you will be able to take a chapter quiz, receive feedback on your answers, and then access Review, Practice, and Enrichment activities to enhance your understanding of chapter content.

# Collaboration and Teaming

## KEY TOPICS

**After reading this chapter you will:**

- Know what to expect regarding collaboration in inclusive classrooms and schools.

- Be able to identify the dispositions and skills needed to effectively collaborate with other professionals.

- Be able to describe the collaborative roles of teachers in inclusive schools.

- Understand how students may be engaged as collaborators to support inclusive programs.

- Understand a series of guided, step-by-step interventions and practices related to working collaboratively to meet the needs of all students.

# chapter 10

# A VIEW FROM TEACHERS

### Why Is Collaboration an Absolute Necessity to Support Inclusion?

We interviewed teachers from Gilpin Manor Elementary and West Hernando Middle School about collaboration. All of the teachers we interviewed said that collaboration was an "absolute necessity" to support effective inclusive programs. Perhaps the main reason for this was that collaboration is used in so many ways to support teachers and inclusive programs. For example, Megan Law, first-grade teacher at Gilpin Manor, emphasized the importance of working with a team of teachers when planning lessons, as teachers provide input regarding how to differentiate instruction. "We work together so we can see which way we need to differentiate the lessons for certain students. It's such a big help because we often just keep doing the same activities . . . so we can get feedback from each other" and learn about new options for differentiation. Similar comments were made by Melissa Pratt, a preschool special education teacher at Gilpin Manor, who "goes back and forth" with teachers she works with as they "constantly modify and differentiate things together. Everybody is on the team, including the paraeducators, and we all have a voice."

Susan Davis and Lisa Hallal, who both work as co-teachers at West Hernando Middle School, elaborated further on how much teachers learn from collaboration when working as co-teachers. "Teachers bring different skills into the classroom, and collaboration provides the opportunity to share that expertise to benefit all students. Subject-matter teachers bring a deep knowledge of the content and strategies for teaching the content in interesting ways. We [special education teachers] often know much less about the content, but bring expertise in making instructional accommodations to make sure that all students learn."

Susan and Lisa continued, "Teachers learn a lot from collaboration. Special education teachers learn a lot about the content, and how to teach it from the content area expert in the general education classroom. We can't know about content in every area in a middle school: English, science, math, social studies. There's no way we can figure out how to make accommodations in instruction or on tests unless we learn about the content of the class. We learn the content by watching the general education teacher, and then we can teach some of the lessons, do re-teaching for students who don't get the information after going over it in class, and work with the classroom teacher to make accommodations in lessons and on tests.

"Content-area teachers also learn from us. One of the most important things they learn is to make accommodations for students. They see us making accommodations to help students learn

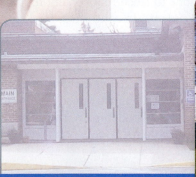

content, or we make suggestions about making accommodations during class lessons—they learn from us and then can do it themselves. We see this because they are comfortable when we have to leave their classroom. They've learned so much about how to make accommodations work. At first they are nervous to have kids with disabilities in their class when they're alone (or the only teacher). After a while they're very comfortable with that, because they've learned so much about accommodations for all of their students."

# Introduction

If you've ever tried to work with peers on a project in a college classroom, you know that collaboration is not a simple task. Some people readily contribute to projects, yet others don't contribute as easily. Some want to complete the project quickly and before the due date, but others want to wait until the last minute. Some attend closely to detail, yet others want to focus on the big picture. Given how difficult and time-consuming collaboration can be, why should teachers or other professionals bother collaborating?

The short answer to that question is "Two (or more) heads are better than one." That is, two or more persons collaborating on a project or activity can often come up with a better project or answer to a problem than a single person can working alone (Bahrami, Olsen, Lathan, Roepstorff, Rees, & Frith, 2010).

Collaboration obviously takes time and effort on the part of all participants. As you reflected on the successful group projects you've worked on in a college classroom, you probably noted that the group members were flexible, cooperative, worked to accommodate the preferences of others, and built on the different areas of expertise that existed in the group. When teachers and other professionals collaborate to solve problems and address student needs, these personal qualities improve the quality of collaboration.

As the teachers from Gilpin Manor Elementary and West Hernando Middle School illustrated in the chapter-opening vignette, "A View from Teachers," collaboration is an "absolute necessity" for effective inclusive programs. They noted that collaboration is essential primarily because general and special education teachers bring different areas of expertise to the general education classroom, and all of these areas of expertise are needed for inclusion to succeed. For example, general education teachers are most often prepared with in-depth knowledge of the content they are teaching and with methods to teach that content to large groups of students. In contrast, special education teachers are typically prepared to differentiate content and adapt instruction to meet the needs of students who struggle to learn the content. Collaboration is all about combining these areas of expertise to meet the needs of *all* students in the general education classroom.

## Pause & Reflect

Consider a group project you completed in a college classroom that was very successful. What qualities of the group made the project successful? Was the content of the project better than any individual could have completed? Does this experience suggest that two heads can often be better than one? Why or why not?

Teachers collaborate to share knowledge and expertise and improve outcomes for students.

# Collaboration: What to Expect

For most of the last century, teachers taught in relative isolation, with their classroom doors closed. They more or less depended on their own knowledge and expertise to address their students' needs. Today, this approach is gradually changing. Two major factors that have contributed to this change are increasing demands for higher levels of student achievement and the increasing diversity of the student population in schools.

Regarding *increased demands for student achievement*, success in the Information Age clearly requires all students to achieve higher levels of knowledge and skills, especially related to literacy and numeracy (Waldron & McLeskey, 2010). States have responded to this need by expecting students to master curriculum at increasingly younger ages. In addition, all states now have accountability measures in place to make certain that students meet expected standards. Thus, teachers are required to ensure that all students achieve at increasingly higher levels.

Part of the accountability system for student achievement is designed to make sure that students who live in poverty, those from different cultural and language backgrounds, and students with disabilities will meet achievement standards. The proportion of school-aged students from *culturally and linguistically diverse backgrounds* has grown substantially over the last decade (NCES, 2010). These data reveal that currently about 45% of students in public schools are from Hispanic, African American, Asian/Pacific Islander, or Native American backgrounds. Perhaps more importantly, students from culturally and linguistically diverse backgrounds make up the majority of students in ten states (Arizona, California, Florida, Georgia, Hawaii, Louisiana, Maryland, Nevada, New Mexico, and Texas). Furthermore, the number of students who live in poverty, and those who speak languages other than English is rapidly growing (Chau, Thampi, & Wight, 2010; NCES, 2010). This increasing diversity, coupled with rising demands for student achievement, makes it important that all teachers collaborate and share expertise with others to make certain that all students succeed in school.

## What Is Collaboration?

Given the higher demands for achievement and related accountability measures, as well as the increasing diversity of schools across the United States, it is incumbent on teachers that they open their classroom doors and begin to collaborate with other professionals to meet students' needs. Teachers have always collaborated with others to some degree. For example, in the past when a teacher had a problem teaching a student, he often asked a fellow teacher for advice during a break between classes, during lunch, or after school. Now collaboration is more structured, it takes more forms (e.g., co-teaching, working in teams), and teachers are expected to collaborate more frequently regarding all aspects of their jobs.

Given the increasing demands for collaboration in schools, many have sought to clearly define collaboration. When we use the term *collaboration* in this book, we refer to "a style of direct interaction between at least two co-equal parties voluntarily engaged in shared decision making as they work toward a common goal" (Friend & Cook, 2010, p. 7). Several defining characteristics of effective collaboration are important to consider and are summarized in Figure 10.1.

When teachers initially begin to collaborate, the success of this activity will vary. However, as collaborators gain trust and respect for one another and learn to work together, collaboration will be more successful. Furthermore, this success will ensure that all participants value collaboration and are motivated to participate, especially as they recognize how much they and their students benefit from these activities.

In any inclusive school, several types of collaboration are needed. As administrators and teachers develop an inclusive school program, they must work together to change their practices, the roles they play, and the very structure of their schools. To achieve these goals, schools develop collaborative teams, which are charged with planning, implementing, monitoring, and supporting the necessary comprehensive changes (McLeskey & Waldron, 2006).

| **Figure 10.1** | **Defining Characteristics of Collaboration** | | |

**Collaboration is based on parity**. Parity suggests that the contributions of everyone involved in collaboration are equally valued. A critical factor that often influences parity is the power collaborators have, or are perceived to have, in decision making. For example, collaborators may go along with suggestions from a principal because of the principal's powerful position and her responsibility for evaluating the performance of teachers. In an effective collaborative relationship, all involved must agree to equally respect the input of others and ensure that all are free to express perspectives on all issues or decisions. Otherwise, collaboration cannot succeed.

**Collaborators share mutual goals**. All participants in collaboration should share specific, common goals, and these goals should be important to everyone. This ensures that the purpose of collaboration is clear to all participants, and that all are motivated to work together to achieve the goals.

**Collaborators share participation, decision making, and accountability**. All collaborators should actively participate in decision making, reach a collective decision that all agree to support, and share accountability for the outcomes of the decision. This does not suggest that all participants should contribute to implementing the decision, which may be an intervention that one participant implements in his classroom. Rather, this suggests a perspective that "we're all in this together" and share responsibility for all aspects of collaborative decision making.

**Collaborators share their resources and expertise**. All participants bring valuable knowledge and skills to a collaborative activity. They also bring resources that others may not have (e.g., time, access to computers or curricular materials). It is important that all participants share their expertise, and that all participants value the expertise of others. This does not imply that an "expert" will come up with a solution to the problem, but rather that all will share suggestions to assure that the best possible information and resources are available to make a good decision. It is also important that all participants share their resources, which are often very limited in a school, to assure that resources are used efficiently and effectively to meet the needs of all students.

**Collaboration is emergent**. If collaboration is to succeed, some positive personal characteristics of participants must be present at the beginning of a collaborative activity, and must grow and flourish over time. These characteristics include:

1. Value collaboration and believe that "two heads are better than one."
2. Participate in collaboration in ways that ensure participants gain trust and respect for one another.
3. Work together to develop a sense of community, where all share expertise, and work together to maximize the strengths and minimize the weaknesses of all participants.

*Sources:* Adapted from P. Dettmer, L. Thurston, A. Knackendoffel, & N. Dyck (2009). *Collaboration, consultation, and teamwork* (6th ed.). Upper Saddle River, NJ: Merrill/Pearson Education; and M. Friend & L. Cook (2010). *Interactions: Collaboration skills for school professionals* (6th ed.). Boston: Allyn & Bacon.

In addition to this role, teachers in inclusive schools often work collaboratively with other teachers, either in a **co-teaching** role or as a **consultant** (i.e., when problems arise, one teacher assists another by problem-solving possible solutions). Still other types of collaborative roles teachers assume include the following:

- Work with other teachers and professionals in **building-based support teams** to solve classroom or school problems.
- Consult with other professionals regarding highly specialized student needs (e.g., consult with school psychologists, behavior specialists, physical therapists, nurses, physicians).
- Collaborate with parents to address student needs.

As you can see, all teachers in an inclusive school work in a range of collaborative roles to ensure that all students are successful. It is safe to say that no single teacher has all the knowledge and skills to address the needs of every student who might enter her classroom. Thus, working collaboratively provides the opportunity for teachers and other professionals to share expertise, learn from one another, and develop strategies that will result in more successful educational experiences for all students.

Although collaboration may seem to be a simple or even a natural skill for a teacher or other professional to engage in, that is often not the case. Understanding the basic components of effective collaboration is an important beginning point for learning to be a successful collaborator. We discuss these key components and provide more background information regarding collaboration in Strategy 10.1 later in this chapter.

# Dispositions and Skills Needed for Successful Collaboration

## Dispositions Needed for Successful Collaboration

Collaboration is not something that comes naturally for most of us. To succeed as collaborators, we need to ensure that we develop and exemplify certain **dispositions** and learn specific skills that lead to success in these roles. See Figure 10.2 for a definition of *dispositions*.

A disposition may be characterized as a habitual inclination, an attitude of mind, or a characteristic tendency. As we attempt to collaborate with others, several dispositions may interfere with collaboration; other dispositions, however, will tend to facilitate the process. Consider the following comments from teachers at Gilpin Manor Elementary and West Hernando Middle School regarding a key disposition for successful collaboration.

Collaboration works better as teachers gain trust and respect for one another.

### Flexibility

When we discussed collaboration with teachers from Gilpin Manor Elementary and West Hernando Middle School, a word that was often used was flexibility. For example, when we asked Jeanne Huskins, a second-grade special education teacher at Gilpin Manor, what it took to be an effective teacher in an inclusive classroom, she replied, "Lots of flexibility." She went on to say that a good, collaborative relationship with a classroom teacher is needed, and this requires that both teachers be flexible to ensure that students' needs are met. Perhaps this flexibility is

## Pause & Reflect

Recall a successful group project you completed in a college classroom. What dispositions of the members of the group contributed to the success of this project? Are the dispositions defined in Figure 10.2 important when working in any collaborative role? Why or why not?

| Figure 10.2 | What Are Dispositions? A Definition from the National Council for Accreditation in Teacher Education (NCATE) |
|---|---|

**Professional dispositions:** Professional attitudes, values, and beliefs demonstrated through both verbal and nonverbal behaviors as educators interact with students, families, colleagues, and communities. These positive behaviors support student learning and development.

The National Council for Accreditation in Teacher Education previously provided a more complete definition of *dispositions*: The values, commitments, and professional ethics that influence behaviors toward students, families, colleagues, and communities and affect student learning, motivation, and development as well as the educator's own professional growth. Dispositions are guided by beliefs and attitudes related to values such as caring, fairness, honesty, responsibility, and social justice. For example, they might include a belief that all students can learn, a vision of high and challenging standards, or a commitment to a safe and supportive learning environment.

*Source:* Reprinted from National Council for Accreditation in Teacher Education. (2011). NCATE Unit Standards: Glossary. Retrieved April 22, 2011, from http://www.ncate.org/

most important when it comes to scheduling. Kim Miller, a third- and fourth-grade special education teacher at Gilpin Manor, elaborated on this idea when she said that all teachers have a schedule that should be respected by all. However, many times teachers need to be flexible regarding their schedule because the needs of students should take priority.

Susan Davis and Lisa Hallal elaborated on the need for flexibility when working in their roles as co-teachers at West Hernando Middle School. They noted that teachers take on many roles when co-teaching in an inclusive classroom—sometimes as an instructor for the entire group and at other times providing additional instruction for a small group. In addition, a co-teacher may work as a floater in class, monitoring student work, providing feedback to students, answering questions, making certain students are on task, managing behavior, and so forth. As Lisa Hallal said, "There's no end to what you do in that room." And so, we see that a key disposition that makes co-teaching successful is flexibility.

"You have to be flexible," continued Lisa Hallal, "that's the number-one thing. Some teachers prefer to do all or most of the instruction, so you have to deal with that teaching style. We've worked with teachers who like total control of dispensing information, and other teachers who are okay with us doing many of the lessons. You have to be flexible enough to say what works in this classroom, what's good for both of us, and what's going to help these kids learn the best, then that's what we'll do. You just have to do whatever it takes to make sure students are a success."

These teacher comments make a compelling case for flexibility as a key disposition for collaboration and co-teaching. Indeed, perhaps one of the most difficult issues that teachers face when collaborating is that both professionals have much knowledge and skill regarding the issue being addressed and have perspectives on how the problem might be addressed. For successful collaboration, professionals must be flexible and willing to:

- Recognize that their solution to a problem may not be the best solution.
- Look at the problem from another person's perspective.
- Compromise regarding an ultimate solution to the problem.

As you reflect on the information we've provided regarding this disposition, you will readily recognize that flexibility is certainly not always easy. All teachers in a collaborative relationship must retain a satisfying professional role and must be treated with respect. At the same time, teachers must be flexible when working with other professionals. Although this is not always easy, teachers are often motivated to be flexible because they know that flexibility leads to more successful collaboration and, most importantly, better outcomes for students.

## Trust

Collaboration requires trust and respect. For example, two teachers who are co-teaching depend on each other for support when behavior management issues arise or to share responsibility for students who do not learn as much as expected. Similarly, when teacher assistance teams make recommendations to teachers who seek support for addressing a concern regarding a student, the teacher must trust that the team has her best interests and those of the student in mind as they work to develop an intervention to address the student's need.

Trust develops over time, as teachers realize that their collaborators (e.g., other teachers) are credible; demonstrate empathy for fellow collaborators (i.e., understand issues from another person's perspective); and accept other team members for who they are (Kampwirth & Powers, 2011; Snell & Janney, 2005). Furthermore, trust develops as collaborators depend on one another, become interdependent, and work to achieve mutual goals by (1) sharing resources, (2) giving help to others, (3) receiving help from others, and (4) dividing the work of the team and taking on a reasonable share of this work (Snell & Janney, 2005). As you consider how collaborators gain trust, you will readily recognize that trust is something that takes time to develop, but it can be lost in a moment (Kampwirth & Powers, 2011) if a collaborator senses that a person is not trustworthy, empathetic, or isn't working in good faith to solve a problem.

## Respectful Interactions

Closely related to the development of trust is the need for collaborators to interact respectfully with one another. This suggests that collaborators will work with each other as equal partners, respecting and attempting to understand the perspectives of others. Factors that potentially interfere with parity, or working as equal partners, may include differences between collaborators related to university degrees; salary; access to resources (e.g., computers, paraeducators); gender; stature; ethnic background; facility with language; positions that differ in status in a school (e.g., principal and teacher); and a range of other factors (Walther-Thomas, Korinek, McLaughlin, & Williams, 2000).

Another aspect of respectful interactions that often influences collaboration is territoriality. That is, a general educator may view co-teaching as an intrusion on her territory because she must share the classroom with a special education teacher (Kochhar-Bryant, 2008). Similarly, a special education teacher may become territorial when others are assigned to teach "her children" in an important content area. Effective collaborators must closely examine their tendency toward protecting territory and share responsibility with other professionals, especially when this collaboration can result in better outcomes for students.

> ### Pause & Reflect
>
> When you interact with others, what are personal qualities that influence how much you respect and listen to the person? Are there certain qualities that cause you to shut down when listening to another? How can you address these biases to make sure that collaboration is effective?

## Frame of Reference

Every collaborator brings a predisposition to respond to professional situations in a certain way, based on his frame of reference. Many factors influence a person's frame of reference, including disciplinary background and preparation (i.e., general education, special education, school psychology, etc.); previous work experience; professional socialization; and a range of other factors (Friend & Cook, 2010). For example, general and special education teachers sometimes differ with respect to how reading should be taught. Teachers and other professionals may have different frames of reference regarding the use of certain instructional strategies (e.g., cooperative learning), how classroom behavior should be managed, or who is responsible and accountable for students with disabilities.

Differing frames of reference can result in difficulty collaborating and can contribute to distortions in communication as collaborative interactions occur (Walther-Thomas et al., 2000). Frame of reference may also be influenced by the cultural identity of collaborators. For example, some cultures place great value on individual goals and achievement; others emphasize interdependence and the well-being of the group as a whole (Friend & Cook, 2010). Reflecting on one's frame of reference, understanding the frames of reference of others, and openly discussing these issues with collaborators are important in ensuring successful collaboration.

## Belief in Collaboration to Meet the Needs of All Students

Beliefs about collaboration and inclusion are important dispositions as you address difficult problems faced by students and attempt to solve these problems. First is the belief that students should be included in general education classes to the maximum extent appropriate. Examining and discussing beliefs regarding what inclusion is, why it is important, and how students benefit from inclusion is an important activity for all teachers and administrators (McLeskey & Waldron, 2002), to ensure that all participants generally agree regarding these issues and support inclusive practices.

Participants in collaboration should also believe in the power of the collaborative process (Kochhar-Bryant, 2008). Confidence that collaboration can improve outcomes for all students is important to convey when working with others, and it can ensure that collaborators take the perspective that even very difficult situations can improve (Kampwirth & Powers, 2011).

## Skills Needed for Successful Collaboration

Effective communication is critical for working with other professionals in a collaborative role. Many factors may interfere with effective communication and result in misunderstandings and poor collaboration. Several of these potential barriers relate to the previously described dispositions. For example, collaborators with different frames of reference will have difficulty communicating and effectively collaborating until they examine and understand the frames of reference that are creating the communication problem. Communication problems can be overcome through the development of effective skills related to listening, verbal communication, nonverbal communication, and addressing conflict. For more information regarding communications skills needed for effective collaboration, see Strategy 10.2 later in this chapter.

### Skills for Managing Difficult Interactions

When collaboration occurs, pairs or teams of professionals can often reach consensus regarding a problem. However, at times, collaborators have very different perspectives on issues, and conflicts arise. When a conflict arises, it is important that collaborators recognize that the problem exists and then actively seek to engage and overcome the problem. Ignoring or avoiding conflict is a sure approach to undermining effective collaboration.

When conflict occurs, it is important to reaffirm the purpose of collaboration—that is, to improve outcomes for students. How collaborators address challenges depends, to a large degree, on the importance they attach to either achieving a professional goal or maintaining a good relationship with collaborators (Walther-Thomas et al., 2000). For example, when neither of these goals is important, the collaborator may simply avoid the conflict by withdrawing, and letting other collaborators make a final decision. This strategy is fine, if the goal is not important to the person who is withdrawing, or if she is not responsible for decision making. If the goal is very important, the collaborator may attempt to force others to accept a solution, which has the potential to produce conflict.

> ### Pause & Reflect
>
> Discuss with a peer how you react to conflict. Do you avoid conflict and withdraw? Confront and compete with others? Accommodate others to escape conflict? Or use a collaborative style to address issues directly and professionally? What style will you use when collaborating with other professionals?

A positive approach to addressing a challenging issue has been described as integrating (Walther-Thomas et al., 2000). When using this strategy, collaborators view the conflict as a problem to solve, and they search for a solution that both addresses the goal of the collaboration and maintains the relationship with collaborators. "This method involves collaboration between people, openness, exchange of information, reduction of tension between parties, and examination of differences to reach a solution acceptable to both parties" (Walther-Thomas et al., 2000, p. 109).

Strategies for addressing conflict include (Correa, Jones, Thomas, & Morsink, 2005):

- Clarify the goal of collaboration.
- Focus on the problem, not the people involved.
- Focus on goals that all collaborators share.
- Insist on using objective criteria to address the problem.
- Examine your feelings, and determine why they differ from others.
- Generate possible solutions collaboratively that benefit everyone.

## Collaborative Roles in Inclusive Schools

As we noted previously, inclusive schools increase the necessity for collaboration by all professionals in a variety of roles and types of collaborative relationships. Three key types of collaborative relationships are working in teams, working as a co-teacher, and consulting with others for assistance.

## Collaborative Teams

Teams of professionals often work together in schools to address a range of different types of issues and concerns. Most inclusive schools use inclusion-support teams to plan, implement, monitor, and evaluate inclusive school programs (McLeskey & Waldron, 2006). These teams consist of a range of professionals in different roles (e.g., teachers, principal, counselor, school psychologist) and other stakeholders (e.g., parents), who all work collaboratively to develop and support an inclusive program.

Inclusion-support teams address school-wide issues as they seek to develop a plan for school change that uses school resources effectively and efficiently to better meet the academic and social needs of all students. These teams often spend several months planning for inclusion, as they visit inclusive schools, examine their own school, plan professional development for teachers and other school staff, and a range of other activities. (For more information regarding how these teams function, see McLeskey & Waldron, 2000, 2006.)

Teachers often work in collaborative teams to address the needs of students who are struggling academically or socially.

Another type of collaborative team addresses individual student needs. Approximately three of every four states require the use of a building-based collaborative support team to provide teachers with direct support in developing interventions to address student needs (Buck et al., 2003). These teams are often referred to as **teacher assistance teams (TATs)**, but also are called *intervention assistance teams, student assistance teams, instructional support teams, school-wide assistance teams*, and *teacher support teams* in some states. Teacher assistance teams are relatively simple to implement, as they are designed to provide teachers with a structure to develop new ideas for their classrooms by brainstorming possible interventions for addressing student academic and social difficulties.

Teachers tend to view TATs very favorably. For example, research has revealed that from 50 to 60% of teachers view interventions developed by teacher assistance teams as using acceptable procedures and feel that the interventions were implemented with a high degree of fidelity (Lane, Pierson, Robertson, & Little, 2004). Furthermore, research on state-wide implementation of teacher support teams in Pennsylvania revealed that these teams were effective in reducing referrals to special education, and resulted in improved measures of student academic learning time (Kovaleski & Glew, 2006). For more information regarding how TATs work, see Strategy 10.3 later in this chapter.

## Co-Teaching

A second type of collaborative role that is common for teachers in inclusive schools is co-teaching. As Susan Davis and Lisa Hallal, teachers from West Hernando Middle School, indicated in the interview in the opening vignette, co-teaching is critical to the success of inclusion in their school. As Susan Davis noted, special education teachers "can't know about content in every area in a middle school: English, science, math, social studies." Similarly, content-area teachers don't know all of the strategies that are needed to adapt for the needs of students with disabilities. Thus, having two teachers with different skills working collaboratively results in a combination of skills that benefits all students.

Co-teaching is the most frequently used model for delivering instruction in inclusive classrooms (Cook, McDuffie-Landrum, Oshita, & Cook, 2011). *Co-teaching* in inclusive classrooms is defined as a general and special education teacher working collaboratively to share responsibility for instructing a diverse group of students in a single classroom. Co-teaching uses the expertise of both general and special education teachers, and when done well provides all students with an improved educational experience.

Several issues are critical to the success of co-teaching (Cook et al., 2011; Friend, Cook, Hurley-Chamberlain, & Shamberger, 2010; Scruggs, Mastropieri, & McDuffie, 2007). For example, co-teachers emphasize the importance of administrative support to make certain that co-teaching is valued and given the resources and support needed to succeed. Co-teachers also emphasize the need for planning time before the school year begins to prepare for co-teaching; professional development to acquire necessary skills; and common planning time during the school year to continue to support co-teaching.

Perhaps most importantly, teachers emphasize the need for compatibility between co-teaching partners (Cook et al., 2011; Mastropieri, Scruggs, Graetz, et al., 2005). When co-teaching relationships work well, they are built on trust and mutual respect for the skills of the co-teaching partner and result in more effective instruction for all students (Mastropieri et al., 2005). Compatibility issues often arise because teachers have different beliefs regarding how to plan for co-teaching, or different beliefs regarding classroom instruction such as classroom routines, discipline, noise levels, and so forth (Friend & Cook, 2010; Mastropieri et al., 2005). We recommend addressing these issues by having frequent "co-teach chats" with your teaching partner. For more information on co-teach chats and ensuring compatibility and avoiding conflict when co-teaching, see Figure 10.3.

---

| **Figure 10.3** | **Supporting Successful Co-Teaching (and Resolving Conflict) Using Co-Teach Chats** |
| --- | --- |

To resolve conflicts that may arise and generally make sure that co-teaching works well, co-teaching partners should regularly schedule meetings to discuss their partnership. We recommend using the following strategies.

1. **Discuss minor issues before they escalate**. Minor issues that occur in co-taught classrooms can escalate if they are not attended to immediately by co-teaching partners. We recommend the use of weekly "co-teach chats" when beginning a co-teaching relationship. These chats should be brief (10 to 20 minutes) and should be structured to address what is working well about co-teaching and what can be improved. These meetings should be less frequent (biweekly, then monthly) as the school year progresses and teachers learn to discuss strengths and challenges of co-teaching more informally.

2. **Reflect on co-taught lessons.** Co-teach chats can be more efficient and beneficial if co-teaching partners focus on a recent co-taught lesson, and reflect on what worked well and what could be improved regarding that lesson. These discussions should begin and end with positive comments regarding the lesson, and at least twice as many positive as negative comments should be made. However, each teacher should contribute at least one area that could be improved when reflecting on each lesson.

3. **Make differences or minor disagreements opportunities to learn**. The fact that co-teaching partners bring different knowledge, skills, instructional approaches, and beliefs to the partnership is a good thing in many ways. Teachers have the opportunity to learn from one another, and experience different approaches to instruction that they may not have considered. Co-teach chats offer the opportunity to build on and discuss these differences as strengths of the partnership. This can be done if both partners remember that the strengths of working as co-teachers emerge from the equal, collaborative partnership, and not from one teacher serving as an expert who advises the other teacher or who has all the right answers.

4. **Use data on student progress to examine how co-teaching may be improved**. As a school year progresses, a source of discussion during co-teach chats should be data regarding student progress. As invariably happens in every classroom, some students will not make sufficient progress over a period of time. Data on the progress of students thus provide objective information regarding an area in which the co-taught classroom needs to improve. This provides a stimulus for discussion regarding how instruction might be altered to improve student outcomes in the co-taught classroom.

5. **Examine your approach to addressing differences, and encourage your co-teaching partner to do the same**. The approaches adults use to address conflict differ with regard to the importance of the relationship, the importance of the outcome, and their willingness to compromise. This may result in avoiding the problem, or one person making all of the decisions. A balance among the use of subsequently described approaches to conflict resolution is needed for successful co-teaching teams. Which of these approaches to conflict resolution do you prefer?

a. **Competitive:** An approach that uses power (knowledge, position, and so forth) to "win" any conflict. This approach emphasizes the importance of the outcome (winning the "battle"), and less emphasis on the relationship with the other person involved, and little emphasis on compromise. Generally, this approach leads to many problems in a co-teaching relationship, and should not be used.

b. **Avoidance:** An approach where one participant avoids or ignores differences. This approach may reflect value for the relationship more than the outcome. At times, especially when very volatile issues are the source of differences, avoidance is advisable. However, some co-teaching partners avoid minor issues, or let the other person make most or all of the decisions. This often leads to problems in the co-teaching relationship and lack of parity.

c. **Accommodation:** An approach where the relationship is valued more than the outcome. This approach results in one co-teaching partner "giving in" and accommodating the other partner to make sure that her needs are met. This approach may be used occasionally in a co-teaching partnership, but the overuse of this approach can produce dissatisfaction in the co-teaching partnership.

d. **Compromise:** The most common approach to addressing conflict is to compromise—when one person gives up some ideas and expects her co-teaching partner to do the same. This approach may be used at times, especially when time is limited. The outcome is often one that all find acceptable, but it may not be the best solution.

e. **Collaboration:** This is often the most satisfying approach to resolving conflict, but it is very time consuming. This occurs when co-teaching partners respect each other's ideas, treat each other respectfully, and consider all information and data to reach the best solution to the conflict that has arisen.

6. **Consider the following tips for constructively using differences between adults:**

a. Respect the many different perspectives that exist between thoughtful, intelligent adults.

b. Listen to your teaching partner and try to understand what she thinks, and why she thinks the way she does.

c. Try not to insist on your favorite method, approach, or preference. Instead, encourage shared or collaborative problem solving to address differences.

d. Seek input from others who are well respected when differences arise that are difficult to resolve.

e. Genuinely care about and respect your co-teaching partner's ideas and perspectives, and show this through your interactions.

*Sources:* P. Dettmer, L. Thurston, A. Knackendoffel, & N. Dyck (2009). *Collaboration, consultation, and teamwork for students with special needs.* Upper Saddle River, NJ: Merrill/Pearson Education; M. Friend & L. Cook (2010). *Interactions: Collaboration skills for school professionals* (6th ed.). Boston: Allyn & Bacon; D. Ploessl, M. Rock, N. Schoenfeld, & B. Blanks (2010). On the same page: Practical techniques to enhance co-teaching interactions. *Intervention in School and Clinic, 45,* 158–168.

When co-teaching is done well, many benefits accrue for students with and without disabilities (Friend et al., 2010; Hang & Rabren, 2008; Scruggs et al., 2007). These benefits include increased student achievement, fewer problems with disruptive behavior, improved student attitudes and self-concepts, and more positive peer relationships.

Co-teaching is effective for students with and without disabilities for three primary reasons. First, co-teaching provides the opportunity to capitalize on the unique knowledge and skills that both teachers bring to the classroom (Ploessl, Rock, Schoenfeld, & Blanks, 2010). Second, two teachers bring an extra pair of hands to the classroom, which provides the opportunity to structure the class and group students in ways that result in more support for students. For example, teachers can more often:

- Use effective, evidence-based instructional practices.
- Differentiate instruction.
- Employ intensive small-group or individual instruction.
- Provide immediate attention to student needs.
- Monitor student on-task behavior and intervene as needed.

Co-teaching is frequently used in inclusive classrooms to meet a diverse range of student needs.

## Pause & Reflect

Examine the dispositions we addressed previously in this chapter. Why are these dispositions especially important for co-teachers? Do you have the necessary dispositions to be a successful co-teacher?

Finally, co-teachers can combine their expertise to determine novel approaches to meet student needs (McLeskey & Waldron, 2000). This is necessary in inclusive classrooms when traditional solutions from general and special education do not readily meet the needs of all students. For example, this may occur as co-teachers determine how to use a specialized method for instruction to meet the needs of a small group of students in the general education classroom, or begin to use student resources to address needs using methods such as class-wide peer tutoring (McMaster, Kung, Han, & Cao, 2008).

Some consider co-teaching as synonymous with inclusion, but this is not the case. Many successful inclusive programs use co-teaching as a core strategy for ensuring student success, and yet others rarely use co-teaching and use other collaborative strategies to support students (e.g., consultative support from a special education teacher or paraeducators). We recommend that teachers in inclusive schools take advantage of co-teaching whenever possible. Co-teaching provides teachers with a powerful opportunity to increase their expertise. For example, special education teachers can learn in-depth information regarding the general education curriculum, methods and grouping strategies that are used in the general education classroom, and which instructional approaches fit into this setting. Similarly, general education teachers can learn methods for making accommodations for diverse student needs, grouping strategies for providing more intensive instruction to students, and so forth. In short, co-teaching provides an excellent opportunity for professional development, and after experiencing co-teaching, teachers often have significantly improved expertise for addressing diverse student needs.

Schools can implement co-teaching in any general education classroom and can use it with any subject matter. Co-teaching takes careful planning because teacher roles and responsibilities change significantly when using this approach. For more information regarding how planning for co-teaching works, see Strategy 10.4 later in this chapter.

## Collaborative Consultation

**Collaborative consultation** involves two persons working together to seek solutions to a mutually agreed on problem or issue. When collaboration involves two professionals, the participants will typically have different areas of expertise and different roles. For example, a special education teacher may consult with a general education teacher regarding methods for making accommodations on tests (e.g., allowing more time, breaking the test into several sessions, providing a calculator) to meet the needs of a student with a disability.

When you teach in an inclusive classroom, you will have students with highly specialized needs that you do not fully understand, regardless of whether you are the general or special education teacher. When this occurs, you will need a specialist to provide information and suggest approaches to meet student needs. For example, a special education teacher may need assistance in addressing the physical needs of a student with a severe physical disability and may seek the consultative assistance of a physical therapist. Others that may provide assistance include school psychologists, behavior specialists, curriculum specialists, speech–language pathologists, social workers, nurses, and so forth.

The steps that are typically included in collaborative consultation include the following:

- Refer a problem or issue to a consultant.
- Identify and clarify the problem to be addressed.
- Brainstorm possible solutions to the problem.
- Select an intervention by the referring teacher.
- Clarify implementation of the intervention.
- Follow up to determine the effectiveness of the intervention.

If the intervention is not effective, or if the collaborators need to address other problems or issues, they repeat the collaborative consultation cycle. Teacher assistance teams (described earlier) use a collaborative consultation approach. For a description of the steps involved in collaborative consultation when using a TAT, see Strategy 10.3 later in this chapter.

As a teacher in an inclusive classroom, you will not only receive assistance from consultants but also serve as a consultant to others. For example, after you have worked in a successful inclusive program for a period of time, you may be asked to consult with other teachers who are developing inclusive programs. In addition, two of the most critical consultative roles for teachers in inclusive classrooms that you will need to address relate to the work you will do with paraeducators and families.

Paraeducators (also called *paraprofessionals, instructional assistants*, or *teacher's aides*) are an important resource for many inclusive classrooms. Paraeducators are individuals who provide instruction and other services to students and who are supervised by teachers responsible for student outcomes (Fisher & Pleasants, 2011). Paraeducators can serve in a variety of roles to support classroom instruction and related activities in an inclusive setting, including the following (Correa et al., 2005):

- Tutor after a teacher provides primary instruction.
- Float in the classroom to check on student progress and respond to questions.
- Provide skill-and-drill activities to individuals or small groups of students.
- Prepare instructional materials, activities, and games.
- Read stories or content-area material.
- Conduct small-group instructional activities.
- Grade, correct homework, and handle other paperwork.
- Work on learning centers, bulletin boards, and so forth.
- Provide support for students with highly specialized needs (e.g., medical or physical needs for students with severe disabilities).

Although paraeducators can be a valuable resource in an inclusive classroom, concerns will arise at times regarding paraeducators' roles and responsibilities. For example, in some classrooms, paraeducators are assigned to one student with a disability. This type of assignment raises the possibility that the paraeducator will take on responsibility for the student (i.e., planning student lessons, assessing student progress) that should reside with the classroom teacher, and the classroom teacher will not be familiar with the student and his needs (French, 2003). In addition, if the paraeducator is "velcroed" to the student and does not work with others in the classroom, difficulty developing social relationships may result for the student.

As a teacher in an inclusive classroom, you will at times supervise paraeducators and ensure that their time is used effectively and efficiently. Some local school districts provide training in working effectively with paraeducators. We provide more information in Strategy 10.5 later in this chapter regarding how teachers may work effectively with paraeducators to improve outcomes for students.

## Families

Two major factors have contributed to the increased involvement of families in the education of students with disabilities. First, the Individuals with Disabilities Education Improvement Act (IDEA, 2004) mandates that parents work with professionals as partners in ensuring an effective education for students with disabilities. This includes parent participation in every decision related to their child with a disability, including identification, assessment, and placement (Rosenberg, Westling, & McLeskey, 2011). Parents also have extensive rights related to the development and approval of the IEP for school-aged students or the individual family service plan (IFSP) for younger children. Parent participation in these activities is designed to ensure that parents and educators work as partners in addressing the needs of students with disabilities and that adversarial relationships are avoided.

A second reason for family involvement is research indicating this involvement can serve to enhance a student's academic achievement and improve behavior and social adjustment.

> More than 30 years of research demonstrate that when families are directly engaged with their children's education, students show increased test scores, higher academic achievement, improved attitudes toward learning, have better social behavior, higher self esteem, fewer placements in special education, higher school attendance rates, and lower dropout rates. (Kochhar-Bryant, 2008, p. 208)

These positive effects have been demonstrated across students from different economic, ethnic, and cultural backgrounds (Kochhar-Bryant, 2008).

Parents and caregivers can be involved in schools in many ways (Correa et al., 2005). For example, families can:

- Share information regarding their children with teachers and other school personnel (e.g., counselor, school psychologist).
- Reinforce and support school programs at home through activities such as a daily report card to address student discipline, or programs to ensure homework completion (Fabiano et al., 2009; Patall, Cooper, & Robinson, 2008).
- Advocate for quality services for their child.
- Volunteer to work in schools for part of the school day or in before- or after-school activities.
- Participate in school decision-making groups, such as a school advisory committee.
- Work in the community with businesses and local government to obtain support for the school.

For teachers in an inclusive classroom, parent support has the potential to significantly enhance student outcomes and increase the resources available to meet student needs. Interventions can be highly effective when teachers and caregivers work collaboratively to develop and implement interventions to address a range of student needs (Fabiano et al., 2009; Patall, Cooper, Robinson, 2008; Whitbread, Bruder, Fleming, & Park, 2007). We provide more information in Strategy 10.6 regarding the development of effective approaches for home–school collaboration.

## Students as Collaborators: Peer Assistance in Inclusive Classrooms and Schools

In many schools, these are days of limited resources, increasing standards for student achievement, and increasing diversity in classrooms. These circumstances require that educators seek cost-effective methods for addressing student needs. Teachers who are effective use all available resources to meet student needs, and one readily available resource is the students themselves (Kauchak & Eggen, 2012). Engaging students in collaborative roles to assist or support peers in addressing the needs of those who are struggling academically or socially is an integral part of many successful inclusive classrooms. Indeed, as we have discussed throughout this text, acceptance and support of students with disabilities is a critical component of any effective, inclusive classroom.

Many **peer-assisted strategies** have been developed to address basic academic skills, higher-level cognitive skills, and social interactions or skill development (McDonnell, 2011). In the following section, we describe a strategy that teachers may use to support students who are struggling academically or socially in inclusive classrooms: the peer buddy program.

## The Peer Buddy Program

Several researchers have found a close relationship between academic achievement and the development of friendship skills, behavior control, and self-esteem (Ginsburg-Block, Rohrbeck, & Fantuzzo, 2006). Peer-assisted learning strategies are an intervention that has the potential not only to improve academic achievement but also to improve social skills. For example, in a review of studies related to peer-assisted learning (Ginsburg-Block et al., 2006), these interventions were found to improve student social and self-concept outcomes. This is an important outcome for inclusive classrooms, because the improvement of social skills and the development of friendships are often goals for students with disabilities, especially those with more severe disabilities in these settings.

The need to improve the social skills and acceptance level of students with disabilities in general education classrooms has led to the development of a peer-assisted learning

In Chapter 13, we discuss how teachers can engage peers in supporting students who are struggling to learn academic skills through the use of strategies such as cooperative learning and peer tutoring.

## A View from Students

### How All Students Benefit from a Peer Support Program

As students with a range of disabilities were being included in general education classrooms at West Hernando Middle School, teachers and administrators recognized that teachers often do not have the time to give every student all the support that they need. To begin to address this issue, the staff developed a Peer Support program, where students volunteer to provide peer support for a student with a disability with elective course credit for this activity. Students are then provided training, and work in a general education classroom with their peer with a disability for one class period each day. Students with a range of disabilities are included in this program, including those with autism, intellectual disabilities, learning disabilities, and physical disabilities.

We discussed the impact of the Peer Support program at West Hernando with two students who have been peer buddies. One of the peer buddies, Emma (pseudonyms are used for all students in this feature), works with a student with an intellectual disability, Melissa, in a U.S. history class. Emma describes that it is "harder for Melissa to learn sometimes, and I have to go over things a few more times with her. It's easier for her if I put tidbits in there, rather than having her always learn from the dryness of the book." Another peer buddy, Susan, works with Lily, a student with autism who was formerly in a self-contained special education class before the Peer Support program started. Susan commented that in her sixth-grade geography class, Lily "likes to do things hands on, and work with other people in class. She doesn't like to be in a self-contained (special education) class because she likes being out and learning different things, not just being in one class and learning the same things over and over again."

Emma commented on the benefits of including students with disabilities in general education classrooms, noting that it is "better for them in regular classrooms because they need the interaction [with typical peers]. They need to talk with kids their age." She went on to comment that at first, "they [students with disabilities] are dependent on you, but as the program gets further along, the peers back off and let [the students with disabilities] do more themselves, helping them become more independent." Emma also commented that students with disabilities benefit from the demands of the general education classroom, because they're going to have these demands in life. "You're going to have deadlines in life. They're going to have to sit there and learn how to do things, how to write, and read. It's going to help them be independent."

Both Emma and Susan commented on how the Peer Support program had changed them and their beliefs and understandings about students with disabilities. Emma explained how she had gotten close to each of the students she had worked with as a peer buddy. "When I go home, if Melissa has had a bad day, then I have a bad day. Because we have that connection, if she's having a good day, it makes my day a lot better."

Susan further explained that working as a peer buddy helped her understand more about students with disabilities, and become more accepting of their differences. She further noted that this made accepting students with disabilities as part of the school community more natural. "I feel different about socializing with students with disabilities. Now I know what to say, if someone in the hallway is upset, I'll go up to him, talk with him, and see what's wrong. You know what to say and won't be nervous."

Susan and Emma both commented that students with disabilities are now a more accepted part of the school community as a result of the Peer Support program. Both also strongly believe that all students at West Hernando Middle School should be part of the Peer Support program. This may happen one day, as the Peer Support program has grown rapidly from 4 students when it began to 114 students who are participating this year. Obviously, many students see how this program benefits the entire school community at WHMS, and want to be part of it.

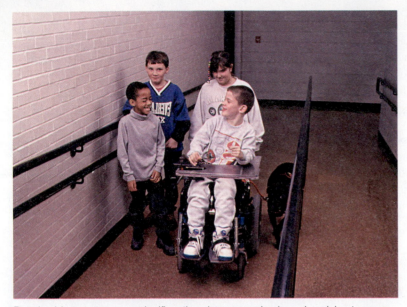

Peer buddy programs can significantly enhance academic and social outcomes for students with disabilities and their peer buddies.

strategy called the peer buddy program (Hughes & Carter, 2008). Although teachers can use the peer buddy program with any student in a classroom who needs academic support and improved social skills, it was initially developed to address the academic and social needs of students with more severe disabilities in middle and high schools (Hughes & Carter, 2008). See the "A View from Students" feature in this chapter for a description of how students provided support and benefited from a peer buddy program at West Hernando Middle School. (Note that this program is called a Peer Support program at WHMS).

As the comments from Emma and Susan regarding the Peer Support program at West Hernando Middle School reveal, these programs can be very successful in improving the acceptance levels of students with disabilities, and providing more opportunities for social interaction with typical peers. This is not always easy to achieve, as students with severe disabilities in secondary schools who are included in general education classes are often isolated and seldom interact with their peers who do not have disabilities. This occurs for many reasons, including the limited social and communication skills of many students with severe disabilities; the structure of the school day in secondary schools (e.g., emphasis on lecture and focus on academic material); and concerns among students without disabilities that they lack the skills and knowledge to interact with peers with severe disabilities. Fostering the interactions of students with severe disabilities and their peers in secondary schools requires intentional efforts by educators, and a peer buddy program provides one approach for addressing this need (Hughes & Carter, 2008). For detailed information regarding the peer buddy program, and how such a program is implemented, see Strategy 10.7 later in this chapter.

## Summary

This chapter addressed the following topics:

### Collaboration: What to expect

- Collaboration refers to "a style for direct interaction between at least two co-equal parties voluntarily engaged in shared decision making as they work toward a common goal" (Friend & Cook, 2010, p. 7).
- Teachers work in a variety of collaborative roles to meet the needs of students in inclusive schools. This collaboration is necessary because no single teacher has all the knowledge and skills necessary to meet the needs of all students. Collaboration thus provides teachers and other professionals with the opportunity to learn from one another as they share knowledge and expertise.

### Dispositions and skills needed for successful collaboration

- Dispositions are characteristic tendencies or habitual inclinations.
- Dispositions necessary for effective collaboration include:
  - Flexibility in adapting to work with others in collaborative roles
  - Trust in collaborative partners to share responsibility for addressing student needs
  - Respectful interactions with collaborators
  - A frame of reference that facilitates collaboration
  - A belief in collaboration to meet the needs of all students

- Communication skills for working effectively with other professionals include:
  - Listening skills
  - Verbal communication skills
  - Nonverbal communication skills
- Skills for managing difficult interactions with other professionals are also needed for effective collaboration.

### Collaborative roles in inclusive schools

- Teachers often work with teams of other professionals (e.g., teacher assistance teams) to collaboratively address student needs.
- Another frequent collaborative role of teachers in inclusive schools is working as a co-teacher.
- Teachers and other professionals may take on a collaborative consultation role. In this role, a professional provides support to another professional to address a specific problem or issue.
- Teachers often work in a collaborative role with paraeducators to provide support for students with disabilities and others who struggle in inclusive classrooms.
- Teachers and other professionals often work collaboratively with families to address the needs of students with disabilities.

### Students as collaborators: Peer assistance in inclusive classrooms and schools

- Engaging students to work collaboratively to address the needs of those who struggle academically or socially can be an integral part of successful inclusive classrooms.
- Two types of peer-assisted learning strategies that are often used in inclusive classrooms are cooperative learning and peer tutoring.
- Another effective strategy for engaging students in providing academic and social support for students with disabilities is a peer buddy program.

## Addressing Professional Standards

Standards addressed in Chapter 10 include:

**CEC Standards:** (4) instructional strategies; (5) learning environments and social interactions; (7) instructional planning; (10) collaboration.

### MyEducationLab

Go to the topic Collaboration, Consultation, and Co-Teaching in the **MyEducationLab** (www.myeducationlab.com) for *Inclusion*, where you can:

- Find learning outcomes for Collaboration, Consultation, and Co-Teaching, along with the national standards that connect to these outcomes.
- Complete Assignments and Activities that can help you more deeply understand the chapter content.
- Apply and practice your understanding of the core teaching skills identified in the chapter with the Building Teaching Skills and Dispositions learning units.
- Examine challenging situations and cases presented in the IRIS Center Resources.
- Check your comprehension on the content covered in the chapter with the Study Plan. Here you will be able to take a chapter quiz, receive feedback on your answers, and then access Review, Practice, and Enrichment activities to enhance your understanding of chapter content.

# EFFECTIVE STRATEGIES FOR COLLABORATION AND TEAMING

## Putting It All Together

Today teachers are opening their classroom doors to others as they collaborate to reach increasingly higher expectations for student outcomes. With this in mind, we hope you will embrace collaboration, but keep the following ideas in mind.

1. **Start slowly.** If you're just beginning to work as a co-teacher in a school, we recommend working with only one or two co-teachers initially. It is important to start slowly with collaborative activities so that you'll have time to develop the skills and reinforce the dispositions you need to make collaboration succeed. Working with a team of teachers to plan instruction or carefully selecting initial co-teachers is often a good way to get started.

2. **Reflect on your strengths and weaknesses as a collaborator.** Every teacher has strengths and weaknesses when working in a collaborative relationship. Some teachers are quick to reach a conclusion regarding a problem, for example, and become impatient when others need more time. There are also some professionals whose perspectives you will not respect as much as the perspectives of others. It is important that you be honest in appraising how others view you as a collaborator, and use that information to improve your skills and dispositions for collaborating with other professionals.

3. **Learn and develop the skills needed for collaboration.** As you reflect on your skills and dispositions as a collaborator, you will certainly recognize some areas that need improvement. Some of these skills or dispositions will improve as you engage in collaborative activities with peers, observe their behavior (and yours) during these interactions, and try out different options to improve communication and decision making. Another critical way of gaining these skills is to take advantage of professional development related to collaboration. This includes working with and observing peers in your school to better understand how they address difficulties when collaborating, and seeking guidance from peers when difficulties arise.

4. **Enjoy the collaborative partnerships you develop.** A major benefit of collaboration for teachers is that it reduces the isolation many feel in their profession. Collaboration allows a group of experienced professionals to share and test ideas in a setting where individual and team efforts are recognized and valued, and all professionals have opportunities for growth and leadership (Waldron & McLeskey, 2010). When collaboration works well, it is very beneficial and enjoyable for all involved and creates a community of support within a school.

5. **Celebrate the successes of collaboration.** When done well, collaboration leads to the synthesis of available expertise and the discovery of new knowledge and teaching approaches that benefit all students (Kochhar-Bryant, 2008). We are sure that you will have many successes as a collaborator—be sure to take the time to recognize and enjoy your successes by celebrating them!

## Strategy Fact Sheet

In the remainder of this chapter, we describe seven effective strategies, which we referred to previously in the chapter, to help you plan effectively to meet the needs of all students.

| STRATEGY | DESCRIPTION | SPECIAL CONSIDERATIONS |
|---|---|---|
| Strategy 10.1: Key Components of Effective Collaboration | Collaboration allows teachers to work with other professionals to improve knowledge, teaching skills, and dispositions. The components of effective collaboration provide teachers with the knowledge and skills needed to confirm that they are well prepared for collaborative roles. | When collaborating regarding inclusion, teachers must work to ensure a respectful, equal partnership with their collaborator. |
| Strategy 10.2: Communication Skills and Successful Collaboration | The most important skills for collaborating successfully with others relate to communication. Communication problems can be overcome through the development of skills related to listening, verbal communication, and nonverbal communication. | Communication is very complex, as it consists of sending and receiving messages simultaneously, sending both verbal and nonverbal messages, and using different types of communication with different people. |
| Strategy 10.3: Teacher Assistance Teams (TATs) | This strategy provides teachers who face problems in their classrooms with a quick, efficient method to seek assistance from well-respected peers. A group of teachers meet with a referring teacher about a specific student problem, brainstorm regarding possible ways to address the problem, and support the teacher in selecting, implementing, and evaluating an intervention. | Most student problems referred to the TAT relate to work habits, classroom behavior, interpersonal behavior, attention problems, and reading difficulties. Recommended interventions are reported to be successful for almost 90% of students. |
| Strategy 10.4: Planning for Co-Teaching | Co-teaching is an approach to collaboration that allows general and special education teachers to share knowledge, dispositions, and skills as they share responsibility for student outcomes in an inclusive classroom. It is important to carefully plan before beginning a co-teaching partnership, and continue planning during the school year as co-teaching roles evolve. | Co-teaching is a dynamic process that requires teachers to change roles often, depending on the content being taught and student needs. Varying teaching roles allows teachers to learn and develop expertise from their teaching partner. |
| Strategy 10.5: Working with Paraeducators | Paraeducators, who work under the supervision of a certified teacher, provide important support for many students in inclusive classrooms. Effectively supervising a paraeducator requires that the teacher collaborate effectively with the paraeducator to be sure that responsibilities are well defined and the paraeducator is well prepared to address these responsibilities. | Paraeducators may provide support such as one-to-one or small-group instruction, support for students with highly specialized needs, grading and other paperwork, and preparation of materials for class lessons. |
| Strategy 10.6: Working with Families: Home–School Collaboration | Effective collaboration between teachers and families can result in significant improvement in student achievement and behavior. Teachers in inclusive classrooms should encourage home–school collaboration and parent involvement in a range of activities. The teacher should get to know parents well and work with parents to determine the types of involvement that will work well for them. | When collaborating with parents, teachers should be knowledgeable regarding the parents' cultural backgrounds. This allows the teacher to understand, respect, and take into account cultural experiences when working with parents. |
| Strategy 10.7: Peer Buddy Programs | Adolescents with moderate-to-severe disabilities benefit from peer interactions, just as other students do. Peer buddy programs are designed to provide academic support, as well as an opportunity for peer interactions to occur in natural school settings. | Peer buddy programs have many benefits for students with and without disabilities, but require careful planning and consistent support to succeed. |

## Strategy 10.1 — KEY COMPONENTS OF EFFECTIVE COLLABORATION

## Rationale

Many professionals take the perspective that collaboration comes naturally, and is a skill that all teachers have (Friend & Cook, 2010). Research evidence indicates that this is often not the case (Correa et al., 2005; Dettmer, Thurston, Knackendoffel, & Dyck, 2009; Friend et al., 2010). Although some teachers may be natural collaborators, many teachers need to learn the skills for working effectively with others. Consideration of key components of collaboration can improve the likelihood that teachers and other professionals will succeed when engaged in these activities. For example, roles should be carefully defined and structured, teachers must understand their roles and be well prepared for them, and outcomes should be evaluated to ensure that collaboration has succeeded (Dettmer et al., 2009; Friend & Cook, 2010).

## Step-by-Step

As you engage in collaboration with other professionals, you should address several key components of these activities to enhance the collaborative activities and improve student outcomes.

**1** *Prepare for collaboration.* Most of us must learn collaboration skills, including those related to effective communication and addressing conflict. Participants in a collaborative relationship should participate in professional development activities together to ensure that they have the knowledge, skills, and dispositions needed for effective collaboration. Possible topics for professional development (addressed later in this chapter) include co-teaching, teaming, working with parents, and working with paraeducators. Other areas of professional development that may be useful include methods for problem solving and working collaboratively to develop inclusive classrooms.

**2** *Define roles.* A key to the success of any collaborative endeavor is ensuring that all participants are clear regarding their roles. For example, co-teachers can take on a range of roles (see Strategy 10.4 for more information on co-teaching roles), and these roles can change over time. Similarly, when professionals work on collaborative teams that address curriculum in a content area or across disciplines, or address individual needs of students and teachers, they must clearly define their roles to ensure that they provide well-coordinated, seamless support for students (Dettmer et al., 2009).

**3** *Achieve role parity.* For collaboration to succeed, all participants must feel that they are important contributors, that they are equal partners in decision making, and that their contributions are valued (Friend & Cook, 2010). This becomes difficult at times when a collaborator is a principal or other professional who is in a supervisory role or is viewed as more knowledgeable than others regarding a particular topic (e.g., inclusion, classroom management). In inclusive settings, professionals often bring different expertise to collaborative deliberations (e.g., a general education teacher may have deep knowledge of a content area, or a special education teacher has skills in adapting and differentiating content). While collaborating, participants must agree to have parity and work as equal partners, even if this is not the case outside of the collaborative relationship (e.g., with a principal) or if knowledge levels regarding the content being addressed differ.

**4** *Address key considerations when collaborating.* As you collaborate with other professionals, keep the following in mind (Kampwirth & Powers, 2011):

- Reach out to your collaborators to make them feel comfortable and accepted as equal partners.
- Make it clear to your collaborators that you strongly prefer to work collaboratively.
- Use time efficiently, so that no one feels that time is being wasted.
- When a problem arises, clearly define the problem and focus on finding solutions.
- Try to understand the collaborative relationship from the perspective of other participants.
- Continue to work on any problems until they are resolved.

**5** *Evaluate the collaborative relationship frequently.* Collaborative relationships change over time, making it important for participants to frequently evaluate whether the relationship is working and how it might be changed to work better. This is true with co-teaching, which may change as student needs evolve over time or as demands on the teacher for content knowledge or differentiation of instruction change. Collaborative colleagues can use discussions to address the evolving nature of collaboration and to ensure that all participants continue to be committed to the collaborative relationship. We previously described co-teach chats (see Figure 10.3), which are an approach that may be used to evaluate and improve co-teaching relationships.

## Applications and Examples

Teachers who are good collaborators continue to gain skills and dispositions that facilitate their work. For example, collaborators must be open to new ideas and demonstrate willingness to others to explore new perspectives, even when they contrast with their point of view. This shows respect for other collaborators and can prevent potential problems with collaborative interactions. Several essential behaviors to consider when working toward a respectful, equal partnership with a collaborator include (Dettmer et al., 2009):

- Really listen, and talk, together with collaborators.
- Describe your perspectives, but give objective examples whenever possible.
- Work toward resolutions or compromises together.
- Provide a collective summary of discussion points and tentative agreements.
- If the process is stalled, seek input from others.
- Talk after completing a collaborative activity, to reflect on outcomes and how to improve collaboration next time.

## Keep in Mind

As you collaborate regarding inclusion, keep in mind that professionals often do not share common definitions of inclusion or inclusive practices. Given this variability, it is important to discuss individual perspectives on inclusion with other collaborators and to ensure that all understand your perspective and that you understand those of others. Successful collaborators determine common ground on which they can focus (e.g., improving outcomes for all students, making all students part of the academic and social community of the school), emphasize similar perspectives, and downplay differences.

**Key References**

Correa, V., Jones, H., Thomas, C., & Morsink, C. (2005). *Interactive teaming: Enhancing programs for students with special needs.* Upper Saddle River, NJ: Merrill/Pearson Education.

Dettmer, P., Thurston, L., Knackendoffel, A., & Dyck, N. (2009). *Collaboration, consultation, and teamwork for students with special needs.* Upper Saddle River, NJ: Merrill/Pearson Education.

Friend, M., & Cook, L. (2010). *Interactions: Collaboration skills for school professionals* (6th ed.). Boston: Allyn & Bacon.

Kampwirth, T., & Powers, K. (2011). *Collaborative consultation in the schools* (4th ed.). Upper Saddle River, NJ: Merrill/Pearson Education.

Kochhar-Bryant, C. (2008). *Collaboration and system coordination for students with special needs.* Upper Saddle River, NJ: Merrill/Pearson Education.

| Strategy 10.2 | # COMMUNICATION SKILLS AND SUCCESSFUL COLLABORATION |

## Rationale

The most important skills for effectively working with others relate to communication (Correa et al., 2005; Friend & Cook, 2010). Collaboration can be effective only if those involved understand each other, convey both verbal and nonverbal (e.g., body language) information intentionally, and avoid misunderstandings. Many factors may interfere with effective communication and result in misunderstandings and poor collaboration. Several of these potential barriers relate to the dispositions we discussed previously in this chapter. For example, collaborators with different frames of reference will have difficulty communicating effectively until they examine and understand the frames of reference that are creating the communication problem. It is therefore important for collaborators to learn effective communication skills to facilitate the best possible collaboration and to improve student outcomes.

## Step-by-Step

Collaborators can substantially reduce communication problems by developing effective communication skills. These skills can be used to make sure that information communicated is the intended information and is understood by collaborators. The most important communication skills for collaborators relate to listening, verbal communication, and nonverbal communication.

**1** *Listen.* Many factors may interfere with effective listening when collaborating (Friend & Cook, 2010). These factors include:

- Filtering certain messages that you do not want to hear. The listener hears the topic of the message and then tunes out.
- Being distracted by details that are tangential to the main point.
- Rehearsing a response while a collaborator is talking.
- Reacting to "hot" words that cause you to react strongly, such as whole language, direct instruction, inclusion, accountability, behaviorism.

Monitoring your reactions to words or topics as communication occurs and recognizing that you are engaging in these behaviors are important steps in moving beyond these barriers to effective communication. Other listening skills that will improve communication include actively listening for the real content of the message you're hearing; attending to the feelings that may be in the message; paraphrasing what you've heard, including the content of the message and the feelings behind the message; and providing the speaker with the opportunity to clarify your perspectives (Vaughn, Bos, & Schumm, 2011; Walther-Thomas, Korinek, McLaughlin, & Williams, 2000).

**2** *Develop verbal communication skills.* Your verbal communication skills are important to consider as you work in a collaborative relationship. You may use several strategies to be clearly understood as you interact with others (Vaughn et al., 2011; Walther-Thomas et al., 2000), including:

- Repeat messages through multiple modes, including restating a message in a different manner (e.g., summarizing the key points of a previous message) and providing a written summary of a message.
- Practice empathy, or place yourself in the other person's shoes, in an attempt to understand your collaborator's frame of reference or perspective on a topic being discussed.
- Ensure understanding by using clear and concise language that is understandable by collaborators (e.g., avoiding the use of professional jargon and acronyms such as IEP, LRE, ASD, IDEA).
- Use questions to clarify, better understand, seek further information, and convey acceptance to the speaker.
- Summarize the content to make certain that all agree regarding what has been discussed.

Michelle Duclos, a seventh-grade science teacher at West Hernando Middle School, notes that at times, she and her co-teacher will have only a few minutes to plan before beginning a team lesson. Frequent, clear, effective communication is needed to ensure that she and her co-teacher share ideas and "play off each other, emphasizing our strengths" during the class. She also emphasizes the importance of teachers reading one another as they move through the class period, by either talking briefly or picking up on nonverbal cues as "an amazing idea comes to one of us during the lesson."

**3** *Address nonverbal communication.* Many teachers who are initially involved in collaboration with other professionals and parents overlook the importance of *nonverbal communication*, which may be a more accurate representation of the intent of what is being communicated than the verbal message (Correa et al., 2005). Certain negative, nonverbal messages are sent to others by appearing to be bored, using a tone of voice that does not match comments, and exhibiting negative behaviors such as inattentiveness to comments made by certain collaborators, facial expressions or eye rolling, sighing, lack of eye contact, and so forth.

Effective collaboration requires that participants use nonverbal communication to convey attention, respect, and understanding when others are speaking. Strategies for conveying positive messages through nonverbal communication include leaning toward the speaker and maintaining eye contact, appearing relaxed and interested in the speaker, maintaining appropriate proximity to the speaker, using an appropriate tone of voice, and monitoring negative nonverbal messages (e.g., sighing, facial expressions) (Correa et al., 2005; Friend & Cook, 2010).

## Applications and Examples

Several issues may result in barriers to effective communication as you work with other professionals. These potential blocks include (Kochhar-Bryant, 2008):

- Verbal or nonverbal messages that convey unequal status or lack of parity. These messages convey the perspective that "I don't view you as an equal partner or respect your point of view."
- A communication mismatch, when one collaborator needs to vent while another wants to discuss how to address a particular child's needs.
- Communications that send mixed messages. For example, a teacher says, "I'm not frustrated," but body language suggests otherwise.
- Distractions or interruptions that convey to a collaborator that his perspective is not respected.
- Focusing on the past with statements such as, "We tried that before, and it didn't work."
- Moralizing, preaching, advising, or conveying that "I know how to solve your problems."

Collaborators need to be vigilant in monitoring their own behavior as well as others' behavior to make sure that these barriers do not arise and have a negative influence or result in a total breakdown of collaboration.

## Keep in Mind

Think for a moment about how difficult it is to communicate effectively. We all have experienced times when we thought we communicated clearly, but the person to whom we were sending the message did not receive the intended message. The complexity of communication is illustrated by several factors, including (Friend & Cook, 2010) the following:

- Communication consists of sending and receiving messages simultaneously.
- Messages are sent using both verbal and nonverbal information.
- The environment in which the message is sent influences communication (e.g., noise or distractions in the setting, others who are present).
- Different types of communication are used by different people.
- Different modes of communication are used to convey information (e.g., verbal, electronic, written messages).

Given the complexity of communication, it is critically important that collaborators frequently check with each other to ensure that they are sending and receiving messages clearly. This requires collaborators to send information in different formats, check understanding by using different words, and ask collaborators to rephrase information to ensure all understand the information.

**Key References**

Correa, V., Jones, H., Thomas, C., & Morsink, C. (2005). *Interactive teaming: Enhancing programs for students with special needs.* Upper Saddle River, NJ: Merrill/Pearson Education.

Friend, M., & Cook, L. (2010). *Interactions: Collaboration skills for school professionals* (6th ed.). Boston: Allyn & Bacon.

Kochhar-Bryant, C. (2008). *Collaboration and system coordination for students with special needs.* Upper Saddle River, NJ: Merrill/Pearson Education.

Vaughn, S., Bos, C., & Schumm, J. (2011). *Teaching students who are exceptional, diverse, and at risk in the general education classroom* (5th ed.). Boston: Pearson.

Walther-Thomas, C., Korinek, L., McLaughlin, V., & Williams, B. (2000). *Collaboration for inclusive education.* Boston: Allyn & Bacon.

| Strategy 10.3 | **TEACHER ASSISTANCE TEAMS (TATS)** |

## Rationale

When teachers need assistance, they have typically sought help from respected colleagues by walking down the hall during a break, or catching the colleague during lunch or after school. Teacher assistance teams (TATs) formalize and simplify this source of assistance. These teams are also a source of professional development, as teachers who participate on the team learn from others about strategies to address a range of student needs.

Teacher assistance teams consist of a group of well-respected professionals who meet two to four times a month to provide assistance using collaborative consultation to other teachers who are having difficulty with a student or group of students. These teams have also been called *intervention assistance teams, student assistance teams,* and *building-based teams.* Research has shown that, when TATs are well designed and supported by teachers and the building principal, referring teachers often receive assistance that they can use in their classroom to address the identified student need (Kovaleski & Glew, 2006; Lane, Pierson, Robertson, & Little, 2004).

## Step-by-Step

Teacher assistance teams typically begin their work when a teacher refers a student with a particular need to the team. Once the referral occurs, the team goes through the following steps (Chalfant & Pysh, 1989):

**1** *Team members read the referral, which includes specific information regarding the child's challenges.* For example, the referral form (see Figure 10.4 for a sample referral form) should include a request for information regarding what the referring teacher wants the student to be able to do that she is not currently doing, what the teacher has already tried to address this problem, and the student's assets and deficits. If team members determine it is needed, one team member observes the child in the referring teacher's class to provide more in-depth information regarding the problem.

| Figure 10.4 | **Teacher Assistance Team Sample Referral Form** |

REQUEST FOR ASSISTANCE—SOUTHSIDE ELEMENTARY SCHOOL

Name of Student     .          Age Grade

Name of Parent

Referred by:

What would you like the student to be able to do that s/he cannot currently do?

Describe what the student does well (assets).

Describe what the student does not do well (deficits).

Additional information that is relevant for the TAT to consider

**2** *The team meets with the teacher for about 30 minutes.* The first step in this meeting is to explicitly identify the problem the team will address. Keep in mind that several problems might be included on the referral form, or the problem might not be clearly defined. The referring teacher is asked to work with the team to determine the most important problem to address. Once this is done, the team discusses the problem until all members agree that the problem is explicitly defined.

**3** *The team, including the referring teacher, brainstorms possible solutions to the problem.* During this time, no comments are made regarding the recommendations or possible solutions to the problem. A recorder lists a recommendation, and then the team moves on to additional recommendations. Teams generate anywhere from 10 to 50 recommendations for addressing most problems.

**4** *The referring teacher selects several of the recommendations.* The recommendations should fit into her classroom and approach to teaching. She may ask for further clarification regarding the recommendations, as necessary.

**5** *The referring teacher selects a recommendation she will use in the classroom to address the student's* problem. The team works with the teacher to clarify any aspects of the recommendation that are unclear and logistics regarding how the intervention may be used in the teacher's classroom.

**6** *The team and the teacher discuss goals for determining the success of the intervention.* This might include a specific reduction in out-of-seat behavior, handing in homework 90% of the time, and so on. The team arranges a time for a follow-up meeting.

**7** *During the follow-up meeting, the teacher provides the TAT with feedback regarding how the recommended intervention worked.* If the intervention did not work, the team has three options regarding how to proceed. First, the teacher might seek additional clarification regarding the intervention that was used. This occurs if the teacher feels that she did not fully understand the intervention, and that additional clarification and support could improve the effectiveness of the intervention. Second, the teacher might select a recommendation from the list generated in the previous meeting, then the team moves though steps 5 and 6 above. Third, the team could begin at step 1 and generate additional recommendations.

## Applications and Examples

Members of TATs may be appointed by the principal, be elected by teachers, or volunteer. No matter how they are selected, all teachers on the TAT should be well-respected members of the faculty who are trusted by other faculty. In most instances principals do not serve on teacher assistance teams because they are in a position to evaluate teachers and this may create parity issues. Another concern related to having a principal on a TAT relates to some teachers' perspectives that a principal may view a referral to a TAT as a sign of weakness on the part of the teacher, and this may result in a reduction in the number of referrals to the team. To make sure teachers were comfortable referring to a TAT, one principal (who was not on the team) was vocal in support of teacher assistance teams and told teachers that referrals to the TAT would be viewed in a positive way for their yearly evaluations, indicating that they were trying to improve their teaching. This resulted in an increase in referrals to the TAT.

Teacher assistance teams are designed to use the time of participants efficiently. For example, the referral form should be one page long and should include only information that is absolutely necessary for team decision making (see Figure 10.4 for a sample referral form). Furthermore, procedures for running the TAT meeting are designed to focus the group quickly on the problem and efficiently brainstorm and select possible interventions to address the problem. For more information regarding this process, see Walther-Thomas and colleagues (2000).

## Keep in Mind

Most student problems that are referred to a TAT relate to work habits, classroom behavior, interpersonal behavior, attentional problems, and reading difficulties. The recommended interventions are reported to succeed for almost 90% of all referrals. Some students for whom recommendations are not successful may be referred to special education (if they are not already identified with a disability) to determine if they need more intensive interventions. It is noteworthy that the TAT process often significantly reduces the number of referrals to special education. Furthermore, when students are referred to special education after being referred to a TAT, they are most often identified with a disability.

**Key References**

Chalfant, J., & Pysh, M. (1989). Teacher assistance teams: Five descriptive studies on 96 teams. *Remedial and Special Education, 10*(6), 49–58.

Kovaleski, J., & Glew, M. (2006). Bringing instructional support teams to scale: Implications of the Pennsylvania experience. *Remedial and Special Education, 27*, 16–25.

Lane, K., Pierson, M., Robertson, E., & Little, A. (2004). Teachers' views of prereferral interventions: Perceptions of and recommendations for implementation support. *Education and Treatment of Children, 27*(4), 420–439.

Snell, M., & Janney, R. (2005). *Collaborative teaming* (2nd ed.). Baltimore: Brookes.

Walther-Thomas, C., Korinek, L., McLaughlin, V., & Williams, B. (2000). *Collaboration for inclusive education*. Boston: Allyn & Bacon.

| Strategy 10.4 | # PLANNING FOR CO-TEACHING |

## Rationale

When used to support inclusion, the primary purpose of co-teaching is to make sure that instruction for students with disabilities (and other students who struggle academically and/or socially) is adapted to meet individual student needs. Co-teaching thus provides students with more intense, differentiated instruction, which is built on the general education curriculum.

Co-teaching has several strengths. When teachers share responsibility for teaching a diverse group of students in one classroom, they can combine their expertise to meet the needs of all students. For students with disabilities, in particular, co-teaching provides access to the general education curriculum, reduces the fragmentation of the curriculum that results when students are pulled out of general education classrooms for instruction, and often results in improved student outcomes. Teachers also report that co-teaching provides a professional support system and leads to less feeling of professional isolation, especially for special education teachers.

## Step-by-Step

During the first year of co-teaching, it is advisable to only develop one or two partnerships. Sufficient time to plan for the co-teaching partnerships should be available during the spring and summer before beginning to co-teach. Planning for co-teaching should address the following:

**1** *Determine common goals for co-teaching that both teachers understand, agree to, and value.* These goals facilitate buy-in from the co-teachers and ensure interdependence in addressing and meeting the goals. Given the emphasis in schools on accountability, a critical factor in determining goals should be data on student needs. This information can be used to make decisions about instructional time, grouping patterns, and instructional methods used in class. Furthermore, data should be used to monitor student progress and make decisions about change that occur in instructional delivery. For example, if co-teachers are engaged in station teaching, it may be necessary to change the size of groups or focus on different goals if some students are not making sufficient progress. This allows co-teachers to provide students who struggle learning academic material with more intensive, direct instruction that will often accelerate learning.

**2** *Discuss the strengths both teachers bring to the classroom, and how these strengths will be used to make co-teaching succeed.* All teachers are better at some things than others, or prefer to engage in certain activities (e.g., large-group instruction, small-group instruction, discussion). It is important to be candid about strengths and preferences in the classroom. Recent research has shown that collaborators are much more successful when they are knowledgeable about their strengths and weaknesses, and are candid with their collaborator about these issues (Bahrami et al., 2010).

Communicating this information during planning for co-teaching allows teachers to share expertise and determine how this expertise can be best used to meet student needs and improve outcomes.

**3** *Define roles and responsibilities for both co-teachers.* Teachers' roles in co-taught classrooms should vary, depending on student needs, the content being taught, and teacher strengths/preferences. Furthermore, it is important that teachers share all roles at times, to make sure that one teacher doesn't always teach the students who are experiencing difficulty. It is also important that both teachers in a co-teaching partnership have professionally fulfilling roles and fully use their expertise. Many types of co-teaching may be used to address student needs.

Figure 10.5 describes several approaches to co-teaching. When planning for co-teaching, teachers should determine which approach to co-teaching will be used for a particular lesson, and the roles of both teachers should be clearly defined. This can become complex because it is typical that more than one type of co-teaching will be used during the school day. For example, with the current emphasis on tiered instructional approaches, many co-teachers use station teaching to provide small-group instruction for students who are struggling to learn academic material (Murawski & Hughes, 2009). This approach is used for part of the school day, and teachers alternate groups to make sure that they share responsibility for teaching students who are struggling. At other times during the school day, teachers may use approaches such as parallel teaching, team teaching, or one teach and one assist, depending on the content being taught, student needs, and teacher preferences.

| Figure 10.5 | Co-Teaching Options |
| --- | --- |

**Team teaching:** Both teachers share equal responsibility for instructing the whole group, and teach the group as equal partners.

**One teach, one support:** One teacher teaches the content of the class, while the other teacher floats, responds to student questions, keeps students on task, addresses management issues, and so forth.

**Complementary teaching:** The class is divided based on student needs, and both teachers teach a group. This may include different content for the groups, review of material that a group of students has not mastered, intensive instruction for a small group of students, and so forth.

**Parallel teaching:** This approach consists of splitting the class into two heterogeneous groups, and one teacher instructs each group using a collaboratively planned lesson. This is designed to reduce the class size or teacher–student ratio, and thus allows the teachers to provide more attention to each student and attend to individual student needs.

**One teach, one observe:** Teachers rarely have the opportunity to observe a student closely during a lesson. Similarly, teachers seldom have the opportunity to observe another teacher during a lesson to learn from another professional. This approach allows these opportunities. It is important to note that this is an approach that should be used infrequently, and should strategically focus on particular opportunities that arise when intensive observation is beneficial.

**Station teaching:** When this approach is used, stations or centers are set up in class that address different content, and students rotate through the stations. Teachers then have the responsibility for a station, and teach all students as they rotate through the station. In many classrooms, students are expected to work independently or cooperatively in one or more stations, or a paraeducator may have responsibility for a station. This approach is used increasingly in elementary and secondary classrooms, given the emphasis on tiered instructional approaches.

**4** *Participate in professional development.* Both co-teaching partners should participate in this professional development, which should address topics such as co-teaching, collaboration, communication skills, problem solving, and instructional strategies. This allows partner teachers the opportunity to develop the common skills they need to enhance the success of co-teaching. These types of activities are beneficial before co-teaching begins, as information is provided regarding the basics of co-teaching, and co-teaching partners are provided the opportunity to discuss this information with others and plan their approach (e.g., definition of roles) to co-teaching. Participating in professional development is also beneficial after beginning co-teaching, as issues invariably arise during implementation of this practice. This professional development should be tailored to the particular needs you face as a co-teacher, and may include visits to other co-taught classrooms for observation, or having a teacher with expertise in co-teaching visit your classroom to provide feedback and coaching regarding areas of concern (McLeskey, 2011).

**5** *Develop a master plan for instruction and a general format for daily lessons that is predictable but flexible.* This can be achieved through initially collaborating to plan a unit of instruction, developing lesson plans that include accommodations for student needs, and determining the type of co-teaching used for different parts of the unit. The approach used by many teachers includes planning curriculum and instruction based on the needs and expected outcomes for all students, most students, and a few students. Using this approach, co-teachers get to know their students well, and they also get to know the preferences of their co-teaching partner. This information is useful in determining the type of co-teaching that will be used for a particular lesson. As the school year progresses, it is important to be flexible in adapting the master plan and format for daily lessons, as the needs of students and preferences of teachers will continue to evolve.

**6** *Develop a plan for classroom management.* The plan should include how to address behavior issues proactively, rules for student behavior, consequences (both positive and negative), and who will handle delivery of consequences. This activity will allow co-teaching partners to begin to learn the preferences of their partner regarding student behavior, and preferences regarding how behavioral issues will be addressed. The plan for classroom management will also continue to evolve through the school year, as student behavior issues change over time. A co-teaching partner in the classroom offers many opportunities to address behavior issues as they arise, as well as opportunities to observe student behavior and better understand why behavior problems may arise and how they may be prevented.

**7** *Create a common planning time for co-teachers during the school year.* During these "co-teach chats," co-teachers address student progress, instructional content, teachers' roles, accountability, and so forth. Teachers should also use this time to reflect on how co-teaching is working and make changes as needed. Teachers should agree on how to efficiently use this planning time. For example, planning routines may be developed to include activities such as the following:

- Celebrate the successes of co-teaching from the previous week's instruction.

- Discuss student needs based on the previous week's instruction and available data.
- Plan instructional content and related student accommodations for the coming week.
- Plan teacher responsibilities for the coming week, to make sure that students receive support as needed.
- Discuss how co-teaching is working, and problem solve regarding areas that need to be improved.

## Applications and Examples

Co-teaching is a dynamic process. You will need to continue to make decisions with your teaching partner regarding a variety of logistical issues over the first year of co-teaching and beyond. As you enter into a co-teaching relationship, continue to acquire skills to support co-teaching and learn about your partner teacher. This makes it important that you and your co-teacher agree that it is fine to ask questions about any issues or misunderstandings that arise. You will likely need to continue to work on sharing responsibility with another professional and communicating effectively regarding student issues, as well as the logistics of co-teaching.

Another issue that you will continue to address is the roles that you and your teaching partner play as co-teachers. Student learning and related needs change over time, and you will find that student-grouping patterns and teacher responsibilities must also change. It is likely that as the year progresses, you will use the one-teach, one-assist model of co-teaching less often, and the station teaching, complementary teaching and team-teaching models more often to ensure that students receive the individual support that they need.

## Keep in Mind

It is easy to fall into a pattern of often grouping low-achieving students together and assuming certain teaching roles that are traditional for general and special education teachers. For example, the general education teacher may always assume the role of content teacher for the large group, and the special education teacher always assumes the role of attending to the needs of low-achieving students. As we've noted previously, a critical aspect of effective inclusion programs is that differences become an ordinary part of the school day. Furthermore, varying the teaching roles allows teachers to learn and develop expertise from their partner teacher and to use their expertise with all students. If co-teaching is to work well, partner teachers must not revert to traditional teaching roles and grouping patterns. Rather, teachers should seamlessly share roles in the classroom, and students who are struggling should be grouped into small, homogeneous groups for only brief periods of intensive instruction. Otherwise, the grouping patterns for these students should be similar to that of their peers.

**Key References**

Bahrami, B., Olsen, K., Lathan, P., Roepstorff, A., Rees, G., & Frith, C. (2010). Optimally interacting minds. *Science, 329*, 1080–1085.

Correa, V., Jones, H., Thomas, C., & Morsink, C. (2005). *Interactive teaming: Enhancing programs for students with special needs* (4th ed.). Upper Saddle River, NJ: Merrill/Pearson Education.

Friend, M. (2008). *Co-Teach!* Greensboro, NC: Marilyn Friend.

Friend, M., & Cook, L. (2010). *Interactions: Collaboration skills for school professionals* (6th ed.). Boston: Allyn & Bacon.

McLeskey, J. (2011). Supporting improved practice for special education teachers: The importance of learner-centered professional development. *Journal of Special Education Leadership, 24*, 26–35.

Murawski, W., & Hughes, C. (2009). Response to intervention, collaboration, and co-teaching: A logical contribution for successful systemic change. *Intervention in School and Clinic, 53*, 267–277.

Villa, R., Thousand, J., & Nevin, A. (2008). *A guide for co-teaching* (2nd ed.). Thousand Oaks, CA: Sage.

Walther-Thomas, C., Korinek, L., McLaughlin, V., & Williams, B. (2000). *Collaboration for inclusive education*. Boston: Allyn & Bacon.

| Strategy 10.5 | **WORKING WITH PARAEDUCATORS** |

## Rationale

The number of paraeducators working in schools has increased dramatically as inclusion has become more prevalent (Fisher & Pleasants, 2011). Many of these paraeducators have been hired to provide support for students with disabilities who require more attention and support than the general education teacher can provide. Paraeducators work under the supervision of a certified teacher and provide support such as one-to-one or small-group instruction (e.g., tutoring or drill and practice) on material already taught by the teacher, support for students with highly specialized needs, grading and other paperwork, preparation of material for class lessons, and so forth. In short, paraeducators provide support for certified teachers in much the same way paralegals provide support to lawyers or paramedics provide medical support.

## Step-by-Step

Paraeducators can provide invaluable assistance in an inclusive classroom if their responsibilities are well defined and they are well prepared for the responsibilities. The supervising teacher is responsible for ensuring that this occurs. When a paraeducator is assigned, the teacher should follow several steps to ensure that she is well prepared. These steps include:

**1** *Welcome and acknowledge the paraeducator.* This includes activities such as introducing the paraeducator to other professionals as part of the teaching team (and not as a helper for a specific student); providing a space for personal belongings; putting the paraeducator's name on the classroom door; and sharing routine responsibilities that communicate authority (e.g., taking roll, writing on the board) (Causton-Theoharis et al., 2007). These types of activities serve to welcome the paraeducator and communicate that she is a valued part of the professional team.

**2** *Orient the paraeducator to the school.* This includes activities such as a thorough tour of the school; introductions to important staff (e.g., office staff, librarian); a review of classroom procedures, policies, and rules; provision of information regarding location of supplies and technology; and access to IEPs and support in reading and interpreting these documents (Causton-Theoharis et al., 2007).

**3** *Provide training related to assigned instructional activities.* Although the school district may provide general professional development for paraeducators, the supervising teacher is in the best position to provide professional development on specific curricular materials and methods, and general procedures used in the inclusive classroom. This may include professional development related to the use of methods for tutoring, packaged programs for reading or math instruction, and so forth. As the year progresses, the supervising teacher monitors the skills of the paraeducator, provides individual professional development and support as needed, and discusses possible training opportunities offered by the district that meet specific needs related to the paraeducator's responsibilities.

**4** *Plan a schedule with the paraeducator.* A critical task of the supervising teacher is to ensure appropriate use of a paraeducator's particular skills in assigned duties. The supervising teacher and paraeducator should discuss these issues and develop a weekly schedule that includes who the paraeducator will support and what the paraeducator's role will be. Addressing what the paraeducator's role should *not* be may also be important. For example, paraeducators should not be fully responsible for any student and should not be responsible for planning programs or lessons, but rather should carry out plans developed by the supervising teacher. The teacher may develop these plans collaboratively with the paraeducator, but ultimately, plans are the responsibility of the supervising teacher. After developing a schedule, the supervising teacher and paraeducator should meet frequently to evaluate how the schedule is working, and make adjustments as necessary.

**5** *Communicate effectively with the paraeducator.* Teachers need regularly scheduled meetings to facilitate effective communication with paraeducators. These meetings may occur during common planning time or at other times during the school day, but they should allow adequate, uninterrupted time to address important issues and concerns. For example, it is important to use the time of the paraeducator effectively, to develop appropriate roles and responsibilities, to address any training needs, and to adjust the paraeducator's schedule as necessary. In addition to regular meetings, communication may be enhanced by the use of daily notebooks, e-mail, and checking in at the beginning and end of each day. Finally, it is important to be open to the ideas and perspectives that the paraeducator provides and to engage in active listening to ensure that these perspectives are clearly understood (Causton-Theoharis et al., 2007).

**6** *Supervise the paraeducator appropriately.* The supervising teacher is responsible for supervising the work of the paraeducator. Roles related to supervision include the following (Friend & Cook, 2010):

- Monitor how well paraeducators are performing assigned tasks.
- Provide feedback, and point out strategies to improve performance.

- Model effective instructional strategies and ways to interact with students.
- Problem solve as disagreements arise with the paraeducator and other teachers.
- Make certain that the paraeducator understands school policies and ethical practices and adheres to these policies and practices.
- Support paraeducators by responding to any questions they may have and providing support and professional development.
- Publicly acknowledge the work of paraeducators.

## Applications and Examples

A key to working effectively with paraeducators is to build a relationship that includes open communication and reflects respect and trust. Collaborating with paraeducators in determining their role, needed training, weekly assignments, and so forth is an important step in ensuring that this occurs. Furthermore, the effective skills for collaboration that we discussed earlier in this chapter are important when working with paraeducators.

Paraeducators were surveyed and asked what is essential for teachers to be good partners with paraeducators (Riggs, 2005). The results of this survey are summarized in Figure 10.6, and provide much insight into how you can work effectively with paraeducators. As we noted previously, key issues seem to be working collaboratively with paraeducators in an atmosphere of trust and respect, clearly defining the paraeducator's role, and ensuring that she receives appropriate professional development to perform assigned tasks and meet students' needs.

## Keep in Mind

Paraeducators can serve in a variety of roles in an inclusive classroom. For example, they can be especially effective in providing tutoring for students using well-structured materials, or engaging students in teacher-developed skill-and-drill activities. Nonetheless, some teachers are hesitant to delegate responsibilities to paraeducators. Some of the reasons this occurs relate to concerns regarding the quality of the paraeducator's work, the need for training if the paraeducator is to engage in certain tasks, the feeling that the teacher doesn't want to be bossy, or the perspective that the teacher can do it faster herself (Friend & Cook, 2010). Teachers should work through these concerns and learn to delegate increasing levels of responsibility to paraeducators. This ensures the efficient use of resources to meet student needs, empowers paraeducators, allows them to learn new skills, and helps to create a team committed to student success (Friend & Cook, 2010).

**Key References**

Causton-Theoharis, J., Giangreco, M., Doyle, M., & Vadasy, P. (2007). Paraprofessionals: The "Sous-Chefs" of literacy instruction. *Teaching Exceptional Children, 40*(1), 56–62.

Fisher, M., & Pleasants, S. (2011). Roles, responsibilities, and concerns of paraeducators: Findings from a statewide survey. *Remedial and Special Education*, published online 7 February 2011, DOI: 10:1177/0741932510397762.

French, N. (2003). Paraeducators in special education programs. *Focus on Exceptional Children, 36*(2), 1–16.

Friend, M., & Cook, L. (2010). *Interactions: Collaboration skills for school professionals* (6th ed.). Boston: Allyn & Bacon.

Riggs, C. (2005). To teachers: What paraeducators want you to know. *Teaching Exceptional Children, 36*(5), 8–12.

| Figure 10.6 | What Paraeducators Want Teachers to Know |

1. **Know and use the paraeducator's name**. Paraeducators are not "Kasey's helper" or invisible! They are a valuable member of the professional staff, and should be recognized and treated as such. This is an important first step in building trust, respect, and good communication.

2. **Be familiar with rules and policies in your district regarding paraeducators**. It is important that the supervising teachers and others understand the ground rules regarding paraeducators. A special education supervisor or school administrator should have this information readily available.

3. **Work with the paraeducator as a valued team member**. The working relationship that develops between a paraeducator and teacher should reflect professionalism, cooperation, and camaraderie. It logically follows that paraeducators should be recognized as a valued member of the professional team.

4. **Explicitly share your expectations**. Paraeducators want to know what to do, as well as what not to do in the classroom. Teachers should explicitly share information regarding expectations regarding classroom management, student behavior, expectations for certain students, and so forth.

5. **Define roles and responsibilities for paraeducators and teachers**. Avoid disagreements and conflicts by explicitly defining the role of paraeducators in a job description and ensuring that their role is clearly differentiated from the role of the teacher.

6. **The teacher should supervise and direct paraeducators**. Paraeducators are often confused regarding who should provide them with direction in a co-taught, inclusive classroom. Teachers should be explicit regarding who provides direction and supervision, and should be clear about what is expected and how to do it.

7. **Ensure effective communication**. Determining effective methods to provide formal and informal feedback to paraeducators regarding their work is a critical role for the supervising teacher. A time should be set aside for discussing how things are working, and improvements that may be needed.

8. **Recognize that paraeducators have knowledge and expertise to share in the classroom**. Paraeducators often gain extensive information regarding students as they perform tasks across a range of settings. Furthermore, paraeducators gain valuable skills as they work with teachers and students over a number of years. Respecting and valuing the knowledge and skills paraeducators bring to their jobs helps to create a good working relationship, and can have a positive effect on student learning.

9. **Take ownership of all students**. Teachers should be classroom leaders for all students, and not put paraeducators in the position of taking responsibility for some students (e.g., a student with a disability). When a paraeducator works individually with a student for a long period of time, the teacher may not be familiar with the student and his needs. It is important to make sure that this does not occur, and the teacher knows and works with *all* students in the classroom.

10. **Respect paraeducators**. If teachers model respect for paraeducators, students will likely model this same behavior. In addition, the job satisfaction and retention of paraeducators are influenced by the extent to which they are valued and respected for the work that they perform.

*Source:* Information adapted from C. Riggs (2005). To teachers: What paraeducators want you to know. *Teaching Exceptional Children, 36*(5), 8–12.

## Strategy 10.6   WORKING WITH FAMILIES: HOME–SCHOOL COLLABORATION

## Rationale

*Home–school collaboration* is defined as a teacher and parent or significant caregiver working collaboratively to develop interventions to address student needs. Interventions that have proven effective related to home–school collaboration include simple activities such as parent monitoring of homework or dispensing consequences based on a daily report card, to more extensive interventions that require parent training, such as parent tutoring in reading and math or improving a student's self-determination skills (Cox, 2005; Fabiano et al., 2009; Kochhar-Bryant, 2008; Patall, Cooper, & Robinson, 2008). Research has shown that home–school interventions are more successful when school personnel collaborate with caregivers and treat them as equals (Cox, 2005).

Family involvement and support are especially important for inclusive programs. Moreover, caregivers for students with disabilities are in a unique position to become involved in their child's education and to work as a partner with educators, given the high level of parent involvement that is required as part of IDEA (Correa et al., 2005; Whitbread et al., 2007). Unfortunately, many parents are not engaged in their child's education. Some of this lack of engagement can be explained by a parent's choice not to become involved, while other parents want to be involved but may have family responsibilities and stressors that make it very difficult to be involved (Kochhar-Bryant, 2008). Still other parents may not be involved because of cultural issues that impede clear, effective communication between school and home (Matuszny, Banda, & Coleman, 2007).

## Step-by-Step

An important responsibility you will have as a teacher in an inclusive classroom is to encourage home–school collaboration and other forms of parent involvement in their children's education. The following steps will help ensure that parents have an opportunity to participate and serve as a resource to improve their children's education.

**1** *Get to know parents as individuals, build trust, and open lines of communication.* Some parents may immediately want to become involved in their child's education, but for others, you will need to get to know the parent before you can develop home–school collaborative interventions. It is important to engage parents in informal settings early in the school year to begin this process. For example, the school might sponsor a kick-off-the-year event that allows teachers and parents to meet in an atmosphere that is informal, comfortable, and stress free (Matuszny et al., 2007). Talking with parents before and after school about topics unrelated to their child is also helpful.

After initially getting to know the parents, you should engage in activities such as inviting parents into the classroom and providing information the parents will find useful to further build a positive relationship. Finally, you could give parents choices regarding alternatives for participating in school-related activities and ask them for input in decision making (Matuszny et al., 2007).

**2** *Try to understand, respect, and take into account the parents' perspective.* Most families have some difficulty adjusting to the needs of a child with a disability. For example, after determining that a child has a disability, some parents may deny that a disability exists and need time before they can accept the disability. Other parents may have stressors in their lives that are exacerbated by having to address the child's disability in home and in school. Understanding the parents' perspectives by talking with them and/or visiting in the home will lead to the conclusion that some parents do not have the time to participate in home–school collaboration, and others choose not to participate, often for very understandable reasons.

**3** *Determine the types of involvement that will work for particular parents.* A group of parents likely will be willing and prepared to engage in home–school collaboration on an intervention that will improve student achievement and/or behavior. We advise beginning with a small group of parents who are interested in using a single intervention. This allows teachers the opportunity to "work out the bugs" with the intervention while working with a group of parents who will provide feedback and aren't likely to be discouraged if some aspects of the intervention need to be adjusted.

**4** *Design, implement, and evaluate the intervention collaboratively with parents.* The intervention should be well structured and easily understood by participating parents, and resources should be available to support the intervention, as needed. Information on possible interventions related to homework, student behavior, tutoring, self-determination, and so forth is widely available. Other teachers in your school and special education consultants are likely to be good sources of information on these types of interventions that have proven to be effective.

More information on working with students and families from culturally and linguistically diverse backgrounds is included in Chapter 13.

## Applications and Examples

When engaging parents in home–school collaboration, or otherwise encouraging parent involvement in school activities, an important consideration is the parents' cultural background(s). To ensure that teachers understand, respect, and take into account parents' cultural background(s), we recommend the following activities (Correa et al., 2005; Harry, Kalyanpur, & Day, 1999):

- Identify cultural values that are embedded in the teacher's interpretation of a student's difficulties or in recommendations for services.
- Explore whether the family understands and values how teachers interpret the student's difficulties, and, if not, have the family share how their values differ from those of the teacher.
- Respect any differences that exist regarding the student that are embedded in the cultural background of the family.
- Determine ways to adapt the teacher's recommendations or interpretations to the value system of the family.

For guidelines regarding how teachers can encourage involvement of parents from culturally diverse backgrounds, see Figure 10.7.

| **Figure 10.7** | **Guidelines for Encouraging Involvement of Parents from Diverse Cultural and Language Backgrounds in Their Child's Education** |
|---|---|

1. **Empower families with knowledge and skills to:**
   - Adapt and cope with the school system, which will likely be very different than their previous experience.
   - Work with their children and reinforce educational programs at home in ways that are natural and functional.

2. **Provide the family with assistance in moving from their native culture to the mainstream culture**, recognizing that cultures vary significantly within such groups. This requires that the teacher learn about the family's cultural experiences, including their expectations regarding schools, interaction patterns with teachers, and desire for involvement in school.

3. **Work as a culture broker** and support the family in contacts with the school. This may involve serving as an advocate or mediator for students from certain ethnic backgrounds, and/or linking with community leaders to enhance home–school collaboration.

4. **When communicating with families, determine the preferred means of communication** that will remove barriers related to cultural, language, and communication differences, and enhance communication between school and home.

5. **Collect information regarding the family related to:**
   - Experiences in their native country
   - The roles of extended family members and siblings
   - The amount of available community support
   - Religious, spiritual, and cultural beliefs
   - Parenting practices related to discipline, independence, and so forth

6. **Provide the family with information** in written and/or oral forms that enables family members to understand exactly what is being conveyed. Ensure that linguistic and cultural barriers do not impede this communication.

*Source:* Adapted from V. Correa, H. Jones, C. Thomas, & C. Morsink (2005). *Interactive teaming: Enhancing programs for students with special needs* (4th ed.). Upper Saddle River, NJ: Merrill/Pearson Education.

## Keep in Mind

Home–school collaboration is especially important for teachers in inclusive settings, but it is only one type of interaction teachers have with parents. Teachers often will be involved in providing information to parents regarding their child's academic and social development, legal issues that influence the child's special education program, and so forth. Teachers may also be involved in reporting and interpreting evaluation and test results for parents; encouraging and preparing parents to work as volunteers in school activities (e.g., working in an after-school tutoring program or participating in a school decision-making group); and/or providing training to build parenting skills (e.g., communicating with children, discipline). Of course, all of these activities are important and should be done while keeping in mind the step-by-step guidelines for effectively working with parents, and information related to working with parents from different cultural backgrounds.

**Key References**

Correa, V., Jones, H., Thomas, C., & Morsink, C. (2005). *Interactive teaming: Enhancing programs for students with special needs* (4th ed.). Upper Saddle River, NJ: Merrill/Pearson Education.

Cox, D. (2005). Evidence-based interventions using home–school collaboration. *School Psychology Quarterly, 20*(4), 473–497.

Fabiano, G., Pelham, W., Coles, E., Gnagy, E., Chronis, A., & O'Connor, B. (2009). A meta-analysis of behavioral treatments for attention-deficit/hyperactivity disorder. *Clinical Psychology Review, 29*, 129–140.

Harry, B., Kalyanpur, M., & Day, M. (1999). *Building cultural reciprocity with families: Case studies in special education*. Baltimore: Brookes.

Kochhar-Bryant, C. (2008). *Collaboration and system coordination for students with special needs*. Upper Saddle River, NJ: Merrill/Pearson Education.

Matuszny, R., Banda, D., & Coleman, T. (2007). A progressive plan for building collaborative relationships with parents from diverse backgrounds. *Teaching Exceptional Children, 39*(4), 24–31.

Patall, E., Cooper, H., Robinson, J. (2008). Parent involvement in homework: A research synthesis. *Review of Educational Research, 78*, 1039–1101.

Whitbread, K., Bruder, M., Fleming, G., & Park, H. (2007). Collaboration in special education: Parent–professional training. *Teaching Exceptional Children, 39*(4), 6–14.

| Strategy 10.7 | **PEER BUDDY PROGRAMS** |

## Rationale

As students enter adolescence, they spend more time with peers, increasing the influence of these interactions on their development (Carter & Hughes, 2005). Adolescents with moderate-to-severe disabilities benefit from peer interactions, just as other students do, while they make friends, learn social skills, and experience an enhanced quality of life. Unfortunately, even when students with moderate-to-severe disabilities are included in general education classes and participate in daily activities in a school (e.g., lunch), they often remain substantially isolated socially from their peers without disabilities. Thus, students with moderate-to-severe disabilities need teachers to intervene and facilitate social interactions with peers (Carter & Hughes, 2005).

Many middle and high schools across the United States have implemented peer buddy programs, which have proven effective in increasing social interactions between students with disabilities and their peers. These programs offer students the opportunity to earn course credit and participate in service learning, as they interact with students with disabilities in school, leisure, and/or work settings.

## Step-by-Step

Peer buddy programs are a strategy for promoting inclusion and "ensuring a positive experience both for the students with severe disabilities and their general education peer buddies" (Hughes, Guth, Hall, Presley, Dye, & Byers, 1999, p. 32). These programs may also be effective for students with mild-to-moderate disabilities. Hughes and colleagues (Hughes & Carter, 2006; Hughes et al., 1999) suggest the following steps in developing a peer buddy program in a middle or high school.

**1** *Develop a course that offers students course credit and an opportunity to fulfill service-learning requirements for participating in the peer buddy program.* This course provides time for peer buddies to spend at least one class period per day with their partners. The content of the course offers participants the opportunity to learn about persons with disabilities and gain knowledge and skills necessary for successfully interacting with and supporting their peer buddies.

**2** *Recruit peer buddies to participate in the program.* This involves promoting the program to teachers, administrators, school staff, and students. Students may be recruited in inclusive classrooms that include a student who would benefit from a peer buddy, or in classes where disability-related issues are being discussed (e.g., health, civics, literature). After the program is in place, peer buddies can provide support in recruitment.

**3** *Screen students who apply to be peer buddies.* Screening criteria may include good attendance (always a key criterion), an adequate grade-point average, recommendations of teachers, written applications, and interviews. Peer buddies should be willing to take the initiative and require minimal supervision, should be open-minded and tolerant regarding individual differences, and they should demonstrate personal qualities such as caring, flexibility, responsibility, and so forth. Keep in mind that peer buddies may not be the highest-achieving students, and students with disabilities may be peer buddies.

**4** *Match students with peer buddies.* Students should be tentatively matched by a teacher or counselor based on common interests, student preferences, and so forth. Students should then have the opportunity to interact, observe in classes, and clarify the role of the peer buddy to determine if the match is a good one. Students, teachers, and/or counselors should participate in making the final matches for peer buddies.

**5** *Develop expectations, and communicate those expectations to peer buddies.* Teachers should communicate expectations to peer buddies through an orientation session. Peer buddies from previous years may assist with this session. Expectations should address attendance, role and responsibilities of the peer buddy, and other program procedures and expectations.

**6** *Prepare peer buddies to ensure success.* Training sessions should address topics such as student information (regarding each student's peer buddy) and confidentiality, disability awareness, instructional strategies, interaction and communication strategies, suggestions for activities, addressing challenging behaviors, and handling emergencies.

# Applications and Examples

On the entrance to West Hernando Middle School is a quote from Booker T. Washington: "If you want to lift yourself up, lift up someone else." The school lives this quote in many ways, including its peer buddy (or Peer Support) program. This was illustrated earlier in this chapter as two students from West Hernando, Emma and Susan, described the benefits of their Peer Support program. West Hernando has 114 peer buddies, making its peer buddy course the second-most popular elective in the school. Students who serve as peer buddies include those with and without disabilities. Maureen Finelli, a teacher who directs the Peer Support program at West Hernando reports that these students supply teachers in inclusive classrooms with invaluable assistance, as they provide support during academic activities and build natural social relationships with students with disabilities.

Benefits of peer buddy programs are included in Figure 10.8. It is noteworthy that these benefits accrue not only for the student with a disability but also for the peer buddy, teachers, and administrators. However, the most important benefits of peer buddy programs are for students with disabilities. As Lisa Hallal, a teacher at West Hernando, noted, "We have

---

| Figure 10.8 | Benefits Associated with Peer Buddy Programs |
|---|---|

**For students who do not have disabilities**
- Friendships develop with students with disabilities.
- Knowledge regarding disabilities increases.
- Advocacy skills are improved.
- Interpersonal skills are enhanced.
- Expectations for peers with disabilities are increased.
- Learn from students with disabilities in areas where they are positive role models.
- Explore careers in human services.
- Experience a sense of accomplishment and personal growth.

**For students with disabilities**
- Develop friendships.
- Engage in more social interactions with peers.
- Acquire new academic, social, and life skills.
- Learn from age-appropriate peers in areas where they are positive role models.
- Receive natural, effective peer support in inclusive settings.
- Increase their independence and self-confidence.

**For teachers**
- Gain assistance to support students with disabilities in learning academic and social skills.
- Provide all students with more opportunities to socialize.
- Increase diversity in the classroom.
- Experience professional growth and personal satisfaction.

**For administrators**
- School climate and sense of school community are improved.
- Gain assistance in supporting students with disabilities in all school settings.
- Support efforts to improve inclusion and align school practices with school reform efforts and legislation related to inclusion

**For parents**
- Their children are more enthusiastic about school.
- Their children have opportunities for new friendships and increased social activities.
- Their children experience academic and social growth.

*Source:* Adapted from C. Hughes & E. Carter (2008). *Peer buddy programs for successful secondary level inclusion.* Baltimore: Brookes.

seen so many benefits. Like Albert, who now goes to the lunchroom. He never went to the lunchroom before. Now he goes with his peers, not his peer buddy. He gets to do what everybody else is doing. That's the beauty of it."

## Keep in Mind

Peer buddy programs have many benefits, but to realize these benefits, the program must be carefully planned and consistently supported. Students who have participated in these programs recommend the following to ensure success (Copeland et al., 2004):

- Offer activities for all students that increase awareness of students with disabilities.
- Ensure that peer buddies receive information about their partner, as well as training regarding how to provide effective support.
- Encourage friendships between students with disabilities and their peers, to increase participation in academic and social activities.
- Provide structures that support the peer buddy program. Sources of structure that are beneficial include a daily schedule of suggested activities, a peer buddy manual that includes information about disabilities, regular conversations with a supervising teacher regarding the peer buddy experience, and writing in a reflective journal.

**Key References**

Carter, E., & Hughes, E. (2005). Increasing social interaction among adolescents with intellectual disabilities and their general education peers: Effective interventions. *Research & Practice for Persons with Severe Disabilities, 30*(4), 179–193.

Copeland, S., Hughes, C., Carter, E., Guth, C., Presley, J., Williams, C., & Fowler, S. (2004). Increasing access to general education: Perspectives of participants in a high school peer support program. *Remedial and Special Education, 25*(3), 342–352.

Hughes, C., & Carter, E. (2008). *Peer buddy programs for successful secondary level inclusion.* Baltimore: Brookes.

Hughes, C., Guth, C., Hall, S., Presley, J., Dye, N. & Byers, C. (1999). "They are my best friends": Peer buddies promote inclusion in high school. *Teaching Exceptional Children, 31*(5), 32–37.

Westling, D., & Fox, L. (2009). *Teaching students with severe disabilities* (4th ed.). Upper Saddle River, NJ: Merrill/Pearson.

# Formal Plans and Planning for Differentiated Instruction

## KEY TOPICS

**After reading this chapter you will:**

- Know about four formal plans required for students who are at risk or who have disabilities, and know the general educator's role in their development.

- Be able to plan for differentiated instruction in a classroom with diverse learners, monitor student progress, use an adaptive grading system, and plan a classroom's physical layout to facilitate inclusion.

- Possess 9 detailed effective strategies to help you when planning to meet the needs of all the students in your classroom.

# chapter 11

# A VIEW FROM FACULTY AND ADMINISTRATORS

### Planning for Inclusion at Gilpin Manor Elementary School

If students are to be taught well in inclusive classrooms, it won't just happen magically. You should understand that by including students with special needs, you create a much more diverse population in terms of educational needs, which means it is not possible to plan for a homogeneous group. To meet the needs of all students, effective planning is essential.

Creating plans is an important part of teaching at schools like Gilpin Manor Elementary School, where inclusion is commonplace. You will find students with IEPs, some with 504 Plans, and others with "Student Success Plans." Kim Miller, the interventionist for grades 3 and 4 at Gilpin Manor, explained the difference between some of the plans. "An SSP is a Student Success Plan. It means that [a child is] having behavioral difficulties, academic difficulties, (or) a combination, but [the child doesn't] have a formal diagnosis . . . so . . . it's a plan just to try different interventions to see what works with this child." On the other hand, Kim added, "504 just means maybe [the child has] ADHD, a formal diagnosis, [or the child is] on medication—[he] could have a couple of accommodations and things." And of course, the IEP is the plan for students eligible for special education services.

In addition to these formal plans, the administration and faculty at Gilpin Manor realize how important it is to plan regularly for instruction to meet the individual needs of their students. Susan Huff, who teaches students in the fifth grade, acknowledges that good planning is essential. To be a good teacher, she said, it takes "content knowledge—being able to know what you're teaching then being able to adapt to meet the needs—and differentiate to meet *all* of the needs in the classroom. That means getting to know the individual child and understanding [her], understanding [her] disability *and* [her] capabilities. Not just 'Oh, that's a kid with ADHD.'" Jenni Hammer, the principal at Gilpin Manor Elementary School, reinforced this idea, saying, "Our county has a really big push over the next three years to really get deep with differentiated instruction." She added that they wanted to learn more about "what differentiation is all about . . . what are the philosophies behind it, what are the fundamentals, what are some of the strategies of differentiation and how do they work and then how do you manage a differentiated classroom?"

Although finding time for planning is critical, it's not always easy. Principal Jenni Hammer explained, "It can certainly be a struggle to find the time to have that collaboration. That's one of our strategies in our school improvement plan: collaboration. And to get as much time as I can—that's the challenge." But it's a challenge that Gilpin Manor tries in earnest to meet. Melissa Pratt, the pre-K interventionist, said, "I love my classroom this year because it's very

much collaborative. . . . In this classroom we're very much a team. We go back and forth—we're constantly, you know, modifying, differentiating things together. . . . Everybody's on the team in the classroom now, even the paraeducators, we're all a team, we all have a voice." Malee Taylor, the SLP on the pre-K team, added, "Good communication, rapport with your teachers, rapport with students, time to collaborate, that's the big thing. Here. . . we all share the same lunch and the same planning time." Without working together in this way, there could not be effective planning, and so there could not be effective inclusion.

# Introduction

If you are looking for effective ways to achieve important goals, planning is an absolute necessity. That is why, as the faculty members at Gilpin Manor explained in their interview, planning is critical if students with disabilities and special needs are to achieve success in inclusive academic settings. These students cannot be expected to achieve sufficiently unless their teachers make plans for it to happen.

Besides direct engagement in teaching and learning activities, teachers' most persistent responsibility is instructional planning. You are probably aware of your state's or school district's general curriculum or **standard course of study (SCOS)** and the grade-level curricular benchmarks that they include. Many of these are online, such as Florida's Sunshine State Standards (http://www.fldoe.org/bii/curriculum/sss/) and North Carolina's Standard Course of Study (http://www.ncpublicschools.org/curriculum/). Standards such as these provide the basis of what students are expected to learn. Planning allows teachers to use their knowledge, experience, and creativity to design effective instruction that will lead to the desired learning outcomes included in the standards. Most students with disabilities or special needs are expected to acquire the same knowledge reflected in the SCOS as students without disabilities, but, in addition, these students may also need to achieve other learning objectives.

## Pause & Reflect

Some teachers and other educational professionals think that schools impose too many "formal" plans that require too many meetings and too much paperwork. What is your thought on this issue? After learning a little more about the plans, decide if you think some can be eliminated.

Teachers may participate with other teachers and administrators in developing four types of formal plans. These plans will be for students who have learning difficulties, or who exhibit challenging behavior, or who have other special needs. They include *response-to-intervention (RTI)* plans, *individualized educational program (IEP)* plans, *Section 504 Plans*, and *behavior intervention plans (BIPs)*. In addition to these plans, teachers must create plans to provide *differentiated instruction* that can effectively meet the needs of all the students in their class, including those students with special educational needs. In this chapter we first explain the rationale and contents of the formal plans, then we address how to develop differentiated instructional plans that will meet the variety of aptitudes and abilities you are likely to find in your classroom.

Plans and planning constitute an important part of a teacher's responsibilities.

# Response-to-Intervention Plans

Today, planning for a student with special needs is likely to begin before the student is referred for special education services. Because many educators believe that every effort must be made to offer effective instruction in the general education classroom *before* a student falls too far behind, and thus prevent the need for special services, many school districts today use a response-to-intervention (RTI) model. (Some state and local education agencies use the term *response to instruction*.)

School districts use RTI primarily for two reasons. The first is to determine if a struggling student might be able to improve performance if a teacher provides more concentrated instruction. As stated above, using RTI means that schools do not have to wait until the student fails, but can try to prevent failure by increasing the intensity or directness of instruction. So, the RTI model allows the school to plan more structured interventions with students even though students have yet to be identified as being eligible for special education (Stuart & Rinaldi, 2009).

A second purpose of RTI is as an alternative means of determining whether a student really needs special education instead of, or in addition to, formal testing. Educators reason that if a student receives increasingly intensive instruction on key areas of weakness and still does not make adequate progress (i.e., does *not* respond to the instruction), then the student probably needs special education services (D. Fuchs & Fuchs, 2006; Hilton, 2007).

Response-to-intervention models usually consist of three "instructional tiers," with each tier requiring more intensive instruction and usually involving more expertise. Often, Tier 1 is considered to be what all students receive. It is presumed to be evidenced-based teaching that should be effective for the majority of students. If, through low performance or screening, it is determined that a student is not succeeding at Tier 1, then one or more Tier 2 interventions may be implemented. At Tier 2, the teacher may meet with the teacher assistance team (TAT; sometimes called a student support team [SST]) to discuss a more intense form of intervention, and this becomes the second tier of intervention, which is provided in addition to Tier 1. The team generally includes a special education teacher, a school guidance counselor, a school psychologist, and perhaps other specialists. The team designs a plan for the student or recommends an existing protocol (a strategy, material, and teaching process) for the general education teacher to implement. If, after a sufficient period of time, the second tier of RTI is not effective, then a decision may be made to refer the student for special education services, which is considered Tier 3. This is usually considered the final or uppermost tier in the RTI model.

The RTI model lends itself well to the type of cooperative planning that occurs in schools like Gilpin Manor, where teachers work together on grade-level teams. In a collaborative planning framework designed by Stuart and Rinaldi (2009), three key components were suggested: planning, execution, and feedback. During the *planning* phase, grade-level teams identify students for different tiers based on screening. This also allows them to identify the specific instructional needs of students and the evidence-based interventions to be used with students. Next, during the *execution* stage, teachers collect baseline data for students in Tiers 2 and 3 and implement differentiated instruction to improve students' weak academic skills. When the interventions are implemented, performance data are collected so that learning can be evaluated. Finally, in the *feedback* stage, teachers make instructional decisions based on students' performance data.

The response-to-intervention model has tremendous implications for general educators because they are the primary instructional agents delivering RTI instruction and must monitor student progress at Tier 1 and Tier 2. As noted, the general educator is supported by members of the school's TAT or SST, who will help in identifying the form of instruction and the instructional targets for monitoring. However, the general educator is expected to work directly with the student under the RTI model.

# Individualized Education Programs

In many cases, one can expect that the RTI approach will result in students learning adequately at Tier 1 or Tier 2, without being identified as a student with a disability. However, if this is not the case, and the student is found to be eligible for special education services, an IEP planning team must create an IEP.

An individualized education program is a document that lists the educational goals for students with special needs, the special education and related services the student is to receive, the educational placement of the student, and other important information. As noted, the IEP team develops and approves the IEP. The team includes professionals, the student's parents, and, whenever possible, the student for whom the IEP is being written. According to IDEA 2004, an IEP must include the following parts:

1. **A statement of the student's present level of educational achievement and functional performance.** The IEP must contain information about the student's educational skills and how they affect her ability to make progress in the general curriculum.

2. **A statement of measurable annual goals and, for students evaluated through alternate assessments, benchmarks, or short-term objectives.** These goals must be related to meeting the student's needs that result from the disability. The goals should enable the student to be involved and progress in the general curriculum or, for a preschool child, to participate in appropriate activities. The goals must also address each of the student's other educational needs related to his disability.

3. **A statement of the special education and related services and supplementary aids and services that teachers will provide to the student.** This part of the IEP must also include a statement of the program modifications or supports that educators will provide to the child. The related services and aids should allow the student to advance appropriately toward attaining annual goals, participate and progress in the general curriculum, and participate in extracurricular and other nonacademic activities with children with and without special needs. The services provided must be based on "peer-reviewed research to the extent practicable" (IDEA 2004, Sec. 614[d][1][a]).

4. **An explanation of the extent, if any, to which the student will *not* participate with students who are not disabled in the general education classroom and in other school activities.** The assumption implicit in IDEA 2004 is that a student with a disability *will* be included in the general education classroom, participate in the general curriculum, and in other ways be involved in school activities. If this is not to occur, educators must include an explanation on the IEP.

5. **A statement about the student's participation in state- or district-wide assessments of student achievement.** This statement must include any individualized modifications in the administration of state- or district-wide assessments that the student needs in order to participate in the assessment. If the IEP team determines that the student will not participate in a particular state- or district-wide assessment, the IEP must state why that assessment is not appropriate for the student and how the student will be assessed.

6. **The projected dates for beginning services and modifications.** These dates refer to services described in item 3 and their anticipated frequency, location, and duration.

7. **A statement of how educators will measure the student's progress toward the annual goals described in item 2 and how the student's parents will be regularly informed.** Parents of students with special needs must be informed of their children's progress at least as often as other

## Pause & Reflect

The laws did not always require classroom teachers to be a part of the IEP team; this requirement was added in a later revision of IDEA because of inclusion. You also saw that teachers were key to the RTI model. With so much involvement by general education teachers with students who have special needs, how do you think this should affect the role of the special educator?

Classroom teachers as well as special education teachers often must participate in IEP planning.

parents are informed of their children's progress. The progress reports must tell parents about their child's progress toward his annual goals and the extent to which that progress is sufficient to enable the student to achieve the goals by the end of the year.

## Section 504 Plans

Most schools and school districts have formal Section 504 Plans for students who, under Section 504 of the Rehabilitation Act or under the Americans with Disabilities Act (ADA) and the ADA Amendments (ADAA) Act of 2008, are considered to be persons with a disability *but* who under IDEA do not qualify for special education services (Madaus & Shaw, 2008). Students who qualify for services under Section 504 will have plans that specify any accommodations or adaptations that they need in order to participate in school activities. The Section 504 Plan ensures that schools respect the civil rights of students with disabilities who are entitled to accommodations so they can participate in school. Under Section 504, individuals with special needs, who are otherwise qualified, cannot be excluded from activities or services that are available to all others.

Because public schools receive federal funds, they must comply with Section 504. However, because a disability is more broadly defined under the Rehabilitation Act and ADAA than under IDEA legislation, many students in public schools who are not in special education may still be considered to have a "mental or physical disability" that "substantially limits a major life activity" and thus require a 504 Plan (Zirkel, 2009).

A 504 Plan requires first that a mental or physical disability be identified, and then the major life activity that it affects. Under the 2008 amendments, major life activities may include seeing, hearing, walking, learning, performing manual tasks, breathing, reading, thinking, concentrating, sleeping, bowel functions, bladder functions, digestive functions, eating, or a condition of equal scope and importance. A school-based 504 team must determine if the condition "substantially" limits one or more of these life activities and, if so, develop a 504 Plan. For example, a student who has asthma may not need special education services because his school performance may be adequate. However, he may still qualify for supports and services under Section 504.

If a student with a disability has been deemed eligible for special education under IDEA, and therefore has an IEP, the IEP will meet the requirement for an intervention plan under both IDEA and Section 504, and so a separate 504 Plan is not required. However, if the student is not in special education but is eligible for services under Section 504, then a 504 Plan *is* required. Therefore, Section 504 of the Rehabilitation Act covers all students with special needs, including those receiving services under IDEA and those who qualify according to the Rehabilitation Act (U.S. Department of Education, Office for Civil Rights, n.d.).

General education teachers often have students with 504 Plans in their classrooms or may have students who should have a 504 Plan. This teacher usually is a part of the IEP planning team, especially if the student receives instruction in the general education classroom. Strategy 11.1 provides some suggestions for being an effective member of the IEP planning team. Strategy 11.2 outlines procedures that schools usually follow when developing a 504 Plan, and Figure 11.1 displays a sample 504 referral form.

## Behavior Intervention Plans

A small number of students exhibit challenging behavior to such an extent that school personnel must develop a formal plan to improve the student's behavior. This plan, called a **behavior intervention plan (BIP)**, is required by law for students with disabilities if the challenging behavior threatens to lead to a more restrictive placement. For example, if a student in a general education classroom exhibits behavior that might require the student to be placed in a separate classroom or school, then educators must write a BIP. Most districts also develop BIPs for any student who regularly engages in inappropriate behavior. The general education classroom teacher is expected to provide information to help develop the plan

| Figure 11.1 | Sample Section 504 Referral Form |
| --- | --- |

Student Information

| Name: | | Date of birth: | |
| --- | --- | --- | --- |
| Address: | | Grade level: | |
| Phone: | | School: | |

Parent Information

| Name: | |
| --- | --- |
| Address: | |
| Phone: | |

Person Making Referral

| Name: | |
| --- | --- |
| Relationship to Student: | |

Reason for Referral

| Identified disability (if any): |
| --- |
| |

Treating Physician

| Name: | |
| --- | --- |
| Address: | |
| Phone: | |

Other persons who may have information that can be used in determining 504 eligibility (e.g., psychologist or counselor)

| Name:<br>Address:<br>Phone: | Name:<br>Address:<br>Phone: |
| --- | --- |
| Name:<br>Address:<br>Phone: | Name:<br>Address:<br>Phone: |

Permission to contact and receive records from the persons listed above should be requested of the student's parent/guardian.

| | |
| --- | --- |
| Principal/Date | Referring Party/Date |

and also is asked to implement the plan as carefully as possible in order to help the student improve the behavior (Crone, Hawken, & Bergstrom, 2007).

The lead person who develops the BIP is usually a school psychologist or behavior specialist who has training in the area of **applied behavior analysis (ABA)** and **positive behavior supports**. This person completes a **functional behavior assessment (FBA)** by interviewing the teacher and directly observing the student. Based on this assessment, the behavior specialist develops a BIP and reviews it with the teacher to determine if the teacher understands the intervention process and feels able to implement it in the classroom.

# Planning for Differentiated Instruction

Although it is important for you to understand and be able to participate in developing and implementing the formal plans we have just described, the most challenging form of planning a classroom teacher will face will be preparing for instruction in the classroom. As you think about planning for classroom instruction, think about how you would plan for an important event. For example, suppose you wanted to throw a party to celebrate graduation. Most likely, you would think about the following:

- Who will come to the party? Should I invite all my friends or keep it small?
- When will the party be? What time will the party start and when should it end? If I'm serving food, when should I do that?
- What kind of supplies will I need? How about food and drinks?
- What kind of music will people like? Should I have the TV on? Should I have a DVD on?
- How should I arrange the furniture, and will I need to borrow some additional tables and chairs?
- Should I try to plan some party games or just let everybody hang out?

Now consider planning for instruction in your classroom, where you are likely to have students with a diverse range of abilities and skills, including some with disabilities or special needs. Here are some questions you will need to answer:

- How big is my class, how many students have disabilities or special needs, and how might their personal conditions affect their participation and learning?
- Will the students with disabilities be in my class all day or part of the day? How will I fill the time with meaningful learning activities for them?
- Do I have all the materials and supplies that I will need to provide instruction and meet students' learning needs? If not, what else will I need? How will I obtain the materials I need?
- What types of instruction and learning activities should I plan? Will students be able to participate and learn like my other students, will they understand my directions and explanations, or do I need to offer some special form of instruction?
- Should I rearrange my furniture and other classroom fixtures in order to better accommodate them? Are different classroom arrangements necessary?

The planning processes we discuss in this section will help you address these issues and help you offer **differentiated instruction** to your students. Differentiated instruction is based on the premise that, within a given group of students, the range of individual strengths, abilities, and needs will preclude a "one size fits all" approach to instruction. Instead, differentiated instruction calls for teachers to offer students different ways to take in information, to process the information so that it makes sense to them, and to demonstrate what they have learned (Tomlinson, 2005). Strategy 11.3 provides a step-by-step process for planning for differentiated instruction.

# Getting to Know Your Students and Their Strengths

In earlier chapters, we discussed various categories of students with disabilities so that you might develop an overview of their conditions. However, getting to know your individual students, including those with special needs, will allow you to develop a much more personalized understanding of their strengths and needs, an understanding that will exceed categories and labels. Although the depth of knowledge that teachers can develop for each student may vary, ultimately, the more you learn about your students, the better you will be able to teach them. By reviewing students' records, including the formal plans discussed previously, talking to the students, and meeting with their other teachers, you will be able to learn important information about each student.

As you learn about your students, try not to focus only on their limitations or special needs but also on their strengths. This will help you develop a positive relationship with the student and thus become a more effective teacher. Tomlinson and Jarvis (2006) suggested five principles for teaching to student strengths:

*Principle 1: Teachers who see the strengths in students teach positively.* Many students with disabilities and special needs have strengths that are not recognized because their strengths are not in the traditional academic areas. Seeing students' strengths allows teachers to create instructional strategies that play to those strengths, like using a student's skill in art to prompt literacy learning. Also, when teachers see a student's strengths, they hold that student in higher regard and have higher expectations, and often that student will achieve more academically.

*Principle 2: Teaching to student strengths helps students see themselves positively.* Students who are challenged by certain academic tasks can easily come to the conclusion that they are simply not able to be successful in particular areas. If success can be achieved by teaching to student strengths, the student may come to realize that her potential is greater than what she thought.

*Principle 3: Teaching to student strengths helps students see strengths in one another.* When some students have weaknesses, others will sometimes tease, ridicule, or even exclude them from the academic and social structure of the classroom. This can make a student who is struggling feel even less able. If teachers can find a student's strength and help the rest of the class learn about it, the student who needs support may find useful encouragement and acceptance from classmates.

*Principle 4: Teaching to student strengths helps students see learning positively.* As interesting and well-designed as a lesson might be, some students will not seem motivated to learn it. However, if you can tie to the lesson or embed something within it that is of personal interest to the student, he is much more likely to see positively what you are trying to teach. This means, of course, that you need to spend the time to determine the interests of your students.

*Principle 5: Teaching to student strengths helps students overcome weaknesses.* Some students' weaknesses tend to dominate their lives. Whether it is a lack of academic skills, social or behavioral weaknesses, or a general lack of interest in all things related to school, their teachers tend to define them by these characteristics. However hard it may be to find, all students have strengths. Finding and reinforcing these early and frequently can be an important initial step in helping students overcome their weaknesses. As Tomlinson and Jarvis (2006) stated, "Teaching to student strengths does not mean ignoring weaknesses. It simply means teaching in a way that takes advantage of student power to energize learning" (p. 21).

Working collaboratively with your colleagues in special education, you can begin planning for differentiated instruction as you acquire important knowledge about your students, their needs, and their strengths. This planning should occur at different levels and at different times (Rosenberg, O'Shea, & O'Shea, 2006). We propose three key levels of planning: a strategic level where you focus on students' learning needs, a tactical level where you plan daily instruction, and an interactive level where you engage in moment-to-moment planning as you teach.

## Level-1 Planning: Identifying Students' Learning Needs

At Level 1, you consider what students are to learn, whether basic skills, such as reading, writing, and math, or specific content areas, such as science and social studies. During this planning, you should look first at the common needs of your whole class and then at the special needs of individual students.

### Focus on the General Curriculum for All Students

The general curriculum, or standard course of study, provides the basis of instruction for all your students, including students with disabilities. According to IDEA and No Child Left Behind, students with disabilities are expected to participate in the general curriculum. Therefore, as a general rule, you should always try to consider how you can apply the principles of differentiated instruction so that all students can learn the material you are presenting to the maximum extent possible. Depending on the nature and degree of students' disabilities, three critical adjustments can help students achieve successful outcomes in the general curriculum: accommodations, supplemental instruction, and modifications of the curriculum. (Note that if a student should receive any of these adjustments, the student's IEP must include them.)

*Accommodations.* Students may receive accommodations or special supports to facilitate learning, as well as supports for evaluation to determine their achievement on general curriculum outcomes. Instructional accommodations might include any number of changes such as using word processing software with spell checkers, listening to audio books, or learning and applying learning strategies. Students may receive testing accommodations for class tests or for end-of-grade or end-of-course assessments. An example of a testing accommodation could be having a paraeducator read the test to a student in order to assess his knowledge of science.

The important thing to remember about an accommodation is that it is not intended to allow the student to achieve an easier standard; rather, it is meant to help the student achieve and demonstrate the same standard as others. Therefore, teachers cannot use an accommodation if it changes the validity of a particular standard. For example, if a standard requires that a student orally read a list of vocabulary words, the teacher cannot read the words for the student. On the other hand, if the standard requires that the student demonstrate an understanding of a key concept in political science, then the student can listen to a lecture or a prerecorded passage about the concept and then verbally explain the concept to demonstrate knowledge.

*Supplemental Instruction.* Teachers can often improve the success of students on academic skills by providing supplemental instruction in key areas. This type of instruction usually focuses on improving

Planning for the use of different accommodations may help students participate in the general curriculum.

basic skills, such as reading, writing, and math skills. These skills would be taught to better help the student be more successful on advanced skills. Alternatively, students may learn to use effective learning strategies, such as note taking and organizational skills, to help them succeed when learning in content areas. Supplemental instruction is not intended to supplant other instructional areas in the general curriculum but to help students better achieve standard outcomes.

*Curriculum Modifications.* In some cases it will not be reasonable to expect students to master the same general curriculum objectives as other students, even if teachers provide one or more accommodations or forms of supplemental instruction. (This will often be true if a student has a more significant degree of intellectual or behavioral disability.) In such cases, the IEP team will probably indicate that the student is to take part in a state's or school district's "alternate-assessment" program. The student will be expected to demonstrate academic skills parallel to or an "extension" of those of same-grade peers, but qualitatively different in nature. A central tenet for making the general curriculum accessible to these students is structuring standards or outcomes within the general curriculum that have been originally developed for students without disabilities so that they may be achieved by learners with more significant disabilities. This process is referred to as *linking* or *aligning* the standards for students with disabilities so that they require a different form or degree of performance but are still based on grade-level standards (Westling & Fox, 2009).

### Identify Nonacademic Goals or Objectives

Although general classroom instruction must focus on academic instruction, some students' formal plans will also include goals or objectives in other areas and instruction such as improving social skills, self-determination skills, and personal-care skills. Level-1 planning, therefore, should include a review of students' IEPs and other formal plans in order to learn not only how the students participate in the general curriculum but also whether they should achieve other important goals or objectives. Strategy 11.4 provides a step-by-step plan for identifying the instructional needs of students with disabilities or special needs.

## Pause & Reflect

Today, the primary focus of education is to achieve important academic outcomes, and teachers have a strong focus on this goal. What is your opinion about general education teachers trying to help students achieve nonacademic goals?

### Person-Centered Planning

All of the preceding approaches to planning may be complemented by a process called *person-centered planning (PCP)*, which is often used to identify activities, daily routines, and learning outcomes for students with more severe disabilities. As the name implies, this planning process looks closely at the needs of an individual through the eyes of those close to him—family, teachers, friends—who then collaborate to plan an appropriate and suitable inclusive life for the target person. Person-centered planning is not a formal plan or a common part of planning for instruction, but it is a valuable process to learn about how a student with more severe disabilities can be meaningfully included in an inclusive community, school, and classroom (Westling & Fox, 2009). Strategy 11.5 provides a process for conducting a person-centered plan.

## Level-2 Planning: Preparing for Daily Instruction

At the second, or tactical, level of planning, you will write detailed plans for daily instruction. This is the most involved part of planning, but it rests greatly on what you learn during Level-1 planning. When at Level 2, your daily plans should cover the following:

- *Who?* Which students will you involve in the lesson? Everyone? A small group? Individual students?
- *What?* What do you want students to learn? What are your instructional objectives?
- *Why?* You should note the source of the objectives such as the standard in the state general curriculum the lesson will address.
- *When?* On what day and at what time of day will the instruction occur? How long will the lesson last?
- *Where?* In what part of your classroom (or elsewhere) will the lesson occur?
- *How?* What will happen during the lesson? What will the teacher, teacher assistant(s), and students do?

The plan will list all teaching and learning activities, including whole-class instruction, group and individual learning activities, instructional materials, and the kinds of educational or assistive technology that some students will be using.

Although no firm guidelines exist, to some extent, the instructional approaches you must plan for depend on the nature of the learning material. If you are planning to teach basic skills, you are more likely to incorporate some tactics, but if you are planning for academic content instruction, you might use others.

## Planning for Basic Skills Instruction

Successful basic skills instruction in inclusive classrooms often incorporates four key tactics: direct instruction, flexible ability grouping, peer tutoring, and the use of assistive and/or educational technology devices and programs. In Figure 11.2, we give an overview of these four components of basic instruction, and in Strategy 11.6, we provide a detailed process for planning for basic skills instruction.

## Planning for Academic Content Instruction

Planning for instruction in academic content areas such as science or social studies is complex when teaching students with mixed academic abilities. Unlike basic skills instruction, during which teachers usually can provide direct instruction to students with similar abilities, content instruction often presents a wide range of information that can be difficult to grasp for many students. Additionally, content instruction often relies on comprehending spoken and written material and demonstrating learning through written tests and papers.

Two strategies can help teachers prepare to teach academic content to students with disabilities or special needs in inclusive classrooms: using principles of universal design for learning (UDL) and using cooperative learning groups. These tactics are described in Figure 11.3. In Strategy 11.7, we provide a detailed process for using planning based on UDL principles.

## Selecting Instructional Materials

The instructional materials that your students use will play an important role in students' success. As you and your colleagues consider the selection of materials, you should keep in mind the appropriateness of the materials for students with special needs. The principles of UDL (see Figure 11.3) are useful when searching for materials. The Center for Applied Special Technology (CAST; www.cast.org) is an important resource for finding and developing instructional materials based on UDL principles. For example, in the online *CAST UDL Book Builder* section, you can "create, read, and share engaging digital books that build reading skills for students. Your universally designed books will engage and support diverse learners according to their individual needs, interests, and skills" (see bookbuilder.cast.org).

| Figure 11.2 | Key Tactics for Planning Basic Skills Instruction |
|---|---|
| **Tactic** | **Description** |
| Direct Instruction | Direct Instruction (DI) is a model for teaching that emphasizes well-developed and carefully planned lessons designed around small learning increments and clearly defined and prescribed teaching tasks. It is based on the theory that clear instruction eliminating misinterpretations can greatly improve and accelerate learning (National Institute for Direct Instruction, n.d.). |
| Flexible Ability Grouping | When teaching basic academic skills, same-ability groups are often very effective and work well with direct instruction. Same-ability grouping allows teachers to focus more intensely on what students need because students within the groups have about the same skill level and thus approximately equal learning needs. Ability groups should be flexible and used for specific targeted learning, such as acquiring reading or math skills. As students demonstrate adequate skill acquisition, teachers should move them from lower groups to higher groups. Ability grouping should not be full time. Students should spend as much time as possible in heterogeneous groups. |
| Peer Tutoring | Peer tutoring, and especially class-wide peer tutoring (CWPT), provides a useful tactic for practicing basic academic skills. CWPT provides students with increased opportunities to improve skills by receiving immediate feedback from a peer tutor. Pairs of students take turns tutoring each other to reinforce concepts and skills initially taught by the teacher. CWPT requires the teacher to instruct all students how to tutor, to give material appropriate for practicing skills, and to allow time on a regular basis (three to five times per week) for tutoring. |
| Educational and Assistive Technology | Educational technology and assistive technology can be used by students with and without disabilities. For example, assistive technology may include the use of word processing software to help students write better and more creatively. Educational technology might be specific computer programs designed to teach select reading and math skills. |

In a recent effort to make traditional text-based material more accessible to all students, CAST has developed the National Instructional Materials Accessibility Standard (NIMAS). According to the National Center on Accessible Instructional Materials at CAST (2011):

> NIMAS is a technical standard used by publishers to produce source files that may be used to develop multiple specialized formats (such as braille or audio books) for students with print disabilities. The source files are prepared using Extensible Markup Language (XML) to mark up the structure of the original content and provide a means for presenting the content in a variety of ways and styles. For example, once a NIMAS fileset has been produced for printed materials, the XML and image source files may be used to create braille, large print, HTML versions, DAISY talking books using human voice or text-to-speech, audio files derived from text-to-speech transformations, and more.

Ultimately, all material that is contained in elementary and high school textbooks will be available to students in forms and formats from which they will be more able to access and learn. Clearly, this will make learning for many students in inclusive settings even more successful.

| Figure 11.3 | Two Tactics for Planning Academic Content Instruction |
|---|---|
| **Tactic** | **Description** |
| Universal Design for Learning (UDL) | The intent of UDL is to create instruction planned from the outset and accessible to learners of different ability levels while maintaining high standards of instructional outcomes. UDL consists of the following key elements:<br>• *Alternative modes of presentation* means that you will plan for different ways to present content to students, so all students will have a better chance of understanding the material you are presenting.<br>• *Alternative modes of responding* suggests that all students will be able to demonstrate their understanding of the material in some fashion consistent with their ability.<br>• *Multiple ways of participation* means that all students can be active learners by engaging in whole-group or small-group discussions, participating on discussion teams, playing educational games, using educational technology, participating in learning centers, being involved in literature circles, or working individually on assignments. |
| Cooperative Learning | Cooperative learning activities, especially using the Jigsaw method (see Chapter 13, Strategy 13.2), involve every participant by providing each one with a unique assignment. Cooperative learning allows students with different abilities to participate in the activity and gain knowledge from it. The important benefit about using cooperative learning groups is that students can help each other and acquire more appropriate social skills. |

For the present, many schools may continue to use more traditional, text-based materials. When these materials are designed to improve reading skills or require reading skills for learning academic content, you should think about the appropriateness of the material for your students who have weak reading skills. Not all such materials that require reading skills are created equally, and some may be more appropriately designed than others (Sperling, 2006; Wanzek, Dickson, Bursuck, & White, 2000).

## Level-3 Planning: Interactive Planning During Instruction

The final aspect of planning is the dynamic creation of plans that usually occur as teachers present lessons and carry out activities. By the time you reach this point, you have carefully considered your students' current learning needs and have created written, detailed lesson plans that choreograph the actions you will take and the ways you expect groups and individual students to participate.

Most effective teachers will use a lesson presentation format such as the following:

- **Introduction.** Tell students what they will learn and why it is important. Motivate students to pay attention and do their best during instruction.
- **Review.** Remind students of previously learned material and show them how it relates to the current lesson.
- **Presentation.** Explain the new material (the concept or the academic skill) and probe students to find out if they are developing an initial understanding of the material.
- **Demonstration.** Show, tell, and give examples of the correct way to perform tasks within the lesson.

Teachers should be adept at dynamic planning to address all learning opportunities.

- **Demonstrate incorrect responses.** Show students examples of incorrect responses and the types of errors they need to avoid.
- **Allow practice.** Give students time to practice their new skills or use their new knowledge.
- **Provide feedback.** As students practice, reinforce correct responses, and correct incorrect responses.
- **Review and summarize.** At the end of the lesson, review what has been learned and summarize the important points.
- **Evaluate.** During some lessons, build in an evaluation process to determine student learning.

## Monitoring Student Progress

Progress monitoring is a procedure that allows teachers to measure regularly and directly how well students are performing on key academic skills. Curriculum-based measurement (CBM) is one of the most common forms of progress monitoring. Teachers use CBM primarily to monitor student progress in key areas, including reading, writing, and math (Deno, 2003). The procedure is based on a simple yet ingenious idea: If teachers can clearly define what students should learn (as contained in the student's curriculum) and create an easy, quick progress-monitoring process, then teachers can make frequent decisions about whether or not progress is occurring. With this knowledge, teachers can decide if their instructional procedures are effective.

Research has shown that CBM is useful for many current trends in general and special education. It is commonly used to measure student performance in RTI models, to determine if students in inclusive or special classes are making adequate progress, and to predict how students will do on end-of-grade assessments (Deno, 2003; Zimmerman & Dibenedetto, 2008).

Curriculum-based management relies on brief, frequent (weekly or biweekly), direct measures of student performance. Using material based on the curriculum in which the student is currently working, or using *general outcome measures*, on a regular basis, the teacher or a paraeducator will sit one-to-one with the student and give the student a brief test or probe. For example, the student will read for 1 minute from a grade-level text while the evaluator marks the words the student misses on a separate data-collection sheet. After the reading session is finished, the teacher will count the number of words read correctly and the number read incorrectly and record the student's performance on a piece of graph paper. Because a similar measure is taken every week from the same-level material (but reading from a different passage), the evaluator can monitor whether or not the student is making progress. If progress is on target, the instruction continues until the student reaches the desired criterion. The student then moves into a higher or more difficult level in the curriculum. If progress is not adequate, the teacher can examine various aspects of the instructional process and make modifications. (In RTI, for example, the Student Support Team may decide to move the student to a higher-intervention tier if progress is insufficient.)

## Pause & Reflect

Monitoring student performance is necessary if you are to really know whether or not students are learning. Are you familiar with ways to monitor student learning other than direct monitoring, such as CBMs? How would you describe them?

Using CBM, teachers can readily evaluate performance on academic objectives for students with disabilities. As part of their collaborative efforts, general education and special education teachers can arrange regular times and conditions to assess student performance. Guidelines for using CBM are contained in Strategy 11.8.

## Grading Students with Disabilities

If teachers use standard grading procedures for students with disabilities as for those without, then, as you might expect, the procedures almost always result in lower grades than other students receive. Traditional grading often reflects a norm-referenced grading system—meaning students are compared to each other—and fails to evaluate the student on other important outcomes such as the amount of effort by the student, the process the student used to reach a correct answer, or the improvement in the student's performance from the previous grading period (Munk & Bursuck, 2004; Silva, Munk, & Bursuck, 2005; Tomlinson, 2005).

When differentiating instruction for students, it is more important that grades reflect individual growth based on predetermined standards rather than reflect the norm-referenced status of the student. According to Tomlinson, "One might think in terms of reporting academic achievement related to a set of clearly defined criteria, plus individual growth along a continuum of clearly defined criteria, plus effort. . . . Such multifaceted reporting can provide information about a student's standing relative to criteria designated as important for a particular class, about that student's degree of progress from the start of the marking period, and about student work habits—three distinct but potentially important messages for students and their parents" (p. 268).

Many school districts have developed grading adaptations for students with disabilities that allow them to be graded based on different criteria. Five types of grading adaptations are relatively common (Silva et al., 2005):

1. Progress on IEP objectives

2. Improvement over past performance

3. Performance on prioritized content and assignments

4. Use of process and effort to complete work

5. Modified weights and scales

By using one or more of these adaptations, teachers may develop a "personalized grading plan" for students and document this plan in the student's IEP (Munk & Bursuck, 2004). Figure 11.4 lists the different types of grading adaptations. Strategy 11.9 provides an outline for developing a personalized grading plan for students with disabilities.

## Arranging the Classroom for Inclusion

As you undertake other parts of planning, it will be very helpful for you to consider the physical arrangements of your classroom and how they might impact students with disabilities or special needs (Wadsworth & Knight, 1999). Here are some of the more important conditions for you to think about:

- **Furniture arrangement and spacing.** Placing furniture too close together can make movement difficult for students with poor motor control or physical disabilities. Remember that all students and teachers need to be able to move about easily in the classroom; make sure there is sufficient space for them to do so.
- **Lighting.** Generally, adequate lighting is necessary for students to learn. Keep in mind, however, that some lighting, and the buzz emitted by fluorescent lights, may be quite bothersome to some students with disabilities. You should make sure all lighting is sufficient, have noisy lights replaced, and, if possible, create some space that uses indirect lighting.
- **Noise control.** Most classrooms can be expected to have a certain level of auditory stimuli. For some students, however, this can be distracting or even lead to challenging behavior.

| Figure 11.4 | Types of Grading Adaptations |
|---|---|

| Adaptation | Example |
|---|---|
| Progress on IEP objectives | *Daily work*<br>If a student's IEP objective states, "The student will use a strategy to solve math problems with 85% accuracy," then the student's use of the math strategy on an assignment with 85% accuracy might result in the student receiving an A on the assignment.<br>*Report card grade*<br>A percentage of a student's report card could be determined by progress on an IEP objective. |
| Improvement | *Daily work*<br>If a student raised his or her test scores average from 50% to 65%, the teacher could add the 15% that would allow the student to raise his or her grade from an F to a D.<br>*Report card grade*<br>A student could be given bonus points for each correct paragraph the student writes beyond the three paragraphs required. So, if the student attempted to write an additional paragraph, he or she could receive bonus points. |
| Prioritization of educational content and assignments | If you believe that one of the two social studies units being covered during the marking period is more important than the other, then the student will spend more time and receive more support on these assignments and they will count more toward the grade. |
| A balanced grading system: processes | Editing is a process that a student might use in the writing process, so a portion of a student's grade could come from the effective use of an editing strategy. |
| A balanced grading system: effort | An example of basing part of a student's grade for an assignment on the student's effort would be to base part of the grade for a math homework assignment on the number of word problems attempted. |
| Modified weights and scales | *Daily work*<br>A teacher could change the grading scale so that a student must earn 90 out of 100 points (90%), rather than the 93 points (93%) indicated in the school-wide grading policy, to earn an A.<br>*Report card grade*<br>A teacher could change the weights assigned to different performance areas by changing the weights assigned to tests and homework to reduce the penalty to a student who struggles with tests but benefits from doing homework. |

A well-planned classroom can be important for including students with special needs.

You can use book cases, room dividers, carpeting, and acoustic tiles to reduce noise levels, as well as set an expectation that students use "indoor voices" in the classroom.

- **Ventilation and temperature.** Although we all desire to be in a space that has a comfortable temperature, for some students with disabilities this can be even more important. Some students may simply be more difficult to manage in extreme temperatures; others may be physically sensitive due to physiological conditions such as hypothermia.
- **Visual accessibility.** As you arrange your classroom, remember that you need to see your students at all times, and they need to see you much of the time. Avoid placing bookcases, room dividers, or other structures that might interfere with making visual contact.
- **Materials storage.** In an orderly classroom, materials and equipment not in use must be stored out of the way so as not to be distracting. For materials that students themselves must retrieve, be sure that they are easily accessible.
- **Plants and animals in the classroom.** Many teachers enjoy using plants and animals for their educational purposes. If you intend to have live creatures in the classroom, remember that some students will need to learn how to interact with them and care for them appropriately. Also remember that you may have some students with allergies or asthma who could be adversely affected by live creatures.

These arrangements will help meet the needs of most students with disabilities in your classroom. In some cases, students with special conditions (either with IEPs or 504 Plans) may require a little more attention. Often, you can find help in meeting the needs of these students in your classroom by consulting with the special education teacher, the school nurse, or the occupational or physical therapist who works in your school.

## Summary

This chapter addressed the following topics:

**Four formal plans required for students who are at risk or who have disabilities**

- *RTI plans.* Students who are having difficulties but who have not yet been placed in special education may require RTI plans.
- *Individualized education program (IEP).* Students in special education require IEPs, which list annual goals, the types of services the student will receive, and other specific components of the special education procedures.
- *Section 504 Plans.* Educators prepare Section 504 Plans for some students who have disabilities as defined by the Rehabilitation Act but are not considered to have disabilities under IDEA. These plans list the accommodations and supports for students.
- *Behavior interventions plans (BIPs).* Educators write BIPs for some students who exhibit significant behavioral issues.

**Planning for differentiated instruction**

- Understanding students and their strengths is a key component of differentiated instruction.
- Level-1 planning requires the teacher to identify learning goals based on the general curriculum and individual goals for students with special needs.
- Teachers should incorporate accommodations, supplemental instruction, and curriculum modifications into Level-1 planning for students with special needs.
- Level-2 planning is planning for two types of daily instruction: basic skills instruction and instruction in academic content areas.
- Level-3 planning is moment-to-moment planning conducted as you provide classroom effective instruction.
- Progress monitoring is a procedure that allows teachers to measure regularly and directly key academic skills.

- Curriculum-based measurement (CBM) is one of the most common forms of progress monitoring.
- Curriculum-based measurement relies on brief, frequent (weekly or biweekly), direct measures of student performance.
- If progress is on target, the instruction will continue; if progress is not adequate, the teacher can make modifications.
- Grades usually fail to evaluate students with disabilities on important outcomes such as amount of effort, the process used to reach a correct answer, or the improvement in the student's performance.
- The following grading adaptations are relatively common:
  - Progress on IEP objectives
  - Improvement over past performance
  - Performance on prioritized content and assignments
  - Use of process and effort to complete work
  - Modified weights and scales

- Personalized grading plans may be created for students using different types of grading adaptations.
- The following physical arrangements of a classroom might impact students with disabilities or special needs and should be modified appropriately:
  - Furniture arrangement and spacing
  - Lighting
  - Noise levels
  - Ventilation and temperature
  - Visual accessibility
  - Materials storage
  - Plants and animals in the classroom

# Addressing Professional Standards

Standards addressed in Chapter 11 include:

**CEC Standards:** (1) foundations; (4) instructional strategies; (5) learning environments and social interactions; (7) instructional planning; (10) collaboration.

## MyEducationLab

Go to the **MyEducationLab** (www.myeducationlab.com) for *Inclusion*, where you can:
- Complete Assignments and Activities that can help you more deeply understand the chapter content.
- Apply and practice your understanding of the core teaching skills identified in the chapter with the Building Teaching Skills and Dispositions learning units.
- Examine challenging situations and cases presented in the IRIS Center Resources.
- Check your comprehension on the content covered in the chapter with the Study Plan. Here you will be able to take a chapter quiz, receive feedback on your answers, and then access Review, Practice, and Enrichment activities to enhance your understanding of chapter content.

# EFFECTIVE PRACTICES
## Putting It All Together

When you have students with disabilities or special needs in your classroom, there is no doubt that your planning responsibilities will increase, but this effort is important. Here are some things effective teachers say about planning.

1. **Collaboration is key.** In this chapter, we have discussed several planning needs for students with disabilities and special needs. As you plan to address these needs, you should seek ongoing input from your colleagues in special education.

2. **Get to know your students.** If you know your students' needs, their strengths, and their unique challenges, your planning is likely to be much more aligned with their needs. You cannot make "generic" plans that will meet all the needs of students who have such diverse characteristics.

3. **Be more detailed in the beginning.** You will find a lot of variation in the detail that different teachers put into their classroom instructional plans. As a general rule, the more complex the learning needs are of a particular student, the more time you will need to plan for those needs.

4. **Look to different sources for plans.** You can find instructional plans and ideas for plans in many sources. Attend conferences and staff development sessions, confer with your colleagues, take additional courses, and search the Internet to obtain multiple sources of information that will help you plan for your students with special needs.

5. **Save your plans, critically evaluate them, and make revisions.** Learn from your plans. Being an effective teacher will always be "a work in progress." Certainly, in the area of planning, you will improve with experience.

## Strategy Fact Sheet

In the remainder of this chapter, we describe nine effective strategies, which we referred to previously in the chapter, to help you plan effectively to meet the needs of all students. The *Strategy Fact Sheet* summarizes these strategies.

| STRATEGY | DESCRIPTION | IMPORTANCE |
|---|---|---|
| Strategy 11.1: Contributing to IEPs | Being an effective member of the IEP team is an important role for the general educator. This strategy offers several ways to help fulfill this important responsibility. | Understanding the required content of an IEP and students' needs will help you be a more effective member of the IEP team. |
| Strategy 11.2: Procedures for Developing a 504 Plan | Section 504 Plans specify accommodations necessary for some students with special needs. This strategy explains how a 504 committee designs such plans. | Section 504 Plans are used for students who have special needs but do not meet criteria for special education under IDEA. |
| Strategy 11.3: Planning for Differentiated Instruction | Planning for differentiated instruction can help meet the needs of students with different abilities. This strategy tells you common ways to vary instructional content and delivery. | Besides planning for how to deliver instruction, it is also important to plan how students can demonstrate what they have learned. |
| Strategy 11.4: Identifying Instructional Needs | This strategy will help you identify the learning needs of students with disabilities based on the general curriculum and also based on their unique learning needs. | Base instructional goals for students with disabilities on the general curriculum, but realize other goals may also be relevant to their needs. |
| Strategy 11.5: Using Person-Centered Plans to Support Inclusion | Person-centered planning is an alternative to traditional planning (IEPs, 504 Plans) that is designed to help identify ways for students with severe disabilities to be included in general education settings. | It is important for students with severe disabilities to be included; however, key people sometimes need to develop innovative ways to achieve inclusion. |
| Strategy 11.6: Planning for Basic Skills Instruction in an Inclusive Classroom | Many students with special needs will need intensive instruction in basic academic skills. This strategy outlines ways to plan for this instruction. | Planning for supplemental forms of instruction can help students learn basic skills. |

| STRATEGY | DESCRIPTION | IMPORTANCE |
|---|---|---|
| Strategy 11.7: Planning for Academic Content Instruction Using UDL Principles | This strategy discusses planning instructional content based on UDL principles in order to teach academic content to students with different ability levels | Universal design for learning provides a planning approach that makes it more possible for all students to benefit from instruction. |
| Strategy 11.8: Using CBM to Measure Student Academic Progress | Evaluating student progress is important for students with special needs. Curriculum-based measurement allows you to closely monitor students' progress and modify your instruction if necessary in order to improve progress. | Unlike grades, CBMs are quantitative measures of the student's performance within the curriculum. |
| Strategy 11.9: Developing a Personalized Grading Plan | Many teachers struggle with deciding how to grade students with disabilities. This strategy provides several useful options. | Parents of students with disabilities are often more interested in learning about factors other than how their child compares to others in the classroom. |

Strategy 11.1 | **CONTRIBUTING TO INDIVIDUALIZED EDUCATION PROGRAMS**

## Rationale

According to IDEA, general education teachers are required to participate as a member of the IEP planning team if all or part of the student's time in school is spent in the general education classroom. The law requires this participation so that the teacher can provide input regarding the curriculum and instruction used in the general education classroom.

Sometimes general education teachers do not like to participate in IEP planning meetings because they do not see the relevance of the process to their job; do not understand the terms, forms, and paperwork; and feel that they are not valued as a team member.

In fact, general educators have a great deal to contribute to planning an IEP. Under current IDEA guidelines, all students with disabilities are expected to participate in the general curriculum, and teachers are held accountable for their learning. Therefore, in order for students to achieve objectives based on the general curriculum, general education teachers should be considered as key partners from the beginning. Their involvement on the IEP team, then, is essential.

## Step-by-Step

**1** *Recognize the importance of your role.* Consider yourself an equal member of the team and a collaborator. General education teachers are expected to participate and contribute, especially with regard to issues related to inclusion and participation in the general curriculum. Many general education teachers feel that they need more preparation in developing IEPs. For this reason, we encourage you to take advantage of all opportunities for staff development in this area.

**2** *Become familiar with the terms, forms, and procedures.* Don't be intimidated by words and acronyms that you do not understand. If you have not developed knowledge through various learning experiences, ask your colleagues to be kind enough to explain the meaning of their statements.

**3** *Be prepared for the IEP meeting.* Your job will be to discuss the student's status and progress in your classroom, or to discuss the curriculum and instruction that will occur and how the student might participate. If the student is currently in your class, collect information and student work samples to demonstrate current skill level. Formal or informal assessments will also be useful. If the student is not in your class, bring examples of the curriculum and work that will be required.

**4** *Involve students in the IEP session.* Whenever possible, students should participate in their own IEP planning meetings. General educators and special educators can help students become involved participants by preparing before the meeting to identify and state their own goals. Available curricular material, such as the *Self-Directed IEP* (Martin, Marshall, Maxson, & Jerman, 1996), can help teachers prepare students for more active participation.

**5** *Leave with a clear understanding of your role and that of others.* After the IEP meeting, you should know the student's goals and how you will address these in the general education classroom. You should also understand the type of instructional interaction you are to have with the student and the support you will receive in the classroom. Additionally, you should know if the student is going to use any assistive technology or other special equipment or material.

**6** *Respect confidentiality.* The material and information discussed in the IEP and other meetings about students are always confidential. Remember to respect this confidentiality after you leave the meeting.

## Applications and Examples

Individualized education program meetings may be scheduled at different times but will generally occur before or after school or during a teacher's planning period if the teacher is expected to attend. Regardless, you should be informed about the meeting far enough in advance so that you are prepared and able to attend. When you learn about the meeting, you should inquire about its purpose (to determine eligibility, to plan goals, to review performance) and what you are expected to contribute. Then you should gather the necessary documentation, review it before the meeting, and make any notes to yourself about issues you feel are most important to remember. When the meeting begins, ask for an agenda. If one is not provided, or if there is none, ask the meeting coordinator to let you know when you will be expected to participate. Be professional, cordial, and attentive throughout the meeting.

## Keep in Mind

Unfortunately, many teachers and school administrators today view the IEP planning process with a degree of disdain, feeling that it requires an unnecessary degree of bureaucracy and paperwork. There is no doubt some truth to this perception, but a well-developed IEP can provide the basis for a meaningful education for a student. Your role in this process can make the difference in simply complying with the law and improving the quality of a student's education.

### Key References

Arndt, S. A., Konrad, M., & Test, D. W. (2006). Effects of the "Self-Directed IEP" on student participation in planning meetings. *Remedial and Special Education, 27*, 194–207.

Barnard-Brak, L., & Lechtenberger, D. (2010). Student IEP participation and academic achievement across time. *Remedial and Special Education, 31*, 343–349.

Jung, L. A., Gomez, C., & Baird, S. M. (2008). Designing intervention plans: Bridging the gap between individualized education programs and implementation. *Teaching Exceptional Children, 41*(1), 26–33.

Kamens, M. W. (2004). Learning to write IEPs: A personalized, reflective approach for preservice teachers. *Intervention in School and Clinic, 40*(2), 76–80.

Konrad, M. (2008). Involve students in the IEP process. *Intervention in School and Clinic, 43*, 236–239.

Martin, J. E., Marshall, L. H., Maxson, L. M., & Jerman, P. L. (1996). *The self-directed IEP.* Longmont, CO: Sopris West.

Martin, J. E., Van Dycke, J. L., Greene, B. A., Gardner, J. E., Christensen, W. R., Woods, L. L., & Lovett, D. L. (2006). Direct observation of teacher-directed IEP meetings: Establishing the need for student IEP meeting instruction. *Exceptional Children, 72*, 187–200.

Meadan, H., Shelden, D. L., Appel, K., & DeGrazia, R. L. (2010). Developing a long-term vision: A road map for students' futures. *Teaching Exceptional Children, 43*(2), 8–14.

Turnbull, A., Zuna, N., Hong, J. Y., Ho, X., Kyzar, K., Obremski, S., Summers, J. A., Turnbull, R., & Stowe, M. (2010). Knowledge-to-Action guides: Preparing families to be partners in making educational decisions. *Teaching Exceptional Children, 42*(3), 42–53.

# PROCEDURES FOR DEVELOPING A 504 PLAN

## Rationale

Millions of public school students in the United States have conditions such as attention-deficit/hyperactivity disorder (ADHD), asthma, epilepsy, or different physical disabilities that present them with unique challenges. They might need extra time to rest, privacy to take their medication, or assistance with personal needs. If their conditions do not interfere with their learning ability, they will not be eligible for, nor do they need, special education services as required under IDEA. However, because in our society we have laws against discrimination, schools must provide these students with reasonable accommodations in the school and classrooms so that their opportunity to participate like other students is not adversely affected.

A Section 504 Plan states the specific accommodations and modifications that a student will receive in order to have equal access to educational services. A school 504 Plan coordinator and an ad hoc committee that includes the student's general education teacher form the plans. All general education teachers, therefore, should be knowledgeable about the contents of 504 Plans and how they are developed.

## Step-by-Step

**1** *Identify the student who may require a 504 Plan.* Any student who has a physical or emotional disability, or who is recovering from a chemical dependency, or who has a condition that interferes with one or more life activity is eligible for a 504 Plan. Major life activities include seeing, hearing, walking, learning, performing manual tasks, breathing, reading, thinking, concentrating, sleeping, bowel functions, bladder functions, digestive functions, eating, or a condition of equal scope and importance. Sometimes students returning to school after a lengthy absence due to illness will require a 504 Plan.

**2** *Identify the 504 Plan coordinator and committee.* Every school must have a 504 Plan coordinator. This is often an assistant principal or guidance counselor, but not a special educator. If you suspect that a student requires a 504 Plan, you should contact the coordinator and complete a referral form. The coordinator should then form a committee to address the student's needs. The committee should include the coordinator, one or more teachers, the parents or guardians, and the student if appropriate. It may also include other personnel with specific knowledge about a student's needs such as a nurse or physician.

**3** *Participate on a 504 planning committee.* As the person referring the student, you should serve on the 504 planning committee so that you can express your concerns about the student's needs. Your focus should be on developing accommodations so the student can participate successfully in your classroom and elsewhere.

**4** *Develop the 504 Plan.* Members of the committee should identify the accommodations the student requires to participate in school activities. Examples of accommodations might include:

- A seat assignment to accommodate the student.
- A diabetic student may be permitted to eat in the classroom.
- A student may be permitted to go to the office for the administration of medication.
- A student's assignments or testing conditions may be adjusted (i.e., extensions of time, modification of test questions).

After developing the plan, all committee members are required to sign it in order to show their agreement with it.

**5** *Inform key persons of the contents of the plan.* Once the plan has been developed, it is important that all key school personnel are aware of its provisions. The plan constitutes a legal document, so teachers and other professionals do not have the option to accept or reject it. The provisions are mandatory, and the 504 Plan coordinator should make sure that all key persons are aware of it.

**6** *Set a review date to review and revise the plan if necessary.* As the plan is approved, it should be scheduled for review at a later time to determine if it is serving its intended purpose. The review date may come at any time, but it should not be longer than 1 year. When the plan is reviewed, if necessary, it should be revised accordingly.

# Applications and Examples

An example of the need for a 504 Plan might be a student with diabetes. Type-1 diabetes, also called *juvenile diabetes* or *insulin-dependent diabetes*, is an autoimmune disease that destroys the cells in the pancreas that produce insulin. Children with Type-1 diabetes require insulin shots. Without medication, the student may become very thirsty, need to urinate often, lose weight, and be very weak. Students with diabetes can participate in most activities with other students but need a few special considerations. They might need privacy to test their blood sugar and inject insulin if necessary, access to the bathroom more frequently than others, and have snacks more often than other students. In the case of hypoglycemia, the student may experience sweating, paleness, trembling, hunger, and weakness, indicating the need for emergency treatment. A 504 Plan for a student with diabetes lists specific supports in the following categories:

- Health-care supervision
- Training of personnel
- Student's level of self-care
- Snacks and meals
- Water and bathroom access
- Treating high or low blood sugar
- Glucose testing
- Insulin injections
- Field trips and extracurricular activities
- Tests and classroom work
- Daily instructions
- Equal treatment and encouragement
- Parental notification and emergency procedures (for a detailed version of a plan for a student with diabetes, see http://www.theparentaladvocate.com/sample-504-plan.htm)

## Keep in Mind

Most students who require 504 Plans will be able to participate in the same school activities as other students, given that educators provide appropriate accommodations. It is important for general educators to refer students for 504 Plans if they believe one may be necessary and to be aware of existing plans and their responsibilities under the plans. Failure to do so could have serious implications for students and teachers.

**Key References**

Madaus, J. W., & Shaw, S. F. (2008). The role of school professionals in implementing Section 504 for students with disabilities. *Educational Policy, 22,* 363–378.

U.S. Department of Education, Office of Civil Rights. (2005). *Questions and answers on disability discrimination under Section 504 and Title II.* Retrieved on March 3, 2011, from http://www2.ed.gov/about/offices/list/ocr/qa-disability.html

Zirkel, P. (2009). What does the law say? New Section 504 student eligibility standards. *Teaching Exceptional Children, 41*(4), 68–71.

## Strategy 11.3 PLANNING FOR DIFFERENTIATED INSTRUCTION

## Rationale

Differentiated instruction is an approach to teaching that is intended to meet the learning needs of students with diverse abilities. It allows teachers to consider different strengths and weaknesses of students and devise instruction based on these characteristics. The instruction is varied so that students can take in information, in various ways, use different approaches to understanding key aspects of the information, and express or demonstrate what they have learned according to their personal skills and abilities.

The differentiated instruction approach assumes that students will learn material to different breadths and depths, but it focuses on all students learning the most essential components, or the most powerful ideas, of the material. To accomplish its desired outcomes, differentiated instruction uses flexible grouping patterns; sometimes whole-class instruction occurs, and sometimes students work in small groups. Groups are never static but may change based on student progress.

Meeting the needs of diverse students during the elementary years is especially important because these young students form critical attitudes about school and its value. This is also the time when it will be most important for students to learn critical foundational skills.

## Step-by-Step

**1** *Get to know your students' strengths and plan to teach to those strengths.* All students may not be equal in all academic areas, but all students have unique strengths. As you get to know your students, learn what they like and what they do well. For example, some students may enjoy playing sports and others may like singing or acting. You can often use students' strengths to find an approach to instruction that will be most appealing to them.

**2** *Vary the instructional content based on student strengths, performance level, and need.* Consider the instructional content and how it might be quantitatively or qualitatively varied based on student entry level. The idea is not to change the essential aspects of the content but to offer it in different ways or degrees based on current student performance. Students must succeed at the building blocks of content before moving on to more complex aspects of the learning material. On the other hand, students who are more advanced should not be held back from more advanced learning. You will often need to conduct some type of preassessment to learn students' familiarity with the content that you are about to teach.

**3** *Vary the instructional approach, lessons, and grouping based on student characteristics and need for support.* The learning processes of students are diverse, and therefore different students need varying amounts and types of support. Teachers should consider how they might modify instruction, or create tiered lessons, and then group students for the different types of instruction to be delivered. Teachers may place students in a whole-class grouping for initial instruction and then in different grouping arrangements based on the nature of the instruction and learning activities. You will derive your knowledge of how students learn from your experience with the students and from reports of previous teachers.

**4** *Consider various ways for students to demonstrate what they have learned.* For some students, more traditional forms of assessment are the best ways to determine their mastery of content knowledge; for others, alternative forms of assessment such as oral assessments or reports might be more appropriate. The important point is that you objectively evaluate how well the student has acquired the desired content through a summative assessment.

**5** *Use formative assessment to monitor student learning.* Although it is important to know if students have acquired the necessary knowledge and skills (determined through summative assessment), it is also important to monitor their progress as instruction is occurring. This is called *formative assessment*. Through monitoring student progress, you can make decisions about current instructional processes and whether certain students might be regrouped for more basic or more advanced forms of instruction. Instructional grouping should be flexible and based on student needs, given the current learning context.

# Applications and Examples

The purpose of differentiated instruction is to maximize learning for each student based on the student's individual characteristics and learning potential. One way to do this is through flexible grouping. For example, a teacher can use whole-class instruction, small-group instruction, and individual instruction, grouping students based on current knowledge, ability, or interests. Care should be taken so that students are challenged to move beyond their current knowledge level but are always given adequate instructional support in order to advance.

One particularly useful approach to differentiated learning is providing tiered activities. The teacher wants all students to learn the same concepts and skills but provides different routes of access that vary in complexity and abstractness. Another way to provide differentiated instruction is through anchor activities, such as journal writing, reading, math games, or vocabulary skills. These are activities that extend the curriculum. Teachers may also use interest centers, learning centers, and learning stations as anchor activities.

A very useful way to provide differentiated instruction is by recognizing and using student strengths and interests. For example, a student may have little interest in learning about geography but may have a lot of interest in trucking. By using this interest, a teacher might find a way to help the student become more interested in geography. For example, the student may be more motivated in learning the cities and states a trucker may have to drive through if moving a load of furniture from Florida to Texas and calculating the distance between key locations.

## Keep in Mind

Differentiated instruction is meant to replace "one size fits all" instruction, but it is clearly a process that requires teacher time, thought, and energy. A beginning point is to examine the curriculum standards for your class, and then see how you might differentiate the content for students at various levels. As you work more with your students, you will come to better understand their abilities, strengths, and needs. Ultimately, you will become more proficient at maximizing learning for *all* of your students.

**Key References**

Broderick, A., Mehta-Parekh, H., & Reid, D. K. (2005). Differentiating instruction for disabled students in inclusive classrooms. *Theory into Practice, 44,* 194–202.

Levy, H. M. (2008). Meeting the needs of all students through differentiated instruction: Helping every child reach and exceed standards. *Clearing House: A Journal of Educational Strategies, Issues and Ideas, 81*(4), 161–164.

Tomlinson, C. A. (1999). *The differentiated classroom: Responding to the needs of all learners.* Alexandria, VA: ASCD.

Tomlinson, C. A. (2003). *Fulfilling the promise of the differentiated classroom. Strategies and tools for responsive teaching.* Alexandria, VA: ASCD.

Tomlinson, C. A. (2005). *How to differentiate instruction in mixed-ability classrooms* (2nd ed.). Upper Saddle River, NJ: Merrill/Pearson Education.

Tomlinson, C. A., & Jarvis, J. (2006). Teaching beyond the book. *Educational Leadership, 64*(1), 16–21.

| Strategy 11.4 | IDENTIFYING INSTRUCTIONAL NEEDS |
|---|---|

## Rationale

If students with disabilities are to be successfully included in general education classrooms, their instructional needs must be met in these classrooms. Some instructional requirements for these students will be like those of other students, but others will extend beyond common learning needs. Working in conjunction with a special educator, your ability to identify and plan for the instructional needs of students with disabilities or special needs is critical to their success. Most of these students should be able to participate in the general curriculum and show progress in it, but to do so, they may need to have special arrangements. In addition, many students with special needs may need instruction in other life areas, such as improving their social skills.

Many students with disabilities and special needs can learn in the general education classroom, but without adequate planning, students may be physically present but not succeeding as learners. The first planning step for successful inclusion is to identify students' instructional needs. This will require that the classroom teacher work with the special education teacher in a continuous, collaborative process to identify students' needs and then plan ways to meet them.

## Step-by-Step

**1** *Participate in the student's IEP meeting.* A good starting point to learning about the educational needs of a student with a disability is to attend the student's IEP meeting. Often, general education teachers are invited to these meetings in order to explain their teaching philosophy, curriculum, or the progress of the student if he is already in the classroom. If you have or will be receiving a student with disabilities, you can learn more about the student and his needs by attending the IEP meeting.

**2** *Study the general curriculum.* You should begin with an assumption that students with disabilities in your classroom will take part in and learn content from the general curriculum. Therefore, as a classroom teacher, your starting point in planning for these students is to study carefully the curriculum required by your local or state education agency for the course(s) and grade level you teach.

**3** *Identify learning goals from the general curriculum for each student with disabilities.* For many students with disabilities, you can expect that they will achieve learning outcomes like students without disabilities. For some students, however, it may be necessary to identify high-priority learning goals from the curriculum. Often, this is done at the IEP planning meeting in conjunction with the special education teacher and the student's parents. As you look at the scope and sequence of the general education curriculum, make sure you know the high-priority outcomes for each student with disabilities in your classroom.

**4** *Decide how students with disabilities can participate in the general curriculum.* Students will be able to participate more fully in the curriculum if teachers provide accommodations (e.g., listening to an audio book if unable to read), use supplemental instruction (e.g., improving basic skills or teaching the student to use strategies), or make curriculum modifications (e.g., learning skills or developing knowledge that reflects a goal in the general curriculum but that the student is more likely to achieve). Collaboration with the special education teacher can help you identify more ways for the student to participate.

**5** *Identify other relevant learning objectives for students with disabilities as listed on their IEPs.* Students with disabilities and special needs, although participating in the general curriculum in an inclusive classroom, often will have other nonacademic learning needs that adults should address. These needs may be identified by parents, special education teachers, or related services professionals such as a speech therapist. You should learn about these other priorities by studying the student's IEP and talking to parents and other professionals.

**6** *Create a classroom list of important IEP goals and objectives for all students with disabilities in your classroom.* A master list of goals and objectives for all the students with disabilities in your classroom, which is accessible and easy to review, will help you keep track of your learning priorities for these students.

# Applications and Examples

Before the beginning of an academic year (and in some schools, as the year is ending), many schools begin assigning students to their next grade. In schools where inclusion is commonly practiced, students with disabilities or with other special needs will be assigned to their classes. Sometimes this occurs as part of the IEP planning process so that the student attends a classroom that parents and teachers believe will be most beneficial.

When you know the students you will have in your class, special planning for those students should begin. You will need to consider (1) how they will be able to learn the same content as other students and (2) other special content they will need to learn. You will find that successful planning for these students will be best done through discussions with the special education teacher about each individual student.

## Keep in Mind

Sometimes teachers believe that they are not adequately prepared to teach students with disabilities in their classrooms, and sometimes this is true. The first step in overcoming this issue is to know what the students should learn. Once you have determined this, then your challenge is to find the best way to teach them.

**Key References**

Browder, D. M., Spooner, F., Wakeman, S., Trela, K., & Baker, J. N. (2006). Aligning instruction with academic content standards: Finding the link. *Research and Practice for Persons with Severe Disabilities, 31,* 309–321.

Garcia, S. B., & Tyler, B. (2010). Meeting the needs of English language learners with learning disabilities in the general curriculum. *Theory Into Practice, 49*(2) 113–120.

Levy, H. M. (2008). Meeting the needs of all students through differentiated instruction: Helping every child reach and exceed standards. *The Clearing House, 81*(4), 161–164.

Maccini, P., Strickland, T., & Gagnon, J. C. (2008). Accessing the general education math curriculum for secondary students with high-incidence disabilities. *Focus on Exceptional Children, 40*(8), 1–32.

Schwarz, P. A. (2007). Special education: A service, not a sentence. *Educational Leadership, 64*(5), 39–42.

Steele, M. (2008). Teaching social studies to middle school students with learning problems. *Clearing House: A Journal of Educational Strategies, Issues and Ideas, 81*(5), 197–200.

| Strategy 11.5 | **USING PERSON-CENTERED PLANS TO SUPPORT INCLUSION** |

## Rationale

Person-centered plans (PCPs) are viewed as alternatives to traditional approaches to planning. They provide an informal approach to determine the best approach to creating meaningful, inclusive activities and routines for persons with severe disabilities. They are called *person-centered* because they do not rely on legal requirements, nor are they necessarily based on existing service models. Instead of documenting an individual's weaknesses, they seek to plan ways to support individuals in natural environments, including communities, schools, and classrooms. There are different types of PCPs. Three that are commonly recognized are *Personal Futures Planning* (Mount & Zwernik, 1988); *Making Action Plans* (MAPs; Forest & Lusthaus, 1987; Vandercook, York, & Forest, 1989); and *Choosing Options and Accommodations for Children* (COACH; Giangreco, Cloninger, & Iverson, 1998). Although somewhat limited, research has been supportive of person-centered planning. Research on COACH has demonstrated that professionals and parents believe it reflects many best practices for teaching students with severe disabilities (Giangreco, Cloninger, Dennis, & Edelman, 1993) and that it leads to the identification of valued life outcomes (Giangreco, Edelman, Dennis, & Cloninger, 1995) and one study found that participating in personal futures planning helped parents be more involved in their child's IEP (Miner & Bates, 1997).

## Step-by-Step

**1** *Form a team.* The team should include the individual with disabilities, family members, friends without disabilities, and general and special education teachers. During the planning sessions, all these individuals gather in one setting to discuss the educational and life needs of the individual with severe disabilities.

**2** *Use a facilitator (often a friend or family member) to coordinate the planning session(s).* This individual begins by asking questions, encouraging open discussion, and writing down the key thoughts of those participating. The facilitator should be a good listener and one who can encourage interaction among those participating in the process. She is responsible for prodding group members to broaden their view of the community and also getting them to offer creative ideas that will allow the individual with disabilities to be a successful participant in integrated settings.

**3** *Seven MAPs questions can serve as a guide to the discussion.* These questions are presented one at a time by the facilitator:

a. What is the individual's history?
b. What is your dream for the individual?
c. What is your nightmare?
d. Who is the individual?
e. What are the individual's strengths, gifts, and abilities?
f. What are the individual's needs?
g. What would the individual's ideal day at school look like and what must be done to make it happen?

**4** *After the facilitator asks each question, participants are asked to respond.* Participants' responses are recorded by the facilitator. There are no rules as to what types of responses should occur. In fact, participants are encouraged to be creative, especially in discussing the individual's potential and future and ways to foster inclusion.

**5** *You should plan for 1 to 3 hours for sessions, and repeat sessions if needed.* The conclusion of the MAPs session is a plan for more participation and inclusion by the student with disabilities, which can be presented in a daily schedule.

## Applications and Examples

Many students with severe disabilities, even when in inclusive classrooms, are not involved in the daily activities of their peers who are not disabled. They may be in an isolated part of the classroom, or may be supported by a one-to-one staff member or a paraeducator. By completing a person-centered plan, different ideas may emerge that will lead to a student being more involved. For example, the student could be supported by peers to participate in regular curricular activities using assistive technology devices such as an augmentative communication device, could join peers during mealtimes in the school cafeteria, could be engaged more in extracurricular activities and at the same time work on social skills, and could work on ambulation and mobility during physical education.

## Keep in Mind

Person-centered planning is not a part of the legally required planning process, so it requires extra energy and commitment from key support persons if it is to occur. Unlike IEPs, PCPs are not legally binding, although they may be useful in informing the outcomes of formal plans like IEPs. Also remember that implementing the plans will take cooperation and commitments from several people and it may be necessary to convince them that these strategies are important.

**Key References**

Forest, M., & Lusthaus, E. (1987). The Kaleidoscope: Challenge to the cascade. In M. Forest (Ed.), *More education/integration* (pp. 1–16). Downsview, Ontario: G. Allen Roeher Institute.

Giangreco, M. F., Cloninger, C. J., Dennis, R. E., & Edelman, S. W. (1993). National expert validation of COACH: Congruence with exemplary practice and suggestions for improvement. *Journal of the Association for Persons with Severe Handicaps, 18,* 109–120.

Giangreco, M. F., Cloninger, C. J., & Iverson, V. S. (1998). *Choosing options and accommodations for children: A guide to planning inclusive education* (2nd ed.). Baltimore: Brookes.

Giangreco, M. F., Edelman, S. W., Dennis, R. E., & Cloninger, C. J. (1995). Use and impact of COACH with students who are deaf–blind. *Journal of the Association for Persons with Severe Handicaps, 20,* 121–135.

Holburn, S. (2002). How science can evaluate and enhance person-centered planning. *Research and Practice for Persons with Severe Disabilities, 27,* 250–260.

Miner, C. A., & Bates, P. E. (1997). The effect of person centered planning activities on the IEP/transition planning process. *Education and Training in Mental Retardation and Developmental Disabilities, 32,* 105–112.

Mount, B., & Zwernik, K. (1988). *It's never too early, it's never too late.* (A booklet about personal futures planning.) St. Paul, MN: Metropolitan Council.

Vandercook, T., York, J., & Forest, M. (1989). The McGill Action Planning System (MAPS): A strategy for building the vision. *Journal of the Association for Persons with Severe Handicaps, 14,* 205–215.

## Strategy 11.6   PLANNING FOR BASIC SKILLS INSTRUCTION IN AN INCLUSIVE CLASSROOM

## Rationale

The most common problem of students with disabilities and students who are at risk is a significant weakness in basic academic skills including reading, writing, and/or math. Students who demonstrate weaknesses in one or more of these areas at a young age often fall further and further behind their peers as they grow older. Without adequate acquisition of these skills, many students will have great difficulty acquiring more advanced knowledge and skills in academic content areas such as science and social studies.

Research has demonstrated that more intense and frequent direct instruction often can help young students improve basic skills. Direct instruction requires that regular scripted interactions occur between the teacher and a small group of students with about the same level of ability. Additionally, students will need the opportunity for increased practice, and teachers should carefully monitor their progress in order to make decisions about the level and form of continued instruction.

## Step-by-Step

**1** *Determine students' current skill level.* Teachers often assess the academic abilities and needs of students at the elementary level through end-of-grade testing or screening assessments. Using these assessments, teachers can identify students who are significantly behind their peers on academic skills. Teachers can then use individual diagnostic assessments to confirm specific weaknesses that will then be the target for remediation.

**2** *Group students into flexible same-ability groups for instructions.* Teachers should place students with similar strengths and weaknesses into small groups of five to seven students for instruction. The groups should not be static. Teachers should move students between groups as performance data indicate changes in their skill level.

**3** *Use direct instruction methods to teach specific skills.* Different formal, commercial instructional programs, such as Reading Mastery, use direct instruction methods. Determine the program(s) used in your district for use in direct instruction. Your district may offer staff development sessions that will help you learn how to use direct instruction. You will need to plan to spend 20 to 30 minutes each day on direct instruction with each group.

**4** *Supplement direct instruction with peer tutoring.* Class-wide peer tutoring (CWPT) provides extra practice time for students to work in pairs on basic skills. Pairs of students take turns tutoring each other to reinforce concepts and skills initially taught by the teacher. The CWPT process requires that the teacher must instruct all students on how to tutor and must give students material appropriate for practicing skills. For optimum success, CWPT should occur three to five times per week.

**5** *Supplement direct instruction with educational technology.* Individual students can work on developing basic skills by using educational technology. Many of these programs allow students to work on individually prescribed skills, provide a great deal of practice and feedback for students, and monitor students' progress.

**6** *Monitor students' progress.* Performance monitoring is important when focusing on basic skills. This process uses brief measures of performance (1 or 2 minutes) called *curriculum-based measures* to directly assess each student's progress. Schools using direct instruction will usually have probe material available to collect performance data. Performance monitoring should occur once a week for each student, but it only takes a few minutes per student.

**7** *Plan for skill maintenance and generalization.* As students show mastery of basic skills, teachers should advance them to higher-skill levels in the curriculum. Students should then practice previously learned skills in the classroom through different exercises so that the skills may be useful and applicable in different ways and at different times.

## Applications and Examples

In inclusive classrooms where teachers must work with some students on basic skills, there will typically be a time when small groups of students huddle with the teacher to receive direct instruction. While the teacher is providing direct instruction to one small group, the other students may be working independently, practicing previously learned skills, or working quietly on a group project for an instructional unit under the supervision of another teacher or an assistant. After the direct instruction for the small group is finished, the students return to the ongoing classroom activities. Another small group, working on different basic skills, then meets with the teacher for instruction. Once a week, such as on Friday, instead of pulling together the small groups, the teacher asks individual students to meet with her for a few minutes so she can administer a performance-monitoring assessment. The teacher records how the students perform on basic skills, such as sounding out letters, within a brief time period (such as 1 minute), and charts their performance on a piece of graph paper in order to watch their progress over time.

## Keep in Mind

Providing direct instruction, using CWPT, and using prescriptive educational technology can be very powerful in improving students' basic skills. The greatest challenge, however, is coordinating all such activities. This requires teachers to conduct a great deal of planning in order to have a smoothly operating classroom.

**Key References**

Deno, S. L. (2003). Developments in curriculum-based measurement. *Journal of Special Education, 37*(3), 184–192.

Glover, P., McLaughlin, T., & Derby, K. M. (2010). Using a direct instruction flashcard system with two students with learning disabilities. *Electronic Journal of Research in Educational Psychology, 8,* 457–472.

Staudt, D. H. (2009). Intensive word study and repeated reading improves reading skills for two students with learning disabilities. *Reading Teacher, 63,* 142–151.

Stecker, P. M., Lembke, E. S., & Foegen, A. (2008). Using progress-monitoring data to improve instructional decision making. *Preventing School Failure, 52*(2), 48–58.

Swain, K., Bertini, T. D., & Coffey, D. (2010). The effects of folding-in of basic mathematics facts for students with disabilities. *Learning Disabilities: A Multidisciplinary Journal, 16,* 23–29.

Viel-Ruma, K., Houchins, D. E., & Jolivette, K. (2010). Direct instruction in written expression: The effects on English speakers and English language learners with disabilities. *Learning Disabilities Research & Practice, 25,* 97–108.

| Strategy 11.7 | # PLANNING FOR ACADEMIC CONTENT INSTRUCTION USING UDL PRINCIPLES |
|---|---|

## Rationale

When students with disabilities or students who are at risk learn academic content, they are often at a disadvantage. They may have difficulty attending to lectures and discussions and comprehending important concepts; reading assignments and comprehending what they read; and writing reports or taking written tests related to the instructional content. For these reasons, many students with disabilities either do not successfully participate in instructional activities to learn specific content or benefit only marginally from their participation.

This situation frustrates many general education teachers. Sometimes they feel that students are not properly motivated to learn, and other times they feel that these students should not participate in general curriculum learning. However, neither of these is necessarily true. If academic content instruction is planned and presented correctly, many students who are challenged by academic content can benefit from instruction and accomplish a number of intended learning outcomes.

Using the principles of universal design to plan instruction can facilitate the ability of students with disabilities to participate in meaningful classroom learning activities. The principles of UDL require that you consider a variety of ways to present material to students, consider different ways for them to show what they have learned, and consider unique ways to motivate them to be engaged.

## Step-by-Step

**1** *Determine what students should learn.* Identify the learning goals that all students should achieve by examining your local or state general curriculum requirements for the content area of interest. What must students know and be able to do, and what is the order of learning? Decide the sequence of instruction and which learning goals students should achieve at what time. Remember the key elements of UDL. You will want to use *various modes of presentation*, allow *alternate modes of responding*, and encourage *multiple ways of participation*.

**2** *Design instruction that is flexible.* Your lesson should allow for a range of student preferences and abilities. For example, some students will require more concrete materials when learning arithmetic skills and some can use virtual materials; some students will want to work alone and some will prefer to work with a partner.

**3** *Present information clearly and in various ways to increase comprehension.* Your verbal presentations should always be as clear as possible in order to increase understanding by students. But comprehension can also be increased by using different media, including visual and physical displays, working with digital and hard copy reading material, clarifying difficult-to-understand information, and focusing on the "big ideas" within a lesson or written material.

**4** *Incorporate appropriate educational and assistive technology into your instruction.* There are a variety of instructional applications that can supplement your instruction. Many of these programs are well sequenced and provide direct feedback to the learner based on his performance. Also, alternative materials such as audio books, text-to-voice software, and video presentations may facilitate learning. The Center for Applied Special Technology (http://www.cast.org/) is a valuable organization where you can find materials that can be accessible for all students.

**5** *Allow different forms of engagement by students.* Students vary a great deal in how they best engage in learning. Some work well in cooperative learning groups, some in pairs, some alone. Some like to listen to a live person lead a discussion, others may wish to read the material independently, and still others may prefer to watch a DVD. Some students will prefer to write using pen and paper, others will use keyboards, and some would rather orally record their message or present information through their artwork. Consider how your students will prefer to engage in learning when arranging activities and allow enough different forms of engagement.

**6** *Use formative evaluation to judge student progress.* Although students may engage in different learning activities, it is important to make sure they are learning critical content. To do this, mini-assessments, or probes, may be conducted once or more per week. For example, in a social studies lesson, teachers may ask most of the class to define key terms in writing, but may meet individually with some students to assess their knowledge orally. It is important that formative assessment occurs throughout the instructional unit so that adjustments may be made in instructional procedures if necessary.

**7** *Use different forms of summative assessment.* Grades should be used to report multiple aspects of student performance at the conclusion of an instructional lesson. These are based on how successfully the student was able to achieve the criteria called for in lessons or by the standard course of study. The assessment on which grades are based can take different forms. As long as it is valid, the student may demonstrate her knowledge through writing, reporting, or in other ways. The grades might reflect not only the learning that occurred but also the student's progress and engagement throughout the learning period.

## Applications and Examples

The following is an abridged statement from an SCOS for sixth-grade social studies:

> The focus for sixth grade is on considering, comparing, and connecting those studies about the United States to the study of South America and Europe, including Russia. As students examine social, economic, and political institutions, they analyze similarities and differences among societies.

To plan lessons to meet this standard so that all students with disabilities could participate, the teacher might begin by thinking about the strengths of students and the materials and activities that would allow all students to participate. Readings, videos, and PowerPoint presentations could be used. Some students might benefit from digital reading material, such as that available from CAST, that could be adjusted to their reading level. Then various activities could be considered that would allow for different groupings and different kinds of involvement that would keep all students engaged. Considering the major learning outcomes, the teacher could then devise formative and summative assessments that would allow all students to be fairly evaluated.

## Keep in Mind

As you learn more about your students with special needs, you will learn more about their strengths and weaknesses. Your goals should be to find the best way to present information to them—and to all students—so that it is most comprehensible; to find activities in which your students will maintain a high degree of engagement; and to develop assessment procedures that will help you best determine what they have learned.

**Key References**

Basham, J. D., Israel, M., Graden, J., Poth, R., & Winston, M. A. (2010). Comprehensive approach to RtI: Embedding universal design for learning and technology. *Learning Disability Quarterly, 33,* 243–255.

Castleberry, G. T., & Evers, R. B. (2010). Incorporate technology into the modern language classroom. *Intervention in School and Clinic, 45,* 201–205.

Elder-Hinshaw, R., Manset-Williamson, G., Nelson, J. M., & Dunn, M. W. (2006). Engaging older students with reading disabilities: Multimedia inquiry projects supported by reading assistive technology. *Teaching Exceptional Children, 39,* 6–11.

King-Sears, M. (2009). Universal design for learning: Technology and pedagogy. *Learning Disability Quarterly, 32,* 199–201.

Kurtts, S. A., Matthews, C. E., & Smallwood, T. (2009). (Dis)solving the differences: A physical science lesson using universal design. *Intervention in School and Clinic, 44,* 151–159.

| Strategy 11.8 | USING CBM TO MEASURE STUDENT ACADEMIC PROGRESS |
|---|---|

## Rationale

Curriculum-based measurements (CBMs) are progress-monitoring tools designed to directly measure academic skills. The value of CBMs and similar progress-monitoring systems is that they allow decisions to be made about changes in instruction before failure occurs. Curriculum-based measurements use repeated measures of student performance over time in order to note progress in the student's performance. The measurement is based on the curriculum the student is working on. For example, if the student is trying to improve oral reading skills, the CBM measures oral reading; if the student is working on improving math computation skills, the CBM measures computational skills. The measurement is also direct. In the reading example, the teacher would listen to the student's oral reading and make a record of the words read correctly and incorrectly; in the math example, the teacher might give the student a page of addition or subtraction problems and record the number of correct and incorrect answers. Research has shown that CBM has a high degree of validity and reliability. A student's performance on CBM correlates with how well she will perform on standardized tests, on end-of-grade tests, and on other measures of academic achievements.

## Step-by-Step

**1** *Identify the students and the learning targets that are to be monitored.* Teachers can use CBM to measure the progress of any student on various tasks. However, CBM is most useful for measuring the performance of students with disabilities or students who are at risk on key academic areas.

**2** *Identify measurement materials to be used, and evaluate their technical quality.* The most common use of CBM is for basic reading skills; however, teachers can also use CBM to measure other skills, including writing and math skills. Some researchers also use CBM to measure performance on academic content at the secondary level. Several commercial measurement systems are available. You can examine several of these at the Website of the National Center on Student Progress Monitoring (www.studentprogress.org). At this same Website, you can also find information about the technical quality (the validity and reliability) of the measurement tools.

**3** *Administer the assessments, score, and graph the outcomes.* If the students have disabilities or are at risk, the teacher should administer the measures once or twice a week. Most measures take only one or a few minutes to administer. It is extremely important that the teacher administer the measures in the same way and for the same amount of time at each occurrence. Only in this way will the observed outcomes maintain their reliability and validity. The teacher records and graphs the results of the student's performance each time a measurement is taken.

**4** *Compare outcomes to target outcomes.* Many school districts maintain the norms of the performance of students without disabilities at the end of the year on the CBMs. If this is the case, the goal will often be for the targeted student to reach this point by the end of the school year. By drawing a line from the beginning level of performance (i.e., the baseline) to the desired outcome across the 36 weeks of the school year, and by noting whether or not performance is keeping up with the target line, the teacher can monitor whether or not progress is sufficient for a particular student. For example, the target line may indicate that every week the student should be able to read two to three more words correctly (see Figure 11.5).

**5** *Evaluate and modify instructional approaches.* If adequate progress is not occurring, the teacher should make changes in the instructional process. This could include a change in skill instruction, the amount of instructional time, the size of the instructional group, the instructional materials, the educational technology program, or the reinforcement strategies. When a teacher makes a change, he should make a notation on the chart in order to determine whether progress has improved. If not, then the teacher should attempt subsequent changes.

**6** *Continue to measure student progress.* Over the course of the school year, the teacher should continue to monitor the student's progress and make any necessary changes.

## Applications and Examples

Direct measurement should occur once or twice a week. As mentioned in step 4, the teacher should then compare the student's outcomes to the target outcomes. The teacher places the measured outcomes on a piece of graph paper in order to see the student's progress (see Figure 11.5). On that same graph paper, the teacher draws a line to indicate the student's learning target. By comparing the student's progress to the target, the teacher (as well as the teacher assistance team, the parents, or other key persons) can determine whether or not to continue with the same instructional procedures (if adequate progress is being made), modify the instruction (if progress is not sufficient), or move on to a higher target (if progress exceeds the current target). To create a CBM for a particular skill, the teacher develops brief oral or written tasks for the student that last about 1 or 2 minutes. Then the teacher (or an assistant) sits one-to-one with the student and gives the student the brief task (which is sometimes called a *probe*). For example, the student reads for 1 minute from grade-level text, while the evaluator marks the words the student misses on a separate data-collection sheet. After the reading session is finished, the teacher counts the number of words read correctly and the number read incorrectly and records the student's performance on a piece of graph paper such as in Figure 11.5.

## Keep in Mind

For CBM to be useful, the teacher must measure the academic skill on a regular basis. Then the teacher must examine the data (as presented on the graph in Figure 11.5) and make decisions about whether or not adequate progress is occurring. If it is not, then a change in instruction may be necessary to improve performance.

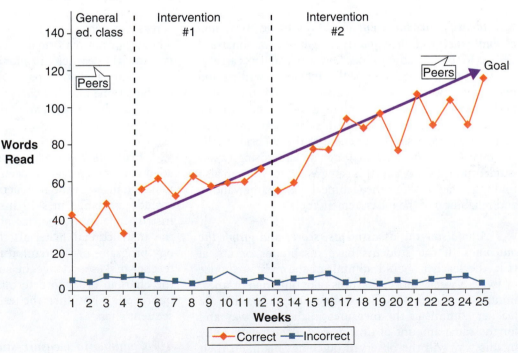

**Figure 11.5** Curriculum-Based Measure Progress Graph

**Key References**

Busch, T. W., & Reschly, A. L. (2007). Progress monitoring in reading: Using curriculum-based measurement in a response-to-intervention. *Assessment for Effective Intervention, 32*(4), 223–230.

Deno, S. L. (2003). Developments in curriculum-based measurement. *Journal of Special Education, 37*(3), 184–192.

Fuchs, L. S., Fuchs, D., & Hamlett, C. L. (2007). Using curriculum-based measurement to inform reading instruction. *Reading and Writing: An Interdisciplinary Journal, 20*(6), 553–567.

Stecker, P. M., Lembke, E. S., & Foegen, A. (2008). Using progress-monitoring data to improve instructional decision making. *Preventing School Failure, 52*(2), 48–58.

| Strategy 11.9 | DEVELOPING A PERSONALIZED GRADING PLAN |

## Rationale and Research

Many students with disabilities will not earn acceptable grades based on traditional grading systems. Their daily grades and report cards will often indicate that they have failed or at least are below average in their performance. Most grades used in public schools are assumed to be norm-referenced; that is, the grades report the status of a student on a particular academic skill in relation to other students. Those who are well above the average earn an A or a B; those below earn a D or an F.

It stands to reason that most students with disabilities or students who are at risk will have below-average grades when considering the population of all of the students in a school. If they did not, it is doubtful that they would be designated with disabilities or at risk. Therefore, what useful purpose comes from giving them a grade based on their performance as it relates to other students, when that grade is usually already highly predictable? Such grades not only tell us little about the students or their work but they can also serve to reduce the students' confidence and punish their efforts to achieve standards that may be very challenging for them. For all of these reasons, educators have developed personalized grading plans (PGPs).

## Step-by-Step

**1** *Review school district policies on adaptive grading.* Many school districts have developed clearly articulated adapted grading standards for students with disabilities. You should inquire about these and determine processes used for grading before giving students assignments that you will evaluate. If the school district does not have its own adapted grading policies, you may work with your school administration and fellow teachers if you think one is necessary.

**2** *Decide if adaptive grading is necessary.* If teachers can provide accommodations or supports in curriculum and instruction for students with disabilities, adaptive grading may not be necessary. The teacher should discuss this issue with the other teachers, parents, and students, who may feel that the playing field has already been sufficiently leveled and no change to the grading process for other students is necessary.

**3** *Decide on the purposes of grading.* Teachers, parents, and students should discuss what they believe grades should mean and come to a common understanding about their meaning. Unless all can agree on what information a grade should convey, then it will be difficult to create a personalized grading plan for a student.

**4** *Examine learner characteristics in the context of classroom demands.* It is important to know the requirements in the classroom that will be especially challenging to the student, given her particular strengths and weaknesses. One outcome of this process may be the identification of an accommodation that might help the student succeed in areas that are known to be difficult.

**5** *Review current class-wide grading practices, and decide if a grading adaptation would be helpful.* By knowing about specific student weaknesses and the class-wide grading practices for forthcoming assignments, teachers, parents, and students can determine their probable impact on the students' grades. If the impact is significant, they may then decide that adaptive grading would be appropriate, in that it might lead to a higher and more meaningful grade.

**6** *Determine the grading adaptation to be used.* A PGP may include adaptations in grading both for individual daily work and assignments, and for report cards. Adaptations may vary depending on what is agreed on, but the most commonly used PGPs base grades on (a) progress on specific IEP objectives; (b) improvement in performance over time; (c) performance on select, prioritized content and assignments; (d) correct procedure use despite an incomplete assignment or test or, similarly, demonstration of a high level of effort although not achieving a desired outcome; or (e) a modified grading scale.

## Applications and Examples

When many students with disabilities advance to more rigorous subject matter, they have difficulty—not because of the material, but because they lack some of the basic skills necessary to perform well. For example, a student in an eighth-grade Algebra I class might have insufficient basic arithmetic skills (memorization of basic facts in addition, subtraction, multiplication, and division). One approach to this problem is to provide the student with a calculator (an accommodation) so that he could work the more complex math problems without relying on memorized facts. However, as trends change, many math teachers are now moving away from the use of such devices, and even though the student has a unique need, the teacher might not feel that the calculator is the answer.

A teacher might develop a PGP that incorporates two adaptations. For example, the teacher could grade based on the extra effort of the student to learn basic math facts during the year, so the student could apply those to the algebra problems. The teacher could also reduce the number of problems required until the student's speed became more comparable to other students'.

## Keep in Mind

The IEP team must specify grading adaptations on an IEP, and grading adaptations should coincide with other curricular and instructional adaptations. In the preceding case, a calculator may have actually eliminated the need for an adaptive grading plan. It is also important at the secondary level to consider postsecondary plans of the student. Grading adaptations will not be recognized by some postsecondary institutions. Finally, it is important to keep the issue of fairness in mind. If the adaptation is viewed as creating an unfair advantage for the student, it will not be well accepted.

**Key References**

Bursuck, W. D., Munk, D. D., & Olson, M. M. (1999). The fairness of report card grading adaptations: What do students with and without learning disabilities think? *Remedial and Special Education, 20*(2), 84–92, 105.

Munk, D. D., & Bursuck, W. D. (1998). Report card grading adaptations for students with disabilities: Types and acceptability. *Intervention in School and Clinic, 33*, 306–308.

Munk, D. D., & Bursuck, W. D. (2001). Preliminary findings on personalized grading plans for middle school students with learning disabilities. *Exceptional Children, 67*, 211–234.

Munk, D. D., & Bursuck, W. D. (2004). Personalized grading plans: A systematic approach to making the grades of included students more accurate and meaningful. *Focus on Exceptional Children, 36*(9), 1–11.

Silva, M., Munk, D. D., & Bursuck, W. D. (2005). Grading adaptations for students with disabilities. *Intervention in School and Clinic, 41*(2), 87–98.

Tomlinson, C. A. (2005). Grading and differentiation: Paradox or good practice? *Theory into Practice, 44*, 262–269.

# Effective Practices for Students from Diverse Backgrounds

## KEY TOPICS

**After reading this chapter you will:**

- Know what to expect with regard to cultural and linguistic diversity in public school classrooms.

- Be able to describe the principles and practices that support effective instruction in culturally responsive classrooms.

- Understand a series of guided, step-by-step interventions and practices to help you meet the needs of students from diverse backgrounds in your classroom.

# chapter 12

## A VIEW FROM THE TEACHER

### Navigating Cultural Responsiveness at Heritage High School

Melanie Buckley knows that cultural diversity is not just an urban issue. As an English teacher and department chair at Heritage High School in suburban (some may even say rural) Leesburg, Virginia, Melanie has observed that too many students from culturally and linguistically diverse (CLD) backgrounds have difficulty meeting academic and behavioral standards. This is a major challenge: Approximately 45% of the Heritage student population comes from CLD backgrounds, with substantial numbers of students (over 10%) from Hispanic, African American, and Asian backgrounds.

Melanie has considerable teaching experience at both the high school and community college levels. Her experience has taught her that "all teachers must be culturally aware and culturally responsive. This means that teachers must be cognizant of their students' lives outside of school, actively learning of their varied cultural backgrounds and the media-saturated popular culture contexts in which they live." She and her team have initiated a number of professional development activities to assist teachers at Heritage. These activities—known as *purposeful pedagogy*—have helped teachers connect elements of the secondary curriculum to the lives of their students from CLD backgrounds. One of the curriculum development sessions, "Beyond Dead White Men and Why You Should Diversify Your Literature Curriculum," was useful and popular with the faculty of the English department.

Melanie recognizes that professional development for teachers must be supplemented by specific actions that engage students and families from culturally and linguistically diverse backgrounds. Recognizing that school personnel need consistent family support to address the learning needs of their students, Melanie and the Heritage team developed "Success Nights," a strategy to involve families that had a history of limited contact with the school. To engage these families, the team used Success Nights to recognize the accomplishments of students and showcase how modest achievements could serve as a foundation for greater academic and social success. In addition to recognizing student accomplishments, guest speakers presented important topical information in an accessible, jargon-free fashion. Instead of being formal and authoritative, Success Nights were social occasions for community team building and letting families know that their input was welcome and needed by the school faculty and administration.

Melanie and her colleagues know that being culturally responsive requires problem solving and experimentation. For example, after reviewing the Heritage standardized test data, it was discovered that a disproportionately high number of students from the English language learner subgroup did not achieve acceptable levels of academic performance. Recognizing that merely assigning more work would not address the challenge, Melanie and the Heritage team wrote a grant

proposal to examine various ways of motivating this group of learners. A similar group process was used to devise a series of ways to increase homework completion among these same students.

Melanie recognizes that far too many students from diverse backgrounds struggle to meet academic expectations. This results in an achievement gap between these students and European American students and higher dropout rates and special education placements for students from CLD backgrounds. Through understanding, reflection, and creative experimentation, Heritage High School remains committed to navigating the intersection of ethnicity, language, and disability, and enhancing cultural responsiveness across all aspects of the school community.

**MyEducationLab**
Visit the MyEducationLab for *Inclusion* to enhance your understanding of chapter concepts with a personalized Study Plan. You'll also have the opportunity to hone your teaching skills through video and case-based Assignments and Activities, Building Teaching Skills and Disposition lessons, and IRIS Case Studies.

# Introduction

Imagine that you are about to begin working in an inclusive school with students who are from diverse backgrounds. In most schools, you will have a significant number of students who come from homes of poverty, and many students of color. Unfortunately, as Melanie Buckley observed in the opening vignette for this chapter, many of these students likely will be behind in both reading and/or mathematics on state assessments (NCES, 2010). Some of these students will be learning English as a second language, others will have disabilities, and some will qualify for gifted and talented programs. Such a diverse classroom context challenges the skills of any teacher who is committed to ensuring that all students achieve at high levels. Success will require finding ways to engage students who may be resistant to learning. Success will also require meeting the individual needs of each student with special needs and finding ways to communicate with students and families whose backgrounds vary considerably from yours.

There is a widespread misconception that diverse schools exist only in urban settings. Heritage High School, in Leesburg, Virginia, is one of many schools that suggest otherwise. In fact, the population of the United States is changing rapidly and dramatically, and understanding the needs of **culturally and linguistically diverse (CLD)** learners is critical to the success of teachers in all settings, particularly teachers with a commitment to inclusive education. Indeed, students with disabilities are just as diverse as—and in some cases more so than—the general population of students. Many students with disabilities are thus from diverse **cultures** and **ethnic groups** (i.e., non-European American backgrounds, where **standard English** is often not spoken in the home), as well as from low-income families.

To better meet the needs of students with disabilities from diverse backgrounds within inclusive schools and classrooms, all teachers should:

- Understand their students' cultural and language backgrounds.
- Learn how they can adapt their teaching based on information about students' cultural and language backgrounds.
- Provide supports to ensure each student's success, and that each student is involved as an active participant in the academic and social community of the school (Banks et al., 2005; Gay, 2010; Ginsburg, 2005; Irvine, 2002).

In this chapter, we begin with a description of students from diverse backgrounds, and what you can expect as you teach these students in an inclusive classroom. Understanding your own background provides a context for reading about and understanding the experiences of students from diverse backgrounds that we discuss in this chapter. Before reading the rest of the chapter, take a moment to reflect on your background in the "Pause & Reflect" exercise.

## Pause & Reflect

Our choice of the words we use to describe ourselves is one way we define our identity. Take a moment and list every word that you would use to describe yourself. Include words that define your physical characteristics, but be sure to go beyond that and list words that describe who you are and the various roles you play. Share your list with a peer, and discuss your commonalities and differences.

# Students from Diverse Backgrounds: What to Expect

Are today's students different from the students who entered school 15 to 20 years ago? Are schools more diverse? To answer these questions we'll need to examine how individual characteristics of the student population have changed and continue to change.

## What to Expect Regarding Student Diversity

Students with disabilities come from a diverse range of cultural, language, and ethnic backgrounds.

Throughout the history of the United States, a substantial majority of the population has been European American (although we use this term, the U.S. Census Bureau and the U.S. Department of Education use the term *non-Hispanic Whites*). This is rapidly changing, especially among school-aged students. Currently, just over 25% of all students are European American in California (NCES, 2010). In nine other states (Arizona, Florida, Georgia, Hawaii, Louisiana, Maryland, Nevada, New Mexico, and Texas), the majority of students are from non-European American backgrounds. Many other states have a large proportion of students from non-European American backgrounds, as about 45% of all students are from diverse backgrounds.

The number of students who speak a language other than English at home continues to increase rapidly across the United States. Today, 1 of every 5 school-aged students (almost 11 million students) speaks a language other than English when they are at home, and about 1 in 10 students is designated as an **English-language learner (ELL)** and entitled to general educational services to address his limited-English proficiency (LEP) (NCES, 2010). As the number of second-language learners increases, the need for services will also increase, and the majority of teachers entering the profession will need to be prepared to meet those students' needs. Indeed, this is already true in some states. For example, in Florida, all teachers are required to have proficiency in addressing the needs of students who are English-language learners.

The poverty rates in the United States may surprise you. About 15 million children under 18 years of age live in families with incomes below the federal poverty level (Chau, Thampi, & Wright, 2010), an increase of 33% since 2000. Even more problematic is how ethnicity is intertwined with poverty, as disproportional percentages of African American, Hispanic, and American Indian children live in poor families (Chau, Thampi, & Wright, 2010). Figure 12.1 gives additional information on ethnic disparities in poverty rates.

## What to Expect Regarding Diversity in Special Education

Understanding the intersection of ethnicity, language, and disability is important, but this issue goes deeper than

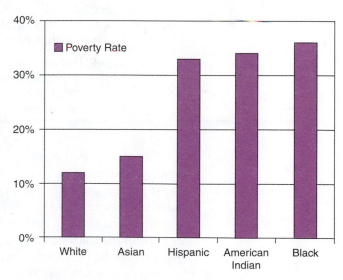

Figure 12.1

Statistics on Children Living in Poverty by Ethnicity in 2009

*Source:* Data from M. Chau, K. Thampi, & V. Wight (2010). Basic facts about low-income children, 2009. The National Center for Children in Poverty. Retrieved January 10, 2011, from http://www.nccp.org/publications/pub_975.html

## Just the Facts

### About Student Diversity and Disability

| What percentage of school-aged students in the United States are from different ethnic groups? | European American 55%<br>Hispanic 21.5%<br>African American 17%<br>Asian/Pacific Islander 5%<br>American Indian/Alaska Native 1% |
| --- | --- |
| What is the prevalence of disability by diversity factors? That is, what percentage of all students from each group is identified with a disability? | • Homeless 30 to 40%<br>• Foster care 16%<br>• English-language learner 8%<br>• American Indian/Alaska Native 12.5%<br>• African American 11.3%<br>• Hispanic 8.6%<br>• European American 7.7%<br>• Asian/Pacific Islander 4.5% |
| Are there differences in ethnicity by disability category? | • Substantially more African American and American Indian/Alaska Native students are identified with disabilities than are students from other ethnic groups.<br>• African American and American Indian/Alaska Native students are overrepresented in the categories of intellectual disability, learning disability, and emotional and behavioral disabilities. |
| How do graduate and dropout rates compare for different ethnic groups? | • Overall, 52% of students with disabilities graduate with a regular diploma. This includes 61.5% of European Americans, 39.2% of African Americans, 47.1% of Hispanics, and 49.4% of American Indian/Alaska Natives. The dropout rate for students with disabilities by ethnic background is 4.8% of European American students, compared to 14.6% of American Indian/Alaska Native students, 9.9% of African American students, and 18.3% of Hispanic students. |
| Where are students educated? | • African American students with disabilities are the least likely of any ethnic group to be educated in a general education classroom. Of these students, 49% are educated in separate settings for much of the school day, compared to 38% of European American students.<br>• African American students with disabilities are also more likely than other ethnic groups to be educated in a separate class or separate school setting. |
| Who is living in poverty? | • Students with disabilities are more likely to be poor than are students in the general population.<br>• About 25% of elementary and secondary students with disabilities live in poverty, compared with 21% of the general population. |

overall statistics. Some groups of students are overrepresented in special education. This means that for some demographic groups, the proportion of students identified for special education is higher than the proportion of that group in the general population. Specifically, African American and American Indian/Alaska Native students with disabilities are overrepresented in the learning disability, intellectual disability, and emotional and behavioral disability categories (U.S. Department of Education, 2011). Overrepresentation of these students has been a longstanding issue and concern for special educators (Skiba, Simmons, Ritter, Gibb, Rausch, Cuadrado, & Chung, 2008).

Further complicating this issue are the specific student placements and outcomes for different demographics. The ethnicity or language of a student strongly influences their classroom placement. For example, African American, Hispanic, American Indian/Alaska Native, and ELL students with disabilities are more likely to be taught in separate classrooms or schools than students who are European American or Asian and Pacific Islander (Skiba, Poloni-Staudinger, Gallini, Simmons, & Feggins-Azziz, 2006). Additionally, although all students with disabilities have low graduation rates, Hispanic, American Indian/Alaska Native, and African American students with disabilities have substantially lower graduation rates than do European American students (U.S. Department of Education, 2010). See "Just the Facts" for more information regarding diversity and students with disabilities.

The population of students entering classrooms today differs substantially from students in the 1990s, and this diversity is predicted to further increase in the future. Moreover, the disproportionate number of these students with disabilities necessitates that educators adapt their inclusive classroom practices to meet the particular needs of students from diverse backgrounds. This need becomes especially obvious when examining the low academic achievement levels and the higher-than-expected dropout rates for many of these students, including both those with and without disabilities.

## What You Need to Know about Student Diversity and Academic Achievement

As the opening vignette with Melanie Buckley revealed, a significant achievement gap was found at Heritage High School, as a large number of students from diverse backgrounds did not meet performance standards. Unfortunately, this finding is common across many schools. For example, the U.S. Department of Education (NCES, 2010) reports that although the achievement gap has narrowed in reading and mathematics, European American students continue to score at higher levels than students from Hispanic and African American backgrounds. This is illustrated by the results from the 2009 administration of the California Standards Test, which revealed large differences in student proficiency by subgroup for third-grade students. In English/language arts, 29% of Hispanic and 29% of African American students were rated proficient or better, compared to 63% of European American students (Kids Data, 2009). Similar achievement gaps were found for high school students in mathematics. Perhaps even more troubling, only 20% of students designated as English-language learners were at or above proficiency.

These gaps also are reflected in the number of students who drop out of school before graduation. For example, in 2008, the percentage of 16- to 24-year-olds who were not enrolled in school and had not earned a diploma was 4.8% for European American students, 9.9% for African Americans, 18.3% for Hispanics, and 14.6% for American Indian/Alaska Native students (NCES, 2010). Data on students with disabilities' graduation rates reveal that about 52% of these students will graduate from high school with a regular diploma (U.S. Department of Education, 2010). Graduation rates for European American students with disabilities were 61.5%, but were considerably lower for African American (39.2%), Hispanic (47.1%), and American Indian/Alaska Native (49.4%) students.

Poverty also poses a serious challenge to children's potential for success in school. Growing up in poverty can negatively impact children's mental and behavioral development as well as their overall health, which can make it more difficult for them to learn (Darling-Hammond, 2010). As such, the achievement gap is often pronounced for students living in poverty. To illustrate, data from the National Assessment of Educational Progress (NCES, 2010) reveal that students in grades 4 and 8 in high-poverty schools from across the United States score substantially lower in reading and mathematics than do students from low-poverty schools.

Given the diversity that currently exists in classrooms across the United States, no matter where you teach, you will have a diverse range of students in your classroom. If you teach in a state that is highly diverse (e.g., Arizona, California, Florida, Georgia, Hawaii, Louisiana, Maryland, Nevada, New Mexico, and Texas), the majority of your students may well be from diverse backgrounds, including those with disabilities. This level of diversity makes it especially important that all teachers who teach in inclusive classrooms know effective principles and practices for addressing the needs of all students. Although many of the practices that we describe throughout this text will often work well with students from diverse backgrounds, in this chapter we provide descriptions of practices that are especially effective for students from culturally and linguistically diverse backgrounds.

## Principles and Practices to Support Effective Instruction

As you may know, the diversity that exists in the student population does not exist in the teaching force. According to data from the National Center for Educational Statistics (2010), the teaching workforce in the United States is largely European American (83%) and female (75%). Furthermore, the percentage of non-European American teachers has increased, but only by about 2% between 1999 and 2008.

This lack of diversity in teacher backgrounds creates a *demographic divide* in many schools. Consider that although 45% of all students are of African American, Hispanic, Asian, and American Indian/Alaska Native descent, only 17% of their teachers are from similar backgrounds (NCES, 2010). This problem is even more extreme in some states, and in many of the nation's largest school systems.

In presenting these data, we do not mean to suggest that teachers from the majority culture cannot successfully teach all students. This is certainly not the case. However, it is important that the teacher workforce include at least a reasonable proportion of teachers who share the cultural and language experiences of their students. These teachers can serve as a rich resource for other teachers and ensure that the diverse backgrounds of students are used to enrich the lives of everyone in the school. Regardless of background, all teachers must bridge the demographic divide by learning about students' backgrounds and experiences, and how these cultural experiences influence student achievement and behavior in school.

## How Teachers Establish Connections across the Demographic Divide

A critical issue related to our ability to accept and teach persons from different cultural groups is whether we view differences as typical and acceptable. All too often, many of us perceive difference as a way of dividing people into two groups: those who are typical (similar to me) and those who are atypical (different from me), rather than seeing human variation along a continuum (Baglieri & Knopf, 2004). We view those who are most like us as being within an acceptable range of typical behavior, while those who differ from us in ways we view as important are viewed as atypical (or even "abnormal"). For most people, these perceptions are implicit feelings. Try a little experiment to help you think about your perceptions of "typical" and how hard it is to alter perceptions.

Cross your arms across your chest in the way that you habitually cross them. Notice which arm is on top. Now cross your arms so that the *other* arm is on top. Many people find

It is important that teachers understand the cultural, ethnic, and language backgrounds of their students.

this so "atypical" that it takes several tries to cross their arms in the nonhabitual way, but there is nothing inherently "typical" about having one's left (or right) arm on top. Yet even when you *know* that there is nothing atypical about the new position, it feels weird. Without deliberate intention, you will habitually return your arms to their accustomed position.

In school, teachers often define "typical" and thus acceptable students as those who come prepared to behave in particular ways and to handle a specific type of academic structure. A number of culturally specific behaviors have been identified that often challenge teachers (Lewis & Doorlag, 2011). Consider whether the following behaviors, which are "typical" behaviors within specific cultural contexts, might seem problematic for you:

- Students talk out, often talking over you or other students in a form of communal participation.
- Students are very reticent to participate, or to ask and answer questions.
- Students come to school or school functions late.

European American, middle-class teachers who have spoken English from birth may expect all students to exhibit behaviors such as taking turns speaking in class, looking teachers in the eye when reprimanded, and asking questions when they don't understand. Yet, each of these behaviors is outside the norm for one or more cultural groups. This can mean that the teacher perceives actions that fall within the norms for a certain student's culture as atypical, and perhaps unacceptable.

These implicit judgments can lead teachers to blame students or their families for lack of success in school, disrupting their connections with students and creating barriers to success. It's important to keep in mind that "what we learn through our culture becomes our reality, and to see beyond that is often difficult" (Chamberlain, 2005, p. 199). *When a teacher's cultural assumptions lead to the conclusion that a student's academic or social behavior is outside the norm of appropriate, the teacher may make well-intended decisions that undermine the student's educational success.*

## What Is Culture and Why Is It So Important?

**Culture** is a concept that helps teachers understand the implicit evaluations they make and the reasons behind some of the student behaviors that "seem" atypical or abnormal. *Culture* has been defined as "the values, traditions, worldview, and social and political relationships created, shared, and transformed by a group of people bound together by a common history, geographic location, language, social class, religion, or other shared identity" (Nieto & Bode, 2008, p. 171). As this definition suggests, culture is dynamic, or changing, and is created or socially constructed by those who participate in it. Culture has also been referred to as an iceberg (Oetzel & Ting-Toomey, 2006). The part that we see and hear on the surface includes such variables as dress, music, food, and language. What is below the surface includes the deeper culture such as traditions, beliefs, values, norms, and worldviews. It is this invisible part of the iceberg that can confuse people as they interact with different cultural groups.

### Some Examples of Cultural Norms in School

Culture can influence how students interact in schools, especially students who are new to the United States. Dimensions of culture include styles of communication and interaction, concepts of self, behavioral expectations and management styles, time, and spatial proximity (Oetzel & Ting-Toomey, 2006). It is important to note that cultural dimensions are not characteristics that students either have or don't have but are aspects that fall along a continuum (Salend & Duhaney, 2005). For example, some groups tend toward an *individualist orientation* in their culture and communication style, but others tend toward a *collectivist orientation*. **Individualist cultures** emphasize individual achievement and initiative and promote self-realization (Gudykunst & Kim, 2003). Students in individualist cultures typically are motivated by individual recognition. For such students, the teacher might create a public display of achievement by hanging stellar student work on the wall. A common manifestation of this orientation in schools is the selection of a citizen of the week.

In collectivist cultures, working for the common good is more highly valued than individual achievement. Students from collectivist cultures may prefer to work in groups, and each member's contribution is judged "successful" only to the degree that it enhances the whole group. Individual awards, praise, or displays of accomplishment may not motivate individuals from collectivist cultures; instead, they may be motivated by group productivity and accomplishment (Trumbull, Rothstein-Fisch, & Greenfield, 2000). Although cultural groups have tendencies toward individualism or collectivism, these cultural traits fall along a continuum, and all cultures have both individual and collective traits. In addition, individuals within cultures differ with regard to these traits.

Cultural tendencies impact the way students participate in education. Figure 12.2 describes several classroom situations and some cultural dimensions to consider. This figure will help you see how a teacher might misinterpret the behavior of a student from a diverse culture. Cultural differences may cause educators to inaccurately judge students as poorly behaved or disrespectful. Consider also that as effective professionals, teachers must be culturally responsive and accept responsibility for learning about cultural differences and helping build bridges between home and school cultures. Because cultural

**Figure 12.2  Cultural Perspectives on Education**

| Classroom Situation | Cultural Dimensions to Consider |
|---|---|
| **Cultural Dimension: Styles of Communication** | |
| A student nods his head "yes" when asked in front of the whole class if he understands the solution to the math problem. Yet the student clearly did not understand the concept as he is unable to even successfully complete any problems on an individual practice assignment. | Consider that the student comes from a culture where he would be embarrassed to admit that he did not know the answer. Direct communication and "calling attention" to individuals may not be encouraged. The teacher could wait and ask the student, individually, to show him how to solve the problem or use response cards during small group. |
| **Cultural Dimension: Concept of Self** | |
| Students in a small group are asked to play "Jeopardy" as a way of solving social studies questions. The winner will receive an award and be allowed to choose a toy from the class store. Lucia, a student from the Ukraine, does not attempt to answer any of the questions. | Consider that the student comes from a culture that promotes collaboration and collectivism. The nature of the competition may make this student uncomfortable. The teacher could set up small teams to work together in answering the Jeopardy questions. |
| **Cultural Dimension: Management Style** | |
| A new student arrives from Central America. The teacher uses a lot of cooperative learning strategies in the classroom. The student seems confused and does not want to leave his desk. | Consider that the student came from a class where the teacher lectures and the students' roles are more passive. The teacher can use a buddy system to help the new student adjust to more "open" classroom activities. |
| **Cultural Dimension: Time** | |
| A student arrives to class late and without his notebook. He's visibly upset. His friend offers to let him borrow a notebook, but the student refuses and remains distracted throughout the class period. | Consider that the student comes from a culture that has a monochromic perspective. Time commitments are taken very seriously and so is personal property Borrowing or lending is seen to intrude on privacy. |
| **Cultural Dimension: Proximity** | |
| A new student who speaks very little English is having a problem getting along with the other students. He has fights on the playground every day, which he seems to provoke by constantly touching the other boys. | Consider that the student comes from a culture where it is appropriate to get close in personal space and touch each other. The other students do not feel comfortable with the close proximity and touching and respond with anger. The teacher needs to speak to the students about personal space and encourage students to express their comfort with proximity. |

differences are implicit, students may have a great deal of difficulty perceiving that their actions are inconsistent with teacher expectations and may find themselves reprimanded by teachers but fail to understand what they did that caused concern.

## Becoming a Culturally Responsive Teacher

Cultural background can influence how students interact and work together in school.

Culturally responsive teachers are simultaneously curious about culture and introspective (Irvine, 2003; Stormont, 2007). They know that culture affects people's perceptions, knowledge, and interactions, and that the impact of cultural assumptions is often implicit. These teachers strive to learn more about themselves, what they believe, and how their beliefs and experiences influence their perceptions of and interactions with students and their families.

### Learning about Culture and Difference

No teacher will possess comprehensive knowledge about all of the possible cultures, languages, disabilities, and economic influences on learning. A teacher's underlying curiosity about individuals, culture, and difference is vitally important (Banks et al., 2005). As Melanie Buckley noted in the opening "A View from the Teacher" feature in this chapter, "All teachers must be culturally aware and culturally responsive. This means they must be cognizant of their students' lives outside of school, actively learning of their varied cultural backgrounds." A teacher who is culturally curious and responsive recognizes that all people are influenced by their background, culture, and experience, and that variations within cultures are as significant as variations across cultures.

While we are all inevitably influenced by our culture, the pervasiveness and dominance of one's own culture (European American, heterosexual, middle-class for a large proportion of teachers) can make certain cultural characteristics invisible to many who have grown up inside that culture. Remember your response to the "Pause & Reflect" exercise that addressed understanding your own background. If you are female, your list may include *sister, friend, sorority member, runner, good student, motivated, strong-willed*. Look back at your list to see if you also listed any descriptive words such as *White, middle class, monolingual, heterosexual, Christian, European American*. Persons from European American, middle-class backgrounds seldom include these terms when describing themselves, suggesting parts of their culture may be invisible to them.

> ## Pause & Reflect
>
> Are certain parts of your culture largely invisible to you or taken for granted? Discuss with a friend or classmate from a different cultural background how this might influence your interactions with friends or your interactions with students in a classroom. Why is it important for a teacher to recognize these aspects of her culture?

### Reflecting on Your Beliefs

Working effectively with students from diverse backgrounds requires you to constantly question your reactions to students and their families and to check the human tendency to judge different as atypical and unacceptable. This is difficult to do. Recall how weird it felt to cross your arms in an uncharacteristic way. Even though you know (a cognitive reaction) that there is nothing abnormal about putting the opposite arm on top, it still feels weird (an affective reaction). Suspending judgment and blame means constantly questioning your reactions to determine when cultural difference might be a factor in your interactions with students.

Unfortunately, there are no road signs to tell you when you are likely to encounter a cultural incongruity with students or with parents. Suspending judgment means you constantly scan your environment through a cultural lens, looking for the possibility that culture could explain a challenge you are facing. Additionally, suspending judgment means you question yourself to identify possible stereotypes that might undermine your expectations for students.

## Demonstrating Care

Most people become teachers because they care about children and youth. For culturally responsive teachers, care means developing comprehensive knowledge about students and their lives so that you are able to link new learning to prior experience and use students' strengths to build their capacity to achieve (Gay, 2010). It also means being tough when you need to be. Teachers who care treat students with respect, require them to treat others with respect, perceive them as capable, and accept them unconditionally, even as they help them change undesirable behavior (Ross, Bondy, Gallingane, & Hambacher, 2008). To do this requires that you know, understand, and value the particular students you teach each year.

### Getting to Know Your Students

Culturally responsive teachers must really *know* their students to teach them effectively. This information is acquired using different strategies. To get to know students, it is important to spend time in their communities, visit homes, interact with families, and attend relevant cultural and family-oriented activities. Even teachers who live outside the community in which they teach find ways to become part of the community. Parents know the teachers and see them in the community, and the teachers know families well enough to know the cultural and experiential resources in students' homes. This has been called knowing the **funds of knowledge** within students' homes (Gonzalez, Moll, & Amanti, 2005).

Other strategies for learning about students include informal conversations with students and parents, observations of student behavior in different settings (i.e., in the classroom, with peers, and with family), and analysis of students' work. Moreover, it is important to become a student of children's culture. What are their favorite television shows? Movies? Music? Video games? Where do they go, and what do they do after school? What significant events have happened in the community? The more you know about the students and their communities, the greater your capacity to link schoolwork to their background knowledge and experience.

### Using an Asset-Oriented Lens

Once you have gotten to know your students, it's important to maintain an "asset-based" view as you teach them (Garcia & Ortiz, 2006). All students present an array of strengths and weaknesses. At times it is challenging to see beyond what students do not know, and take an "asset-based" perspective on the strengths that might be used in teaching them. For example, one teacher encountered a fifth-grade student who had mastered few basic math facts. Previous teachers had tried numerous strategies to get him to learn—urging him to practice, requiring him to complete mad-minute practices, drilling him on flash cards, testing him, providing peer tutoring, and failing him. The teacher learned that the student loved video and computer games and enjoyed being a leader. She used these assets to engage the student as she created a series of games for the Smartboard focused on math facts. As the student worked with the teacher to develop the games and helped to guide others in playing the games, he learned the math facts.

Taking an asset-oriented approach may seem obvious, but it is often not easy. As teachers work to develop an asset orientation, they must spend time investigating students' assets. For example, teachers may learn whether students have significant home responsibilities for younger siblings, if they provide translation assistance for adults in their families, or if they have

### Pause & Reflect

Adopting an asset orientation matters a great deal. Consider how your interactions with a student would be different if you believed the student to be stubborn (a deficiency) versus determined (an asset), wild versus energetic, or whiny versus sensitive? How can we teach ourselves to see assets instead of deficits?

It is important that teachers learn about the lives of their students outside of school.

outside jobs or activities. Teachers can then make a list of the skills required to succeed in each academic content area. This type of information helps identify strengths that will be useful in reaching every student.

### Becoming a Warm Demander

Research suggests that teachers support the achievement motivation of culturally diverse students by adopting the stance of a *warm demander.* Teachers who are warm demanders are culturally responsive, do not lower their standards, and are viewed as willing to help students (Ware, 2006). See the following "A View from a Teacher" feature for a perspective from warm demander Jan Patterson, an eighth-grade language arts teacher at West Hernando Middle School with a reputation for working successfully with students from diverse backgrounds.

## A View from a Teacher

### Jan Patterson Embraces the Role of a Warm Demander

Jan Patterson is an eighth-grade language arts and reading teacher at West Hernando Middle School. She has a reputation among her fellow teachers for being demanding, and also for working well with students from diverse backgrounds. We interviewed Ms. Patterson about her approach to teaching, and discovered that her beliefs align well with the characteristics of a warm demander. She is supportive of her students and she treats them respectfully, but she demands that they meet performance expectations for their behavior and academic achievement.

Ms. Patterson began by stating that she looks at "inclusion as affecting every student. They all come in as individuals." She goes on to note that all her students come into her classroom as teachers: "They bring in their culture, and I honor that. If there's a topic going on and it's something that is relevant to a student, then they become a teacher." She describes an example of a student in her class from Haiti who returned to her homeland during the holiday break, and experienced firsthand the devastation from an earthquake. "What a good source of information [she was. Students] have background and experience that none of us will ever have. I tell their parents too, 'You're all teachers. If you have something to bring [into the classroom], please feel free to come in, keep us company, and add to the classroom.'"

There are many other ways in which Ms. Patterson shows respect and warmth for students. For example, she states, "I believe all my students are young adults, so I address them as 'Mr.' and 'Ms.' to show them respect. That applies to all students. How you handle and address that [respect for students] often takes care of the rest of the issues. I respect them all as unique individuals." She also is very supportive of students who need additional assistance to master their academic work. She tells her students, "I'm here on Tuesday, Wednesday, and Thursday after school for tutoring. What we are looking at is skill building, not the grade. You can retake anything you want as many times as you want for full credit. I don't care how many times you want to take that test. Because you're going to eventually master the skills. You take the responsibility of retaking that test, and you need my individual attention, I'm right there for you, my door is always open if you need me."

Clearly respectful and supportive of her students, Ms. Patterson is also steadfastly demanding that they master academic material and behave appropriately. She clearly articulated her "no excuses" perspective when she said, "An adolescent sentence structure is this—Truth, Conjunction, and Excuse. I stop listening at the conjunction. In a nice way, I'm saying, 'Come on, I don't need to hear an excuse.' A student's background is never an excuse for bad behavior or not mastering skills." She goes on to say that in her classroom, a student can't give up. "No! I can't help you if you tell me 'I don't get it' or 'I don't know where to start.' That tells me that you've given up. You can't give up. You need to do this one way or another!"

Ms. Patterson believes in working closely with parents to provide students with support to learn and behave appropriately. "I make a call to their house when they misbehave or don't do their homework. I really believe in having contact with the parents because we're working for the same cause. They want their children to be successful, and so do we. When they do something extremely creative, I also call the house. Why should I deny their parents the opportunity to know what's happening, [so] I call the house!"

According to Ms. Patterson, no matter what the student's background is, everyone must behave appropriately and master academic content in her classroom. Culture or disability or family background is never an excuse. "You still have to do what's required. You still have to do your work. I don't ever want to be in a position where I have to excuse somebody because of who [he or she is]!" She emphasizes with students and their families that she accepts no excuses because her job is to "teach students how to be successful in the real world. You need to understand the power of language, the power of body language, you need to understand people's immediate perceptions of you as an adult."

Ms. Patterson's success with students from a broad range of backgrounds attests to the success of her warm-demander philosophy. Students respect her and the demands that she makes on them, while at the same time they realize that she returns that respect, and will do anything she can to help them succeed.

Research on positive classroom environments (Patrick, Turner, Meyer, & Midgley, 2003), the development of resilience (Benard, 2004), culturally relevant pedagogy (Gay, 2010), and culturally relevant classroom management (Weinstein, Tomlinson-Clarke, & Curran, 2004) reflects many of the perspectives that Jan Patterson shares regarding her role as a warm demander. This research and Jan's comments indicate that there are three characteristics of classroom environments that support academic achievement (Ross et al., 2008): (1) a respectful, caring relationship between students and the teacher; (2) respectful relationships among peers; and (3) clear and high expectations for behavior and achievement. These are consistent with the characteristics of warm demanders.

***Care Is the Foundation for the Warm Demander.*** The foundation of any effective classroom is that students know the teacher cares about them. This is the "warm" part of being a warm demander. Keep in mind the previous discussion of what it means to care. *Warm* doesn't mean being nice, and it isn't about gentle nurturing, which often becomes benign neglect (Gay, 2002). As noted previously, *warm* means the teacher believes in students and cares enough about their futures to create a community where it is safe to take risks, where achievement is valued, where support is provided, and where students are never "let off the hook." Most importantly, it means caring enough to demand that students behave and achieve.

***Warm Demanders Create a Respectful Community.*** Community is a key part of many cultural groups. Within a community, each member's individual needs are met (Gay, 2002). A key task for a culturally responsive teacher is building a community so that it is safe for every student to take the risks necessary to learn. Culturally responsive teachers bring themselves into the classroom and enable students to do the same. To do this, teachers share their families, their interests, and their lives with their students and use structures such as class meetings to enable students to share information and get to know one another. They communicate that respect for others is highly valued by respecting and listening to students and teaching students to respect and listen to one another. As Jan Patterson from West Hernando Middle School noted, all students should be shown respect as unique individuals.

These classrooms are the opposite of a "collection of strangers," a description that unfortunately fits many classrooms. When students are strangers, it is impossible to create a network of caring peers who support one another through learning challenges. In addition, classroom-management problems escalate when students do not know one another. Yet, the significance of creating community is often forgotten, particularly in secondary classrooms. For example, a high school teacher initiated a community-building class meeting with a group of ninth-grade students who were in a transition classroom because of poor performance on the eighth-grade state assessment test. Within two meetings, students began to share personal information, and after the second session, the teacher overheard a student say, "Going to this class is like being in a club." The fact that the student saw this class as so different from his other classes suggests how rare it is that some high school students feel a true sense of belonging.

***Warm Demanders Explicitly Teach Classroom Rules, Routines, and Procedures.*** It is critically important to teach expectations, particularly social skills, in diverse, inclusive classrooms (Harriott & Martin, 2004). This means that culturally responsive teachers *never* assume that students know what is expected. Even when teaching in high school, culturally responsive teachers teach the behaviors they expect students to demonstrate. In fact, explicitly teaching specific rules and procedures is a long-established principle of effective classroom management (Evertson & Emmer, 2009). If rules and procedures are not taught, classroom management can become an escalating sequence of consequences and punishments. The result is the development of a negative, often punitive, classroom environment where many fail to thrive.

The following principle may help you: Assume that students will behave respectfully and appropriately if they know and remember what the teacher expects. Culturally responsive classroom teachers teach their academic and behavioral expectations using multiple strategies (Bondy et al., 2007). These strategies include:

- Stating their expectations
- Providing models and demonstrations
- Providing humorous negative examples
- Requiring student restatement of expectations
- Providing opportunities for practice with feedback
- Repeating instructions as necessary
- Reminding students of and reinforcing appropriate behavior

***Protecting the Classroom Community through Teacher Insistence.*** A key difference between teachers who establish environments that support achievement motivation and those who do not is that effective teachers strategically and respectfully insist that students abide by rules and procedures and that they respect one another and the teacher (Patrick et al., 2003). Yet in their "insistence," effective teachers always preserve the respectful and caring connection to each student. As one middle school student commented, "She's mean out of the kindness of her heart" (Wilson & Corbett, 2001, p. 91). The view that Jan Patterson provided earlier in this chapter reflects this perspective well.

All teachers want their students to abide by classroom rules. Yet, some give multiple "chances" that send inconsistent messages to students. Others become punitive and threatening. These responses undermine the expectation that students must be respectful of one another—the former by allowing disrespectful behavior, and the latter by treating students disrespectfully. Charney (2002) provides guidelines to help teachers say what they mean. In addition to keeping demands simple and short, she directs teachers to clearly communicate what is negotiable and what is not and to remind only twice. An effective "reminder" strategy that she suggests is to ask students to "rewind" when inappropriate behavior surfaces. This gives the student a clear directive and a chance to correct inappropriate behavior but maintains a lighter tone likely to be effective particularly with secondary-level students.

## High Expectations: What Does "No Excuses" Really Mean?

We've already noted that culturally responsive teachers convey a belief in the potential of students that enables them to transcend barriers to learning. Enacting this belief requires that teachers view student learning as a puzzle that they are constantly striving to solve (Banks et al., 2005; Corbett et al., 2002). They use a variety of activities and strategies for instruction and work to match their methods to students (Cole, 2001).

### Teaching Is Guided by Assessment and a Problem-Solving Approach

Culturally responsive teachers use a continual assessment system to determine who is and who isn't learning. They also constantly search for another way to make learning comprehensible (Gay, 2002). If one way isn't working, they modify instruction and reteach (Garcia & Ortiz, 2006). These are teachers who simply refuse to believe there is any student who cannot be reached, and they actively communicate this belief to students. This belief is a guiding principle of inclusive practice and differentiated instruction.

> The basic premise of differentiated instruction is to systematically plan curriculum and instruction that meets the needs of academically diverse learners by honoring each students' learning needs and maximizing each student's learning capacity. (Van Garderen & Wittacker, 2006, p. 12)

In short, instruction should be culturally responsive for all students in inclusive classrooms. The central theme here is that teaching and learning are not culture free, and therefore student failure should initially be viewed as a mismatch between the school's culture and environment and the student's needs (Garcia & Ortiz, 2006).

### Insisting on Completion and Quality

Insistence is just as important in establishing high academic expectations as it is in establishing a respectful learning community. Culturally responsive teachers do not allow students to do less than their best (Corbett et al., 2002). They insist that students complete and revise their work until it meets high standards. In a study of urban middle school students' perspectives about effective teachers, students valued teachers who made them do their work, even when they didn't want to do it (Wilson & Corbett, 2001). Others have made the same point in stressing that important learning inevitably involves struggle (Weinstein, 2002). Effective teachers not only convey that the struggle is important but insist that students persist through barriers and provide them with support until they succeed. They encourage students to try, refuse to allow them to get by with incomplete or sloppy work, give them opportunities to make up work, provide tutoring, make work relevant to students' lives, and reteach using varied strategies until everyone understands and succeeds (Wilson & Corbett, 2001).

> ## Pause & Reflect
>
> Mr. Newsome believes he has high standards. As evidence, he reports that his tenth-grade math students get zeros if they do not turn in homework. He says with pride that he does not just "pass students through." One third of his class got D's or F's last term, and he says, "They earned them." Do these practices suggest that Mr. Newsome has high expectations?

## Using a Diverse Curriculum

Motivation to achieve is influenced by factors such as culture, values, and language (Ginsberg, 2005). It also is influenced by the nature of the curriculum. The school curriculum is not culturally neutral. The curriculum as represented in texts, national and state standards, and the experience of most teachers, is a reflection of the European American culture. The school curriculum "promotes its own (a) cultural values, practices and perceptions; (b) psychological, social, economic, and political needs; and (c) elevated status within the larger society" (Hollins, 1996, p. 82).

Teachers should view their curricular materials with a critical eye (Gay, 2002). The text may include a few multicultural historic figures, but that is often not enough. Gay cautions that when the same few figures are taught repeatedly, students learn that their ancestors really did not contribute much. Similarly, she notes that it is inappropriate to focus more attention on African Americans than on other ethnic groups. In addition, the fiction and nonfiction that students read needs to be diverse so that they see their lives and cultures reflected in the characters, setting, and plot of the stories. When students see themselves in their books, they are more likely to enjoy reading, make a connection to literature, and build vocabulary and language skills that assist them academically. To be effective, teachers need "wide ranging knowledge of subject matter content, so that they can construct a curriculum that includes multiple representations addressing the prior experiences of different groups of students" (Banks et al., 2005, p. 251).

Literature is not the only strategy to broaden the curriculum. Teachers should draw on their communities for curricular content and take a risk and teach controversial topics such as ethnicity and poverty (Gay, 2002). Additional strategies for incorporating diversity in the curriculum include

Using material from different cultural groups for instruction can motivate students to learn.

ideas such as teaching thematic units organized around countries or languages; studying and comparing fashion, religious and marriage customs, games, and hair styling from around the world; and subscribing to magazines from around the world that help teachers and students learn about students' cultures and provide possible curricular topics (Jones, 2005).

## Summary

This chapter addressed the following topics:

**Students from diverse backgrounds: What to expect**

- The demographics of public school students are rapidly changing in terms of ethnicity, language, poverty, and disability as classrooms across the United States become more diverse.
- Although about 55% of school-aged students are European American, in 10 states the majority of students are from non-European Americans backgrounds.
- Students with disabilities include students from all ethnicities, language backgrounds, and socioeconomic levels.
- Some groups of students are overrepresented in special education. For example, students who live in poverty and those from ELL backgrounds are more likely to be in special education. African American and American Indian/Alaska Native students are also over-represented in special education.
- A significant achievement gap exists across students from different ethnic, language, and socioeconomic backgrounds.
- The lack of connection between teachers' and students' background knowledge, experience, and culture (i.e., the demographic divide) is a key contributing factor to this achievement gap.

**Principles and practices to support effective instruction**

- Culturally responsive teaching is designed to foster resilience in students, improve student outcomes, and enhance the educational futures of students.
- Culturally responsive teachers are those who
  - Study culture and the ways that students differ.
  - Believe that every student has the capacity to succeed.
  - Learn to suspend judgment and blame when interacting with students and families.
  - Show students that they sincerely care about them.
  - Develop depth of knowledge about their students.
  - Develop the skills and stance of a warm demander.
  - Hold students to high expectations.
  - Make the curriculum meaningful.
  - Connect instruction to students' interests and experiences.

## Addressing Professional Standards

Standards addressed in Chapter 12 include:

**CEC Standards:** (1) foundations, (2) development and characteristics of learners, (3) individual learning differences, (4) instructional strategies, (5) learning environments and social interactions, (6) language, (9) professional and ethical practice.

---

### MyEducationLab

Go to the topic Cultural and Linguistic Diversity in the **MyEducationLab** (www .myeducationlab.com) for *Inclusion,* where you can:

- Find learning outcomes for Cultural and Linguistic Diversity, along with the national standards that connect to these outcomes.
- Complete Assignments and Activities that can help you more deeply understand the chapter content.
- Apply and practice your understanding of the core teaching skills identified in the chapter with the Building Teaching Skills and Dispositions learning units.
- Examine challenging situations and cases presented in the IRIS Center Resources.
- Check your comprehension on the content covered in the chapter with the Study Plan. Here you will be able to take a chapter quiz, receive feedback on your answers, and then access Review, Practice, and Enrichment activities to enhance your understanding of chapter content.

# EFFECTIVE PRACTICES FOR STUDENTS FROM DIVERSE BACKGROUNDS

## Putting It All Together

No matter where the school, almost all teachers in the United States have a diverse range of students in their classrooms. Although many of the evidenced-based practices that we discuss throughout this text are effective with these students, they often need more than this. Several considerations to keep in mind when working with students from diverse backgrounds include:

1. **Know yourself.** To work effectively with students from different cultural backgrounds, you must be intimately aware of your own cultural background, and how this background influences your expectations of students in your classroom. Most teachers take for granted that they understand their cultural backgrounds, but evidence from classrooms reveals that this is all too often not the case.

2. **Know your students.** Throughout this text, we've emphasized the need to get to know your students' academic and social-behavioral strengths and weaknesses. This is especially important when teaching students from diverse backgrounds. Get to know them personally, including information about their family background, cultural experiences, and interests.

3. **Use this knowledge.** Knowing your students' backgrounds can provide many benefits for an effective teacher in an inclusive classroom. This knowledge helps build rapport with students, and conveys to students that you value and care about them. This information can also be used as a foundation for instructional experiences in class, and improves the likelihood that students will be engaged in these activities.

4. **Keep learning about all your students.** Although in this chapter we have emphasized students from culturally diverse backgrounds, it is also important to apply these principles to *all* students in your classroom. All students benefit from teachers who are warm demanders—teachers who care about them, respect them, provide them with needed supports, and demand success from them.

In the remainder of this chapter, we describe five effective strategies to help you meet the needs of students from culturally and linguistically diverse backgrounds. The *Strategy Fact Sheet* summarizes these strategies.

## Strategy Fact Sheet

| STRATEGY | DESCRIPTION | SPECIAL CONSIDERATIONS |
|---|---|---|
| Strategy 12.1: Culturally Responsive Teaching | Culturally responsive teaching involves providing supports to students from culturally and linguistically diverse backgrounds to make sure they are active participants in the academic and social communities of the school, and have a successful school experience. | All too often, an achievement gap exists between students from CLD backgrounds and their European American peers. Culturally responsive teaching is needed to address this gap and improve academic outcomes for students from CLD backgrounds. |
| Strategy 12.2: Teaching Reading to Students who are English-Language Learners (ELLs) | Research has identified five components of instruction that lead to improved reading outcomes for students who are English-language learners. | Many students who are English-language learners lag behind their peers in learning to read. As part of this instruction, it is important to focus on developing academic language or the language of schools. |
| Strategy 12.3: Highly Effective Instructional Practices for Students from CLD Backgrounds | Highly effective instructional practices have been identified that ensure that students from CLD and high poverty backgrounds do not continue to fall further behind in learning the skills needed for school success. | Closing the achievement gap for students from CLD and high poverty backgrounds should have a positive impact on dropout rates, and should also reduce discipline referrals for many students. |

*(Continued)*

| STRATEGY | DESCRIPTION | SPECIAL CONSIDERATIONS |
|---|---|---|
| Strategy 12.4: Culturally Responsive Classroom Management | Expectations for appropriate behavior are often influenced by culture. A cultural divide between teachers and their students makes this problem even worse. To address this issue requires the use of culturally responsive forms of classroom management. | The achievement gap for many students from CLD backgrounds is significantly influenced by a discipline gap, as students from diverse backgrounds are more frequently subjected to school disciplinary sanctions. Culturally responsive classroom management can be effective in reducing this discipline gap as well as improving achievement. |
| Strategy 12.5: Double-Check: A Culturally Responsive Approach to Classroom Management | Double-check is a framework to support teachers in delivering culturally responsive classroom management. This approach uses evidence-based components to address culturally responsive practices in the classroom. | Professionals agree that there is a need to provide more culturally responsive approaches to classroom management, but few alternatives are available. The Double-check framework begins to address this need. |

Strategy 12.1 | # CULTURALLY RESPONSIVE TEACHING

## Rationale

As you learned earlier in this chapter, an achievement gap exists in reading and math between students from culturally and linguistically diverse backgrounds (including students who are African American, Hispanic, and American Indian/Alaska Natives) and European American students (NCES, 2010). Although this gap has narrowed in recent years, it remains substantial. Providing instruction to students from CLD backgrounds that significantly improves achievement has proven to be more difficult than many expected. To effectively address the needs of students from CLD backgrounds, teachers must be responsive to students' cultural and linguistic backgrounds, and adapt their instruction based on this information. Furthermore, culturally responsive teachers must provide supports to students from CLD backgrounds to make sure that they are active participants in the academic and social communities of the school (Gay, 2010; Sheets, 2005).

## Step-by-Step

Culturally responsive teaching is designed to improve the achievement of all students in a learner-centered, culturally supported context that recognizes student strengths and uses these strengths to improve achievement (Richards, Brown, & Forde, 2006). Recent research has identified critical components of effective instruction in culturally responsive classrooms (Cartledge & Kourea, 2008).

**1** *Identify and address the academic needs of CLD students.* Evidence indicates that many students from CLD backgrounds begin school behind their European American counterparts (NCES, 2010). These differences are often greatest among students from low socioeconomic backgrounds. This suggests the importance of a sense of urgency in identifying areas of academic weakness as early as possible, and intervening with intensive instruction to ensure that academic deficits do not increase (Cartledge & Kourea, 2008). More specifically, when high-quality instruction is delivered to small groups of three to five students who have similar needs for short periods of time, evidence reveals that this instruction often significantly reduces the achievement gap, and may prevent the labeling of students with disabilities (Cartledge, Gardner, & Ford, 2009; Fletcher et al. 2007; Torgesen, 2009).

**2** *Provide frequent academic monitoring.* Given the difficulty professionals have had in closing the achievement gap for students from CLD backgrounds, it is especially important to monitor student academic progress often (Cartledge & Kourea, 2008). For example, curriculum-based measures (Deno, 2007) should be used to determine student skill development in reading and mathematics as they begin school. For students who have areas of weakness, more intensive instruction should be provided to address these needs, and student progress should be frequently monitored using curriculum-based measures to determine whether the student's academic progress is accelerating. Providing tiers of increasingly focused, intensive instruction for students who do not make sufficient academic progress has been shown to be highly effective in improving academic outcomes for students from CLD backgrounds in reading (Torgesen, 2009) and math (Fuchs, Fuchs, Craddock, et al., 2008).

**3** *Engage students in a high level of academic responding.* An academic achievement gap exists between students from CLD backgrounds and their European American peers at least in part because CLD students lack opportunities for active academic responding in most classrooms (Cartledge & Kourea, 2008). Furthermore, for many students from culturally and linguistically diverse backgrounds, learning is not just cognitive and technical; it is also active and emotional (Gay, 2010). Thus, instruction should often reflect novelty, variability, and active participation. To support active student engagement, the following strategies should be considered (Boykin & Bailey, 2000).

- Use movement that is expressive and purposeful.
- Encourage open expression of thoughts, ideas, and emotions.
- Use activities that encourage or support high levels of physical stimulation.

- Use music, dance, and rhythm when teaching academic tasks.
- Include multiple stimuli and activities when teaching.
- Use cultural practices originating in the home as part of academic tasks.
- Encourage student bonding or interconnectedness.

**4** *Use an appropriate pace of instruction.* Instructional pace relates to the speed at which academic information is presented. Obviously, a faster pace influences the amount of content that is covered in a class, allowing more opportunities to learn. This is an important consideration for students from CLD backgrounds who may have had more limited opportunities to learn academic content than their European American peers. A brisk academic pace also is more likely to keep students actively engaged and reduce off-task and disruptive behavior (Cartledge & Kourea, 2008). Thus, use a brisk pace of instruction whenever possible. It is important to note that the effectiveness of a brisk pace is dependent on the provision of high-quality instruction that is carefully planned and structured. In addition, this type of instruction provides the opportunity to build on cultural themes that relate to improved instruction for students from CLD backgrounds, including active engagement and movement as part of instruction, and having students engage in more than one task simultaneously (Boykin, Tyler, & Miller, 2005).

**5** *Develop a community of learners to support the learning of all students.* A key component of culturally responsive instruction is the development of a supportive learning environment that employs a community of learners to support the learning of all students. Such a learning environment has been shown to be effective in working with students from a wide range of cultural backgrounds. As Gay (2010) noted, "Underlying values of human connectedness and collaborative problem solving are high priorities in the cultures of most groups of color in the United States" (p. 187). Thus, developing a learning community and actively engaging students in working with one another is especially effective for students from cultural groups that emphasize a collectivist or communal orientation (Boykin, Tyler, & Miller, 2005).

Involving students in their own learning using strategies such as cooperative learning and peer tutoring are approaches that may be used to develop a community of learners. For example, research has shown that peer tutoring improves student motivation, creates more opportunities for teacher–student interactions, provides a framework that teaches students that they need to work collaboratively to meet instructional goals, increases student engaged time, and often results in significantly improved academic outcomes for students from CLD backgrounds (Cartledge & Kourea, 2008).

Cooperative learning and peer tutoring strategies are discussed in more detail in Chapter 13.

# Applications and Examples

When cooperative groups are used in classrooms, teachers often control the groups by determining group membership, assigning roles to group members (leader, note-taker), and encouraging competition within and across groups (Sheets, 2005). When this occurs, the cohesiveness and engagement of cooperative groups is decreased. A collaborative approach should be used when students work cooperatively in small groups. This approach enhances group responsibility, focuses participation more on learning and sharing, and results in a process that is more natural and communal. To prepare students for collaborative group work, teachers attend to the following (Sheets, 2005):

- Keep competition to a minimum.
- Focus responsibility for the learning of all group members on the group.
- Provide for self-selection of group members by students.
- Encourage students to develop social bonds.
- Work to ensure that students equally participate in group activities.
- Support students in developing communication, negotiation, problem solving, and self-evaluation skills.
- Employ some open-ended learning activities.

# Keep in Mind

As we have noted previously, a demographic (or cultural) divide often exists between teachers and their students. Given the diverse range of students that currently are in classrooms in most parts of the United States, it is important that all teachers develop their knowledge and skills to provide more culturally responsive instruction. Several activities that may be useful in this regard include (Richards, Brown, & Forde, 2006):

- *Learn about the experiences and history of persons from CLD groups.* This provides perspective on how different historical experiences have influenced attitudes and values of different groups. This type of activity also will allow teachers to begin to see how their values differ from those of other cultural groups. This learning can be facilitated by interacting with members of cultural groups, or by reading literature written by member of a cultural group.
- *Visit students' families and communities.* This activity helps teachers get to know their students as part of their cultural world outside of school. More specifically, it helps teachers develop the perspective that a student is not just another person in the classroom, but is part of a complex social and cultural network that likely has a significant influence on the student's attitudes and values.
- *Read about teachers who have been successful working in diverse settings.* Books, articles, blogs, or other writing by these teachers can provide insight into effective, culturally responsive methods (e.g., see Codell, 2009; Esquith, 2007). To learn even more, visiting the classroom of a teacher who has been highly successful working with students from CLD backgrounds can provide firsthand knowledge of how culturally responsive instruction is provided.
- *Develop an appreciation of diversity.* To be effective in a culturally diverse setting, a teacher must come to view differences as a typical part of society, and actively reject the notion that any one group is more competent than another. To do this, teachers might examine their affiliations with different groups (e.g., gender, ethnicity) and the advantages or disadvantages that come from this membership. Developing an appreciation of diversity results in a respect for differences, and provides a clear understanding regarding why it is important to teach from this perspective. The key to this understanding will likely be the realization that the teacher's views of the world are not the only views, and cannot always be the most important views.

**Key References**

Cartledge, G., Gardner, R., & Ford, D. (2009). *Diverse learners with exceptionalities: Culturally responsive teaching in the inclusive classroom.* Upper Saddle River, NJ: Pearson Education.

Cartledge, G., & Kourea, L. (2008). Culturally responsive classrooms for culturally diverse students with and at risk for disabilities. *Exceptional Children, 74*(3), 351–371.

Gay, G. (2010). *Culturally responsive teaching: Theory, research, and practice.* New York: Teachers College Press.

Richards, H., Brown, A., & Forde, T. (2006). *Addressing diversity in schools: Culturally responsive pedagogy.* Tempe, AZ: National Center for Culturally Responsive Educational Systems, Arizona State University.

Sheets, R. H. (2005). *Diversity pedagogy.* Upper Saddle River, NJ: Pearson Education.

## Strategy 12.2 | TEACHING READING TO STUDENTS WHO ARE ENGLISH-LANGUAGE LEARNERS (ELLS)

## Rationale

Many students who are English-language learners lag behind those who are not ELL in the development of reading skills. Although this achievement gap has narrowed in recent years (NCES, 2010), it remains substantial. Fortunately, evidence now exists to shed some light on instructional methods that are most likely to increase reading achievement levels for English-language learners at the elementary level (Gersten et al., 2007; Kamps et al., 2007). This research has identified five components of reading instruction that are particularly important for teaching reading to students from ELL backgrounds.

## Step-by-Step

**1** *Assess students who are English-language learners using English-language measures on the components of early reading instruction (i.e., phonological awareness, alphabetic knowledge, reading words, and reading text).* As with other students who struggle with learning to read, curriculum-based measures should be used to (a) screen for reading problems, (b) assess reading skills, and (c) monitor reading progress over time. The same measures can be used with students who are native English speakers and those who are English-language learners, and the same standards or performance benchmarks can be used for both groups.

**2** *Provide explicit, direct instruction to students who are at risk for reading problems in the five core areas of beginning reading (i.e., phonological awareness, phonics, reading fluency, vocabulary, and comprehension).* Areas of focus for the instruction should be determined by assessment measures, and intensive instruction should be provided to small groups of students who have similar educational needs. Provide this small group instruction daily for at least 30 minutes in groups of three to five students. Consider intervention programs such as Read Well (Sprick, Howard, & Fidanque, 1998) or SRA Reading Mastery (Engelmann & Bruner, 2003) to deliver this instruction. These programs may be used as a central component of reading instruction for 30 to 50 minutes of intensive, small-group instruction per day, as both employ the principles of direct, explicit instruction and address core areas of beginning reading instruction.

**3** *Throughout the school day, provide students high-quality vocabulary instruction.* This should include in-depth instruction related to content words that are frequently used as part of instruction. Ideally, these words should be from the student's reading program, and from texts used in other content areas (i.e., mathematics, science, social studies). Use instructional time to teach the meanings of common or everyday English words, phrases, and expressions that are known to most students who are native English speakers, but that ELL students may not have yet learned.

**4** *Provide students with support to develop formal or academic English, especially related to reading and mathematics.* Daily English instruction should be part of the core curriculum at the earliest grades, preferably for a specified block of time each day. This instruction should begin before students learn to read and write, and should be focused on the development of age-appropriate English morphology, syntax, and vocabulary. Focus this instruction on the use of appropriate verb tense, plurals, and the use of adverbs and adjectives. Offer opportunities to practice these features of English in natural, meaningful contexts of oral and written communication, and in a range of situations (e.g., describing events, summarizing content, telling stories).

**5** *Have students work in pairs for approximately 90 minutes a week.* Use these activities to allow students the opportunity to practice and extend material already taught. Students at different levels of academic ability should be paired, or at different levels of English proficiency. Peer-assisted strategies such as class-wide peer tutoring (CWPT) (Greenwood, Arreaga-Mayer, Utley, Gavin, & Terry, 2001) and peer-assisted learning strategies (PALS) (Saenz, Fuchs, & Fuchs, 2005) have been demonstrated as effective with students across a range of age levels and content areas.

These strategies may be used with English-language learners for instruction related to basic skills in reading and language, or for older students to provide feedback regarding vocabulary and comprehension. Students may also work in pairs to support English-language development. For example, students could work together reading text, and discussing this text using a structured format (e.g., practice summarizing the text with feedback).

Peer-assisted strategies are described in more detail in Chapter 13.

## Applications and Examples

Vocabulary instruction for students from ELL backgrounds should be more explicit and structured than instruction that is typically provided in general education classrooms (Gersten et al., 2007). Furthermore, the goal of this instruction is to provide students with an understanding of words so that this vocabulary can be used in natural communication and as a basis for further language learning. Vocabulary instruction for students from ELL backgrounds should be intense and rich. It should also:

- Include multiple exposures to the selected vocabulary words over time, and across opportunities to read, write, and speak.
- Place an emphasis on definitions that are student friendly.
- Engage students in the use of word meanings in natural contexts related to reading, writing, speaking, and listening.
- Include regular review across these contexts.

## Keep in Mind

Many potential barriers may impede the use of effective strategies for teaching ELL students. Some particular barriers to keep in mind include:

- Some teachers believe that reading problems may resolve themselves after oral language proficiency is attained by ELL students.
- Some instruction focuses too much on what is tested, and too little on vocabulary development and comprehension.
- Teachers may not be comfortable identifying students for additional reading instruction if the student's English-language skills are low.
- Developing a grade-level or building-level schedule to deliver the instruction needed by ELL students may be difficult, and requires the involvement of all teachers and administrators.

For additional information regarding these and other barriers to providing instruction to ELL students in reading and English language instruction, see Gersten and colleagues (2007), which is available from the U.S. Department of Education, Institute for Education Sciences as part of their "Practice Guides" series at http://ies.ed.gov/ncee/wwc/publications/practiceguides/.

### Key References

August, D., & Siegel, L. (2006). Literacy instruction for language-minority children in special education settings. In D. August & T. Shanahan (Eds.), *Developing literacy in second-language learners: Report of the National Literacy Panel on Language-Minority Children and Youth* (pp. 523–553). Mahwah, NJ: Erlbaum.

Gersten, R., Baker, S., Shanahan, T., Linan-Thompson, S., Collins, P., & Scarcella, R. (2007). *Effective literacy and English language instruction for English learners in the elementary grades.* NCEE-2007-4011. Washington, DC: U.S. Department of Education-Institute for Education Sciences.

Greenwood, C., Arreaga-Mayer, C., Utley, C., Gavin, K., & Terry, B. (2001). Classwide Peer Tutoring learning management system: Applications with elementary-level English language learners. *Remedial and Special Education, 22*(1), 34–47.

Kamps, D., Abbott, M., Greenwood, C., Arreaga-Mayer, C., Wills, H., Longstaff, J., Culpepper, M., & Waiton, C. (2007). Use of evidence-based, small-group reading instruction for English language learners in elementary grades: Secondary-tier intervention. *Learning Disability Quarterly, 30*(3), 153–168.

Vaughn, S., & Linan-Thompson, S. (2007). *Research-based methods of reading instruction for English language learners, grades K–4.* Alexandria, VA: ASCD.

| Strategy 12.3 | **HIGHLY EFFECTIVE INSTRUCTIONAL PRACTICES FOR STUDENTS FROM CLD BACKGROUNDS** |

## Rationale

Highly effective instructional practices are needed to ensure that students from CLD backgrounds do not continue to fall further behind in learning basic skills that are needed for school success. Several research-based practices have been identified that are particularly effective for students from CLD and high-poverty backgrounds (Borich, 2011; Cartledge, Gardner, & Ford, 2009). Using these practices should result in many benefits for students from CLD backgrounds. For example, narrowing of the achievement gap should have a significant and positive influence on student dropout rates, and should reduce discipline referrals for many students (Gregory, Skiba, & Noguera, 2010).

## Step-by-Step

**1** *Ensure that the qualities of effective instruction are used to guide classroom instruction.* Although many research-based practices have been shown to work with students across cultural and language groups, some practices are particularly effective, given the diverse backgrounds and life experiences of many students from CLD backgrounds. Borich (2011) recommends the following practices as particularly effective for students from high-poverty backgrounds.

- Use progress monitoring to ensure that students are learning the material and making adequate academic progress. Charts and graphs should be used to illustrate the progress that is being made by the student.
- Begin by teaching the most concrete information, then move to applications of this information, followed by teaching patterns and abstractions.
- Provide immediate assistance to students who indicate a need for help in the classroom. The use of peer assistants or peer tutoring may be useful in providing this assistance.
- Provide time for practice with feedback immediately after material has been learned.
- Plan transitions from one activity to another in advance, to maintain the structure and flow of activities and to maintain momentum.

**2** *Provide appropriate praise.* Much research evidence has documented that teachers are less likely to praise low-achieving students for their academic performance, and are more likely to praise those achieving at high levels (Rodriguez & Bellanca, 2007). Furthermore, teachers tend to give fewer reasons for praise to low achievers, with typical responses such as "OK" or "Good job." Teachers should provide praise to low-achieving students when they make significant progress, especially when the student fails to recognize this progress. This praise should be natural, sincere, private, and focused on a specific accomplishment (Rodriguez & Bellanca, 2007).

As students are receiving high levels of intensive instruction in the classroom, provide both praise for student progress, as well as corrective feedback for responses that are incorrect. High levels of academic responding are worthwhile only if students receive feedback to correct inaccurate responses, preventing continued practice of incorrect responses (Rodriguez & Bellanca, 2007). Provide feedback by using a graph of the student's progress, which can be reinforcing and instructive for the student, especially when corrective feedback is provided (Cartledge & Kourea, 2008).

**3** *Treat students respectfully.* Research has shown that teachers tend to be less respectful and courteous to low-achieving students, yet demand respect from these students (Rodriguez & Bellanca, 2007). These negative teacher behaviors often consist of sarcasm, put-downs, and interruption of student responses in class. These behaviors tend to produce a group of "low-status" students in the classroom, reduce the students' interest in academic content, and may lead to behavior problems as students express frustration over their low status. Furthermore, when a teacher engages in these behaviors, higher-achieving students who receive more respectful treatment are likely to model the teacher's behavior toward these so-called low-status students.

In contrast to a classroom that produces a group of low-status students, research from a range of sources has shown the power of culturally responsive caring in the classroom (Gay, 2010). When teachers take this approach, all students are valued and treated with respect and courtesy, and teachers are characterized as warm demanders (Ross et al., 2008). These teachers develop a respectful relationship with students, ensure that students treat one another respectfully, develop a task-oriented environment in the classroom, and have clear and high expectations for all students. In short, they are caring for all students, while also demanding high levels of achievement from all students.

④ *Ensure that students are asked high-level questions and are engaged in high-level material.* Students who are perceived by teachers as low performing are often asked low-level, factual questions during classroom discussions, but students perceived as higher performing are asked questions that require the application and evaluation of ideas (Rodriguez & Bellanca, 2007). Asking high-level questions has been shown to improve students' critical thinking and formation of concepts (Borich, 2011).

Teachers who successfully use questions to facilitate discussion in diverse, inclusive classrooms provide an appropriate wait-time for a student response to a question. Rather than expecting an immediate response, effective teachers wait at least 2 to 3 seconds, or more, and don't immediately respond to questions or add additional questions (Rodriguez & Bellanca, 2007). Increase the effectiveness of questions in facilitating discussions by having students engage in discussions in settings that are similar to their sociocultural experiences. For example, some students are more comfortable responding to questions and engaging in discussions in small groups with informal structures (Borich, 2011).

Research has shown that teachers tend to call on high-achieving students more often than they call on low-achieving students (Rodriguez & Bellanca, 2007). This research has also revealed that teachers tend to call on students in the front row and in seats toward the middle of the classroom more often than they call on students in the back of the room. To address this issue, monitor your behavior to ensure that questions are equally distributed across all students in the classroom, thus ensuring that all students have the opportunity to engage in high-level classroom discussions.

⑤ *Provide opportunities for student self-regulation.* To achieve academic success, all students benefit from activities that are self-directed. These activities tend to increase the confidence of students, and improve student motivation, especially for students from diverse backgrounds (Borich, 2011; Rodriguez & Bellanca, 2007). Self-regulated strategies have been developed for teaching students mathematics (Montague, 2008) and writing (Mason, Harris, & Graham, 2011).

Strategies that may be used to promote self-regulated instruction for students from CLD backgrounds include (Borich, 2011):

- *Provide the student with a choice regarding learning activities.* When students pursue topics on their own, they will often choose topics that are culturally relevant. In addition, these activities allow students to construct their own meaning and interpretations related to classroom activities, as they participate in and direct their own learning.
- *Use challenging problems for instruction.* These problems should be focused so that the student must make decisions regarding what is important for a solution. This allows the student to have control over problem solving, and provides an opportunity to see learning as self-directed.
- *Include problems from the real world that require problem solving.* This allows learners to become investigators in their communities as they solve actual problems. As students engage in these activities, they must apply classroom knowledge to a practical problem, thus increasing their interest in the problem while reinforcing information they have learned.
- *Use group activities to support self-directed instruction.* These group activities may add to the comfort level of some students as they begin to engage in self-directed learning. Furthermore, working in groups allows students the opportunity to gain information from others, and then create new or unusual variations on this knowledge that can be applied during self-directed learning.

More information regarding these self-regulation strategies is provided in Chapter 13.

## Applications and Examples

One approach that can be used to develop self-directed learning for students from CLD backgrounds is cooperative learning. This approach to learning has been shown to be effective for students from a range of culture and language backgrounds (Gay, 2010). However, when students work in cooperative groups, it becomes obvious that there is great variety among students with regard to independence, persistence, and flexibility (Borich, 2011). These characteristics are influenced, at least to some degree, by a student's cultural background, and may influence the quality of each student's participation in a cooperative group (Gay, 2010). To ensure that all students engage in high-quality activities in cooperative groups, teachers should attend closely to students who need more

More information on cooperative learning is provided in Chapter 13.

structure (i.e., shorter attention span, tend to ask fewer questions), and those who need less structure (i.e., enjoy discussion, want to solve problems). Teachers should also monitor student persistence in working on activities and flexibility in working with others to solve problems (Borich, 2011). Adjusting the cooperative group structure and process to accommodate student preferences ensures that all students are actively engaged in these groups, and learn to work well with others who may have different approaches to learning.

## Keep in Mind

A key consideration for teachers when using effective instructional strategies to improve educational outcomes for students from diverse backgrounds relates to teacher expectations. Research has revealed that teachers may have low expectations for academic success for students who are from CLD backgrounds, those from high-poverty backgrounds, students with disabilities, and students who have not achieved at expected levels in the past. Teachers who have these low expectations tend to hold on to them tenaciously, and, as might be expected, these low expectations influence the quality of learning opportunities that are provided to certain students (Gay, 2010). Recent research reveals that a combination of high expectations and high-quality instruction can significantly increase academic achievement levels for many of these students (Borich, 2011; Gay, 2010; Rodriguez & Bellanca, 2007; Torgesen, 2009). Thus, it is important that all teachers closely examine their expectations for student success, and adjust low expectations so that *all* students are given an equitable opportunity to receive high-quality instruction and achieve at a high level.

### Key References

Borich, G. (2011). *Effective teaching methods: Research-based practices* (7th ed.). Upper Saddle River, NJ: Pearson Education.

Cartledge, G., Gardner, R., & Ford, D. (2009). *Diverse learners with exceptionalities: Culturally responsive teaching in the inclusive classroom.* Upper Saddle River, NJ: Pearson Education.

Cartledge, G., & Kourea, L. (2008). Culturally responsive classrooms for culturally diverse students with and at risk for disabilities. *Exceptional Children, 74*(3), 351–371.

Gay, G. (2010). *Culturally responsive teaching: Theory, research, and practice.* New York: Teachers College Press.

Rodriguez, E., & Bellanca, J. (2007). *What is it about me you can't teach? An instructional guide for the urban educator.* Thousand Oaks, CA: Corwin Press.

# CULTURALLY RESPONSIVE CLASSROOM MANAGEMENT

## Rationale

The achievement gap that exists for many students from diverse backgrounds may be significantly influenced by a discipline gap; that is, students from diverse backgrounds are more frequently subjected to school disciplinary sanctions, including removal from the classroom or school (Gregory, Skiba, & Noguera, 2010; Wallace, Goodkind, Wallace, & Bachman, 2008). This discipline gap is likely influenced by the demographic divide that exists between teachers and many of their students, who often are from different cultural backgrounds that reflect different expectations for student behavior (Cartledge, Gardner, & Ford, 2009; Gay, 2010; Weinstein, Curran, & Tomlinson-Clarke, 2003). These differences become a problem at times because expectations for appropriate behavior are often influenced by culture, "and conflicts are likely to occur when teachers and students come from different cultural backgrounds" (Weinstein, Tomlinson-Clarke, & Curran, 2004, p. 26). Culturally responsive classroom management is needed to reduce the discipline gap and provide a more equitable classroom experience for students from CLD backgrounds.

## Step-by-Step

Culturally responsive classroom management is designed to create a setting in which student behavior is appropriate—not because of fear of punishment or a desire for a reward, but because students have a sense of personal responsibility (Weinstein, Tomlinson-Clarke, & Curran, 2004). The teacher therefore places an emphasis on teaching students to make good decisions about their behavior, rather than emphasizing an overreliance on external control. Research provides support for several key components of culturally responsive classroom management (Cartledge & Kourea, 2008; Weinstein, Curran, & Tomlinson-Clarke, 2003; Weinstein, Tomlinson-Clarke, & Curran, 2004).

**1** *Recognize your own biases and ethnocentrism (Weinstein, Curran, & Tomlinson-Clarke, 2003; Weinstein, Tomlinson-Clarke, & Curran, 2004).* We are all cultural beings who have assumptions, beliefs, and biases related to human behavior. It is critical that teachers recognize that cultural differences exist, and that schools often reflect some of these biases. More specifically, schools most often adopt a European American, middle-class worldview that influences how most classrooms operate (i.e., placing an emphasis on efficiency, independence, and individual achievement). By examining your own cultural, ethnic, and socioeconomic class biases, you are much less likely to misinterpret the behavior of students from different cultural backgrounds and treat them inequitably.

**2** *Be aware of and knowledgeable about the cultural backgrounds and related behavior patterns of your students (Weinstein, Curran, & Tomlinson-Clarke, 2003;* *Weinstein, Tomlinson-Clarke, & Curran, 2004).* Many classrooms include students from a range of cultural backgrounds. At least some of these students are likely to have patterns of behaviors and beliefs that vary from the expectations in a typical classroom. For example, Delpit (1995) has pointed out that many African American students from working-class families are accustomed to experiencing very direct language from authority figures (e.g., "Sit in your seat and get to work"), rather than the indirect, or polite language that is often used in classrooms (e.g., "Are you ready to get in your seat and get to work?"). Teachers can learn about students' backgrounds and gain valuable information that informs culturally responsive classroom management by learning about (a) the experiences and history of persons from CLD backgrounds; (b) students' families and communities; (c) interpersonal relationship styles and discipline practices; and (d) cultural conceptions of time and space (e.g., how students think about punctuality).

**3** *Establish clear expectations for behavior (Cartledge & Kourea, 2008; Weinstein, Curran, & Tomlinson-Clarke, 2003; Weinstein, Tomlinson-Clarke, & Curran, 2004).* As we noted previously, different cultures may have different views regarding appropriate behavior. For example, in some cultures, making eye contact is a sign of respect for authority figures, yet in other cultures, averting the eyes is viewed as more appropriate. In many classrooms, teachers expect students to sit and listen while others speak. This expectation may be inadvertently disregarded by some African American students who are more accustomed to being active participants by using a call-response pattern of interaction. When using this interaction style, there are frequent interactions between the speaker and others (e.g., responses are often provided when the speaker makes statements).

It is important to note that when a mismatch occurs between a student's cultural background and classroom rules, the teacher must make a decision regarding whether or not this difference should be accommodated. This practice of mutual accommodation (Nieto & Bode, 2008) suggests that at times teachers should adjust rules based on students' cultural backgrounds, while at other times they should maintain rules that are needed to meet the requirements of school (e.g., attendance, punctuality, homework completion), and that are important to ensure academic progress and success.

Any good classroom management system is built on clear rules for behavior that students from all cultural groups understand. Typically, classrooms have three to six rules that are stated in a positive way (e.g., "follow teacher directions," "complete assignments on time") and are associated with success in the classroom. To ensure that students understand and have ownership for the rules, the teacher and students should develop these rules collaboratively. Students should also be engaged in discussions regarding the rules, and opportunities should be provided for modeling and practice to ensure understanding.

**4** *Organize the classroom to support culturally responsive practices (Weinstein, Curran, & Tomlinson-Clarke, 2003).* The physical environment of the classroom can be used to convey respect for cultural diversity. This may be done in many ways, including the following:

- Display a map of the world that highlights students' countries of origin.
- Use different languages on signs and posters in the classroom that welcome students.
- Depict persons from different cultural groups in pictures that are displayed.

- Emphasize literature from different cultures, and ensure that books promoting diversity are prominently displayed.

The physical environment of the classroom can also be used to affirm connectedness among students and a sense of community that accepts and supports all students. For example, arranging desks in clusters that allow students to work together, engage in discussions, share materials, and assist one another on academic tasks can be done to facilitate the connectedness among students and the development of a sense of community.

**5** *Create a caring setting (Cartledge & Kourea, 2008; Weinstein, Curran, & Tomlinson-Clarke, 2003).* In any classroom, management of student behavior is more successful when a climate of trust, respect, and caring is developed. This is especially important when students are from a different cultural background than the teacher. Developing a sense of community within the classroom can be an important component of a caring classroom. Teachers can begin to develop a sense of classroom community by having students explore how they are similar and different. Other activities such as morning meetings and cooperative learning activities allow students to get to know one another better and highlight students' unique backgrounds and abilities.

The teacher can play a key role in developing a sense of caring and respect for others within the classroom by engaging in activities that model these behaviors. This can be done by (a) greeting students in their native language and having other students learn words or phrases in this language; (b) modeling respect for diversity by including examples from different cultures in instructional activities; and (c) taking on the role of a warm demander (Ross et al., 2008) by not only caring for the students but also having high expectations and holding students accountable for their behavior and the quality of their work.

## Applications and Examples

A critical element of culturally responsive classroom management is fairness (Cartledge & Kourea, 2008). There are many ways teachers can ensure fairness in a culturally diverse classroom. One important consideration is to ensure that behavioral consequences match any violation of rules that may occur, and are not viewed by students as an overreaction to an infraction. Another critical consideration is that disciplinary actions should not be discriminatory against any group of students or individual, or allow privileges for certain groups. For example, Weinstein and colleagues describe the dress code at a school where European American students were allowed to wear pants with holes in the thighs, while African American students were punished with 10-day suspensions for not snapping the straps on their overalls (Weinstein, Tomlinson-Clarke, & Curran, 2004).

A key concern that arises regarding fairness in the classroom is when students begin to discern unfairness, they not only become angry but they may also begin devaluing the importance of education and disengage from school (Cartledge & Kourea, 2008). These behaviors are more likely to occur if classes seem to have standards that favor the advantaged group, and thus reflect ethnic injustice.

## Keep in Mind

Teachers may engage in many actions and activities that promote culturally responsive caring and respect for all students. Caring in action may be reflected in behaviors such as the following (Gay, 2010).

- Ensure that students from different ethnic groups feel valued, recognized, respected, seen, and heard in the classroom.
- Demonstrate personal and academic knowledge of culturally diverse students.
- Be confidants, resources, and advocates for culturally diverse students.
- Help students develop a sense of who they are, what they value, and what they can accomplish.
- Support students to develop competence, confidence, compassion, courage, and courtesy.
- Be academically demanding and personally supportive.
- Treat each student in the classroom with equal human worth.
- Acknowledge differences among students without making judgments.

**Key References**

Cartledge, G., Gardner, R., & Ford, D. (2009). *Diverse learners with exceptionalities: Culturally responsive teaching in the inclusive classroom.* Upper Saddle River, NJ: Pearson Education.

Cartledge, G., & Kourea, L. (2008). Culturally responsive classrooms for culturally diverse students with and at risk for disabilities. *Exceptional Children, 74*(3), 351–371.

Gay, G. (2010). *Culturally responsive teaching: Theory, research, and practice.* New York: Teachers College Press.

Hoover, J., Klingner, J., Baca, L., & Patton, J. (2008). *Methods for teaching culturally and linguistically diverse exceptional children.* Upper Saddle River, NJ: Pearson Education.

Weinstein, C., Curran, M., & Tomlinson-Clarke, S. (2003). Culturally responsive classroom management: Awareness in action. *Theory into Practice, 42*(4), 269–276.

Weinstein, C., Tomlinson-Clarke, S., & Curran, M. (2004). Toward a conception of culturally responsive classroom management. *Journal of Teacher Education, 55*(1), 25–38.

# DOUBLE-CHECK: A CULTURALLY RESPONSIVE APPROACH TO CLASSROOM MANAGEMENT

## Rationale

Professionals are in agreement that more culturally responsive approaches to classroom management are needed to address the needs of students from culturally and linguistically diverse backgrounds (Gay, 2010). These practices should be based on current evidence regarding effective practices, and must address the needs of teachers and students from a diverse range of cultural backgrounds. The double-check framework has been developed to support teachers in delivering culturally responsive behavior management (Hershfeldt, Sechrest, Pell, Rosenberg, Bradshaw, & Leaf, 2009; Rosenberg, 2007). This approach uses evidence-based components to address culturally responsive practices in the classroom.

## Step-by-Step

Double-check is a five-step framework for supporting teachers in developing more culturally responsive classroom management strategies.

**1** *Engage in reflective thinking about cultural group membership.* Double-check begins by having teachers examine their own cultural group membership, as well as those of their students. As this is done, teachers begin to understand the concept of culture, and recognize why culture is important to understand for effective classroom practice. Teachers examine their thinking regarding culture by (a) being aware of their own group membership and history; (b) being aware of their students' group memberships and histories; (c) considering how classroom behaviors of students are influenced by past and present circumstances (e.g., life experiences, cultural practices); (d) examining their own (the teacher's) biases, and how these biases might influence the interpretation of classroom behavior; and (e) making efforts to reach out to students and understand differences. These activities are best completed in collaboration with other teachers. We later describe a self-assessment instrument that can be used to facilitate this process.

**2** *Develop sensitivity to students' cultural and situational messages.* As we noted previously, getting to know your students' cultural backgrounds and histories, as well as examining your own cultural history and biases are important steps in developing sensitivity to students' cultural experiences and practices. Given the many different cultural backgrounds of students, and the differences that exist within a given cultural group (Gay, 2010), it is important that teachers interpret student behavior based on the student's cultural background. For example,

Townsend (2000) has noted that some teachers respond negatively to a communication style of some African American students that is viewed as argumentative during classroom discussions. Interpreting this communication style through a cultural lens allows the teacher to realize that viewing this behavior as argumentative is a misinterpretation, as the students are expressing a passionate feeling about the topic being discussed—a behavior that is highly valued and appreciated by most teachers.

**3** *Develop an authentic, caring relationship with students.* In any classroom, fewer behavior problems occur when the teacher and students have a positive relationship. This is especially important when working with students from a range of cultural backgrounds, as most students value a caring relationship with their teacher. Teachers who demonstrate caring for their students are interested not only in the students' academic achievement but also their social and emotional well-being. Moreover, when a teacher has a caring, authentic relationship with a student, the teacher is in a better position to address any behavior issues with a plan that aligns with the student's cultural background.

Indicators that teachers are initiating and maintaining authentic, caring relationships with students include:

- Examples of the teacher's involvement in the student's personal life
- Discussion of the student's behavior rather than reacting immediately to behavior
- Examples of recognition that situational factors (e.g., need to save face) influence behavior

- Increased levels of positive attention directed toward the student (e.g., engagement during instructional activities)
- Evidence of caring and trust directed toward the student

④ *Develop effective communication with students from CLD backgrounds.* As we noted previously, many students from CLD backgrounds have distinctive communication styles that may not be a good fit for typical expectations of teachers. Teachers who have a culturally responsive approach to addressing these communication styles should seek to understand the intended communicative function of the student's behavior. Furthermore, the teacher's behavior should reflect civility and respect, even when this may be difficult to do. Finally, culturally responsive teachers should recognize that some issues that arise may be explained by the student's lack of facility with code-switching (Gay, 2010)—that is, the student may not recognize that different contexts require different types of communication.

⑤ *Connect the student's experiences with the curriculum.* Using examples from a student's cultural background in classroom lessons and activities tangibly demonstrates that the teacher values the student's background. Furthermore, these experiences help the teacher develop more authentic relationships with students, and model acceptance of diversity to all members of the class. This connection to the curriculum should occur on an ongoing basis, and should be reflected in books that are read in class, coverage of historical events from different cultural perspectives, and so forth. This ensures that the value of different cultures permeates the curriculum, and that the cultural backgrounds of all students are represented in the curriculum.

## Applications and Examples

Examining one's cultural background and experiences is not an easy task. This is especially true when a person is from the majority or dominant culture (i.e., European American in most U.S. schools). We would recommend that as teachers examine their cultural group membership and their biases, they should work collaboratively with other teachers. Ideally, some of these teachers should be from different cultural backgrounds. To facilitate this process, we recommend using the self-assessment from Hershfeldt and colleagues (2009) or a brief, adapted version of that self-assessment in Figure 12.3 as a starting point for this examination and discussion. All school personnel should complete the assessment anonymously. Each item in the assessment should be interpreted individually. This assessment can be used as a catalyst for discussion among small groups of school professionals or at faculty meetings, or the data may be aggregated to provide a building-level needs assessment and suggest possible directions for professional development.

Figure 12.3 Double-Check Self-Assessment

Review and provide a rating for each item below

| | Evidence | | | | |
|---|---|---|---|---|---|
| **Program Components** | 4—See regularly in my school or classroom | 3-See most of the time | 2-Rarely see | 1-Never see | U-Does not apply in my school |
| **Reflection on students' group memberships** | | | | | |
| I understand culture and why it is important. | | | | | |
| I reflect on how my actions contribute to student behavior. | | | | | |
| My views of differences are positive and constructive. | | | | | |
| **Developing authentic relationships with students** | | | | | |
| I encourage positive interactions among all students. | | | | | |
| I display to students tangible evidence of caring and trust. | | | | | |
| I am genuinely interested in the personal lives and activities of my students. | | | | | |
| **Effective communication** | | | | | |
| I have high expectations for all of my students. | | | | | |
| I am civil and respectful in all of my communications with students. | | | | | |
| I am not judgmental in my communications with students. | | | | | |
| I know about and recognize "code switching." | | | | | |
| **Connections to the curriculum** | | | | | |
| I use examples from students' cultural backgrounds in my lessons. | | | | | |
| I use activities in instruction that reflect the cultural backgrounds of my students. | | | | | |
| I highlight cultural differences in a positive way. | | | | | |
| **Sensitivity to cultural and situational messages** | | | | | |
| I know how situations related to health, poverty, dress, and so forth may influence behavior. | | | | | |
| I am aware that students need to address multiple groups. | | | | | |
| I am aware of students' social and political consciousness. | | | | | |

Open ended questions. Review the items above that were rated below a "4". Those rated "3" may require additional practice or attention. Those rated "2" or "1" may require additional instruction and practice. Please respond to the items below by prioritizing the areas in which you would like resources and support to address cultural responsiveness to students.

**Additional professional development in the following areas would be useful:**

**Additional practice (e.g., role play, coaching) in the following areas would be useful:**

*Note:* This assessment is abbreviated and adapted from Rosenberg (2007) and Hershfeldt et al. (2009). For the full Self-Assessment, see Hershfeldt et al. (2009).

## Keep in Mind

Current research evidence strongly supports a positive system of behavior support for all students, and suggests that negative responses to behavior and punishment can quickly become ineffective when addressing the behavior of any student. To keep classroom management as positive as possible, and to address student discipline and the occasional need for punishment, Cartledge, Gardner, and Ford (2009) recommend the following:

- Avoid disproportionate use of disciplinary actions for certain cultural or ethnic groups.
- Keep punishment to a minimum, and ensure that consequences directly relate to the infraction and are fair and brief.
- Emphasize positive relationships and show respect for all students, even when punishment is being used.
- Communicate high expectations for social behavior for all students.
- Appeal to students' backgrounds and integrity as reasons for behaving appropriately.

**Key References**

Cartledge, G., Gardner, R., & Ford, D. (2009). *Diverse learners with exceptionalities: Culturally responsive teaching in the inclusive classroom*. Upper Saddle River, NJ: Pearson Education.

Cartledge, G., & Kourea, L. (2008). Culturally responsive classrooms for culturally diverse students with and at risk for disabilities. *Exceptional Children, 74*(3), 351–371.

Gay, G. (2010). *Culturally responsive teaching: Theory, research, and practice*. New York: Teachers College Press.

Hershfeldt, P., Sechrest, R., Pell, K., Rosenberg, M., Bradshaw, C., & Leaf, P. (2009). Double-check: A framework of cultural responsiveness applied to classroom behavior. *Teaching Exceptional Children Plus, 6*(2), Article 5. Retrieved January 21, 2011, from http://escholarship.bc.edu/education/tecplus/vol6/iss2/art5

Rosenberg, M. (2007, September). *Double check: Application of culturally responsive behavior management principles*. Paper presented at the initial training for PBIS Plus, Baltimore, MD.

# Effective Instruction in Core Academic Areas: Teaching Reading, Writing, and Mathematics

## KEY TOPICS

**After reading this chapter you will:**

- Know what to expect regarding effective instruction in inclusive classrooms.

- Be able to describe principles and practices to support effective instruction in inclusive classrooms.

- Understand principles and practices related to effective instruction in reading, writing, and mathematics.

- Understand a series of guided, step-by-step interventions and practices to help you provide effective instruction to students in inclusive classrooms.

# chapter 13

# A VIEW FROM TEACHERS

### What Is Effective Instruction?

We interviewed several teachers from Gilpin Manor Elementary and West Hernando Middle School regarding effective instruction in inclusive classrooms. Here's what they had to say.

A sixth-grade teacher, Lisa Grover, emphasized the importance of getting to know your students. "We do pretesting, talk with the students, review their work, for much of the first month of school. We look at what kind of work they hand in, what type of motivation they have. We look at whether they have a behavior problem as well. You really need to get to know them and their levels and what they understand." Lisa also stressed the importance of communication with parents as she gets to know her students. "I send a letter to the parents at the beginning of the year, and say, 'In a million words or less, tell me about your child.' This is a very good learning opportunity for me. The parents really open up more when they're writing something down about the child. I get to know about their child's strengths and weaknesses, and what the family relationships are. I keep the letters on file all year, and go back to them often."

Susan Huff, a fifth-grade teacher, discussed the importance of content knowledge for effectively teaching all students. She commented that it is "important to know what you're teaching." This deep knowledge of content helps a teacher to better "adapt and differentiate to meet all the needs of students in the classroom." Susan concurs with the previous comments from Lisa Grover about getting to know your students to make this occur. Teachers need to know more than simply "That's a kid with ADHD. They have to get to know the individual child and understand their disability and their capabilities."

Laura Scott, a seventh-grade teacher, talked about the need for planning a lesson well and letting students know what's coming. "It's good to give students a heads up in the morning about the schedule for the day to keep them focused. For some children, it's really important for them to know what's going to happen during a class period, even if it's written on an index card that says we're going to do 1, 2, and then 3, so that they see what's coming and know what the period looks like. Sometimes it's a matter of having very specific expectations for the student, and they know they have to work for a certain amount of time."

Melissa Pratt, a preschool teacher at Gilpin Manor, and Eileen Walls, a behavior specialist at West Hernando, both discussed the importance of using different approaches to presenting information to students so that students get to see the information, hear about it, and experience it, which result in multiple opportunities to learn. Melissa said that students "need models, they need visuals. A multisensory approach works best. And although this may be a special

education approach, it works well for everybody, and all children benefit." Eileen Walls extended this idea by saying, "Visual aids are very powerful, when they can look at it, touch it, pass it around. That helps. We do charts and maps. Sometimes we have students draw their own map, and a lot of other 'do-it-yourself' activities. When we're talking about weather, in the book is a weather map from years ago in another part of the country. I'll tell them, when you go home, look at the weather outside, and make yourself a weather map. Why is the weather like it is now?"

Finally, Vicki Eng, a seventh-grade teacher at West Hernando Middle School, noted the importance of having a classroom where expectations are clear and lessons are carefully planned and well organized. "It helps students to have guidelines and rules posted. This helps get the class under control, and they know what to expect. Lessons also need to be well planned—what you're going to teach them and how. Then they can make progress in learning, and I can make a real difference in their lives."

**MyEducationLab**

Visit the MyEducationLab for *Inclusion* to enhance your understanding of chapter concepts with a personalized Study Plan. You'll also have the opportunity to hone your teaching skills through video and case-based Assignments and Activities, Building Teaching Skills and Disposition lessons, and IRIS Case Studies.

# Introduction

When you complete the Pause & Reflect exercise below and reflect with a peer on effective and ineffective teachers you have had, the importance of an effective teacher will likely be obvious. You may be surprised to know that it has only been in recent years that educators have realized just *how* important an effective teacher is, especially for students who struggle to learn core academic skills (i.e., reading, writing, and arithmetic). Research has shown that students who are assigned to the most effective teachers three years in a row score as many as 50 percentile points higher on achievement tests when compared to students who are assigned to the least effective teachers (Rivers & Sanders, 2002).

For students with less effective teachers, this level of difference in achievement is sufficient to lead to failing statewide accountability measures, grade retention, and even, in some extreme cases, a label of learning disability. Over a period of years, the quality of the teacher contributes more to student achievement than any other factor, including class size, class composition, or student background (Rivkin, Hanushek, & Kain, 2005).

Fortunately, research has documented many of the effective practices that teachers may employ to make sure that students who struggle academically learn to read, write, and use math skills. Some of these practices may be new to you; others are surprisingly simple and obvious, as the interview with teachers from Gilpin Manor Elementary and West Hernando Middle School at the beginning of this chapter illustrated. For example, Laura Scott said that lessons should be carefully planned so students know what is expected of them, and students should be actively involved in the lessons whenever possible. A related part of effective instruction was described by both Lisa Grover and Susan Huff, as they noted that the teacher needs to know her students well, and understand what they know and don't know. This information, along with deep knowledge of the content being taught provides a teacher with the needed information to successfully differentiate instruction to meet the needs of all students.

## Pause & Reflect

Discuss with a peer your experiences in a class in which you learned a lot. What factors contributed to this effective instruction? What were the characteristics of a class in which you learned very little? How did these classes differ?

The most important single factor influencing student learning is an effective teacher.

A key concept that we often use when describing effective instruction is that many students seem to learn basic skills in reading, writing, and math by osmosis; they just soak up this information and readily learn it. However, students who struggle to learn these skills, including many who have disabilities, are different. It seems that they must be taught everything, using direct, explicit methods. This is a bit of an oversimplification (i.e., all students struggle at times, and all students seem to learn at least some things by osmosis), but we have found this concept useful as we consider what works when teaching students who struggle to learn basic academic skills.

In this chapter, we address effective instruction for core academic skills in reading, writing, and mathematics. We do this by addressing high-quality **core instruction** in general education classrooms (or Tier-1 instruction in response-to-intervention [RTI] models), as well as supplementary instruction that teachers may provide in general education classrooms when students struggle to learn this content (i.e., Tier-2 instruction). These instructional practices provide a critical foundation of knowledge and skills that you will need to effectively meet the needs of all students and to ensure that they learn basic academic skills in reading, writing, and mathematics, and make adequate yearly progress as they move through school.

# Effective Instruction in an Inclusive Classroom: What to Expect

As you know from your years in school, students in *any* classroom have skill levels in reading, writing, and mathematics that vary dramatically. It is not uncommon to have some students who read well above grade level, while others struggle to read and learn from material presented in class. This same range of skill levels is also common in writing and mathematics. Providing effective instruction for the full range of students in a classroom while addressing the needs of students who struggle to learn basic skills is not a simple matter.

However, the importance of providing instruction to ensure that students learn basic skills in early elementary school is widely recognized by elementary teachers, parents, and policy makers (i.e., by the U.S. Congress in the No Child Left Behind Act of 2001). More specifically, basic skills in reading, writing, and mathematics are building blocks for later learning, and students must master these skills to ensure success as they move through school and learn more complex content.

Providing effective instruction for all students is a major purpose of inclusion, and is why most general education teachers support well-designed inclusive programs. These teachers realize that they will be much more successful in providing effective instruction to all students if they have collaborative support from special education staff. To make inclusion successful, general and special education teachers share their skills and knowledge of students, instructional methods, and classroom organization. This collaboration provides the opportunity to group students creatively and differentiate instruction so that teachers can more effectively address the needs of all students.

The reality of all classrooms is that teachers engage in what one teacher called a juggling act, trying to figure out how to distribute their time among various students. As Susan Huff, a fifth-grade teacher at Gilpin Manor Elementary School said, one of her biggest challenges is finding the time to meet the needs of all of students. "It takes a lot of time to differentiate instruction, and create support materials." Working with a special education teacher or paraeducator may address this issue to some degree, because this allows teachers to regroup students and provide intensive, small-group instruction to those who struggle to learn basic skills. But even under the best of circumstances, time is at a premium in a general education classroom. Given this shortage of time, many teachers in inclusive programs use strategies such as cooperative learning and peer tutoring to engage students in learning together collaboratively to better address student needs.

Finally, a reality of many classrooms is that instructional services are being reorganized to provide seamless tiers of instruction to better meet student needs as part of RTI models. These models are designed to provide high-quality, effective core instruction in the general education classroom (Tier-1 instruction), and supplementary instruction in the general education classroom for students who struggle to learn basic skills (Tier-2 instruction). Well-designed RTI models can provide the foundation for effective instruction in inclusive schools and classrooms, ensuring that all students have the necessary supports to learn basic skills in reading, writing, and mathematics.

# Principles and Practices to Support Effective Instruction

Delivering effective instruction in core academic areas is not a simple task. In this section, we present information on research-based practices for delivering instruction that improves academic achievement for many students who struggle to learn basic skills in reading, writing, and mathematics. We begin by addressing teacher behaviors in delivering instruction, and then describe grouping practices that may be used to deliver effective instruction.

## Effective Instruction: Teacher Behaviors in Delivering Instruction

Research and the experiences of teachers have shown that when a teacher engages in effective instruction in teaching basic skills in reading, writing, and mathematics (or teaching new skills in any content area), certain instructional behaviors are consistently observed (Borich, 2011; Kauchak & Eggen, 2012; McLeskey & Waldron, 2011; Rosenshine & Stevens, 1986). These behaviors relate to the teacher's actions when beginning a lesson, presenting information during the lesson, guiding student practice after instruction, correcting student work and providing feedback, planning and carrying out student seatwork, and following up the lesson. Each of these components is briefly described in Figure 13.1.

You will note from Figure 13.1 that effective instruction is well organized; focuses student attention on well-defined, critical information; provides multiple opportunities to learn material with feedback; and includes follow-up monitoring to ensure that the information is retained over time. These components of effective instruction and related lesson structure provide a foundation for high-quality core instruction in the general education classroom. If you review the interview with teachers from Gilpin Manor Elementary and West Hernando Middle School that was presented at the beginning of this chapter, you'll see that they address many of these principles, including providing clear expectations, ensuring that lessons are well organized, and varying activities during a lesson. Although these components do not include everything a teacher needs to know about effective instruction, they provide a good foundation, especially for teaching basic skills in reading, writing, and mathematics. For a review of the principles of research-based instruction in core content areas, see Strategy 13.1 later in this chapter.

Educators have incorporated the components of effective instruction in Figure 13.1 into materials that use **direct instruction** or an explicit approach to instruction. This approach has been demonstrated to be highly effective for students who struggle learning basic skills (Borich, 2011). *Direct instruction* is defined as "a model that uses teacher demonstration and explanation combined with student practice and feedback to help learners acquire well-defined knowledge and skills needed for later learning" (Eggen & Kauchak, 2012, p. 266). For example, Reading Mastery (Engelmann & Bruner, 2003) is a complete

Effective instruction requires careful planning and organization of classroom activities.

| Figure 13.1 | Components of Effective Instruction: Lesson Delivery and Follow-Up |
|---|---|

1. Review and check homework
   - Develop routines for students to check each other's homework.
   - Review and question students regarding past learning.
   - Review relevant prerequisite skills before instruction.
   - Reteach when necessary.
2. Presentation of material, information
   - Provide a short statement of objectives and an overview or advance organizer.
   - Present ideas so that they are clear to students at different levels of understanding.
   - Highlight main points.
   - Provide concrete examples and illustrations.
   - Provide models and demonstrations.
   - Proceed at a rapid pace, but in a logical, step-by-step order.
   - Frequently check for understanding by asking questions.
   - As necessary, provide detailed and redundant instruction, including examples.
3. Guided practice following instruction
   - Initial practice is closely monitored or guided by the teacher.
   - Evaluate student responses and ask questions to check for understanding.
   - Ensure that all students respond and receive feedback.
   - As needed, provide additional instruction.
   - Guided practice continues until students firmly grasp content, a success rate of at least 80% is achieved, and students can work independently.
4. Correctives and feedback
   - Follow a quick, firm, correct response with another question or a brief acknowledgment of correctness (e.g., "That's right").
   - Follow a hesitant correct response with process feedback (e.g., "Yes, Linda, that's right because . . .").
   - When the first response in incorrect, try to elicit an improved response.
   - Corrections can include feedback (i.e., simplifying the question, giving clues), explaining or reviewing steps, giving process feedback, or reteaching.
   - Student errors indicate a need for more practice; monitor student work for systematic errors.
   - Use praise in moderation; specific praise is more effective than general praise.
   - Continue guided practice and corrections until all students meet the objectives of the lesson.
5. Independent practice (seatwork)
   - Provide sufficient practice.
   - Practice should be directly relevant to the skills/content being taught.
   - Practice to overlearning, when responses are firm, quick, and automatic.
   - During independent practice, the correct response rate should be 95% or better.
   - Students should be held accountable for seatwork.
   - Seatwork should be actively supervised, whenever possible.
6. Weekly and monthly review
   - Systematically review material previously learned.
   - Include review in homework.
   - Test frequently.
   - Reteach material missed on tests.

*Sources:* Adapted from Borich, 2011; Kauchak & Eggen, 2012; Rosenshine & Stevens, 1986.

instructional program to teach reading that is built on the principles of direct instruction. This program includes highly structured material for students in grades K–6, with related scripts for teachers as they teach material to students. Similar programs are available to teach reading to older students (e.g., Corrective Reading [Engelmann, Hanner, & Johnson, 2008] for students in grades 4–12); writing (e.g., Reasoning and Writing [Englemann, 2001] for students in grades K–12); and mathematics (e.g., Connecting Math Concepts [Engelmann, Carnine, Bernadette, & Engelmann, 2003] for grades K–8 and Corrective Math [Carnine, Engelmann, & Steely, 2003] for grade 4 to adult). For a description of a lesson using direct instruction to teach mathematics in a first-grade classroom, see Strategy 13.2 later in this chapter.

# Grouping Students to Support the Delivery of Effective Instruction

As you reflected on your experiences with grouping arrangements in school, you likely recalled many examples when a teacher provided instruction to an entire class. This approach to instruction is efficient, as the teacher conveys information to a large number of students quickly. You (and most teachers) very likely have been quite successful in learning information using this grouping format. However, for some students, especially those who struggle to learn basic academic content, this approach often does not work well.

## Pause & Reflect

Consider the ways you were grouped for instruction when you were in school. What were the most common grouping arrangements in elementary school? Secondary school? Which grouping arrangements made it easier for you to learn content? Why?

In recent years, many teachers have begun to use alternatives to whole-group instruction in general education classrooms to ensure that they better meet the needs of all students (Eggen & Kauchak, 2012; Good & Brophy, 2008). This change in practice has occurred as teachers have recognized that if only whole-class instruction is used, "individual student needs are not met or, worse yet, that selected children, often the most needy, may be denied access to knowledge, instruction, and an opportunity to learn" (Reutzel, 2003, p. 243).

These **alternative grouping strategies** are designed to allow teachers to use components of effective instruction (see Figure 13.1) that may be difficult to employ when using whole-group instruction. For example, teachers may use these grouping strategies to reduce the number of students being taught and offer the teacher the opportunity to provide intensive, explicit instruction that is tailored to the individual needs of students and closely monitored to ensure effectiveness (Gersten et al., 2009; McLeskey & Waldron, 2011).

Options for grouping students who do not learn content via whole-group instruction include homogeneous ability groups; mixed-ability groups (e.g., cooperative groups); individual tutoring; and **peer tutoring**. These grouping options may be used in a general education classroom or in a separate classroom. To determine whether groups of students require instruction in the general education classroom or in separate locations, teachers should address logistical considerations related to the size of the general education classroom, the type of activities that are occurring across groups, student characteristics (e.g., attention to task), and similar issues.

## Skill-Based Grouping

Perhaps the most intuitively appealing approach for grouping students who struggle to learn academic content, and indeed the most widely used strategy in schools for most of the last century (Haager & Klingner, 2005), has been to group students based on their perceived ability or skill level. This **ability grouping**, or tracking strategy, has been (and continues to be) an appealing approach because it ostensibly allows teachers to group students based on common needs, and it simplifies planning and teaching so that teachers may focus on specific student needs.

Much evidence indicates that when students are in low-skill or low-ability groups *for much or all of the school day,* they often do not benefit academically (Freeman & Alkin, 2000; Good & Brophy, 2008; McLeskey & Waldron, 2011; Reutzel, 2003; Salend & Garrick Duhaney, 2007). This type of ability grouping has been particularly negative for students from low socioeconomic status backgrounds and those with disabilities (Freeman & Alkin, 2000; Good & Brophy, 2008; McLeskey & Waldron, 2011; Salend & Garrick Duhaney, 2007). The lack of effectiveness of this type of grouping has been attributed to a number of factors (Good & Brophy, 2008; McLeskey & Waldron, 2011; Reutzel, 2003), including:

- Fewer students assume leadership roles.
- More students engage in disruptive behavior.
- Contact between students across different skill levels is limited.
- The quality of instruction in these groups tends to be poor.

| **Figure 13.2** | **Guidelines for Student Grouping** | | |
|---|---|---|---|

1. The number, size, and composition of groups should be flexible, and vary according to content and student needs.
2. Groups should be periodically created, modified, and disbanded depending on student needs.
3. Groups should vary in size, from 2 to 10 students, depending on the purpose and format of instruction.
4. Grouping should lead to more effective instruction and improved achievement, not simply differential pacing through the curriculum.
5. Group scheduling and instruction should be flexible, and should depend on the content of instruction and students' instructional needs.
6. Students should spend the majority of the day in mixed ability groups.
7. Teachers should limit the extent to which membership in an ability group determines other school experiences.
8. Groups should be organized so that struggling learners receive the extra instruction they need. Groups for these students should typically be smaller (e.g., 3–5 students), and meet for more instructional time with the teacher.
9. An explicit strategy should be used for closely supervising the work of groups.

*Sources:* Adapted from Good & Brophy, 2008; McLeskey & Waldron, 2000; Unsworth, 1984.

Although long-term ability groups are often not effective, this does not mean that students should never be grouped by skill or ability for instruction. When used appropriately, this type of instruction has been demonstrated to be highly effective. For example, teachers may use skill-based grouping to provide struggling readers the intensive instruction they need to make adequate academic progress. However, when using skill-based grouping, teachers should attend to guidelines for effective use of groups (summarized in Figure 13.2) that help to avoid many of the pitfalls that have arisen in the past.

### Mixed-Ability Grouping Using Cooperative Learning

At least partially in response to problems that exist when grouping students with similar skills or ability, educators developed strategies for delivering instruction using mixed-ability groups (Borich, 2011; Eggen & Kauchak, 2012). These strategies are primarily based on the use of small groups of students (usually two to six) who work in cooperative groups to learn academic content. **Cooperative learning** involves students working together to learn and to ensure that others in their group learn as well (Eggen & Kauchak, 2012). Cooperative learning groups vary widely in type, but they share common characteristics that are described in Figure 13.3. For a description of cooperative learning, see Strategy 13.3 later in this chapter.

## Individual Tutoring

Several researchers contend that individualized tutoring is the optimal instructional method for meeting the needs of students who are struggling academically (D'Agostino & Murphy, 2004; Elbaum, Vaughn, Hughes, & Moody, 2000; Good & Brophy, 2008). Tutoring is especially effective when done by teachers who are highly skilled and can engage in flexible decision making to meet individual student needs. Classroom teachers routinely provide brief, short-term tutoring to students in inclusive classrooms, but

Cooperative learning is an alternative grouping strategy that can lead to improved student learning.

| Figure 13.3 | Common Characteristics of Cooperative Learning Groups |
| --- | --- |

- **Positive interdependence:** The accomplishment of the group goal depends on all group members working together. Thus, each group member must be concerned about the performance of all of the other group members. Students are not successful until the group has achieved its goal, and each individual has attained his or her goal.
- **Individual accountability:** All students are held individually accountable for their own learning, as well as for their contributions to the group. Individual evaluations are used to determine if each student has mastered the content being learned.
- **Cooperative skills:** Students must learn and practice social and cooperative skills within the group. These are social skills that are commonly used in group activities, such as sharing materials, taking turns, and encouraging others.
- **Face-to-face interaction:** In cooperative learning groups, students interact with one another as they are working. They may seek assistance from others, offer assistance, plan activities, learn different aspects of the content, teach content to others, and so forth.
- **Student reflection and goal setting:** At the end of a cooperative activity, students evaluate how the group functioned, and whether the group's goals were met. Students then engage in reflective discussion and individual goal setting to improve their work in cooperative groups.
- **Heterogeneous grouping:** Most often, cooperative groups should be heterogeneous, as students are mixed based on ability, skills, interests, and student characteristics (e.g., gender, ethnicity, ability or disability, language spoken in the home). However, at times, homogeneous groups are formed based on student interest (e.g., students interested in a particular topic in science might work together) or for instruction related to particular skills.

*Sources:* Marzano, Pickering, & Pollock, 2001; Putnam, 1998.

## Pause & Reflect

Cooperative learning groups are at times frustrating for students. Have you experienced this frustration? In what ways? How might you minimize frustrating experiences of students when using cooperative groups?

long-term, intensive teacher tutoring is most often used as a Tier-3 intervention when a student has not responded well to previous interventions.

Several teacher tutoring programs have been developed that focus on helping students develop early reading skills (Clay, 2001; Hayes, Lane, & Pullen, 2005; Hoover, 2001). The most widely used of these programs is Reading Recovery (Clay, 2001), which has been documented as effective for many students. This program is highly specialized and requires extensive training and related materials. For more information on Reading Recovery, see Strategy 13.4 later in this chapter.

Peer tutoring can be a highly effective instructional strategy.

## Peer Tutoring

Peer-assisted tutoring strategies are a cost-effective approach to providing individual tutoring for students who struggle to learn academic content. These strategies consistently increase the academic achievement of struggling readers and are academically beneficial for the tutor as well (Bond & Castagnera, 2006; Fuchs, Fuchs, Craddock, Hollenbeck, Hamlett, & Schatschneider, 2008). Furthermore, teachers have effectively used these activities across grade levels and content areas (Bond & Castagnera, 2006; Stenhoff & Lignugaris/Kraft, 2007).

Peer-assisted learning strategies entail the use of same-age or cross-age peers to provide academic and/or social assistance to students who are struggling in school (Fuchs et al., 2008). The most widely used and thoroughly researched peer-assisted learning strategy is class-wide peer tutoring (CWPT) and a variation on this strategy, peer-assisted learning strategies (PALS) (Abbott, Greenwood, Buzhardt, & Tapia, 2006; Fuchs et al., 2008; McMaster et al., 2006). For more information regarding a form of peer tutoring that is used to teach reading in grades 2–6, see Strategy 13.5, "Peer-Assisted Learning Strategies."

To ensure that peer tutoring is effective, tutors require training, and teachers must address other procedural guidelines. Good and Brophy (2008) have provided guidelines for implementing peer-tutoring programs. These guidelines begin by noting that the learning outlook in the class must change to a "we learn from one another" mind-set. They also describe several important procedural matters, including:

1. Provide clearly specified times of the day for tutoring.
2. Clearly describe specific assignments, and provide related materials for tutors.
3. Tutors should work with tutees long enough to complete a sequence of assignments (over 1 to 2 weeks), rather than starting anew each day with a new tutee.
4. Change the tutoring assignments every couple of weeks to prevent developing an "I'm your teacher" perspective.
5. Tutors should not administer tests or be responsible for other student evaluation.
6. Allow students to be tutors and tutees.
7. Peer-tutoring programs take time. Spend the first week or so modeling tutoring behaviors, making sure instructions for tutoring are clear, having students model appropriate tutoring, and so forth.
8. Let parents know that peer tutoring will be used and that all students will be both tutors and tutees.

# Effective Instruction in Reading, Writing, and Mathematics

In the sections that follow, we address high-quality, effective core instruction (i.e., Tier 1) in the general education classroom in reading, writing, and mathematics. This instruction forms the foundation of any effective, inclusive classroom, and it ensures that students have the opportunity to learn basic skills that form the foundation for later learning in school. However, as we've discussed previously, even with high-quality core instruction, some students continue to struggle to learn basic skills in reading, writing, and/or mathematics. We also address more intensive, research-based instructional strategies and programs that enable teachers to meet the needs of these students in the general education classroom.

## Reading Instruction

Many students seem to learn to read with little effort, but in all schools there are some students who struggle to learn to recognize words, read fluently, and comprehend what they read. Students who struggle with learning how to read often experience difficulty in two areas (Torgesen, 2000). First, they encounter difficulty in understanding how words they know orally are represented in print. This problem is often manifested in connecting sounds and letters in words, and it results in difficulty sounding out words. For example, a child may not recognize a beginning sound in a word, or that beginning sounds in two words match (e.g., *dog* and *duck*, or *fat* and *fox*).

Many children who struggle learning to read also often have a second problem related to a limited sight vocabulary. That is, the words they recognize immediately by sight are limited in number and range (Torgesen, 2000). For example, students in first grade may have difficulty quickly recognizing high-frequency words such as *him, walk,* and *open,* even after often reviewing the words over a period of several weeks.

These difficulties must be addressed explicitly if beginning readers are to make adequate progress in learning to read. Research related to why children struggle as they learn to read has led to a better understanding of critical components of beginning reading instruction and how teachers should address these difficulties.

### Effective Beginning Reading Instruction

Most educators agree on the crucial components of beginning reading instruction that are needed to address the difficulties faced by children who struggle learning to read (National Reading Panel, 2000; Pressley, 2002). These components address learning the sounds of letters in spoken words (**phonological awareness**), learning how letters correspond to sounds and applying this information (**phonics**), learning to read quickly and accurately (**fluency**), and understanding what is read, including single words (**vocabulary**) and the text (**comprehension**). These components of beginning reading are included in many beginning reading programs and basal reading series.

Students who struggle learning to read often have difficulty with these components of reading. **Explicit instruction** that focuses on these components and uses effective instructional strategies can significantly reduce the number of students who struggle when learning to read (Foorman, 2007; Torgesen, 2009). Many activities that teachers may use in the general education classroom to address each of these areas have been developed by the Florida Center for Reading Research (FCRR) and are available at www.fcrr.org/. Teachers can use activities from the FCRR Website to address problems with beginning reading related to phonological awareness, phonics, fluency, vocabulary, and comprehension. See Figure 13.4 for examples of these activities.

| Figure 13.4 | Activities to Support Student Learning of Critical Skills in Beginning Reading Instruction |
|---|---|

- **Phonological awareness:** Rhyme recognition—The student is shown a picture and then names the object in the picture ("A box"). The student is then shown a second picture, names the object ("A fox"), and is asked if the words rhyme.
- **Phonological awareness:** Syllables segmenting and blending—Students working in pairs are given a picture of a harmonica and the written word *harmonica.* One student says the word *harmonica*, and pauses between syllables. The second student counts the syllables and says, "*Harmonica* has four syllables." The students then exchange roles and complete another word.
- **Phonological awareness:** Phoneme matching—Students are given pictures of three objects and are asked to match initial sounds in the words. The student names each object, then marks the object that does not have the same initial sound as the other two objects.
- **Phonics:** Letter recognition—Students are given a board with a grid of letters of the alphabet and magnetic letters. The student is asked to choose a magnetic letter, say the letter name, and match the letter to the grid.
- **Phonics:** Letter/sound correspondence—The student is given several objects and a grid of letters that match the initial sound of each object. The student chooses an object and places the object on the letter that matches the initial sound (e.g., "glove" /g/).
- **Fluency:** Fast match of high frequency words—Students working in pairs are given 20 cards with high-frequency words. One student says a word, *large,* and counts to five while the second student finds the matching word. Students then reverse roles.
- **Vocabulary:** Word identification, memory word match—Students are given 20 words on cards, placed face down on a table. One student turns over two cards. If the cards match, the student keeps them for her pile. If they do not match, the cards are turned face down in their original place, and the other student turns over two cards. Students continue until matches are found for all cards.
- **Comprehension:** Sentence structure and meaning—Students are given sentences written on strips of paper. One student reads the sentence and then matches the meaning of the sentence to one of the pictures. This continues until all sentences and pictures are matched.

*Source:* Adapted from Florida Center for Reading Research. (2011). *Curriculum and instruction: Student center activities, grades K–1.* Retrieved April 11, 2011, from www.fcrr.org/

Beginning reading instruction is typically delivered to whole groups. This strategy is appropriate for many students (Reutzel, 2003), especially if lessons are well designed and the components of effective instruction that we discussed previously in this chapter are used in the lesson. These strategies ensure that information is taught explicitly and that teachers provide students with supports or scaffolding as they learn to read.

In addition, during whole-class instruction, teachers can use several activities that engage students who struggle learning to read. These activities include storytelling, reading aloud, sharing student-authored material (stories, poems, songs), and reading books together (Reutzel, 2003). Other strategies to engage students who struggle during large-group instruction include asking questions regarding reading material and pairing students to discuss the answer; having students provide a summary of the main points of a presentation; and checking frequently with students to determine if they have a question about a point made or material presented (Vaughn, Hughes, Moody, & Elbaum 2001).

After completing a lesson, it is important that students who struggle learning the content are given high-quality feedback, based on their specific needs, and are given the opportunity to practice (Coyne, Zipoli, & Ruby, 2006). This may occur as part of instruction on specific skills in a small group, which provides students opportunities to respond and interact with the teacher that were not available during large-group instruction. Another strategy for feedback involves pairing students or having them work in cooperative groups to ensure that everyone has mastered lesson content.

## Supporting Students Who Struggle Learning to Read

If students continue to struggle after they've been provided high-quality, effective core instruction, it may be necessary to provide additional instruction that is explicit, intensive, and systematic (Harlacher, Walker, & Sanford, 2010; Mellard, McKnight, & Jordan, 2010; Ritchey, 2011). Explicit instruction uses the approach to instruction that is described in Figure 13.1, and includes explicit presentation of information, guided practice following instruction, corrective feedback to students, and independent practice. Furthermore, this instruction should focus on the specific skills that students are struggling to learn. Intensive instruction includes providing more time for instruction (e.g., a second time for reading instruction during the day in addition to core instruction), providing instruction in a small group (e.g., three to five students), or using instructional methods such as choral responses or peer interaction to increase students' interaction with the content (Harlacher, Walker, & Sanford, 2010; Ritchey, 2011). Finally, systematic instruction is provided to make sure that the content being taught or goals of instruction are clear, that students who are taught in small groups have similar instructional needs, that the material is broken down and taught sequentially, and that this content is closely coordinated with the general education curriculum (Ritchey, 2011).

One of the most widely researched areas in education is beginning reading instruction. This research has resulted in a number of research-based programs that teachers can use for instruction to improve student skills in phonological awareness and phonics (also called *alphabetics*), fluency, comprehension, and general reading achievement (Institute of Education Sciences, 2011). Several of these programs are briefly described in Figure 13.5.

### Pause & Reflect

How were you taught to read? Discuss this topic with a peer. If you learned to read with ease, how do the structured, intensive methods of reading instruction described here differ from how you were taught? Why are these methods needed for students who struggle?

Teachers often use the types of research-based programs that are described in Figure 13.5 as they deliver high-quality, intensive instruction (often Tier 2) to students who struggle learning to read. This instruction is provided *in addition to* core (Tier 1) instruction. Educators develop these instructional tiers to provide high-quality instruction as part of a school's RTI program and as a framework for identifying students with disabilities (Fletcher

| Figure 13.5 | Research-Based Programs for Providing Beginning Reading Instruction |
| --- | --- |

**Effective addressing alphabetics (phonological awareness and phonics), fluency, and comprehension**

- **SpellRead,** formerly known as *SpellRead Phonological Auditory Training*, is designed for students in grades 2 and above who are 2 or more years below grade level in reading. The SpellRead program emphasizes mastering specific skills through explicit instruction, consists of 130 lessons, and takes from 5 to 9 months to complete (Kaplan K12 Learning Services, 2008). The program is offered for 60 to 90 minutes a day to groups of five students.
- **Ladders to Literacy** has been documented as effective for kindergarten students, and includes 20 activities addressing each of three areas: print awareness, phonological awareness, and oral language (Ladders to Literacy, 2008). This program is published as part of *Ladders to Literacy: A Kindergarten Activity Book.*
- **Peer-Assisted Learning Strategies (PALS)** (Fuchs, Fuchs, & Burish, 2000) is a peer-tutoring program that incorporates the existing curriculum to address student needs in reading. Students typically participate in PALS tutoring three times a week for 30 to 35 minutes. For more information regarding PALS, see Strategy 13.5.

**Effective for alphabetics and fluency**

- **Corrective Reading** (Engelmann, Hanner, & Johnson, 2008) is a direct-instruction program that is designed to address alphabetics, fluency, and comprehension for students in grades 3 and higher. Lessons are highly structured and scripted, and can be used with an entire class or a small group of four or five students. This program is used four to five times a week for 45 minutes.

**Effective for alphabetics and comprehension**

- **Reading Intervention for Early Success** (formerly called *Early Intervention in Reading [EIR]*) (Houghton Mifflin, 2006) is used with the entire class or with small groups to address the needs of students who are struggling with learning to read. *Early Success* uses picture books to provide instruction related to phonemic awareness, fluency, sight vocabulary, and reading comprehension for students in grades K–4.

**Effective for alphabetics**

- **Lindamood Phonemic Sequencing Program (LIPS)** (Lindamood & Lindamood, 1998), formerly called *Auditory Discrimination in Depth*, is designed for use with a small group or one child in grades K–4. The program offers direct instruction regarding decoding words, identifying individual sounds and blends in words, letter patterns, sight words, and using context clues. The program is used for one hour a day, and lasts for 4 to 6 months.
- **Earobics** (Houghton Mifflin, n.d.) is used to supplement a language arts program. The program uses interactive software for students in pre-K through grade 1 (*Earobics Foundations*) and grades 2 and 3 (*Earobics Connections*) to provide systematic instruction in basic literacy skills, including phonemic awareness, phonics, and comprehension. Multimedia support materials for the software are available, as well as books, leveled readers, manipulatives, and card sets.

*Source:* Information on selected programs adapted from Institute of Education Sciences (2011). *What works clearinghouse.* Retrieved April 11, 2011, from http://ies.ed.gov/

& Vaughn, 2009). For more information regarding the development of an RTI program and tiers of instruction for reading, see Strategy 13.6.

## Writing Instruction

Writing is a very complex process that requires the integration of many skills related to content knowledge, the mechanics of writing (i.e., handwriting, spelling, punctuation), **self-regulation**, attention, and planning and organization. When teaching writing, most teachers focus on the *process* of writing rather than the end product (Cutler & Graham, 2008). Thus, students learn to write by engaging in planning, writing, revising, and editing their work.

### Effective Beginning Writing Instruction

The stages of process writing typically include the following (Gardner & Johnson, 1997; Lipkewich & Mazurenko, 2008):

1. **Prewriting.** This stage provides the writer with the opportunity to gain information regarding the topic through a review of written material (e.g., magazines, books, newspapers), online information, media, personal experiences, class discussion, and so forth. Students may also collaborate with other students to discuss and brainstorm regarding a topic or content area. To assist students in organizing information during prewriting, teachers often use strategies such as graphic organizers or brainstorming webs. Prewriting prepares students with the information needed to write about a topic and organizes information to facilitate writing.

2. **Writing a draft.** Students learn to write by writing. At this stage, teachers encourage students simply to get something on paper. In other words, teachers emphasize producing content—not the mechanics of writing. Students will need a nonthreatening setting so that they may begin exploring a content area without fear that they lack the skills to write. Teachers encourage students to choose their best ideas to write about and to continue writing rather than stopping to edit (that comes later).

3. **Revising the draft.** Initially, teachers encourage students to read their drafts aloud for flow and content. Students then work with a peer or in a small group to obtain feedback on their draft by reading their draft to others and noting if the writing is clear, logical, contains sufficient detail, and so forth. Teachers may provide students with a framework for reviewing the draft. For example, students may review the draft using the following rubric:

Students should write each day in a setting where they are comfortable and motivated to write.

   a. Is the information in a logical, effective order?
   b. What information or details are not needed?
   c. Does the reader need to know any additional information?
   d. What words or details could you replace with better or clearer words?

4. **Editing the draft.** After receiving feedback, the student then edits the draft for content and organization. Students work together to edit for mechanics (spelling, punctuation, capitalization). The teacher may provide assistance to students, as needed. Revision and editing continue until the student has a final draft that is acceptable to the student and the teacher.

5. **Publishing.** The students publish the final draft of their work, and then may read their work aloud and share the final product with peers, parents, and others.

Several additional features of exemplary writing instruction are included in Figure 13.6. These features emphasize that students learn to write by writing each day in a setting where they are comfortable and motivated to write and where they receive the supports necessary to succeed in the writing process.

### Supporting Students Who Struggle Learning to Write

Many students learn to write successfully using process writing in a setting that emphasizes the features of exemplary writing instruction, yet many students with disabilities who receive this effective instruction continue to struggle. These students produce written products that are less coherent, expansive, polished, and effective than those produced by peers without disabilities (Harris, Graham, Mason, & Friedlander, 2008).

To teach students with disabilities who struggle as they learn to write, research suggests that an effective teacher should develop the attitudes and practice the behaviors described next (Graham, Harris, & Larsen, 2001; Harris et al., 2008):

| Figure 13.6 | Features of Classrooms with Effective Writing Instruction |
|---|---|

- Student work is displayed prominently; writing and reading material is abundant.
- Students work on a range of writing activities daily.
- Students are motivated to write by a risk-free setting, as well as by selecting their own topics for writing or modifying teacher assignments, and being reinforced for their writing accomplishments.
- The teacher has a positive attitude that all students can learn to write successfully, and makes sure that all students are aware of this positive attitude.
- The teacher regularly meets with students concerning their writing, and establishes goals and criteria to guide the students' work.
- Students use a predictable writing routine as they reflect on and revise their work.
- The teacher models the process of writing and a positive attitude toward writing.
- Students work cooperatively with others to assist with the writing process. Students present their work in progress or completed work to peers for feedback.
- The teacher provides instruction that addresses necessary skills, including phonological awareness, handwriting, spelling, writing conventions, sentence-level skills, text structure, the functions of writing, and planning and revising.
- The teacher provides follow-up, targeted instruction to ensure that all students master necessary writing skills.
- Writing skills are integrated across the curriculum.
- Teachers provide students opportunities to self-regulate writing by working independently, arranging their own space, and seeking help from others.
- The teacher frequently assesses writing progress, strengths, and needs.
- Teachers conduct conferences and communicate with parents regarding the writing program and students' progress as writers.

*Source:* Adapted from Graham, Harris, & Larsen (2001).

1. **Expect that every child will learn to write.** When a student has problems with learning to read and experiences difficulty with the mechanics of writing, it may not be easy for a teacher to remain optimistic that the student will succeed in learning to write. Negative attitudes might result in less interaction and feedback with students, more criticism, and less praise. Children with disabilities can be taught to write, but they need added support to succeed. It is important to focus on what the student can do as the writing process progresses and to build on the student's strengths.

2. **Identify and address obstacles that impede the student's success.** Students with disabilities may minimize the role of planning in writing, use ineffective strategies when revising their writing (e.g., focus on mechanical errors and not the content), struggle with the mechanics of writing, or place too much emphasis on handwriting, punctuation, or spelling. The particular obstacles that face a student who is learning to write should be identified so that writing instruction can be tailored to the student's individual needs.

3. **Intervene early.** Providing supplemental instruction addressing areas of weakness as students begin to learn to write can prevent or reduce the effects of difficulties later on. For example, research has shown that early instruction in areas such as spelling and handwriting can have a positive impact on a student's compositional fluency later on.

4. **Provide balanced instruction.** Students who struggle with learning to write need a balance of informal instructional methods (i.e., process writing) and formal instruction in specific skill areas that are weak (e.g., writing form and structure, strategies for planning). Students need a balance because too much formal instruction can have a negative impact on their motivation to write, whereas too much emphasis on informal methods may leave students without the skills that are critical to success.

5. **Use technology to support writing.** The writing of many students with disabilities can be significantly facilitated and enhanced by using technology. For example, the use of word processing reduces the need to recopy when revising, reduces demands related to

For more information on the use of technology to support instruction, see Chapter 16.

handwriting for students with motor problems, and results in papers produced in attractive, professional formats.

Perhaps the most important skill for students who have problems with learning to write relates to strategies for regulating their own writing, from prewriting activities through the finished product. For example, some students benefit from explicit instruction in an approach to improve planning as they are writing. **Self-regulated strategy development (SRSD)** is an instructional approach that teachers can use to formally teach students strategies that improve writing (Graham, Harris, & MacArthur, 2006; Harris et al., 2008; Harris, Graham, & Mason, 2003). For more information regarding this approach to writing instruction, see Strategy 13.7 later in this chapter.

## Mathematics Instruction

Many students with disabilities have difficulty keeping up with grade-level peers in math. This occurs for a range of reasons, depending on the characteristics of the disability and the nature of the mathematics content. For example, some students with reading problems do not have difficulty with math until later elementary grades, when word problems are prevalent and the demands of reading make it difficult for them to make adequate progress. Other students with disabilities have difficulty learning basic math skills because of memory problems, and some have difficulty with math concepts (e.g., number sense) that may occur because of a mathematics disability or a cognitive deficit. Of course, some students with disabilities do quite well in math, so you'll see a wide variation of strengths and weaknesses when working with students with disabilities in mathematics.

### Effective Beginning Mathematics Instruction

As you know, mathematics is a unique subject matter in that content is relatively simple to sequence, with skills building on one another. Thus, if a student misses information regarding one aspect of division, she will likely have difficulty with higher-level division skills until mastery of the prerequisite skill occurs or accommodations are provided.

Given the nature of mathematics content, effective mathematics instruction depends on lessons that are well designed, using the effective instructional practices that we discussed previously in this chapter. Key components of effective instruction in mathematics include ensuring that students have prior or prerequisite knowledge, teacher modeling, and providing sufficient time for student practice with teacher feedback.

Researchers have examined mathematics basal series that are widely used in elementary schools to determine if important features of instructional design that support effective instruction are built into these materials (Jitendra, Salmento, & Haydt, 1999). These features of instructional design are included in Figure 13.7.

| Figure 13.7 | **Features of Instructional Design That Support Effective Instruction in Mathematics** |
|---|---|

- Objectives that state what students will do are included and address behaviors that are observable, clear, and complete.
- One new concept or skill is taught at a time.
- Sufficient review activities are provided related to background knowledge.
- Explicit explanations of problems or concepts to be learned are provided.
- Lessons are carefully constructed that lead to efficient use of instructional time and maximum student achievement.
- Sufficient and appropriate teaching examples are provided.
- Adequate opportunities for practice are provided.
- Reviews of skills learned are appropriately distributed over time.
- Feedback procedures allow for quick, effective feedback when errors are made.

*Source:* Adapted from Jitendra, Salmento, & Haydt (1999).

These instructional design features are included in most basal mathematics series. However, at times a text may place insufficient emphasis on one of the criteria (e.g., not enough distributed practice on skills learned), making it necessary for the teacher to add instructional activities to ensure that students learn and retain the skills taught (Jitendra et al., 1999).

## Supporting Students Who Struggle Learning Mathematics

Even with highly effective core or Tier-1 instruction in the general education classroom, some students will continue to struggle in learning mathematics. When this occurs, several research-based strategies are available for teaching these students more effectively and efficiently, including the following:

1. **Teachers should instruct students in small groups or individually, using systematic, explicit instruction.** *Explicit instruction* in math has been defined as "a teacher demonstrating a specific plan (strategy) for solving the problem types and students using this plan to think their way through a solution" (Gersten & Clarke, 2007). This type of instruction works most efficiently when used with a small group of students (no more than two to six) who need to learn the same skill. The teacher should present instruction using the components of effective instruction that we discussed previously in this chapter. Instruction should provide highly explicit modeling of the steps needed to solve problems (Gersten et al., 2009).

2. **Instruction should be carefully planned, be fast paced, use varied activities, and ensure student engagement** (L. Fuchs & Fuchs, 2001; Gersten et al., 2009). Lessons should include thoughtful selection and sequencing of instructional examples, especially during the early stages of instruction when scaffolding is needed for student success. Using rapid pacing in a lesson ensures that students will complete more activities in a lesson. Likewise, using varied instructional activities (e.g., modeling, discussion, hands-on examples, problem solving) and quick pacing increases the level of student involvement and engagement in the lesson.

3. **Teachers should use concrete, representational (pictures), and abstract examples of problems in lessons** (L. Fuchs & Fuchs, 2001; Gersten et al., 2009; Miller & Hudson, 2007). Students with disabilities and others who struggle to learn math skills and concepts benefit from using manipulatives as they are learning concepts that underlie math problems (e.g., bundles of 10 sticks to illustrate regrouping). Using manipulatives to help students learn math concepts facilitates mastery of the concepts and improves maintenance of the skills learned (L. Fuchs & Fuchs, 2001). Mathematics instruction is most effective when teachers provide multiple graphic or manipulative examples that are specific to a set of problems and when students then practice using their own graphic organizers with teacher guidance (Gersten et al., 2009).

4. **Teachers should encourage students to use self-questioning or think-aloud strategies** (L. Fuchs & Fuchs, 2001; Gersten et al., 2009; Montague, 2007). Students with disabilities and others who struggle to learn math often have difficulty with multistep problems. When this occurs, these students may randomly use strategies rather than using a step-by-step approach. Research has demonstrated that encouraging students to verbalize their thinking (i.e., talking through a problem) is consistently effective in improving math problem solving (Gersten et al., 2009). For a detailed example of the use of self-talk as a self-regulation strategy in math instruction, see Strategy 13.8 later in this chapter.

## Summary

This chapter addressed the following topics:

**Effective instruction in an inclusive classroom: What to expect**

- Effective instruction is well organized; focuses student attention on well-defined, critical information; provides multiple opportunities to learn material with feedback; and includes follow-up monitoring to ensure that the information is retained over time.
- The components of effective instruction have been incorporated into materials that use an explicit or direct instruction approach.
- Effective instruction requires well-planned instructional content, with adaptations for individual student needs.

**Principles and practices to support effective instruction**

- Alternatives to whole-group instruction are needed to meet the needs of some students.
- Alternative grouping strategies allow teachers to use components of effective instruction that they may not be able to use during whole-group instruction.
- Grouping alternatives include homogeneous ability groups, mixed-ability groups (e.g., cooperative groups), individual tutoring, and peer tutoring.
- Long-term ability groups are often ineffective. However, short-term, small-group, intensive instruction using ability groups may be very effective.

**Effective instruction in reading, writing, and mathematics**

- When students struggle learning to read, critical components of beginning reading programs include phonological awareness, phonics, fluency, and comprehension (including understanding both single words and the text).
- Students who continue to struggle when provided high-quality core instruction in reading should be provided intensive, explicit, systematic instruction in small groups or individually. This also should occur when students struggle to learn writing or mathematics.
- After a group reading lesson, it is important that students who struggle learning to read have opportunities for high-quality feedback based on their specific needs.
- Stages of effective writing instruction include prewriting, writing a draft, revising the draft, editing the draft, and publishing.
- For struggling writers, teachers should identify obstacles to learning to write, intervene early, provide balanced instruction, and use technology to support writing.
- Key components of effective mathematics instruction include ensuring that students have prerequisite knowledge, teacher modeling of information being taught, and providing sufficient time for student practice with teacher feedback.
- High-quality instruction in mathematics should be fast paced, use varied activities, and ensure student engagement; present concrete, representational (pictures), and abstract examples of problems during lessons; and encourage students to use self-questioning or think-aloud strategies.

# Addressing Professional Standards

Standards addressed in Chapter 13 include:

**CEC Standards:** (3) individual learning differences; (4) instructional strategies; (5) learning environments and social interactions; (7) instructional planning.

## MyEducationLab

Go to the topic Reading Instruction in the **MyEducationLab** (www.myeducationlab .com) for *Inclusion,* where you can:

- Find learning outcomes for Reading Instruction, along with the national standards that connect to these outcomes.
- Complete Assignments and Activities that can help you more deeply understand the chapter content.
- Apply and practice your understanding of the core teaching skills identified in the chapter with the Building Teaching Skills and Dispositions learning units.
- Examine challenging situations and cases presented in the IRIS Center resources.
- Check your comprehension on the content covered in the chapter with the Study Plan. Here you will be able to take a chapter quiz, receive feedback on your answers, and then access Review, Practice, and Enrichment activities to enhance your understanding of chapter content.

# EFFECTIVE INSTRUCTION IN CORE ACADEMIC AREAS

## Putting It All Together

Delivering effective instruction in core academic areas involves not just knowledge of practices but also much additional information related to collaboration, planning, classroom management, and the use of technology, among other things. With this in mind, we offer several suggestions for your consideration.

1. **Effective instruction depends on collaboration.** In an inclusive setting, a general education teacher often brings a deep knowledge of the content, whereas a special education teacher brings a toolbox of strategies to ensure that all students learn the material. When teachers combine these areas of expertise, they learn valuable new skills and provide more effective instruction. Thus, all students learn more. Collaboration is often essential to provide support for effective instruction in inclusive classrooms.

2. **Effective instruction is well organized.** Vicki Eng, a teacher from West Hernando Middle School, made this point well: "When you walk into a class with kids with LD or students who struggle, you need to be well organized; you can't wing it, or you lose control of your class. You need to have guidelines, rules posted early, so issues don't become problems you can't control." The information we presented previously on effective instruction clearly demonstrates that instruction for students who struggle should be explicit, intensive, and systematic. Furthermore, this information should be presented in a classroom where instruction is predictable, and disruptions to instruction are kept to a minimum.

3. **Effective teachers have a toolbox of strategies that work.** No effective practice works every time for every student. Effective teachers monitor the effectiveness of instructional approaches and have alternatives available when a strategy does not work with a student. These strategies are obtained from many places, including from other teachers, online resources, textbooks, professional development activities, and so forth. Teachers improve their practice by adding effective instructional strategies to their toolbox that can be used to meet the needs of all their students.

4. **Effective teachers are lifelong learners.** The best teachers are those who continue to improve and are constantly adding new strategies to help their students who struggle. These are teachers who reflect on their practice, use progress-monitoring data to determine if students are making sufficient progress, and change instructional strategies as necessary to improve outcomes for students. Teachers who continue to learn new practices observe effective practices in other teachers' classes whenever possible. They also welcome observation in their own classrooms, as well as coaching support from peers when they are learning new practices (McLeskey, 2011).

## Strategy Fact Sheet

In the remainder of this chapter, we describe eight effective strategies, which we referred to previously in the chapter, to help you plan effectively to meet the needs of all students.

| STRATEGY | DESCRIPTION | SPECIAL CONSIDERATIONS |
|---|---|---|
| Strategy 13.1: Principles of Research-Based Instruction in Core Content Areas | Most states and local school districts emphasize the use of instructional practices that have been demonstrated effective. Here, we describe general principles of instruction that have been proven effective for students who struggle with learning academic content. | Principles of research-based instruction provide a general framework for delivering high-quality core instruction in the general education classroom. |

*(Continued)*

| STRATEGY | DESCRIPTION | SPECIAL CONSIDERATIONS |
|---|---|---|
| Strategy 13.2: Direct Instruction of Core Academic Skills | As students learn basic academic skills, a direct, systematic approach to instruction is needed, especially for those who struggle. Direct instruction provides such an approach, which has been demonstrated effective in teaching core academic skills. | A direct instruction approach is used to teach facts, rules, and action sequences that are building blocks for later learning. The more time students spend actively being taught, reviewing, and practicing these skills, the more information they will retain. |
| Strategy 13.3: Cooperative Learning | A grouping strategy that uses mixed-ability groups for instruction. The goal is to ensure that all students learn assigned content, which may range from basic academic skills to complex group projects. | Formal cooperative learning approaches may be used for an extended period of time. However, more informal approaches to cooperative learning may be used to work on specific tasks for brief periods of time. |
| Strategy 13.4: Reading Recovery | A tutoring approach for beginning readers that employs effective instructional strategies to reduce the number of students who have difficulty learning to read. | Reading Recovery requires special, extensive training for tutors, and it can be expensive to implement. Students can be taught in pairs to reduce costs. Reading Recovery may be used as a Tier-3 approach to instruction. |
| Strategy 13.5: Peer-Assisted Learning Strategies | Peer tutoring that offers an efficient, cost-effective method for providing students with independent practice on the skills they need in order to develop in-depth knowledge of content. | Peer-tutoring programs such as PALS can be used in any subject area, and they are flexible, easy to implement, cost-effective, and time efficient. These qualities likely account for the acceptance and use of these interventions by many teachers in elementary and secondary classrooms. |
| Strategy 13.6: Beginning Reading: Tiers of Instruction & RTI | Assumes that a student should be identified with a disability only after high-quality instruction has been provided, and the student has continued to struggle to learn. | In an RTI model, high-quality, effective instruction includes core instruction in the general education classroom (Tier 1), instruction in small groups (Tier 2), and intensive, individualized instruction focusing on specific student needs (Tier 3). |
| Strategy 13.7: Self-Regulated Strategy Development and Writing Instruction | An approach used to support students in using writing strategies effectively and independently. Teachers provide explicit instruction as students learn the strategy and how it can be applied. | Many elementary students with disabilities have difficulty planning and regulating writing strategies. SRSD may be used to improve student planning and self-regulation as they learn to write. |
| Strategy 13.8: Cognitive Strategy Instruction for Mathematics Problem Solving | An approach to support students who struggle to learn mathematics by scaffolding instruction. Includes built-in cues and prompts for students as they engage in strategies for self-regulation, self-instruction, self-monitoring, and self-checking. Supports are gradually faded. | Teachers have developed strategies for solving mathematics problems by talking through how they solve a particular type of problem, or by talking with proficient students to better understand how they solve problems. |

| Strategy 13.1 | **PRINCIPLES OF RESEARCH-BASED INSTRUCTION IN CORE CONTENT AREAS** |

## Rationale

Many students readily learn core academic skills in reading, writing, and mathematics, but some students struggle to learn these skills. This is especially true for many students with disabilities, students from culturally and linguistically diverse backgrounds, and those from high-poverty backgrounds. For students who struggle to learn academic skills, prevention is the best approach. That is, students should be provided with high-quality core instruction (Tier 1) in the early elementary grades to make sure that they learn basic academic skills. This is true for all content areas, but it is especially important in reading, writing, and mathematics, which are building blocks for later learning.

## Step-by-Step

The following are research-based general principles that have proven useful when providing instruction to students who struggle to learn academic content.

**1** *Provide high-quality core instruction in the general education classroom.* This instruction should be well organized, explicit, and routinely provide students with opportunities for cumulative review of content that was previously mastered (Fletcher, Lyon, Fuchs, & Barnes, 2007). High-quality core instruction in general education classrooms is characterized by good classroom management; balanced teaching of skills; student supports or scaffolding for learning new content; integration of curriculum across content areas (e.g., teaching reading vocabulary in science) whenever possible; and support for students in developing skills for self-regulation (Foorman, 2007).

**2** *Increase the time students spend learning key academic content.* The time students spend learning academic content has a significant impact on how much they learn (Borich, 2011). In spite of this finding, students who struggle to learn core academic content are often pulled out of elementary reading instruction and placed in a separate setting for instruction. In most, if not all, instances, students who are struggling with reading should participate in general education reading instruction (e.g., a 90-minute reading block). This instruction should be differentiated to meet the needs of students who are struggling to learn the content. More intensive instruction (Tier 2) should be provided in the general education classroom during this reading block using methods such as peer-assisted learning strategies (PALS). (See Strategy 13.5 later in this chapter.) Still more intensive interventions (Tier 3) that are needed and that cannot be provided in the general education classroom should be delivered in addition to this instruction, and should not supplant high-quality general education instruction. An example of this type of reading instruction is described later in this chapter when we discuss Reading Recovery in Strategy 13.4.

**3** *Differentiate instruction in the general education classroom to meet student needs.* All students, including those who struggle learning academic content, will benefit from lessons that provide background information regarding material to be learned (e.g., review of background information and content before reading), or exercises that build skills (e.g., steps for regrouping in math) related to content. Teachers should also provide some instruction in inclusive classrooms that differentiates activities or instruction based on individual student needs using activities such as peer tutoring, cooperative learning structures, center-based instruction, and small-group instruction (L. Fuchs & Fuchs, 2007; Vaughn & Roberts, 2007). For example, consider the range of tasks that students might need to work on in a kindergarten class. While some students might work with a general education teacher to practice phoneme segmenting and blending, others might work with a special education co-teacher to identify parts of a book, while more advanced students might work with a paraeducator or in small cooperative groups to decode simple words.

**4** *Closely integrate interventions with general education practices and curricular content* (Fletcher et al., 2007). The same curriculum that is used in the general education classroom should be used when providing an intervention in reading, writing, or math for a student who is struggling to learn this content. Interventions are thus used that complement and build on the curriculum of the general education classroom. This results in a "double dose" of instruction across settings, increases the probability that the skills will be learned, and ensures that these students are making progress in learning the general education curriculum (Mellard, McKnight, & Jordan, 2010).

**5** *Employ strategies to increase student attention to and engagement in tasks.* Teachers can support increased attention and engagement using strategies such as the following (Lerner & Johns, 2009):

- Break a long task into shorter parts.
- Reduce the length of homework assignments.
- Use distributed practice (i.e., short periods of practice spread over time).
- Use strategies to make tasks more interesting, such as building on student interests, using novel activities, or providing students opportunities to work in small groups.
- Alternate tasks that are high interest for students with those that are low interest.

**6** *Frequently monitor student progress.* This should be done using measures that directly relate to the content being taught. Educators have developed **curriculum-based measurement (CBM)** techniques to provide an efficient and effective measure of student progress in basic content areas (Deno, 2003, 2007). The academic progress of students who are struggling should be monitored frequently to determine the effectiveness of instructional strategies and interventions. If students are not making sufficient progress, interventions should be adapted or changed based on data collected from the curriculum-based measures.

## Applications and Examples

Over the last decade, coordinating curriculum for students across settings has been simplified by the adoption of state-wide curriculum standards in most states. For example, in Florida, the Next Generation Sunshine State Standards (see www.floridastandards.org/) are used for all students as they are taught core content skills in reading, math, and writing (as well as other content areas). Furthermore, the standards have been extended through the use of *access points*, which provide access to the general education curriculum for students with the most significant cognitive disabilities by extending and capturing the essence of the standards at reduced levels of complexity. The access points are provided at three levels: Independent—the highest level of the access points; Supported—the middle level of the access points; and Participatory—the lowest level of the access points. Figure 13.8 provides an example of a Next Generation Sunshine State Standard in reading/language arts at the kindergarten level that includes access points.

For more information on CBMs, see Strategy 11.8, page 229, in Chapter 11.

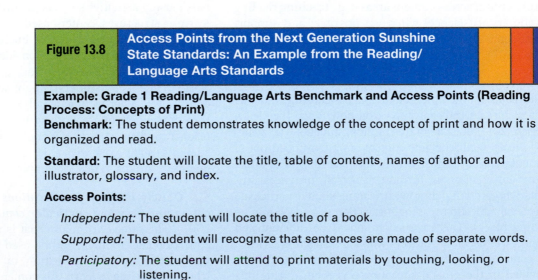

| Figure 13.8 | Access Points from the Next Generation Sunshine State Standards: An Example from the Reading/Language Arts Standards |
| --- | --- |

**Example: Grade 1 Reading/Language Arts Benchmark and Access Points (Reading Process: Concepts of Print)**

**Benchmark:** The student demonstrates knowledge of the concept of print and how it is organized and read.

**Standard:** The student will locate the title, table of contents, names of author and illustrator, glossary, and index.

**Access Points:**

*Independent:* The student will locate the title of a book.

*Supported:* The student will recognize that sentences are made of separate words.

*Participatory:* The student will attend to print materials by touching, looking, or listening.

*Source:* Florida Department of Education, retrieved March 15, 2011, from www.floridastandards.org

## Keep in Mind

Unfortunately, some students continue to struggle, even when provided high-quality core instruction in the general education classroom. For these students, many of the principles of effective instruction that we discussed earlier in this chapter will be useful to consider when teaching basic academic skills. Furthermore, more intensive instructional approaches will be available in most schools to provide these students with additional support. We provide descriptions of more intensive strategies that may be useful when high-quality core instruction does not lead to desired results. This includes approaches such as direct instruction, peer-assisted learning strategies, and Reading Recovery.

**Key References**

Fletcher, J., Lyon, R., Fuchs, L., & Barnes, M. (2007). *Learning disabilities: From identification to intervention*. New York: Guilford.

Foorman, B. (2007). Primary prevention in classroom reading instruction. *Teaching Exceptional Children, 39*(5), 24–30.

Fuchs, L., & Fuchs, D. (2007). A model for implementing responsiveness to intervention. *Teaching Exceptional Children, 39*(5), 14–20.

Mellard, D., McKnight, M., & Jordan, J. (2010). RTI tier structures and instructional intensity. *Learning Disabilities Research & Practice, 25*, 217–225.

Vaughn, S., & Roberts, G. (2007). Secondary interventions in reading: Providing additional instruction for students at risk. *Teaching Exceptional Children, 39*(5), 40–46.

## Strategy 13.2 | DIRECT INSTRUCTION OF CORE ACADEMIC SKILLS

# Rationale

Effective instructional approaches differ, depending on the nature of the content being taught. As elementary students learn to read or learn basic math skills, a more direct, systematic approach to instruction is needed by many students to ensure content mastery. This type of direct instruction "is indispensible for achieving content mastery and overlearning of fundamental facts, rules, and action sequences that may be essential to subsequent learning and remembering what was learned long afterwards" (Borich, 2011, p. 226). The more time students spend being actively taught, reviewing, and practicing basic facts and skills, the more information they will retain. *Direct instruction* is defined as "a model that uses teacher demonstration and explanation combined with student practice and feedback to help learners acquire well-defined knowledge and skills needed for later learning" (Eggen & Kauchak, 2012, p. 266).

# Step-by-Step

A direct-instruction lesson focuses on one clearly defined learning objective. Before beginning the lesson, it is important to identify the objective of the lesson, identify topics that will be addressed related to the objective, and prepare examples (to illustrate and model the problem and for student practice) related to the objective. Once the lesson is carefully planned, the following steps are typically included in a direct-instruction lesson.

**1** *Introduction and review.* The lesson should begin with an introduction to the topic, including the purpose of the lesson and an advance organizer so that students will know what content will be addressed and what activities will be used. This is then followed by a review of background information and prerequisite skills. For example, if first-grade students are being taught adding two-digit whole numbers without regrouping, topics addressed might include presenting example word problems that include this type of addition problem; reviewing single-digit addition and having students use manipulatives to represent the addition; and having students use manipulatives to represent two-digit numbers (this example is adapted from Eggen & Kauchak, 2012).

**2** *Presentation.* The lesson is then presented by explicitly walking students through how to solve a problem, one step at a time, and is designed to provide them with a thorough understanding of the skill. Continuing with the math example related to adding two-digit whole numbers without regrouping, this might include presenting a word problem that requires this type of operation, walking students through the process for solving this problem using questioning and modeling, and repeating this process with one or more additional problems as needed. The lesson should include information regarding the difference between the ones column and the tens

column. This might begin with a demonstration of the difference between ones and tens using manipulatives, followed by questioning students regarding the difference in digits in the ones and tens columns. Finally, students should be engaged in the lesson to ensure that they understand the content. This can be done by responding to students' questions about the problems, and/or by teacher questioning of students regarding each step involved in solving the problem.

**3** *Provide guided practice.* After completing the previous step and ensuring that students have an understanding of two-digit addition without regrouping, problems should be provided that allow students to practice with close supervision. This might initially occur as students work at their desks. After practicing several problems, one student could then be chosen to model how to solve the problem for the rest of the class. This student should be asked to explain the difference between digits in the ones and tens columns, and talk through how the problem is solved. This process should then be repeated with another student and a second problem, and repeated by a third student, as necessary.

**4** *Independent practice.* Students should then be given problems for independent practice, followed by work with a peer to check answers and provide feedback. It is best to provide opportunities for independent practice for short periods of time over several days to ensure student understanding of the problems. This type of distributed practice has been shown to be very effective in helping students learn basic skills. As most students in class are engaged in independent practice, the teacher then has time to provide additional instruction to students who are having difficulty with the skill being taught.

**5** *Assessment.* Students should be given problems to solve on their own. This will provide information regarding how many students have successfully mastered this content, and which students require additional instruction and/or practice to master the skill. It is important to note that many students will likely require at least some additional guided and independent practice to learn this skill to a level of automaticity, which allows them to solve such problems with little thought and fosters the use of this skill in solving more advanced problems (i.e., transfer of the skill to new math problems).

## Applications and Examples

Many classrooms include students with significant intellectual disabilities who are expected to make progress in the general education curriculum (Westling & Fox, 2009). As we noted previously, goals for these students may include mastering content related to access points that provide access to the general education curriculum by extending and capturing the essence of the standards at reduced levels of complexity. Figure 13.9 addresses the example used previously related to two-digit addition without regrouping from the Next Generation Sunshine State Standards at the first-grade level, and includes access points that may be used for including students with significant intellectual disabilities in this direct-instruction lesson. Direct instruction has proven to be a very effective strategy for these students. When providing academic skill instruction for students with significant intellectual disabilities, it is important to keep in mind the importance of teaching all students information that will lead to a more meaningful and productive life, as these skills are made meaningful for students and connected to their everyday lives (Westling & Fox, 2009).

| Figure 13.9 | Access Points from the Next Generation Sunshine State Standards: An Example from the Math Standards |
|---|---|

**Example: Grade 1 Mathematics Benchmark, Standards, and Access Points**
**Benchmark:** Represent two-digit numbers in terms of tens and ones.

**Standards:** MA.1.A.1.1. Model addition and subtraction situations using the concepts of "part–whole," "adding to," "taking away from," "comparing," and "missing addend."

MA.1.A.2.2. Represent two-digit numbers in terms of tens and ones.

**Topic addressed:** Adding two-digit whole numbers without regrouping.

**Access Points:**

*Independent:* Identify the meaning of addition as adding to and subtraction as taking away from. (Note that the student may use objects or pictures to demonstrate understanding.)

*Supported:* Demonstrate understanding of the meaning of joining (putting together) and separating (taking apart) sets of object.

*Participatory:* Recognize when an object or person is added to (addition) or is taken away from (subtraction) a situation.

*Source:* Standards are from the Florida Department of Education, retrieved March 17, 2011, from www.floridastandards.org/

## Keep in Mind

Although this direct-instruction lesson may seem simple and straightforward, difficulties may arise for teachers, especially at Step 2—Presentation. Difficulties arise here for three reasons (Eggen & Kauchak, 2012). First, it is often difficult to take a skill that is so understandable and automatic (i.e., you don't have to think about it, and haven't in many years), and make it understandable for children in first grade. This may result in difficulty in verbalizing how a problem is solved, or modeling problem solving, as steps are taken for granted and skipped or described superficially. A second problem with the presentation step relates to this first difficulty, as teachers rush through the modeling or description of the problem and provide a very brief or superficial explanation. This results in many students not understanding the problem, and difficulty in practicing the skill. Finally, for many teachers direct instruction suggests that the teacher is doing all the instruction as part of this teacher-centered model, and questioning students is not important. This is obviously not the case, as questioning students and encouraging students to ask questions should be an integral part of direct instruction. This process helps ensure that students understand the skill being taught and lets the teacher know if this is not the case. Furthermore, student questioning and having students model and describe how they solved a problem may be helpful for other students in the classroom, as such descriptions by novice problem solvers may be easier to understand than the teacher's description.

### Key References

Borich, G. (2011). *Effecting teaching methods: Research-based practices* (7th ed.). Upper Saddle River, NJ: Pearson Education.

Carnine, D., Silbert, J., Kame'enui, E., & Tarver, S. (2010). *Direct instruction reading* (5th ed.). Upper Saddle River, NJ: Pearson Education.

Coyne, M., Kame'enui, E., & Carnine, D. (2007). *Effective teaching strategies that accommodate diverse learners.* Upper Saddle River, NJ: Pearson Education.

Eggen, P., & Kauchak, D. (2012). *Strategies and models for teachers: Teaching content and thinking skills* (6th ed.). Upper Saddle River, NJ: Pearson Education.

Stein, M., Kinder, D., Silbert, J., & Carnine, D. (2006). *Designing effective mathematics instruction: A direct instruction approach* (4th ed.). Upper Saddle River, NJ: Pearson Education.

| Strategy 13.3 | **COOPERATIVE LEARNING** |

## Rationale

*Cooperative learning* is a grouping strategy that uses mixed-ability groups for instruction. The goal of this strategy is to ensure that all students learn assigned content, which may range from basic academic skills to complex content that involves group projects. Teachers can use two general types of cooperative groups in general education classrooms, depending on the purpose of the lesson and student needs (Marzano, Pickering, & Pollock, 2001). Teachers may use informal groups (Ask Your Neighbor, Think-Pair-Share) to work on specific, well-defined tasks for brief periods of time. These groups help students understand expectations, provide additional time for learning content with support, and focus students' attention on important content (Marzano et al., 2001). Teachers may use more formal cooperative groups for several days or weeks to complete a complex task or to learn more extensive content.

Research on cooperative learning has revealed that this approach may be used to improve the achievement of students across a range of content areas and often results in greater achievement gains than traditional, whole-group instruction (Good & Brophy, 2008; Slavin & Madden, 2006). Other benefits of cooperative learning include improved prosocial interactions among students who differ with regard to achievement, gender, or ethnicity; improved acceptance of students with disabilities among peers without disabilities; and improved effective outcomes related to student self-esteem, academic self-confidence, motivation for learning, and value for shared academic work (Good & Brophy, 2008; Slavin & Madden, 2006).

## Step-by-Step

Jigsaw (Aronson, 2004, 2011) is a cooperative learning strategy that is widely used by teachers. This strategy uses mixed-ability groups to learn content, solve a problem, or complete a project. Each member of the group is given an assignment or assigned to specialize in one aspect of a unit of instruction. Each assignment is a piece of the overall puzzle required to solve the problem, complete the project, or learn the content. Thus, each student's contribution is critical, and assignments are tailored to the strengths of the particular student. Teachers typically implement Jigsaw using the following steps, which are adapted from Aronson (2011).

**1** *The teacher divides the class into four- to six-person Jigsaw groups.* Group composition should be based on the individual strengths of each student, and groups should be diverse in relation to gender, ethnicity, and ability. One person should be appointed as the group leader, typically a responsible, mature student.

**2** *The teacher divides the day's lesson into four to six components.* A history lesson in which students are to learn about Eleanor Roosevelt might consist of the following independent segments: (1) her childhood, (2) her family life with Franklin Roosevelt and their children, (3) her life after Franklin Roosevelt contracted polio, (4) her work in the White House as First Lady, and (5) her life and work after Franklin Roosevelt's death.

**3** *Each student is then assigned to learn one segment.* The teacher ensures that each student has access only to information regarding her segment of the assignment.

**4** *Each student reads her assignment at least twice* and becomes familiar with the information. Students then form temporary expert groups, by having one student from each group join other students who are assigned to learn the same segment. Students in these expert groups then discuss their segment, and rehearse the presentations they will make to their Jigsaw group.

**5** *Students return to their Jigsaw groups* and present information regarding their segments to the other group members. All group members are encouraged to ask questions for clarification.

**6** *During these activities, the teacher floats from group to group,* observes, and intervenes if any group is having difficulty (e.g., one group member is dominating or disruptive).

**7** *At the end of the session,* students may be required to produce a product with their completed work or take a quiz regarding the content of the lesson.

# Applications and Examples

Cooperative learning methods are often adapted to meet particular classroom needs. For example, Jigsaw has been adapted for use with narrative material that all students are assigned to learn (Slavin, 1990). When using this Jigsaw II approach, heterogeneous groups of students all receive the same assignment (e.g., reading a section of a chapter in a history class that addresses the Civil War). The teacher selects topics from the assignment, and each student from a group is assigned to become an expert on one topic. After reviewing the material, students across groups meet to discuss and learn about their topic with others who have the same assigned topic. After all become experts on their topics, they return to their Jigsaw II group and teach the information to their peers. Students are then prepared to take individual tests on the content (Slavin, 1990).

## Keep in Mind

Many informal structures are also available for using cooperative learning (Good & Brophy, 2008; Kagan, 1994). For example, when using Think-Pair-Share (Good & Brophy, 2008), the teacher asks a question, students are given time to think individually, and then the students discuss their ideas with a partner. Next, the teacher asks some students to share their ideas with the class. Another cooperative structure is called Numbered Heads Together (Kagan, 1994). When using this structure, students are assigned to small groups of three or four, and each student in the group is given a number. The teacher then asks a question or poses a problem, students think about the problem individually, and then put their heads together to discuss the problem. Finally, the teacher asks all students with a certain number to stand. He then asks some of these students to share and discuss their answer with the class. This strategy is good for reviewing and checking student understanding of material (Good & Brophy, 2008).

**Key References**

Aronson, E. (2011). *Jigsaw classroom: Jigsaw in 10 easy steps.* Retrieved July 27, 2011, from www.jigsaw.org

Good, T., & Brophy, J. (2008). *Looking in classrooms* (9th ed.). Boston: Allyn & Bacon.

Kagan, S. (1994). *Cooperative learning.* San Diego, CA: Kagan Cooperative Learning.

McMaster, K., & Fuchs, D. (2005). *Cooperative learning for students with disabilities.* Retrieved February 20, 2008, from www.teachingld.org

Slavin, R., & Madden, N. (Eds.). (2006). *Success for all: Summary of research on achievement outcomes.* Baltimore: Johns Hopkins University, Center for Data-Driven Reform in Education.

| Strategy 13.4 | **READING RECOVERY** |

## Rationale

Some professionals have contended that the most effective approach to rapidly increasing student academic achievement in basic content areas is having a well-trained teacher work with a student one-on-one using highly effective instructional materials and strategies (D'Agostino & Murphy, 2004; Good & Brophy, 2008). Reading Recovery is this type of tutoring approach for beginning readers. It employs effective instructional strategies with a goal of reducing the number of students who have severe difficulty learning to read. Typically, this type of approach is delivered outside the general education classroom, and is often considered to be an intensive Tier-3 intervention. Reading Recovery is presented here to provide an example of the type of more intensive instruction students may receive when interventions in the general education classroom do not produce desired results.

Reading Recovery was developed in New Zealand by Marie Clay in 1976 (Clay, 1993). It has since spread to the United States and is widely used in most states. Research on Reading Recovery reveals that this approach is highly effective in improving the reading skills of many struggling beginning readers, and these improvements are sustained beyond the tutoring sessions and at least until the end of second grade (D'Agostino & Murphy, 2004).

## Step-by-Step

Teachers offer Reading Recovery to students who are among the lowest 10 to 20% of struggling readers. The approach involves daily tutoring sessions that continue for 12 to 20 weeks, or until the student meets program criteria for discontinuation (that is, his reading improves significantly, closing the achievement gap with peers). Students who struggle the most with reading are the first to receive tutoring in a school. Reading Recovery is built on several assumptions, including (1) reading is more than reading words; (2) reading is a social activity; (3) children begin to read by attending to various aspects of printed text; and (4) the tasks children must attend to most closely when they are learning to read require less attention as their reading improves (Clay, 2001; D'Agostino & Murphy, 2004). Reading Recovery is typically implemented with the following steps:

**1** *Students who are identified by teachers as struggling readers in the first grade are assessed* on their skills related to letter identification, hearing and recording sounds in words, print concepts, word skills, writing, and text reading. Typically, students who score at or below the 20th percentile on a test of these skills are eligible for Reading Recovery tutoring.

**2** *Selected students receive tutoring daily for 30 minutes,* for as many as 20 weeks or until each student's reading achievement improves to a level similar to peers, and the child is discontinued.

**3** *Tutoring sessions for the first 2 weeks consist of "roaming around the known,"* including activities such as sharing reading and writing, building trust, and determining the student's strengths.

**4** *Reading Recovery lessons then begin* and include a fixed set of activities, as the child (a) reads from one or more familiar books; (b) independently reads the previous day's book as the teacher keeps a running record of student responses (e.g., miscues, omissions); (c) identifies letters and engages in a word making/breaking activity using plastic letters and a magnetic board; (d) writes a sentence or brief story, which is cut into pieces; (e) reassembles the cut-up sentence or story; and (f) reads a new book with teacher support.

**5** *Children are discontinued when they read at an average level for their grade.* Other students continue for up to 20 weeks of tutoring.

## Applications and Examples

Reading Recovery is only one of several approaches to tutoring that teachers may use with students who are struggling to learn to read. Another approach that is used in some states is Reading Rescue (Hoover, 2001; Hoover & Lane, 2001). Reading Rescue is similar to Reading Recovery, except that it places more emphasis on teaching phonemic awareness and phonics (Ehri, Dreyer, Flugman, & Gross, 2007). Research has revealed that Reading Rescue is an effective intervention for struggling readers, and paraeducators may implement this approach with results that are nearly as effective as when teachers conduct the tutoring (Ehri et al., 2007). Other tutoring programs are available that use volunteers who are not fully certified teachers as tutors, and research has shown that these programs are effective with many students who struggle learning to read (Baker, Gersten, & Keating, 2000; Hayes et al., 2005; Pullen, Lane, & Monaghan, 2004).

## Keep in Mind

Some educators have criticized Reading Recovery and other teacher tutoring programs because of the high cost of these interventions (Grossen, Coulter, & Ruggles, 1996; Mathes & Denton, 2002). The estimates of the cost per student vary widely, from $2,500 to $10,000. A related consideration is that as many as 50% of students who complete Reading Recovery continue to struggle learning to read (Mathes & Denton, 2002). Some evidence indicates that the expense of Reading Recovery may be reduced by teaching students in pairs (Iversen, Tunmer, & Chapman, 2005). However, there is no doubt that individual tutoring by a teacher is expensive and that tutoring by peers or volunteers and small-group instruction may be more cost-effective. Still other evidence has shown that small, homogeneous groups of students (from two to five) who are taught using highly effective instructional methods learn as much as students who are taught using one-to-one tutoring (Elbaum et al., 2000). The key issues in this research seem to relate to the quality and the intensity (brief, focused on specific skills) of the instruction.

**Key References**

Clay, M. (1993). *Reading recovery: A guidebook for teachers in training.* Portsmouth, NH: Heinemann.

D'Agostino, J., & Murphy, J. (2004). A meta-analysis of reading recovery in United States schools. *Educational Evaluation and Policy Analysis, 26*(1), 23–38.

Ehri, L., Dreyer, L., Flugman, B., & Gross, A. (2007). Reading rescue: An effective tutoring intervention model for language-minority students who are struggling readers in first grade. *American Educational Research Journal, 44*(2), 414–448.

Elbaum, B., Vaughn, S., Hughes, M., & Moody, S. (2000). How effective are one-to-one tutoring programs in reading for elementary students at risk for reading failure? A meta-analysis of the intervention research. *Journal of Educational Psychology, 92*(4), 605–619.

Iversen, S., Tunmer, W., & Chapman, J. (2005). The effects of varying group size on the Reading Recovery approach to preventive early intervention. *Journal of Learning Disabilities, 38*(5), 456–472.

# PEER-ASSISTED LEARNING STRATEGIES

## Rationale

An issue teachers often face in inclusive classrooms is having enough time and hands to provide students with the instruction they need, especially in basic skill areas (i.e., reading and math). Once a teacher has initially taught new material, peer tutoring offers an efficient, cost-effective method for providing students with independent practice on the skills that are needed to develop in-depth knowledge regarding the content. Extensive research has revealed that peer tutoring has positive academic and social outcomes for both the tutor and tutee across grade levels and content areas (McMaster, Fuchs, & Fuchs, 2006; Stenhoff & Lignugaris/Kraft, 2007).

Peer-assisted learning strategies (PALS) is one form of peer tutoring that researchers have demonstrated to be effective, and many teachers have found that it fits well into their classroom routines. This method uses "structured activities that require peers to engage in frequent interaction, provide each other with immediate corrective feedback, and take turns as tutor and tutee" (D. Fuchs, Fuchs, & Burish, 2000, p. 85). Teachers have used PALS with students from kindergarten through grade 12, in the areas of reading and math.

## Step-by-Step

The use of peer tutoring in reading is one example of the PALS approach. Teachers use this particular strategy with students in grades 2–6, and it addresses activities to increase student fluency and comprehension. This program is implemented using the following steps:

**1** *The teacher provides an orientation and teaches students how to use peer-tutoring strategies.* PALS materials (available at http://kc.vanderbilt.edu/pals/) provide structured lessons lasting from 30 to 60 minutes that teachers can use to prepare students. Teachers instruct students regarding how to use the PALS instructional strategies, how and when to respond to peers when errors are made, and so forth. They are also informed that two teams will be formed, each with one half of the tutoring pairs, and the teams will be awarded points.

**2** *The teacher selects pairs of students* based on their reading level, matching higher- and lower-level readers. For example, the teacher might rank-order all students based on their reading level, split the list in half, and pair the student on top of the first list with the student on top of the second list. Some variation in this procedure may occur based on teacher judgment regarding students who are a good match and those who are not.

**3** *The teacher schedules* three, 35-minute PALS sessions per week. These sessions may be in addition to current reading instructional time or could take the place of reading activities that are currently used.

**4** *PALS sessions begin with partner reading.* For this activity, the student with the higher reading level always initially reads a selected reading passage that is at the reading level of the lower reader. The lower-level reader then reads the passage. As the passage is read, the tutor notes when a reading error occurs, stops the reader, points out the word that was missed, and asks the reader to figure out the word. If the reader does not respond within 4 seconds, the tutor provides the word, and reading continues.

**5** *Students engage in paragraph shrinking.* This activity requires readers to monitor their comprehension and make judgments regarding the selection and reduction of the material being read. More specifically, students read a paragraph and stop to identify the main idea. They are assisted by tutors, who guide main idea statements by asking who or what the paragraph is mainly about, and provide support in identifying the most important thing related to the *who* or *what*. Students then express the main idea in 10 words or less.

**6** *Prediction relay* is the final PALS activity. In this activity, the reader makes a prediction about the information on the next one-half page, reads this information aloud as the tutor corrects errors, confirms or disconfirms the prediction, and summarizes the main idea. The tutor provides feedback regarding the prediction and summarizes the main idea.

**7** *Points are awarded* by students for correct responses and by the teacher as students demonstrate appropriate tutoring behavior. At the end of the week, the points for each team are tallied, and the winning team is announced. Thus, PALS combines competition among teams with cooperation as pairs of students work together.

# Applications and Examples

Several forms of peer tutoring are available, but PALS and a very similar approach, Classwide Peer Tutoring (Fulk & King, 2001), are the most widely used and have been demonstrated as effective by extensive research. Teachers can use these approaches to peer tutoring with any subject area. Both approaches are flexible, easy to implement, cost-effective, and time-efficient. These qualities likely account for the acceptance and use of these interventions by many teachers in elementary and secondary classrooms.

An important research finding to note is that the effectiveness of peer tutoring is significantly enhanced if tutors are thoroughly prepared before the intervention. In addition, it is important that teachers monitor the behavior of tutors to ensure that appropriate procedures are consistently used (Stenhoff & Lignugaris/Kraft, 2007). Research has also revealed that peer tutoring can have a positive effect on student social skills and self-concept (Ginsburg-Block et al., 2006).

## Keep in Mind

In spite of increasing emphasis on accountability measures and ensuring that all students learn to read by grade 3, evidence suggests many students do not meet this goal (McLeskey & Waldron, 2011). The most effective method for rapidly bringing these students up in basic skills is one-to-one or small-group instruction (Elbaum et al., 2000). Unfortunately, most schools do not have the resources to provide this type of instruction to students on a regular basis. Peer tutoring offers an excellent alternative to small-group or one-to-one instruction provided by teachers or paraeducators. Students who provide peer tutoring are a readily available resource, and with appropriate preparation, they can provide peer tutoring that will often significantly improve student outcomes.

### Key References

Fuchs, D., Fuchs, L., & Burish, P. (2000). Peer-assisted learning strategies: An evidence-based practice to promote reading achievement. *Learning Disabilities Research and Practice, 15*(2), 85–91.

Fuchs, D., Fuchs, L., Shamir, A., Dion, E., Saenz, L., & McMaster, K. (2010). Peer mediation: A means of differentiating classroom instruction. In R. Allington & A. McGill-Franzen (Eds.), *Handbook of reading disabilities* (pp. 362–372). Mahwah, NJ: Erlbaum.

Fulk, B., & King, K. (2001). Classwide peer tutoring at work. *Teaching Exceptional Children, 34*(2), 49–53.

Ginsburg-Block, M., Rohrbeck, C., & Fantuzzo, J. (2006). A meta-analytic review of social, self-concept, and behavioral outcomes of peer-assisted learning. *Journal of Educational Psychology, 98*, 732–749.

Stenhoff, D., & Lignugaris/Kraft, B., (2007). A review of the effects of peer tutoring on students with mild disabilities in secondary settings. *Exceptional Children, 74*, 8–30.

# BEGINNING READING: TIERS OF INSTRUCTION AND RESPONSE TO INTERVENTION

## Rationale

As we noted previously, response to intervention (RTI) was included in IDEA 2004 as an alternative for identifying students with disabilities. Student identification using RTI is based on the assumption that a student should be identified with a disability only after high-quality instruction has been provided and the student has continued to struggle to learn. This high-quality instruction typically includes core instruction in the general education classroom (Tier 1), instruction in small groups (Tier 2), and intensive, individualized instruction focusing on specific student needs (Tier 3) (Fletcher & Vaughn, 2009). Research indicates that the use of tiered interventions for students who struggle with learning to read are effective in preventing reading difficulties for many students who are at risk or who struggle in the early elementary grades (Torgesen, 2009; Vellutino, Scanlon, Small, & Fanuele, 2006).

(For more information on CBMs, see Strategy 11.8 in Chapter 11.)

## Step-by-Step

The primary purpose of RTI is to provide high-quality early intervention for students who are at risk for academic difficulties; a related purpose is more valid identification of students with disabilities (Fletcher & Vaughn, 2009). The advantages of an RTI approach "include earlier identification, a stronger focus on prevention, and assessment with clearer implications for academic programming" (L. Fuchs & Fuchs, 2007, p. 14). Many approaches to implementing RTI are available. One such approach (adapted from recommendations by L. Fuchs and Fuchs [2007] and Vaughn and Roberts [2007]) includes the following steps:

**1** *The foundation for an effective RTI approach is high-quality core instruction in the general education classroom.* In reading, this instruction is typically built on a curriculum that includes the basic components of early reading instruction (i.e., phonemic awareness, phonics, reading fluency, and comprehension). Many schools use a basal reading series such as *Open Court Reading* (SRA/McGraw-Hill, 2005), a "phonics-based K–6 curriculum that is grounded in the research-based practices cited in the National Reading Panel Report" (Borman, Dowling, & Schneck, 2007), to provide a framework for high-quality instruction. Other schools use a whole-school improvement program such as Success for All (Slavin, 2004). We described effective instructional practices to meet student needs previously in this chapter.

**2** *Teachers use a universal screening of all students to identify those who struggle to learn to read when provided high-quality instruction in the general education classroom.* Teachers then monitor the reading progress of those identified with possible reading problems on a weekly basis using a curriculum-based measure (CBM). Students identified with a reading problem based on the

CBM results then receive a Tier-2 intervention (L. Fuchs & Fuchs, 2007).

**3** *A Tier-2 intervention is more intensive than instruction that is typically provided in the general education classroom.* Teachers deliver these interventions in small groups (e.g., three to six students) for brief periods of time (e.g., 15 to 30 minutes) each day, for up to 20 weeks. Tier-2 interventions should be provided in addition to core instruction in the general education classroom, coordinated with the curriculum of the general education classroom, targeted to specific student skill deficits, and include progress monitoring two to four times per month to ensure adequate progress (L. Fuchs & Fuchs, 2007; Vaughn & Roberts, 2007).

**4** *Although many students with early reading difficulties have skill deficits, others may have motivational problems.* For these students, a school psychologist may work with the teacher to problem solve regarding individualized interventions that the teacher can use to increase the student's motivation (L. Fuchs & Fuchs, 2007). Interventions may include the use of books or other reading material addressing topics that are high interest for the student, group reading activities with peers, or employment of reinforcement systems that reward the student for reading.

**5** *During Tier 2, teachers monitor student progress on targeted skills using a CBM system or other measure of student progress from two to four times per month.* Teachers use these measures to determine if a student has progressed sufficiently to ensure success in the general education classroom. For students who continue to struggle, a multidisciplinary team meets to discuss the student's eligibility for special education, and, as appropriate, to develop a Tier-3 intervention.

**6** *A Tier-3 intervention consists of instruction delivered by special education.* This intervention should be more intensive and focused on individual student needs than instruction provided in Tier 2; closely coordinated with general education instruction; provided in addition to general education reading instruction; and frequently monitored using CBM to ensure that the intervention is working (L. Fuchs & Fuchs, 2007; Vaughn & Roberts, 2007). Teachers should deliver Tier-3 instruction in groups of two or three students, and it should last longer than Tier-2 instruction (for 50 minutes or more) (Vaughn & Roberts, 2007).

## Applications and Examples

Two important characteristics of well-designed tiers of instruction are coordination of curriculum across tiers, and close alignment of instruction with the general education curriculum. Curriculum coordination has often presented difficulty across general and special education classrooms, because different materials are used and different student skills are emphasized across settings. Well-aligned instruction provides the student with multiple opportunities to master needed skills and increases the effectiveness of interventions.

For example, *Reading Intervention for Early Success* (formerly called *Early Intervention in Reading EIR)* (Houghton Mifflin, 2006) is designed to use with basal reading series that emphasize evidence-based instructional practices. Teachers can use *Reading Intervention for Early Success* with small groups (five to seven students) to address reading weaknesses as a Tier-2 intervention. Research has proven this program to be effective in addressing early reading difficulties (Wahl, 2003). Teachers use *Early Success* for 30 minutes a day to address skill development related to phonics, fluency, sight vocabulary, and reading comprehension.

## Keep in Mind

Response to intervention is an approach to delivering effective instruction in other basic skill areas (e.g., mathematics or writing), and teachers can also use RTI to provide support for students with behavior problems (Fairbanks, Sugai, Guarding, & Lathrop, 2007; Sugai & Horner, 2009). The use of RTI in writing or mathematics is similar to the steps used with reading intervention. The use of this framework to address student behavior problems is somewhat different. For example, a Tier-1 intervention for students with possible emotional and behavioral problems might consist of a school-wide system that requires schools to "identify and explicitly teach school-wide expectations; implement a system to acknowledge expectation-compliant behavior; define and consistently apply consequences for inappropriate behavior; and regularly review progress towards school-wide goals. Such a universal system reflects the features of positive behavior support" (Fairbanks et al., 2007, p. 289). Teachers then use Tier-2 interventions to develop specific social behavior and skills for small groups of students; while Tier-3 addresses individualized intervention.

### Key References

Fuchs, L., & Fuchs, D. (2007). A model for implementing responsiveness to intervention. *Teaching Exceptional Children, 39*(5), 14–20.

Harlacher, J., Walker, N., & Sanford, A. (2010). The "I" in RTI: Research-based factors for intensifying instruction. *Teaching Exceptional Children, 42*(6), 30–38.

Ritchey, K. (2011). The first "R": Evidence-based reading instruction for students with learning disabilities. *Theory into Practice, 50,* 28–34.

Sugai, G., & Horner, R. (2009). Responsiveness-to-intervention and school-wide positive behavior supports: Integration of multi-tiered system approaches. *Exceptionality, 17,* 223–237.

Vaughn, S., & Roberts, G. (2007). Secondary intervention in reading: Providing additional information for students at risk. *Teaching Exceptional Children, 39*(5), 40–46.

| Strategy 13.7 | **SELF-REGULATED STRATEGY DEVELOPMENT AND WRITING INSTRUCTION** |

## Rationale

Many elementary students with disabilities have difficulty planning and regulating the strategies they use as they write (Harris, Graham, Mason, & Friedlander, 2008). Strategies have been developed that teachers may use to improve student planning and self-regulation as students learn to write. One of these strategies begins with a three-step framework for planning and writing called POW (**P**ick my idea; **O**rganize my notes; **W**rite and say more). The POW activity may be coupled with a strategy for composing called TREE (**T**opic sentence— Tell what you believe; **R**easons—three or more, Why do I believe this? Will my readers believe this? etc.; **E**nding—Wrap it up right; **E**xamine—Do I have all my parts?). The POW and TREE strategies provide students with a framework for both planning and composing as they learn to write.

Research has revealed that self-regulation strategies can be successfully taught, are used by students in their writing, and result in improved written products (Baker, Chard, Ketterlin-Geller, Apichatabutra, & Doabler, 2009). Teachers have successfully used self-regulated strategy development (SRSD) with classes, small groups, and individual students to develop writing strategies for a range of genres (Harris et al., 2008).

## Step-by-Step

Teachers use SRSD to support students in using writing strategies effectively and independently. The teacher provides explicit instruction as the students learn the strategy and then provides the students with instruction related to how they can apply the strategy. Instruction in these strategies entails the use of six steps adapted from Graham, Harris, and MacArthur (2006); Harris, Graham, and Mason (2003); and Harris, Graham, Mason, and Friedlander (2008).

**1** *Ensure background knowledge.* Initially, the teacher determines the background knowledge and skills (e.g., vocabulary, concepts) the student needs in order to learn and use the strategy. The teacher presents this information to the student and determines how to organize and structure instruction, given the particular student who is being taught. The student is also typically given one or more self-statements or self-speech, which is a powerful form of self-regulation, and then begins learning to use this powerful form of self-regulation. For example, the student may use a self-statement such as "I can do this if I use my strategy and take my time." The teacher discusses with the student why these statements are important, as well as how and when they should be used.

**2** *Discuss the strategy.* The teacher and student then discuss the strategy to be learned. For example, the teacher describes the POW + TREE strategies and how the student can use them to guide her writing. The teacher explains each step in the strategies as well as how the mnemonics can help the student to remember the strategies. The teacher may also examine with the student her current level of writing performance, and how the strategy might help improve her writing.

**3** *Model the strategy.* The teacher or a peer then models the use of the strategy for the student, using self-instruction while writing for a class assignment. The modeling and self-instruction should be spontaneous and natural.

**4** *Memorize the strategy.* The student then memorizes the steps in the strategy and the mnemonic that facilitates learning. Memorization typically begins in the previous two steps and may continue into the next step. This repetition and distributed practice is important for the student who is having difficulty remembering information, because she can't use the strategy if she can't remember it.

**5** *Provide support.* The student then uses the strategy as she plans, composes, writes, revises, and edits class writing assignments. The student uses the self-regulation strategy to support her work, while the teacher provides support or scaffolding as needed through prompts, interactions, and guidance.

**6** *Student independent use.* The teacher should fade or discontinue use of supports as quickly as possible, so that the student independently uses the self-regulation strategy. The teacher should plan to periodically review the strategy with the student to ensure continued use. Over time, the teacher and student may determine that the self-regulation strategy should be discontinued as the student's writing skills and self-regulation skills improve.

## Applications and Examples

Another strategy that is used for writing instruction is W-W-W WHAT=2 HOW=2 (Mason, Harris, & Graham, 2011). Teachers use this strategy as a framework for students who are engaged in story planning. This framework includes the following:

Who is the main character?
When does the story take place?
Where does the story take place?
What does the main character do or want to do? What do other characters do?
What happens then?
How does the story end?
How does the main character feel? How do the other characters feel?

Teachers can pair this strategy with the POW strategy and use graphic organizers to outline the information produced as prewriting planning takes place. For more information regarding this strategy, see Mason, Harris, and Graham (2011).

## Keep in Mind

The overall goals of SRSD relate to assisting students in developing skills and strategies to support planning, writing, revising, and editing; to support students in monitoring and managing their own writing; and to promote positive attitudes toward writing. To ensure effective use of SRSD, teachers have noted several important considerations (Harris et al., 2003). First, these activities should be collaborative among teachers and students. As instruction continues, students should take increasing responsibility for self-regulation strategies. Second, teachers should tailor strategy instruction to the individual student's approach to writing. Strategies will work well with some students but not others. Teachers should adapt strategies to fit an individual student's needs. Third, the teacher should give each student the time he needs to master a strategy, rather than only a fixed amount of time to teach a strategy. Finally, to teach a strategy well, teachers should help students understand the meaning and significance of the strategy.

**Key References**

Baker, S., Chard, D., Ketterlin-Geller, L., Apichatabutra, C., & Doabler, C. (2009). Teaching writing to at-risk students: The quality of evidence for self-regulated strategy development. *Exceptional Children, 75,* 303–318.

Graham, S., & Harris, K. (2006). Cognitive strategy instruction. In C. MacArthur, S. Graham, & K. Harris (Eds.), *Handbook of writing research* (pp. 187–207). New York: Guilford.

Graham, S., Harris, K., & MacArthur, S. (2006). Explicitly teaching struggling writers: Strategies for mastering the writing process. *Intervention in School and Clinic, 41*(5), 290–294.

Harris, K., Graham, S., Mason, L., & Friedlander, B. (2008). *Powerful writing strategies for all students.* Baltimore: Brookes.

Mason, L., Harris, K., & Graham, S. (2011). Self-regulated strategy development for students with writing difficulties. *Theory into Practice, 50,* 20–27.

| Strategy 13.8 | COGNITIVE STRATEGY INSTRUCTION FOR TEACHING MATHEMATICS PROBLEM SOLVING |
| --- | --- |

## Rationale

The most powerful interventions for students who struggle to learn mathematics are the use of direct instruction (discussed previously in this chapter) and cognitive strategy instruction (Montague, 2007). Cognitive strategy instruction can be as simple as a teacher modeling and encouraging students to verbalize their thinking as they work on a math problem (self-talk) or having students draw a graphic representation of the steps needed to solve a computation problem (Gersten & Clarke, 2007). Still other self-regulation strategies consist of teaching students several steps to follow when solving word problems (L. Fuchs & Fuchs, 2001; Montague, 2007).

Researchers suggest that the use of strategy instruction such as think-alouds or self-regulation is often effective because this approach helps students control the impulsive, often random approach they use to problem solving (Gersten & Clarke, 2007). This instruction is also useful in teaching students the steps needed to solve a problem and ensuring that students maintain this information over time (Montague, 2007).

## Step-by-Step

Strategy instruction is designed to support students who struggle to learn mathematics by scaffolding instruction so that students can think and respond like successful learners. This instruction includes built-in cues and prompts for students as they engage in strategies for self-regulation, self-instruction, self-monitoring, and self-checking (Montague, 2007). Teachers gradually fade supports as students become proficient. The major components of strategy instruction are described in the following example, which has been adapted from Dunlap and Dunlap (1989); Montague (2007); and Montague, Warger, and Morgan (2000):

**1** *Assess the student* to determine if he has mastered the prerequisite knowledge and skills. For example, if completing subtraction problems with regrouping, the student must understand the concepts underlying addition, subtraction, and place value. The student also must either know basic math facts or be able to use a fact chart efficiently (Fahsl, 2007).

**2** *Develop and explicitly teach the student a strategy for problem solving.* For example, for solving subtraction problems, the teacher could provide the following steps to the student, who checks off the strategies as they are completed (Dunlap & Dunlap, 1989):

- Did I copy the problem correctly?
- Did I regroup when needed?
- Did I borrow correctly?
- Did I subtract all the numbers?
- Did I subtract correctly?

**3** *Model the strategy.* As part of explicit instruction of the problem-solving strategy, the teacher should model the strategy while engaging in self-talk through each step. The student then repeats this process with support from the teacher. The student may also practice the problem-solving strategy with peers, who provide feedback as needed.

**4** *Fade the prompts.* As students practice the problem-solving strategy, they become more proficient, and the teacher may fade the prompts (e.g., verbal cues, checklist of strategies).

**5** *Provide students with specific feedback* regarding their performance as they use the problem-solving strategy. Teachers should also praise students for their performance, as appropriate, to maintain motivation and convey that they are making progress and can learn to successfully solve problems.

## Applications and Examples

Educators have begun to place more emphasis on solving mathematics problems that are applicable to the students' real world (Montague et al., 2000). Many students struggle to solve complex mathematics word problems and benefit from strategies that provide a systematic structure for addressing such problems. Self-regulation strategies help students control their own actions and become more independent as they learn to solve complex problems (Montague, 2007). Steps used in a self-regulation strategy for mathematics word problems may include the following (Montague, 2007; Montague et al., 2000):

- Read the problem for understanding, then ask if you understand the problem.
- Put the problem into your own words. First underline important information, then ask yourself if you understand this information.
- Make a drawing or diagram of the problem. As needed, teachers may use a graphic organizer with built-in prompts (i.e., some of the information provided) to support students (Maccini & Gagnon, 2005).
- Develop a plan to solve the problem by deciding the operations that should be used and how many steps are needed, then check to see if the plan makes sense.
- Predict the answer by rounding numbers and doing the problem in your head. Check to make sure you used the important information in the problem.
- Complete the operations in the problem in the correct order. Does your answer compare to your estimate?
- Check to see if you correctly completed all the computation steps and in the correct order.
- Ask for help if needed.

## Keep in Mind

A number of sources may be useful for a wide range of strategies for solving particular types of mathematics problems. Elementary and secondary mathematics texts are sources of these strategies. Another option is applying general problem-solving strategies that have proven useful for students in other academic areas. For example, SRSD (described previously as a strategy for improving written expression in Strategy 13.7) has also proven useful as a strategy for improving student skill development in mathematics (Montague, 2008).

Many teachers have developed their own problem-solving strategies by engaging in self-talk as they solve a particular type of mathematics problem or by talking with proficient students to better understand how they solve problems. (Try Googling "math problem-solving strategies," and you'll find the results of this work.) Remember, think-alouds or problem-solving strategies are simply how proficient learners solve mathematics problems. Sharing these strategies with students who struggle learning mathematics is a powerful approach to improving skill development.

**Key References**

Fuchs, L., & Fuchs, D. (2001). Principles for the prevention and intervention of mathematics difficulties. *Learning Disabilities Research and Practice, 16*(2), 85–95.

Gersten, R., & Clarke, B. (2007). *Effective strategies for teaching students with difficulties in mathematics: Instruction research brief.* Reston, VA: National Council for Teachers of Mathematics.

Maccini, P., & Gagnon, J. (2005). *Math graphic organizers for students with disabilities.* Retrieved March 11, 2008, from www.K8accesscenter.org

Montague, M. (2007). Self-regulation and mathematics instruction. *Learning Disabilities Research and Practice, 22*(1), 75–83.

Montague, M., Warger, C., & Morgan, T. (2000). Solve it! Strategy instruction to improve mathematical problem solving. *Learning Disabilities Research and Practice, 15*(2), 110–116.

# Teaching Students in Secondary Content Areas

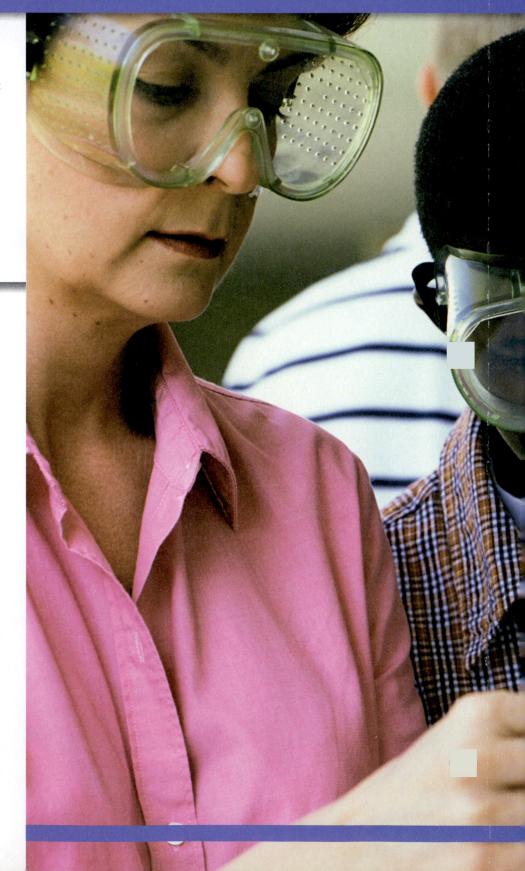

## KEY TOPICS

**After reading this chapter you will:**

- Know what to expect with regard to content learning differences among students with disabilities.

- Be able to identify and describe a range of models and approaches for inclusive content-area instruction.

- Possess a series of guided step-by-step effective practices for teaching students with disabilities in content-area classes.

# chapter 14

# A VIEW FROM A TEACHER-LEADER

### Susan Hill Addresses the Challenges of Teaching Secondary Content to Students with Disabilities

Susan Hill, Dean of Special Education at Heritage High School, is always on the move. With her active involvement in almost all aspects of special education at the school, it is rare when Ms. Hill has time to sit down and catch her breath. She would have it no other way: Ms. Hill spends considerable time on important legal and compliance issues, ensuring that parents understand and remain part of their child's special education program. Still, she is primarily an instructional leader, devoting most of her efforts to coaching and providing consultative service to content-area general educators, special education teachers, and co-teaching teams. Being the instructional resource person is among the most rewarding aspects of her position. Ms. Hill receives great satisfaction suggesting evidence-based practices to her colleagues, and she enjoys having opportunities to model specific techniques that help students with disabilities succeed in their subject-area classrooms. Along with the many rewards, however, Ms. Hill feels that developing and implementing instructional supports for her students are also among the most challenging and frustrating aspects of her job.

What is so challenging? Ms. Hill has observed that many ninth-grade students with disabilities enter Heritage with a wide diversity of background knowledge, academic skills, and learning strategies. As a result of this diversity, students require significant amounts of remedial instruction in how to access, engage, and use secondary content material. Some students lack the reading skills to benefit fully from established textbooks and cannot prepare written assignments that reflect understanding of the curriculum. In fact, the level of skill deficiencies—in reading, writing, and math—are so severe that Heritage has developed a highly structured elective course to remediate basic skills for all ninth graders with disabilities. Recognizing that a special course in skills is necessary but clearly not sufficient, Ms. Hill and her general and special education colleagues regularly assess the learning needs of individual students, determine which elements of each subject-area curriculum are essential for the student to acquire, and find methods that can help students learn that content. The overwhelming challenge is to ensure that the content deemed essential is not watered down, or weakened. Students must receive rigorous instruction in much of the standard curriculum in order to pass the state-mandated exit exams, Standards of Learning Tests (SOLs), required for students seeking an academic diploma.

How do Ms. Hill and her team meet these challenges? As with most activities at Heritage, collaborative planning teams determine how teachers can best address the content learning of

the students. For some students, Ms. Hill and other special educators provide consultative services to general education content specialists. In other cases, co-teaching teams coordinate the delivery of instruction and support. For students with more severe cognitive disabilities, content-area specialists assist special education teachers to identify elements of the curriculum that can be presented in a more functional and concrete fashion.

In terms of specific techniques, Ms. Hill urges her teachers to augment their instruction with content enhancements—explicit tools that help organize lessons and assist when demonstrating difficult concepts to struggling learners. She also recognizes the need to reduce the reliance on textbooks for students with disabilities. Many have difficulty reading and comprehending high-level textual material and benefit from alternative high-interest, easier-readability reading materials as well as technology-based supports such as audio recordings and white boards. Ms. Hill has also observed the value of universally designed instructional techniques, and she urges all of her teachers to use routines that help students organize their daily class notes and assignments. For students with more severe cognitive impairments, she urges care in selecting the aspects of the curriculum to emphasize and the increased amounts of teacher-directed instruction. Although this often requires novel ways of deploying personnel, both teachers and paraprofessionals, she has noted that increased adult support results in fewer behavioral disruptions and greater academic performance.

Susan Hill recognizes that aligning essential elements of the secondary curriculum and specific instructional supports to the learning needs of individual students is not a perfect science. It is detective work, an exercise of daily problem solving to determine which evidence-based practices work for specific students. More often than not, the process works. Assisted considerably by the work of Ms. Hill and her colleagues, students at Heritage High School, those with and without disabilities, continue to perform well on their SOLs and have achieved adequate yearly progress for the past 7 years.

# Introduction

When presented with effective, motivating instruction, most secondary students learn their subject-area content material: science, history, math, and so on. Although students vary in their acquired levels of proficiency, they succeed, in large part, because they read fluently, attend to presentations selectively, and devise strategies to organize and remember major elements of their lessons. They perform well on assessments (papers and exams) because they know how to access and retrieve what they have learned. Moreover, in seemingly automatic fashion, these students organize new learning; connect new content to old; store material in ways that make future use easy; and take time to actually *think about their thinking* (Bransford, Brown, & Cocking, 2000; Ellis, 1993).

Unfortunately, not all students experience content-area learning in this way. As observed by Susan Hill, the Dean of Special Education at Heritage High School, in our opening feature, some students enter secondary classrooms lacking the basic skills—often reading and writing—and strategies to benefit fully from the curriculum. In some circumstances, students present themselves as unorganized, unmotivated, uninterested, and disruptive. More often than not, these behaviors are the result of a learning problem or disability, and reflect years of frustration being unable to understand important and interesting subject matter.

In addition to their need for motivating material, these students need explicit guidance and support in how best to access subject-area content. Moreover, they need clear instruction in how to organize and manage their own learning. Meeting the instructional needs of these students is the challenge facing content-area general and special education teachers in inclusive settings. Nonetheless, by pooling their efforts and expertise, teachers can make secondary content subjects (e.g., biology, history, physics, and geometry) interesting and accessible to all levels and types of learners (Scruggs, Mastropieri, Berkeley, & Graetz, 2010).

How can teachers identify students who lack adequate information processing skills? How can subject-area content be made accessible to students with learning differences and disabilities? Is it possible to differentiate content instruction for such students and still maintain high standards for other students in the classroom? Many teachers, such as those on the faculty at Heritage High School, recognize that universal and individualized instructional practices help all students access and acquire subject-area knowledge. These instructional practices are *engineered* (Dukes & Lamar-Dukes, 2009)—designed and delivered collaboratively by general and special education teachers. In this chapter, we focus on strategies and techniques that provide students with explicit strategies for reading, organizing, storing, and retrieving content—practices that result in enhanced subject-area achievement.

## Content Learning Differences: What to Expect

Consider what it is like for learners who lack the skills to learn the material presented in secondary-content classes. First and foremost, many of these students have difficulty understanding incoming information because of receptive language difficulties, reading comprehension problems, organization deficits, as well as shortcomings in short- and long-term memory functioning (Anderson-Inman, Knox-Quinn, & Horney, 1996; Vaughn et al., 2011). Along with poor spelling, handwriting skills, and a tendency toward easy distractibility, essential skills such as note taking, studying, and test taking fail to develop adequately. Not surprisingly, frustration builds, motivation falls, and students experiencing continued failure often engage in inappropriate behaviors to mask their academic weaknesses.

Many of these learners also lack the tools for approaching and managing the complex requirements of academic tasks. They either lack specific strategies for dealing with subject matter, or select—sometimes randomly—approaches that are inappropriate for the assigned task. When facing complex content, these students do not actively engage the learning process. Specifically, they do not reflect on previous lessons, rarely think of alternative ways to think about the content, or seldom evaluate and revise their initial thinking (Wery & Nietfeld, 2010).

As these issues often involve **metacognition**, or *the thinking about thinking*, you should anticipate that content-area instruction goes beyond curriculum standards and basic skills. To reach all students, teachers need to enrich lessons and learning resources with strategic enhancements and provide instruction that is sensitive to information processing. How do teachers make these adjustments to lesson development? Research has found that successful teachers differentiate instruction to best meet the needs of individual learners. At the same time, successful teachers ensure that instruction sensitive to individual learners is also appropriate for the entire class (Lenz, Bulgren, Kissam, & Taymans, 2004; Walker-Dalhouse, Risko, Eswothy, Grasley, Kaisler, McIlvain, & Stephen, 2009).

No one understands the need to provide supports and accommodations for challenging content more than Jon Pruess, a general science and physics teacher at Heritage High School. Identified as having a learning disability for most of his middle and high school years, Mr. Pruess had few

### Pause & Reflect

Think back to a situation where you were unable to perform a skill, complete a task, or engage in an activity to your (or another's) satisfaction. Describe your frustrations, and identify several of the feelings you experienced in relation to your inability to meet the requirements adequately. What could have been done to help you?

Secondary students who have learning problems and disabilities often mask their inability to content area instruction by appearing uninterested or being disruptive.

teachers who understood the way he processed their subject-area lessons. Currently, along with special education co-teacher Tracey Ludwig, Mr. Pruess sees firsthand that stimulating content and enthusiastic presentations are not enough for some of his students. Every day, Mr. Pruess and Mr. Ludwig make critical decisions as to which elements of the curriculum to emphasize and how much of their instruction should target specialized methods and supports that help students connect with the content. To make these types of instructional decisions general and special education subject-area teachers must first understand the nature of curriculum and what it takes to work collaboratively in the delivery of the curriculum.

## Understanding Curriculum

Among the most critical decisions made by parents, educators, and policy makers is the composition of the curriculum: the content, skills, and processes students learn in school. With state government policy makers mandating core curricular standards for schools, teachers in recent years have had reduced say in the selection of course content. However, teachers remain central in the placement of topics emphasized in their classes, as well as the materials, resources, and methods used to deliver the content. More important, teachers make daily decisions regarding adaptations and accommodations to the curriculum to address the individual needs of their students.

What do teachers of inclusive content-area classes need to understand about curriculum? First, with federal (e.g., No Child Left Behind [NCLB]) and state-wide accountability systems, most students with disabilities are expected to make progress in all aspects of the general education curriculum. Second, because students vary in their ability to learn, retain, and apply information, not all students will learn all aspects of a given subject area. Specifically, some core elements of subject material must be learned to proficiency by all students, while other aspects of the material will be learned by only a smaller proportion of students. Finally, teachers typically need structured routines (e.g., planning pyramids) for instructional planning in order to determine which elements of the curriculum specific students require (Schumm, 1999; Vaughn, Bos, & Schumm, 2007).

## Working Collaboratively

Throughout this text, we discuss repeatedly the importance of collaboration in the delivery of inclusive educational programs. Not surprisingly, when teaching subject-area content, a solid working partnership between the content-area expert and the special educator is essential. How do such partnerships work? At Heritage High School, for example, the nature and style of collaborative teaming arrangements vary from class to class, often a function of the teachers' expertise, instructional styles, comfort levels, and, of course, the needs of the students. For example, in the inclusive physics class co-taught by Jon Pruess and Tracey Ludwig, Mr. Pruess, a natural storyteller and accomplished scientist, delivers the majority of the large-group direct instruction. Mr. Ludwig, the special educator, circulates among the students, providing efficient and timely support in the form of suggested strategies, content enhancements, and encouragement. In the geometry class co-taught by Anthony Long and Shana Watson, Ms. Watson, the special educator, assumes a greater share of the large-group direct-instruction responsibilities. Ms. Watson,

Teachers work collaboratively to make curricular adaptations that address the individual needs of students.

certified in both math and special education, also provides guided notes and individualized support to students when Mr. Long provides the direct instruction.

Each of these co-teaching teams uses a slightly different collaborative approach to instruction and support. Still, each of their collaborative efforts is effective because they orchestrate their planning and instruction in ways that maximize individual pedagogical strengths, they are sensitive to preferred instructional roles, and they address the needs of students. Although roles and responsibilities change, the co-teaching partners make sure that they plan lessons together as well as review their instructional processes and student outcomes frequently. Most important, regardless of their co-teaching approach, the special educators are not put in the position of being classroom assistants. They regularly provide substantial instruction and support, to the entire group, small groups, or individual students.

# Models and Approaches for Inclusive Content-Area Instruction

When teaching secondary content in inclusive classes, successful teachers select from a variety of evidence-based models and approaches. Typical practices include universal design for learning, direct instruction, guided discovery learning, cooperative learning, strategy instruction, and content enhancements.

## Universal Design for Learning

**Universal design for learning (UDL)** is a way of making instruction accessible to all students by building supports and accommodation into the original mode of teaching rather than making adaptations after the fact. Universal design is all around us, most noticeably in architecture and product development (Edyburn, 2010; Hitchcock, Meyer, Rose, & Jackson, 2002). Currently, it is typical practice for architects to use universal design to build in accommodations to buildings from their initial design phases, including ramps for wheelchair users as an essential part of a building's design. Similarly, closed captioning, originally intended to benefit people who cannot hear the sound from a television because of a disability, benefits many others (e.g., those in noisy bars, health clubs, or bedrooms when another person is sleeping) who do not have problems hearing.

Merely a decade ago, universal design for learning was the domain of a few instructional technology experts. However, given the rapid advances in technology and curriculum design, universal design is a reality that pervades schools and enhances teachers' delivery of content-area instruction (King-Sears, 2009; McLeskey & Waldron, 2002). At Heritage High School, geometry co-teachers Anthony Long and Shana Watson have integrated a number of "special" universal techniques into their usual lesson plans. For example, they begin every class with a display of an advance graphic organizer of the lesson content. Guided notes help students keep up with the main points of the lesson, and calculators prevent calculation difficulties from interfering with conceptual understanding of the content.

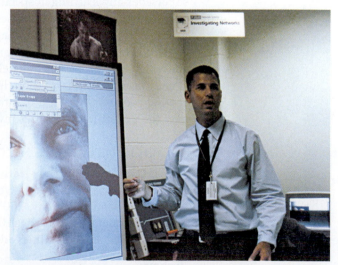

Universal design for learning is a way of making instruction accessible by building supports and accommodation into typical modes of instructional delivery.

## Direct Instruction

Typically appropriate for learners of all ages, **direct instruction (DI)** refers to a set of specific teacher behaviors and curriculum materials that correlate with increased levels of student academic achievement. Known for its high degree of structure and predictability, DI contains three principal components: demonstration, guided practice, and independent practice. During the *demonstration* stage of a lesson, the teacher explicitly presents elements of the instructional material or models methods for applying a skill or solving a particular problem. Consider how students apply DI in secondary settings: In their geometry class, Anthony Long or Shana Wheeler demonstrate explicitly the formula for determining the degree of an interior angle of a parallelogram when the degrees of three of the other angles are known. Using a direct instruction sequence, they present the formula and model the steps in solving several examples.

*Guided practice* is a closely supervised application of the demonstrated content supplemented by teacher cues, prompts, and corrective feedback. Often indistinguishable from interactive demonstrations, guided practice is most effective when students have numerous and varied opportunities to interact with the content of the lesson. Examples of guided practice activities in secondary content-area classes include small groups of students solving algebra or geometry problems on the board, working together to apply a chemistry or physics laboratory concept, or replying in unison fashion to questions about characteristics of governments.

*Independent practice* typically follows guided practice, but only when students are ready to engage the content on their own. Teachers can and should deliver independent practice through creative instructional activities and cooperative group projects. Most content-area classrooms, however, typically rely on seatwork and homework. Because many students spend as much as 70% of an instructional period in seatwork activities, it is essential that the activities be age and subject appropriate, be consistent with the goals of the lesson, have multiple response formats, and contain components that students can complete with a high degree of success (Gaffney, 1987). Like seatwork, students should be able to complete homework assignments independently. Effective assignments emphasize information already learned and set the stage for the acquisition of new content. When integrating homework into lessons, teachers should ensure they do not use it to punish students or to replace school-based instruction (Cooper, 2001).

## Guided Discovery Learning

The primary goal of *guided discovery learning (GDL)* is to teach students to be independent problem solvers— in other words, to learn the generic steps to scientific inquiry and logical thinking. By learning the generic process of problem solving, students can acquire and master information from a number of content areas. Guided discovery learning applies problem-solving strategies to new material and situations. Students learn specific content information through the introduction of novel problems requiring similar problem-solving strategies and involving new but similar information. In essence, with GDL, the problem-solving process supersedes any learning of specific content material (Rosenberg et al., 2006).

For students with disabilities included in content-area classes, the guided portion of GDL must be prominent. Teachers accomplish this by emphasizing different ways to solve content-specific problems and presenting a specific sequence of questions and actions for addressing the problem. A model of instruction that carries many of these general features is *problem-centered learning* (Borich, 2010; Cote, 2011). Teachers develop an explicit problem-solving process through a natural dialogue with students, with students gradually taking over the steps and procedures involved in the task at hand (see Strategy 14.7).

## Cooperative Learning

See **Chapter 13** for detailed information on cooperative learning.

Applications of **cooperative learning** vary widely in type yet share some common beneficial characteristics, including positive interdependence, individual accountability, and cooperative skills (Good & Brophy, 2003; Putnam, 1998; Slavin, 1999). Teachers use cooperative learning frequently in Heritage High School, with secondary content-area co-teaching teams often selecting and sometimes adapting the following evidence-based applications.

### Jigsaw

Three to five students form heterogeneous groups. Each team member is assigned a part (piece) of the assignment (puzzle). Students from the different groups who are assigned to the same part form expert groups. The expert groups meet to review information regarding their part, determine the most important information, and then return to their teams. The teams then review the important information from each part and synthesize the information (Aronson, Stephen, Sikes, Blaney, & Snapp, 1978; Slavin, 1990).

### Student Teams—Achievement Divisions (STAD)

Students are arranged into heterogeneous teams of four to six. Following a pretest, the teacher presents content, and teams work together on worksheets, study guides, or other practice activities. Students take individual tests on the material, and scores are compared with their pretest scores to derive a gain score. The gain scores are averaged for a team gain score. Points are awarded for individual and team gains (Slavin, 1990).

## Learning Strategies

**Learning strategies** are a broad array of techniques that help students access and use higher-order secondary-content knowledge. Strategies work because they focus directly on what students can do to improve their performance, facilitate comprehension, allow for active student engagement in instruction, and promote the active creation of rules for using instructional presentations and materials (Berkeley, Mastropieri, & Scruggs, 2011; Rogan, 2000). Effective strategies focus on content (what to teach) and design (how to teach) (Ellis & Lenz, 1996). The content of strategies includes explicit instructional steps that help students organize, store, and ultimately express elements of their lessons and activities. For example, with the DEFENDS writing strategy (see Strategy 14.2), teachers present a series of seven steps for writing persuasive essays: (1) **D**ecide on goals and theme; (2) **E**stimate main ideas and details; (3) **F**igure best order of main ideas and details; (4) **E**xpress the theme in the first sentence; (5) **N**ote each main idea and supporting points; (6) **D**rive home the message in the last sentence; and (7) **S**earch for errors and correct.

The design, or "how-to-teach," component requires teachers to model, lead, and test students in the acquisition of the strategies. This instruction usually consists of eight steps:

1. Teacher pretests and obtains student commitment to learn.
2. Teacher describes the new strategy.
3. Teacher models the new strategy.
4. Teacher and students verbally rehearse strategy steps.
5. Student practices on controlled materials.
6. Student practices on grade-appropriate classroom materials.
7. Teacher posttests and obtains student commitment to generalize.
8. Student generalizes.

> ### Pause & Reflect
>
> Think back to your days as a secondary student. What learning strategies did you use in your content-area classes? Which of the strategies did you find to be most effective?

During strategy acquisition, steps are taken to facilitate generalization by having students apply learned strategies across content areas.

## Content Enhancements

**Content enhancements** are instructional techniques that teachers use to help academically diverse learners understand, store, and access secondary subject-area material. These techniques help teachers think about and organize content as well as present and explain difficult concepts to struggling learners. When using content enhancements, teachers ensure that (1) group and individual needs are met; (2) the integrity of content is maintained; (3) critical elements of content are translated in ways that promote learning; and (4) an instructional partnership exists between teacher and student (Lenz et al., 2004). Because there are many different ways to enhance content, it is useful to think of content enhancements in three major categories: redesigned instruction and materials, devices, and routines (King-Sears & Mooney, 2004).

### Redesigned Instruction and Materials

Educators usually design teaching sequences and instructional materials to match the profiles of "average" students. However, few if any students meet all elements of these profiles, and it is not unusual for teachers to find it necessary to adapt certain lessons or the materials they use. Earlier in this chapter, we talked about universal design for learning, a proactive way of making instruction accessible to all students by building supports and accommodations into the original mode of teaching. Although this is a preferable mode of adapting instruction, teachers sometimes must differentiate instruction or make adaptations to existing methods and materials. Teachers usually choose among nine types of instructional adaptations (see Table 14.1; Cole et al., 2000). The most frequently used adaptations tend to be the more obvious—adaptations in size (e.g., the number of items that a student is expected to complete) and time (e.g., time allocated for completing a task). However, other adaptations include (1) adjusting the difficulty level of lessons, (2) structuring how students participate and provide responses, (3) providing encouragement and support, (4) recognizing the individual student's success in large-group lessons, and (5) facilitating peer-driven, content-focused reciprocal questioning.

**Table 14.1**   Nine Types of Adaptations

| Adaptation | Definition | Example |
|---|---|---|
| **Input** | The instructional strategies used to facilitate student learning | Use videos, computer programs, field trips, and visual aids to support active learning. |
| **Output** | The ways learners can demonstrate understanding and knowledge | Students write a song, tell a story, design a poster or brochure, or perform an experiment. |
| **Size** | The length or portion of an assignment, demonstration, or performance learners are expected to complete | Reduce the length of report to be written or spoken, reduce the number of references needed, reduce the number of problems to be solved. |
| **Time** | The flexible time needed for student learning | Individualize a time line for project completion, allow more time for test taking. |
| **Difficulty** | The varied skill levels, conceptual levels, and processes involved in learning | Provide calculators, and tier the assignment so that the outcome is the same but with varying degrees of concreteness and complexity. |
| **Level of support** | The amount of assistance to the learner | Students work in cooperative groups or with peer buddies, mentors, cross-age tutors, or paraeducators. |
| **Degree of participation** | The extent to which the learner is actively involved in the tasks | In a student-written, -directed, and -acted play, a student may play a part that has more physical action rather than numerous lines to memorize. |
| **Modified goals** | The adapted outcome expectations within the context of a general education curriculum | In a written language activity, a student may focus more on writing some letters and copying words than composing whole sentences or paragraphs. |
| **Substitute curriculum** | Significantly differentiated instruction and materials to meet a learner's identified goals | In a foreign language class, a student may develop a play or script that uses both authentic language and cultural knowledge of a designated time period rather than reading paragraphs or directions. |

*Source:* Information adapted from Cole et al. (2000).

### Devices

By *devices,* we are referring to the range of concrete prompts and cues that help students understand content material and relationships among concepts. Graphic organizers, for example, are very useful for representing relationships between and among critical elements typical of content-area instruction. Graphic representations help make abstract concepts and complicated relationships (e.g., cause–effect, compare–contrast, hierarchy, cycle, etc.) concrete and tangible, allowing for easier application to the content being studied. Equally useful are mnemonic and key-word strategies (see Strategy 14.3), tools that help students with disabilities as well as other students to access content information when needed (Wolgemuth, Cobb, & Alwell, 2008).

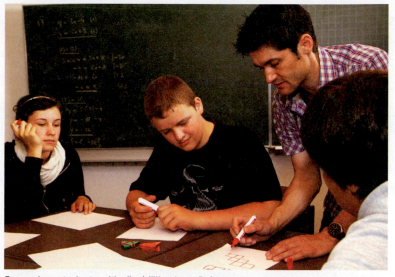

Secondary students with disabilities benefit from content enhancements such as graphic organizers when learning advanced academic content.

### Routines

A *teaching routine* is a series of steps and procedures that guides the introduction and learning of content knowledge (King-Sears & Mooney, 2004). Some routines assist teachers in organizing and presenting content that helps students see both the big picture and the details of what they will learn. Other routines serve as supports for teaching difficult concepts and operations. The primary purpose in using a specific routine is to proactively structure a portion of instruction in ways that identify and address potential obstacles to learning (Bulgren & Lenz, 1996).

Earlier, we introduced two universal design routines (the unit and lesson organizer routines) that help organize and present content. An example of a routine that assists in the actual teaching of concepts is the concept diagram (see Figure 14.1). Notice how the graphic explicitly guides students in considering similarities and differences among key elements of higher-order math. Keep in mind, however, that routines are complex and often require some degree of training and practice if they are to be implemented effectively. Routines will not be effective if they are simply distributed to students without adequate instruction. Detailed manuals are published by the Center for Learning at the University of Kansas, Center for Research on Learning (http://www.ku-crl.org), and extensive descriptions of these routines are available in the literature (e.g., Bulgren & Lenz, 1996; Bulgren, Schumaker, & Deshler, 1988, 1993; Lenz et al., 2004; Sabornie & deBettencourt, 2009).

## Content Survival Strategies

The successful acquisition of content-area knowledge requires that students learn and apply a series of survival strategies. Four of the more important strategies are content-area reading, note taking, test taking, and time management.

### Content-Area Reading

For Susan Hill, Dean of Special Education at Heritage High School, one of the major challenges in providing secondary content instruction is that many students lack the reading skills to benefit fully from textbooks. Because a large part of secondary-content instruction involves the independent reading of textbooks, it is essential that teachers use a range of strategies to facilitate content-area reading for students with disabilities. Keep in mind that secondary textbooks contain more than just narrative text. Students must also be able to understand and make use of maps, graphs, charts, and tables that augment and reinforce critical content (Sabornie & deBettencourt, 2009).

### Pause & Reflect

What changes need to be made to current textbooks if they are to contain supports and accommodations for students with learning problems? Identify ways that technology can help provide these supports.

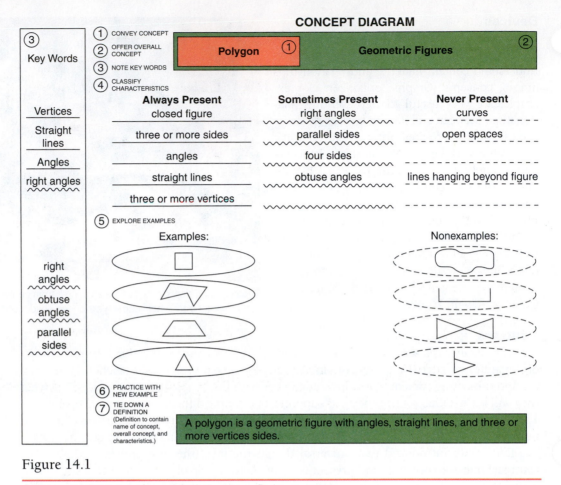

**Figure 14.1**

A Concept Diagram for a Math Lesson: Polygons

*Sources:* Adapted from J. A. Gorman & K. Lysaght. (1996). *Accommodating diversity in a general education math class in a middle school.* Presentation at Boston College, School of Education and from *The Concept Mastery Routine* by J. A. Bulgen, J. B. Schumaker, & D. D. Deshler. (1993). Lawrence, KS: Edge Enterprises.

Providing supports for content-area reading requires a multifaceted approach, including textbook exploration activities, intensive vocabulary instruction, comprehensive comprehension strategies, self-questioning strategies, audio-texts, study guides and focused chapter questions, as well as the identification of supplemental Web-based resources (Berkeley, Marshak, Mastropieri, & Scruggs, 2011; Conderman & Elf, 2007; Steele, 2007; Vaughn et al., 2011). For students with more severe challenges, teachers can, depending on the cognitive characteristics of students, replace and/or supplement text by priming background knowledge, using **picture walks** (pictures that preview lesson content), and integrating think-alouds in their instruction (Gately, 2008). Detailed descriptions of several of these content-area reading techniques are provided in Strategy 14.4.

## Note Taking

Students who have effective note-taking skills perform better on content-area assessments than those students who have difficulty with the process (Boyle, 2007, 2010). Unfortunately, few students receive direct instruction in how best to record the important points of classroom lectures and presentations. Many students with disabilities are at increased risk for failure because they are unable to

Because textbooks are a large part of secondary instruction, it is essential that students learn strategies for successfully using textbook features that facilitate understanding and application of content.

apply the complex processes associated with recording their thoughts. Specifically, students with disabilities often have trouble deciding what points to record; keeping up with the constant flow of lecture material; shifting back and forth between the process of listening and writing; and reviewing the information they record (Porte, 2001; Suritsky & Hughes, 1996).

Teachers can develop, improve, and support note-taking skills in four general ways: (1) accommodations, (2) techniques that facilitate note taking, (3) directly teaching note taking, and (4) note-taking strategies (Suritsky & Hughes, 1996). Note-taking accommodations include using strategic forms and guided notes, which are explicit supports that cue the student to elements of the recording process (Konrad, Joseph, & Itoi, 2011). Ways to facilitate note taking include teachers' changing the presentation rate of the lectures, using visual aids, and inserting questions and cues into their lessons. Direct teaching of note taking is the explicit delivery of lessons on how best to address content before the presentation, during the lesson, and after the lesson. Finally, using a specific note-taking strategy (e.g., LINCS and AWARE) involves the teaching and application of highly structured packages of note-taking processes. Detailed descriptions of these methods are provided in Strategy 14.5.

### Test Taking

Traditional pencil-and-paper tests are the most common method of measuring student performance in most content-area classes. Unfortunately, many low-achieving students, including students with disabilities, fail to use the effective test-taking strategies employed by their higher-achieving peers (Hong, Sas, & Sas, 2006). These students are not *test-wise*: They often fail to attend to test directions, lack persistence in considering multiple-choice options, have difficulty constructing written text, and are easily misled by irrelevant and distracting information on the test form (Scruggs & Mastropieri, 1990; Therrien, Hughes, Kapelski, & Mokhtari, 2009). Because they tend not to use deductive reasoning, they fail to eliminate similar and absurd options when considering response options (Hughes, 1996). Similar to note taking, teachers can improve students' test-taking skills by providing accommodations on the test, directly teaching effective test-taking techniques, or employing a comprehensive test-taking strategy. Detailed techniques are provided in Strategy 14.6.

### Pause & Reflect

Describe the feelings you experience when getting ready to take a "big" test. How can having a test-taking strategy reduce nervousness and anxiety and facilitate clear thinking?

### Time and Assignment Management

To succeed in content-area classes, students need to organize their time and efforts, ultimately completing homework and other assignments accurately and on time. One way students organize time and manage their assignments is by using planners and agenda books. These tangible organizers provide a structure for listing and prioritizing assignments, as well as a way for scheduling short- and long-term academic activities and events (Scott & Compton, 2007). Unfortunately, too many students do not make full use of the planners because they have difficulty recording assignments, detailing the requirements of multicomponent tasks, and estimating the amount of time needed to complete tasks (Salend & Gajria, 1995). Other students just forget to use their planners and agenda books. As with the other content survival strategies, teachers can provide direct instruction and support for the use of planners for assignment and time management through strategic instruction (see Figure 14.2). For example, researchers found that the mnemonic strategy PROJECT increased homework rate completion, assignment quality, and grades among students with disabilities in inclusive content-area classes (Hughes, Ruhl, Schumaker, & Deshler, 2002).

## Content-Area Instruction for Students with Severe Disabilities

Until recently, educators assumed that individuals whose measured intelligence fell below an IQ of 55 were incapable of content-area learning. This thinking has changed. Although students with severe disabilities will not acquire academic skills at the same levels as students with less severe disabilities, research has shown that many can benefit from access to the general education

**TRICK BAG** (Scott & Compton, 2007)
  **T**—Take out agenda book.
  **R**—Record assignment.
  **I**—Insert important details.
  **C**—Circle materials you need.
  **K**—Keep materials in homework folder.
  **B**—Be sure you can read it.
  **A**—Ask a partner to check it.
  **G**—Go put it in your backpack.

**PROJECT** (Hughes et al., 2002)
  **P**—Prepare your forms.
  **R**—Record and ask.
  **O**—Organize
      **B**—Break assignment into parts.
      **E**—Estimate the number of study sessions.
      **S**—Schedule the sessions.
      **T**—Take your materials home.
  **J**—Jump to it.
  **E**—Engage in the work.
  **C**—Check your work.
  **T**—Turn in your work.

Figure 14.2

Two Strategies for Assignment Management

## Pause & Reflect

Where students with severe disabilities receive instruction remains highly controversial. In your view, in what setting should teachers deliver secondary-content instruction? What challenges must teachers meet in order to provide this instruction in general education classrooms?

curriculum and strategically enhanced content instruction (Knight, Browder, Agnello, & Lee, 2010; Browder & Spooner, 2006). Encouraged by this research and spurred on by federal legislation requiring an increased focus on academic instruction, content-area instruction at some level is expected practice for students with severe disabilities (Westling & Fox, 2009).

What does this mean for general and special education teachers who already work collaboratively in inclusive content-area classrooms, but with students whose disabilities are less severe? In some respects, teaching content to students with severe disabilities requires many of the same processes used with other students. Units and lessons need to be designed and delivered with an understanding of curriculum, collaboration, and instructional methods if all students are to benefit from the instruction. Universal design principles that employ multiple means of presentation, expression, and engagement are necessary if students are to truly participate during lessons (Wehmeyer & Agran, 2006). Finally, working with peer tutors or friends without disabilities increases involvement with the content as well as fostering greater opportunities for social interaction (Carter, Cushing, Clark, & Kennedy, 2005).

Teachers' achievement expectations for students with disabilities may differ in depth and complexity from those for students without disabilities; however, expectations must be true to grade-level content (Browder et al., 2007). Consider how Dymond and colleagues (2006) developed a universally designed high school science course responsive to needs of all students, including those with severe disabilities. Initially, the researchers developed a series of questions to address modification of key areas of curriculum and instructional delivery. The researchers made major changes to the course by adapting materials and modes of student participation, adjusting instructional delivery, and having alternate forms of assessment. Specifically, large-print reading material and laptops with Internet connections and LCD projectors were added to the more traditional materials. Students were given a range of choices of how they would like to participate, ranging from interactive lessons to hands-on activities, team projects, and peer tutoring. Finally, a range of assessments such as rubrics and checklists were used to evaluate student outcomes during presentations and hands-on work sessions.

**Table 14.2** Redesigning Content Lessons for Students with Severe Disabilities

| Design Need | Action Steps |
|---|---|
| Curriculum | • Identify curriculum standards addressed and the big ideas to be taught.<br>• Add and delete content to match the learning needs of students.<br>• Sequence content appropriately.<br>• Ensure content relates to outcomes that can be applied out of school. |
| Instructional delivery/ organization | • Provide a variety of hands-on learning activities.<br>• Ensure that activities allow for opportunities to make choices.<br>• Allow for numerous opportunities for repeated practice.<br>• Incorporate heterogeneous grouping arrangements.<br>• Have explicit roles for all adults in the provision of academic and behavioral supports.<br>• Program activities that call for a full range of student participation and responses. |
| Materials | • Incorporate assistive technology support to facilitate participation and understanding of material.<br>• Modify instructional materials to make them more concrete and functional (e.g., color-code equipment, label equipment with symbols, etc.). |
| Assessment | • Have multiple methods available to assess performance.<br>• Allow students to choose assessment method.<br>• Use assessment data to evaluate and refine instruction. |

*Source:* Information adapted from Dymond et al. (2006).

As a result of the UDL process, general education and special education teachers began to collaborate more and share more instructional responsibilities, and they became more concerned that the students with severe disabilities participated meaningfully during instruction. Frequency of teacher interactions with students increased, and student participation in lessons grew from an afterthought to a part of the planning process. Although the greatest gains were in personal and social skills, Dymond and colleagues (2006) found notable gains in the understanding of the science content. Table 14.2 contains a series of action steps teachers can apply when redesigning secondary content for students with severe disabilities.

## Summary

Effective teachers can teach content in inclusive classes by understanding the learning characteristics of their students and working collaboratively to implement proactive strategies that support higher-order learning. This chapter addressed the following topics:

**Content area learning: What to expect**

- Unlike their normally achieving peers, many students with disabilities included in content-area classes do not have the basic reading, writing, or math skills necessary for academic success.
- Students have problems acquiring content due to organizational deficits, problems in self-regulation, and deficits in short- and long-term memory.
- Because deficits are largely in skill and metacognitive ("the thinking about thinking") areas, content instruction must address both skills issues and strategic learning.
- Although state and local policy makers are prominent in the composition of subject-area curriculum, teachers remain central decision makers in how topics are emphasized and taught.
- Because students vary in their ability to learn new information, teachers must decide which elements of their subject area are essential for all students to know.
- Content-area instruction in inclusive settings requires active collaboration among subject-area experts and special education learning specialists.

**Models and approaches for inclusive content-area instruction**

- Universal design for learning, a proactive way of making instruction accessible for all students, minimizes the need to make adaptations in methods and materials after the fact.
- Direct instruction—known for its structure, predictability, and correlation with high levels of student achievement—comprises three principal components: demonstration, guided practice, and independent practice.
- Guided discovery learning focuses on applying problem-solving strategies to a range of subject areas and situations.
- Although they vary by type, cooperative learning approaches are defined by three common beneficial characteristics: positive interdependence, individual accountability, and cooperative practices.
- Learning strategies guide students as they interface with higher-order content material. Areas emphasized in the approach include what to teach (content), how to teach (design), and transferability across subject areas.
- Content enhancements are instructional techniques that assist all learners while maintaining the integrity of the subject-area material. The three major categories of content enhancements are redesigned instruction and materials; devices such as graphic organizers and mnemonics; and routines that proactively structure segments of instruction to avoid obstacles to learning.
- Because many students with disabilities have problems reading text, a multifaceted series of supports is necessary, including textbook exploration activities, intensive vocabulary instruction, comprehensive comprehension strategies, audio-texts, study guides and focused chapter questions, and supplemental Web-based resources.
- Students with disabilities included in content-area classes benefit from note-taking accommodations, techniques that facilitate note taking, and direct instruction in note-taking techniques and comprehensive strategies.
- Because many students with disabilities are not test-wise, explicit test-taking strategies can help students demonstrate a true measure of their academic performance.
- Students with disabilities can increase their time and assignment management through explicit instruction on how to use planners and agenda books.
- Although students with severe disabilities will not acquire the depth and complexity of subject-area curricula, they can benefit from strategically enhanced content instruction.

## Addressing Professional Standards

Standards addressed in Chapter 14 include:
**CEC Standards:** (3) individual learning differences, (4) instructional strategies, and (7) instructional planning.

### MyEducationLab

Go to the topic Content Area Teaching in the **MyEducationLab** (www.myeducation.lab) for *Inclusion*, where you can:

- Find learning outcomes for Content Area Teaching, along with the national standards that connect to these outcomes.
- Complete Assignments and Activities that can help you more deeply understand the chapter content.
- Apply and practice your understanding of the core teaching skills identified in the chapter with the Building Teaching Skills and Disposition learning units.
- Check your comprehension on the content covered in the chapter with the Study Plan. Here you will be able to take a chapter quiz, receive feedback on your answers, and then access Review, Practice, and Enrichment activities to enhance your understanding of chapter content.

# EFFECTIVE STRATEGIES FOR TEACHING SECONDARY CONTENT AREAS

## Putting It All Together

With increased academic standards required of all students, more students with disabilities are being included in high-demand content-rich classes and many arrive unable to respond to the academic demands. Teams of general and special education teachers are required to design and apply instructional procedures that simultaneously meet the individual needs of students with learning differences as they deliver engaging, challenging, and provocative lessons to entire classes.

To maximize your efforts, we recommend that you keep in mind the following factors—central to successful student outcomes:

1. **Content-area instruction in inclusive settings is a team effort** requiring the active participation of subject-area experts and special education learning specialists.

2. **The primary role of the content-area specialist is to select carefully the subject matter** that is essential for all students to learn and to format the material for access and acquisition; the role of the special education specialist is to provide supports and teach students the strategies and skills to enhance their effectiveness as efficient learners (Deshler & Putnam, 1996).

3. **When presented well, content-area subject matter is interesting, engaging, and motivating.** Consequently, if provided with opportunities and support for interacting with the material, students will respond positively and participate in class discussions and activities.

4. **Methods that support and enhance accessibility** such as universal design, content enhancements, and learning strategies can be integrated into classroom activities with positive impact on the instruction of other learners.

5. **Remember the affective elements of teaching when providing specialized supports.** Encouragement, positive self-statements, and skills for coping with difficult situations should always supplement content and strategy instruction.

## Strategy Fact Sheet

In the remainder of this chapter, we describe seven effective strategies, which we referred to previously in the chapter, to help you plan effectively to meet the needs of all students.

| EFFECTIVE PRACTICE | TYPE OF STRATEGY/BRIEF DESCRIPTION | SPECIAL CONSIDERATIONS |
|---|---|---|
| Strategy 14.1: Content Enhancements: Unit and Lesson Organizers | A universal design instructional support that highlights unit and lesson content, how elements of the content are related, and the knowledge and assignments required for success. | Components of the organizers must be taught explicitly to mastery; without such instruction, students may be confused by the graphical components. |
| Strategy 14.2: Improving Expository Writing across Content-Area Classes | The most important skills for writing thoughtful and informative narratives involve an awareness and strategic application of the three-stage writing process: prewriting, production, and reviewing. | Writing is very complex, and students need to understand that it is a process that cannot be completed thoughtlessly. Successful writing is focused, multiphased, and iterative, requiring considerable planning, adequate source material, and an organizational framework. |
| Strategy 14.3: Mnemonic Strategies | A versatile series of techniques that produce meaningful recall-enhancing connections that do not exist naturally in content. | Mnemonics can be a labor-intensive, time-consuming instructional activity, and the relative cost-benefit of using the technique needs to be monitored regularly. |

| EFFECTIVE PRACTICE | TYPE OF STRATEGY/BRIEF DESCRIPTION | SPECIAL CONSIDERATIONS |
|---|---|---|
| Strategy 14.4: Content-Area Reading | A series of supports and strategies that assist students in understanding textbook content. Specific techniques include textbook exploration activities, adapted vocabulary, structured comprehension strategies, study guides, and visual maps. | The development of effective reading accommodations for secondary content can be challenging. However, the extent of text-driven content instruction necessitates that teachers devote time to the development of these supports and accommodations. |
| Strategy 14.5: Developing and Supporting Note Taking | To facilitate the coordination of the myriad skills required for effective note-taking, teachers provide explicit instruction in specific techniques and strategies as well as infuse supports in their lessons. | The complexity of skills required for successful note taking may require that some students receive intensive practice in small groups with enhanced teacher guidance. |
| Strategy 14.6: Developing Effective Test Taking | A series of strategies that ensure that student test performance reflects true understanding, including appropriate test accommodations and the direct teaching of test-taking skills and strategies. | In addition to teaching test-taking strategies, it is important to ensure that test accommodations provided are acceptable and appropriate for individual students. |
| Strategy 14.7 Problem-Centered Learning (PCL) | An inquiry-based instructional method that provides students with strategic supports and explicit steps for solving problems, resulting in increased motivation to engage in group problem-solving work. | Because a number of components of PCL are open-ended and inductive, it is essential that teachers provide tangible supports to students with disabilities throughout the instructional process. |

| Strategy 14.1 | CONTENT ENHANCEMENTS: UNIT AND LESSON ORGANIZERS |

## Rationale

The major concepts, activities, and requirements for a subject-area unit or lesson can be represented in a user-friendly graphic organizer. Both unit and lesson organizers contain elements of universal design and they assist students with and without disabilities. Both organizers provide explicit visual supports reflecting (1) essential content, (2) how elements of the content are related and fit into the "big picture" of the task, (3) ways for self-monitoring progress, and (4) the knowledge and assignments that are required for success. A number of research efforts have demonstrated that students of teachers who use these organizers improve their academic performance (Gajria, Jitendra, Sood, & Sacks, 2007).

## Step-by-Step

**1** *Convert elements of the curriculum into tangible unit and lesson learning segments, determine relationships among the segments, and identify supports needed for students to learn segmented material.*

- Engage in ReflActive planning, and use the acronym SMARTER to guide actions.
  a. *Shape the content:* Focus on the material that is critical for all students to understand.
  b. *Map the critical content:* Graphically represent connections between and among elements of the material.
  c. *Analyze difficulties:* Determine the content that may prove difficult for students to understand.
  d. *Reach enhancement decisions:* Decide how to best organize, sequence, and support instruction.
  e. *Teach strategically:* Explicitly cue students to important information, and directly teach alternative ways to think about and apply the content.
  f. *Evaluate the enhancements,* and *Revisit the outcomes:* Ensure that students can learn the material (Bulgren, Deshler, & Lenz, 2007).

- Incorporate unit and lesson segments into organized graphic devices that students can readily understand.

**2** *Deliver direct instruction related to the various components of graphic unit and lesson organizers.*

- Explain the purpose of the organizer, and clarify the actions that both students and teachers need to take to ensure successful learning.
- Focus on new vocabulary and the organization that links the elements of the content.
- Demonstrate graphically how content is organized, and relate to "big-picture" issues (Lenz et al., 2004).

**3** *Actively engage students in the continued use of the organizers.*

- Articulate cooperative teacher and student responsibilities when using the organizers.
- Cue components of organizers, demonstrating how they work with specific content, and regularly review effectiveness.
- Analyze student errors and make adjustments in instruction.

## Applications and Examples

Sample unit and lesson organizers are provided in Figures 14.3 and 14.4. The two examples represent how the unit, *Causes of the Civil War,* can be represented and how one lesson, *Economic Differences,* is organized. Pay particular attention to the many supports provided on the organizers. Specifically, the unit organizer shows how the current learning segment is related to previous and future units and graphically illustrates how elements of the unit are related. A schedule of activities is provided, and self-test questions related to the "big ideas" of the unit are prominently displayed. The lesson organizer reviews the big picture of the unit and provides a graphic representation of the content being presented, self-test questions, and lesson-related tasks.

**Figure 14.3**

Unit Organizer

*Source:* Reprinted with permission from J. Bulgren & B. K. Lenz. (1996). Strategic instruction in content areas. In D. D. Deshler, E. S. Ellis, & B. K. Lenz (Eds.), *Teaching adolescents with learning disabilities* (p. 437). Denver: Love. Copyright 1996 by Love Publishing Company.

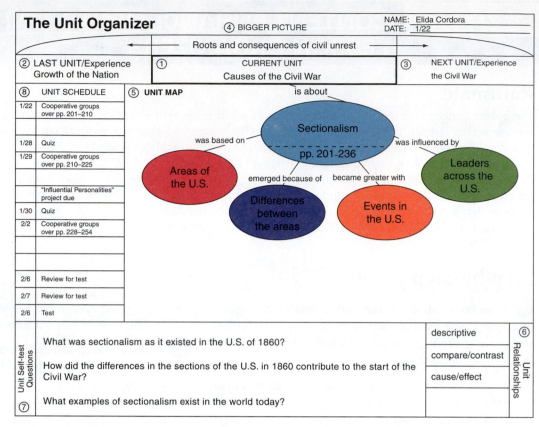

**Figure 14.4**

Lesson Organizer

*Source:* Reprinted with permission from J. Bulgren & B. K. Lenz. (1996). Strategic instruction in content areas. In D. D. Deshler, E. S. Ellis, & B. K. Lenz (Eds.), *Teaching adolescents with learning disabilities* (p. 439). Denver: Love. Copyright 1996 by Love Publishing Company.

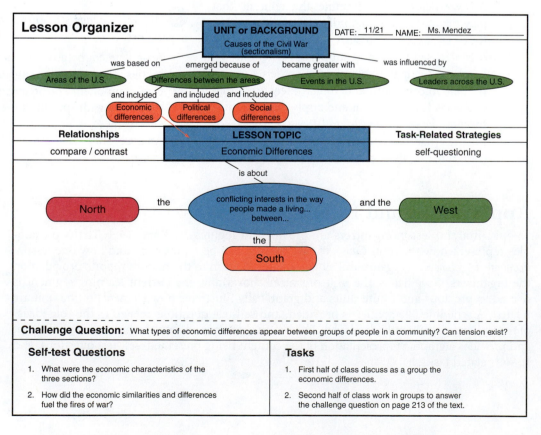

## Keep in Mind

Unit and lesson organizers are excellent classroom applications of universal designs for learning. They are useful for most learners, as they correspondingly provide support for students with disabilities. For students with learning problems, however, it is important that elements of the organizers be taught to mastery. Without adequate explicit instruction and supervised practice, students may be confused by the interplay of the graphical supports and fail to use them.

**Key References**

Boudah, D. J., Lenz, B. K., Bulgren, J. A., Schumaker, J. B., & Deshler, D. D. (2000). Don't water down! Enhance content through the unit organizer routine. *Teaching Exceptional Children, 32*(3), 48–56.

Bulgren, J., Deshler, D. D., & Lenz, B. K. (2007). Engaging adolescents with LD in higher order thinking about history concepts using integrated concept enhancement routines. *Journal of Learning Disabilities, 40,* 121–133.

Bulgren, J., & Lenz, B. K. (1996). Strategic instruction in content areas. In D. D. Deshler, E. S. Ellis, & B. K. Lenz (Eds.), *Teaching adolescents with learning disabilities* (pp. 409–473). Denver: Love.

Fisher, J. B. (1995). Searching for validated inclusive practices: A review of the literature. *Focus on Exceptional Children, 28,* 1–16.

| Strategy 14.2 | **IMPROVING EXPOSITORY WRITING ACROSS CONTENT-AREA CLASSES** |

## Rationale

Expository writing is the primary way that secondary students communicate their conceptual understanding of subject-area content. In most content-area classes, students are expected to compose thoughtful, persuasive, and informational narratives that reflect their integration and synthesis of required content (Chalk, Hagan-Burke, & Burke, 2005). This type of writing is highly complex and demanding. To succeed, students must adhere to the mechanics of writing, as well as focus on organization, purpose, and communication of intent (Harris, Graham, & Mason, 2003). Unfortunately, many students with disabilities in content-area classes do not fully grasp the writing process and experience great difficulty when required to write narrative essays (Englert et al., 2009). Teachers of content-area classes likely will encounter students whose writing difficulties range from lower-order mechanical difficulties to higher-order organizational and conceptual problems. Fortunately, general and special education teachers can turn to a solid body of research that has improved the writing performance of students in content-area classes.

## Step-by-Step

**1** *Have students develop an awareness of the writing process* by presenting the questions effective writers ask themselves when writing. Questions fall in three areas: prewriting, production, and reviewing (Ellis & Colvert, 1996).

- **Prewriting**
  - Who will read my work?
  - What is the reader's frame of reference?
  - Do I have enough information?
  - What is the theme of my effort, and what are the main ideas I want to express?
  - What details can I provide for each of the main ideas?
  - How can I best organize all of these details?
- **Production**
  - What more can I add to my effort?
  - Does each sentence make sense?
  - Does each sentence relate to the ones that precede and follow it?
- **Reviewing**
  - Did I tell the readers what I planned to tell them?
  - Are the paragraphs purposeful, coherent, and unified?
  - Is everything I wrote needed?
  - Did I fully convey my ideas?

**2** *Directly teach students to be content-rich, strategic writers* by delivering Self-Regulated Strategy Development (SRSD) instruction (Harris et al., 2003).

- Step 1: Have students identify and generate the basic parts of an essay. Consider having students vocalize positive self-statements (e.g., "I can do this if I use a strategy") and practice the DARE mnemonic:
  - D—Develop topic sentence.
  - A—Add supporting detail.

- R—Reject arguments from the other side.
- E—End with a conclusion.
- Step 2: Discuss the writing strategy to be used, and set goals.
  - Think, "Who will read this and why am I writing this?"
  - Plan what to say using DARE.
  - Write and say more (Chalk et al., 2005).
- Step 3: Model the strategy using a think-aloud or self-instructional sequence.
- Step 4: Have students memorize the steps in the strategy.
- Step 5: Provide collaborative practice and support, shifting more of the writing and strategy use to the student.
- Step 6: Have students practice the strategy independently.

**3** *Consider teaching a comprehensive writing strategy* such as DEFENDS to help students develop essays that stress a specific point of view (Ellis & Colvert, 1996).
- **D**—Decide on goals and theme.
- **E**—Estimate main ideas and details.
- **F**—Figure best order of main ideas and details.
- **E**—Express the theme in the first sentence.
- **N**—Note each main idea and supporting points.
- **D**—Drive home the message in the last sentence.
- **S**—Search for errors and correct.
  - **S**—Set editing goals.
  - **E**—Examine essay to see of it makes sense.
  - **A**—Ask yourself if message is clear.
  - **R**—Reveal picky errors (capitalization, punctuation, etc.).
  - **C**—Copy over neatly.
  - **H**—Have a last look for errors.

**4** *Provide a self-editing checklist* that allows students to review their written output (Guzel-Ozmen, 2009).

- Remind students to review their work in terms of content and organization.
- Model self-edits by considering critical elements of the paper using checklist components such as:
  - Was a title provided?
  - Was a theme or topic introduced?
- Were supporting points made explicit?
- Were transition sentences employed when needed?
- Did the conclusions make sense?
- Was the writing grammatically correct?

- Provide explicit prompts and cues to remind students to maintain use of the self-editing checklist when writing across content area classes.

## Applications and Examples

Charts and tangible graphics are excellent ways of organizing expository writing. For secondary students who have to justify and support their ideas, a format that allows for structuring main and supportive ideas is useful for developing essay themes. A graphic tool adopted from Ellis and Colvert (1996) is provided in Figure 14.5.

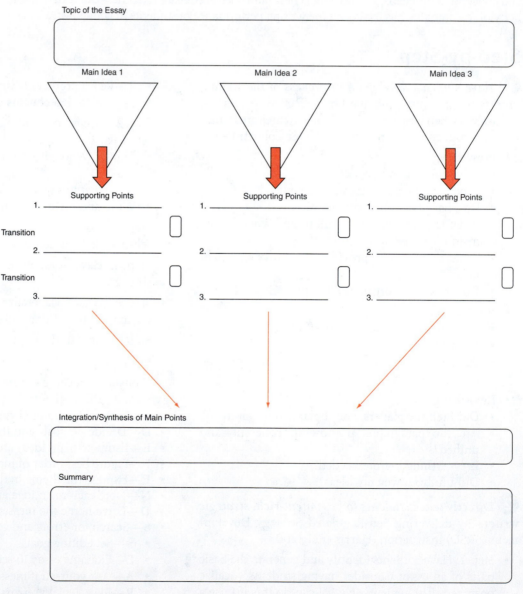

Figure 14.5

Essay Development Planning Tool

*Source:* Information adapted from Ellis & Colvert (1996).

## Keep in Mind

When presenting writing strategies, it is imperative that students understand that it is a multiphased process that goes beyond just putting words to paper (or machine). Successful writers spend substantial amounts of time on structured prewriting activities such as planning, the gathering of source material, and content organization.

**Key References**

Chalk, J. C., Hagan-Burke, S., & Burke, M. D. (2005). The effects of self-regulated strategy development on the writing process for high school students with learning disabilities. *Learning Disability Quarterly, 28,* 75–87.

Ellis, E. S., & Colvert, G. (1996). Writing strategy instruction. In D. D. Deshler, E. S. Ellis, & B. K. Lenz (Eds.), *Teaching adolescents with learning disabilities* (pp. 127–207). Denver: Love.

Harris, K. R., Graham, S., & Mason, L. H. (2003). Self-regulated strategy development in the classroom: Part of a balanced approach to writing instruction for students with disabilities. *Focus on Exceptional Children, 35*(7), 1–16.

Monroe, B. W., & Troia, G. A. (2006). Teaching writing strategies to middle school students with disabilities. *The Journal of Educational Research, 100*(1), 21–33.

Schumaker, J. B., & Deshler, D. D. (2003). Can students with LD become competent writers? *Learning Disability Quarterly, 26,* 129–141.

Sundeen, T. (2007). So what's the big idea? Using graphic organizers to guide secondary students with learning and behavioral issues. *Beyond Behavior, 16*(3), 29–34.

## Strategy 14.3  MNEMONIC STRATEGIES

## Rationale

Remembering subject-area information and having ways of applying what one has learned are essential for success in school. *Mnemonic strategies* are procedures that enhance memory by forming associations that do not exist naturally in the content. Mnemonic techniques form associations by building meaningful connections to seemingly unconnected concepts by recoding, transforming, and elaborating on existing material (Hughes, 1996; Mastropieri, Sweda, & Scruggs, 2000). To readily retrieve the content, students need to be explicitly taught effective ways to input (or encode) information. Mnemonic instruction and materials have produced significant gains in content-area instruction for students with and without disabilities (e.g., Marshak, Mastropieri, & Scruggs, 2011). Mnemonics are versatile techniques, easily implemented in secondary-content classes, and applicable to a wide range of subject-area curricula. They are not, however, a specific curricular approach, educational philosophy, or even a method of improving comprehension. Mnemonics are embedded in instructional sequences and simply help students remember things.

## Step-by-Step

**1** *Help students develop an understanding of mnemonics* by demonstrating how first-letter strategies help organize and retrieve information through the acronyms FIRST and LISTS (Hughes, 1996).

- FIRST is used to help design the mnemonic by:
  - **F**—Form a word.
  - **I**—Insert a letter.
  - **R**—Rearrange the letters.
  - **S**—Shape a sentence.
  - **T**—Try combinations.
  - *Sample:* HOMES = First letters of the Great Lakes (Huron, Ontario, Michigan, Erie, Superior)

- LISTS for making and designing lists:
  - **L**—Look for clues.
  - **I**—Investigate the items.
  - **S**—Select a mnemonic using FIRST.
  - **T**—Transfer information to a card.
  - **S**—Self-test.

**2** *Demonstrate how keyword mnemonics enhance associations, making information to be learned meaningful.*

- Transform an unfamiliar concept to a word or phrase (keyword) that the student knows. For example, the keyword for barrister would be *bear*, represented in a picture of a bear acting as a lawyer (Mastropieri & Scruggs, 1998).
- Provide a strategy for and practice retrieval of the concept. When asked to define *barrister*, students should think of the picture of the keywords. This facilitates the association and assists in the retrieval of the definition.

**3** *Promote generalization across subject areas* by embedding mnemonics in various instructional situations (e.g., peer tutoring) and teaching students to generate their own keywords using a specific strategy such as IT–FITS (King-Sears, Mercer, & Sindelar, 1992; Marshak et al., 2011).

- **I**—Identify the term.
- **T**—Tell the definition of the term.
- **F**—Find a keyword.
- **I**—Imagine the term doing something with the keyword.
- **T**—Think about the term doing something with the keyword.
- **S**—Study what you imagine and think until you know the definition.

**4** *Actively teach independent mnemonic use.*

- Alert students as to the purpose of mnemonic strategies and how practice will improve academic performance.
- Model mnemonic use, and reinforce correct applications.
- Be explicit in your thinking processes in developing and using the mnemonics; have students explain their own thinking when using the technique.
- Provide adequate opportunities for generalization across topics and subject areas.

# Applications and Examples

Teachers have used keyword mnemonic instruction to help students with disabilities to learn SAT vocabulary words (Terrill, Scruggs, & Mastropieri, 2004). At the conclusion of a 6-week instructional period, students with learning disabilities learned 92% of the words taught with the mnemonic, compared to only 49% of the words taught traditionally. Note how Terrill and colleagues (2004) connected vocabulary to keywords:

| WORD | KEYWORD | MEANING | ILLUSTRATION |
|---|---|---|---|
| **Abhor** | Horrible | Regard with horror; hate deeply | A monster regarded with horror |
| **Extant** | Ant | Still existing | Ants continue to come to picnics over the years |
| **Turbulent** | Turtle | Violent, stormy | A turtle swimming through a violent storm |

# Keep in Mind

Like all instructional techniques, the effectiveness of mnemonic use should be monitored regularly. Specifically, mnemonics can be a time-consuming activity and the relative cost-effectiveness of the technique needs to be considered in terms of student outcomes. In some cases, the addition of keywords to an already burgeoning curriculum can frustrate students and actually detract from lessons and units. Also, several research efforts (e.g., King-Sears et al., 1992; Marshak et al., 2011) indicate that teacher-provided keywords and pictures are more effective than requiring students to generate their own. With limited instructional time, decisions as to when to use mnemonics must be made judiciously, considering student characteristics and actual measures of performance.

**Key References**

Hughes, C. A. (1996). Memory and test taking skills. In D. D. Deshler, E. S. Ellis, & B. K. Lenz (Eds.), *Teaching adolescents with learning disabilities* (pp. 209–266). Denver: Love.

Marshak, L., Mastropieri, M. A., & Scruggs, T. E. (2011). Curriculum enhancements in inclusive secondary classrooms. *Exceptionality, 19*, 61–74.

Mastropieri, M. A., & Scruggs, T. E. (1998). Enhancing school success with mnemonic strategies. *Intervention in School and Clinic, 33*(4), 201–208.

Mastropieri, M. A., Sweda, J., & Scruggs, T. E. (2000). Putting mnemonic strategies to work in an inclusive classroom. *Learning Disabilities Research & Practice, 15*(2), 69–74.

Sabornie, E. J., & deBettencourt, L. (2009). *Teaching students with mild and high-incidence disabilities at the secondary level.* Upper Saddle River, NJ: Merrill/Pearson Education.

| Strategy 14.4 | CONTENT-AREA READING |
|---|---|

## Rationale

Large numbers of students with disabilities lack the reading skills to benefit fully from their subject-area textbooks (Gajria, Jitendra, Sood, & Sacks, 2007; Vaughn et al., 2011). A big part of secondary content instruction is textbook driven, and students are frequently required not only to use their textbooks in class but also to complete their homework assignments. Textbooks across content areas have been simplified to adjust to students' lowered reading levels and short attention spans, and organizational features have been added to help students focus on essential content (Sabornie & deBettencourt, 2009). Still, many students with learning problems and disabilities fail to succeed with these resources. Teachers assist with content-area reading in a number of ways, including textbook exploration activities, intensive adaptation of vocabulary, structured comprehension strategies and study guides, as well as visual maps and think-alouds.

## Step-by-Step

**1** *Have students become acquainted with the critical features of their textbooks.*

- Explain the purpose of the text, and demonstrate how the organization of the text aligns with the sequence of course activities.
- Provide explicit instruction about specific features of the textbook, including the table of contents, index, glossary, and organizational cues such as introductory overviews and paragraph headings, as well as specialized print and font alternatives.
- Demonstrate how content-related features such as charts, graphs, and other visuals augment narrative text.

**2** *Provide enhanced support for new vocabulary.*

- Identify, list, and define all boldfaced and italicized words in assigned chapters.
- Develop anticipation guides—brief, interesting lesson starters—that link prior knowledge to new vocabulary words (Hairrell et al., 2011).
- Provide students with lists, or word banks, of vocabulary words and their corresponding definitions. Schedule time for structured peer-based cooperative activities (e.g., flash-card practice) that promote understanding.
- Audio-record persistently difficult words and their definitions, and provide time for students to listen and apply them in practice activities.

**3** *Teach structured comprehension strategies, and provide study guides.*

- Teach students to apply the learning strategy SCROL for increased success with their textbooks (Reid & Ortiz-Lienemann, 2006):
  - **S**—Survey: Review the headings of the assigned reading selection, and ask "What do I know

about this topic?" and "What information will be presented?"
  - **C**—Connect: Determine how the headings in the chapter relate to each other.
  - **R**—Read: Read the headings and attend to bold-faced or italicized words and phrases.
  - **O**—Outline: Record the headings and outline the major ideas and supporting details without looking back at the text.
  - **L**—Look-Back: Review the text and then check and correct outlines.
- Provide study guides to clarify text material.
  - Effective study guides can include succinct summaries of the content, graphic organizers representing relationships among sections of the reading selection, definitions of difficult vocabulary, and key questions.
  - Explain the importance of study guides, model effective use, and provide immediate assistance to students if and when required.

**4** *Supplement text material with visual maps and think-aloud activities (Gately, 2008).*

- Prepare "story" maps that reflect the content of the reading selection.
- Ensure that story maps contain adequate background information as well as the actions and events currently being taught.
- Use arrows to reflect the direction of actions occurring in the reading selection.
- Have students think aloud, or talk through, the content presented on the visual map.
- Ask questions to ensure that students understand the content and the relationship among critical concepts presented in the reading selection.

**5** *Include after-reading strategies to review and consolidate content-area learning (Hairrell et al., 2011).*

- After reading, have students review vocabulary to ensure students' understanding of definitions.

- Ensure students understand new vocabulary and content by having them provide overviews of reading selections.
- Assess depth of understanding by having students discuss the important elements of the reading selection.

## Applications and Examples

Conderman and Elf (2007) developed an exploration activity for students to discover clues for using their social studies textbook. The activity, called A History Mystery, prompts students to access the basic and specialized features of the textbook. First, students must identify the name and author(s) of the text. Second, students find their way around the book by identifying the number of chapters and reviewing how features of the text (e.g., advance organizers, illustrations, glossary, index, and different-colored text) help facilitate information collection and assignment completion. Most important, the activity provides frequent opportunities for students to practice application of the text's features, either independently or in cooperative workgroups.

## Keep in Mind

Constructing effective content reading accommodations can be difficult and time-consuming. However, with secondary-content instruction in science, history, and math using text material on a daily basis, we recommend that teachers allocate sufficient time for these essential activities. Remember to save hard and electronic copies of all of your text adaptations so that you might apply them with other groups of students.

**Key References**

Conderman, G., & Elf, N. (2007). What's in this book? Engaging students through a textbook exploration activity. *Reading and Writing Quarterly, 23,* 111–116.

Gately, S. E. (2008). Facilitating reading comprehension for students on the autism spectrum. *Teaching Exceptional Children, 40*(3), 40–45.

Hairrell, A., Simmons, D., Swanson, E., Edmonds, M., Vaughn, S., & Rupley, W. H. (2011). Translating vocabulary research to social studies instruction: Before, during, and after text-reading strategies. *Intervention in School and Clinic, 46*(4), 204–210.

Sabornie, E. J., & deBettencourt, L. U. (2009). *Teaching students with mild and high-incidence disabilities at the secondary level.* Upper Saddle River, NJ: Merrill/Pearson Education.

Steele, M. M. (2007). Teaching social studies to high school students with learning problems. *The Social Studies, 98*(2), 59–63.

**Strategy 14.5** | # DEVELOPING AND SUPPORTING NOTE TAKING

## Rationale

The ability to take notes in content-area classes requires students to coordinate a number of complex skills and cognitive processes, including listening, auditory discrimination, short-term memory, prioritizing, and transcribing for later use. Moreover, when making use of their notes, students need to recollect what they represent about the important content of the lesson. The ability to take notes is critical in secondary-content classes. Several studies (e.g., Boyle, 2010) have found that active independent note taking results in increased class participation, improved recall of information, and higher rates of achievement. Unfortunately, many students with learning problems and disabilities do not take notes nor do they rely on others (e.g., peers and teachers) to take notes for them or to provide them with preexisting "canned" products. Teachers promote and support independent note taking by providing accommodations, adapting their instructional delivery, and directly teaching note-taking techniques and comprehensive mnemonic strategies.

## Step-by-Step

**1** *Provide within-lesson adaptations and accommodations for note taking.*

- Decrease the speed of presentations and inject pauses during logical breaks in lessons.
- Integrate verbal prompts, cues, and questions that signal the need for note taking.
- Supplement presentations with user-friendly visual aids such as charts, tables, and handouts.
- Provide detailed outlines that (a) contain an advance organizer for note taking, (b) help students identify key information in the presentation, and (c) result in products for future use.
- Prepare guided notes—to prompt student attention to critical aspects of the presentation (Konrad et al., 2011).

**2** *Directly teach students components of effective note taking.*

- Highlight note-taking preparation strategies such as securing a seat with a good view of the teacher, reviewing previous days' notes on the topic, identifying unfamiliar vocabulary, and having all necessary materials (e.g., paper, pencil).
- Demonstrate specific "in-lecture" note-taking skills such as (a) recognizing cues that signal important information, (b) using a personalized system of abbreviations, (c) selecting user-friendly frameworks for organizing and recording notes, and (d) paraphrasing critical information summaries.
- Model and provide practice in post-presentation activities such as reviewing, editing, and studying notes.

**3** *Provide intensive instruction in a comprehensive note-taking strategy.*

- The LINKS strategy (Suritsky & Hughes, 1996) provides students with instruction in specific note-taking steps and practice activities:
  - **L**—Listen
  - **I**—Identify verbal cues
  - **N**—Note
  - **K**—Key words
  - **S**—Stack information in outline form

- The AWARE strategy (Suritsky & Hughes, 1996) teaches students note-taking skills needed before, during, and after the content presentations:
  - **A**—Arrange to take notes by
    - Arriving early
    - Taking seat front and center
    - . Having materials
    - . Noting date
  - **W**—Write quickly, making sure to
    - Indent minor points
    - Record some words without vowels
    - Abbreviate whenever possible
  - **A**—Apply cues by
    - Attending to all verbal cues
    - Recording cued lecture points
    - Accentuating cued material
  - **R**—Review notes as soon as possible
  - **E**—Edit notes, remembering to
    - Add information not recorded
    - Add personal details

## Applications and Examples

Figure 14.6 contains a sample strategic note-taking form. Pay particular attention to how the form focuses student thinking about the content as well as provides a structure to organize, use, and develop questions about the information.

**Preclass Information**

    **Class or Lecture Topic:** _____

    **What Do You Know About Topic?** _____

_____

_____

_____

**During Class**

    **Put Class/Lecture Notes Here:**

_____

_____

_____

_____

_____

_____

    **List New Vocabulary Here:**

_____

_____

    **List Questions and Things You Are Unsure of Here:**

_____

_____

_____

**After Class**

    **Write three to five main points of the lecture here:**

_____

_____

_____

_____

    **Identify areas in need of more information here:**

_____

_____

_____

Figure 14.6

Strategic Note-Taking Activity Form

*Source:* Information adapted from Weishaar & Boyle (1999).

## Keep in Mind

Teaching and supporting note taking are appropriate instructional activities for most inclusive content-area classes. Some students with disabilities, however, will need additional practice to attain competence. One way of providing additional opportunities is to have small groups of students practice the various steps cooperatively, supplemented with teacher guidance and feedback.

**Key References**

Boyle, J. R. (2007). The process of note taking: Implications for students with mild disabilities. *The Clearing House, 80*(5), 227–230.

Boyle, J. R. (2010). Note-taking skills of middle school students with and without learning disabilities. *Journal of Learning Disabilities, 43*(6), 530–540.

Konrad, M., Joseph, L. M., & Itoi, M. (2011). Using guided notes to enhance instruction for all students. *Intervention in School and Clinic, 46*(3), 131–140.

Lazarus, B. (1993). Guided notes: Effects on secondary and post secondary students with mild disabilities. *Education and Treatment of Children, 16,* 272–289.

Suritsky, S., & Hughes, C. A. (1996). Notetaking strategy instruction. In D. D. Deshler, E. S. Ellis, & B. K. Lenz (Eds.), *Teaching adolescents with learning disabilities* (pp. 267–312). Denver: Love.

| Strategy 14.6 | DEVELOPING EFFECTIVE TEST TAKING |

## Rationale

As students with disabilities participate in secondary-content classes, they will also be subject to rigorous performance assessments. Unfortunately, a large proportion of students with disabilities lack adequate test-taking skills and strategies. Several options are available for teachers to ensure that student test performance reflects true understanding of the material. First, teachers can provide test modifications and accommodations. Second, teachers can directly teach specific test-taking skills or a comprehensive test-taking strategy. Research (e.g., Carter et al., 2005) has demonstrated that the teaching of techniques and strategies can raise scores on various types of classroom and school-based assessments.

## Step-by-Step

**1** *Use a range of accommodations when assessing content-area knowledge and performance.*

- *Setting accommodations:* Change the location or environmental conditions of the assessment.
- *Timing accommodations:* Allow more time for the test, or alter how the time is organized.
- *Scheduling accommodations:* Change when the test occurs and how it is administered.
- *Response accommodations:* Change the format of how the student responds to items, and allow for use of assistive devices when appropriate.

**2** *Directly teach students to be "test-wise" when being assessed.*

- Demonstrate how to eliminate absurd and similar options on multiple-choice tests.
- Illustrate how absolute words such as *always* and *never* are options to be avoided on multiple-choice tests.

- Emphasize the importance of reading all instructions carefully and managing time during test situations.

**3** *Make the test environment conducive for success* (Conderman & Pedersen, 2010).

- Arrange furniture, room temperature, and lighting to maximize comfort and minimize distractions.
- Create a "do not disturb" atmosphere by turning off intercom and phones.
- Have test materials organized and ensure students have enough space for working on the test materials.
- Prompt students to relax, to do their best, and to apply their test-taking strategies.

**4** *Provide intensive instruction in comprehensive test-taking packages such as the ANSWER strategy for essay tests (described next).*

## Applications and Examples

The ANSWER strategy (Hughes, 1996), a mnemonic systematic way of approaching essay items, uses the following steps and substeps:

**A**—Analyze the situation.
- Read the question carefully.
- Underline key words.
- Gauge the time you need.

**N**—Notice requirements.
- Scan for and mark the parts of the question.
- Ask and say what is required.
- Tell yourself you will write a quality answer.

**S**—Set up an outline.
- Set up main ideas.
- Assess whether they match the question.
- Make changes if necessary.

**W**—Work in details.
- Remember what you learned.
- Add details to the main ideas using abbreviations.
- Indicate order.
- Decide if you are ready to write.

**E**—Engineer your answer.
- Write an introductory paragraph.
- Refer to your outline.
- Include topic sentences.
- Tell about details for each topic sentence.
- Employ examples.

**R**—Review your answer.
- Look to see if you answered all parts of the question.
- Inspect to see if you included all main ideas and details.
- Touch up your answer.

## Keep in Mind

A student's performance on content-area assessments is a function of what he has learned as well as how skillful or "test-wise" he is in navigating the test-taking process. One way to obtain an accurate measure of student knowledge in content-area classrooms is by providing test accommodations. Although the provision of accommodations during tests is believed to "level the playing field" for students with disabilities, teachers should carefully consider which accommodations are acceptable and appropriate for individual students. When teaching test-wise techniques or comprehensive test-taking strategies, it is not enough merely to present the mnemonic steps. Students who need test-taking strategies require explicit instruction, models of effective application, and ample opportunities to practice the process.

**Key References**

Carter, E. W., Wehby, J., Hughes, C., Johnson, S. M., Plank, D., Barton-Arwood, S., & Lunsford, L. (2005). Preparing adolescents with high incidence disabilities for high stakes testing with strategy instruction. *Preventing School Failure, 49,* 55–62.

Conderman, G., & Pedersen, T. (2010). Preparing students with mild disabilities for taking state and district tests. *Intervention in School and Clinic, 45,* 232–241.

Hong, E., Sas, M., & Sas, J. C. (2006). Test-taking strategies of high and low math achievers. *Journal of Educational Research, 99,* 144–155.

Hughes, C. A. (1996). Memory and test taking skills. In D. D. Deshler, E. S. Ellis, & B. K. Lenz (Eds.), *Teaching adolescents with learning disabilities* (pp. 209–266). Denver: Love.

Thurlow, M. L., Elliott, J. L., & Ysseldyke, J. E. (2003). *Testing students with disabilities* (2nd ed.). Thousand Oaks, CA: Corwin.

| Strategy 14.7 | **PROBLEM-CENTERED LEARNING (PCL)** |

# Rationale

Many students with disabilities do not succeed in secondary content classes because they are unable to solve multifaceted problems that require higher-order thinking. Difficulties arise because students are unable to identify the nature of the problem and/or to apply strategies needed to solve the problem. Problem-centered learning (PCL)—sometimes referred to as problem-based learning or problem solving—provides students with strategic supports and explicit steps for solving problems, resulting in increased motivation to engage in group problem-solving work. Complex, real-world dilemmas or challenges are prepared that require students to integrate, synthesize, and apply diverse streams of content knowledge (Belland, Glazewski, & Ertmer, 2009; Levin, Hibbard, & Rock, 2002). During problem-centered learning activities, students typically work in small groups and are prompted to (1) define the nature of the problem, (2) devise a strategy for solving the problem, (3) implement the approach, and (4) evaluate and discuss the results of their efforts (Eggen & Kauchak, 2012). To support students with learning difficulties, tangible prompts and cues that guide the development and application of higher-order problem-solving skills are embedded in lesson materials (Cote, 2011).

# Step-by-Step

**1** *Plan PCL learning activities to meet the needs of students (Borich, 2011).*

- Identify topic areas of study: Clearly define the challenge, dilemma, or problem to be solved.
- Ensure that the task is meaningful to the students and that they have enough prerequisite knowledge to participate in the activity.
- Integrate supports (e.g., advance organizers, graphic organizers) that prompt students to access, critically evaluate, and utilize data from a variety of sources.
- Develop a detailed problem-solving unit plan that outlines a structured schedule for instruction and group activities.
- Ensure that there is enough time for group discussions and that each student has an opportunity to access materials and share her thinking.

**2** *Implement PCL activities in logically sequenced phases (Eggen & Kauchak, 2012).*

- Present problem/challenge: Prompt students' attention, provide advance organizers, and review lesson prerequisites.

- Encourage strategy development: Have students generate possible approaches to problem solution and model selected fruitful approaches.
- Employ explicit dialogues (e.g., talk-alouds reflecting how one thinks about the problem) when modeling possible solutions.
- Have students select and implement a strategy.
- Provide opportunities for students to evaluate and present their outcomes.
- Deliver directed feedback on students' strategies and outcomes.

**3** *Use a variety of strategies to teach PCL components (Cote, 2011).*

- Use brainstorming to encourage student generation of possible solutions: Emphasize that there is no one correct approach.
- Demonstrate and model effective problem-solving thinking.
- Promote discussions that encourage students to justify and defend their contributions.
- Employ small peer-assisted groups; these groupings allow students to practice in an open and supportive atmosphere.

# Applications and Examples

Although PCL is a fairly open-ended inquiry approach to learning, comprehensive planning is needed to ensure that all students can benefit from this type of instruction. Use the following checklist, adapted from Cote (2011) and Eggen and Kauchauk (2012) to ensure that your planning is all that it can be:

- Identify the **topic** for investigation.
- Develop specific **objectives** for the unit.
- Identify the **problems** that are relevant to the students.
- Employ instructional sequences that explicitly **demonstrate** and **model** selected strategies.
- Ensure access to **materials** that are needed for students to solve the problems.
- Program time for **guided practice** of possible problem solutions.
- Ensure that students **justify** and **defend** their solutions.
- Deliver constructive **feedback** throughout the process.

## Keep in Mind

Problem-centered learning is an inquiry-based approach to instruction that has a number of components that are open-ended and inductive. Therefore it is essential that teachers provide tangible supports to students with disabilities throughout the instructional process. One method of integrating supports in busy inclusive classrooms is PCL software (Cote, 2007). These programs help students define the problems to be solved by infusing hints and feedback through a structured problem-solving sequence. Interactive methods for accessing information are also provided, along with prompts on how best to evaluate the information.

**Key References**

Borich, G. D. (2011). *Effective teaching methods: Research-based practice.* Upper Saddle River, NJ: Pearson.

Cote, D. (2007). Problem-based learning software for students with disabilities. *Intervention in School and Clinic, 43*(1), 29–37.

Cote, D. (2011). Implementing a problem-solving intervention with students with mild to moderate disabilities. *Intervention in School and Clinic, 46*(5), 259–265.

Eggen, P., & Kauchak, D. (2012). *Strategies and models for teachers: Teaching content and thinking skills.* Upper Saddle River, NJ: Pearson.

Levin, B., Hibbard, K., & Rock, T. (2002). Using problem-based learning as a tool for learning to teach students with special needs. *Teacher Education and Special Education, 25*(3), 278–290.

# Effective Practices for All Students: Classroom Management

## KEY TOPICS

**After reading this chapter you will:**

- Know what to expect with regard to the range of student behaviors (and misbehaviors) typical of most classrooms.

- Be able to identify, describe, and apply core readiness and "tiered" behavior management strategies that contribute to successful classroom management.

- Possess a series of guided step-by-step effective practices for the prevention and reduction of challenging student behavior.

# A VIEW FROM A TEACHER

**Eileen Walls Describes the Success of West Hernando Middle School's Tiered Classroom Management System**

At West Hernando Middle School, students manage their behavior by using their WINGS. WINGS is an acronym that refers to the school-wide expectations that form the core of the school's structured-management (or tiered-management) program. Students are required to (1) make **W**ise choices, (2) engage in **I**nnovative learning, (3) accept **N**ew challenges, (4) engage in **G**ood citizenship, and (5) demonstrate **S**trong positive behavior. According to Eileen Walls, the behavior specialist at West Hernando, "All teachers, at the beginning of the year, are charged with explaining what constitutes using one's WINGS. Each of the WINGS expectations is operationally defined and modeled so students know what specific classroom behaviors the teachers are looking for to reinforce." Teachers post the WINGS acronym in every classroom and hallway, as well as in the gym and cafeteria. Teachers also use it as a streamlined method for verbally reminding students to behave appropriately.

The WINGS program is an application of positive behavior support (PBS). Students are provided positive consequences when they choose to meet the behavioral expectations. In addition to receiving positive attention from adults, students who earn a set number of positive bookmarks—the tangible method of recording appropriate student behavior—can attend a kid-friendly movie with popcorn and a drink.

For students who have difficulty meeting the WINGS standards, teachers provide supports and reminders designed to redirect behavior. For those who continue to be inappropriate, teachers use a hierarchy of negative consequences to decrease future occurrences of specific misbehaviors. These negative consequences include brief lunch detentions, in-school time-out and suspension, and after-school detention. Each of these negative consequences provides opportunities to teach students replacement behaviors—alternative ways of addressing their behavioral needs—in socially and school-appropriate ways. Teachers provide a range of supports and interventions before removing any student from the learning environment. Like most PBS systems, the great majority of students at West Hernando respond positively to WINGS. A second tier of interventions is available for those students whose extreme and persistent patterns of misbehavior require specialized supports and interventions.

According to Ms. Walls, WINGS works because everyone in the school is involved in its implementation. "Everyone—paraeducators, custodians, front office staff, teachers, and administrators—is committed to the system and expects WINGS behavior from students." The initial

data on this comprehensive behavior management system have been impressive. West Hernando has a lower rate of discipline referrals and suspensions than any other middle school in the county. Ms. Walls credits the PBS team and its reliance on data-based decision making for these impressive outcomes. The team meets regularly, reviews the discipline data, and proposes changes as necessary. The team addresses problem areas and regularly provides staff members with updated booster sessions in classroom management techniques.

## MyEducationLab

Visit the MyEducationLab for *Inclusion* to enhance your understanding of chapter concepts with a personalized Study Plan. You'll also have the opportunity to hone your teaching skills through video and case-based Assignments and Activities, Building Teaching skills and Disposition lessons, and IRIS Case Studies.

# Introduction

Consider this nightmare experienced, in one form or another, by many beginning teachers (and even some veteran educators): It is the first day of school, and the first-period, sixth-grade language arts class is filing into the classroom. Rather than any semblance of order, most of the 27 students, 9 with identified disabilities, run into the room and upset the neatly arranged materials prepared for distribution on your desk. When the students reach their seats, two of the tallest young men refuse to remove their headgear, claiming that they belong to a strict religious order forbidding the exposure of an uncovered scalp. When you distribute the course overview, two girls in the back of the room crumple up the papers and throw them across the room, claiming that they don't care about the work. After you've spent 10 minutes trying to restore order, three students move to the back of the room and seem to be throwing the handouts, now paper airplanes, out the window. The two boys with headgear issues are trying to sneak out the back door. To cap off this nightmare, the principal is at the front door inquiring about your willingness to accommodate the special needs of a new student with a severe attention-deficit disorder.

Rarely do nightmares like this approximate the behavior in actual classrooms. Still, levels of concern and anxiety about classroom management among teachers, particularly those new to the field, are quite high. This anxiety is not surprising, because the ability to manage student behavior is a clear marker of teaching success: Effective discipline, classroom control, and organizational skills are associated with positive student outcomes and increased teacher ratings. Conversely, one of the main reasons beginning teachers leave the field is poor or inadequate discipline in the classroom (Kauchak & Eggen, 2010; Vittetoe, 1997).

What types of behaviors do teachers in inclusive settings encounter? How do they manage simultaneously the range of generic problem behaviors typical of most developing students as well as the more intensive challenging behaviors exhibited by others with behaviorally involved disabilities (i.e., attention deficits, emotional and behavioral disabilities)? Many teachers, like those on the faculty of West Hernando Middle School and Heritage High School, actively address the behavior of all of their students by adopting an approach to discipline that is *systematic*, *proactive*, *supportive*, and *responsive*.

As noted by Eileen Walls in our opening feature, being *systematic* means that effective discipline is much more than having a *bag of tricks*. As we discuss later in this chapter, management is a tiered and sequential process that requires careful and logistical thinking about all school and classroom activities and events (Sprague & Walker, 2005; Yell, Meadows, Drasgow, & Shriner, 2009). Being *proactive* means taking carefully considered actions (e.g., adjusting the traffic flow in hallways and the cafeteria, making use of specific transition cues) that minimize and often prevent the occurrence of problem behaviors. Being *supportive* refers to the range of positive teacher attitudes that drive successful behavior management activities. As Susan Hill, the Dean of Students at Heritage High School knows, successful classroom teachers convey genuine concern for students by (1) having periodic private interactions that reflect a desire to know and understand students individually; (2) employing verbal and nonverbal communication techniques that indicate civility, respect, and patience; and (3) willingly making adjustments that assist students in meeting behavioral expectations. Finally, being *responsive* refers to teachers providing positive recognition for students who behave as expected and a willingness to try a variety of interventions to redirect problem behaviors when they occur.

# Student Behavior: What to Expect

A broad consensus exists as to what constitutes appropriate student behavior. Most teachers believe that self-control and cooperation skills minimize disruption and foster the self-discipline necessary for academic success (Lane, Givner, & Pierson, 2004). Consequently, similar to many teachers in our featured schools, you will want students to (1) comply in an appropriate fashion to teacher requests and academic tasks; (2) have impulse control; (3) deal with problems, anger, and negative feedback in developmentally appropriate ways; (4) be cooperative and courteous with peers; (5) stay attentive, involved, and productive during classroom activities; and (6) follow rules, recognizing the contexts for different types of behaviors (Trenholm & Rose, 1981; Walker, 1995).

Obviously, you will not always experience these desired behaviors from your students, and so it becomes your job to address and redirect misbehavior. What types of discipline issues do educators typically encounter? The popular media would have us believe that most misbehaviors faced by teachers are severe—aggression, bullying, theft, and vandalism. Fortunately, this is not accurate. As is the case in our three featured schools, most school and classroom misbehavior is related to inattention to task, crowd-control issues during transitions, getting work accomplished in a timely fashion, and students acting *cool* by creatively testing limits. Specifically, the most common misbehaviors exhibited by students include tardiness, being unprepared, not attending, talking, calling out, and mild forms of verbal and physical aggression (Kulinna, Cothran, & Regualos, 2006). Some students may even swear, run in the hallway, tell off-color jokes, and show arrogance toward and disrespect for peers and adults. As we will discuss later, teachers can prevent many of these behaviors through proactive structuring of the school and classroom environment. Misbehaviors that are not preempted typically stop when they are brought to the attention of teachers, administrators, and/or parents.

Some students, however, exceed these mild forms of challenging behavior and repeatedly disrupt the flow of school and classroom events. Others respond defiantly when asked to participate appropriately in activities and hurt others both physically and emotionally when frustrated. The number of such students and the frequency of their behaviors often vary according to the levels of structure and consistency in specific schools and individual classrooms. Still, even in the most positive and structured schools and classrooms, you will encounter students who, for any number of reasons, pose challenges because of their behavior. These students stand out from other students because of their *significant behavioral excesses* and *behavioral deficits*. Not surprisingly, many require supports that go beyond typical practice and could require individualized services outside the general education classroom.

When we speak of *significant behavioral excesses*, we are referring to behaviors that, because of their high rate, frequency, duration, or intensity, interfere with opportunities to achieve academic success and/or social competence. For example, consider the student who spends far too much time out of her seat or argues vehemently and relentlessly when being directed by a teacher. *Significant behavioral deficits* refers to specific behaviors and actions students lack that are required for academic and social competence. For example, it is not unusual for teachers to note that several of their students lack appropriate social skills. Significant numbers of students with behavioral deficits in social skills simply don't know, or have not been taught, how to behave in certain situations; others may have acquired the skills but do not perform them at acceptable levels. When encountering students with persistent challenging behaviors, you will likely conclude that most troubling patterns of misbehavior are a dynamic combination of behavioral excesses and deficits.

Most student misbehavior is related to inattention, unstructured transitions, and a desire to act "cool" with peers.

# Behavior Management Readiness and Tiered Management Strategies

Successful teachers' behavior management efforts begin long before students enter the classroom. Like the preparation efforts of a professional athlete or master craftsman, preparation of the work environment, organization of equipment, and mental self-preparation for the task at hand require considerable attention of the teacher. Specific critical areas of concern for teachers are (1) classroom organization, (2) effective instruction, and (3) creating a climate of care and respect.

## Classroom Organization

Regardless of the subject area being taught or the age of the students, most classrooms are busy, energetic places that have a variety of instructional and noninstructional events occurring simultaneously for all students. For example, consider biology class at Heritage High School. During the fifth period, Gina Craun directs an active, hands-on laboratory class to 22 students who require intensive instruction if they are to meet the state's standards of learning. Eight of the students are conducting independent laboratory experiments. The remaining 14, having completed the experiments, are writing up their results. Six of these students have identified individualized education program (IEP) goals related to written expression. Denise Pohill, the special education teacher, therefore provides them additional supports and accommodations. At the rear of the room, a one-to-one instructional assistant from the "school within the school" program for students with behavioral needs monitors a student as he completes independent seatwork.

### Pause & Reflect

Successful behavior management requires considerable planning and preparation. What steps would you take to get your classroom *management ready* before the arrival of your students?

If you were to review a slow-motion video of a typical day in that classroom (or most other classrooms), you would see with pinpoint clarity how successful teachers recognize and address organizational pressures (see Table 15.1 for listing and definitions). Consider the following preventive practices that help address these ever-present demands:

- Arranging the physical environment.
- Valuing instructional time.
- Being prepared.
- Coordinating resources.

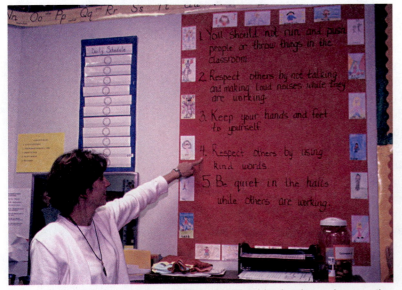

Successful behavior management requires considerable planning and preparation before the arrival of students.

### Arranging the Physical Environment

Successful behavior managers make effective use of the physical dimensions of their room, and arrange furniture and materials for accessibility, instructional effectiveness, appropriate social interactions, and safety. How teachers actually design the classroom varies as a function of (1) layout and location; (2) age, number, and behavioral profiles of the students; and (3) levels of supports required by students with disabilities (Capizzi, 2009; Paine, Radicci, Rosellini, Deutchman, & Darch, 1983; Rosenberg et al., 2006).

### Valuing Instructional Time

Effective behavior management and student learning is contingent on treating instructional

**Table 15.1** Organizational Pressures of Classrooms

| Organizational Pressure | Definition |
| --- | --- |
| Immediacy | Many events require immediate attention or action. |
| Publicness | The teacher is always on stage. |
| Multidimensionality | Classrooms are crowded and busy places in which limited resources are used to achieve a wide range of goals. |
| Unpredictability | Events in classrooms change daily and many occurrences are difficult to predict. |
| History | Events that occur early in the school year set the tone for later happenings. |
| Simultaneity | Many things happen at the same time in classrooms. |

*Source:* Adapted from Doyle (1980).

time as a valuable resource and, correspondingly, maximizing opportunities for teaching and learning (Vannest & Hagen-Burke, 2010). Specific strategies include (1) highlighting policies that encourage and reinforce attendance and punctuality; (2) ensuring that adequate time is devoted (and actually delivered) to task-relevant activities; and (3) explicitly teaching and conducting transitions between and among activities efficiently with little disruption (Nix, 2008).

**Being Prepared**

Teachers who are prepared have organized and easy-to-follow lesson plans, start lessons promptly, have materials close by, and maintain a consistent schedule. This preparation allows teachers to focus their efforts exclusively on the instructional and behavioral flow of their lessons.

**Coordinating Resources**

Effective behavior managers address the immediacy and connectivity of classroom events by developing time-saving organizational resources. Several of the more useful resources include (1) an IEP-monitoring procedure that promotes instructional support and accountability, (2) a substitute teacher packet that highlights the essential information one would need to teach and manage the class during short-term absences, and (3) a readily available resource guide of school and community services that can address critical needs presented by students and their families.

## Effective Instruction

A major prerequisite for the success of any behavior management plan is the delivery of accessible and motivating instruction. Regardless of how interesting or topical a lesson might be, a precursor to disruptive behavior is a student's inability to understand academic content and his frustration with the ways the content is presented. Rather than being perceived as being "dumb," some students, particularly those who have experienced repeated academic failure, find it easier to act up or be the class clown. During later interactions with peers, these inappropriate behaviors are easier to explain than the lack

**Pause & Reflect**

Consider the relationship between instruction and student behavior. How can instruction that lacks supports and accommodations contribute to the disruptive behavior of students with learning problems and disabilities?

of integration or problem-solving skills. Clearly, instructional supports and accommodations within the context of interesting, motivating lessons can reduce the frequency and intensity of disruptive behaviors.

## A Climate of Care and Respect

Many of the guidelines for effective behavior management presented thus far are methodical, scientifically validated, systematic procedures applied in a seemingly mechanistic step-by-step fashion. Recognize, however, that these technical aspects of classroom discipline are only part of the process—clearly necessary, but not sufficient. The success of behavior management techniques is also contingent on the ways in which teachers communicate with their students and engage in culturally responsive practices. Similar to instruction, teachers deliver behavior management through a series of person-to-person interactions that involve a number of intangible (i.e., difficult to operationalize) dispositions, behaviors, and personal qualities (Hershfeldt, Sechrest, Pell, Rosenberg, Bradshaw, & Leaf, 2009; Rosenberg et al., 2006).

### Authentic Relationships

Most interpersonal relationships are built on trust and require adequate time to develop. Solid relationships between teachers and students typically grow from a foundation of brief contacts and interactions, such as greeting students at the start of the day and giving special attention to their interests and personal lives. Relationships evolve when teachers present themselves in engaging and appealing ways, revealing that they are considerate, ethical, friendly, enthusiastic, and caring. Helpfulness is a characteristic that most students value, particularly those who require additional academic and behavioral supports. Moreover, positive interactions with teachers help students adjust to the pressures of school environment and promote social competence (Scott, Alter, Rosenberg, & Borgmeier, 2010). Teachers demonstrate helpfulness by (1) highlighting the collaborative nature of classrooms, (2) emphasizing trust between themselves and students, (3) promoting positive and productive communication, and (4) teaching self-control strategies that help students take responsibility for their behaviors (Charles, 2002; Koenig, 2000).

### Civility and Respect

*Civility* means that a person is cognizant that her behaviors have consequences for others and anticipates what those consequences may be (Forni, 2002). *Respect* refers to the basic human right to be acknowledged and treated with dignity (Rosenberg et al., 2011). Teachers model civility and respect by (1) communicating through body language and a vocal tone that reflects support, patience, and understanding; (2) listening actively to students and maintaining appropriate eye contact; (3) having private interactions with students that reflect a genuine interest in their opinions, concerns, and well-being; and (4) communicating appropriate, positive expectations for student performance and behavior (Kauffman, Mostert, Trent, & Hallahan, 2002; Rosenberg et al., 2006; Thorson, 1996).

### Culturally Responsive Practices

Teachers communicate care and respect for all students by adhering to culturally responsive instructional and behavior management practices. These practices are built on the assumptions that one's culture influences perceptions and knowledge, and that aspects of that culture manifest themselves, directly

Support, helpfulness, and a desire to develop authentic relationships with students enhance behavior management efforts.

and indirectly, during teacher–student interactions (Ford & Kea, 2009). Successful teachers maintain a healthy curiosity about cultural differences and are introspective about how their typical practices affect those from differing backgrounds. Keep in mind that this awareness and analysis are not excuses for student failure. Culturally responsive teachers believe they can help every student achieve. They do so by reducing judgmental attitudes and reactions of those who struggle in school and highlighting examples of diverse students who succeed in school despite experiencing poverty, language differences, and/or disabilities (Ross, Kamman, & Coady, 2011). Specifically, Hershfeldt et al. (2009) suggest that teachers double-check on five core components of culturally responsive practices as they develop and apply behavior management strategies:

1. Reflect on your own cultural group membership as it relates to the group membership of students.

2. Make every effort to form an authentic relationship with students.

3. Recognize that some students have distinctive communication styles that do not conform to typical norms and expectations.

4. Ensure that exemplars from students' backgrounds are integrated into instruction.

5. Be aware that students' behaviors in school can be a way to respond to multiple community constituencies (e.g., community and peer expectations).

See **Chapter 12** for detailed information on the double-check framework.

## Tiered Management

As we noted earlier, successful behavior management in inclusive schools and classrooms requires the use of a systematic, tiered system of behavior management (Dwyer & Osher, 2000; Rosenberg & Jackman, 2003; Scott et al., 2010). Tiered systems (see Figure 15.1) allow educators to address the behavioral needs of all students by addressing universal, inclusive management concerns typical of most students and by using a continuum of individualized planning and interventions for those students who do not readily respond to elements of the universal management system.

> ### Pause & Reflect
>
> Why is it important to begin tiered management efforts at the universal level? Why not focus initial efforts on the most intensive interventions for students who are misbehaving?

In the first tier, often referred to as *universal inclusive practices and supports*, teachers emphasize classroom policies and processes (e.g., mission statements, rules, procedures, consequences for appropriate and inappropriate behaviors, crisis procedures, etc.). Approximately 80 to 85% of students respond positively to these universal practices. The second tier of interventions is for the 5 to 15% of students whose extreme, frequent, persistent patterns of misbehavior require targeted or specialized supports and interventions (Hawken & Horner, 2003; Scott et al., 2010). These **targeted interventions** are typically powerful, focused, school-based efforts designed to reduce frequent and intensive problem behaviors. **Wraparound interventions** are more intensive and extensive, involving the integrated efforts of a multidisciplinary team of professionals from both within and outside the school (Eber, Sugai, Smith, & Scott, 2002).

## Universal Inclusive Practices and Supports

At the core of effective universal practices is a comprehensive management plan, an explicit representation of behavioral expectations and what happens when students either comply to or violate the standards. Generally, five core elements are included in successful plans: (1) mission statement, or statement of purpose; (2) rules, procedures, and behavioral supports; (3) surface management and consequences; (4) crisis considerations; and (5) documentation that makes the plan accessible to students, families, and colleagues (e.g., Curwin & Mendler, 1999; Lewis & Sugai, 1999; Nelson, 1996; Rosenberg & Jackman, 2003; Simonsen, Fairbanks, Briesch, Myers, & Sugai, 2008; Walker, Colvin, & Ramsey, 1995; Yell & Bradley, 2009).

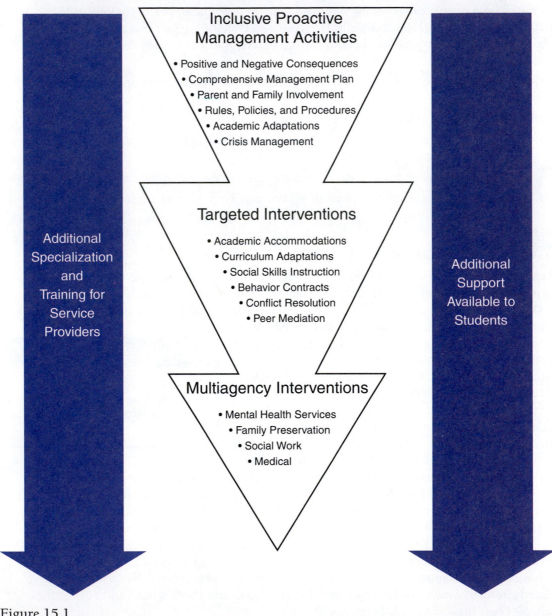

Figure 15.1

Comprehensive Behavior Management: Levels of Intervention and Inclusive Support Model

*Sources:* Adapted from Nelson, 1996; and Walker et al., 1996. Reprinted with permission from M. S. Rosenberg & L. A. Jackman. (2003).

### Mission Statement or Statement of Purpose

A *mission statement*, or *statement of purpose*, is a brief declaration that represents your approach to teaching and learning with a particular emphasis on expected school and classroom behavior. Effective statements seek to inspire, have a positive focus, and reflect a respect for the dignity of all students and a commitment to helping students perform to their highest level (White, 1996).

## Rules, Procedures, and Behavioral Supports

Rules and procedures communicate behavioral standards and expectations. *Rules* define acceptable behavior; *procedures* delineate the steps required for the successful completion of a task, activity, or operation. Well-articulated rules and procedures are particularly important for students who need explicit supports. Rules and procedures serve as discriminative stimuli and overt guides; teachers can use them to prompt and cue students throughout their daily multi-tasking. Rules and procedures also serve as specific behavioral targets that effective teachers reinforce with attention and praise (see Strategy 15.1).

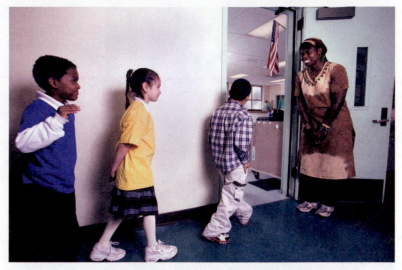

A major component of successful behavior management is having routines and procedures that guide students through school and classroom activities.

## Surface Management and Consequences

Rather than being authoritative and coercive, an effective teacher structures her behavior management system so that students recognize that it is *their* choice to either comply or not comply with the stated expectations. As you can imagine, the way in which a teacher responds to student choices has an enormous impact on subsequent student behavior. Typically, a teacher's response to student behavior falls into three major categories: surface management techniques, consequences for rule and procedure compliance, and consequences for noncompliance.

**Surface management techniques** are the range of commonsense measures that address minor instances of misbehavior quickly, efficiently, and, for the most part, with little disruption of ongoing instruction (see Strategy 15.2). Although the names for these techniques may seem novel and unusual, in action, they are clearly familiar. Generations of educators have used surface management techniques, often in an automatic, intuitive fashion.

Consequences are teacher-initiated verbalizations and actions that follow students' behaviors, both appropriate and inappropriate (see Strategy 15.3). When employing consequences, it is important to consider their impact. For a consequence to be effective, student behavior must change. Teachers use positive consequences to increase levels of appropriate behavior and use negative consequences to reduce the frequency and intensity of troublesome inappropriate behaviors.

Unfortunately, some consequences, particularly those applied to student misbehavior, are delivered in anger and frustration, with little thought given to their influence on students' behaviors. One way to avoid this scenario is to apply consequences in an educative rather than vindictive fashion. Clearly, some classroom behaviors can get you angry, and instead of presenting consequences in a thoughtful manner, you might deliver them in a vengeful, almost menacing fashion. To minimize these situations, it is important to attend to your own feelings regularly and to keep frustration and resentment in check (Curwin & Mendler, 1999).

### Pause & Reflect

Why is it important that consequences, particularly those directed to inappropriate behavior, be delivered in an educative rather than vindictive fashion? What strategies can be used to help during these often stressful situations?

## Crisis Considerations

Fortunately, in most schools, crisis situations—instances when students present extreme physical and emotional behaviors responses—are rare. However, it is important for teachers to know what to do if and when such actions occur. The most challenging aspect of a crisis is that the student appears to have little or no control over the behavior, and management techniques and consequences designed to reduce problem behavior have little or no effect (see Strategy 15.4).

Although extreme physical and emotional student behaviors are rare, it is essential that teachers know what to do if such crisis situations occur.

During the crisis, the primary task is to assist the student through the crisis in a safe, nonthreatening, and non-punitive fashion while maintaining the safety of others in the immediate environment. The recommended course of action for schools is to develop crisis-response teams of four to five people who are trained in both verbal intervention techniques and safe, nonaversive methods of physical restraint (Johns & Carr, 1995). Other adults in the school are instructed in decision rules to determine if the team is to be called in as well as the code for accessing the team. However, when faced with a crisis, teachers should

1. Remain calm, remove dangerous items from the area, and send someone for assistance.

2. Avoid body language and verbalizations that escalate situations.

3. Instruct other students to vacate the crisis area.

4. Plan for the student in crisis to reenter class after the crisis (Albert, 2003; Johns & Carr, 1995; Jones & Jones, 2004; Yell et al., 2009).

### Documentation for Access

After you have developed the components of your comprehensive behavior management plan, it is essential to share it with students, their families, administrators, and related-service providers. Some school-wide teams and individual teachers create full-sized manuals that articulate the major components (mission statement, rules, procedures, consequences) of the management plan (see Dwyer & Osher, 2000; Jones & Jones, 2004; Rosenberg et al., 2006; Walker, Colvin, & Ramsey, 1995). Other schools develop user-friendly brochures and Web pages that highlight the major components of the plan. Figure 15.2 illustrates a sample brochure. Regardless of the format you choose, use of a summary checklist, such as shown in Figure 15.3, can ensure that your behavior plan presents the essential components in the correct manner.

## Targeted Interventions

Even with the best planning and implementation of a well-conceived comprehensive management plan, some students (approximately 10 to 15% of the student population), with and without disabilities, will require additional school-based behavioral supports and accommodations. *Targeted interventions* are intensive actions directed toward chronic, repetitive, and pervasive problem behaviors presented by these students. Typically, the design of individualized targeted interventions involves completing a functional behavioral assessment (FBA) (described in the next section) and using the results to develop an individual plan of action. However, before engaging in the labor-intensive process of an FBA, it is often useful to engage in function-based thinking (FBT) and implement certain resource-efficient generic targeted interventions that researchers have found reduce a range of disruptive classroom behaviors (Hawken & Horner, 2003; Hershfeldt, Rosenberg, & Bradshaw, 2010; Park, 2007). Function-based thinking and two interventions (check-in, connect, check-out systems and behavioral contracting) are detailed in Strategies 15.5 and 15.6.

## Functional Behavioral Assessment

For those students who do not respond to generic targeted interventions, teachers should conduct a functional FBA. The FBA is a powerful problem-solving process that identifies

This is a sample of the consequences used in my class. For a complete list, please reference the student handbook.

## Positive Consequences

(To Increase Appropriate Behavior)

- Line Leader
- Verbal praise
- Positive note home
- Positive phone call
- Stickers
- School supplies
- Healthy treats
- Lunch with teacher/administrator
- Extra computer time
- Homework pass
- Ice cream social
- Extended recess

## Negative Consequences

(To Decrease Inappropriate Behavior)

Nonverbal cues/warnings
- Verbal cues
- Time-out with written reflection
- Loss of recess
- Note or phone call home
- Parent conference
- Office referral
- In-school suspension
- Out-of-school suspension

Mrs. Marquis's contact information:
Marquis@omail.com

We welcome your comments and feedback. Feel free to contact me by e-mail at any time or by phone after 3:00 PM and before 7.00 PM.

## Plan for Success

Mrs. Marquis's Third-Grade Class

**Parent Guide**

2009–2010

## Mission Statement

To provide a safe and nurturing environment, which fosters creativity, academic achievement, and cooperation. With the support of families, staff, and community members, our students will reach their full potential.

Please help us achieve our goals! Volunteer to be a class helper.

## Rules for
## Stars

**S**how respect; Keep yourself to yourself.

**T**ruly be prepared for class.

**A**dhere to directions the first time given.

**R**aise your hand, and wait to be recognized.

**S**how up on time.

Figure 15.2

Sample Brochure for a Comprehensive Behavior Management Plan

| Figure 15.3 | Measure to Assess Quality of Comprehensive Plan |
|---|---|

**How Evident?** Read each statement and circle the most appropriate rating in regard to the manual being evaluated.

| 1—Not evident | 2— | 3—Evident | 4— | 5—Extremely evident |
|---|---|---|---|---|

| Mission Statement | Rating |
|---|---|
| The mission statement clearly states a vision reflecting student outcomes. | 1    2    3    4    5 |
| The mission statement clearly states expectations for students. | 1    2    3    4    5 |
| The mission statement has direct, clear statements that are focused and behaviorally used. | 1    2    3    4    5 |
| **Rules and Expectations** | |
| The rules are stated positively and defined clearly. | 1    2    3    4    5 |
| There are six or fewer rules. | 1    2    3    4    5 |
| Rules are observable and measurable. | 1    2    3    4    5 |
| Rules are jargon free and age appropriate for students. | 1    2    3    4    5 |
| Supports for rule success are articulated (supports need to be in place prior to failure). | 1    2    3    4    5 |
| **Positive Consequences** | |
| Positive consequences can be implemented easily at both team and classroom level. | 1    2    3    4    5 |
| Positive consequences contain a balance of praise, nontangible reinforcement, and tangible reinforcement that can be easily delivered. | 1    2    3    4    5 |
| The positive consequences include a mix of desirable tangible reinforcements and big ticket items (e.g., social and physical activities). | 1    2    3    4    5 |
| **Negative Consequences** | |
| The consequences are natural, logical, and have an established hierarchy (e.g., rule reminder, warning, action plan). | 1    2    3    4    5 |
| The consequences are related to mission statement, rules, and procedures. | 1    2    3    4    5 |
| The consequences preserve a student's dignity and help to promote an internal locus of control. | 1    2    3    4    5 |
| The negative consequences reduce instances of secondary gain. | 1    2    3    4    5 |
| Intervention for problem behavior is not viewed as a negative consequence (e.g., referral to guidance, SIT team). | 1    2    3    4    5 |
| **Procedures** | |
| Procedures are positively stated and are age appropriate. | 1    2    3    4    5 |
| Each procedure is developed in a logical, step-by-step fashion. | 1    2    3    4    5 |
| The terms used in procedures are simple (as short as possible), specific, and jargon free. | 1    2    3    4    5 |
| Procedures are observable and measurable. | 1    2    3    4    5 |

| | | | | | |
|---|---|---|---|---|---|
| Procedures promote increased efficiency and effectiveness of the instructional environment. | 1 | 2 | 3 | 4 | 5 |
| There are at least three different school procedures (e.g., hallway, bathroom, late, cafeteria, nurse). | 1 | 2 | 3 | 4 | 5 |
| **Crisis Intervention** | | | | | |
| Crisis is defined in terms of students. | 1 | 2 | 3 | 4 | 5 |
| There is a plan for responding to and dealing with a crisis. | 1 | 2 | 3 | 4 | 5 |
| **Additional Factors for Success** | | | | | |
| The plan outlines target dates for staff implementation, evaluation, and student and parent education. | 1 | 2 | 3 | 4 | 5 |
| The supports for student noncompliance clearly divide faculty and administrative expectations and responsibilities. | 1 | 2 | 3 | 4 | 5 |
| Members of the crisis team are identified, and a plan for responding to a crisis developed. | 1 | 2 | 3 | 4 | 5 |
| Rules are jargon free and can be readily understood by parents, staff, and faculty. | 1 | 2 | 3 | 4 | 5 |
| Guidelines promote, encourage, and recognize compliance of procedures. | 1 | 2 | 3 | 4 | 5 |
| Documents reflect that the school values positive behavior. | 1 | 2 | 3 | 4 | 5 |
| The faculty has created unique forms, checklists, and lesson plans for teaching the plan, specific to the needs of their school. | 1 | 2 | 3 | 4 | 5 |

*Note:* These statements reflect effective characteristics of a school-wide comprehensive behavior management plan.

*Source:* Reprinted with permission from M. S. Rosenberg & L. A. Jackman. (2003). Development, implementation, and sustainability of comprehensive school-wide behavior management systems. *Intervention in School and Clinic, 39*(1), 10–21.

the function or purpose of an individual student's inappropriate behavior patterns. The results of the FBA provide a more precise road map for the design and implementation of methods that help students reduce their troubling behaviors and engage in alternative positive behaviors. Three key assumptions serve as the foundation for the FBA process. First, all behavior, appropriate and inappropriate, is learned and supported by current environment conditions. Second, all behavior is purposeful, meaning that people behave in ways that satisfy their needs or that help achieve a specific outcome. Finally, FBAs are most effective when a team of professionals collaborate in the process (Scott & Kamps, 2007). Typically, these are professionals from diverse fields who provide input and suggestions from their areas of expertise. As a classroom teacher, you may be required to serve as case manager for the team, organizing the information and coordinating communication among team members.

## Behavior Intervention Plans

Successful behavior intervention plans (BIPs) are characterized by (1) the simultaneous strengthening and reducing of targeted behaviors through the application of behavioral techniques, (2) direct teaching of social skills, and (3) emphases on self-management, self-control, and student independence.

### Strengthening and Reducing of Targeted Behaviors

When implementing behavioral intervention programs, the teacher's goal is to replace instances of disruptive classroom behaviors with more appropriate alternatives (Gongola & Daddario, 2010). This step requires that teachers implement techniques that simultaneously reduce and strengthen targeted behaviors. Increasing behavior involves the process of reinforcement. Positive reinforcement occurs when the presentation of an environmental consequence results in a corresponding increase in the frequency or intensity of a behavior. Negative reinforcement (often confused incorrectly with punishment) occurs when the removal of an unpleasant event results in an increase in the target behavior. Teachers have three behavioral options to decrease behavior: extinction, differential reinforcement, and punishment. The diversity of behavioral methods to strengthen appropriate classroom behavior and decrease problem behavior is summarized in Tables 15.2 and 15.3.

**Table 15.2**  Procedures for Increasing Appropriate Behaviors

| Type | Definition | Advantages | Disadvantages |
|---|---|---|---|
| Edible | A primary reinforcer. Potency varies as a function of deprivation and satiation. | • Potency with students who possess severe handicaps.<br>• Useful in establishing reinforcing properties of other events (e.g., praise, smiles). | • Delivery disrupts classroom functioning.<br>• Difficult to dispense in busy classroom settings.<br>• Need to be constantly aware of student allergies. |
| Praise and attention | Conditioned social reinforcers that can be delivered verbally and nonverbally (e.g., smiles, winks, physical contact). | • Easily and quickly administered.<br>• Unobtrusive during classroom activities.<br>• Little preparation required. | • Because the reinforcement values of praise and attention needs to be learned, some individuals may not respond.<br>• Limited potency with inappropriate behaviors that have high secondary reinforcing properties (e.g., theft, substance abuse). |
| High-probability behaviors | The preferred activities of students can be used as reinforcers for low-probability behaviors. | • Schools have many desirable activities available.<br>• Powerful and cost free.<br>• Low probability of satiation. | • Difficulty in delivering activity reinforcers immediately.<br>• Disruptions may occur during transitions between activities.<br>• Delivery mode tends to be all or none; little opportunity to portion out activities. |
| Performance feedback | Using the knowledge of progress or results to reinforce a target behavior. | • Easily initiated in setting where performance criteria are explicitly stated.<br>• Low cost and motivating. | • Effectiveness of feedback alone has been equivocal. |
| Tokens | Conditioned, generalized reinforcers whose strength is derived from items, activities, and desirable consequences they present. | • Combat satiation in that a number of backups can be employed.<br>• Easily dispensed.<br>• Serve to bridge the period of time between the occurrence of a behavior and the delivery of a primary reinforcer.<br>• Allow for gradations of reinforcement. | • Requires effort in record keeping and other management activities.<br>• Fading of tokens often neglected. |

*Source:* Reprinted with permission from M. S. Rosenberg, L. J. O'Shea, & D. J. O'Shea. (2006). *Student teacher to master teacher: A practical guide for educating students with special needs* (4th ed., p. 272). Upper Saddle River, NJ: Merrill/Pearson Education.

**Table 15.3**   Three Commonly Used Punishment Techniques

| Type | Definition | Advantages | Disadvantages |
|---|---|---|---|
| Reprimand | A verbal statement or nonverbal gesture that expresses disapproval. | • Easily applied with little or no preparation required.<br>• No physical discomfort to students. | • Sometimes not effective. Can serve as positive reinforcement if this is a major source of attention. |
| Response cost | A formal system of penalties in which a reinforcer is removed, contingent upon the occurrence of an inappropriate behavior. | • Easily applied with quick results.<br>• Does not disrupt class activities.<br>• No physical discomfort to students. | • Not effective once student has "lost" all reinforcers.<br>• Can initially result in some students being more disruptive. |
| Time-out | Limited or complete loss of access to positive reinforcers for a set amount of time. | • Fast acting and powerful.<br>• No physical discomfort to students. | • Difficult to find secluded areas where students would not be reinforced inadvertently.<br>• May require physical assistance to the time-out area.<br>• Overuse can interfere with educational and prosocial efforts. |

*Source:* Reprinted with permission from M. S. Rosenberg, L. J. O'Shea, & D. J. O'Shea. (2006). *Student teacher to master teacher: A practical guide for educating students with special needs* (4th ed., p. 273). Upper Saddle River, NJ: Merrill/Pearson Education.

## Direct Teaching of Social Skills

Some students misbehave because they lack the specific behavioral skills to act productively in the school and classroom environment. For these students, direct instruction in such skills would improve social competence and reduce problem behavior. Some teachers provide instruction in social skills by using commercially prepared social skills curricula (e.g., the Skillstreaming series; Goldstein & McGinnis, 1997, McGinnis & Goldstein, 1997). These programs cluster specific skills into domains (e.g., dealing with feelings, friendship-making skills, coping skills) and provide instructional sequences for teaching the skills. Effective curricula typically include validated instructional components (e.g., direct instruction, modeling, coaching, reinforcement, controlled practice), assessment instrumentation, and the flexibility to address the needs of individual students as well as small groups (Carter & Sugai, 1989; Sugai & Lewis, 1996). Other teachers choose to create their own activities to teach replacement behaviors and can benefit from combining low-cost multimedia technology with structured social skills lessons (Cumming, 2010).

## Self-Management, Self-Control, and Independence

The ultimate goal of any behavioral intervention is for a student to regulate his own behavior independently. Teaching self-management and self-control allows students in need of behavior change to assume larger roles in their behavior change efforts. Programs typically consist of four components: self-assessment, goal setting, evaluation, and self-determination of reinforcement (Polsgrove & Smith, 2004; Vannest, Reynolds, & Kamphaus, 2008). In self-assessment, a student reflects on her own behavior and determines if the behavior is inadequate or inappropriate. Next, the student identifies the behaviors required, sets goals, and selects strategies that help regulate behavior. Then, through the process of self-determination, the student evaluates her performance. Finally, the nature and scope of reinforcement that she should receive to perform the target behavior is determined.

Classroom implementation of self-management typically follows a sequence. First, the teacher introduces the procedure by informing a student (or a small group of students) that it is important to keep track of the occurrence and nonoccurrence of his target behavior. The teacher then introduces the student to a cuing mechanism. This could be a "low-tech" tool such as a self-monitoring card (Kamps, 2010) or a technologically enhanced device such as a smart phone or tablet (e.g., Kramer, 2004). Every time the student is cued, he should ask himself, "Was I engaging in the target behavior?" and mark the monitoring device appropriately. The instructor should model the procedures, and the student should practice initially to ensure that the student can reliably differentiate between the occurrence and nonoccurrence of the target behavior. After the procedure succeeds in teaching a student to monitor and record his own behavior, procedures designed to teach the self-determination of reinforcement can begin (Rosenberg et al., 2006). When the student reaches an acceptable level of performance, it may be time to carefully wean the student from the external aspects of the procedure. However, if student performance begins to deteriorate, the teacher should not hesitate to resume using the external prompts.

## Wraparound Supports

A small percentage of students, usually no more than 1 to 3%, requires a series of intensive, highly structured behavioral supports that involve the coordinated efforts of families, educators, and community-based professionals. Educators often use the term *wraparound* or *system of care* to describe these interventions because they reflect three essential elements associated with this type of service delivery. First, rather than conforming to existing service-delivery alternatives, these are integrated educational and community services designed to meet the unique needs of children and their families. Second, services are provided in the local neighborhood. Finally, services are responsive to the culture of the child and family. It is not unusual for wraparound systems of care to include professionals from the fields of mental health, medicine, social work, substance abuse, law enforcement, and vocational rehabilitation (Eber, Breen, Rose, Unizycki, & London, 2008).

What do teachers need to know about wraparound programming, and how can they contribute to the success of such programs? First, recognize that the community school is the most effective place for service coordination. It is a centrally located setting that can provide convenient access to a range of services with reduced stigma (Cullinan, 2002). Second, use positive strength-based commentary during conversations with family members. This will help ascertain, with minimal defensiveness, the ideas, values, frustrations, and dreams family members have about their child. Clearly, to attain increased family participation and trust, members of the school community must project an encouraging and supportive attitude toward behavioral improvement. Finally, as a teacher, recognize that you contribute to the school-based wraparound team process by (1) helping identify, clearly defining, and prioritizing needs; (2) developing action plans and interventions that cross disciplines; and (3) collecting data that assist in the evaluation of interventions geared toward measurable outcomes (Duckworth et al., 2001; Eber, Sugai, Smith, & Scott, 2002; Scott et al., 2010).

Consider how Susan Hill, the Dean of Special Education at Heritage High School, participates in her school's system of care. Ms. Hill often facilitates the student support team, which is a group of administrators, teachers, and related service personnel who together consider the needs of students who require integrated social, behavioral, and medical supports in order to fully benefit from educational programming. The team serves as a focal point for reviewing student progress and responding to needs as expressed by the students and their families. Ms. Hill readily admits that this is challenging work: Services are difficult to access, and teachers experience an emotional toll in seeing so many families in pain and dire circumstances.

Fortunately, Ms. Hill has witnessed many successes such as (1) securing needed mental health and therapeutic treatments for students and (2) accessing in-home social work support for several single mothers who were having difficulty managing the behavioral demands of their nonverbal and very active adolescents with developmental delays.

Ms. Hill believes that much more work remains to be done. At the top of her list of frustrations are those few families who are reluctant to become involved in the process and tend to avoid contacts with school personnel. Ms. Hill is always looking for novel ways to increase involvement.

## Summary

Effective teachers manage the behavior of all of their students by developing procedures that are systematic, proactive, supportive, and responsive.

### Student behavior: What to expect

- Most school and classroom misbehavior is related to tardiness, inattention, crowd-control issues, and students testing the limits.
- Students who exceed these mild forms of misbehavior stand out from their peers due to their behavioral excesses and behavioral deficits.
- Students with behavioral excesses engage in high rates and frequencies of disruptive behaviors that interfere with academic performance; those with behavioral deficits lack specific skills necessary for academic and social competence.

### Behavior management readiness and tiered management strategies

- Successful behavior managers organize their environments by making effective use of the physical dimensions of their classroom, valuing instructional time, being prepared, and coordinating resources.
- An essential prerequisite for effective behavior management is the delivery of accessible, motivating, and supportive instruction.
- Successful behavior management is contingent on developing authentic relationships with students, modeling civility and respect, and employing culturally responsive practices.
- Tiered management allows teachers to meet the needs of all students by first addressing universal concerns—the typical needs of most students—and then using a continuum of interventions for those students who don't respond to the system.
- At the center of universal practices is a comprehensive management plan containing five core domains: (1) mission; (2) rules, procedures, and supports; (3) surface management and consequences; (4) crisis considerations; and (5) accessible documentation.
- Targeted interventions are intensive actions directed toward chronic and pervasive problem behaviors.
- For students who do not respond to generic targeted interventions, teachers may need to complete a functional behavior assessment (FBA) and develop a structured behavior intervention plan (BIP).
- Successful BIPs focus on the simultaneous strengthening and reducing of targeted behaviors; direct teaching of specific skills; and student self-management and independence.
- A small percentage of students will require wraparound supports—intensive, highly structured supports that require the coordinated efforts of families, educators, and community-based health professionals.

## Addressing Professional Standards

Standards addressed in Chapter 15 include:

**CEC Standards:** (3) Individual learning differences, (4) instructional strategies, (5) learning environments and social interactions, and (7) instructional planning.

## MyEducationLab

Go to the topic Classroom/Behavior Management in the **MyEducationLab** (www
.myeducationlab.com) for *Inclusion*, where you can:

- Find learning outcomes for Classroom/Behavior Management, along with the national standards that connect to these outcomes.
- Complete Assignments and Activities that can help you more deeply understand the chapter content.
- Apply and practice your understanding of the core teaching skills identified in the chapter with the Building Teaching Skills and Dispositions learning units.
- Examine challenging situations and cases presented in the IRIS Center Resources.
- Get practice considering classroom management with our online simulations.
- Check your comprehension on the content covered in the chapter with the Study Plan. Here you will be able to take a chapter quiz, receive feedback on your answers, and then access Review, Practice, and Enrichment activities to enhance your understanding of chapter content.

# EFFECTIVE PRACTICES FOR CLASSROOM MANAGEMENT

## Putting It All Together

At times, particularly early in your career, you will find the process of managing student behavior challenging. You may encounter colleagues who hold flawed views of how best to manage behavior, parents who fail to respond to your well-intentioned efforts to address persistent troubles, and administrators who fall short in supporting your structured management system. If and when these events occur, it is best, of course, if you respond in a professional manner:

1. **Remain patient, keep things in perspective, and be aware of the big picture.** Schools are a microcosm of society, and you should not take it personally if events do not go as planned.

2. **Practice diplomacy.** Consider the perspective of those who you find frustrating, and identify the functions of their actions. Try to understand why they believe and act as they do, and seek to negotiate win-win resolutions to conflicts.

3. **Remain poised.** Your comportment during stressful and frustrating circumstances is a reflection of your competence and professionalism. Students look to adults as models of desired behavior, and they will learn from your actions.

4. **Reflect on your own actions, and get help when needed.** Consider how your own actions and belief systems contribute to the development and maintenance of challenging situations. Do not be reluctant to ask for help and support from friends and colleagues.

5. **Show your pleasure when helping your students.** Educators choose to teach because they enjoy it and derive satisfaction in seeing their students overcome challenges and grow socially. Recognize when challenges are met, and celebrate when students succeed as a result of your efforts.

## Strategy Fact Sheet

In the remainder of this chapter, we describe eight effective strategies, some of which we referred to previously in the chapter, to help you plan effectively to meet the needs of all students.

| EFFECTIVE PRACTICE | TYPE OF STRATEGY/BRIEF DESCRIPTION | SPECIAL CONSIDERATIONS |
|---|---|---|
| Strategy 15.1: Developing and Maintaining Rules and Procedures | A universal design behavioral support that communicates and defines acceptable behavior and efficient routines associated with success in the classroom. | Rules and procedures must be taught explicitly as well as reviewed and practiced throughout the school year, particularly after breaks for holidays and vacations. |
| Strategy 15.2: Surface Management Techniques | Commonsense behavior management methods for minor disruptive behaviors; surface management techniques overlap with elements of teaching with little disruption to the instructional process. | Surface management requires an awareness of classroom activities and events, multitasking skills that increase with time and experience. |
| Strategy 15.3: Developing Consequences and Delivering Them with Consistency | A series of teacher-directed events and behaviors that are used to promote compliance to behavioral expectations and to reduce the frequency and intensity of inappropriate behaviors. | For classroom management systems to succeed, it is essential that students complying with expectations are recognized and reinforced for their efforts. |
| Strategy 15.4: Defusing Confrontations and Responding to Dangerous Behavior | A series of interpersonal communication techniques that can defuse confrontational situations and maintain the safety of students and staff. | Some students use the shock value of extreme behaviors to intimidate and coerce others. It is important to minimize instances of these students attaining desired outcomes through such behaviors. |
| Strategy 15.5: Check-In, Connect, and Check-Out Systems | Targeted low-cost interventions that provide students with immediate feedback on behavior, supportive relationships with school personnel, and increased recognition contingent on improvements in appropriate behavior. | The success of check-in systems depends on the quality of adults who coordinate the program. Specifically, coordinators need to interact well with students, work closely with families, proactively address conflict, and believe that positive changes will occur. |

| EFFECTIVE PRACTICE | TYPE OF STRATEGY/BRIEF DESCRIPTION | SPECIAL CONSIDERATIONS |
|---|---|---|
| Strategy 15.6: Behavioral Contracts | Formal documents that detail the elements of specific, realistic individualized behavior change initiatives. | Because contracts require students to wait for a specific "payoff," it is important to gauge how long students can maintain their behavior without tangible reinforcement. |
| Strategy 15.7: Function-Based Thinking, Functional Behavior Assessments, and Behavior Intervention Plans | A process designed to identify possible linkages between student behavior and the events and conditions in classroom and school environments; information identified is used to develop a behavior intervention plan (BIP). | Keep it simple and straightforward: The key element of functional thinking is to identify and intervene on factors that contribute to a student's inappropriate behaviors. |
| Strategy 15.8: Direct Teaching of Social Skills: Social Stories | Written from the student's perspective, social stories explicitly highlight a course of action that one could take when encountering a challenging social situation. | Social stories work best when they are implemented along with other methods of evidence-based social skill instruction, including modeling, role playing, and practice in naturalistic settings. |

| Strategy 15.1 | **DEVELOPING AND MAINTAINING RULES AND PROCEDURES** |

## Rationale

Teacher expectations regarding classroom organization and behavior management are communicated most effectively to students through rules and procedures. *Rules* are explicit definitions of acceptable behavior in your classroom; *procedures* are the routines or series of behaviors that students follow in order to complete a task, activity, or operation such as eating lunch in the cafeteria or requesting a pass to the lavatory. When introduced correctly, rules and procedures prompt, motivate, and guide students to adhere to classroom behavioral standards. Moreover, posting, teaching, and reviewing these expectations leads to reductions in disruptive behavior and improvements in academic engagement and conflict resolution (Capizzi, 2009; Simonsen, Fairbanks, Briesch, Myers, & Sugai, 2008).

## Step-by-Step

The steps for developing and maintaining rules and procedures are:

**1** *Know local community and school district expectations regarding the behavior of students.* Consider the community context of your expectations for discipline. Design your classroom rules and procedures to be congruent with the prevailing legal requirement and school board expectations.

**2** *Articulate the specific behaviors and procedures associated with success in your classroom.* Reconstruct these expectations into explicit statements that will enable you and the students to agree about the occurrence or nonoccurrence of the behavioral expectations.

**3** *Involve students in the development of the rules and procedures:*

- Solicit input as to the importance of classroom rules and how they should be enforced.
- Generate procedural solutions for classroom processes that contribute to disruption and disorder.

**4** *Keep rules and procedures accessible.*

- Limit the number of rules to five or six, and ensure that procedures are phrased in a task-analyzed, easy-to-follow sequence of steps.
- Keep the wording of rules and procedures simple and jargon free.
- Phrase rules and procedures positively rather than negatively, focusing on what students should do rather than not do.
- Provide supports for those students who have difficulty meeting expectations.

**5** **Maintain the potency of rules and procedures.**

- Keep rules and procedures posted in areas where students can see them.
- Teach and provide extensive practice with rules and procedures during the first week of school.
- Model desired student responses, and provide booster sessions on the rules and procedures at regularly scheduled intervals throughout the school year.
- Monitor your own level of consistency in adhering to the classroom rules and procedures.

## Applications and Examples

To assist in the development of rules, make use of the Rules Development Worksheet (see Figure 15.4) (Rosenberg et al., 2006), a format that allows for (1) the articulation of a general case rule, (2) the definition of the rule in your classroom or setting, (3) plans for teaching the rule, and (4) methods to provide supports for those students who have difficulty complying with the rule. We recommend that you use this format to fully develop each of your classroom rules.

**Directions:** List the school-wide rules in the first column. Think about what each rule will look like and mean in your classroom. Record these points in the second column. Next, list a variety of methods for "teaching the rule" to your students. Finally, generate a list of possible supports for helping *all* students achieve success with the school-wide rules in *your* classroom.

| School-Wide Rule | Meaning of the Rule in My Class | Teaching the Rule | Available Supports |
|---|---|---|---|
| *The students will be prepared.* | *The students will be in their seats at the ringing of the bell with books, writing tools, drills, and homework.* | • *Elicit rationale for the rule.*<br>• *Role-play "the prepared student."*<br>• *Display "being prepared materials" visually.* | 1. *Set up pencil & pen loaner box.*<br>2. *Praise students who are prepared.*<br>3. *Provide visual and verbal cues to prompt preparedness.* |
|  |  |  |  |

### Figure 15.4

---

Rules Development Worksheet

*Note:* This figure may be photocopied for noncommercial use only. ©PRO-ED, Inc., 2003.
*Source:* Reprinted with permission from M. S. Rosenberg, L. J. O'Shea, & D. J. O'Shea. (2006). *Student teacher to master teacher: A practical guide for educating students with special needs* (4th ed., p. 18). Upper Saddle River, NJ: Merrill/Pearson Education.

Successful behavior managers also know how to facilitate the completion of daily procedural routines such as morning arrival, trips to the rest-room, and transitioning to the cafeteria. Consider the following two sample procedures as possible models for use in your own classrooms:

**Morning Arrival**

- Students enter building after 8:15.
- Check schedule: A or B Day.

- Go to locker and retrieve supplies.
- Deposit all hats and personal items in locker.
- If you eat breakfast, report directly to cafeteria.
- When the warning bell rings, report directly to class.
- Upon arrival to classroom, complete your morning log.

### CAFÉ (Care About Food Enjoy lunch) Procedures

- Join the END of ONE line, ONE time.
- Sit in your assigned area.
- Respect each other's space, feelings, and property.
- Use appropriate language and tone.
- Remain seated until the teacher signals for you to dispose of waste correctly and return to class.

## Keep in Mind

For compliance to rules and procedures to maintain throughout the school year, it is essential to teach, practice, and reinforce them with regularity and consistency (Morrissey, Bohanon, & Fenning, 2010). It is also important to provide consistent and active supervision regularly, as well as structured booster sessions at various times of the year, particularly after holidays and vacations.

### Key References

Capizzi, A. M. (2009). Starting the year off right: Designing and evaluating a supportive class room management plan. *Focus on Exceptional Children, 42*(3), 1–12.

Curwin, R. L., & Mendler, A. N. (1999). *Discipline with dignity* (2nd ed.). Alexandria, VA: ASCD.

Evertson, C., Emmer, E. T., & Worsham, M. (2006). *Classroom management for elementary teachers* (7th ed.). Boston: Allyn & Bacon.

Rademacher, J. E., Callahan, K., & Pederson-Seelye, V. A. (1998). How do your classroom rules measure up? Guidelines for developing an effective rule management routine. *Intervention in School and Clinic, 33*(5), 284–289.

Rosenberg, M. S., O'Shea, L., & O'Shea, D. J. (2006). *Student teacher to master teacher* (4th ed). Upper Saddle River, NJ: Merrill/Pearson Education.

Simonsen, B., Fairbanks, S., Briesch, A., Myers, D., & Sugai, G. (2008). Evidence-based practices in classroom management: Considerations for research to practice. *Education and Treatment of Children, 31*(3), 2008.

# SURFACE MANAGEMENT TECHNIQUES

## Rationale

Surface management techniques are commonsense "stop-gap" methods that teachers use intuitively to deal with relatively minor instances of disruptive behaviors. The strength of these techniques is that they overlap elements of the teaching process and can be applied with minimal disruption to the instructional process. Although they are not a substitute for a well-planned comprehensive management program, they do allow teachers to return students to the instructional flow of the classroom with finesse, "with-it-ness," grace, and, sometimes, good humor.

## Step-by-Step and Applications and Examples

Surface management techniques are best viewed as a menu of alternatives in which specific techniques align with the intensity of the behaviors and match the presenting behaviors. We identify presenting behaviors that are typically served by each technique and highlight how it is best applied.

| TECHNIQUE | BEHAVIORS | APPLICATION |
|---|---|---|
| **Planned ignoring** | Minor attention-seeking behaviors such as pencil tapping or making noises. | When teachers do not feed in, or reinforce, a student's need for immediate gratification, minor disruptive behaviors will eventually stop. |
| **Signal interference** | Off-task behaviors such as talking with or annoying peers. | Use of nonverbal gestures, eye contact, noise, or body posture prompts students to redirect their inappropriate behaviors. |
| **Proximity control** | Minor disruptive behavior such as talking and socializing with others during task-oriented activities. | Close physical presence to the student serves to deter disruptive behaviors and promotes greater task orientation. |
| **Changing the pace** | Off-task behaviors such as staring out windows, resting head on desk, and talking to neighbors. | Infusing the lesson with a game, personal anecdote, story, or even a change in vocal tone revitalizes lessons and keeps students attending to work. |
| **Removal of seductive objects** | Disruptive and off-task behaviors associated with task-irrelevant objects. | Objects that co-opt student attention are removed without incident and returned at an appropriate time. |
| **Interest boosting** | A student's flagging interest (and corresponding inappropriate behavior) in activity. | Interest heightened by teacher noting the unique and challenging qualities of the activity as well as indicating personal interest in the content. |
| **Tension decontamination through humor** | Tense or anxiety-filled classroom situations. | Diplomatic use of humor, mostly the self-deprecating type, can preempt confrontational and counterproductive situations. |
| **Antiseptic bouncing** | A student who is on the verge of a potentially serious, highly disruptive behavioral event. | Safely and nonpunitively removing a student from the classroom (e.g., delivering a message to the school nurse, running an errand). |

## Keep in Mind

Some teachers develop a surface management routine rapidly and can orchestrate the overlapping nature of behavioral prompting, redirection, and interruption-free instruction instinctively, with little apparent forethought. Most teachers, however, require practice in this multi-tasking. With experience and time, successful teachers develop the seamless awareness of everything that is going on in the classroom, and they are characterized by their students as "having eyes in the back of their heads."

**Key References**

Beck, M. A., Roblee, K., & Johns, C. (1982). Psychoeducational management of disturbed children. *Education, 102*(3), 232–235.

Kounin, J. S. (1970). *Discipline and group management in classrooms*. New York: Holt, Rinehart and Winston.

Levin, J., & Nolan, J. (2007). *Principles of classroom management* (5th ed.). Boston: Allyn & Bacon.

Long, N., & Newman, R. G. (1965). Managing surface behavior of children in school. In N. Long, W. Morse, & R. Newman (Eds.), *Conflict in the classroom: The education of emotionally disturbed children* (pp. 233–240). Belmont, CA: Wadsworth.

Olive, E. C. (2004). Practical tools for positive behavior facilitation. *Reclaiming Child Youth, 13*(1), 43–47.

| Strategy 15.3 | DEVELOPING CONSEQUENCES AND DELIVERING THEM WITH CONSISTENCY |

# Rationale

Consequences promote compliance to behavior expectations and reduce the frequency and intensity of inappropriate behaviors. Consequences work best when they (1) are clear and related to class rules and procedures, (2) possess a range or hierarchy of alternatives, (3) are natural and logical for the school environment (4) serve an educative rather than vindictive function, (5) are delivered with consistency and care, and (6) maintain students' dignity.

# Step-by-Step

The steps for developing consequences and delivering them with consistency are:

**1** *Develop a system of positive consequences to recognize and reinforce appropriate behaviors.*

- Generate a menu of desirable products, actions, and events that can be integrated into the daily routine of the classroom. This menu can include
  - Privileges such as first choice of games, computers, and athletic equipment during free time
  - Certificates and awards recognizing periods of appropriate behavior and initiating positive social initiations toward others
  - Notes, phone calls, or e-mails home recognizing desired changes in behavior
  - Ways for students to be a class/teacher helper such as tutoring younger students, grading papers, or serving as a messenger
- Target the specific behaviors you seek to enhance or increase. A good rule of thumb when targeting is to ensure that the behaviors are consistent with class rules and procedures, overt, and easy to determine if they occur (i.e., contain movement).
- Ensure that you deliver points and tokens in a systematic and logically appropriate fashion. For some students, delivery of points can wait for the end of the instructional period; others, because of the intensity of the presenting behaviors, require more frequent recognition.
- Make sure to record points and tokens easily and accurately. Whenever appropriate, allow students to manage and keep track of their own points and tokens.
- Develop an array of desirable and school-appropriate back-up reinforcers. Have several activities or items that students can earn in a short period of time; highly regarded, larger items or events should require savings over time.

- Consider a response–cost system, a method for deducting points if students engage in intensive disruptive and aggressive behaviors.

**2** *Develop a hierarchy of negative consequences that provide a range of options to decrease rates of inappropriate behavior.*

- Consider the use of least intrusive generic consequences that do not interrupt the flow of classroom activities. These include surface management techniques, indirect class reminders and restatement of the rules and procedures, and directed verbal reminders of expectations.
- Use, when necessary, more intensive directed consequences:
  - Student "quiet time" to calm down
  - Teacher-directed time-out
  - Reflection time in class or other classroom
- Refer students to the appropriate administrator for behaviors such as fighting and bullying; contact parents for design of a coordinated action plan.

**3** *Initiate a self-check system that promotes delivery of consequences with respect and consistency:*

- Stay close to the student and make direct eye contact, using a soft voice. Do not embarrass the student in front of peers. Always implement the consequence, and do not accept excuses or bargaining.
- Monitor your delivery of consequences, making sure that you maintain consistency. Remain calm, professional, and fair to all students in the classroom (not inadvertently picking on a few who act out).
- Avoid power struggles with confrontational students:
  - Knowing how power struggles develop and entrap (Curwin & Mendler, 1999)
  - Being firm and anger free rather than defensive
  - Not giving in to coercion, whining, or emotionality
  - Having private discussion with the student about her frustrations and alternatives to her behavior

## Applications and Examples

Some teachers remain concerned that giving students rewards for appropriate behavior can be seen as "bribery." Consider using positive reinforcers that are natural to the school and classroom environment. Rhode, Jenson, and Reavis (1993) provide several suggestions in their classic resource, *The Tough Kid Book*. Here is a listing of several of the natural reinforcers:

- Being line leader, team captain, or paper monitor
- Helping the custodian, feeding the fish and other class pets, or serving as class messenger
- Tutoring younger students
- First choice of activity, art supplies, or PE equipment
- Free time with specific activities, favorite peers, or adults
- Lunch with principal or related service personnel

## Keep in Mind

The delivery of consequences for enhancing rule compliance and decreasing instances of noncompliance is at the heart of successful behavior management. Unfortunately, many teachers deliver negative consequences far more frequently than positive recognitions. For discipline systems to be effective, it is essential to maintain a focus on positive behaviors; students who are doing the right things need to be recognized and reinforced. When delivering consequences to reduce inappropriate behaviors, it is critical to maintain an educative and professional manner instead of presenting an angry, menacing, and vindictive demeanor. Attend to your feelings when you are managing student behavior, and recognize that it is your professional responsibility to keep frustration and anger in check. Treats, yelling, and making demands when students are upset and agitated will not work, and may actually serve to escalate problem student behavior.

### Key References

Curwin, R. L., & Mendler, A. N. (1999). *Discipline with dignity* (2nd ed.). Alexandria, VA: ASCD.

Jones, V., & Jones, L. (2007). *Comprehensive classroom management: Creating communities of support and solving problems.* Upper Saddle River, NJ: Pearson/Allyn & Bacon.

Rhode, G., Jenson, W. R., & Reavis, H. K. (1993). *The tough kid book: Practical classroom management strategies.* Longmont, CO: Sopris West.

Rosenberg, M. S., O'Shea, L., & O'Shea, D. J. (2006). *Student teacher to master teacher* (4th ed). Upper Saddle River, NJ: Merrill/Pearson Education.

Sprick, R., Sprick, M., & Garrison, M. (1993). *Interventions: Classroom management strategies.* Longmont, CO: Sopris West.

Taylor-Greene, S., et al. (1997). School-wide behavioral support: Starting the year off right. *Journal of Behavioral Education, 7*(1), 99–112.

Yell, M. (2009). Classroom and behavior management II: Responding to behavioral skills instruction and generalization strategies. In M. L. Yell, N. B. Meadows, E. Drasgow, & J. G. Shriner (Eds.), *Evidence-based practices for educating students with emotional and behavioral disorders* (pp. 261–281). Upper Saddle River, NJ: Merrill/Pearson.

**Strategy 15.4**   ## DEFUSING CONFRONTATIONS AND RESPONDING TO DANGEROUS BEHAVIOR

## Rationale

Consider this strategy: "An ounce of prevention is worth a pound of cure." It is unlikely that you will have to deal with aggressive confrontational behaviors that threaten the safety of students and staff in your classroom. However, you should be aware of interpersonal communication techniques that can defuse some situations and of rapidly implemented procedures that maintain the safety of students and staff. Rather than fear these unfortunate circumstances, it is best to view them as manageable challenges and part of a complex process of assisting students in need and crisis. This type of mind-set is a prime example of a positive approach to the resolution of behavioral flare-ups. It allows students in vulnerable situations to get the help and support they need, as others in the immediate environment are kept safe and secure.

## Step-by-Step

**1** *Be aware of atypical signs of agitation.*

- Signs of agitation can include distractible behaviors such as darting eyes, nonconversational language, out-of-context outbursts, and intermittent starting and stopping several activities.
- Other signs include significant decreases in academic and social behaviors such as staring into space, withdrawal from typical peer groups and activities, and lack of eye contact.

**2** *Attempt to defuse the confrontational or dangerous behavior:*

- Communicate your support and concern for the student by remaining calm and acknowledging the critical nature of the situation.
- Minimize chances of escalating the situation. Lower your voice, slow your rate of speech, adjust your body stance, keep your arms at your side and avoid face-to-face positioning, and do not back the student into a corner (figuratively or literally).
- Allow the student to vent, but redirect the student to focus on the current situation; do not respond to irrelevant comments.
- Provide the student with choices (and limits) for resolution of the situation. Remind the student that the choices have corresponding and varying consequences.

**3** *Take charge of your own emotions.*

- Respond but do not react to the student's verbalizations and behaviors.

- Deal in the moment, yet be aware of the importance of maintaining the relationship.
- Release your emotions at the end of the situation.

**4** *If the student escalates into physically violent or dangerous behaviors, engage in preplanned safety procedures.*

- Signal a "room-clear," removing all other students from the immediate environment to a predetermined location with adequate supervision.
- Remove, or clear, the audience from the emotional event, thereby reducing the emotional intensity of the situation and the reinforcing properties of the behavioral event.
- Get assistance: Contact the school crisis support team (or designated individual) immediately to provide emergency physical restraint (only when deemed necessary) and crisis intervention procedures.

**5** *After the event, complete all necessary follow-up procedures.*

- Maintain a running record of the event and any relevant antecedent and/or consequent actions.
- Notify parents or guardians of the event, and involve them in problem solving and intervention planning.
- Plan instructional efforts to teach the student alternatives to the problem behavior.

# Applications and Examples

Defusing confrontations and managing physically aggressive behaviors involves minimization or avoidance of certain behaviors and verbalizations. To identify those actions that should be avoided, Albert (2003) surveyed teachers to determine actions that failed to work and even made things worse. Consider this list as behaviors to avoid when seeking to defuse confrontational situations.

**Behaviors to Avoid**

- Raising voice, preaching, and insisting on the last word
- Tense body language
- Sarcasm and degrading or embarrassing put-downs
- Questioning student's character
- Acting superior, and insisting on being correct
- Drawing unrelated persons into the conflict
- Backing the student into a corner
- Pleading, nagging, or bribing
- Bringing up unrelated events
- Commanding, demanding, and/or dominating communication style

## Keep in Mind

Aggressive and confrontational student behaviors are frightening, and, although infrequent, teachers unfortunately must be aware of how to manage them. Some students have learned to use the shock value of extreme behaviors to intimidate and coerce others. These inappropriate behaviors are reinforced when peers and adults acquiesce to aggressive students' demands. The chain of aggression and intimidation can be broken when students learn that they cannot get desired outcomes through threatening and confrontational behavior.

**Key References**

Albert, L. (2003). *Cooperative discipline*. Circle Pines, MN: AGS.

Colvin, G., Ainge, D., & Nelson, R. (1997). How to defuse confrontations. *Teaching Exceptional Children, 29*(3), 47–51.

Johns, B. H., & Carr, V. G. (1995). *Techniques for managing verbally and physically aggressive students*. Denver: Love.

Jones, V., & Jones, L. (2007). *Comprehensive classroom management: Creating communities of support and solving problems*. Boston: Pearson/Allyn & Bacon.

Sprick, R., Sprick, M., & Garrison, M. (1993). *Interventions: Managing physically dangerous behavior*. Longmont, CO: Sopris West.

Yell, M. (2009). Classroom and behavior management II: Responding to behavioral skills instruction and generalization strategies. In M. L. Yell, N. B. Meadows, E. Drasgow, & J. G. Shriner (Eds.), *Evidence-based practices for educating students with emotional and behavioral disorders* (pp. 261–281). Upper Saddle River, NJ: Pearson.

| Strategy 15.5 | **CHECK-IN, CONNECT, AND CHECK-OUT SYSTEMS** |

## Rationale

Check-in, connect, and check-out systems, sometimes referred to as *behavior education programs*, are targeted interventions for students who do not respond to typical classroom behavior management approaches. These low-cost prevention approaches provide additional supports in the form of more immediate feedback on behavior, sustained positive relationships with school personnel, and increased positive attention contingent on positive behavior change. A number of research efforts have found that the system is an easily administered, cost-effective means of reducing the frequency of problem behaviors, particularly those that are initiated and maintained by peer and adult attention (e.g., Cheney, Stage, Hawken, Lynass, Mielenz, & Waugh, 2009; Lehr, Sinclair, & Christenson, 2004).

## Step-by-Step

**1** *Before the start of each school day, students identified as being in need of specialized behavior supports check in with a coordinator or monitor.*

- The coordinator/monitor, a paraprofessional or trained volunteer, must have the flexibility to check students in and out of school (committing to approximately 10 hours per week).
- Successful coordinators/monitors interact well with students and believe they can succeed; work closely with families and other teachers; negotiate, compromise, and proactively address conflict; and apply solid organizational and recording skills.

**2** *During check-in, the coordinator or monitor:*

- Ensures students are prepared for the school day (e.g., necessary materials and completed homework assignments).
- Reviews the student's individualized daily progress feedback (DPF) form, an easy-to-complete feedback mechanism that allows teachers and other school personnel to connect with students, prompt target behaviors, and rate student performance (see a sample on the next page).

- Dispatches students to class with good cheer, positive statements, and high expectations for meeting the day's goals.

**3** *Throughout the day, teachers and other school staff:*

- Greet students and prompt appropriate behavior.
- Provide directed verbal feedback regarding behavioral goals.
- Complete the DPF form at natural transitions (e.g., hourly, end of instructional period, after lunch).

**4** *At the end of the day, the coordinator or monitor:*

- Computes student points and provides performance feedback.
- Gives students a copy of the DPF form for parents to review and sign.
- Enters student data into a database for weekly and monthly performance reviews.
- Considers if the student needs additional supports if goals are not being met.

## Applications and Examples

A sample DPF form is provided here. Note how the teacher, paraeducators, and related-service provider have the opportunity to provide feedback on the identified goals throughout the school day.

**Sample DPF Form Skeet Ulrich's Daily Progess Feedback Form**

| PERIOD | GOAL 1: USING APPROPRIATE LANGUAGE IN APPROPRIATE TONE | GOAL 2: KEEPING HANDS AND FEET TO SELF | GOAL 3: RAISING HAND AND BEING RECOGNIZED BEFORE SPEAKING OUT | SIGN-OFF |
|---|---|---|---|---|
| Arrival/Morning Activities 8:10–8:30 | | | | |
| Reading Group and Follow-Up Activities 8:30–9:45 | | | | |
| Written Language 9:50–11:00 | | | | |
| Speech/PE 11:05–11:45 | | | | |
| Lunch 11:50–12:30 | | | | |
| Math 12:35–1:35 | | | | |
| SS/Science/Activity Time 1:40–2:45 | | | | |
| End-of-Day Activities 2:50–3:10 | | | | |

## Keep in Mind

Teachers often use check-in, connect, and check-out systems in conjunction with token and point systems. It is therefore essential that teachers plan programs with "fading" in mind. Teachers should view the fading of specialized supports as celebratory and should recognize appropriate behavior maintenance recognized through school and classroom events. For students who do not respond to these programs, teachers often need to conduct an in-depth functional behavioral assessment in order to supplement or adapt intervention procedures.

**Key References**

Cheney, D., Lynass, L., Flower, A., Waugh, M., Iwaszuk, W., Mielenz, C., & Hawken, L. (2010). The Check, Connect, and Expect Program: A targeted, tier 2 intervention in the schoolwide positive behavior support model. *Preventing School Failure, 54*(3), 152–158.

Crone, D. A., Horner, R., & Hawken, L. S. (2004). *Responding to behavior in schools: The Behavior Education Program.* New York: Guilford.

Hawken, L. S. (2006). School psychologists as leaders in the implementation of a targeted intervention: The Behavior Education Program. *School Psychology Quarterly, 21*(1), 91–111.

Lehr, C. A., Sinclair, M. F., & Christenson, S. L. (2004). Addressing student engagement and truancy prevention during the elementary years: A replication study of the Check & Connect model. *Journal of Education for Students Placed at Risk, 9*(3), 279–301.

# BEHAVIORAL CONTRACTS

## Rationale

Behavioral contracts are formal, tangible documents that clearly specify the specific elements of an individualized behavior change program. They are advantageous because they allow students to work at their own pace and, most importantly, remain involved in the planning and ongoing monitoring of interventions. Well-planned behavioral contracts also guide students in realistic goal setting and help those who lack motivation to attain fair, reasonable, and worthwhile benchmarks.

## Step-by-Step

**1** *Meet with the student to discuss the need for the contract and the advantages of mutual negotiation.*

**2** *Define the specific behaviors required of the student.*

- State in positive, observable, and measurable terms all elements of the expected behaviors.
- Articulate contract criteria such as starting and ending dates as well as daily time periods and locations in which contract provisions will be enforced.
- Ensure that student goals are reasonable and attainable and, if necessary, open to renegotiation.
- Consider including a bonus clause for students who "overachieve" and/or a penalty clause for those who fail to meet the contract's conditions in a timely fashion.

**3** *Negotiate contract reinforcers.*

- Identify privileges that the student would like to attain.
- Negotiate a point system in which cumulative instances of appropriate behavior lead to the reinforcer.
- Consider adding in bonus clauses for exceptionally high rates of compliance to contract criteria.

**4** *Formalize the contract and monitor data.*

- Put all negotiated elements in writing.
- Develop a plan to monitor how the contract is working.
- Sign the document.
- Share the contract with parents and school administrators.

## Applications and Examples

A sample generic behavioral contract follows. Note that the contract (1) is stated in positive terms, (2) promotes success through modest gradations of behavior change, (3) provides frequent and predictable reinforcement, and (4) reflects that the conditions were developed through negotiations between the teacher and student.

## Keep in Mind

Because contracts work on a "delayed-payoff" system, you will need to gauge how long students are willing to go without reinforcement. Students having to wait too long often dooms well-developed contracts. Also, during the negotiation phase, students are likely to overestimate what they can accomplish during the contract period. It is often necessary to review the behavioral criteria expected of students to ensure that modest degrees of success can be attained. Finally, like many behavioral techniques, contracts may take some time to "kick in." Some students will test the system and will need time to trust that the adults are truly interested in helping them succeed rather than just developing another technique for highlighting their shortcomings.

**Key References**

Hall, R. V., & Hall, M. C. (1982). *How to negotiate a behavioral contract.* Lawrence, KS: H & H Enterprises.

Lovett, T. C. (1995). *Tactics for teaching.* Upper Saddle River, NJ: Merrill/Pearson Education.

Rhode, G., Jenson, W. R., & Reavis, H. K. (1993). *The tough kid book: Practical classroom management strategies.* Longmont, CO: Sopris West.

Sprick, R., Sprick, M., & Garrison, M. (1993). *Interventions: Goal setting and contracting.* Longmont, CO: Sopris West.

Yell, M. (2009). Classroom and behavior management II: Responding to behavioral skills instruction and generalization strategies. In M. L. Yell, N. B. Meadows, E. Drasgow, & J. G. Shriner (Eds.), *Evidence-based practices for educating students with emotional and behavioral disorders* (pp. 261–281). Upper Saddle River, NJ: Merrill/Pearson.

**FUNCTION-BASED THINKING, FUNCTIONAL BEHAVIOR ASSESSMENTS, AND BEHAVIOR INTERVENTION PLANS**

## Rationale

Function-based thinking (FBT) is designed to serve the needs of students who are not responding to universal interventions but whose behaviors have not yet evolved to the point of requiring intensive intervention. When faced with students who repeatedly misbehave and fail to respond to typical management structures, teachers use FBT to consider the function of the presenting behavior and plan a classroom-based intervention accordingly. The goal is to identify possible linkages between student behavior and events/conditions in the immediate environment. Functional-based thinking is not designed as a replacement for functional behavior assessments (FBAs); it is a less intrusive and user-friendly examination of how a student's behavior problem may be caused and sustained by classroom events (Hershfeldt, Rosenberg, & Bradshaw, 2010; Park, 2007). Although similar in approach, FBAs are more powerful problem-solving processes that teachers use when students do not respond to FBT-based generic interventions. Often, FBAs require a team of professionals to collaborate in observation and data analysis. The outcome of the FBA process is the development of a behavior intervention plan (BIP) that focuses on the simultaneous strengthening and reduction of target behaviors identified by the FBA.

## Step-by-Step

**1** *Engage in functional-based thinking by using the ERASE strategy to understand the relationship between presenting problem behavior and the school/classroom environment* (Park, 2007; Scott et al., 2010).

- **E**xplain the presenting problem behavior by identifying it and specifying events that occur before and after it.
- **R**eason: Hypothesize what the student may be gaining or avoiding by the problem behavior. Specifically consider antecedents to the behavior and the outcomes of the behavior. This leads to identification of possible functions (e.g., attention, avoidance, etc.) of the behavior.
- **A**ppropriate: Identify the appropriate behaviors that will take the place of the problem behavior. Ensure that the desired behaviors to be taught and/or reinforced serve the same function as the problem behavior but are suitable for the classroom environment.
- **S**upport: Identify the instructional accommodations, behavioral interventions, and implementation supports necessary to prompt and sustain the developing appropriate behavior.
- **E**valuate: Define criteria for success, and evaluate the success of your efforts.

**2** *For more intensive behavioral problems and those behaviors that remain unresponsive to generic targeted interventions, conduct a functional behavior assessment.* Effective FBAs can be conducted through a five-step process (Center for Effective Collaboration and Practice, 1998; McConnell, Hilvitz, & Cox, 1998; Rosenberg et al., 2008; Ryan, Halsey, & Matthews, 2003; Shippen, Simpson, & Crites, 2003):

- *Step 1: Describe and assess the significance of the behavior.* Consider how much the student's behavior differs from that of his classmates, whether it is chronic and a threat to others, and whether the behavior may be a function of a cultural difference.
- *Step 2: Refine the definition of the problem behavior.* Enhance your knowledge of the behavior by noting (1) when and where the behavior occurs; (2) the conditions (e.g., certain students present or during large-group instruction) in which the behavior occurs; (3) activities that occur both before and after the behavior; and (4) common setting events—situations or contexts that can influence behavioral events (e.g., when late to school, after missing breakfast).
- *Step 3: Collect and analyze information on the environment, setting demands, and possible functions of the problem behavior.* Employ multiple methods to collect information on the behavior and the student. Useful artifacts include archival records, evidence of academic work, interviews with parents and relevant school personnel, descriptions of instructional and social environments, and direct observations. Characterize the behavior of interest by function or whether the problem is a skill deficit (not knowing how to behave) or a

performance deficit (knowing how to behave but not performing it under specific conditions).

- *Step 4: Generate a hypothesis statement and plan for intervention.* Develop a concise summary of information, focusing on factors surrounding the student's behavior, including both the antecedents and consequences. The hypothesis—a best guess as to why the behavior is occurring—guides the development of the intervention.
- *Step 5: Develop, implement, and evaluate the intervention plan.* Develop an intervention plan that includes positive behavior-change strategies, program modifications, and behavior supports necessary to address the problem behavior. Implement the plan with fidelity, and collect data consistently on the targeted behavior in order to evaluate the efficacy of your intervention plan.

**3** *Develop behavior intervention plans that simultaneously strengthen and reduce targeted behaviors* through the application of behavioral techniques, self-management and self-control, and student independence. As suggested by Gable and colleagues (2001), plans should include activities that:

- Teach acceptable replacement behaviors that serve a similar function as the inappropriate behavior.
- Teach students to cope with typical and difficult-to-alter settings or events such as the physical arrangement of the classroom, scheduling, and classmates.
- Replace antecedents that may prompt the occurrence of the problem behavior with events that set the occasion for appropriate behaviors.
- Employ positive consequences that reinforce desired behaviors.

## Applications and Examples

Albert (2003) provides a useful framework for understanding the functions or goals of student misbehavior. Students often choose to misbehave in order to get attention, exercise power, obtain revenge, or avoid failure. In Table 15.4, we define these functions of misbehavior and indicate how knowledge of these goals is the first step in designing successful interventions.

**Table 15.4**   Understanding the Goals of Misbehavior

| | Attention-Seeking Behavior | Power Behavior |
|---|---|---|
| Active Characteristics | Student does all kinds of behaviors that distract teacher and classmates. | *Temper tantrums and verbal tantrums:* Student is disruptive and confrontive. |
| Passive Characteristics | Student exhibits one-pea-at-a-time behavior, operates on slow, slower, slowest speeds. | *Quiet noncompliance:* Student does his or her own thing, yet often is pleasant and even agreeable. |
| Students' Legitimate Needs | Positive recognition. | Personal autonomy. |
| Silver Lining | Student wants a relationship with the teacher (and classmates). | Student exhibits leadership potential, assertiveness, and independent thinking. |
| | **Revenge Behavior** | **Avoidance-of-Failure Behavior** |
| Active Characteristics | *Physical and psychological attacks:* Student is hurtful to teacher, classmates, or both. | *Frustration tantrum:* Student loses control when pressure to succeed becomes too intense. |
| Passive Characteristics | Student is sullen and withdrawn, refusing overtures of friendship. | Student procrastinates, fails to complete projects, develops temporary incapacity, or assumes behaviors that resemble a learning disability. |
| Students' Legitimate Needs | Safety and security. | Success. |
| Silver Lining | Student shows a spark of life by trying to protect self from further hurt. | Student may want to succeed if [he or she] can be assured of not making mistakes and of achieving some status. For some severely discouraged students, there is no silver lining. |

*Source:* Reprinted with permission from L. Albert. (2003). *Cooperative discipline: A teacher's handbook* (pp. 178–179). Circle Pines, MN: AGS Publishing.

## Keep in Mind

As you approach the FBT, FBA, and BIP processes, don't be overwhelmed by the variety of methods and the host of instruments, tools, and techniques used to obtain critical information. If you experience any confusion, remember that, regardless of the professional jargon employed, the key element in the process is simply *identifying factors that may contribute to a student's misbehavior*. Once identified, you can develop a realistic positive intervention plan that includes program modifications, direct instruction, behavior-change strategies, and behavioral supports needed to sustain desired changes in behavior.

**Key References**

Center for Effective Collaboration and Practice. (1998). *Functional behavioral assessment*. Retrieved June 6, 2011, from http://cecp.air.org/fba/problembehavior/main.htm

Chandler, L. K., & Dahlquist, C. M. (2002). *Functional assessment: Strategies to prevent and remediate challenging behaviors in school settings*. Upper Saddle River, NJ: Merrill/Pearson Education.

Hershfeldt, P. A., Rosenberg, M. S., & Bradshaw, C. P. (2010). Function-based thinking: A systematic way of thinking about function and its role in changing student behavior problems. *Beyond Behavior, 19*(3), 12–21.

Park, K. L. (2007). Facilitating effective team-based functional behavioral assessments in typical school settings. *Beyond Behavior, 17*(1), 21–31.

Scott, T. M., Liaupsin, C. J., Nelson, C. M., & Jolivette, K. (2003). Ensuring student success through team-based functional behavioral assessment. *Teaching Exceptional Children, 35*(5), 16–21.

Shippen, M. E., Simpson, R. G., & Crites, S. A. (2003). A practical guide to functional behavioral assessment. *Teaching Exceptional Children, 35*, 36–44.

| Strategy 15.8 | **DIRECT TEACHING OF SOCIAL SKILLS: SOCIAL STORIES** |

## Rationale

*Social stories* are short, simple narratives written from the perspective of the student. They explicitly highlight a course of action for students to take when they encounter challenging social situations. Generally, the stories comprise concrete, developmentally appropriate cues, thoughts, and responses typical of targeted social situations, using six specific types of statements:

- *Descriptions:* Information centering on contextual factors such as the setting, required actions, and participants
- *Directives:* Descriptions of desired actions in response to social cues or specific situations
- *Perspectives:* Descriptions of the feelings and reactions of others in the social situation
- *Affirmations:* Statements that reassure the student by reinforcing the desired action
- *Control statements:* Words that assist the student to recall important information
- *Cooperative statements:* Descriptions of how assistance will be provided.

Teachers use social stories to teach a range of social behaviors, including sportsmanship, appropriate greeting behaviors, reducing talking out during lessons, and minimizing frustration during homework time.

## Step-by-Step

**1** *Identify the target behaviors in need of intervention.*

- Assess behaviors needed by students for success in the classroom, including getting along with others, controlling anger, following directions, responding to others, requests, and using free time appropriately.
- Consult family members to assist in prioritizing social behavior needs.

**2** *Identify the key features of the problematic social situation.*

- Identify where the situation occurs, who is involved, and what occurs, as well as how it starts and ends.
- Survey teachers and relevant service providers to ascertain what is prompting and maintaining the problem behaviors.
- Interview the student regarding her views of the situation.

**3** *Write the social story.*

- Create the story from the perspective of the student.
- Emphasize the behavioral steps needed to address the presenting social situation.
- Consider the comprehension level of the student and include descriptions, directives, perspectives, affirmations, control sentences, and cooperative sentences.
- Ensure that the emphasis of the story is on description rather than direction.
- Consider integrating social networking environments into the training (e.g., Morgan, 2010).
- Use visuals whenever possible.

**4** *Evaluate the effectiveness of the social story.*

- Have the student respond to questions about what she will do the next time the situation occurs.
- Monitor the student's behavior in natural social situations.

## Applications and Examples

Following is a sample social story adapted from Toplis and Hadwin (2006) to teach appropriate lunchtime behaviors. Note that elements of the story are more descriptive and affirmative than directive.

**Sample Social Story: Things to Do at Lunchtime**

The buzzer for lunch goes at ten past twelve. It rings three times. (Descriptive)

That means we go to our seats and sit down. (Descriptive)

When everyone at my table is sitting, our teacher tells us to go. We can wash our hands in the sink at the back of the room if we have been doing messy stuff. (Descriptive)

The locker area is busy with lots of children. We get our lunch boxes there. (Descriptive)
Some children are talking to each other. (Descriptive)
I try to walk past them and into the dining room. Sometimes I say "excuse me" and wait for them to move. (Directive)
I sit at table number three by the door. (Descriptive)
Eating lunch is good. (Affirmative)
Then it is time for play. Playtime is a good time to spread out and get rid of my energy that builds up when I am sitting. (Descriptive and Affirmative)
In the playground, many children run and shout. They are loud because they are having fun. (Descriptive and Perspective)

## Keep in Mind

Smaller-scale evaluations of social story interventions have been generally positive, and the popularity of the technique among teachers is growing (e.g., Sansoti et al., 2004; Toplis & Hadwin, 2006). However, several recent research efforts (e.g., Chan et al., 2011; Reynhout & Carter, 2011) have raised questions regarding the immediate effect of the intervention on student behavior and, more important, how well modest outcomes generalize to other settings and maintain over time. Consequently, consider this caution: Social stories should not be the *only* social-skills intervention introduced to students. Teachers should implement social stories only in tandem with other evidence-based instructional practices (Sansoti et al., 2004).

### Key References

Crozier, S., & Tincani, M. J. (2005). Using a modified social story to decrease disruptive behavior of a child with autism. *Focus on Autism and Other Developmental Disabilities, 20*(3), 150–157.

Gray, C. A., & Garand, J. D. (1993). Social stories: Improving responses of students with autism with accurate social information. *Focus on Autistic Behavior, 8*(1) 1–10.

Kamps, D. (2010). Social skills instruction and generalization strategies. In B. Algozzine, A. P Daunic, & S. Smith (Eds.), *Preventing problem behaviors* (pp. 71–111). Thousand Oaks, CA: Corwin.

More, C. (2008). Digital stories targeting skills for children with disabilities: Multidimensional learning. *Intervention in School and Clinic, 43*(3), 168–177.

Sansoti, F. J., Powell-Smith, K. A., & Kincaid, D. (2004). A research synthesis of social story interventions for children with Autism Spectrum Disorders. *Focus on Autism and Other Developmental Disabilities, 19*(4), 194–204.

Toplis, R., & Hadwin, J. A. (2006). Using social stories to change problematic lunchtime behaviour in school. *Educational Psychology in Practice, 22*(1), 53–67.

# Using Technology to Support Inclusion

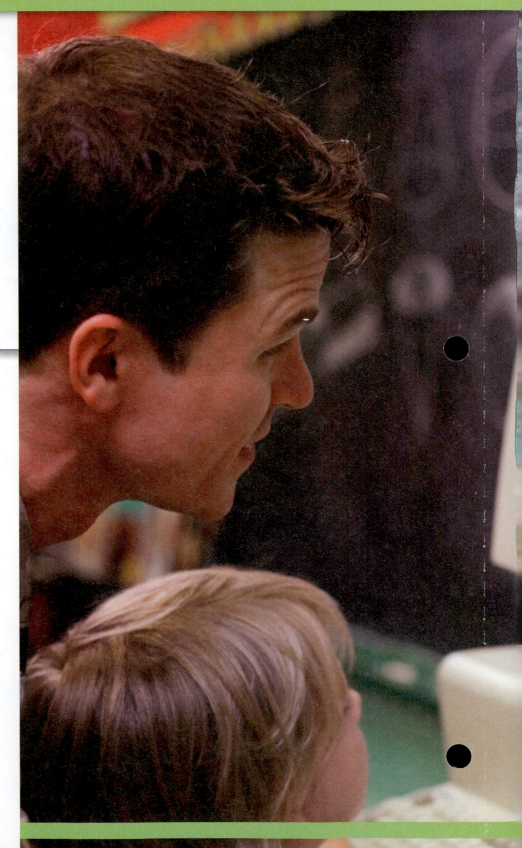

# A VIEW FROM AN ASSISTIVE TECHNOLOGY SPECIALIST

### Allison McMahon Explains How AT Facilitates Inclusion

Allison McMahon is the assistive technology (AT) resource teacher for Cecil County, Maryland, the home county of Gilpin Manor Elementary School. She started her career as an adaptive physical education teacher, but in the 1990s she attended several workshops on assistive technology and, in her words, she "was hooked." As the assistive technology resource teacher for the county, Allison works with students with disabilities who might benefit from AT devices and services.

Because Cecil County is committed to inclusion, Allison sees a big part of her job as finding ways to use assistive technology devices so that students can have better access to the general curriculum. How does AT facilitate inclusion? "Well," Allison says, "I believe that with kids in general education classrooms, I think that the use of assistive technology facilitates access to the curriculum. I mean, its basically what my job is—to help kids access the curriculum through the use of AT—to try to close the gap. Or for some kids, to modify the curriculum so that they're still following the curriculum but it's at an appropriate level for them. We try to modify the materials so that teachers can use them." Allison points out that many assistive technology devices enable students to be more involved in learning. For example, "If they have Kurzweil or Victor Reader to use to have text read aloud . . . that builds independence and [the students] don't have to have a person sitting next to them."

Providing students with effective AT devices and services requires a carefully planned process. Allison explained this process: "With assistive technology, we try to follow a protocol so if a teacher has a student who she feels would benefit from assistive technology, she fills out a consultation request form. Either the teacher fills it out and sends it to me or the special education building coordinator at the school will send it to me. Sometimes it's generated right at the IEP meeting by the IEP team. The team lists what assistive technology the student is currently using and what assistive technology might benefit the student, whether it be for written expression, communication, or whatever. And that kind of gives me a background of the student and I can follow up from there and go make observations and spend time with the student."

There are many different types of assistive technology devices and Allison collaborates with teachers and other professionals to find the best fit for each student. "When we're working with students, we try to use a team approach whenever possible. . . . If it's a written expression issue, the teacher and the occupational specialist and myself might get together and talk about that student. Or if it's a communication issue, the speech pathologist and [I] will meet."

The value of Allison's work with her team members recently was realized when Ryley, a little boy with autism spectrum disorders (previously introduced in Chapter 8) began using an iPod with a communication application called Proloquo2Go. His progress on the device was so fast that his mother was overwhelmed. Allison described the mom's reaction: "It's pretty amazing when somebody's mother, and I'd never met Ryley's mom, . . . [came up to me] at a parent resource fair, and she [was] crying and gave me a hug. You know, it was just—I mean, that's the kind of stuff that just makes you feel that what you're doing is so important. So, yeah, Ryley is a huge success story."

## MyEducationLab

Visit the MyEducationLab for *Inclusion* to enhance your understanding of chapter concepts with a personalized Study Plan. You'll also have the opportunity to hone your teaching skills through video and case-based Assignments and Activities, Building Teaching Skills and Disposition lessons, and IRIS Case Studies.

# Introduction

The use of technology to help students learn to communicate, or have more success in their academic work, or for various other reasons, can be powerful, as Allison McMahon described. But this may not be much of a surprise to most people because today's world has simply become saturated with technology. We would guess that it's probably hard for many young adults today to remember a time without all the convenience brought to us by modern technology: We talk and text on our cell phones to friends and family between classes, watch Web-based presentations while sitting in the student union, listen to our iPods while exercising, and use our laptops or iPads to buy e-tickets for a trip to a sunny place for spring break. We play electronic games with our fingers while sitting down and do arithmetic problems with calculators on our cell phones. MapQuest and the GPS on our dashboards mean never having to ask for directions again; but these will soon be outdated because our smart phones will have the apps we need to show us where we are and how to get to where we are going. People who previously earned a living typing term papers have mostly gone out of business, and if we don't have time to read, there are plenty of audio books that we can download and listen to while driving home.

New personal technology devices are appearing faster than we can learn how to use the ones we have, and the Internet puts just about every kind of information only a few mouse clicks away. Because technology makes so many tasks so much easier and faster, because we can do things sooner rather than later, and because so much of our work and play is of a higher quality, we readily pursue the benefits technology provides. In a recent study of college students, Kvavik (2011) found that more than 93% of the students owned a computer, all students accessed the Internet, and almost all used applications primarily for education and communication.

Given the ubiquity of technology and the roles it plays in people's lives, it cannot be surprising that technology can also fill an important role in the lives and learning of public school students, especially those with special needs. For many of these students, technology can provide a shortcut to learning and participation that otherwise would be even more challenging without it.

## Pause & Reflect

What type of technology devices do you and your friends use? Do these devices and the connections they allow make your communication and learning easier? How would your student and social life be different without them? How would you survive?

Technology makes life more convenient.

# Educational Technology and Assistive Technology

Because of the rapid growth of technology, we understand that in a book on inclusion, a chapter devoted specifically to this topic is essential. Although various chapters in the book have alluded to different technology programs, we believe that separate treatment of the topic will help teachers realize the powerful tools that are emerging to help students with special needs be more successful learners. As you begin or continue your work as a teacher, we want you to be supportive of students in your classroom who have disabilities or exhibit special learning needs. We want these students, like others, to succeed in both the classroom and throughout the school. Whether you are trying to help a student develop basic literacy or math skills, write a daily journal, create a report, or navigate a wheelchair through your classroom, technology can help you and your students be more successful.

**Educational technology** is a term used for technology that is used in general educational systems for all students, including students with disabilities. On the other hand, **assistive technology devices** are specifically designed devices that meet unique needs of students with disabilities (i.e., those who have met the eligibility criteria for special education services under IDEA). Students who use assistive technology devices, and often their teachers and parents, are also provided *assistive technology services* to help them use the devices correctly and effectively.

In this section, we will examine some types of educational technology and assistive technology devices. Then, in the next section, we will discuss principles for using these technologies effectively and also discuss the principles of **universal design for learning (UDL)**, an approach to designing instructional materials, usually using technology, so that more students may have access to them.

## Types of Educational Technology

There is a wide selection of educational technology tools that may assist teachers in the classroom. The following types are commonly used in schools and classrooms and will often be helpful to students with special needs.

### Interactive Whiteboards (Smart Boards)

One of the more popular teaching tools used in schools today is the interactive whiteboard, the most common of which is the Smart Board (http://smarttech.com/smartboard). Smart Boards are particularly useful because, unlike individual computers or other devices (iPods or iPads), teachers can use them to work with groups of students because of the large screen. They let teachers project digital material from their computers (including from the Internet, PowerPoints, or documents) onto the whiteboard and allow teachers and students to write or draw on the board to add to the projected material, to highlight it, to emphasize certain points, or to change it. The Smart Board tends to easily gain students' attention and then lets the teacher make important points. Students can also "write" on the Smart Board to show an answer or demonstrate that they understand something. Smart Boards can be used in a variety of curriculum areas.

### Drill-and-Practice Software

Unlike the Smart Board, most educational applications are delivered through individual computers. Drill-and-practice software is presented this way and provides individual learners with the opportunity to increase instructional time working on specific academic skills such as computing arithmetic answers, solving math word problems, or learning letter–sound correspondence. These applications often use interesting formats to keep

Smart Boards can increase student collaboration and engagement.

students' attention, present instructional items sequentially, and provide feedback either by telling the student the response is correct or by giving the student an opportunity to correct an incorrect response. Students may stop the program at any point and resume where they left off at their next session. Instructional games are similar to drill-and-practice software, except they have game formats and rules and allow students to compete with themselves or each other.

### Integrated Learning Systems

Integrated learning systems are more comprehensive instructional programs that educators may network throughout a school or school district. They are intended to incorporate instruction for an entire range of objectives tied to national, state, or district standards. According to Bitter and Legacy (2008), these systems are "generally intended to stand alone as a sole source of instruction" (p. 179). The material is presented in a linear format, and as with drill-and-practice software, the student may proceed at his or her own pace. The system manages data on student performance, and reports can be generated for teachers, schools, or school districts to monitor the progress of students. Although integrated learning systems software purports to offer complete instruction, most students, especially those with special needs, will need support from teachers in order to achieve academic success.

### Reading and Math Programs

Students with disabilities and special needs in regular classrooms, as well as some other students, will often need more intense instruction in two areas: reading and math. A number of commercially available, technology-based or technology-enhanced programs can help teachers in these areas. These programs usually cover several grades, are sequentially presented, and allow the student to progress at his or her own pace. Most of them also assess the student's progress through the program. Although we cannot tell you about all such programs, Figure 16.1 provides some examples of popular commercial technology products for teaching reading and math skills.

## Types of Assistive Technology Devices

Whereas the purpose of educational technology is to provide teachers with tools to help students learn or improve academic knowledge and skills, the purpose of **assistive technology** is to help students who lack specific skills or abilities engage in activities that they otherwise could not do or could not do very well. For example, a student who cannot read may listen to an audio book; someone who can't speak could use an **augmentative or alternative communication (AAC)** device; and a student who has poor writing skills could use word processing to write an essay. As you can certainly imagine, assistive technology and educational technology often overlap. For example, word processing software can be considered assistive technology because it helps improve written output for a student with writing difficulties, but it might also help the student learn how to spell or use better grammar and thus be considered educational technology.

According to IDEA 2004, an AT device is "any item, piece of equipment, or product system, whether acquired commercially off the shelf, modified, or customized, that is used to increase, maintain, or improve functional capabilities of a child with a disability" (*excluding* "a medical device that is surgically implanted, or the replacement of such device") (IDEA 2004, Section 602). Additionally, the law does not simply recognize the importance of AT devices but also the critical need for providing AT services that are discussed later.

Thousands of AT devices are available, far too many to completely list, so the selection of the type of device a student may need, or a specific AT device, can be challenging. One way to determine the sort of device that would be useful is to consider different learning needs of a student and then think of the type of AT device that might be useful (Best, Reed, & Bigge, 2005; Wisconsin Assistive Technology Initiative, 2004). In the following sections, we discuss the types of AT devices available and how they help meet students' needs.

| Figure 16.1 | Commercially Available Educational Software for Teaching Reading and Math Skills |
|---|---|
| **Reading and Math Programs and Purposes** ||
| Destination Reading Series by Riverdeep | Four courses cover emergent literacy, phonemic awareness, fluency, comprehension, and vocabulary. For grades pre-K–8. |
| Waterford Early Reading Program by Waterford | Systematic and explicit instruction in phonemic awareness, phonics, text comprehension, vocabulary, print concepts, readiness skills, writing, and oral fluency provide a comprehensive foundation for reading. For grades pre-K–2. |
| PLATO Elementary Language Arts by PLATO Learning | An online language arts curriculum for elementary students develops skills in reading, writing, speaking, and listening. For grades K–6. |
| Academy of Reading by School Specialty | An online reading program helps students who are at risk and English language learners achieve rapid, permanent gains in reading. For grades 2–12. |
| Leap Track Reading Pro by Leap Frog School | Multisensory instruction, direct instruction, and high-interest nonfiction text develop reading comprehension, word knowledge, and vocabulary skills. For grades 3–8. |
| READ 180—Next Generation by Scholastic | Individualized instruction is provided in areas of phonemic and phonological awareness, fluency, vocabulary, comprehension, spelling, and writing. For elementary–high school. |
| Achieve Now Mathematics by PLATO Learning | Over 2,100 hours of instruction are provided in math skills with over 1,000 learning objectives. For grades K–6. |
| iPass by iLearn | A fully automated, Web-based math curriculum and instruction system provides individualized instruction to meet the identified needs of each student. For grades 3–8. |
| Cognitive Tutor Algebra by Carnegie Learning | A combination of collaborative, student-centered textbook lessons and adaptive Cognitive Tutor software lessons are provided. |
| PLATO Algebra 1 by PLATO Learning | An online curriculum aligns to the Common Core state standards as well as supports the Standards for Mathematical Practice. |

### Assistive Technology Devices to Support Reading

In the area of reading, technology may help students by providing them with visual and auditory supports. Technology can highlight certain words to improve visual discrimination, provide picture cues, and even convert written text to speech that the student can listen to. Using text-to-speech software, and compatible hardware, students can scan printed materials and read using digitalized speech, a great support for students with significant reading difficulties. Programs can also modify the speed of the reading, spell words for students, or even read in different languages or different voices. E-books and e-texts can be downloaded to help students with reading difficulties acquire content that they might otherwise not be able to access (Beard, Carpenter & Johnston, 2011). Figure 16.2 provides a list of AT reading resources to assist students with reading difficulties.

**Pause & Reflect**

Do you prefer to read a book or to listen to an audio version? Can you imagine what you would choose if you experienced serious reading problems? E-books can open a big world to many people who have difficulty reading print due to learning disabilities or visual disabilities.

### Assistive Technology Devices to Support Writing and Spelling

Technologies also can help students who have difficulty writing and spelling. If handwriting presents a challenge to students and it is important for the student to improve this skill,

| **Figure 16.2** | **Assistive Technology Reading Resources** |
|---|---|
| **Edmark Reading Program**<br>http://www.donjohnston.com/catalog/edmarkdtxt.htm | This software uses a whole word, multisensory approach to teach comprehension and recognition. Users of this software learn sight recognition and meaning of a word, practice comprehension, and use the word in story content. Repetition and short instructional steps are used. |
| **Homework Wiz Plus and Speaking Homework Wiz**<br>http://www.donjohnston.com/catalog/homeworkd.htm | Franklin's nonspeaking speller and dictionary program helps students spell-check words and includes 40,000 basic definitions. Confusable Checker helps students distinguish homophones to make correct word choices. The Speaking Homework Wiz allows students to enter a word phonetically, then the correct spelling will be displayed along with an audio pronunciation of the word. |
| **IntelliTools Reading: Balanced Literacy**<br>http://www.intellitools.com/Products/Balanced_Literacy | This is a nine-unit program that provides literacy instruction at the first-grade skill level. It incorporates reading, phonics, and writing. Included are 142 lessons, nine full-color storybooks, 212 phonics activities, a CD with more than 500 activities, and 27 structured writing exercises. This program uses a mouse and IntelliKeys. |
| **Key Skills for Reading: Letters and Words**<br>http://store.sunburst.com/Search.aspx? | Five multilevel activities provide animated practice. Students learn the order of the alphabet, to organize words and objects by initial consonant sounds, to identify short and long vowel sounds, and lots more. The program has clear auditory support to help in reading success. |
| **Kurzweil 3000**<br>http://www.kurzweiledu.com/products_k3000win_features.asp | Kurzweil offers printed or electronic text for the computer screen with visual and audible assistance. The program includes many features to help with study skills, writing, and test taking. It adapts to each learning style. Kurzweil 3000 offers an audible assistant to help with spell-checking and word prediction as students type. |
| **WYNN 3.1 Freedom Scientific's Learning Systems Group**<br>http://freedomscientific.com | This software solution transforms printed text into understandable text and reads it aloud while simultaneously highlighting it. |
| **Let's Go Read**<br>http://www.sunburst-store.com/cgi-bin/sunburst.storefront/EN/Catalog/1244 | Lessons offered in this software help students learn to read through interactive stories and sequenced lessons. Vocabulary skills are expanded, as is comprehension. |
| **Picture It**<br>http://www.slatersoftware.com/pit.html | This software includes more than 6,000 pictures that can be incorporated to text so that the reader can see picture-supported material to better understand the text. Students can listen to stories and read along with highlighted words. |

| | |
|---|---|
| **Quicktionary II, Reading Pen II**<br>http://www.donjohnston.com/<br>catalog/quicktionarytxt.htm | These handheld scanners allow students to simply scan over a word that is not understood. The word is then read out loud back to the student and the dictionary definition is provided. |
| **ScreenReader**<br>http://www.brighteye.com/texthelp.htm | Allows a PC to read out loud words that appear in any Windows-based application. |
| **Recordings for the Blind and Dyslexic**<br>http://www.rfbd.org | RFB&D's library contains more than 104,000 titles in a broad variety of subjects, from literature and history to math and sciences, at all academic levels, from kindergarten through postgraduate and professional. |
| **SoothSayer Word Prediction**<br>http://www.enablemart.com/<br>productdetail.aspx?store-10&<br>pid-356&dept-22 | Many features of this program help students type more accurately and more quickly. AutoType completes a word once the student starts to type it. SoothSayer can correct spelling errors and also comes with a built-in dictionary of more than 11,000 words. A speech voice option is available. |
| **TextHelp Read and Write Gold**<br>http://www.brighteye.com/texthelp.htm | This software offers a range of helpful tools for special education in reading and writing. Some of these include word prediction, dictionary, spell-checker, RealSpeak voice providing a humanlike voice, and a pronunciation tutor. |
| **WordSmith**<br>http://www.brighteye.com/texthelp.htm | WordSmith provides visual reinforcement and helps to develop recognition of new words and vocabulary through color highlights and reading of words, sentences, and paragraphs. WordSmith helps with pronunciation as it breaks words into syllables, and it includes a moving mouth to aid in more accurate speech. Also included are word prediction, spell-checker, thesaurus, and homonym support. |
| **CAST eReader**<br>http://www.cast.org | This text-to-speech software tool is designed to support users who have difficulty reading. |

*Source:* Reprinted from L. A. Beard, L. B. Carpenter, & L. J. Johnston. (2011). *Assistive technology: Access for all students* (2nd ed., pp. 75–76). Upper Saddle River, NJ: Merrill/Pearson. Used with permission.

then various low-tech to high-tech approaches might be useful. Low-tech strategies can help structure the student's writing environment to produce better handwritten work. For example, securing the paper with a clipboard or tape, providing clear boundaries with heavy lines, or adapting the writing tool by using pencil grips might be helpful. Occupational therapists can usually offer assistance to teachers to help in this area. If the student will be better facilitated by using a keyboard to write, the student can use a personal computer or portable word processor. Students can travel with these devices and use them to produce written work whenever necessary (Beard et al., 2011).

Besides circumventing handwriting problems, word processing can also be helpful in other ways. Many students with mild disabilities will have difficulty using spelling and grammar correctly to produce written documents. To help them overcome this challenge, word processing can provide spell checking and grammar checking and can facilitate editing a paper by providing tools such as cutting, copying, and pasting. Related hardware and software can also be helpful. Handheld devices can help students find and correct spelling errors and define words. Word prediction software aids students who have difficulty spelling

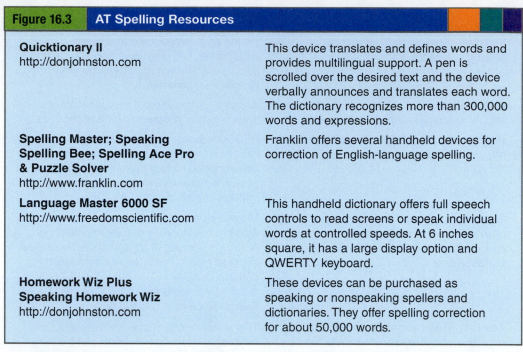

| Figure 16.3 | AT Spelling Resources |
| --- | --- |
| **Quicktionary II**<br>http://donjohnston.com | This device translates and defines words and provides multilingual support. A pen is scrolled over the desired text and the device verbally announces and translates each word. The dictionary recognizes more than 300,000 words and expressions. |
| **Spelling Master; Speaking Spelling Bee; Spelling Ace Pro & Puzzle Solver**<br>http://www.franklin.com | Franklin offers several handheld devices for correction of English-language spelling. |
| **Language Master 6000 SF**<br>http://www.freedomscientific.com | This handheld dictionary offers full speech controls to read screens or speak individual words at controlled speeds. At 6 inches square, it has a large display option and QWERTY keyboard. |
| **Homework Wiz Plus**<br>**Speaking Homework Wiz**<br>http://donjohnston.com | These devices can be purchased as speaking or nonspeaking spellers and dictionaries. They offer spelling correction for about 50,000 words. |

*Source:* Reprinted from L. A. Beard, L. B. Carpenter, & L. J. Johnston. (2011). *Assistive technology: Access for all students* (2nd ed., p. 77). Upper Saddle River, NJ: Merrill/Pearson. Used with permission.

a word by providing several words that might be meaningful in the context of the sentence. The students can then look at the list of words and select the one that is most appropriate. Technologies that are useful for helping students with spelling and writing appear in Figures 16.3 and 16.4.

### Assisstive Technology Devices to Support Math

Students who have difficulty with mathematics can also be helped by AT devices. These devices can help students whose challenges are associated with completing calculations or who have difficulty with problem solving due to language and comprehension problems. Students who have difficulty functioning due to weaknesses in basic calculations may use calculators to help them circumvent these problems. Students who must focus on solving more complex word problems will often find that using calculators will allow them to focus more on reasoning and less on arithmetic operations. Figure 16.5 lists several AT devices that will help students who have difficulty with math.

### Augmentative and Alternative Communication Devices

Some students, especially those with intellectual, physical, or multiple disabilities, require augmentative and alternative communication (AAC) devices to help compensate for their lack of verbal communication ability. Specially trained speech–language pathologists are best prepared to provide support for these students so they can learn to use these special AT devices. However, educators should also be aware of these students and their communicative needs and should know how to promote the use of the AAC devices so students can communicate effectively in natural environments.

Students may use a variety of AAC devices. These range from being fairly simple (producing single words) to being capable of producing synthesized speech. Examples of AAC devices include the following:

- Communication boards or books with pictures, objects, letters, and/or words
- Eye-gaze boards or frames
- Simple voice-output devices (e.g., BIGmack, Cheap Talk, Voice in a Box, MicroVoice, Talking Picture Frame)

| Figure 16.4 | AT Writing Resources |
|---|---|
| **Co:Writer**<br>http://www.donjohnston.com/catalog/cow4000d.htm | This program adds word prediction, grammar, and vocabulary to word processors. FlexSpell helps those students who spell phonetically by recognizing and predicting words consistent with the actual letters and sounds of the letters. Grammar support helps correct such errors as subject–verb agreement, spelling, customary word usage, and proper noun usage. |
| **EZ Keys**<br>http://www.freedomofspeech.com/wordsplus.html | Uses dual word prediction that displays a table of the six most frequently used words that begin with the letters that the student types when beginning to type a word. EZ Keys provides alternatives to using a mouse: expanded keyboard, joystick, single and multiple switch scanning. |
| **Gus! Word Prediction**<br>http://www.enablemart.com/productdetail.aspx?store-10&pid-576&dept-22 | Improves typing speed by offering word completion and word prediction. Offers a list of words based on what keys the user has already typed. The list changes according to keys typed and then predicts the current and the subsequent words. This helps slow or one-finger typists. Abbreviation expansion, speech output, and dictionary are also provided. |
| **WordQ Writing Aid Software**<br>http://www.enablemart.com/productdetail.aspx?store-10&pid-104&dept-22 | This writing tool is used with standard word processors. It provides spoken feedback and suggests words to use through word prediction. Students can hear each word spoken so that it is easier to differentiate words. It is simple to use and transparent to all Windows applications. |
| **Write:Outloud**<br>http://www.donjohnston.com/catalog/writoutd.htm | Immediate speech feedback is given as students type words, sentences, and paragraphs. Students can listen for proper word usage, grammar, and misspellings. Students with disabilities can correct their work independently from hearing and seeing what they write. |
| **Draft:Builder**<br>http://www.donjohnston.com | This tool leads students through three key steps in creating a first draft: organizing ideas, taking notes, and writing the draft. The display gives students a framework to generate, manipulate, and connect ideas and information. |

*Source:* Reprinted from L. A. Beard, L. B. Carpenter, & L. J. Johnston. (2011). *Assistive technology: Access for all students* (2nd ed., p. 79). Upper Saddle River, NJ: Merrill/Pearson. Used with permission.

- Voice-output devices with different communication levels (e.g., 6 Level Voice in a Box, Macaw, Digivox)
- Voice-output devices with icon sequencing (e.g., AlphaTalker II, Vanguard, Chatbox)
- Voice-output devices with dynamic display (e.g., Dynavox, Speaking Dynamically with laptop computer, Freestyle)
- Devices with speech synthesis for typing (e.g., Cannon Communicator, Link, Write: Out Loud with laptop) (Best et al., 2005)

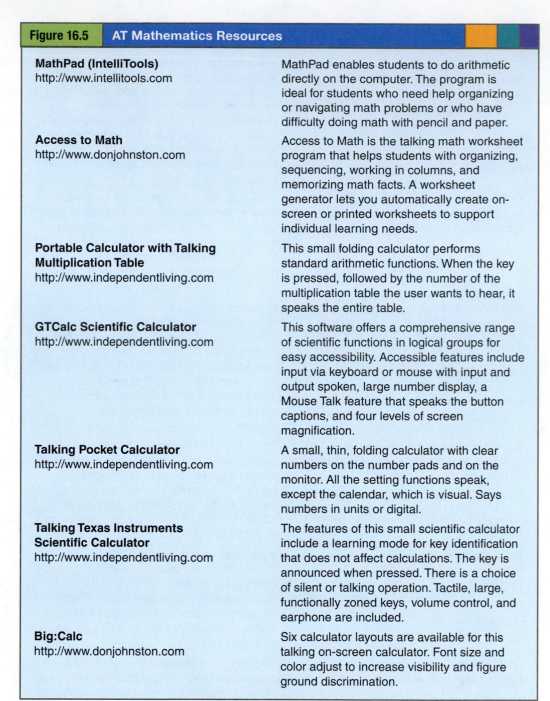

| Figure 16.5 | AT Mathematics Resources |
|---|---|
| **MathPad (IntelliTools)**<br>http://www.intellitools.com | MathPad enables students to do arithmetic directly on the computer. The program is ideal for students who need help organizing or navigating math problems or who have difficulty doing math with pencil and paper. |
| **Access to Math**<br>http://www.donjohnston.com | Access to Math is the talking math worksheet program that helps students with organizing, sequencing, working in columns, and memorizing math facts. A worksheet generator lets you automatically create on-screen or printed worksheets to support individual learning needs. |
| **Portable Calculator with Talking Multiplication Table**<br>http://www.independentliving.com | This small folding calculator performs standard arithmetic functions. When the key is pressed, followed by the number of the multiplication table the user wants to hear, it speaks the entire table. |
| **GTCalc Scientific Calculator**<br>http://www.independentliving.com | This software offers a comprehensive range of scientific functions in logical groups for easy accessibility. Accessible features include input via keyboard or mouse with input and output spoken, large number display, a Mouse Talk feature that speaks the button captions, and four levels of screen magnification. |
| **Talking Pocket Calculator**<br>http://www.independentliving.com | A small, thin, folding calculator with clear numbers on the number pads and on the monitor. All the setting functions speak, except the calendar, which is visual. Says numbers in units or digital. |
| **Talking Texas Instruments Scientific Calculator**<br>http://www.independentliving.com | The features of this small scientific calculator include a learning mode for key identification that does not affect calculations. The key is announced when pressed. There is a choice of silent or talking operation. Tactile, large, functionally zoned keys, volume control, and earphone are included. |
| **Big:Calc**<br>http://www.donjohnston.com | Six calculator layouts are available for this talking on-screen calculator. Font size and color adjust to increase visibility and figure ground discrimination. |

*Source:* Reprinted from L. A. Beard, L. B. Carpenter, & L. J. Johnston. (2011). *Assistive technology: Access for all students* (2nd ed., p. 81). Upper Saddle River, NJ: Merrill/Pearson. Used with permission.

Finding an appropriate AAC device for a student and teaching him how to use it are only the beginning to helping the student to achieve communicative success. Many students with AAC devices will be more successful if they have support and instruction to use the device in the classroom and other areas around the school and community.

## Personal Support Technologies

Handheld devices such as personal digital assistants (PDAs), iPhones, iPods, and iPads are becoming more and more popular as AT devices. Many people, for example, use their iPhones to help them manage personal needs. Depending on their specific capabilities, these devices can help with various chores such as managing an appointments calendar, writing documents, reading e-mails, accessing the Internet, or listening to downloaded books. Over the last several years, researchers have demonstrated that specially configured PDAs can help persons with intellectual disabilities perform various activities that they could do not alone or without extensive training (Wehmeyer, Palmer, Smith, Parent, Davies, & Stock, 2006). For example, in a 2003 study, individuals with intellectual disabilities used a palm-top computer called a Pocket Compass (designed by Wehmeyer and colleagues) to help them decide what steps they should take on vocational tasks that required decision making. The Pocket Compass was preprogrammed with audio and visual cues to remind participants what actions they should take (after initial instruction) at certain decision-making points in the task. For example, when the individual had to make a decision, the computer displayed up to four pictures, each representing a different possible decision at the decision-making point. As the pictures were displayed, an audio instruction stated, "Touch the picture on the screen that matches the number shown on the second page of the invoice" (Davies, Stock, & Wehmeyer, 2003, p. 184). When the individual tapped the number, the program continued to provide audio and visual cues to direct the participant to the appropriate action. Davies and co-workers (2003) found that study participants using the Pocket Compass required fewer prompts from their support person, had fewer decision errors, and had fewer errors on completing the steps in the task. Personal digital assistants have been used in various other studies to help students with intellectual disabilities learn vocational skills, transition skills, and domestic skills (e.g., Chihak, Kessler, & Alberto, 2007, 2008; Mechling, Gast, & Seid, 2009; Riffel et al., 2005).

Like PDAs, and maybe even more, we are beginning to see an increase in the use of iPods and iPads as AT devices. More and more apps are becoming available for iPods and iPads that allow them to function as effective AT devices (Shah, 2011). There are several advantages to using these devices over more traditional AT devices. They are lighter and therefore easier to handle, and the touch screen on the iPad is easier for many students with disabilities to interact with as compared to a keyboard and mouse. They are also less expensive and can accommodate a number of different applications, many of which are free or inexpensive. For example, Proloquo2Go, the communication app that was mentioned earlier in the chapter, costs a little under $200, which is not free, but more sophisticated communication systems will cost much more, some around $10,000 or more. For these reasons, many school districts around the country are now starting to purchase iPads for use by students with special needs (Kaufenberg, 2010; Shah, 2011). Sailers (2010) provides a list of iPod, iPad, and iPhone apps available for students with disabilities (see: http://www.scribd.com/doc/24470331/iPhone-iPad-and-iPod-touch-Apps-for-Special-Education). Additionally, a visit to Apple's special education Website will provide you with an up-to-date view of apps for students with disabilities (see: http://www.apple.com/education/special education/).

At Gilpin Manor Elementary School and throughout Cecil County, Maryland, iPods and iPads are used in several ways, according to Allison McMahon, the district's AT resource specialist. Allison reported, "The big trend this year has been using iPods and iPads. . . . We're using them in four different ways in our county. We're using them for academic support. We're using them for communication with a program called Proloquo2Go. We're using them in our STEP program, which is our student transition employability program. It's a program at our school of technology where students go for prevocational training and use the iPods with an app (for the students to learn different work skills) to become more independent. They can refer to the iPod instead of having to have a teacher right next to them to guide them to the next step. And then we're using them for kids who need social stories, like video social stories and also for students with autism who need to take breaks and . . . need [a] calming or some kind of sensory activity."

Personal devices like iPads can often serve as inexpensive AT devices.

**Assistive Technology Devices for Daily Living**

Many additional AT devices can help meet a variety of daily needs. Many of these will be useful for students with physical or multiple disabilities. These include devices for mobility, such as powered wheelchairs or scooters; or for activities of daily living, such as adaptive eating utensils or adapted toothbrushes. To review many of the available AT devices that can be useful for students with disabilities, you can visit ABLEDATA at www.abledata.com, a Website that provides information about thousands of AT devices.

# Principles and Practices for Effectively Using Educational Technology and Assistive Technology

## Use of Educational Technology to Facilitate Inclusion

For all students, educational technology in the general education classroom facilitates learning in several ways. For example, many students will use technology to gather information through the Internet, analyze data by using spreadsheets, or create and share information by using word processing and presentation software. When used effectively, technology can help learners direct more of their own learning, be more engaged in participatory and authentic learning processes, think more critically, and work more cooperatively with others (Bitter & Legacy, 2008; Jonassen, Howland, Marra, & Crismond, 2008). In this way, educational technologies support "meaningful learning when they fulfill a learning need—when interactions with technologies are learner initiated and learner controlled, and when the interactions with the technologies are conceptually and intellectually engaging" (Jonassen et al., 2008, p. 7). In Strategy 16.1, at the end of this chapter, we provide directions to help teachers teach students how to use educational technology in the classroom.

Many of the technology tools used by students without disabilities can be used in similar ways by students with disabilities. That is, many students with disabilities become more engaged and can work more effectively and efficiently when they use interactive whiteboards, word processing programs, spreadsheets, presentation software, the Internet, or other types of technology. Research has demonstrated how different types of educational technology impact students with disabilities or special needs.

In an early analysis of studies in which computers were used to help improve the reading skills of students with learning disabilities, Hall, Hughes, and Filbert (2000) found that students demonstrated improvement in 13 of 17 studies. In another review, MacArthur, Ferretti, Okolo, and Cavalier (2001) found that computer programs were especially useful for teaching phonological awareness and decoding skills. A later study found that adolescents with learning disabilities had fewer spelling errors and reading errors, and had better structure and organization in their written work when they used word processing software instead of writing with pencil and paper (Hetzroni & Shrieber, 2004). Other researchers have reported similar outcomes (e.g., Blackhurst, 2005; Hasselbring & Bausch, 2005; MacArthur, 2000; Wanzek, Vaughn, Wexler, Swanson, Edmonds, & Kim, 2006).

Some recent studies have examined how e-texts and text-to-voice applications can help students better comprehend written material. In these studies, students with learning disabilities and students with moderate intellectual disabilities performed better on comprehension assessments when text-to-speech was provided to help them understand the written

## Pause & Reflect

What role has educational technology played in your learning? Did you use specific software programs when you were in school? Have you often used word processing, presentation, or spreadsheet software for your academic work? And speaking of technology and education, how important is the Internet to you?

material (Douglas, Ayres, Langone, Bell, & Meade, 2009; Izzo, Yurick, & McArrell, 2009). Comprehension has also been improved by students with learning disabilities when Kidspiration© was used to create story maps (Wade, Boon, & Spencer, 2010).

Other studies have looked at how educational technology can help students with disabilities become more engaged to improve academic or social behavior. A few of these studies have used Smart Boards. In one, students with learning disabilities were able to learn their own targeted letter sounds, but also learned some of the letter sounds of other students, demonstrating that Smart Boards are helpful for facilitating *incidental learning* (Campbell & Mechling, 2009). Similarly, in another study, students with moderate intellectual disabilities were able to learn their own sight words on a Smart Board, but also some of the words of other students in the group (Mechling, Gast, & Thompson, 2008–2009). And in yet another, teachers used Smart Boards to present social stories to students with ASD. Students looked at pictures on the Smart Board of children engaging in socially appropriate behavior and pointed out what they were doing correctly (Xin & Sutman, 2011). In Strategy 16.2 we discuss ways to use Smart Boards effectively with mixed ability groups of students.

Other instructional technology tools can also help students with disabilities be engaged learners. Bouck and Flanagan (2010) discussed how "virtual manipulatives" could be used by teachers to teach math skills and Parette, Hourcade, and Blum (2011) explained how Microsoft PowerPoint offers features such as pictures, sounds, and animations that will better hold students' attention.

## Teaching Students to Use Educational Technology

Many students with disabilities or special needs will enjoy working at a computer and will need little prompting to do so. It is important to realize, however, that most students will require initial instruction, modeling, and prompting in order to learn to use the software. Afterward, you may find that students can work independently on the computer for periods ranging from 10 to 20 minutes. Once you have learned for yourself how the software operates, you will be ready to introduce it to your students. As mentioned previously, Strategy 16.1 provides general guidelines for teachers to use when teaching students to use educational technology. Strategy 16.3 outlines how to teach using READ 180, a popular program used to teach reading skills to students between the fourth and twelfth grades. You will see that the program provides a very comprehensive approach that not only uses technology but also requires direct instruction from the teacher and reading narratives from leveled readers. In Strategy 16.4, we explain how to use PLATO® Achieve Now on PSP® (Mathematics) to improve students' math skills in different areas.

Teachers often use educational technology to complement or supplement instruction rather than replace it. This means that the students in your classroom with special needs will still require direct instruction in order to develop critical skills in reading, math, and other curricular areas. What you can expect from many educational technology programs, however, is an initial and periodic assessment of key skills, an opportunity to practice those skills, and an ongoing record of how students are progressing on skills. Programs will also often use thematic devices, graphics, and feedback to students to help motivate them to achieve the objectives of the program. Strategy 16.5 offers a procedure for evaluating educational software that you will find helpful. We also encourage you to examine the Websites of specific products, keeping in mind that the technology producers may be biased when promoting their own products.

### Pause & Reflect

If a technology device helps you do something that you cannot do without it, you might consider it an AT device. Navigational devices (e.g., GPS) are quite popular. Have you ever used one of these, and did it help you get somewhere? If it did help you, you were using an AT device.

## Use of Assistive Technology to Facilitate Inclusion

Just as different types of educational technology can facilitate learning in inclusive settings, various types of assistive technology can help students gain access to different learning opportunities. It is important to keep in mind, though, that assistive technology devices are intended to meet a specific need for a student with a disability. This means that AT devices will not be used by all students, but that you may have one or two students in a classroom with his or her unique AT device.

During an IEP session, IDEA 2004 requires that the planning committee must consider whether the student with a disability can benefit from a specific device and related AT services. This can be interpreted to mean that the IEP team must especially consider an AT device when reviewing the present level of performance, during the development of annual goals and objectives or benchmarks, and when determining the appropriate placement of a student (Bausch, Quinn, Chung, Ault, & Behrmann, 2009; Parette & Peterson-Karlan, 2007). An AT device that would better allow a student to function in a general education classroom would certainly merit consideration by the IEP team. However, the decision-making process for determining whether or not a specific AT device is appropriate for a student with a disability is complex. In Strategy 16.6 we provide a practical process for deciding about the appropriateness of specific AT devices and questions that the IEP team should answer when considering an AT device.

As seen previously in this chapter, assistive technology devices vary greatly in their purposes and designs and may be used with students whose disabilities range from mild to severe. A sample of the research on the use of assistive technology devices demonstrates that it can be successful in helping bridge the gap between current student abilities and student participation and involvement. These studies have included students with mild disabilities who have achieved greater academic success using AT devices (e.g., Anderson, Anderson, & Cherup, 2009; Bouck & Flanagan, 2009; Hetzroni & Shrieber, 2004; Kim, Woodruff, Klein, & Vaughn, 2006; MacArthur & Cavalier, 2004; Montgomery, Karlan, & Coutinho, 2001; Wanzek et al., 2006; Williams, 2002) as well as students with more significant disabilities who have learned to communicate and control their environment using AT devices (e.g., Carey & Sale, 1994; Cavalier & Brown, 1998; Cosbey & Johnston, 2006; Daniels, Sparling, Reilly, & Humphry, 1995; Hutinger, Johanson, & Stoneburner, 1996; Lancioni et al., 2002; Reichle, 2011; Todis, 1996). Although most research on assistive technology has looked at the effectiveness of devices specifically designed to be AT equipment, recent research has evaluated more commonly available, and thus less expensive, hardware and how it can be used to meet the unique needs of students with disabilities. This research has shown the utility of iPads and iPods on teaching functional skills such as work skills, transitioning, and pedestrian navigation (e.g., Cihak, Fahrenkrog, Ayres, & Smith, 2010; Kelley, 2011; Van Laarhoven et al., 2009). In these studies, the devices are used to present the learners with visual and/or auditory cues that direct them through a series of steps so that they may perform a task independently. For example, in one study, five out of six young adults with autistic spectrum disorders learned to follow directions for performing a fire safety demonstration by using a performance cue system contained on their iPhones (Burke, Andersen, Bowen, Howard, & Allen, 2010). In another, four young adults with mild to moderate intellectual disabilities were able to use picture cues presented on a video iPod to learn to find their way around a college campus (Kelley, 2011).

## Teaching Students to Use Assistive Technology

The process for initiating and using assistive technology with a student with disabilities requires collaboration, as was pointed out by Allison McMahon at the beginning of the chapter. Usually the decision regarding the use of a specific assistive technology device will occur at the IEP meeting. In other cases, parents, teachers, or related services professionals (e.g., speech/language pathologists, physical or occupational therapists) may recognize that a student might benefit from a device and suggest its use to the IEP team. For example, Allison McMahon learned about Proloquo2Go and suggested its use to Mallee Taylor, who then tried it out with Ryley and found it worked well for him.

Classroom teachers often show a mixed level of commitment to using an AT device with students who have one. This is often related to their educational background, their understanding of the device, and their general comfort with technology (Connor, Snell, Gansneder, & Dexter, 2010; Sze, 2009). This is one of the reasons that collaboration is important. This situation can also be addressed, somewhat, through the provision of assistive technology services carried out by AT resource teachers like Allison McMahon. It is not enough simply to provide AT *devices*, but IDEA also requires providing

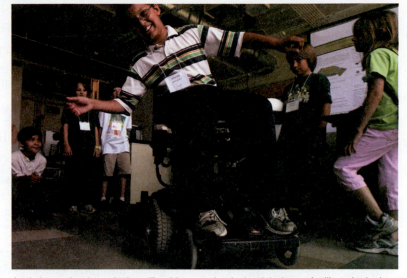

Assistive technology devices like this motorized wheelchair can facilitate inclusion in daily life.

AT *services*. *Assistive technology services* are defined under IDEA as "any service that directly assists a child with a disability in the selection, acquisition, or use of an assistive technology device" (§ 602(2)). These services may include evaluating the needs of the student, acquiring the device, implementing the use of the device, and providing training and assistance to teach teachers and others how to use the device (Westling & Fox, 2009).

As technology in general continues to expand in our lives, we can expect AT devices to become more common and more user-friendly, suggesting that teachers will become more and more comfortable with their use. At the end of this chapter, we provide a few strategies to help teachers use some of the more common AT devices, including using word processing to help with students' writing needs (Strategy 16.7), using calculators to solve math problems (Strategy 16.8), supporting students who use augmentative/alternative communication (AAC) devices (Strategy 16.9), and supporting students in motorized wheelchairs (Strategy 16.10).

# Universal Design for Learning

Universal design for learning (UDL) is a curriculum design process called for in IDEA 2004 that provides guidelines for designing curriculum in a way that will make it more accessible to more learners with various ability levels. Although UDL is not synonymous with assistive technology, it is often made more feasible because of advances in technology tools.

## Principles and Guidelines of UDL

One way to enhance the opportunity for students with disabilities to participate in inclusive classrooms and the general curriculum is to design a curriculum based on the principles of universal design for learning. These principles begin with the notion that key elements of instruction can be varied to allow learning by students with a range of abilities. The Center for Applied Special Technology (CAST, 2011) proposed three principles of UDL—and within them nine guidelines—necessary for a universal curriculum. The principles and guidelines are as follows:

- **Principle I: Provide Multiple Means of Representation.** Alternative means of presenting instructional material can reduce perceptual or learning barriers and can improve students' ability to recognize things. Digital format is the most flexible means for presenting curricular materials because it makes material transformable, transportable, and recordable. The guidelines for Principle I are:

- Guideline 1: Provide options for perception.
- Guideline 2: Provide options for language, mathematical expressions, and symbols.
- Guideline 3: Provide options for comprehension.

- **Principle II: Provide Multiple Means of Action and Expression.** Universal design for learning allows students to respond with their preferred means of control. Different strategic and motor systems of students can be accommodated. Principle II has the following guidelines:

- Guideline 4: Provide options for physical action.
- Guideline 5: Provide options for expression and communication.
- Guideline 6: Provide options for executive functions.

- **Principle III: Provide Multiple Means of Engagement.** Finally, students' interests in learning, as indicated by their engagement, can be matched with the modes of presentation and response and can increase student motivation. Three guidelines are used with Principle III:

- Guideline 7: Provide options for recruiting interest.
- Guideline 8: Provide options for sustaining effort and persistence.
- Guideline 9: Provide options for self-regulation.

## Applying Principles and Guidelines of UDL

Many of the materials for creating UDL-based curricula are available from the Center for Applied Special Technology (CAST). For example, CAST (2011) provides "checkpoints" which suggest materials that help achieve the principles and guidelines presented above, and for each checkpoint. CAST suggests a variety of online resources, most of which are free. For example, under the first principle and the first guideline, text-to-speech software might be considered for a student who doesn't access information through reading. For another student who needs to strengthen his or her vocabulary, CAST's *UDL Editions* includes a "multimedia glossary" in all of its texts. A student can click on a word and can read the definition, listen to it through text-to-speech, and see a visual image of it. Additionally, CAST provides a "free technology toolkit" (http://udltechtoolkit.wikispaces.com/) and invites teachers to join its wiki to offer ideas and comments.

## Example of the Effectiveness of UDL Applications

There are a number of ways that UDL has been applied to improve student learning. Three examples in which UDL principles were applied in classrooms are illustrative.

Dymond and colleagues (2006) reported an example of a comprehensive instructional unit using UDL principles. These researchers used the principles to design a high school science course that would be accessible to students without disabilities, students with mild disabilities, and students with more severe intellectual disabilities. The authors developed a set of questions to address as they redesigned traditional course lesson plans. The questions helped them consider how key areas could be modified, including the curriculum, instructional delivery and organization of the learning environment, student participation, materials, and assessment. The major changes made to the course included the following:

- **Materials:** Large-print reading material and laptops with Internet connections and LCD projectors were added to the more traditional materials.
- **Forms of student participation:** Students were given choices of how they would participate. For example, active, interactive, and leadership types of participation were offered, including more hands-on activities, team projects, and students teaching students.

- **Instructional delivery:** A variety of instructional methods occurred during daily instruction, including more student-directed instruction and technology-driven instruction.
- **Assessment:** Forms of assessment increased, including reading tests to students and using rubrics and checklists to evaluate students during presentations and hands-on work sessions.

Dymond and colleagues (2006) reported that as a result of the UDL process, many changes occurred in the teachers and their students. The general education and special education teachers began to collaborate more, shared more instructional responsibilities, and became more concerned that the students with disabilities be able to participate meaningfully during instruction.

In another study, researchers used an online tool called the Virtual History Museum (VHM; http://vhm.msu.edu/site/default.php) to increase the learning outcomes in social studies for all students (Bouck, Courtad, Heutsche, Okolo, & Englert, 2009). Virtual History Museum was developed at the University of Michigan and allows teachers to create different kinds of exhibits using text or artifacts that they create or import. Artifacts may include pictures or documents as well as audio or video clips. Students may read the text displays or use a text-to-speech screen reader. This gives students an option of reading the text, listening to it, or doing both. The VHM lets students who had not been able to participate in social studies because of their learning disabilities to become engaged learners.

In the third study, the researchers wanted to increase participation by students with multiple disabilities in shared story learning activities (Browder, Mims, Spooner, Ahlgrim-Delzell, & Angel, 2008). To do this, the researchers considered the key principles of UDL and asked these key questions: "Is there a better way to present this opportunity to respond?" "Is there an alternative way the student could respond?" and "What prompt can be used to make the response?" Based on consideration of each student's characteristics, the researchers then designed different instructional procedures. For example, they displayed some objects on a bulletin board as a different form of representation; changed the type of switch a student was using in order to allow a different type of response; and used low lighting in the room to increase engagement time. As a result of such design decisions, all students increased their participation in the activity.

## Summary

This chapter addressed the following topics:

### Types of educational technology

- Interactive whiteboards (Smart Boards) are popular teaching tools because, unlike individual computers or other devices, teachers can use them to work with groups of students.
- Drill-and-practice software provides individual learners with the opportunity to increase instructional time working on specific academic skills.
- Integrated learning systems are instructional programs networked throughout a school or school district intended to incorporate instruction to meet national, state, or district standards.
- Reading and math programs offer technology-based or technology-enhanced programs that cover learning objectives for several grades and allow the student to progress at his or her own pace.

### Types of assistive technology devices

- Assistive technology devices to support reading may help students by providing them with visual and auditory supports, highlighting certain words to improve visual discrimination, provide picture cues, and even convert written text to speech.

- Assistive technology devices can help students who have difficulty writing and spelling by using a keyboard on a personal computer or a portable word processor; providing spell checking and grammar checking; and providing word prediction software.
- Assistive technology devices to support math can help students with calculations and word problems.
- Augmentative/alternative communication (AAC) devices can help students with intellectual, physical, or multiple disabilities communicate. These can range from producing single words to producing synthesized speech.
- Personal support technologies are handheld devices such as personal digital assistants, iPhones, iPods, and iPads that can help guide students through different activities such as daily living skills, vocational skills, or pedestrian skills using visual and auditory cues.
- Assistive technology devices for daily living are used by students with physical or multiple disabilities and include devices such as powered wheelchairs or scooters or adaptive eating utensils or adapted toothbrushes.

### Use of educational technology to facilitate inclusion

- Research supports the use of educational technology to improve reading skills, reduce spelling errors, and improve writing.
- E-texts and text-to-voice applications can help students better comprehend written material.
- Smart Boards have been found to help students learn letter sounds and site words and for facilitating incidental learning. They have also been used to present social stories to students with autism spectrum disorders.

### Teaching students to use educational technology

- Most students with disabilities will require initial instruction, modeling, and prompting in order to learn to use educational technology tools.
- Teachers should become familiar with the technology and then support students as they gradually learn to use it.

### Use of assistive technology to facilitate inclusion

- Assistive technology devices are intended to meet a specific need for a student with a disability so a teacher may have one or two students in a classroom with their own unique AT device.
- IDEA 2004 requires that, during an IEP session, the IEP planning committee must consider whether the student with a disability can benefit from a specific device and related AT services.
- Research on the use of AT devices demonstrates that it can be successful in helping bridge the gap between current student abilities and student participation and involvement for students with mild disabilities and for students with more significant disabilities.
- iPads and iPods have been found effective for teaching work skills, transitioning, and pedestrian navigation. The devices are used to present the learners with visual and/or auditory cues that direct them through a series of steps so that they may perform a task independently.

### Teaching students to use assistive technology

- Usually the decision regarding the use of a specific assistive technology device will occur at the IEP meeting.
- Parents, teachers, or related services professionals may recognize that a student might benefit from an AT device.
- Teachers' educational backgrounds, their understandings of the device, and their general comfort with technology will affect how well they work with students with AT devices.
- Assistive technology services are required when AT devices are provided to a student and may include evaluating the needs of the student, acquiring the device, implementing the use of the device, and providing training and assistance to teach teachers and others how to use the device.

**Universal design for learning (UDL)**

- Universal design for learning is a curriculum design process that provides principles and guidelines for designing curriculum in a way that will make it more accessible to more learners.
- The three principles of UDL are (1) provide multiple means of representation, (2) provide multiple means of action and expression, and (3) provide multiple means of engagement.
- The Center for Applied Special Technology provides resources and materials for designing universal curricula.
- Research has supported the use of UDL with students of different ability levels.

## Addressing Professional Standards

Standards addressed in Chapter 16 include:

**CEC Standards:** (3) individual learning differences; (4) instructional strategies; (5) learning environments and social interactions; (7) instructional planning.

### MyEducationLab

Go to the topic Instructional Practices and Learning Strategies in the **MyEducationLab** (www.myeducationlab.com) for *Inclusion*, where you can:

- Find learning outcomes for Instructional Practices and Learning Strategies, along with the national standards that connect to these outcomes.
- Complete Assignments and Activities that can help you more deeply understand the chapter content.
- Apply and practice your understanding of the core teaching skills identified in the chapter with the Building Teaching Skills and Dispositions learning units.
- Check your comprehension on the content covered in the chapter with the Study Plan. Here you will be able to take a chapter quiz, receive feedback on your answers, and then access Review, Practice, and Enrichment activities to enhance your understanding of chapter content.

# EFFECTIVE STRATEGIES FOR USING TECHNOLOGY TO SUPPORT INCLUSION

## Putting It All Together

Teachers will find that including students with disabilities can be more successful if you and your collaborators in special education take advantage of different forms of technology. We suggest that you reflect on the following suggestions:

1. **Learn about what is available.** Technology is so abundant it seems to be outdated before we can learn to use it. Thus, knowing what is available requires teachers to access information through the Web, books, or journals. Attending conferences or workshops can also be useful, as is talking to the school district's assistive technology consultant to keep up with newly developing products.

2. **Work with technology and assistive technology specialists and other team members.** As we discussed in Chapter 11, collaboration with others is critical for successfully teaching students with special needs. All team members should be involved in identifying, selecting, and implementing the use of technology to ensure that devices will be used appropriately and in settings that will maximize potential.

3. **Focus on the students' needs.** We recommend the use of educational or assistive technology tools only when they contribute to the ability of students to do something, or help the students learn better or faster. Although technology can be used for entertainment, in instructional settings, technology should help students achieve specific goals or perform important skills.

4. **Monitor students' progress.** Many educational technologies incorporate assessment probes into the program and create reports for teachers so they can assess students' progress. You should use these reports and modify instruction as necessary to improve your students' performance. With AT devices, you can observe how often a student uses the device, if the student uses it as designed, and if it helps meet the objective for which it was designed.

## Strategy Fact Sheet

In the remainder of this chapter, we describe ten effective strategies about the use of technology to help you plan effectively to meet the needs of all students. The Strategy Fact Sheet summarizes these strategies.

| STRATEGY | DESCRIPTION | IMPORTANCE |
|---|---|---|
| Strategy 16.1: Teaching Students to Use Educational Technology Programs | This classroom instruction strategy provides a step-by-step process for teaching students to effectively use educational software to improve basic academic skills. | A great deal of educational technology is available today that teachers can use to their advantage as a complement to direct instruction. |
| Strategy 16.2: Using the Smart Board to Teach in an Inclusive Classroom | This strategy provides information about how to engage students with disabilities when using a Smart Board. | Smart Boards are popular learning tools and some research shows they can be effective with students with disabilities. |
| Strategy 16.3: Using READ 180 in the Classroom | A popular program that addresses critical reading skills for students in grades 4–12. This strategy provides an overview of how to use this program. | Read 180 will work best if teachers are adequately prepared to use it. Materials and workshops are available from the producer to teach teachers about the material. |

| STRATEGY | DESCRIPTION | IMPORTANCE |
|---|---|---|
| Strategy 16.4: Using the Computer Game PLATO® Achieve Now on PSP® (Mathematics) to Improve Students' Homework Performance | Motivating students to learn math skills can be challenging. This strategy describes how this PSP-based game can help individual students in this area. | Although electronic games are more fun than more traditional approaches to learning, close teacher monitoring of assignments is still important. |
| Strategy 16.5: Evaluating Educational Technology | This strategy will help teachers decide the value of various educational technology products. The step-by-step guide will better ensure that students will benefit from the selected program. | Although much educational technology software is available, it is not all equal. Careful review of different products will lead to a better selection for your students with special needs. |
| Strategy 16.6: A Decision-Making Process for Selecting Assistive Technology Devices | Assistive technology can help students accomplish various tasks and assignments. But you must be able to decide what will be most effective for individual student needs. | Many students with disabilities can benefit from assistive technology, but much of it can be expensive. Teachers must always take care to select devices that students will use. |
| Strategy 16.7: Using Word Processing and Related Software to Support Student Writing | Offers guidance for teaching students with writing difficulties how to use word processing to produce better-written papers and reports. | Word processing allows many students with learning disabilities to better express their thoughts. An important tool for many teachers. |
| Strategy 16.8: Teaching Students with Disabilities to Use Calculators | Provides a step-by-step instructional process for teaching students to use calculators to solve math problems in school and in the real world. | There is some debate among experts as to the extent that students should use calculators to solve arithmetic problems, but for some students, they can be an important tool. |
| Strategy 16.9: Supporting Students Who Use Augmentative/Alternative Communication Devices | Relatively speaking, few students will require AAC devices to communicate. When the need arises, however, this strategy will help IEP team members select the best device for the student. | A few students with disabilities will require the support of AAC devices to communicate. Used correctly, these devices can enhance their ability to participate in daily life. |
| Strategy 16.10: Supporting Students Who Use Motorized Wheelchairs | Some students with special needs will require wheelchairs for mobility. This strategy helps teachers understand how wheelchairs operate and how to help students use them. | Students who use wheelchairs must learn how to navigate them in a way that helps them fit into the flow of daily life. A little instruction and direction may sometimes be necessary. |

**Strategy 16.1** | **TEACHING STUDENTS TO USE EDUCATIONAL TECHNOLOGY PROGRAMS**

## Rationale

Studies have shown that educational technology can improve academic skills, especially reading skills (Hall, Hughes, & Filbert, 2000). MacArthur and colleagues (2001) found that computer programs were especially useful for teaching phonological awareness and decoding skills. A study by Hetzroni and Shrieber (2004) showed that adolescents with learning disabilities had fewer spelling errors and reading errors, and had better structure and organization in their written work when they used word processing software instead of writing with pencil and paper. Other researchers have reported similar outcomes (e.g., Blackhurst, 2005; Hasselbring & Bausch, 2005; MacArthur, 2000; Wanzek et al., 2006). More recent studies have examined how e-texts and text-to-voice applications can help students better comprehend written material (Douglas et al., 2009; Izzo, Yurick, & McArrell, 2009).

## Step-by-Step

**1** *Become knowledgeable about the program you are using.* Before exposing any of your students to the program, make sure you understand its features, how it operates, how the student uses it, and how the program directs the student through its activities. If staff development sessions are available on use of the program, take advantage of the opportunity to participate.

**2** *Identify appropriate objectives and activities within the software program.* The advantage of most educational technology programs is that they allow differentiated instruction for students with different skill levels. The program itself may identify specific student needs if a diagnostic component is built into it. Regardless, you will want the student to focus on those areas of the program that will help meet academic needs.

**3** *Provide adequate supervision and support as each student begins to use the software program.* Each student must learn to use the program correctly to use it successfully. Students who are younger, who have less experience working on computers, or who have intellectual or learning disabilities likely will require more direct instruction and more support in using the program. This phase may take several sessions until the student is comfortable operating the program.

**4** *Maintain an awareness of students' level of comfort and frustration with the program.* If too many failures occur, you should move the student to a lower level of the program to ensure more success. If the student is using different programs, proportionally distribute the student's time so that the student spends more time on the program that addresses the student's greatest need.

**5** *Reinforce students for correctly using the software program.* You may reinforce correct use of the program by letting students engage in another preferred educational program, or you may let them play another computer game. Of course, you can also use more traditional types of reinforcement, such as extra playground time or token reinforcement. Many educational reading and math software programs have games built into them that are related to the learning objectives. Students may play these and still practice important skills.

**6** *Monitor the student's progress in the program.* You need to examine the reports provided by the program and make sure the student is making adequate progress on the program's probes. If not, the student should not move forward in the program until better performance indicates that she should do so. The student may require more direct instruction from you to help her acquire some specific skills.

**7** *Monitor the student's progress independently of the program's evaluation.* Performance on the program should not be assumed to equate with performance under other conditions, such as on curriculum-based evaluation in the classroom. Therefore, you should always have off-program tests to make sure the student can demonstrate skills under different conditions.

## Applications and Examples

When schools decide they will acquire new educational technology, they begin by developing a plan as to how they will implement the technology. The goal is to make the classroom a more effective learning environment by offering students more effective learning tools. The new technology will also have an impact on how teachers teach. Therefore teachers need to plan how the technology will become a part of the instructional process. They need to consider what learning objectives it will help students reach, how students will be able to interact with the technology, how they will prepare students to use the technology, and how and when students will use the technology. For these reasons, most educational technology programs require staff development in order for teachers to use it effectively; teachers need to take advantage of this learning opportunity (Pohlmann, 1999–2011).

## Keep in Mind

Many of your students, like yourself, will already come to you with advanced computer usage skills. Their experience with different types of technology will be an advantage and may reduce the amount of time it will take them to learn how to use a program. Likewise, the quality and user-friendly features of a program can also affect a student's learning curve.

**Key References**

Hall, T. E., Hughes, C. A., & Filbert, M. (2000). Computer-assisted instruction in reading for students with learning disabilities: A research synthesis. *Education and Treatment of Children, 23,* 173–193.

Hetzroni, O. E., & Shrieber, B. (2004). Word processing as an assistive technology tool for enhancing academic outcomes of students with writing disabilities in the general classroom. *Journal of Learning Disabilities, 37,* 143–154.

Izzo, M. V., Yurick, A., & McArrell, B. (2009). Supported eText: Effects of text-to-speech on access and achievement for high school students with disabilities. *Journal of Special Education Technology, 24*(3), 9–20.

MacArthur, C. A., Ferretti, R. P., Okolo, C. M., & Cavalier, A. R. (2001). Technology applications for students with literacy problems: A critical review. *Elementary School Journal, 101,* 273–301.

Pohlmann, B. (1999–2011). *Strategies to implement technologies in a classroom.* Retrieved June 5, 2011, from: http://www.ehow.com/way_5984431_strategies-implement-technology-classroom.html

| Strategy 16.2 | USING THE SMART BOARD TO TEACH IN AN INCLUSIVE CLASSROOM |
|---|---|

## Rationale

Smart Boards, generically known as interactive whiteboards, are a relatively recent development in education but one that has become ubiquitous in classrooms throughout the United States. Teachers can use them like a traditional blackboard or whiteboard, but the Smart Boards also work like a computer screen, only much larger. As something is projected on them like it might be on a computer screen—for example, a Website or a PowerPoint presentation—teachers or students can write or draw on the screen with special pens, and then save the screen image in a file for later reuse. Smart Boards have several benefits: They are interactive, increase engagement, maintain attention, allow students to focus better, allow teacher-made or predeveloped lessons to be presented, and are appropriate for use with the whole class, groups, pairs, or individual students. Some recent research has demonstrated benefits of using Smart Boards with students with disabilities.

## Step-by-Step

**1** *Make sure you are familiar with how the Smart Board operates.* Know how to turn it on, connect to the Internet, navigate the Internet, use different colored Smart Board pens and the eraser when the Digital Ink Layer is open, save your notes in a notebook file using the Capture Writing button, and close the Digital Ink Layer.

**2** *Select an appropriate lesson for your class or for the group.* The lesson should be based on local, state, or national standards. You can create your own lessons or you might visit the Smart Exchange (http://exchange.smarttech.com/search.html?m=01) to see and download lessons suggested by other teachers. You can also submit lessons.

**3** *Think about the students with special needs in your classroom or group and how you might need to accommodate them.* Smart Boards have been shown to be effective tools for students with intellectual disabilities, learning disabilities, and autism spectrum disorders. Other students with special needs, like ADHD, might also benefit. Considering the needs of students, you might

- Arrange their seating to be closer to the Smart Board.
- Make sure they are attending when directing your instruction to other students so they can take advantage of incidental learning opportunities.

- Embed material appropriate to their level in the lesson and call on them to respond—for example, vocabulary words or comprehension questions.
- Provide gestures or verbal or physical prompts to get them to respond appropriately.
- Pair them with a peer buddy to help them respond and create.
- Provide extra time for them to respond.

**4** *At the completion of the Smart Board activity, follow up with written or verbal assessment activities* to determine if students have learned what you have taught.

**5** *You can also use the Smart Board for "show and tell."* Let students prepare their presentations individually or in pairs and groups using PowerPoint, then ask them to share it with the class. Students can be more creative and expressive and will not have to physically manage posters or large displays.

**6** *The Smart Board can serve as a great tool for preparing for tests* by reviewing facts, playing games, or presenting problems. Let students work individually or together as they prepare.

## Applications and Examples

At Gilpin Manor Elementary School in Elkton, Maryland, you will find Smart Boards in nearly every classroom; there is even a plan to install one in the gym. Teachers stand in front of the room, projecting different types of materials onto the Smart Board and highlight the material in different ways. Gilpin Manor's students with disabilities enjoy lessons from the Smart Board. Melissa Pratt, the pre-K interventionist at Gilpin Manor, said, "With the implementation of the Smart Board—because we know our kids are bombarded with video games and movies— . . . we can make it interactive, we can have animation. I did the story of Goldilocks and we actually got to see Goldilocks eat the different things, break the chairs, run away when the bears came home—and those kids . . . they saw the movement and were engaged and they can answer some questions. So I think technology is going to be the gateway, especially for your nonverbal children, it's giving them another way to communicate." Allison McMahon, the AT specialist added, "It's multisensory. They're touching, they're seeing, they're moving, so yeah, absolutely."

## Keep in Mind

Smart Boards can be powerful learning tools, but like other types of technology, they should not be used simply for entertainment, but for meaningful instruction. Although they will be effective for much instruction, for individual students with disabilities, there is always a need to fit the instruction to meet the student's needs.

**Key References**

Campbell, M. L., & Mechling, L. C. (2009). Small group computer-assisted instruction with SMART Board technology: An investigation of observational and incidental learning on nontarget information. *Remedial and Special Education, 30*(1), 47–57.

Mechling, L. C., Gast, D. L., & Krupa, K. (2007). Impact of SMART Board technology: An investigation of sight word reading and observational learning. *Journal of Autism and Developmental Disorders, 37,* 1869–1882.

Mechling, L. C., Gast, D. L., & Thompson, K. L. (2008–2009). Comparison of the effects of SMART board technology and flash card instruction on sight word recognition and observational learning. *Journal of Special Education Technology, 23*(1), 34–46. http://www.eric.ed.gov/ERICWebPortal/search/detailmini .jsp?_nfpb=true&_&ERICExtSearch_SearchValue_0=EJ861024&ERICExtSearch_SearchType_0 =no&accno=EJ861024

Xin, J. F., & Sutman, F. X. (2011). Using the SMART Board in teaching social stories to students with autism. *Teaching Exceptional Children, 43*(4), 18–24.

| Strategy 16.3 | USING READ 180 IN THE CLASSROOM |
|---|---|

## Rationale

READ 180 is Scholastic's comprehensive reading intervention program for students reading below the proficient level in grades 4–12. According to its Website,[1] READ 180 underwent an extensive research and developmental process that began in 1985 and continued through 1999. A recently produced *Compendium of READ 180 Research* (Scholastic, Inc., 2006), provided by the publisher, offers the results of extensive evaluation analyses and research conducted in school districts throughout the United States. Among the findings reported are the following:

- All struggling readers need to be engaged and given incentive to learn to read.
- The READ 180® program and services are strongly aligned with the 15 elements (necessary to improve reading skills) cited in the *Reading Next* report (Biancarosa & Snow, 2004).
- READ 180 is the result of many years of educational research and development (Scholastic, Inc., 2006, *Compendium of READ 180 Research*, pp. 4–5).

## Step-by-Step

**1** *Become knowledgeable about the material.* READ 180 requires teachers to begin by studying the comprehensive teacher's material that comes with the product. The publisher offers teachers printed materials and also a two-day staff development session to learn to use its materials.

**2** *Allocate adequate instructional time.* READ 180 is designed for use in 90-minute blocks of time per day, 5 days a week. During the 90-minute instructional period, the teacher uses the READ 180 materials to provide systematic instruction in reading, writing, and vocabulary.

**3** *Start with whole-group instruction.* The first component of daily instruction includes 20 minutes of instruction to the whole class. Students then break into three smaller groups that rotate through three 20-minute small-group rotations.

**4** *Divide the class into three small groups of comparable ability.* The small-group rotations include the following grouping patterns:

- *Small-group instruction:* The teacher works with one small group using the READ 180 book (rBook) and

*Resources for Differentiated Instruction.* In this group the teacher focuses on individual student needs and provides differentiated instruction.
- *Computer instruction:* In a second group, students use the READ 180 Software independently, which provides intensive, individualized skills practice.
- *Independent reading:* In a third group rotation, students build reading-comprehension skills through modeled and independent reading of the READ 180 paperbacks and audiobooks.

**5** *End the daily instruction with whole-group instruction.* The 90-minute session ends with 10 minutes of whole-group instruction.

**6** *Evaluate individual and group performance.* The teacher can use the READ 180 built-in assessment to gauge the progress of each student. The results of the assessment allow teachers to group students for small-group instruction and to assign leveled READ 180 paperback books for independent reading.

## Applications and Examples

The Charleston County School District (2006) described how several schools in its district used READ 180 and some of the results of its usage. Here is how the program was used in two schools:

In Chicora Elementary School, one fifth-grade teacher used READ 180 during her daily reading block. The teacher used the basal reader during whole-group instruction and then

---

[1]READ 180 is produced by Scholastic, Inc. Much of the content reported here is based on the publisher's Website at http://teacher.scholastic.com/products/read180/.

rotated only the lowest-performing students through the READ 180 stations. The remaining students worked on other reading-related projects during these rotations. Teachers at Goodwin Elementary School used READ 180 in the three fifth-grade classes during reading block. Goodwin had one full set of READ 180 materials and one partial set of materials that the three fifth-grade teachers shared. The lack of materials made it challenging for all three teachers to fully implement READ 180. Two teachers therefore used the READ 180 materials to augment their reading instruction, primarily using the computer component of READ 180. The third teacher used all components of READ 180, implementing it in a fashion similar to that of the fifth-grade teacher at Chicora, using the basal reader during whole-group instruction, and then rotating the lowest-performing students through the READ 180 stations while the other students worked on other reading-related projects. (Charleston County School District, 2006, pp. 1–2)

## Keep in Mind

The value of READ 180 to students may depend on how well teachers are prepared to use it and how well they adhere to the recommended instructional practices. Teachers are likely to use the program more effectively if they have attended the in-service sessions provided by the publisher, are knowledgeable about how the instruction is to be provided, and can implement the program in the prescribed manner. Even so, there is always the chance of technical glitches occurring. Adequate technical support therefore should be available either from the publisher or from the school district's instructional technology department.

**Key References**

Charleston County School District. (2006). *Implementation of READ 180 (Reading Intervention Program) in CCSD schools.* Retrieved May 21, 2008, from http://www.ccsdschools.com/CCSD_Reports/Program _Evaluation_Reports/CCSD_Implementation_of_READ_180_July_2006.pdf

Hasselbring, T. S., & Bausch, M. E. (2005). Assistive technologies for reading. *Educational Leadership, 63*(4), 72–75.

Hasselbring, T. S., & Goin, L. I. (2004). Literacy instruction for older struggling readers: What is the role of technology? *Reading and Writing Quarterly, 20*(2), 123–144.

Scholastic, Inc. (2006). *Compendium of READ 180 research.* Retrieved May 21, 2008, from http://teacher .scholastic.com/products/read180/research/pdfs/READ180_Compendium_6_26_06.pdf

Scholastic, Inc. (2008). *READ 180.* Retrieved May 21, 2008, from http://teacher.scholastic.com/products/ read180/

Strategy 16.4

# USING THE COMPUTER GAME PLATO® ACHIEVE NOW ON PSP® (MATHEMATICS) TO IMPROVE STUDENTS' HOMEWORK PERFORMANCE

## Rationale

With the development of Achieve Now on the PSP (PlayStation® Portable) system produced by Sony, PLATO Learning is attempting to provide a medium to students in elementary and middle school grades that will motivate them to engage in learning math and other subjects. PLATO maintains that by providing the opportunity to learn math skills through a popular medium such as the PSP, students will be more likely to increase their learning time, family support for educational activities will increase, and student attitudes and motivation will improve.

On its Website, PLATO presents three evaluation reports (not true experimental studies) that show improvement in students' performance over time when the Achieve Now program was used. Because of other possible sources of influence, however, it is not possible to determine that the gains could be attributed solely or primarily to the product. Other researchers, however, have shown some support for the idea that students will learn more when they are using computer games (see "Key References").

## Step-by-Step

**1** *Determine students' current skill level and needs.* In order to benefit the most from the Achieve Now program, the teacher will need to identify the student's current instructional needs and assign the appropriate lesson for the student.

**2** *Review available lessons.* A variety of lessons are presented in game form for students to practice on the PSP. Sample games and their contents follow:

- *Cali's Geo Tools™:* This is an open-ended program for practicing and mastering basic mathematics concepts. Various activities allow students to explore concepts of congruence, symmetry, and spatial relationships.
- *Math Gallery™:* This program provides multimedia mathematics manipulatives that allow students to acquire a concrete understanding of mathematics. Areas covered: geometry, measurement, probability, statistics, rational numbers, number sense, and computation.
- *P.K.'s Math Studio™:* This collection allows students to master basic mathematics concepts by solving word problems, applying concepts and strategies to build expressions, and analyzing and discovering rules that govern patterns and functions.
- *P.K.'s Place™:* This set of lessons provides practice in mathematics and problem solving. Areas covered are concepts of operations, experiments, number theory, computation, geometry, statistics and probability, and integration of concepts across strands (e.g., algebra patterns, estimation, and estimates).

- *The Quaddle Family Mysteries®:* This program helps students develop their mathematics skills and become active problem solvers. Areas covered: concepts of measurement such as length, area, perimeter, weight and capacity, volume, time, and temperature.
- *The Secret of Googol®:* These lessons help children develop a strong foundation in mathematics. Areas covered are geometry and spatial sense, concepts of whole numbers and groups, concepts of operations, computation, and problem solving.
- *Timeless Jade Trade®:* This program engages students in concentrated study of mathematical concepts such as fractions, decimals, and percentages.
- *Timeless Math®:* This is a series of mathematics challenges that broaden students' awareness of other cultures while strengthening their mathematics skills. Areas covered are rational numbers, concepts of operations, geometry and measurement, statistics and probability, relations, functions, and number theory.

**3** *Allow students to practice in the classroom. Observe students' abilities to use games appropriately.* Although many elementary and middle school students today can easily handle PlayStation technology, it will be important to allow them to practice the math lessons under supervision in order to ensure that they are attending to the problems and attempting to find the correct responses.

**4** *Create additional homework assignments.* Direct students to the appropriate lessons for homework assignments.

**5** *Probe students' skills to ensure learning.* As with all academic learning activities, it is important that teachers use individual probes or curriculum-based assessments to assess student progress. Students may enjoy engaging with the programs and the PSP, but this does not guarantee that learning is occurring. To know this requires an independent evaluation.

## Applications and Examples

Here is a report taken from the PLATO Learning (2008) Website describing how one school in Mississippi used the PLATO system: Holly Springs Intermediate served over 500 students in grades 4 through 6 and had a 97% African American student population. In 2002, Holly Springs began using PLATO Achieve Now, The PLATO Network, and PLATO eduTest Assessment in a special, grant-funded project. The school district selected 120 fourth graders to learn using The PLATO Achieve Now Program; students were pretested in September and posttested in May. As part of the project, teachers attended staff development sessions to analyze pretest results and to determine greatest areas of need. Subsequently, The PLATO Achieve Now Program was aligned with the district's curriculum and the Mississippi State Standards. During the year, teachers provided direct instruction in the classroom, and students were allowed to check out PlayStations for use outside the classroom.

## Keep in Mind

Students in elementary and middle schools are likely to find game-based activities on a PSP very attractive and fun to play. But be warned: Learning will not automatically improve when students are provided with these games. It is critical that you provide instruction in the classroom, that students know how to use the devices and can use them independently, and that you evaluate their learning in a traditional way.

**Key References**

Ford, M., Poe, V., & Cox, J. (1993). Attending behaviors of ADHD children in math and reading using various types of software. *Journal of Computing in Childhood Education, 4*, 183–196.

MacKenty, B. (2006). All play and no work: Computer games are invading the classroom—And not a moment too soon. *School Library Journal, 52*(9), 46–48.

Ota, K. R., & DuPaul, G. J. (2002). Task engagement and mathematics performance in children with attention-deficit hyperactivity disorder: Effects of supplemental computer instruction. *School Psychology Quarterly, 17*, 242–257.

PLATO Learning. (2008). *PLATO® Achieve Now on PSP® (Mathematics)*. Retrieved May 23, 2008, from http://www.plato.com/Products/PLATO-Achieve-Now-on-PSP/PLATO-Achieve-Now-on-PSP-Mathematics.aspx

# EVALUATING EDUCATIONAL TECHNOLOGY

## Rationale

Various educational technology programs allow students to work independently on computers to develop or improve basic skills. The advantage of this technology is that students can work on required skills while the teacher provides direct instruction to other students. As the student engages with the program, she is presented reading or math activities that require a response. Depending on the program, a variety of features may be included, such as attractive graphics, game-like formats, visual and auditory prompts, feedback to the student's responses, and directions for more practice. Programs can also monitor student progress and provide reports to the teacher on this progress.

The issue, then, is which program(s) to select. Usually, programs are not decided by an individual teacher but by a school district technology director working in concert with a district-wide committee. At times, however, you may need to play a role in the decision-making process or be asked to provide feedback about a program you are currently using.

## Step-by-Step

1️⃣ *Determine classroom needs.* Identify which students will use the program, their ages or grade levels, specific skills they need more work on, their cognitive and learning abilities, any sensory and physical limitations, and their ability to interact with a program independently.

2️⃣ *Determine if the program addresses classroom needs.* Note the grade levels the program covers, the objectives addressed, and if they are linked to national, state, or local standards.

3️⃣ *Evaluate the interface design and user appeal.* Does it appear pleasant and engaging from your students' point of view? Does it enhance engagement rather than interfere with learning? Are the screen layouts, graphics, colors, and auditory stimuli pleasing, or might they detract from the content?

4️⃣ *Consider the instructional design aspects of the program.* Determine if the program can diagnose current academic ability and if lessons are structured and presented in a systematic manner based on a hierarchy of objectives. Also assess the amount of practice the program allows and if it provides practice for skill generalization.

Determine if the program provides immediate feedback to students, if it monitors progress, and if it provides reports to the teacher.

5️⃣ *Determine whether the program can be used in different locations.* Find out if the program can be used only in the classroom or if it can be transported to other places such as the computer lab or the student's home.

6️⃣ *Determine the technical features and requirements of the program.* Is the program Web-based or stand-alone? Will you have sufficient hardware and technical support? You will need to determine if you have adequate memory, workstation networking, or Internet connectivity. You should also find out if the vendor will provide training and technical support.

7️⃣ *Look for information about the effectiveness of the program.* Look at the vendor's Website for reviews provided by professional organizations and for published studies in professional journals. Ask vendors to tell you who is using the program, and then contact these users. Ask about teacher satisfaction with the product as well as improvement in student performance outcomes.

## Applications and Examples

Teachers who successfully incorporate educational technology into their instructional activities tend to do so in the following ways:

- They work with other teachers who are also using technology and are supportive of each other.
- They are supported by their schools and school districts and often supported by a technology coordinator or director.

- They receive adequate staff development and in-class support to help them use the technology.
- They often work for principals who are knowledgeable about technology and who provide leadership for its use.
- They generally have good relationships with their students and use effective classroom management practices.

## Keep in Mind

Educational technology can add an important element to the instruction of students in many ways. Most importantly, the teacher needs to understand how the software works and in what ways it will address student needs. At that time, a valuable tool may be available to assist students with their academic challenges.

**Key References**

Bishop, M. J., & Santoro, L. E. (2006). Evaluating beginning reading software for at-risk learners. *Psychology in the Schools, 43*(1), 57–70.

Bitter, G. G., & Legacy, J. M. (2008). *Using technology in the classroom* (7th ed.). Boston: Pearson/Allyn & Bacon.

Dynarski, M., Agodini, R., Heaviside, S., Novak, T., Carey, N., Campuzano, L., Means, B., Murphy, R., Penuel, W., Javitz, H., Emery, D., & Sussex, W. (2007). *Effectiveness of reading and mathematics software products: Findings from the first student cohort*. Washington, DC: U.S. Department of Education, Institute of Education Sciences.

Shakeshaft, C., Mann, D., Becker, J., & Sweeney, K. (2002). Choosing the right technology. *School Administrator, 59*(1), 34–37.

| Strategy 16.6 | A DECISION-MAKING PROCESS FOR SELECTING ASSISTIVE TECHNOLOGY DEVICES |

## Rationale

Assistive technology devices can be useful to many students with disabilities; however, many times the student may not benefit from the device as intended. Several reasons can explain this lack of benefit: The device may not match the student's need, the student may not have the necessary skills to use the device, use of the device may not be acceptable to the student or the student's family, or the device may not operate as intended. For AT devices to be used most effectively, it is critical that the most appropriate device be found to meet the student's need in the context in which the student will use the device. Because so many devices exist, it may be tempting to simply select a device "off the shelf" or recommend a device because it seems as though it would be useful to the student. However, several authorities have noted the importance of undergoing a thoughtful and detailed process to find the most appropriate device and to put it into service with the student in a way that best ensures its correct use. Next we provide recommendations for correctly selecting and appropriately using AT devices.

## Step-by-Step

**1** *Involve the IEP team in the decision-making process.* When considering the need for an AT device, the IEP team should collectively have enough knowledge to make a decision. At least one person on the team should have some knowledge about available devices, and other members of the team should have knowledge about the student's curriculum and functioning in different areas including physical ability, language development, and any other area that may be pertinent.

**2** *Determine the specific needs of the student.* The IEP team should select an AT device in response to clearly defined goals and objectives with the intention of enhancing skills.

**3** *Consider student characteristics and abilities.* Different AT devices have different levels of complexity and different use requirements that the IEP team should consider in light of the student's abilities. The team must take into consideration the student's intellectual, physical, sensory, and social abilities. Whenever possible, the team should also attend to the student's preference for a device.

**4** *Determine where the student will use the device.* Although some devices may be appropriate for use in only one setting, others may be useful or necessary for several settings. The IEP team therefore must consider the transportability of the device, its size, and its durability, among other factors.

**5** *For AAC devices, determine with whom the device will be used.* The team should consider the targets of the individual when he uses an AAC device. If the target audience is limited, the select individuals can be instructed in the meaning of the signs, icons, or expressions that the device indicates. If the audience is broader, the production of the device must be relatively clear and unambiguous.

**6** *Determine how well the device must operate.* Consider how fast and durable a device must operate and to what degree or breadth it must perform. A device in need of constant repair will not be often used or will soon be abandoned.

**7** *Consider practical constraints in acquiring the device, and determine if they can be adequately addressed.* Specifically, the team must consider different funding sources for the device, the availability of the device or equipment, and how long it may take to arrive. Team members should also consider who will teach the student to use the device and should interact with others, such as family members, about the use of the device.

**8** *Consider the response to the device within the student's family and cultural contexts.* Finally, the IEP team must give a great deal of thought as to how the AT device will affect the family of the individual with disabilities on a daily basis. The team should also consider how the student will use the AT device within the family and what effect it might have on family activities, routines, and resources.

## Applications and Examples

The selection of an AT device requires an IEP team to consider many issues. As one authority stated, "To most effectively match assistive technology devices and services with any individual with a disability, team members must consider five parallel domains: (a) user characteristics, (b) family issues, (c) cultural factors, (d) technology features, and (e) service system considerations" (Parette, 1997, p. 271).

An often overlooked but important factor when selecting an AT device is the possible impact of a device within the family routine. For example, the device can affect communication within the family, change family members' roles and activities, and create new demands for family members. Additionally, many AT devices require parents or caregivers to learn how they operate and how to maintain them. This instruction of family members is considered an essential AT support service, but it requires additional time and effort on the part of family members.

## Keep in Mind

Assistive technology devices can be very useful, but many are sitting on shelves in schools and are not being used. Some are ordered and then never used; others are used briefly and then left on the sideline. This means there is a loss of both money and a student's potential—because the student did not use an appropriate device. Adhering to the guidelines presented in this strategy can help avoid these costly mistakes.

**Key References**

Best, S. J., Reed, P., & Bigge, J. L. (2005). Assistive technology. In S. J. Best, K. Wolff Heller, & J. L. Bigge (Eds.), *Teaching individuals with physical or multiple disabilities* (5th ed., pp. 179–226). Upper Saddle River, NJ: Merrill/Pearson Education.

Parette, H. P., & Peterson-Karlan, G. R. (2007). Facilitating student achievement with assistive technology. *Education and Training in Developmental Disabilities, 42,* 387–397.

Parette, P., & McMahan, G. A. (2002). What should we expect of assistive technology? Being sensitive to family goals. *Teaching Exceptional Children, 35*(1), 56–61.

Todis, B. (1996). Tools for the task? Perspectives on assistive technology in educational settings. *Journal of Special Education Technology, 13*(2), 49–61.

| Strategy 16.7 | **USING WORD PROCESSING AND RELATED SOFTWARE TO SUPPORT STUDENT WRITING** |
|---|---|

## Rationale

Many students with learning disabilities have difficulty with written expression. When asked to write, they may try to avoid the task, and sometimes exhibit behavior problems, or simply not comply with the teacher's request. When they do try to work on a written assignment, they may not organize or plan their assignment very well; may produce written work full of spelling, punctuation, and grammatical errors; will likely use fewer words than their peers without disabilities and not vary their vocabulary; and then turn in an unedited, illegible paper.

Such outcomes as these may be avoided if teachers invest adequate time teaching students strategies to use word processing and related software to plan, create, and edit written products. Research has shown that when students use word processors to produce written documents, they tend to write more, have fewer errors, and produce written documents of higher quality (see "Key References," following).

## Step-by-Step

**1** *Using selected software, teach students writing skills using the following steps:*

- **Help students organize their written assignment.** Students can use programs such as Inspiration to help them brainstorm and create the major components of their writing assignment and synthesize the contents into related categories. Students need teacher instruction in how to create and complete their organization. Teacher-provided models and feedback on their creations will be helpful.

- **Teach students to use word prediction to help with spelling weaknesses.** Word-prediction software allows students to type in the first few letters of a word and then offers the student a list of words to select to insert. The dictionaries included in many word-prediction software programs allow teachers to add custom words for special topics such as science projects.

- **Use voiced text to allow students to review what they have written.** Voiced software converts written text into spoken words and will often highlight the written text as the voicing of each word occurs. This process allows students to listen to their written work and make corrections as necessary.

- **As students write, teach them to use spell checkers.** Spell checkers are not perfect, but they may be helpful to students. Problems with spell checkers include failing to identify words that are misspelled for their context (e.g., homonyms), not identifying the correct spelling of a misspelled word in the correction list, and the inability of the student to identify the correctly spelled word from the list. Teachers need to carefully monitor the use of spell checking in order to ensure correct usage.

- **Encourage the use of a thesaurus to help students build and use different vocabulary.** A thesaurus offers students alternative vocabulary to help eliminate the overuse of certain words. However, teachers should carefully monitor the use of alternate words to make sure they fit the context of the written material.

- **Help students review and edit their work using grammar checkers.** We all know that grammar checkers can be both a help and a hindrance. Students may use them to find errors, but sometimes they may work against the writer's purpose. If students use grammar checkers, the teacher needs to support students in understanding the grammatical error that is identified.

**2** *Evaluate the student's work, and provide feedback.* Feedback to the student should address the written product, the components of the product (organization, grammar, spelling, etc.), and the use of the software as part of the writing process. The teacher should point out areas of weakness to the student and provide opportunities to improve on those areas.

## Applications and Examples

Here is how one student benefited from the use of AT software to facilitate writing:

> With the use of an organizational program, Joe is able to enter his research into a semantic web and then convert the web into an outline. Using the outline and a word-processing program, Joe pairs a verbal rehearsal strategy with word prediction. For each component of the outline, he generates a sentence aloud before typing it. He then uses the voice output feature to read back what he has written, at first, sentence by sentence, but then less often as his self-confidence grows (Montgomery and Marks, 2006).

After Joe finishes his draft with the help of AT software, he uses word programs to polish his effort. The thesaurus helps him replace some words he uses repeatedly in the document, and then spell-check and grammar check features allow him to produce a final product.

## Keep in Mind

The software discussed here will not improve students' writing without sufficient direction from the teacher. For success to occur with writing, students need much practice with feedback. As students find that the software can accommodate their weaknesses, the quality of their writing content may improve. As with all learning, the more time invested in the process, the better the outcome.

**Key References**

Bryant, D. P., Bryant, B. R., & Raskind, M. H. (1998). Using assistive technology to enhance the skills of students with learning disabilities. *Intervention in School and Clinic, 34*(1), 53–58.

Hetzroni, O. E., & Shrieber, B. (2004). Word processing as an assistive technology tool for enhancing academic outcomes of students with writing disabilities in the general classroom. *Journal of Learning Disabilities, 37,* 143–154.

MacArthur, C. A. (2000). New tools for writing: Assistive technology for students with writing difficulties. *Topics in Language Disorders, 20*(4), 85–100.

Montgomery, D. J., & Marks, L. J. (2006). Using technology to build independence in writing for students with disabilities. *Preventing School Failure, 50*(3), 33–38.

Quenneville, J. (2001). Tech tools for students with learning disabilities: Infusion into inclusive classrooms. *Preventing School Failure, 45*(4), 167–170.

Strategy 16.8 | # TEACHING STUDENTS WITH DISABILITIES TO USE CALCULATORS

## Rationale

Educators continue to debate the use of calculators by students who are learning math skills. One side takes the position that calculators can allow students to deal easily with simple calculations, focusing their mental energy more on using reasoning to solve problems. The other side maintains that students should learn basic arithmetic facts so they can apply them automatically when needed. Many experts feel the argument is not needed and maintain that although it is important for students to learn basic math facts, they also should be allowed to save time by using calculators (see "Key References," following).

For some students with disabilities, calculators are a helpful tool that allows them to overcome a serious weakness. Even though these students can often improve their math skills, the issue is often one of finding the correct answer in a short period of time. In these cases, their calculating abilities may be inadequate, so that without the use of a calculator, they may not be able to handle the immediate situation. A calculator, therefore (and sometimes a talking calculator), becomes an important AT device.

## Step-by-Step

**1** *When students can memorize math facts, they should.* Many students with learning disabilities and other mild disabilities can learn math facts, including addition, subtraction, multiplication, and division facts, and various drill-and-practice games will help them do so. Teachers, especially those teaching younger students, should not avoid teaching facts with an assumption that the students will always be able to use a calculator.

**2** *Begin teaching the use of calculators as students learn math facts.* As students learn basic facts, teach them simultaneously how to use calculators. Create games that allow students to respond as fast as possible (in writing or orally) to math fact quizzes, then let them check their answers with calculators.

**3** *Teach students to estimate the correct answers to problems.* Even when students use calculators, it is easy to make keying errors that lead to incorrect calculations. For this reason, students should learn to estimate the answer when the problem uses large numbers. They can then compare their estimated answers to the calculated answers in order to determine if the latter are probably correct.

**4** *Teach students to use appropriate operations (+, −, ×, ÷) to find answers.* If the value of the calculator is to help students find answers quickly, it is essential that they learn which math operations are necessary to solve particular specific problems. It is critical that students learn what math operations mean and when to apply them.

**5** *Younger children can use calculators to play games to learn math functions and facts.* Allowing younger elementary-age students to play games with the calculator will help them learn the meaning of operations. These games should include items that can be manipulated while calculations are being conducted so that the children can see the relationship.

**6** *Apply skills using calculators to solve word problems.* Solving word problems presents a great challenge for many students with disabilities. Teachers should place a great deal of focus on reading and understanding these problems and using calculators to solve them.

**7** *Teach students to use calculators in real-world applications.* Particularly as students grow older and must learn to operate in the real world, it is important for them to have practice using the calculator in community settings. At this time, it is also important to focus on estimating.

**8** *Some students benefit from talking calculators.* Students with visual problems and some students with learning disabilities benefit from talking calculators. These calculators allow the user to enter numbers (usually the keys are quite large and easy to see) and hear the answers to their calculations.

## Applications and Examples

When working on skills with students using calculators, the first thing to remember is that the skills should not be dissimilar to skills being learned by other students. The best guide for teachers are the curriculum standards used for other students. Most states have such standards, and most often these are based on the standards of the National Council of Teachers of Mathematics.

Some students with disabilities are at a disadvantage in achieving higher-level standards because they lack basic skills that they have not been able to adequately master. For those students, the IEP team should consider the calculator to be an AT device that will allow the students to master these skills.

## Keep in Mind

Even with calculators, many students with disabilities are at a disadvantage because of their difficulties in translating information provided in a word problem or in a contextual situation into knowing the math operations that they should conduct. The calculator is helpful in arriving at correct answers only if the students can enter numbers and operations appropriately. As with other skills learned by students with disabilities, practice is necessary for them to learn to use calculators effectively.

**Key References**

Huinker, D. (2002). Calculators as learning tools for young children's explorations of number. *Teaching Children Mathematics, 8*, 316–321.

Judd, W. (2007). Instructional games with calculators. *Mathematics Teaching in the Middle School, 12*, 312–314.

Mittag, K. C., & Van Reusen, A. K. (1999). One fish, two fish, pretzel fish: Learning estimation and other advanced mathematics concepts in an inclusive class. *Teaching Exceptional Children, 31*(6), 66–72.

National Council of Teachers of Mathematics. (2004). *Overview: Standards for school mathematics: Pre-kindergarten through grade 12.* Retrieved on December 15, 2007, from http://standards.nctm.org/document/chapter3/index.htm

| Strategy 16.9 | SUPPORTING STUDENTS WHO USE AUGMENTATIVE/ALTERNATIVE COMMUNICATION DEVICES |

## Rationale

The development of augmentative/alternative communication (AAC) devices has opened up the door of communication for people who years ago could not express their needs, wishes, and thoughts. These devices range from something as simple as a board with small objects, pictures, or symbols for a student to point to, to a very sophisticated (and expensive) device that will produce completely synthesized speech when the person types letter keys, or touches words, symbols, or pictures.

The identification of an appropriate AAC device, the interface the individual will have with it, and the range of the vocabulary for the device are among the issues that the IEP team needs to address before a student can acquire and learn to use a device. This assessment process often is conducted by a speech–language pathologist (SLP) with specialized preparation. However, this person needs assistance from other key individuals, such as the classroom teacher, in making many of these decisions. Additionally, the SLP seeks the cooperation of these individuals in providing supports for the student using the AAC device so that the student will achieve improved communication.

## Step-by-Step

**1** *Develop a communicative rapport with the student.* The best communication is natural communication. Develop a comfortable rapport with the student so that your interactions do not seem strained or artificial. Always assume that the student can understand what you are saying, but at the same time, try to say what you mean in a way that is most likely to be understood. Having a good sense of humor and joking around are always good ways to build rapport.

**2** *Make sure the student has continued access to the device and that it is functioning appropriately.* Students who use an AAC device need to have as much access to it as possible, and the teacher should make sure that the device is working appropriately. It is not the teacher's responsibility to fix a broken AAC device, but it is important to let the SLP know if the device is not working as it should.

**3** *Encourage the student to communicate at natural times.* The more opportunities a person has to use an AAC device, the better he will be able to do so. All teachers and other key people in the AAC user's environment should not let him fade to the communication background but should encourage his communication whenever the chance occurs.

**4** *Promote interactions with other students.* Interaction with peers is perhaps the best way to promote communication, and students with disabilities often improve their communication skills in contexts where peer interaction is promoted. However, because AAC devices can inhibit the initiation of communication, prompting peer interactions can be very important.

**5** *Ask open-ended questions, and encourage questions from the student.* Often, when people use AAC devices, others tend to limit the nature of verbalizations with them, such as asking yes or no questions. It is better for students if others ask questions or elicit comments that might require them to stretch their ability so they can develop more elaborate responses.

**6** *Be aware of issues related to handling, maintenance, transportation, and storage of the device.* As we've said, AAC devices can range from very simple to very elaborate. Those that are more sophisticated can be quite expensive to purchase and repair. It would be a good idea for you to understand any appropriate procedures and cautions that you should take when you must handle the device.

## Applications and Examples

Chloe is a 10-year-old fourth grader with multiple disabilities. She uses a digitized AAC device that includes pictures of food and activities to state her wishes for snacks and different choices throughout the day. When it is time to make a choice, Chloe's teacher prompts her to look at her device and indicate her selection. If she does not respond, the teacher physically prompts her by moving her hand part of the way toward the board while asking her what she would like. When Chloe pushes the button, the communication device sounds out the word or the phrase that she has pressed, and the teacher (or others) responds. For example, if the teacher asks Chloe if she would like something to drink, Chloe responds by pressing the button for "juice, please" if she is thirsty. Other AT devices allow Chloe to participate in other ways during the day.

## Keep in Mind

Having an AAC device does not mean that the student will be able to overcome all communication limitations, nor does it mean the device will be the sole manner in which the student communicates. As with other AT devices, an AAC device is only another tool that helps the student bridge the gap between current ability level and achieving a useful outcome. The efforts of the classroom teacher, along with the expertise of the SLP and the involvement of the family, increase the chance of a successful outcome.

**Key References**

Beukelman, D. R., & Mirenda, P. (2005). *Augmentative and alternative communication: Supporting adults and children with complex communication needs* (3rd ed.). Baltimore: Brookes.

Downing, J. (2005). *Teaching communication skills to students with severe disabilities* (2nd ed.). Baltimore: Brookes.

Hunt, P., Soto, G., Maier, J., Muller, E., & Goetz, L. (2002). Collaborative teaming to support students with augmentative and alternative communication needs in general education classrooms. *Augmentative and Alternative Communication, 18,* 20–35.

Kent-Walsh, J. E., & Light, J. C. (2003). General education teachers' experiences with inclusion of students who use augmentative and alternative communication. *Augmentative and Alternative Communication, 19,* 104–124.

TherapyTimes. (2006). *Back to school tips for AAC devices.* Retrieved May 29, 2008, from http://www.therapytimes.com/content=5601J64E48769C841

**Strategy 16.10**  # SUPPORTING STUDENTS WHO USE MOTORIZED WHEELCHAIRS

## Rationale

A person's ability to move around serves many important purposes. Early in life, movement is a critical part of learning and development, and young children who have limited mobility are at a disadvantage. Movement allows children to develop cognitive and perceptual abilities as well as communication and social skills. Impaired mobility therefore not only limits a child's movement from one place to another but has an overall detrimental effect on her general development.

Including students in wheelchairs in regular classrooms allows them to maintain their social relationships with their classmates and gives them the chance to participate in the general curriculum. Inclusion, however, may require that teachers are aware of accommodations for the student and some basic conditions necessary to facilitate the student's involvement and mobility. These are discussed next.

## Step-by-Step

**1** *Discuss the student's needs with a physical therapist, and evaluate your classrooms accommodations for the student.* Physical therapists (PTs) are key professionals who can help design classroom arrangements and conditions that can allow physical closeness and participation by students in motorized wheelchairs. It is also important for the PT to discuss with you any discomfort of the student so that he is not distracted from learning activities. In the classroom, the teachers should ensure ready access to all parts of the room, including centers and materials.

**2** *Monitor the student's position in the wheelchair, and be aware of comfort level.* The PT should provide you with instructions about the correct positioning of the student in the wheelchair, and you may need to monitor the student to make sure that this position is maintained. Sometimes it will be important for the student to be repositioned in order to be more comfortable.

**3** *Know when the student may leave the wheelchair and how to assist with the transition.* The student will sometimes need assistance to get out of the wheelchair and into another position. At times, you, and perhaps another teacher or an assistant, may need to help the student move. The PT can provide you with instruction regarding the correct way to move someone.

**4** *Be aware of the basic operating procedure of the wheelchair.* You do not need to be a mechanic, but you should be aware of some of the basic parts and procedures that operate the wheelchair. At a minimum, you should know about the on-off switch, the chair lock, the control device used to direct the chair, the clutch for engaging the wheel, and the belt used to drive the wheel. Generally, in order for the wheelchair to move, plugs must be tightly plugged in, the brakes off, the clutch engaged, and the power turned on.

**5** *Make sure the student operates the wheelchair safely and correctly.* Like other students, those in wheelchairs will sometimes want to show off, move too fast, or not follow common classroom rules. Students in wheelchairs should know how to operate their wheelchairs safely and follow the rules for doing so.

## Applications and Examples

When Jason was 4 years old, he was diagnosed as having Duchenne muscular dystrophy. The condition resulted in a gradual loss of muscle control and ultimately in the loss of Jason's ability to walk. Although his parents were devastated by his condition, they wanted to make sure that he remained a full participant in all life activities including school. At first, Jason was mobile in a manual wheelchair, but as his arm muscles began to weaken, he required the use of a motorized wheelchair. Now 11 years old and in the fifth grade, Jason is involved as much as possible in regular class activities. He continues to have a positive outlook and is supported by his family, friends, and teachers. Jason's chair is an important form of assistive technology that facilitates inclusion.

## Keep in Mind

Misbehavior may be occasionally acceptable, but when the student is powering a device that may weigh up to 400 or 500 pounds, acting out can potentially cause serious harm to the driver or other students in the area. Students should be disciplined to be careful.

**Key References**

Best, S. J., Heller, K. W., & Bigge J. L. (Eds.). (2005). *Teaching individuals with physical or multiple disabilities* (5th ed.). Upper Saddle River, NJ: Merrill/Pearson Education.

National Institute for Rehabilitation Engineering. (2003). *Power wheelchairs and user safety.* Retrieved May 29, 2008, from http://www.abledata.com/abledata_docs/PowerChair-Safety.htm

Wadsworth, D. E., & Knight, D. (1999). Preparing the inclusion classroom for students with special physical and health needs. *Intervention in School and Clinic, 34*(3), 170–175.

# Glossary

**Ability grouping:** An instructional arrangement that allows students with common learning characteristics to benefit from targeted instruction.

**Absence seizures:** Also referred to as *petit mal seizures,* these seizures are very brief, lasting perhaps 1 to 10 seconds, with the person experiencing a loss of consciousness but otherwise remaining fixed in position.

**Accommodations:** Changes in curriculum, instruction, and/or grouping arrangements to meet the needs of students with disabilities in general education classrooms.

**Acoustical amplification system:** A device that serves to increase the volume and intensity of sound directed toward a student or group of students.

**Adequate yearly progress (AYP):** The No Child Left Behind Act mandates that all students make AYP. Each state defines AYP, which is intended to measure student progress and ensure that all students experience continuous and substantial growth in academic achievement.

**Advance organizer:** Information that is used to introduce a new topic that may include an overview of the topic, goals for learning, how the new information is organized, and connections of the new information to previous knowledge.

**Aggression:** Physical or verbal attacks that use intimidation and manipulation to get one's own way.

**Alternate assessments:** The use of nontraditional methods of measurement to judge student performance.

**Alternative grouping strategies:** Used to support students who do not make adequate progress using whole-group instruction. Includes a range of small-group alternatives for instruction that reduce the number of students being taught and facilitate the use of effective instruction.

**Alternative routes to certification:** Nontraditional approaches to teacher preparation of varying length and intensity that circumvent traditional university training efforts.

**Americans with Disabilities Act (ADA):** An act that requires nondiscriminatory protection of civil rights and accessibility to physical facilities and applies to all segments of society with the exception of private schools and religious organizations.

**Amphetamines:** A type of stimulant medication used to treat the symptoms of attention-deficit/hyperactivity disorder (ADHD). Amphetamines include Adderall and Dexedrine.

**Anxiety:** Uncomfortable physical and mental signs of distress concerning our daily life challenges.

**Applied behavior analysis (ABA):** The application of the scientific method and behavioral principles to the observation, study, and modification of behavior.

**Asperger's disorder:** An autism spectrum disorder characterized by qualitative impairments in nonverbal behaviors, social relationships, interests, and social and emotional reciprocity, but, unlike autism, it involves no delays in language or cognitive development.

**Assistive technology (AT):** Technology that helps individuals with disabilities function more like those without disabilities by helping to bridge the gap between what a person can do and what he or she may need to do.

**Assistive technology devices:** Any item, piece of equipment, or product system used to increase, maintain, or improve functional capabilities of a student with a disability.

**Assistive technology services:** Any service that directly assists in the selection, acquisition, or use of an assistive technology device.

**Asthma:** A chronic lung condition that can result in attacks and difficult breathing, wheezing, coughing, excess mucus, sweating, and chest constriction.

**Ataxia:** A form of cerebral palsy characterized by lack of balance and uncoordinated movements.

**Athetosis:** A form of cerebral palsy characterized by involuntary muscle movements.

**Attention-deficit/hyperactivity disorder (ADHD):** "A persistent pattern of inattention and/or hyperactivity-impulsivity that is more frequently displayed and more severe than is typically observed in individuals at a comparable level of development" (APA, 2000, p. 85).

**Augmentative/alternative communication (AAC):** Simple or technologically advanced methods that support or enhance oral and mechanical modes of communication.

**Autism spectrum disorders (ASD):** ASD, also referred to as pervasive developmental disorders (PDD), are a group of developmental disorders that share common social, communicative, and stereotyped and ritualistic behavioral similarities, varying in age of onset and severity of symptoms. The group includes autism, Asperger's syndrome, pervasive developmental disorder—not otherwise specified (PDD-NOS), Rett syndrome, and childhood disintegrative disorder (CDD).

**Autistic disorder:** Sometimes referred to as early infantile autism, childhood autism, or Kanner's autism, it is characterized by marked impairments in social interactions and communication, and restrictions in activities or interests.

**Autoimmune disease:** A condition in which the body attacks its own cells due to an overactive immune response against substances and tissues normally present in the body.

**Balanced instruction:** In reading, balanced instruction means using components of both whole-language and phonics or skills approaches to instruction. This instruction in mathematics consists of an emphasis on both skills instruction and knowledge of underlying mathematical concepts.

**Behavior intervention plan (BIP):** An individual plan to improve a student's behavior based on an assessment of personal or environmental conditions hypothesized to influence the occurrence of the behavior.

**Bilingualism:** The ability to speak two languages. (*Multilingualism* refers to the ability to speak more than two languages.)

**Blind:** Lack of ability to see light and form.

**Blindness:** The condition of being without vision.

**Bone tuberculosis:** A rare condition in which an infectious disease (tubercle bacillus) attacks bones or joints.

**Building-based support teams:** Groups of professionals who work with teachers to address student academic or behavior difficulties.

**Central auditory processing disorder:** A disorder related to the processing of auditory information in the brain that is characterized by difficulty recognizing and interpreting sounds.

**Cerebral palsy (CP):** A nonprogressive neurological disorder caused by brain damage before, during, or after birth that impairs a person's posture and movement ability.

**Child Find services:** Services provided by a state to identify children with disabilities in order to provide them with educational and related services.

**Childhood disintegrative disorder:** Following 2 years of relatively normal development, the child develops a severe loss of functioning.

**Chromosomal anomalies:** A condition in which strands of chromosomal material within cells are not arranged in their normal pattern. Anomalies often result in syndromes such as Down syndrome.

**Civil rights movement:** A particularly active period from the late 1950s to the early 1990s that advocated for the application of the Bill of Rights to all disenfranchised persons, whether by race, gender, or disability.

**Clubfoot:** A congenital anomaly in which the foot points downward and inward.

**Co-existing conditions:** The co-occurrence of two or more disorders, disabilities, or diseases that are not caused by each other. Sometimes called *co-morbidity*.

**Collaboration:** Teachers' and other professionals' working together to achieve common goals.

**Collaborative consultation:** A formal process that includes (1) specific problem identification and goal setting; (2) analysis of factors contributing to the problem and brainstorming possible problem-solving interventions; (3) planning an intervention; and (4) evaluating the outcomes.

**Collectivist cultures:** Cultures in which working for the common good is more highly valued than individual achievement.

**Communication disorders:** Language disorders or speech disorders that interfere with communication.

**Comprehension:** Understanding and remembering what is read.

**Conductive hearing loss:** Locus of hearing loss in the outer and/or middle ear.

**Congenital anomaly:** A physical disability apparent at the time of birth.

**Congenital hip dislocations (dysplasia):** At birth, the ball at the top of the thighbone does not sit securely in the socket of the hip joint.

**Consultant:** A teacher (or other professional) who provides assistance to another teacher by problem solving possible solutions to a classroom problem.

**Content disorders:** See *semantic disorders*.

**Content enhancements:** Instructional techniques that help academically diverse learners understand, store, and access academic content.

**Content maps:** Visual representations that students may use to understand relationships among ideas or information. Maps explicitly present important information and make this content accessible to all students.

**Continuum of services:** A requirement of IDEA 2004; students with disabilities must be offered a continuum of placement options for service delivery, including both general education and special class placements.

**Cooperative learning:** Involves a range of strategies in which students work together to learn and to ensure that others in their group learn.

**Core instruction:** Instruction provided to the whole class based on the general education curriculum.

**Co-teaching:** When used in inclusive classrooms, co-teaching is defined as a general and special-education teacher working collaboratively to share responsibility for instructing a diverse group of students in a single classroom.

**Culturally and linguistically diverse (CLD):** Backgrounds that are non–European American and, in some instances, non–English speaking, including African American, Hispanic, Native American/ Alaskan Native, and Asian/Pacific Islander.

**Culturally responsive classroom management:** Built on the assumption that culture impacts people's perceptions, knowledge, and interactions, and that the impact of cultural assumptions is often implicit. Culturally responsive teachers strive to learn more about who they are, what they believe, and how their beliefs and experiences influence their perceptions of and interactions with students and their families from a range of cultural backgrounds. Teachers use this knowledge of self and others' cultural backgrounds to guide culturally responsive classroom management.

**Culturally responsive teaching:** Built on the assumption that culture impacts people's perceptions, knowledge, and interactions, and that the impact of cultural assumptions is often implicit. Culturally responsive teachers strive to learn more about who they are, what they believe, and how their beliefs and experiences influence their perceptions of and interactions with students and their families from a range of cultural backgrounds. Teachers use this knowledge of self and others' cultural backgrounds to guide culturally responsive teaching.

**Culture:** The values, beliefs, traditions, and behaviors associated with a particular group of people who share a common history.

**Curriculum-based measurement (CBM):** A systematic approach for monitoring student progress in reading, mathematics, writing, and spelling by directly assessing academic skills.

**Curvature of the spine (scoliosis):** Abnormal spinal growth with convexity to the right or left side.

**Cystic fibrosis:** A disease that affects major body organs that secrete fluids. It primarily affects the lungs and the digestive system.

**Deaf:** With a capital *D*, used to describe a particular group of people who share a language (American Sign Language) and a culture (Deaf culture).

**Deaf-blind:** Concomitant hearing and visual impairments, the combination of which causes severe communication and other developmental and educational needs.

**Decibels (dBs):** Unit of measure used to report degree of hearing loss.

**Deinstitutionalization:** The policy of releasing people, particularly those with disabilities of the mind, from institutions and into community settings.

**Depression:** A pervasive and insidious series of symptoms that influences mood, thought, and carriage.

**Developmental aphasia:** A language impairment that is assumed to be the result of some type of neurological dysfunction.

**Developmental milestones:** Characteristics and abilities of infants, toddlers, and children that commonly appear within a specific range of time (e.g., sitting up or rolling over).

**Diabetes:** A disease in which the body does not produce or properly use insulin to convert sugar, starches, and other food into energy.

**Differentiated instruction:** An approach to instruction that includes proactive planning to meet diverse students' needs. Differentiated instruction is student centered, based on student assessment data, and includes multiple approaches to content, process, and product to ensure that all students learn.

**Diplegia:** A physical disability in which the legs are more affected than the arms.

**Direct instruction (DI):** "A model that uses teacher demonstration and explanation combined with student practice and feedback to help learners acquire well-defined knowledge and skills needed for later learning" (Eggen & Kauchak, 2012, p. 266).

**Dispositions:** One's temperament or tendency, generally learned over time, to act or respond in a certain way, given a certain situation.

**Distributed practice:** The distribution of instruction or study of information over time. For example, it is often more effective to distribute the study of spelling words during 10-minute sessions over several days than massing practice over one or two longer periods.

**Down syndrome:** A condition due to chromosomal anomaly in which three chromosome strands (instead of two) occur at pair 21 (trisomy 21). Children with Down syndrome are usually smaller than average and have slower physical, motor, language, and mental development.

**Duchenne muscular dystrophy:** A commonly genetically inherited form of muscular dystrophy.

**Dyslexia:** A reading disability that is assumed to be the result of some type of neurological dysfunction.

**Echolalia:** Repeating words and parts of or whole sentences spoken by other people, with little understanding.

**Educational technology:** Technology used to facilitate learning academic skills.

**Emotional and behavioral disabilities (EBD):** Refers to students who exhibit inappropriate personal or social behavior that interferes with learning.

**English-language learner (ELL):** Includes students who are learning English as a second language or those previously called students with limited English proficiency.

**Entrepreneurial supports:** Supportive, self-sustaining, for-profit corporations built on the skills and interests of those with disabilities.

**Epilepsy:** A neurological condition that makes people prone to having seizures.

**Ethnic group:** A group in which individual members identify with one another, usually based on ancestry. Ethnic groups often share common practices related to factors such as culture, religion, and language.

**Evidence-based practices:** Teaching approaches that have been repeatedly demonstrated through research to result in improved student learning.

**Exclusion clause:** Often included in the definition of learning disabilities to ensure that the primary reason for a student's academic difficulty is a learning disability and not another disability (e.g., intellectual disability or emotional and behavioral disability) or environmental conditions (e.g., poor teaching).

**Executive functions:** Thinking processes that are used to engage in a range of activities, including planning, organizing, attending, strategizing, and remembering details. These functions allow students to manage their behavior as they evaluate their actions and make adjustments if they are not achieving desired results.

**Explicit instruction:** When instructional content is explicitly taught using systematic instructional methods, often based on behavioral theory.

**Externalizing behavior problems:** Overt manifestations of problem behaviors typically characterized by defiance and disruption.

**Figurative language:** A variety of figures of speech such as idioms, metaphors, analogies, similes, hyperbole, understatement, jokes, allusions, and slang.

**Fluency:** The rate and smoothness of reading, demonstrated by reading text quickly and accurately.

**Fluency disorders:** Interruptions in the normal flow of speech.

**Form disorders:** Problems in creating sounds used to make words and word parts.

**Foster care:** A state-run system of support in which children are removed from birth or custodial parents and placed with certified foster or stand-in parents under state authority.

**Full inclusion:** The perspective taken by some disability advocates that all students with disabilities should be educated in general education classrooms for the full school day.

**Functional behavioral assessment (FBA):** A systematic, highly structured method of gathering information to determine the purpose or function of observed behaviors.

**Functional language:** Communicating with a purpose, such as being able to communicate basic wants and needs.

**Funds of knowledge:** The cultural and experiential resources within a student's home that a culturally responsive teacher may use to provide effective, successful curriculum and instruction.

**Genetic inheritance:** A condition that is genetically transmitted from one or two parents to a child.

*Grand mal seizure:* See *tonic-clonic seizure.*

**Graphic organizers:** Visual representations or aids that may be used to organize and facilitate learning of information.

**Hearing impairment:** An impairment in hearing, whether permanent or fluctuating, that adversely affects a child's educational performance but that is not included under the IDEA definition of deafness.

**Hemiplegia:** A physical disability in which the limbs on one side of the body are more affected.

**Hemophilia:** A rare inherited disorder in which the blood does not clot normally and may lead to dangerously excessive bleeding.

**Hyperactivity:** A characteristic used to identify students with ADHD. Students who are hyperactive exhibit a high level of activity that is not appropriate in a particular setting and is not age appropriate.

**Impulsivity:** A characteristic used to identify students with ADHD. Students who are impulsive respond without thinking at a level that is not age appropriate.

**Inclusion:** Students with disabilities are included as valued members of the school community. This suggests that they belong to the school community and are accepted by others; that they actively participate in the academic and social community of the school; and that they receive supports that offer them the opportunity to succeed.

**Individualist cultures:** Cultures that value individual achievement and initiative and promote self-realization.

**Individualized education program (IEP):** A detailed, structured plan of action required by IDEA that informs and guides the delivery of instruction and related services.

**Individualized health care plan (IHCP):** A student plan that specifies health and medically related activities that must

occur to maintain the student's health or to provide in the case of a medical emergency that may arise from the student's condition.

**Individuals with Disabilities Education Improvement Act of 2004 (IDEA 2004):** Landmark legislation, originally enacted in 1975 as the Education for All Handicapped Children Act, that guides how states and school districts must educate children with disabilities.

**Insulin:** A hormone that affects metabolism and other body systems. It causes the body's cells to take glucose from blood.

**Intellectual disability (ID):** Subaverage general intellectual functioning, existing concurrently with deficits in adaptive behavior and manifested during the developmental period, that adversely affects a child's educational performance.

**Internalizing behavior problems:** Inwardly directed problem behaviors typically characterized by social withdrawal, anxiety, and depression.

**Juvenile arthritis:** A broad term that encompasses different types of chronic diseases that result in damage to the joints in children.

**Juvenile diabetes:** See *Type 1 diabetes.*

**Language disorders:** Conditions in which a person has difficulty sharing thoughts, ideas, and feelings completely, including disorders of form, content (or semantics), and use (or pragmatics).

**Learning strategies:** Approaches to planning, executing, and evaluating a task that enhance student learning. Learning strategies are learned and used naturally by some students and must be taught to others.

**Least restrictive environment (LRE):** A mandate of IDEA that requires that students with special needs are educated with children without disabilities to the maximum extent appropriate.

**Legal blindness:** A central acuity of 20/200 or less in the better eye with the best possible correction; is used to determine eligibility for various legal purposes such as taxation.

**Leukemia:** A cancer of the blood or bone marrow.

**Limb deficiencies:** Lack of fully developed arms or legs at birth.

**Limited English proficiency (LEP):** Describes individuals who do not speak English as their primary language, and who have limited ability to read, write, speak, or understand English.

**Linguistic schema:** A cognitive construct that allows for the organization of language information in long-term memory.

**Litigation:** A lawsuit or other action in the courts that seeks to resolve a legal disagreement about an issue.

**Mediation:** A voluntary process in which a qualified, impartial facilitator works with families and school districts to resolve issues related to the identification, assessment, and placement of a student with disabilities.

**Metacognition:** An awareness of thinking processes and how individuals monitor and use these processes.

**Mixed hearing loss:** Both a conductive and sensorineural hearing loss.

**Mnemonic devices:** Memory aids that teachers use to assist students in remembering information. For example, HOMES is a mnemonic device used to aid in learning the names of the Great Lakes (Huron, Ontario, Michigan, Erie, and Superior).

**Motor speech disorders:** Neurological conditions that affect a person's speech.

**Muscular dystrophy:** A progressive physical disability that results in ongoing muscle weakness.

**Myelomeningocele:** The most severe form of spina bifida; loss of sensation and muscle control occur in parts of the body below the lesion.

**Negative reinforcement:** The removal of events or activities following a behavior that serves to increase the rate of frequency or the behavior.

**Nephritis:** Inflammation of one or both kidneys.

**Neurological disorder:** A condition involving the nervous system.

**No Child Left Behind (NCLB) Act:** Federal legislation requiring that states (1) assess student performance in reading, math, and science; (2) ensure that all students have highly qualified teachers; and (3) provide public school choice and supplemental services to students unable to meet adequate yearly progress (AYP) for 2 years.

**Noncompliance:** Instances when students choose not to respond to instructions or requests.

**Normalization:** Suggests that persons with disabilities should have the opportunity to live their lives as independently as possible, making their own life decisions regarding work, leisure, housing, etc.

**Occupational therapy:** Delivered by an occupational therapist who has knowledge and skills similar to the physical therapist's but has an orientation toward purposeful activities or tasks such as the use of fine-motor skills related to daily living activities.

**Orthopedic and musculoskeletal conditions:** Conditions that affect bones or muscles within the limbs.

**Osteogenesis imperfecta:** A genetic disorder characterized by bones that break easily.

**Paraeducator:** A person who assists a teacher in a special education or general education classroom. Also called a paraprofessional, teacher assistant, or teacher's aide. Peer-assisted strategies: Engage peers in supporting students using activities such as peer tutoring or peer buddy systems.

**Peer tutoring:** A series of grouping alternatives that allow same-age or cross-age peers to assist classmates who are struggling with specific academic content.

**People-first language:** Emphasizes that persons with disabilities are just that: people who happen to have a disability. This language is respectful of people with disabilities, puts the person first (*person with a disability,* and not *disabled person*), and avoids the use of negative terms (*handicapped, wheelchair bound, retard*) to describe people with disabilities.

**Pervasive developmental disorder—not otherwise specified (PDD-NOS):** Individuals who do not meet the criteria or the degree of severity that characterizes the four other disorders in the PDD group but who still show a pattern of impairments in social interaction, verbal and nonverbal communication skills, and stereotypical or restricted interests.

*Petit mal* **seizure:** See *absence seizure.*

**Phonemic awareness:** The ability to hear, identify, and manipulate sounds (phonemes) in words. Phonemic awareness is a basic prerequisite skill needed to use phonics in learning to read. Phonics: The relationship between the sounds of oral language and the symbols (letters) of written language.

**Phonological and articulation disorders:** Difficulties using the mouth movement, lips, tongue, and voice box to produce speech sounds.

**Phonological awareness:** Understanding how oral language can be separated into smaller or component sounds and manipulated.

**Phonological processing:** The ability to use sound–symbol correspondences to sound out words. Many students with reading disabilities have problems with phonological processing.

**Physical therapists:** A professional who evaluates, plans, and develops interventions to improve posture and balance; to prevent bodily malformations; and to improve walking ability and other gross-motor skills.

**Physical therapy:** Provided by a physical therapist who evaluates, plans, and develops interventions to improve posture and balance; to prevent bodily misformations; and to improve walking ability and other gross-motor skills. The physical therapist works primarily with students who have significant disabilities.

**Picture Exchange Communication System (PECS):** An augmentative and alternative communication system that uses pictures to systematically teach people to initiate communication.

**Picture walks:** Using pictures to provide a preview of lesson content.

**Poliomyelitis:** An acute viral disease spread from person to person that can lead to muscle weakness and paralysis. Often referred to as "polio."

**Positive behavior management (PBS):** An applied science that uses educational methods to expand an individual's behavior repertoire and systems change methods to redesign an individual's living environment to, first, enhance the individual's quality of life and, second, to minimize his or her problem behavior (Carr et al., 2002).

**Pragmatic disorders:** See *usage disorders.*

**Pragmatics:** The rules that govern and describe how language is used in different contexts and environments.

*Prenatal causes:* Conditions that result in a disability that originate before birth.

**Proleptic teaching:** A guided discovery model of instruction in which teachers provide a strategy and then allow students to apply the strategy to unique situations.

**Prosthetic devices:** Artificial devices or extensions used to replace missing body parts.

**Pseudohypertrophy:** A condition that appears in children with muscular dystrophy in which the calves seem to be growing larger.

**Psychological processing:** Often included as part of the definition of learning disabilities. A psychological processing problem suggests that an underlying psychological difficulty may cause an academic problem. For example, difficulty with phonological processing may contribute to a problem learning to read.

**Quadriplegia:** A physical disability in which all four limbs are affected as well as the trunk and the muscles that control the neck, mouth, and the tongue.

**Regular education initiative (REI):** A policy initiative formally introduced in the mid-1980s calling for general educators to become more involved in and responsible for the education of students with disabilities.

**Replacement behaviors:** A series of positive actions that help students achieve the same functions or outcomes as do the challenging behaviors of concern.

**Resilience:** Not an innate ability, but a capacity available to all students that results in successful adaptation in school (or other settings) in spite of threatening or challenging circumstances.

**Response to intervention (RTI):** An approach to the identification of special education needs that is based on the assumption that students who struggle academically should be identified with a learning disability only if they do not respond to effective and intensive levels of instruction. It is also a tiered service-delivery approach in which teachers provide more intensive levels of service to students only when lower levels of instructional intensity fail to succeed.

**Rett disorder:** A neurodevelopmental disorder characterized by seizures and mental retardation as well as a loss of functional or purposeful use of hands.

**Rheumatic fever:** An inflammatory disease that can develop as a complication of untreated or poorly treated strep throat.

**Scaffolding:** The temporary support that teachers give students as they learn academic content.

**Screening:** Determining whether a child has a broad set of behavioral characteristics that suggest the possibility of a disability and the need for further assessments.

**Section 504 of the Rehabilitation Act:** Civil rights legislation that provides protections for those whose disabilities do not match the definitions under IDEA, including communicable diseases; temporary disabilities; and allergies, asthma, or illnesses due to the environment. Under Section 504, a student has a disability if that student functions as though disabled. Section 504 extends protections against discrimination beyond schools to employment and social and health services.

**Self-determination:** Assumes that persons with disabilities will act as the primary decision makers in their lives and make choices free from undue influence.

**Self-injurious behaviors (SIBs):** These are behaviors such as hitting your own head or biting your own hand that can be potentially dangerous. They are sometimes exhibited by students with severe disabilities.

**Self-management:** A range of actions, such as self-instructing, monitoring, evaluation, reinforcement, graphing, and advocacy, by which a student can increase independence by increasing positive behaviors and skills.

**Self-regulated strategy development (SRSD):** A systematic approach to teaching students strategies for learning academic content, often in writing and mathematics.

**Self-regulation:** Strategies that students use to monitor and control their own behavior (e.g., to decrease inappropriate behaviors, increase appropriate behaviors, and/or increase academic accuracy and productivity).

**Semantic disorders:** Difficulty using specific words or word combinations required by language rules. Also called *content disorders*.

**Sensorineural hearing loss:** Locus of hearing loss in the cochlea, inner ear, or eighth cranial nerve.

**Sensory disabilities:** Visual disabilities, including blindness; hearing impairments, including deafness; and deaf-blindness.

**Severe discrepancy:** The primary criterion that educators use to identify students with learning disabilities in many states. Defined as a severe discrepancy between expected achievement (typically based on an IQ score) and actual achievement.

**Sheltered workshops:** Segregated facilities that provide noncompetitive training and employment opportunities for individuals with disabilities.

**Sickle cell anemia:** A disease in which a block in normal blood flow causes pain and can damage most organs. The condition is most common among those with sub-Saharan African ancestry.

**Sickle cell disease:** See *sickle cell anemia*.

**Social stories:** An instructional technique in which students create or interpret narrative or visual illustrations that reflect typical social encounters.

**Social withdrawal:** A tendency to spend excessive amounts of time in solitary activities with low rates of verbalizations and interactions with others.

**Spasticity:** A form of cerebral palsy characterized by stiff muscles. Specific language impairment: A particular profile of language difficulty that an individual may exhibit; comprises various disorders.

**Speech disorders:** Conditions in which a person cannot produce speech sounds correctly or fluently, or has problems with his or her voice. Most common are phonological and articulation disorders, fluency disorders, voice disorders, and motor speech disorders.

**Spina bifida:** A break in the spinal cord that can leave a person with a loss of physical ability below the break.

**Standard course of study (SCOS):** A curriculum guide prepared by a local or state education agency that specifies learning objectives or benchmarks for subjects in all grade levels.

**Standard English:** A controversial term that is most often used to refer to the dialect of English spoken by educated people.

**Stereotyped behaviors:** Repetitive behaviors (e.g., hand flapping) seen among some individuals with disabilities.

**Stereotypies:** Also called *stereotyped behaviors,* these are repetitive behaviors (e.g., hand flapping) seen among some individuals with disabilities.

**Stimulant medications:** Frequently used to treat students with ADHD. These medications have been found to be highly effective for many students with ADHD because they increase attention and reduce restlessness. Stimulant medications include Ritalin and Concerta.

**Supported employment:** A range of supports that enable people with disabilities to work in natural environments.

**Surface management techniques:** A series of teacher-based actions that address minor instances of misbehavior with little disruption to the instructional environment.

**Targeted interventions:** Powerful school-based actions directed toward the chronic and persistent problem behaviors of those students who do not respond to school-wide methods of discipline and behavior management.

**Teacher assistance team (TAT):** A widely used form of building-based support that uses a systematic approach to identify student difficulties and generate possible solutions for referring teachers.

**Time-out:** A disciplinary behavior reductive technique in which a student is removed from a reinforcing environment following an undesired behavior.

**Tonic-clonic seizure:** Also referred to as a *grand mal* seizure, a seizure during which the person loses awareness, ceases to engage in any activity, loses consciousness, becomes stiff (tonic), and then engages in jerking (clonic) movements.

**Type 1 diabetes:** Also called juvenile diabetes or insulin-dependent diabetes; an autoimmune disease that destroys the cells in the pancreas that produce insulin.

**Universal design for learning (UDL):** A method of making curriculum and instructional activities accessible to all students by including supports and accommodations in the original design rather than making alterations after the fact.

**Universal precautions:** Guidelines provided by the Centers for Disease Control and Prevention to prevent the transmission of communicable diseases.

**Usage disorders:** Difficulty using language that is appropriate for the social context.

**Visual acuity:** Quality of ability to see, usually reported as a fraction (e.g., 20/20); the top number states the distance from the object, and the bottom number states the distance at which a person with normal vision could see the same object or figure that is 20 feet away.

**Visual disabilities:** See *visual impairment.*

**Visual field:** The area in front of a person that can be seen while looking forward and not moving the head.

**Visual impairment:** An impairment in vision that, even with correction, adversely affects a student's educational performance. The term includes both partial sight and blindness.

**Vocabulary:** In reading instruction, often refers to words that are quickly recognized in print. Also often called *sight vocabulary.*

**Voice disorders:** Inappropriate pitch, loudness, or sound quality during speech.

**Voice-output communication aids (VOCA):** Portable devices that allow people with difficulty in speech to communicate through the use of graphic symbols and words on computerized displays.

**Working memory:** Temporarily stores and uses information. Working memory allows an individual to see something, think about it, and then act on this information.

**Wraparound interventions:** Intensive interventions that are grounded in values of family empowerment and cultural competence, which typically require the coordinated and integrated efforts of teams of professional service providers.

# References

Abbott, M., Greenwood, C., Buzhardt, J., & Tapia, Y. (2006). Using technology-based support tools to scale up the class-wide peer tutoring program. *Reading and Writing Quarterly, 22*(1), 47–64.

Achenbach, T. M., & Rescorla, L. (2001). *Manual for the ASEBA school-age forms and profiles.* Burlington: University of Vermont, Research Center for Children, Youth, and Families.

ADA Amendments Act of 2008, Public Law 110-325. Retrieved February 22, 2011, from http://www.access-board.gov/about/laws/ada-amendments.htm

Albert, L. (2003). *Cooperative discipline: A teacher's handbook.* Circle Pines, MN: American Guidance Service.

Allbritten, D., Mainzer, R., & Ziegler, D. (2004). Will students with disabilities be scapegoats for school failure? *Teaching Exceptional Children, 36*(3), 74–75.

American Academy of Asthma Allergy and Immunology. (2005). *Pediatric asthma: Feature article.* Retrieved July 1, 2008, from http://www.aaaai.org/

American Academy of Pediatrics. (2000). Clinical practice guideline: Diagnosis and evaluation of the child with attention-deficit/hyperactivity disorder. *Pediatrics, 105*(5), 1158–1170.

American Association on Intellectual and Developmental Disabilities. (2007). *AIDD/ARC position statement on sexuality.* Retrieved January 6, 2012, from http://www.aamr.org/content_154.cfm?navID=40

American Association on Intellectual and Development Disabilities. (2010). *Definition of intellectual disability.* Retrieved January 6, 2012, from http://www.aamr.org/content_100.cfm?navID=21

American Federation of Teachers. (2006). *Let's get it right: AFT's recommendation for No Child Left Behind.* Retrieved January 6, 2012, from http://www.aft.org.

American Foundation for the Blind. (2005). *Statistical snapshots.* Retrieved February 5, 2011, from http://www.afb.org/SectionID=15&Mode=Print

American Psychiatric Association. (2000). *Diagnostic and statistical manual of mental disorders* (4th ed., text rev.). Washington, DC: Author.

American Speech-Language-Hearing Association. (2010). *Roles and responsibilities of speech-language pathologists in schools* [Professional Issues Statement]. Retrieved February 5, 2011, from http://www.asha.org/docs/html/PI2010-00317.htm#sec1.2

Americans with Disabilities Act of 1990, Pub. L. No. 101-336, §2, 104 Stat. 328 (1991).

Anderson, C. L., Anderson, K. M., & Cherup, S. (2009). Investment vs. return: Outcomes of special education technology research in literacy for students with mild disabilities. *Contemporary Issues in Technology and Teacher Education, 9,* 337–355.

Anderson-Inman, L., Knox-Quinn, C., & Horney, M. A. (1996). Computer-based study strategies for students with learning disabilities: Individual differences associated with adoption level. *Journal of Learning Disabilities, 29*(5), 461–466.

Arndt, S. A., Konrad, M., & Test, D. W. (2006). Effects of the "Self-Directed IEP" on student participation in planning meetings. *Remedial and Special Education, 27,* 194–207.

Aronson, E. (2004). Building empathy, compassion, and achievement in the Jigsaw classroom. In J. Aronson (Ed.). Improving academic achievement: Impact of psychological factors on education (pp. 213–227). Bingley, UK: Emerald Group Publishing.

Aronson, E. (2011). Jigsaw classroom: Jigsaw in 10 easy steps. Retrieved July 27, 2011, from http://www.jigsaw.org

Aronson, E., Stephan, C., Sikes, J., Blaney, N., & Snapp, M. (1978). *The Jigsaw classroom.* Beverly Hills, CA: Sage.

August, D., & Siegel, L. (2006). Literacy instruction for language-minority children in special education settings. In D. August & T. Shanahan (Eds.), *Developing literacy in second-language learners: Report of the National Literacy Panel on Language-Minority Children and Youth* (pp. 523–553). Mahwah, NJ: Erlbaum.

Austin, J. L., & Agar, G. (2005). Helping young children follow their teachers' directions: The utility of high probability command sequences in pre-K and kindergarten classrooms. *Education and Treatment of Children, 28,* 222–236.

Autism Information Center. (2008). *Frequently asked questions: Prevalence.* Retrieved July 2, 2008, from http:/www.cdc.gov.

Baglieri, S., & Knopf, J. H. (2004). Normalizing difference in inclusive teaching. *Journal of Learning Disabilities, 37*(6), 525–529.

Bahr, M. & Kovaleski, J. (2006). The need for problem-solving teams. *Introduction to the special issue, 27,* 2–5.

Bahrami, B., Olsen, K., Latham, P., Roepstorff, A., Rees, G., & Firth, C. (2010). Optimally interacting minds. *Science, 329* 1080–1085.

Baird, G., Charman, T., et al. (2000). A screening instrument for autism at 18 months of age: A 6-year follow-up. *Journal of the American Academy of Child and Adolescent Psychiatry, 29,* 694–702.

Baker, S., Chard, D., Ketterlin-Geller, L., Apichatabutra, C., & Doabler, C. (2009). Teaching writing to at-risk students: The quality of evidence for self-regulated strategy development. *Exceptional Children, 75,* 303–318.

Baker, S., Gersten, R., & Keating, T. (2000). When less may be more: A 2-year longitudinal evaluation of a volunteer tutoring program requiring minimal training. *Reading Research Quarterly, 35*(4), 494–519.

Baker, S. K., Fien, H., & Baker, D. L. (2010). Robust reading instruction in the early grades: Conceptual and practical issues in the integration and evaluation of tier 1 and tier 2 instructional supports. *Focus on Exceptional Children, 42*(9), 1-20.

Banks, J. A. (1988). *Multiethnic education: Theory and practice* (2nd ed.) Boston: Allyn & Bacon. Banks, J., Cochran-Smith, M., Moll, L., Richert, A., Zeichner, K., LePage, P., Darling-Hammond, L., Duffy, H., with McDonald, M. (2005). Teaching diverse learners. In L. Darling-Hammond

& J. Bransford (Eds.), *Preparing teachers for a changing world: What teachers should learn and be able to do* (pp. 232–273). San Francisco: Jossey-Bass.

Barkley, R. (2006a). Comorbid disorders, social and family adjustment. In R. Barkley (Ed.), *Attention-deficit hyperactivity disorder: A handbook for diagnosis and treatment* (3rd ed., pp. 184–218). New York: Guilford.

Barkley, R. (2006b). Primary symptoms, diagnostic criteria, prevalence, and gender differences. In R. Barkley (Ed.), *Attention-deficit hyperactivity disorder: A handbook for diagnosis and treatment* (3rd ed., pp. 76–121). New York: Guilford.

Barnard-Brak, L., & Lechtenberger, D. (2010). Student IEP participation and academic achievement across time. *Remedial and Special Education, 31,* 343–349.

Basham, J. D., Israel, M., Graden, J., Poth, R., & Winston, M. (2010). A comprehensive approach to RTI: Embedding universal design for learning and technology. *Learning Disability Quarterly, 33*(4), 243–255.

Bausch, M. E., Quinn, B. S., Chung, Y., Ault, M. J., & Behrmann, M. M. (2009). Assistive technology in the individual education plan: Analysis of policies across ten states. *Journal of Special Education Leadership, 22*(1), 9–23.

Beard, L. A., Carpenter, L. B., & Johnston, L. J. (2011). *Assistive technology: Access for all students* (2nd ed.). Upper Saddle River, NJ: Merrill/Pearson.

Beirne-Smith, M., Patton, J. M., & Kim, S. H. (2006). *Mental retardation: An introduction to intellectual disability* (7th ed.). Upper Saddle River, NJ: Merrill/Pearson Education.

Belland, B. R., Glazewski, K. D., & Ertmer, P. A. (2009). Inclusion and problem-based learning: Roles of students in a mixed ability group. *Research in Middle Level Education Online, 32*(2), 1–19.

Benard, B. (2004). *Resiliency: What we have learned.* San Francisco: WestEd.

Benner, G. J., Nelson, J. R., & Epstein, M. H. (2002). Language skills of children with EBD: A literature review. *Journal of Emotional and Behavioral Disorders, 10,* 43–59.

Bennett, C. I. (2006). *Comprehensive multicultural education: Theory and practice* (6th ed.). Boston: Allyn & Bacon.

Berkeley, S., Marshak, L., Mastropieri, M. A., & Scruggs, T. E. (2011). Improving comprehension of social studies text: A self-questioning strategy for inclusive middle school classes. *Remedial and Special Education, 32*(2), 105–113.

Berkeley, S., Mastropieri, M. A., & Scruggs, T. E. (2011). Reading comprehension strategy instruction and attribution retraining with secondary students with learning and other mild disabilities. *Journal of Learning Disabilities, 44*(1), 18–32.

Best, S. J. (2010a). Physical disabilities. In S. J. Best, K. W. Heller, & J. L. Bigge (Eds.), *Teaching individuals with physical or multiple disabilities* (6th ed., pp. 32–58). Upper Saddle River, NJ: Merrill/Pearson Education.

Best, S. J. (2010b). Health impairments and congenital infections. In S. J. Best, K. W. Heller, & J. L. Bigge (Eds.), *Teaching individuals with physical or multiple disabilities* (6th ed., pp. 82–109). Upper Saddle River, NJ: Merrill/Pearson Education.

Best, S. J., & Bigge, J. L. (2010). Cerebral palsy. In S. J. Best, K. W. Heller, & J. J. Bigge (Eds.), *Teaching individuals with physical or multiple disabilities* (6th ed., pp. 59–81). Upper Saddle River, NJ: Merrill/Pearson Education.

Best, S. J., Reed, P., & Bigge, J. L. (2005). Assistive technology. In S. J. Best, K. W. Heller, & J. L. Bigge (Eds.), *Teaching individuals with physical or multiple disabilities* (5th ed., pp. 179–226). Upper Saddle River, NJ: Merrill/Pearson Education.

Biancarosa, C., & Snow, C. E. (2004). *Reading Next—A vision for action and research in middle and high school literacy: A report to Carnegie Corporation of New York* (2nd ed.). Washington, DC: Alliance for Excellent Education. Retrieved January 6, 2012, from *www.all4ed.org/files/ReadingNext.pdf.*

Biklen, D. (1985). *Achieving the complete school: Strategies for effective mainstreaming.* New York: Teachers College Press.

Bitter, G. G., & Legacy, J. M. (2008). *Using technology in the classroom* (7th ed.). Boston: Pearson/Allyn & Bacon.

Blackhurst, A. E. (2005). Perspectives on applications of technology in the field of learning disabilities. *Learning Disability Quarterly, 28,* 175–179.

Bond, R., & Castagnera, E. (2006). Peer supports and inclusive education: An underutilized resource. *Theory into Practice 45*(3), 224–229.

Bondy, E., Ross, D., Gallingane, C., & Hambacher, E. (2007). Creating environments of success and resilience: Culturally responsive classroom management and more. *Urban Education, 42*(4), 326–348.

Borich, G. (2010). *Effective teaching methods: Research-based practices* (7th ed.). Upper Saddle River, NJ: Pearson Education.

Borman, G., Dowling, N., & Schneck, C. (2007). *The national randomized field trial of Open Court Reading.* Retrieved January 6, 2012, from https://www.sraonline.com/download/News/PressRelease/National_OCR_Study.pdf

Bouck, E. C., Courtad, C. A., Heutsche, A., Okolo, C. M., & Englert, C. S. (2009). The virtual history museum: A universally designed approach to social studies instruction. *Teaching Exceptional Children, 42*(2), 14–20.

Bouck, E. C., & Flanagan, S. M. (2010). Virtual manipulatives: What are they and how teachers can use them. *Intervention in School and Clinic, 45,* 186–191.

Boudah, D. J., Lenz, B. K., Bulgren, J. A., Schumaker, J., B., & Deshler, D. D. (2000). Don't water down! Enhance content learning through the unit organizer routine. *Teaching Exceptional Children, 32*(3), 48–56.

Boutot, E., & Bryant, D. (2005). Social integration of students with autism in inclusive settings. *Education and Training in Developmental Disabilities, 40*(1), 14–24.

Bower, E. M. (1960). *Early identification of emotionally handicapped children in school.* Springfield, IL: Charles C. Thomas.

Boykin, A. W., & Bailey, C. (2000). *The role of cultural factors in school relevant cognitive functioning: Description of home environmental factors, cultural orientations, and learning preferences* (Report 43). Washington, DC, and Baltimore: Howard University and Johns Hopkins University, Center on the Education of Students Placed at Risk (CRESPAR).

Boykin, A. W., Tyler, K., & Miller, O. (2005). In search of cultural themes and their expressions in the dynamics of classroom life. *Urban Education, 40*(5), 521–549.

Boyle, J. R. (2007). The process of note taking: Implications for students with mild disabilities. *The Clearing House, 80*(5), 227–232.

Boyle, J. R. (2010). Note-taking skills of middle school students with and without learning disabilities. *Journal of Learning Disabilities, 43*(6), 530–540.

Bransford, J. D., Brown, A. L., & Cocking, R. R. (Eds.). (2000). *How people learn.* Washington, DC: National Academy Press.

Bricker, D. (2000). Inclusion: How the scene has changed. *Topics in Early Childhood Special Education (TECSE), 20*(1), 14–19.

Broderick, A., Mehta-Parekh, H., & Reid, D. K. (2005). Differentiating instruction for disabled students in inclusive classrooms. *Theory into Practice, 44,* 194–202.

Browder, D. M., Mims, P. J., Spooner, F., Ahlgrim-Delzell, L., & Angel, L. (2008). Teaching elementary students with multiple disabilities to participate in shared stories. *Research and Practice for Persons with Severe Disabilities, 33,* 3–12.

Browder, D. M., & Spooner, F. (Eds.). (2006). *Teaching language arts, math, & science to students with significant cognitive disabilities.* Baltimore: Brookes.

Browder, D. M., Spooner, F., Wakeman, S., Trela, K., & Baker, J. N. (2006). Aligning instruction with academic content standards: Finding the link. *Research and Practice for Persons with Severe Disabilities, 31,* 309–321.

Browder, D. M., Wakeman, S. Y., Flowers, C., Rickelman, R. J., & Pugalee, D. (2007). Creating access to the general curriculum with links to grade-level content for students with significant cognitive disabilities: An explication of the concept. *Journal of Special Education, 41*(1), 2–16.

*Brown v. Board of Education,* 347 U.S. 483 (1954).

Brown, D. F. (2004). Urban teachers' professed classroom management strategies: Reflections of culturally responsive teaching. *Urban Education, 39*(3), 266–289.

Brown, L., Shiraga, B., & Kessler, K. (2006). The quest for ordinary lives: The integrated post-school vocational functioning of 50 workers with significant disabilities. *Research and Practice for Persons with Severe Disabilities, 31,* 93–121.

Bruce, C. D., Esmonde, I., Ross, J., Dookie, L., & Beatty, R. (2010). The effects of sustained classroom-embedded professional learning on teacher efficacy and related student achievement. *Teaching and Teacher Education, 26*(8), 1598–1608.

Bryan, T., Burstein, K., & Ergul, C. (2004). The social-emotional side of learning disabilities: A science-based presentation of the state of the art. *Learning Disability Quarterly, 27*(1), 45–51.

Bryant, D. P., Bryant, B. R., & Raskind, M. H. (1998). Using assistive technology to enhance the skills of students with learning disabilities. *Intervention in School and Clinic, 34*(1), 53–58.

Buck, G., Polloway, E., Smith-Thomas, A., & Cook, K. (2003). Prereferral intervention processes: A survey of state practices. *Exceptional Children, 69*(3), 349–360.

Bulgren, J. (2006). Integrated content enhancement routines: Responding to the needs of adolescents with disabilities in rigorous inclusive secondary content classes. *Teaching Exceptional Children, 38*(6), 54–58.

Bulgren, J., Deshler, D. D., & Lenz, B. K. (2007). Engaging adolescents with LD in higher order thinking about history concepts using integrated content enhancement routines. *Journal of Learning Disabilities, 40*(2), 121–133.

Bulgren, J., & Lenz, K. (1996). Strategic instruction in the content areas. In D. D. Deshler, E. S. Ellis, & B. K. Lenz (Eds.), *Teaching adolescents with learning disabilities* (pp. 409–473). Denver: Love.

Bulgren, J., Schumaker, J. B., & Deshler, D. D. (1988). The effectiveness of a concept teaching routine in enhancing the performance of students with learning disabilities in secondary mainstream classes. *Learning Disability Quarterly, 11*(1), 3–17.

Bulgren, J., Schumaker, J. B., & Deshler, D. D. (1993). *The concept mastery routine.* Lawrence, KS: Edge Enterprises.

Burke, R. V., Andersen, M. N., Bowen, S. L., Howard, M. R., & Allen, K. D. (2010). Evaluation of two instruction methods to increase employment options for young adults with autism spectrum disorders. *Research in Developmental Disabilities: A Multidisciplinary Journal, 31,* 1223–1233.

Burns, B. J., & Goldman, S. K. (1998). *Promising practices in wraparound for children with serious emotional disturbance and their families: Vol. 4. Systems of care: Promising practices in children's mental health 1998 series.* Washington, DC: Georgetown University, Child Development Center, National Technical Assistance Center for Children's Mental Health.

Burns, M. K., Deno, S. L., & Jimerson, S. R. (2007). Toward a unified response-to-intervention model. In S. R. Jimerson, M. K. Burns, & A. M. VanDerHeyden (Eds.), *Handbook of response to intervention: The science and practice of assessment and intervention* (pp. 428–440). New York: Springer.

Burstein, N., Sears, S., Wilcoxen, A., Cabello, B., & Spagna, M. (2004). Moving toward inclusive practices. *Remedial and Special Education, 25*(2), 104–116.

Busch, T. W., & Reschly, A. L. (2007). Progress monitoring in reading: Using curriculum-based measurement in a response-to-intervention. *Assessment for Effective Intervention, 32*(4), 223–230.

Campbell, M. L., & Mechling, L. C. (2009). Small group computer-assisted instruction with SMART Board technology: An investigation of observational and incidental learning on nontarget information. *Remedial and Special Education, 30*(1), 47–57.

Capizzi, A. M. (2009). Starting the year off right: Designing and evaluation of a supportive classroom management plan. *Focus on Exceptional Children, 42*(3), 1–12.

Carey, D. M., & Sale, P. (1994). Notebook computers increase communication. *Teaching Exceptional Children, 27*(1), 62–69.

Carlson, E., Lee, H., & Schroll, K. (2004). Identifying attributes of high quality special education teachers. *Teacher Education and Special Education, 27,* 350–359.

Carnine, D., Engelmann, S., & Steely, D. (2003). *Corrective math.* Chicago: Science Research Associates.

Carnine, D., Silbert, J., Kame'enui, E., & Tarver, S. (2010). *Direct instruction reading* (5th ed.). Upper Saddle River, NJ: Pearson Education.

Carr, E. G., Dunlap, G., Horner, R. H., Koegel, R. L., Turnbull, A. P., Sailor, W., Anderson, J. L., Albin, R. W., Koegel, L. K., & Fox, L. (2002). Positive behavior support: Evolution of an applied science. *Journal of Positive Behavior Interventions, 4,* 4–16, 20.

Carr, E. G., Horner, R. H., Turnbull, A. P., Marquis, J. G., McLaughlin, D. M., McAtee, M. L., Smith, C. E., Ryan, K. A., Ruef, M. B., & Doolabh, A. (1999). *Positive behavior support for people with developmental disabilities: A research synthesis.* Washington, DC: American Association on Mental Retardation.

Carter, E., & Hughes, C. (2006). Including high school students with severe disabilities in general education classes: Perspectives of general and special educators, paraprofessionals, and administrators. *Research & Practice for Persons with Severe Disabilities, 31*(2), 174–185.

Carter, E., Sisco, L., Brown, L., Brickham, D., Al-Khabbaz, Z., & MacLean, W. (2008). Peer interactions and academic engagement of youth with developmental disabilities in inclusive middle and high school classrooms. *American Journal on Mental Retardation, 113,* 479–494.

Carter, E. W., Cushing, L. S., Clark, N. M., & Kennedy, C. H. (2005). Effects of peer support interventions on students' access to the general curriculum and social interactions. *Research and Practice for Persons with Severe Disabilities, 30,* 15–25.

Carter, E. W., Wehby, J., Hughes, C., Johnson, S. M., Plank, D. R., Barton-Arwood, S. M., & Lunsford, L. B. (2005). Preparing adolescents with high-incidence disabilities for high-stakes testing with strategy instruction. *Preventing School Failure, 49*(2), 55–62.

Carter, J., & Sugai, G. (1989). Survey on prereferral practices: Response from state departments of education. *Exceptional Children, 55,* 298–302.

Cartledge, G. W., Gardner, R., & Ford, D. Y. (2009). *Diverse learners with exceptionalities: Culturally responsive teaching in the inclusive classroom.* Upper Saddle River, NJ: Merrill/Pearson.

Cartledge, G. W., & Kourea, L. (2008). Culturally responsive classrooms for culturally diverse students with and at risk for disabilities. *Exceptional Children, 74*(3), 351–371.

Caruso, A., & Crawford, S. (2011). Transitioning and post-secondary life. In K. M. McCoy (Ed.), *Autism from the teacher's perspective: Strategies for classroom instruction* (pp. 395–430). Denver: Love.

CAST. (2011). *Universal design for learning guidelines version 2.0.* Wakefield, MA: Author. Retrieved June 4, 2011, from http://www.udlcenter.org/aboutudl/udlguidelines

Caterino, L. C., & Mahoney, J. M. (2011). Evidence-based procedures for the assessment of children with autism. In K. M. McCoy (Ed.), *Autism from the teacher's perspective: Strategies for classroom instruction* (pp. 83–124). Denver: Love.

Causton-Theoharis, J., Giangreco, M., Doyle, M., & Vadasy, P. (2007). Paraprofessionals: The "Sous-Chefs" of literacy instruction. *Teaching Exceptional Children, 40*(1), 56–62.

Cavalier, A. R., & Brown, C. C. (1998). From passivity to participation: The transformational possibilities of speech-recognition technology. *Teaching Exceptional Children, 30*(6), 60–65.

Center for Effective Collaboration and Practice. (1998). *Functional behavioral assessment.* Retrieved June 6, 2011, from http://cecp.air.org/fba/problembehavior/main.htm

Centers for Disease Control. (2010, November). *Increasing prevalence of parent-reported attention deficit/hyperactivity disorder among children—United States, 2003 and 2007.* Morbidity and Mortality Weekly Report (MMWR). Retrieved February 18, 2011, from http://www.cdc.gov/mmwr/preview/mmwrhtml/mm5944a3.htm

Centers for Disease Control. (2011, February). *Prevalence of autism spectrum disorders—Autism and developmental disabilities monitoring network, United States.* Morbidity and Mortality Weekly Report (MMWR) Surveillance Summaries. December 18, 2009/58(SS10); 1–20. Retrieved January 6, 2012, from http://www.cdc.gov/ncbddd/autism/data.html

Chalfant, J., & Pysh, M. (1989). Teacher assistance teams: Five descriptive studies on 96 teams. *Remedial and Special Education, 10*(6), 49–58.

Chalk, J. C., Hagan-Burke, S., & Burke, M. D. (2005). The effects of self-regulated strategy development on the writing process for high school students with learning disabilities. *Learning Disability Quarterly, 28,* 75–87.

Chamberlain, S. P. (2005). Recognizing and responding to cultural differences in the education of culturally and linguistically diverse learners. *Intervention in School and Clinic, 40*(4), 195–221.

Chan, J., O'Reilly, M. F., Lang, R. B., Boutot, E. A., White, P. J., Pierce, N., & Baker, S. (2011). Evaluation of a Social Stories intervention implemented by pre-service teachers for students with autism in general education settings. *Research in Autism Spectrum Disorders, 5,* 715–721.

Charles, C. M. (2002). *Essential elements of discipline.* Boston: Allyn & Bacon.

Charleston County School District. (2006). *Implementation of READ 180 (Reading Intervention Program) in CCSD schools.* Retrieved January 6, 2012, from http://www.ccsd-schools.com.

Charney, R. (2002). *Teaching children to care.* Greenfield, MA: The Northeast Foundation for Children.

Chau, M., Thampi, K., & Wright, V. (2010). *Basic facts about low-income children, 2009. Children under age 18. Fact sheet.* New York: National Center for Children in Poverty, Columbia University.

Chawarska, K., & Volkmar, F. R. (2005). Autism in infancy and early childhood. In F. R. Volkmar, R. Paul, A. Klin, & D. Cohen (Eds.), *Handbook of autism and pervasive developmental disorders: Vol. 1. Diagnosis, development, neurobiology, and behavior* (4th ed., pp. 223–246). Hoboken, NJ: Wiley.

Cheney, D., & Bullis, M. (2004). The school-to-community transition of adolescents with emotional and behavioral disorders. In R. B. Rutherford, Jr., M. M. Quinn, & A. R. Mathur (Eds.), *Handbook of research in emotional and behavioral disorders* (pp. 369–384). New York: Guilford.

Cheney, D., Flower, A., & Templeton, T. (2008). Applying response to intervention metrics in the social domain for students at risk for developing emotional or behavioral disorders. *The Journal of Special Education, 42*(2), 108–126.

Cheney, D., Lynass, L., Flower, A., Waugh, M., Iwaszuk, W., Mielenz, C., & Hawken, L. (2010). The Check, Connect, and Expect Program: A targeted, tier 2 intervention in the schoolwide positive behavior support model. *Preventing School Failure, 54*(3), 152–158.

Cheney, D., Stage, S. A., Hawken, L., Lynass, L., Mielenz, C., & Waugh, M. (2009). A 2-year outcome student of the Check, Connect, and Expect intervention for students at risk for severe behavior problems. *Journal of Emotional and Behavioral Disorders, 17*(4), 226–243.

Cihak, D., Fahrenkrog, C., Ayres, K. M., & Smith, C. (2010). The use of video modeling via a video iPod and a system of least prompts to improve transitional behaviors for students with autism spectrum disorders in the general education classroom. *Journal of Positive Behavior Intervention, 12,* 103–115.

Cihak, D., Kessler, K. B., & Alberto, P. A. (2007). Generalized use of a handheld prompting system. *Research in Developmental Disabilities, 28,* 397–408.

Cihak, D. F., Kessler, K., & Alberto, P. A. (2008). Use of a handheld prompting system to transition independently through vocational tasks for students with moderate and severe intellectual disabilities. *Education and Training in Developmental Disabilities, 43,* 102–110.

Clark, G. M., & Bigge, J. L. (2005). Transition and self-determination. In S. J. Best, K. W. Heller, & J. L. Bigge (Eds.), *Teaching individuals with physical or multiple disabilities* (5th ed., pp. 367–398). Upper Saddle River, NJ: Merrill/Pearson Education.

Clay, M. (1993). *Reading recovery: A guidebook for teachers in training.* Portsmouth, NH: Heinemann.

Clay, M. (2001). *An observation survey of early literacy achievement* (2nd ed.). Portsmouth, NH: Heinemann.

Codell, E. (2009). *Educating Esme: Diary of a teacher's first year* (expanded edition). Chapel Hill, NC: Algonquin.

Cole, C., Horvath, B., Chapman, C., Deschenes, C., Ebeling, D., & Sprague, J. (2000). *Adapting curriculum & instruction in inclusive classrooms: A teachers' desk reference* (2nd ed.). Bloomington: Indiana Institute on Disability and Community.

Cole, C., Waldron, N., & Madj, M. (2004). Academic progress of students across inclusive and traditional settings. *Mental Retardation, 42*(2), 136–144.

Cole, R. W. (2001). *More strategies for educating everybody's children.* Alexandria, VA: Association for Supervision and Curriculum Development.

Coleman, M., & Vaughn, S. (2000). Reading interventions for students with emotional/behavioral disorders. *Behavioral Disorders, 25*(2), 93–104.

Conderman, G., & Elf, N. (2007). What's in this book? Engaging students through a textbook exploration activity. *Reading and Writing Quarterly, 23,* 111–116.

Conderman, G., & Pedersen, T. (2010). Preparing students with mild disabilities for taking state and district tests. *Intervention in School and Clinic, 45*(4), 232–241.

Connor, C., Snell, M., Gansneder, B., & Dexter, S. (2010). Special education teachers' use of assistive technology with students who have severe disabilities. *Journal of Technology and Teacher Education, 18,* 369–386.

Connor, D. (2006). Stimulants. In R. Barkley (Ed.), *Attention-deficit hyperactivity disorder: A handbook for diagnosis and treatment* (3rd ed., pp. 608–647). New York: Guilford.

Conroy, M. A., Strichter, J., & Gage, N. (2011). Current issues and trends in the education of children and youth with autism spectrum disorders. In J. M. Kauffman & D. P. Hallahan (Eds.), *Handbook of special education* (pp. 277–290). New York: Routledge.

Cook, B., McDuffie-Landrum, K., Oshita, L., & Cook, S. (2011). Co-teaching for students with disabilities. A critical analysis of the empirical literature. In J. Kauffman & D. Hallahan (Eds.), *Handbook of Special Education* (pp. 147–159). New York: Routledge.

Cook, L. H., & Boe, E. E. (2007). National trends in the sources of supply of teachers in special and general education. *Teacher Education and Special Education, 30*(4), 217–232.

Coonrod, E. E., & Stone, W. L. (2005). Screening for autism in young children. In F. R. Volkmar, R. Paul, A. Klin, & D. Cohen (Eds.), *Handbook of autism and pervasive developmental disorders: Vol. 2. Assessment, interventions, and policy* (4th ed., pp. 707–729). Hoboken, NJ: Wiley.

Cooper, H. (2001). *The battle over homework* (2nd ed.). Thousand Oaks, CA: Corwin.

Copeland, S., Hughes, C., Carter, E., Guth, C., Presley, J., Williams, C., & Fowler, S. (2004). Increasing access to general education: Perspectives of participants in a high school peer support program. *Remedial and Special Education, 25*(3), 342–352.

Corbett, D., Wilson, B., & Williams, B. (2002). *Effort and excellence in urban classrooms.* New York: Teachers College Press.

Corbett, W. P., Clark, H. B., & Blank, W. (2002). Employment and social outcomes associated with vocational programming for youths with emotional or behavioral disorders. *Behavioral Disorders, 27,* 358–370.

Correa, V., Jones, H., Thomas, C., & Morsink, C. (2005). *Interactive teaming: Enhancing programs for students with special Needs* (4th ed.). Upper Saddle River, NJ: Merrill/Pearson Education.

Cosbey, J. E., & Johnston, S. (2006). Using a single-switch voice output communication aid to increase social access for children with severe disabilities in inclusive classrooms. *Research and Practice for Persons with Severe Disabilities, 31,* 144–156.

Costello, J., Mustillo, S., Erkanli, A., Keeler, G, & Angold, A. (2003). Prevalence and development of psychiatric disorders in childhood and adolescence. *Archives of General Psychiatry, 60,* 837–844.

Cote, D. (2007). Problem-based learning software for students with disabilities. *Intervention in School and Clinic, 43*(1), 29–37.

Cote, D. (2011). Implementing a problem-solving intervention with students with mild to moderate disabilities. *Intervention in School and Clinic, 46*(5), 259–265.

Council for Exceptional Children. (1999). *Universal design: Ensuring access to the general education curriculum.* Research Connections in Special Education. Arlington, VA: Author.

Council for Exceptional Children. (2007). *Position on response to intervention (RTI): The unique role of special education and special educators.* Arlington, VA: Author.

Coutinho, M. J., Oswald, D. P., & Forness, S. R. (2002). Gender and sociodemographic factors and the disproportionate identification of culturally and linguistically diverse students with emotional disturbance. *Behavioral Disorders, 27*(2), 109–125.

Cox, D. (2005). Evidence-based interventions using home–school collaboration. *School Psychology Quarterly, 20*(4), 473–497.

Coyne, M., Kame'enui, E., & Carnine, D. (2007). *Effective teaching strategies that accommodate diverse learners* (3rd ed.). Upper Saddle River, NJ: Pearson Education.

Coyne, M., Zipoli, R., & Ruby, M. (2006). Beginning reading instruction for students at risk for reading disabilities: What, how, and when. *Intervention in School and Clinic, 41*(3), 161–168.

Crawford, J. (2002). *Census 2000: A guide for the perplexed.* Retrieved January 6, 2012, from *www.languagepolicy.net/articles/census02.htm*

Crone, D. A., Hawken, L. S., & Bergstrom, M. K. (2007). A demonstration of training, implementing, and using functional behavioral assessment in 10 elementary and middle school settings. *Journal of Positive Behavior Interventions, 9,* 15–29.

Cullinan, D. (2002). *Students with emotional and behavioral disorders.* Upper Saddle River, NJ: Merrill/Pearson Education.

Cullinan, D. (2004). Classification and definition of emotional and behavioral disorders. In R. B. Rutherford, Jr., M. M. Quinn, & A. R. Mathur (Eds.), *Handbook of research in emotional and behavioral disorders* (pp. 32–53). New York: Guilford.

Cullinan, D., & Sabornie, E. J. (2004). Characteristics of emotional disturbance in middle and high school students. *Journal of Emotional and Behavioral Disorders, 12,* 157–167.

Cumming, T. (2010). Using technology to create motivating social skills lessons. *Intervention in School and Clinic, 45*(4), 242–250.

Curwin, R. L., & Mendler, A. N. (1999). *Discipline with dignity* (2nd ed.). Alexandria, VA: Association for Supervision and Curriculum Development.

Cutler, L., & Graham, S. (2008). Primary grade writing instruction: A national survey. *Journal of Educational Psychology, 100*(4), 907-919.

D'Agostino, J., & Murphy, J. (2004). A meta-analysis of Reading recovery in United States schools. *Educational Evaluation and Policy Analysis, 26*(1), 23–38.

Dalston, R. M. (2000). Voice disorders. In R. B. Gillam, T. P. Marquardt, & F. N. Martin (Eds.), *Communication sciences and disorders: From science to clinical practice* (pp. 283–312). San Diego: Singular.

Daniels, L. E., Sparling, J. W., Reilly, M., & Humphry, R. (1995). Use of assistive technology with young children with severe and profound disabilities. *Infant–Toddler Intervention, 5,* 91–112.

Darling-Hammond, L. (2010). *The flat world of education: How America's commitment to equity will determine our future.* New York: Teachers College Press.

Davies, D., Stock, S., & Wehmeyer, M. L. (2003). A palmtop computer-based intelligent aid for individuals with intellectual disabilities to increase independent decision making. *Research and Practice for Persons with Severe Disabilities, 28,* 182–193.

deBettencourt, L. (2002). Understanding the differences between IDEA and Section 504. *Teaching Exceptional Children, 34*(3), 16–23.

Delpit, L. (1995). *Other people's children: Cultural conflicts in the classroom.* New York: New Press.

Deno, E. (1970). Special education as developmental capital. *Exceptional Children, 37*(3), 229–237.

Deno, S. (2003). Developments in curriculum-based measurement. *Journal of Special Education, 37*(3), 184–192.

Deno, S. (2007). Curriculum-based measurement. In J. McLeskey (Ed.), *Reflections on inclusion: Classic articles that shaped our thinking* (pp. 221–249). Arlington, VA: Council for Exceptional Children (CEC).

Deshler, D. (2005). Adolescents with learning disabilities: Unique challenges and reasons for hope. *Learning Disability Quarterly, 28,* 122–124.

Deshler, D. D., & Putnam, M. L. (1996). Learning disabilities in adolescents: A perspective. In D. D. Deshler, E. S. Ellis, & B. K. Lenz (Eds.), *Teaching adolescents with learning disabilities* (pp. 1–7). Denver: Love.

Dettmer, P., Thurston, L., Knackendoffel, A. & Dyck, N. (2009). *Collaboration, consultation, and teamwork for students with special needs.* Upper Saddle River, NJ: Merrill/Pearson Education.

de Valenzuela, J. S., Copeland, S., Huaqing Qi, C., & Park, M. (2006). Examining educational equity: Revisiting the disproportionate representation of minority students in special education. *Exceptional Children, 72*(4), 425–441.

Dexter, D. D., Hughes, C. A., & Farmer, T. W. (2008). Responsiveness to intervention: A review of field studies and implications for rural special education. *Rural Special Education Quarterly, 3*(4), 3–9.

Diamond, K. E., & Hong, S-Y. (2010). Young children's decisions to include peers with physical disabilities in play. *Journal of Early Intervention, 32,* 163–177.

Division for Learning Disabilities. (2007). *Thinking about response to intervention and learning disabilities: A teacher's guide.* Arlington, VA: Author.

Doll, B., Sands, D. J., Wehmeyer, M. L., & Palmer, S. (1996). Promoting the development and acquisition of self-determined behavior. In D. J. Sands & M. L. Wehmeyer (Eds.), *Self-determination across the lifespan: Independence and choice for people with disabilities* (pp. 65–90). Baltimore: Brookes.

Dore, R., Dion, E., Wagner, S., & Brunet, J. (2002). High school inclusion of adolescents with mental retardation: A multiple case study. *Education and Training in Mental Retardation and Developmental Disabilities, 37*(3), 253–261.

Doubt, L., & McColl, M. A. (2003). A secondary guy: Physically disabled teenagers in secondary schools. *Canadian Journal of Occupational Therapy, 70*(3), 139–151.

Douglas, K. H., Ayres, K. M., Langone, J., Bell, V., & Meade, C. (2009). Expanding literacy for learners with intellectual disabilities: The role of supported eText. *Journal of Special Education Technology, 24*(3), 35–44.

Doyle, W. (1980). Classroom management. West Lafayette, IN: Kappa Delta Pi.

Doyle, W. (1986). Classroom organization and management. In M. C. Wittrock (Ed.), *Handbook of research on teaching* (pp. 392–431). New York: Macmillan.

Duckworth, S., Smith-Rex, S., Okey, S., Brookshire, M. A., Rawlinson, D., Rawlinson, R., Castillo, S., & Little, J. (2001). Wraparound services for young schoolchildren with emotional and behavioral disorders. *Teaching Exceptional Children, 33*(4), 54–60.

Duhaney, L. M. G., & Salend, S. J. (2000). Parental perceptions of inclusive educational placements. *Remedial and Special Education, 21*(2), 121–128.

Dukes, C., & Lamar-Dukes, P. (2009). Inclusion by design: Engineering inclusive practices in secondary schools. *Teaching Exceptional Children, 41*(3), 16–23.

Dunlap, L., & Dunlap, G. (1989). A self-monitoring package for teaching subtraction with regrouping to students with learning disabilities. *Journal of Applied Behavior Analysis, 22*(3), 309–314.

Dunn, L. M. (1968). Special education for the mildly retarded—Is much of it justifiable? *Exceptional Children, 35,* 5–22.

DuPaul, G. (2007). School-based interventions for students with attention deficit hyperactivity disorder: Current status and future directions. *School Psychology Review, 36*(2), 183–194.

DuPaul, G., Barkley, R., & Connor, D. (1998). Stimulants. In R. Barkley (Ed.), *Attention deficit hyperactivity disorder: A handbook for diagnosis and treatment* (2nd ed., pp. 510–551). New York: Guilford.

Dwyer, K., & Osher, D. (2000). *Safeguarding our children: An action guide.* Washington, DC: U.S. Department of Education and Justice, American Institutes for Research.

Dymond, S. K., Renzaglia, A., Rosenstein, A., Chun, E. J., Banks, R. A., Niswander, V., & Gilson, C. L. (2006). Using a participatory action research approach to create a universally designed inclusive high school science course: A case study. *Research & Practice for Persons with Severe Disabilities, 31*(4), 293–308.

Dymond, S., & Russell, D. (2004). Impact of grade and disability on the instructional context of inclusive classrooms. *Education and Training in Developmental Disabilities, 39*(2), 127–140.

Dynarski, M., Agodini, R., Heaviside, S., Novak, T., Carey, N., Campuzano, L., Means, B., Murphy, R., Penuel, W., Javitz, H., Emery, D., & Sussex, W. (2007). *Effectiveness of reading and mathematics software products: Findings from the first student cohort.* Washington, DC: U.S. Department of Education, Institute of Education Sciences.

Eber, L., Breen, K., Rose, J., Unizycki, R. M., & London, T. H. (2008). Wraparound as a tertiary level intervention to students with emotional/behavioral needs. *Teaching Exceptional Children, 40*(6), 16–22.

Eber, L., Sugai, G., Smith, C., & Scott, T. (2002). Wraparound and positive behavior interventions and supports in the schools. *Journal of Emotional and Behavioral Disorders, 10,* 171–180.

Edyburn, D. L. (2009). RTI and UDL interventions. *Journal of Special Education Technology, 24*(2), 46–47.

Edyburn, D. L. (2010). Would you recognize universal design for learning if you saw it? Ten propositions for new directions for the second decade of UDL. *Learning Disability Quarterly, 33*(1), 33–41.

Eggen, P., & Kauchak, D. (2012). *Strategies and models for teachers: Teaching content and thinking skills* (6th ed.). Upper Saddle River, NJ: Pearson Education.

eHow. (1999–2008). *How to use educational software for students with learning disabilities.* Retrieved February 6, 2008, from http://www.ehow.com/how_2091734_use-educational-software-students-learning-disabilities.html

Ehri, L., Dreyer, L., Flugman, B., & Gross, A. (2007). Reading Rescue: An effective tutoring intervention model for language-minority students who are struggling readers in first grade. *American Educational Research Journal, 44*(2), 414–448.

Elbaum, B., Vaughn, S., Hughes, M., & Moody, S. (1999). Grouping practices and reading outcomes for students with disabilities. *Exceptional Children, 65*(3), 399–415.

Elbaum, B., Vaughn, S., Hughes, M., & Moody, S. (2000). How effective are one-to-one tutoring programs in reading for elementary students at risk for reading failure? A meta-analysis of the intervention research. *Journal of Educational Psychology, 92*(4), 605–619.

Elder-Hinshaw, R., Manset-Williamson, G., Nelson, J. M., & Dunn, M. W. (2006). Engaging older students with reading disabilities: Multimedia inquiry projects supported by reading assistive technology. *Teaching Exceptional Children, 39,* 6–11.

Elliott, S. N., & Busse, R. T. (2004). Assessment and evaluation of students' behavior and intervention outcomes: The utility of rating scale methods. In R. B. Rutherford, Jr., M. M. Quinn, & A. R. Mathur (Eds.), *Handbook of research in emotional and behavioral disorders* (pp. 54–77). New York: Guilford.

Ellis, E. S. (1993). Integrative strategy instruction: A potential model for teaching content area subjects to adolescents with learning disabilities. *Journal of Learning Disabilities, 26*(6), 358–383, 398.

Ellis, E. S., & Colvert, G. (1996). Writing strategy instruction. In D. D. Deshler, E. S. Ellis, & B. K. Lenz (Eds.), *Teaching adolescents with learning disabilities* (pp. 127–207). Denver: Love.

Ellis, E. S., & Lenz, B. K. (1996). Perspectives on instruction in learning strategies. In D. D. Deshler, E. S. Ellis, & B. K. Lenz (Eds.), *Teaching adolescents with learning disabilities* (pp. 9–60). Denver: Love.

Engelmann, S. (2001). *Reasoning and writing.* Chicago: Science Research Associates. Engelmann, S., & Bruner, E. (2003). *Reading mastery classic.* Chicago: Science Research Associates.

Engelmann, S., Carnine, D., Bernadette, K., & Engelmann, O. (2003). *Connecting math concepts.* Chicago: Science Research Associates.

Engelmann, S., Hanner, S., & Johnson, G. (2008). *Corrective reading.* Chicago: Science Research Associates.

Englert, C. S., Mariage, T. V., Okolo, C. M., Shankland, R. K., Moxley, K. D., Courtad, C. A., Jocks-Meier, B. S., O'Brien, J. C., Martin, N. M., & Chen, H. (2009). The learning to learn strategies of adolescent students with disabilities. *Assessment for Effective Instruction, 34*(3), 147–161.

Epstein, M. H., & Sharma, J. M. (1998). *Behavioral and emotional rating scale.* Austin, TX: Pro-Ed.

Erwin, E. J., & Soodak, L. C. (2000). Valued member or tolerated participant: Parents' experiences in inclusive early childhood settings. *The Association for Persons with Severe Handicaps Journal (JASH), 25*(1), 29–41.

Escolar, D. M., Tosi, L. L., Tesi Rocha, A. C., & Kennedy, A. (2007). Muscles, bones, and nerves. In M. L. Batshaw, L. Pellegrino, & N. J. Roizen (Eds.), *Children with disabilities* (6th ed., pp. 203–215). Baltimore: Brookes.

Esquith, R. (2007). *Teach like your hair's on fire: The methods and madness inside room 56.* New York: Penguin.

Evertson C., & Emmer, E. (2009). *Classroom management for classroom teachers* (8th ed.). Upper Saddle River, NJ: Pearson Education.

Evertson, C. M., Emmer, E. T., Sanford, J. P., & Clements, B. S. (1983). Improving classroom management: An experiment in elementary school classrooms. *The Elementary School Journal, 84*(2), 172–188.

Fabiano, G., Pelham, W., Coles, E., Gnagy, E., Chronis, A., & O'Connor, B. (2009). A meta-analysis of behavioral treatments for attention-deficit/hyperactivity disorder. *Clinical Psychology Review, 29,* 129–140.

Fahsl, A. (2007). Mathematics accommodations for all students. *Intervention in School and Clinic, 42*(4), 198–203.

Fairbanks, S., Sugai, G., Guardino, D., & Lathrop, M. (2007). Response to intervention: Examining classroom behavior support in second grade. *Exceptional Children, 73*(3), 288–310.

Feifer, S. (2011). How SLD manifests in reading. In D. Flanagan & V. Alfonso (Eds.), *Essentials of specific learning disabilities identification* (pp. 21–41). Hoboken, NJ: Wiley.

Ferguson, D. L. (1995). The real challenge of inclusion: Confessions of a "rabid inclusionist." *Phi Delta Kappan, 77*(4), 281–287.

Fields, J. (2004). *America's families and living arrangements. U.S. Census Bureau.* Retrieved January 6, 2012, from http://www.census.gov/prod/2004pubs/p20-553.pdf

Fisher, J. B. (1995). Searching for validated inclusive practices: A review of the literature. *Focus on Exceptional Children, 28*(4), 2–23.

Fisher, M., & Meyer, L. H. (2002). Development and social competence after two years for students enrolled in inclusive and self-contained educational programs. *Research and Practice for Persons with Severe Disabilities, 27*(3), 165–174.

Fisher, M., & Pleasants, S. (2011). Roles, responsibilities, and concerns of paraeducators: Findings from a statewide survey. *Remedial and Special Education,* published online 7 February 2011, DOI: 10:1177/0741932510397762.

Fletcher, J., Denton, C., & Francis, D. (2005). Validity of alternative approaches for the identification of learning disabilities: Operationalizing unexpected underachievement. *Journal of Learning Disabilities, 38*(6), 545–552.

Fletcher, J., Lyon, R., Fuchs, L., & Barnes, M. (2007). *Learning disabilities: From identification to intervention.* New York: Guilford.

Fletcher, J., & Vaughn, S (2009) Response to intervention: Preventing and remediating academic difficulties. *Child Development Perspectives, 3*(1), 30–37.

Fletcher, J. M., & Vaughn, S. (2009). Response to intervention models as alternatives to traditional views of learning disabilities: Response to commentaries. *Child Development Perspectives, 3*(1), 48–50.

Florida Center for Reading Research. (2008). *Curriculum and instruction: Student center activities, grades K–1.* Retrieved January 6, 2012, from http://www.fcrr.org/curriculum/studentCenterActivities2005.shtm

Fombonne, E. (2003, January). The prevalence of autism. *Journal of the American Medical Association, 289*(1), 87–89.

Foorman, B. (2007). Primary prevention in classroom reading instruction. *Teaching Exceptional Children, 39*(5), 24–30.

Foorman, B., & Torgesen, J. (2001). Critical elements of classroom and small-group instruction to promote reading success in all children. *Learning Disabilities Research & Practice, 16*(4), 203–212.

Ford, D. Y., & Kea, C. D. (2009). Creating culturally responsive instruction: For students' and teachers' sakes. *Focus on Exceptional Children, 41*(9), 1–16.

Foreman, P., Arthur-Kelly, M., Pascoe, S., & King, B. S. (2004). Evaluating the educational experiences of children with profound and multiple disabilities in inclusive and segregated classroom setting: An Australian perspective. *Research and Practice for Persons with Severe Disabilities, 29,* 183–193.

Forest, M., & Lusthaus, E. (1987). The Kaleidoscope: Challenge to the cascade. In M. Forest (Ed.), *More education / integration* (pp. 1–16). Downsview, Ontario: G. Allen Roeher Institute.

Forness, S. R., & Kavale, K. A. (2000). Emotional or behavioral disorders: Background and current status of the E/BD terminology and definition. *Behavioral Disorders, 25*(3), 264–269.

Forni, P. M. (2002). *Choosing civility: Twenty-five rules of considerate conduct.* New York: St. Martin's Griffin.

Foster, B., & King, B. H. (2003). Asperger syndrome: To be or not to be? *Current Opinion in Pediatrics, 15*(5),491–494.

Fox, N., & Ysseldyke, J. (1997). Implementing inclusion at the middle school level: Lessons from a negative example. *Exceptional Children, 64*(1), 81–98.

Freeman, S., & Alkin, M. (2000). Academic and social attainments of children with mental retardation in general education and special education settings. *Remedial and Special Education, 21*(1), 3–18.

French, N. (2003). Paraeducators in special education programs. *Focus on Exceptional Children, 36*(2), 1–16.

Friend, M., & Bursuck, W. D. (2006). *Including students with special needs: A practical guide for classroom teachers* (4th ed.). Boston: Allyn & Bacon.

Friend, M., & Cook, L. (2007). *Interactions: Collaboration skills for school professionals* (5th ed.). Boston: Allyn & Bacon.

Friend, M., & Cook, L. (2010). *Interactions: Collaboration skills for school professionals* (6th ed.). Upper Saddle River, NJ: Pearson.

Friend, M., Cook, L., Hurley-Chamberlain, D., & Shamberger, C. (2010). Co-teaching: An illustration of the complexity of collaboration in special education. *Journal of Educational and Psychological Consultation, 20,* 9–27.

Fuchs, D., & Fuchs, L. (1994). Inclusive schools movement and the radicalization of special education reform. *Exceptional Children, 60*(4), 294–309.

Fuchs, D., & Fuchs, L. S. (2006). Introduction to Response to Intervention: What, why, and how valid is it? *Reading Research Quarterly, 41,* 93–99.

Fuchs, D., Fuchs, L., & Burish, P. (2000). Peer-assisted learning strategies: An evidence-based practice to promote reading achievement. *Learning Disabilities Research and Practice, 15*(2), 85–91.

Fuchs, D., Fuchs, L., Shamir, A., Dion, E., Saenz, L., & McMaster, K. (2010). Peer mediation: A means of differentiating classroom instruction. In R. Allington & A. McGill-Franzen (Eds.), *Handbook of reading disabilities* (pp. 362–372). Mahwah, NJ: Erlbaum.

Fuchs, L., & Fuchs, D. (2001). Principles for the prevention and intervention of mathematics difficulties. *Learning Disabilities Research and Practice, 16*(2), 85–95.

Fuchs, L., & Fuchs, D. (2007). A model for implementing responsiveness to intervention. *Teaching Exceptional Children, 39*(5), 14–20.

Fuchs, L., Fuchs, & Compton, D. L. (2010). Rethinking response to intervention at middle and high school. *School Psychology Review, 39*(1), 22–28.

Fuchs, L., Fuchs, D., Craddock, C., Hollenbeck, K., Hamlett, C., & Schatschneider, C. (2008). Effects of small-group tutoring with and without validated classroom instruction on at-risk student's math problem solving: Are the two tiers of prevention better than one? *Journal of Educational Psychology, 100*(3), 491–509.

Fuchs, L., Fuchs, D., Karns, K., Yazdian, L., & Powell, S. (2001). Creating a strong foundation for mathematics learning with kindergarten peer-assisted learning strategies. *Teaching Exceptional Children, 33*(3), 84–87.

Fuchs, L. S., Fuchs, D., & Hamlett, C. L. (2007). Using curriculum-based measurement to inform reading instruction. *Reading and Writing: An Interdisciplinary Journal, 20*(6), 553–567.

Fulk, B., & King, K. (2001). Classwide peer tutoring at work. *Teaching Exceptional Children, 34*(2), 49–53.

Gable, R. A., Hendrickson, J. M., & Van Acker, R. (2001). Maintaining the integrity of FBA-based interventions in schools. *Education and Treatment of Children, 24*(3), 248–260.

Gaffney, J. S. (1987). *Seatwork: Current practices and research implications.* Paper presented at the 64th meeting of the Council for Exceptional Children, Chicago.

Gajria, M., Jitendra, A. K., Sood, S., & Sacks, G. (2007). Improving comprehension of text in students with LD: A research synthesis. *Journal of Learning Disabilities, 40*(3), 210–225.

Galea, J., Butler, J., Iacono, T., & Leighton, D. (2004). The assessment of sexual knowledge of people with intellectual disability. *Journal of Intellectual & Developmental Disability, 29,* 350–365.

García, S., & Ortiz, A. (2006). Preventing disproportionate representation: Culturally and linguistically responsive prereferral interventions. *Teaching Exceptional Children, 38*(3), 64–68.

García, S. B., Méndez Pérez, A., & Ortiz, A. A. (2000). Mexican American mothers' beliefs about disabilities. *Remedial and Special Education, 21*(2), 90–100.

García, S. B., & Tyler, B. (2010). Meeting the needs of English language learners with learning disabilities in the general curriculum. *Theory into Practice, 49*(2), 113–120.

Gardner, A., & Johnson, D. (1997). *Teaching personal experience narrative in the elementary and beyond.* Flagstaff, AZ: Northern Arizona Writing Project Press.

Gately, S. E. (2008). Facilitating reading comprehension for students on the autism spectrum. *Teaching Exceptional Children, 40*(3), 40–45.

Gay, G. (2002). Preparing for culturally responsive teaching. *Journal of Teacher Education, 53*(2), 106–116.

Gay, G. (2010). *Culturally responsive teaching: Theory, research, & practice.* New York: Teachers College Press.

Geary, D., Hoard, M., & Bailey, D. (2011). How SLD manifests in mathematics. In D. Flanagan & V. Alfonso (Eds.), *Essentials of specific learning disabilities identification* (pp. 43–64). Hoboken, NJ: Wiley.

Gersten, R., Baker, S., Shanahan, T., Linan-Thompson, S., Collins, P., & Scarcella, R. (2007). *Effective literacy and English language instruction for English learners in the elementary grades.* NCEE-2007-4011. Washington, DC: U.S. Department of Education, Institute for Education Sciences.

Gersten, R., Chard, D., Jayanthi, M., Baker, S., Morphy, P., & Flojo, J. (2009). Mathematics instruction for students with learning disabilities: A meta-analysis of instructional components. *Review of Educational Research, 79,* 1202–1242.

Gersten, R., & Clarke, B. (2007). *Effective strategies for teaching students with difficulties in mathematics: Instruction research brief.* Reston, VA: National Council for Teachers of Mathematics.

Giangreco, M. F., Cloninger, C. J., Dennis, R. E., & Edelman, S. W. (1993). National expert validation of COACH: Congruence with exemplary practice and suggestions for improvement. *Journal of the Association for Persons with Severe Handicaps, 18,* 109–120.

Giangreco, M. F., Cloninger, C. J., & Iverson, V. S. (1998). *Choosing options and accommodations for children: A guide to planning inclusive education* (2nd ed.). Baltimore: Brookes.

Giangreco, M. F., & Doyle, M. B. (2002). Students with disabilities and paraeducator supports: Benefits, balance, and Band-Aids. *Focus on Exceptional Children, 34*(7), 1–12.

Giangreco, M. F., Edelman, S. W., Dennis, R. E., & Cloninger, C. J. (1995). Use and impact of COACH with students who are deaf–blind. *Journal of the Association for Persons with Severe Handicaps, 20,* 121–135.

Giangreco, M. F., Suter, J., & Doyle, M. (2010). Paraprofessionals in inclusive schools: A review of recent research.

*Journal of Educational and Psychological Consultation, 20,* 41–57.

Gillam, R. B. (2000). Fluency disorders. In R. B. Gillam, T. P. Marquardt, & F. N. Martin (Eds.), *Communication sciences and disorders: From science to clinical practice* (pp. 313–339). San Diego: Singular.

Ginsberg, M. G. (2005). Cultural diversity, motivation and differentiation. *Theory into Practice, 44*(3), 218–225.

Ginsburg-Block, M., Rohrbeck, C., & Fantuzzo, J. (2006). A meta-analytic review of social, self-concept, and behavioral outcomes of peer-assisted learning. *Journal of Educational Psychology, 98*(4), 732–749.

Glover, P., McLaughlin, T., & Derby, K. M. (2010). Using a direct instruction flashcard system with two students with learning disabilities. *Electronic Journal of Research in Educational Psychology, 8,* 457–472.

Goldstein, A. P., & McGinnis, E. (1997). *Skillstreaming the adolescent: New strategies and perspectives for teaching prosocial skills.* Champaign, IL: Research Press.

Gongola, L. C., & Daddario, R. (2010). A practitioner's guide to implementing a differential reinforcement of other behaviors procedure. *Teaching Exceptional Children, 42*(6), 14–20.

Gonzalez, N., Moll, L. C., & Amanti, C. (2005). *Funds of knowledge: Theorizing practices in households and classrooms.* Mahwah, NJ: Erlbaum.

Good, T., & Brophy, J. (2003). *Looking in classrooms* (9th ed.). Boston: Allyn & Bacon.

Good, T., & Brophy, J. (2008). *Looking in classrooms* (10th ed.). Boston: Allyn & Bacon.

Graham, S., & Harris, K. (2006). Cognitive strategy instruction. In C. MacArthur, S. Graham, & K. Harris (Eds.), *Handbook of writing research* (pp. 187–207). New York: Guilford.

Graham, S., Harris, K., & Larsen, L. (2001). Prevention and intervention of writing difficulties for students with learning disabilities. *Learning Disabilities Research & Practice, 16*(2), 74–84.

Graham, S., Harris, K., & MacArthur, S. (2006). Explicitly teaching struggling writers: Strategies for mastering the writing process. *Intervention in School and Clinic, 41*(5), 290–294.

Green, F., Schleien, S., Mactavish, J., & Benepe, S. (1995). Nondisabled adults perceptions of relationships in the early stages of arranged partnerships with peers with mental retardation. *Education and Training in Mental Retardation and Developmental Disabilities, 30,* 91–108.

Greenwood, C., Arreaga-Mayer, C., Utley, C., Gavin, K., & Terry, B. (2001). Classwide Peer Tutoring learning management system: Applications with elementary-level English language learners. *Remedial and Special Education, 22*(1), 34–47.

Gregory, A., Skiba, R., & Noguera, P. (2010). The achievement gap and the discipline gap: Two sides of the same coin? *Educational Researcher, 39*(1), 59–68.

Gresham, F. (2002). Responsiveness to intervention: An alternative approach to the identification of learning disabilities. In R. Bradley, L. Danielson, & D. Hallahan (Eds.), *Identification of learning disabilities: Research to practice* (pp. 467–519). Mahwah, NJ: Erlbaum.

Gresham, F. M.(2007). Evolution of the response-to-intervention concept: Empirical foundations an recent developments. In S. R. Jimerson, M. K. Burns, & A. M. VanDerHeyden (Ed.), *Handbook of response to intervention: The science and practice of assessment and intervention* (pp. 10–24). New York: Springer.

Gresham, F. M., & Elliott, S. N. (1990). *The social skills rating system (SSRS).* Circle Pines, MN: American Guidance Service.

Gresham, F. M., & Kern, L. (2004). Internalizing behavior problems in children and adolescents. In R. B. Rutherford, Jr., M. M. Quinn, & A. R. Mathur (Eds.), *Handbook of research in emotional and behavioral disorders* (pp. 54–77). New York: Guilford.

Gresham, F. M., Lane, K. L., MacMillan, D. L., & Bocian, K. M. (1999). Social and academic profiles of externalizing and internalizing groups: Risk factors for emotional and behavioral disorders. *Behavioral Disorders, 24,* 231–245.

Gresham, F. M., & Vellutino, F. (2010). What is the role of intelligence in the identification of specific learning disabilities? Issues and clarification. *Learning Disabilities Research & Practice, 25*(4), 194–206.

Griffin, H. C., Fitch, C. L., & Griffin, L. W. (2002). Causes and interventions in the area of cerebral palsy. *Infants and Young Children, 14*(3), 18–23.

Grinker, R. R. (2008). What in the world is autism: A cross-cultural perspective. *Zero to Three, 28,* 5–10.

Grossen, B., Coulter, G., & Ruggles, B. (1996). Reading recovery: An evaluation of benefits and costs. *Effective School Practices, 15*(3), 6–24.

Gruwell, E. (1999). *The freedom writers diary.* New York: Broadway Books.

Gudykunst, W. B., & Kim, Y. Y. (2003). *Communicating with strangers: An approach to intercultural communication.* New York: McGraw-Hill.

Gun Han, K., & Chadsey, J. (2004). The influence of gender patterns and grade level on friendship expectations of middle school students toward peers with severe disabilities. *Focus on Autism and Other Developmental Disabilities, 19*(4), 205–214.

Guzel-Ozmen, R. (2009). Modified cognitive strategy instruction: An expository writing strategy. *Intervention in School and Clinic, 44*(4), 216–222.

Haager, D., & Klingner, J. (2005). *Differentiating instruction in today's schools: The special educator's guide.* Upper Saddle River, NJ: Pearson Education.

Hairrell, A., Simmons, D., Swanson, E., Edmonds, M., Vaughn, S., & Rupley, W. H. (2011). Translating vocabulary research to social studies instruction: Before, during, and after text-reading strategies. *Intervention in School and Clinic, 46*(4), 204–210.

Hale, J., Alfonso, V., Berninger, V., et al. (2010). Critical issues in response-to-intervention, comprehensive evaluation, and specific learning disabilities identification and intervention: An expert white paper consensus. *Learning Disabilities Quarterly, 33,* 1–14.

Hall, M., Kleinert, H. L., & Kearns, J. F. (2000). Going to college! Postsecondary programs for students with moderate and severe disabilities. *Teaching Exceptional Children, 32*(3), 58–65.

Hall, T. E., Hughes, C. A., & Filbert, M. (2000). Computer-assisted instruction in reading for students with learning disabilities: A research synthesis. *Education and Treatment of Children, 23,* 173–193.

Hampton, E. O., Whitney, D. W., & Schwartz, I. S. (2002). Weaving assessment information into intervention ideas: Planning communication interventions for young children with disabilities. *Assessment for Effective Intervention, 27,* 49–59.

Handleman, J. S., Harris, S. L., & Martins, M. P. (2005). Helping children with autism enter the mainstream. In F. R. Volkmar, R. Paul, A. Klin, & D. Cohen (Eds.), *Handbook of autism and pervasive developmental disorders: Vol. 2. Assessment, interventions, and policy* (4th ed., pp. 1029–1042). Hoboken, NJ: Wiley.

Hang, Q., & Rabran, K. (2008). An examination of co-teaching: Perspectives and efficacy indicators. *Remedial and Special Education, 30,* 259–268.

Hanley, G. P., Iwata, B. A., & McCord, B. E. (2003). Functional analysis of problem behavior: A review. *Journal of Applied Behavior Analysis, 36,* 147–185.

Hardman, M. L., & Mulder, M. (2004). Federal education reform: Critical issues in public education and their impact on students with disabilities. In L. M. Bullock & R. A. Gable (Eds.), *Quality personnel preparation in emotional/behavioral disorders: Current perspectives and future directions.* Denton, TX: Institute for Behavioral and Learning Differences at the University of North Texas.

Hardman, M. L., Rosenberg, M. S., & Sindelar, P. T. (2004). Preparing highly qualified teachers for students with emotional or behavioral disorders: The impact of NCLB and IDEA. *Behavioral Disorders, 29*(3), 266–278.

Harlacher, J., Walker, N., & Sanford, A. (2010). The "I" in RTI: Research-based factors for intensifying instruction. *Teaching Exceptional Children, 42*(6), 30–38.

Harriott, W., & Martin, S. (2004). Using culturally responsive activities to promote social competence and classroom community. *Teaching Exceptional Children, 37*(1), 48–54.

Harris, K., Graham, S., & Mason, L. H. (2003). Self-regulated strategy development in the classroom: Part of a balanced approach to writing instruction for students with disabilities. *Focus on Exceptional Children, 35*(7), 1–16.

Harris, K., Graham, S., Mason, L., & Friedlander, B. (2008). *Powerful writing strategies for all students.* Baltimore: Brookes.

Harry, B., Kalyanpur, M., & Day, M. (1999). *Building cultural reciprocity with families: Case studies in special education.* Baltimore: Brookes.

Hartshorne, N. (2001/2002). It sounds nice, but is inclusion really worth it? *Deaf-Blind Perspectives, 9*(2), 12–13.

Hasselbring, T. S., & Bausch, M. E. (2005). Assistive technologies for reading. *Educational Leadership, 63*(4), 72–75.

Hawken, L. S., & Horner, R. H. (2003). Evaluation of a targeted intervention within a schoolwide system of behavior support. *Journal of Behavioral Education, 12*(3), 225–240.

Hawken, L. S., Vincent, C. G., & Schumann, J. (2008). Response to intervention for social behavior: Challenges and opportunities. *Journal of Emotional and Behavioral Disorders, 16*(4), 213–225.

Hayes, L., Lane, H., & Pullen, P. (2005). *University of Florida reading initiative (UFRI): Tutoring for beginning readers.* Gainesville, FL: College of Education, University of Florida.

Heflin, L., & Alaimo, D. (2007). *Students with autism spectrum disorders: Effective instructional practices.* Upper Saddle River, NJ: Merrill/Pearson Education.

Heller, K. W. (2004). Integrating health care and educational programs. In F. P. Orelove, D. Sobsey, & R. K. Silberman (Eds.), *Educating children with multiple disabilities: A collaborative approach* (2nd ed., pp. 379–424). Baltimore: Brookes.

Hershfeldt, P., & Rosenberg, M. S. (2008, November). *Beyond universal management: What developing teachers need to know about managing problem behaviors.* Paper presented at the annual conference of the Teacher Education Division of the Council for Exceptional Children, Dallas, TX.

Hershfeldt, P., Rosenberg, M. S., & Bradshaw, C. P. (2010). Function-based thinking: A systematic way of thinking about function and its role in changing student behavior problems. *Beyond Behavior, 19*(3), 12–21.

Hershfeldt, P., Sechrest R., Pell, K., Rosenberg, M., Bradshaw, C., & Leaf, P. (2009). Double-Check: A framework of culturally responsiveness applied to classroom behavior. *Teaching Exceptional Children Plus, 62*(2), Article 5. Retrieved January 21, 2011, from http://escholarship.bc.edu/education/tecplus/vol16/iss2/art5/

Hetzroni, O. E., & Shrieber, B. (2004). Word processing as an assistive technology tool for enhancing academic outcomes of students with writing disabilities in the general classroom. *Journal of Learning Disabilities, 37,* 143–154.

Hilton, A. (2007). Response to intervention: Changing how we do business. *Leadership, 36*(4), 16–19.

Hitchcock, C., Meyer, A., Rose, D., & Jackson, R. (2002). Providing new access to the general curriculum: Universal design for learning. *Teaching Exceptional Children, 35*(2), 8–17.

Holburn, S. (2002). How science can evaluate and enhance person-centered planning. *Research and Practice for Persons with Severe Disabilities, 27,* 250–260.

Holler, R., & Zirkel, P. (2008). Section 504 and public schools: A national survey concerning "Section 504-only" students. *NASSP Bulletin, 92,* 19–43.

Hollins, E. R. (1996). *Culture in school learning: Revealing the deep meaning.* Mahwah, NJ: Erlbaum.

Hong, E., Sas, M., & Sas, J. C. (2006). Test taking strategies of high and low mathematics achievers. *Journal of Educational Research, 99*(3), 144–155.

Hoover, J., Klingner, J., Baca, L., & Patton, J. (2008). *Methods for teaching culturally diverse exceptional children.* Upper Saddle River, NJ: Pearson Education.

Hoover, J. J., & Patton, J. R. (2008). The role of special educators in a multitiered instructional system. *Intervention in School and Clinic, 43*(4), 195–202.

Hoover, N. (2001). *Reading Rescue: A handbook for tutors.* Gainesville, FL: Literacy Trust.

Hoover, N., & Lane, H. (2001). *Preventing literacy failure through cost-effective tutoring: A report on outcomes in high-poverty and rural schools.* Paper presented at the annual meeting of the American Educational Research Association, New York.

Houghton Mifflin. (2006). *Reading intervention for early success.* Boston, MA: Author. Houghton Mifflin. (n.d.). *Earobics.* Boston, MA: Author.

Hughes, C., & Carter, E. (2006). *Success for all students: Promoting inclusion in secondary programs through peer buddy programs.* Upper Saddle River, NJ: Prentice Hall.

Hughes, C., & Carter, E. (2008). *Peer buddy programs for successful secondary school inclusion.* Baltimore: Brookes.

Hughes, C., Guth, C., Hall, S., Presley, J., Dye, M., & Byers, C. (1999). "They are my best friends": Peer buddies promote inclusion in high school. *Teaching Exceptional Children, 31*(5), 32–37.

Hughes, C. A. (1996). Memory and test taking strategies. In D. D. Deshler, E. S. Ellis, & B. K. Lenz (Eds.), *Teaching adolescents with learning disabilities* (pp. 209–266). Denver: Love.

Hughes, C. A., & Maccini, P. (1997). Computer-assisted mathematics instruction for students with learning disabilities: A research review. *Learning Disabilities: A Multidisciplinary Journal, 8*(3), 155–166.

Hughes, C. A., Ruhl, K. L., Schumaker, J., & Deshler, D. D. (2002). Effects of instruction in an assignment completion strategy on the homework performance of students with learning disabilities in general education classes. *Learning Disabilities Research & Practice, 17*(1), 1–18.

Hutinger, P., Johanson, J., & Stoneburner, R. (1996). Assistive technology applications in educational programs of children with multiple disabilities: A case study report on the state of the practice. *Journal of Special Education Technology, 13*(1), 16–35.

Hyman, S., & Towbin, K. E. (2007). Autism spectrum disorders. In M. L. Batshaw, L. Pelligrino, & N. Roizen (Eds.), *Children with disabilities* (pp. 325–343). Baltimore: Brookes.

Idol, L. (2006). Toward inclusion of special education students in general education. *Remedial and Special Education, 27*(2), 77–94.

Individuals with Disabilities Education Act, Public Law 105-17. (1997). Retrieved January 6, 2012, from http://www.ed.gov/offices/OSERS/Policy/IDEA/index.html

Individuals with Disabilities Education Improvement Act (IDEA) of 2004, Public Law 108-446 (2004). Retrieved January 6, 2012, from http://idea.ed.gov/download/statute.html

Institute for Children and Poverty. (2007). *Quick facts*. Retrieved May 17, 2008, from http://www.icphusa.org

Institute of Education Sciences. (2008, 2011). What works clearinghouse. Retrieved March 12, 2008, from http://ies.ed.gov/ncee/wwc/

Irvine, J. J. (2002). *In search of wholeness: African American teachers and their culturally specific practices*. New York: Palgrave/St. Martins Press.

Irvine, J. J. (2003). *Educating teachers for diversity: Seeing with a cultural eye*. New York: Teachers College Press.

Iversen, S., Tunmer, W., & Chapman, J. (2005). The effects of varying group size on the Reading Recovery approach to preventive early intervention. *Journal of Learning Disabilities, 38*(5), 456–472.

Izzo, M. V., Yurick, A., & McArrell, B. (2009). Supported eText: Effects of text-to-speech on access and achievement for high school students with disabilities. *Journal of Special Education Technology, 24*(3), 9–20.

Jitendra, A., Salmento, M., & Haydt, L. (1999). A case analysis of fourth-grade subtraction instruction in basal mathematics programs: Adherence to important instructional design criteria. *Learning Disabilities Research & Practice, 14*(2), 69–79.

Johns, B. H., & Carr, V. G. (1995). *Techniques for managing verbally and physically aggressive students*. Denver, CO: Love.

Johnson, D. W., Johnson, R., & Holubec, E. (1998). *Cooperation in the classroom* (7th ed.). Edina, MN: Interaction Books.

Johnson, G. O. (1962). Special education for the mentally handicapped: A paradox. *Exceptional Children, 29*(2), 62–69.

Johnson, J., & Reid, R. (2011). Overcoming executive function deficits with students with ADHD. *Theory into Practice, 50,* 61–67.

Jonassen, D. H., Howland, J., Marra, R. M., & Crismond, D. P. (2008). *Meaningful learning with technology* (3rd ed.). Upper Saddle River, NJ: Merrill/Pearson Education.

Jones, T. (2005). Twenty ways to incorporate diversity into your classroom. *Intervention in School and Clinic, 41*(1), 9–12.

Jones, V. (1993). Assessing your classroom and school-wide student management plan. *Beyond Behavior, 4*(3), 9–12.

Jones, V., & Jones, L. (2004). *Comprehensive classroom management: Creating communities of support and solving problems* (7th ed.). Boston: Pearson.

Jung, L. A., Gomez, C., & Baird, S. M. (2008). Designing intervention plans: Bridging the gap between individualized education programs and implementation. *Teaching Exceptional Children, 41*(1), 26–33.

Justice, L. M. (2010). *Communication sciences and disorders: A contemporary perspective* (2nd ed.). Upper Saddle River, NJ: Allyn & Bacon/Pearson Education.

Kagan, S. (1994). *Cooperative learning*. San Diego, CA: Kagan Cooperative Learning.

Kamens, M. W. (2004). Learning to write IEPs: A personalized, reflective approach for preservice teachers. *Intervention in School and Clinic, 40*(2), 76–80.

Kamps, D. (2010). Social skills instruction and generalization strategies. In B. Algozzine, A. P. Daunic, & S. Smith (Eds.), *Preventing problem behaviors* (pp. 71–111). Thousand Oaks, CA: Corwin.

Kamps, D., Abbott, M., Greenwood, C., Arreaga-Mayer, C., Wills, H., Longstaff, J., Culpepper, M., & Waiton, C. (2007). Use of evidence-based, small-group reading instruction for English language learners in elementary grades: Secondary-tier intervention. *Learning Disability Quarterly, 30*(3), 153–168.

Kamps, D., & Greenwood, C. (2005). Formulating secondary-level reading interventions. *Journal of Learning Disabilities, 38*(6), 500–509.

Kampwirth, T., & Powers, K. (2011). *Collaborative consultation in the schools: Effective practices for students with learning and behavior problems* (4th ed.). Boston: Pearson Education.

Kanner, L. (1943). Autistic disturbances of affective contact. *The Nervous Child, 2,* 217–250.

Kaplan K12 Learning Services. (2008). *SpellRead services*. Retrieved May 13, 2008, from http://www.KaplanK12.com

Kauchak, D., & Eggen, P. (2010). *Introduction to teaching: Becoming a professional* (4th ed.). Upper Saddle River, NJ: Pearson Education.

Kauchak, D., & Eggen, P. (2012). *Learning and teaching: Research-based methods* (6th ed.). Upper Saddle River, NJ: Pearson Education.

Kaufenberg, J. (2010, May). *iPad apps for kids with special needs*. Retrieved May 27, 2011, from http://blog.easystand.com/2010/05/ipad-apps-for-kids-with-special-needs/

Kauffman, J. (1993). How we might achieve the radical reform of special education. *Exceptional Children, 60*(1), 6–16.

Kauffman, J., & Hallahan, D. (2005). *Special education: What is it and why we need it? Boston*: Pearson Education.

Kauffman, J. M. (1981). Introduction: Historical trends and contemporary issues in special education in the United States. In J. M. Kauffman & D. P. Hallahan (Eds.), *Handbook of special education* (pp. 3–23). Upper Saddle River, NJ: Prentice Hall.

Kauffman, J. M. (2001). *Characteristics of emotional and behavioral disorders of children and youth* (7th ed.). Upper Saddle River, NJ: Merrill/Pearson Education.

Kauffman, J. M. (2005). *Characteristics of emotional and behavioral disorders of children and youth* (8th ed.). Upper Saddle River, NJ: Merrill/Pearson.

Kauffman, J. M., Mostert, M. P., Trent, S. C., & Hallahan, D. P. (2002). *Managing classroom behavior: A reflective case-based approach* (3rd ed.). Boston: Allyn & Bacon.

Kavale, K., & Forness, S. (2000). History, rhetoric, and reality: Analysis of the inclusion debate. *Remedial and Special Education, 21*(5), 279–296.

Kavale, K. A., Mathur, S. R., & Mostert, M. P. (2004). Social skills training and teaching social behavior to students with emotional and behavioral disorders. In R. B. Rutherford, Jr., M. M. Quinn, & A. R. Mathur (Eds.), *Handbook of research in emotional and behavioral disorders* (pp. 446–461). New York: Guilford.

Kelley, K. R. (2011). Effects of a video iPod with picture prompts on pedestrian navigation and route completion on a college campus. Unpublished doctoral dissertation, University of North Carolina at Charlotte.

Kelley, M., & Herrick, C. L. (2011). Bridging the social disconnect: Social characteristics of ASD. In K. M. McCoy (Ed.), *Autism from the teacher's perspective: Strategies for classroom instruction* (pp. 63–80). Denver: Love.

Kennedy, C. H., & Shukla, S. (1995). Social interaction research for people with autism as a set of past, current, and emerging propositions. *Behavioral Disorders, 21,* 21–35.

Kids Data. (2009). *Kidsdata.org data groups.* Retrieved January 25, 2011, from http://www.kidsdata.org/data/demographic/

Kim, A., Woodruff, A. L., Klein, C., & Vaughn, S. (2006). Facilitating co-teaching for literacy in general education classrooms through technology: Focus on students with learning disabilities. *Reading & Writing Quarterly, 22,* 269–291.

King-Sears, M. (2009). Universal design for learning: Technology and pedagogy. *Learning Disability Quarterly, 32*(4), 199–201.

King-Sears, M. E., Mercer, C. D., & Sindelar, P. T. (1992). Toward independence with keyword mnemonics: A strategy for science vocabulary instruction. *Remedial and Special Education, 13,* 22–33.

King-Sears, M. E., & Mooney, J. F. (2004). Teaching content in an academically diverse class. In B. K. Lenz, D. D. Deshler, & B. Kissam (Eds.), *Teaching content to all: Evidence-based inclusive practices in middle and secondary schools* (pp. 221–251). Boston: Pearson.

Klin, A., McPartland, J., & Volkmar, F. R. (2005). Asperger syndrome. In F. R. Volkmar, R. Paul, A. Klin, & D. Cohen (Eds.), *Handbook of autism and pervasive developmental disorders: Vol. 1. Diagnosis, development, neurobiology, and behavior* (4th ed., pp. 88–125). Hoboken, NJ: Wiley.

Knight, V., Browder, D., Agnello, B., & Lee, A. (2010). Academic instruction for students with severe disabilities. *Focus on Exceptional Children, 42*(7), 1–16.

Kochhar-Bryant, C. (2008). *Collaboration and system coordination for students with special needs.* Upper Saddle River, NJ: Merrill/Pearson Education.

Koenig, L. (2000). *Smart discipline for the classroom: Respect and cooperation restored* (3rd ed.). Thousand Oaks, CA: Corwin Press.

Koh, M., & Robertson, J. (2003). School reform models and special education. *Education and Urban Society, 35*(4), 421–442.

Konrad, M. (2008). Involve students in the IEP process. *Intervention in School and Clinic, 43,* 236–239.

Konrad, M., Joseph, L. M., & Itoi, M. (2011). Using guided notes to enhance instruction for all students. *Intervention in School and Clinic, 46*(3), 131–140.

Kovaleski, J., & Glew, M. (2006). Bringing instructional support teams to scale: Implications of the Pennsylvania experience. *Remedial and Special Education, 27,* 16–25.

Kramer, C. (2004). *The effects of a self-management device on the acquisition of social skills in adolescent males with SED.* Unpublished doctoral dissertation, Johns Hopkins University, Baltimore.

Kulinna, P. H., Cothran, D. J., & Regualos, R. (2006). Teachers' reports of student misbehavior in physical education. *Research Quarterly for Exercise and Sports, 77*(1), 32–41.

Kvavik, R. B. (2011). *Convenience, communications, and control: How students use technology.* EDUCAUSE Center for Applied Research and University of Minnesota, Twin Cities. Retrieved May 17, 2011, from http://www.educause.edu/Resources/EducatingtheNetGeneration/ConvenienceCommunicationsandCo/6070

Ladders to Literacy. (2008). *Ladders to literacy outreach.* Retrieved May 13, 2008, from www.wri-edu.org/ladders

Lancioni, G. E., Singh, N. N., O'Reilly, M. F., Oliva, D., Baccani, S., & Canevaro, A. (2002). Using simple hand-movement responses with optic microswitches with two persons with multiple disabilities. *Research and Practice for Persons with Severe Disabilities, 27,* 276–279.

Landrum, T. J. (2011). Emotional and behavioral disorders. In J. M. Kauffman & D. P. Hallahan (Eds.), *Handbook of special education* (pp. 209–220). New York: Routledge.

Lane, K. L. (2004). Academic instruction and tutoring interventions for students with emotional and behavioral disorders: 1990 to the present. In R. B. Rutherford, Jr., M. M. Quinn, & A. R. Mathur (Eds.), *Handbook of research in emotional and behavioral disorders* (pp. 462–486). New York: Guilford.

Lane, K. L., Carter, E. W., Pierson, M. R., & Glaeser, B. C. (2006). Academic, social, and behavioral characteristics of high school students with emotional disturbances or learning disabilities. *Journal of Emotional and Behavioral Disorders, 14*(2), 108–117.

Lane, K. L., Givner, C. C., & Pierson, M. R. (2004). Teacher expectations of student behavior: Necessary success in elementary school classrooms. *Journal of Special Education, 38*(2), 104–110.

Lane, K., Pierson, M., Robertson, E., & Little, A. (2004). Teachers' views of prereferral interventions: Perceptions of and recommendations for implementation support. *Education and Treatment of Children, 27*(4), 420–439.

Lang, H. G. (n.d.). *Science education for deaf students: Priorities for research and instructional development.* Retrieved January 6, 2012, from *www.deafed.net/PublishedDocs/LANGScienceelitreview5.doc*

Lawrence-Brown, D. (2004). Differentiated instruction: Inclusive strategies for standards-based learning that benefit the whole class. *American Secondary Education, 32*(3), 34–62.

Lazarus, B. D. (1993). Guided notes: Effects with secondary and postsecondary students with mild disabilities. *Education and Treatment of Children, 16*(3), 272–289.

Lee, H. J. (2011). Cultural factors related to the hidden curriculum for students with autism and related disabilities. *Intervention in School and Clinic, 46*(3), 141–149.

Lee, S., Yoo, S., & Bak, S. (2003). Characteristics of friendships between children with and without disabilities. *Education and Training in Developmental Disabilities, 38*(2), 157–166.

Lee, S. H., Soukup, J. H., Little, T. D., & Wehmeyer, M. L. (2009). Student and teacher variables contributing to access to the general education curriculum for students with intellectual and developmental disabilities. *The Journal of Special Education, 43*(1), 29–44.

Lehr, C. A., Sinclair, M. F., & Christenson, S. L. (2004). Addressing student engagement and truancy prevention during the elementary years: A replication study of the Check & Connect model. *Journal of Education for Students Placed at Risk, 9*(3), 279–301.

Lenz, K., & Deshler, D. (2004). *Teaching content to all: Evidence-based inclusive practices in middle and secondary schools.* Boston: Allyn & Bacon.

Lenz, K., Bulgren, J., Kissam, J., & Taymans, J. (2004). SMARTER planning for academic diversity. In K. Lenz & D. Deshler (Eds.), *Teaching content to all: Evidence-based inclusive practices in middle and secondary schools* (pp. 47–77). Boston: Allyn & Bacon.

Lerner, J., & Johns, B. (2009). *Learning disabilities and related mild disabilities* (11th ed.). Belmont, CA: Wadsworth.

Lesseliers, J., & Van Hove, G. (2002). Barriers to the development of intimate relationships and expression of sexuality among people with developmental disabilities: Their perceptions. *Research and Practice for Persons with Severe Disabilities, 27,* 69–81.

Levin, B., Hibbard, K., & Rock, T. (2002). Using problem-based learning as a tool for learning to teach students with special needs. *Teacher Education and Special Education, 25*(3), 278–290.

Levy, H. M. (2008). Meeting the needs of all students through differentiated instruction: Helping every child reach and exceed standards. *The Clearing House, 81*(4), 161–164.

Lewis, R., & Doorlag, D. (2011). *Teaching students with special needs in general education classrooms* (8th ed.). Upper Saddle River, NJ: Pearson Education.

Lewis, T. J., & Sugai, G. (1999). Effective behavior support: A systems approach to proactive school-wide management. *Focus on Exceptional Children, 31*(6), 1–24.

Lindamood, P., & Lindamood, P. (1998). *Lindamood phonemic sequencing program (LIPS).* San Luis Obispo, CA: Lindamood-Bell Learning Processes.

Lindsay, G. (2007). Educational psychology and the effectiveness of inclusive education/mainstreaming. *British Journal of Educational Psychology, 77,* 1–24.

Linn, A., & Smith-Myles, B. (2004). Asperger syndrome and six strategies for success. *Beyond Behavior, 14*(1), 3–9.

Lipkewich, A., & Mazurenko, R. (2008). *ABC's of the writing process.* Retrieved January 6, 2012, from http://www.angelfire.com/wi/writingprocess/

Little, M. (2009). *Response to intervention (RtI) for teachers: Classroom instructional problem solving.* Denver: Love.

Loeber, R. & Burke, J. D. (2011). Developmental pathways in juvenile externalizing and internalizing problems. *Journal of Research on Adolescence, 21*(1), 34–46.

Loveland, K. A., & Tunali-Kotoski, B. (2005). The school-age child with an autistic spectrum disorder. In F. R. Volkmar, R. Paul, A. Klin, & D. Cohen (Eds.), *Handbook of autism and pervasive developmental disorders: Vol. 1. Diagnosis, development, neurobiology, and behavior* (4th ed., pp. 247–287). Hoboken, NJ: Wiley.

Luckner, J. L., & Muir, S. (2002). Suggestions for helping students who are deaf succeed in general education settings. *Communication Disorders Quarterly, 24,* 23–30.

Luckner, J. L., Sebald, A. M., Cooney, J., Young, J., & Muir, S. G. (2006). An examination of the evidence-based literacy research in deaf education. *American Annals of the Deaf, 150,* 443–456.

Maag, J. (2002). A contextually based approach for treating depression in school-age children. *Intervention in School and Clinic, 37*(3), 149–155.

Maas, E., & Robin, D. A. (2006). Motor speech disorders: Apraxia and dysarthria. In L. M. Justice (Ed.), *Communication sciences and disorders: An introduction* (pp. 180–211). Upper Saddle River, NJ: Merrill/Pearson Education.

MacArthur, C. A. (2000). New tools for writing: Assistive technology for students with writing difficulties. *Topics in Language Disorders, 20*(4), 85–100.

MacArthur, C. A., & Cavalier, A. R. (2004). Dictation and speech recognition technology as test accommodations. *Exceptional Children, 71,* 43–58.

MacArthur, C. A., Ferretti, R. P., Okolo, C. M., & Cavalier, A. R. (2001). Technology applications for students with literacy problems: A critical review. *Elementary School Journal, 101,* 273–301.

Maccini, P., & Gagnon, J. (2005). *Math graphic organizers for students with disabilities.* Retrieved March 11, 2008, from www.K8accesscenter.org

Maccini, P., Strickland, T., & Gagnon, J. C. (2008). Accessing the general education math curriculum for secondary students with high-incidence disabilities. *Focus on Exceptional Children, 40*(8), 1–32.

Madaus, J. W., & Shaw, S. F. (2008). The role of school professionals in implementing section 504 for students with disabilities. *Educational Policy, 22,* 363–378.

Maheady, L., Harper, G., & Mallette, B. (2001). Peer-mediated instruction and interventions and students with mild disabilities. *Remedial and Special Education, 22*(1), 4–14.

Marks, D. (2005). *Culture and classroom management: Grounded theory from a high poverty predominately African American elementary school.* Unpublished doctoral dissertation University of Florida, Gainesville, FL.

Marshak, L., Mastropieri, M. A., & Scruggs, T. E. (2011). Curriculum enhancements in inclusive secondary classrooms. *Exceptionality, 19,* 61–74.

Martin, J. E., Marshall, L. H., Maxson, L. M., & Jerman, P. L. (1996). *The self-directed IEP.* Longmont, CO: Sopris-West.

Martin, J. E., Van Dycke, J. L., Greene, B. A., Gardner, J. E., Christensen, W. R., Woods, L. L., & Lovett, D. L. (2006). Direct observation of teacher-directed IEP meetings: Establishing the need for student IEP meeting instruction. *Exceptional Children, 72,* 187–200.

Martinez, R. S., Nellis, L. M., & Prendergast, K. A. (2006). Closing the achievement gap series: Part II. Response to Intervention (RTI)—Basic elements, practical applications, and policy recommendations. *Center for Evaluation & Education Policy, 4*(8).

Martinussen, R., & Major, A. (2011). Working memory weaknesses in students with ADHD: Implications for instruction. *Theory into Practice, 50,* 68–75.

Marzano, R., Pickering, D., & Pollock, J. (2001). *Classroom instruction that works.* Alexandria, VA: Association for Supervision and Curriculum Development.

Mason, L., Harris, K., & Graham, S. (2011). Self-regulated strategy development for students with writing difficulties. *Theory into Practice, 50*(1), 20–27.

Mastropieri, M. A., & Scruggs, T. E. (1998). Enhancing school success with mnemonic strategies. *Intervention in School and Clinic, 33*(4), 201–208.

Mastropieri, M. A., & Scruggs, T. E. (2005). Feasibility and consequences of response to intervention: Examination of the issues and scientific evidence as a model for the identification of individuals with learning disabilities. *Journal of Learning Disabilities, 38*(6), 525–531.

Mastropieri, M. A., Scruggs, T. E., Graetz, J., et al. (2005). Case studies in co-teaching in the content areas: Successes, failures, and challenges. *Intervention in School and Clinic, 40*(5), 260–270.

Mastropieri, M. A., Sweda, J., & Scruggs, T. E. (2000). Putting mnemonic strategies to work in an inclusive classroom. *Learning Disabilities Research & Practice, 15*(2), 69–74.

Mathes, P., & Denton, C. (2002). *Reading Recovery: Current practice alerts.* Retrieved March 12, 2008, from www.TeachingLD.org

Mattison, R. E. (2004). Psychiatric and psychological assessment of emotional and behavioral disorders during school mental health consultation. In R. B. Rutherford, Jr., M. M. Quinn, & A. R. Mathur (Eds.), *Handbook of research in emotional and behavioral disorders* (pp. 163–180). New York: Guilford.

Matuszny, R., Banda, D., & Coleman, T. (2007). A progressive plan for building collaborative relationships with parents from diverse backgrounds. *Teaching Exceptional Children, 39*(4), 24–31.

McConnell, M. E., Hilvitz, P. B., & Cox, C. J. (1998). Functional assessment: A systematic approach for assessment and intervention in general and special education classrooms. *Intervention in School and Clinic, 34,* 10–20.

McCoy, K. M. (Ed.). (2011). *Autism from the teacher's perspective: Strategies for classroom instruction.* Denver: Love.

McDonnell, J. (2011). Instructional contexts. In J. Kauffman & D. Hallahan (Eds.), *Handbook of special education* (pp. 532–543). New York: Routledge.

McGinnis, E., & Goldstein, A. P. (1997/2003). *Skillstreaming in early childhood: New strategies and perspectives for teaching prosocial skills.* Champaign, IL: Research Press.

McLeskey, J. (Ed.). (2007). *Reflections on inclusion: Classic articles that shaped our thinking.* Arlington, VA: Council for Exceptional Children.

McLeskey, J. (2011). Supporting improved practice for special education teachers: The importance of learner-centered professional development. *Journal of Special Education Leadership, 24,* 26–35.

McLeskey, J., Landers, E., Hoppey. D., & Williamson, P. (2011). Learning disabilities and the LRE mandate: An examination of national and state trends. *Learning Disabilities Research & Practice, 26*(2), 60–66.

McLeskey, J., Landers, E., Williamson, P., & Hoppey, D. (2011). The Least Restrictive Environment mandate of IDEA: Are we moving toward educating students with disabilities in less restrictive settings? *The Journal of Special Education,* first published online as doi:10.1177/0022466910376670

McLeskey, J., & Pacchiano, D. (1994). Mainstreaming students with LD: Are we making progress? *Exceptional Children, 60,* 508–517.

McLeskey, J., & Waldron, N. (2000). *Inclusive schools in action: Making differences ordinary.* Alexandria, VA: Association for Supervision and Curriculum Development.

McLeskey, J., & Waldron, N. (2002, September). School change and inclusive schools: Lessons learned from practice. *Phi Delta Kappan, 84*(1), 65–72.

McLeskey, J., & Waldron, N. (2006). Comprehensive school reform and inclusive schools: Improving schools for all students. *Theory into Practice, 45*(3), 269–278.

McLeskey, J., & Waldron, N. (2011a). Educational programs for elementary students with learning disabilities: Can they be both effective and inclusive? *Learning Disabilities Research and Practice, 26*(1), 48–57.

McLeskey, J., & Waldron, N. (2011b). *Are full inclusion programs for elementary students with LD justifiable?* Paper presented at the Council for Exceptional Children Convention, National Harbor, MD.

McLeskey, J., Henry, D., & Axelrod, M. (1999). Inclusion of students with LD: An examination of data from Reports to Congress. *Exceptional Children, 65,* 55–66.

McLeskey, J., Tyler, N. C., & Flippin, S. S. (2004). The supply of and demand for special education teachers: A review of research regarding the chronic shortage of special education teachers. *Journal of Special Education, 38*(1), 5–21.

McLeskey, J., Waldron, N., So, T. H., Swanson, K., & Loveland, T. (2001). Perspectives of teachers toward inclusive school programs. *Teacher Education and Special Education, 24,* 108–115.

McMaster, K., & Fuchs, D. (2005). *Cooperative learning for students with disabilities.* Retrieved February 20, 2008, from www.teachingld.org

McMaster, K., Fuchs, D., & Fuchs, L. (2006). Research on peer-assisted learning strategies: The promise and limitations of peer-mediated instruction. *Reading & Writing Quarterly, 22*(1), 5–25.

McMaster, K., Kung, S., Han, I., & Cao, M. (2008). Peer-assisted learning strategies: a "Tier 1" approach to promoting English learners' response to intervention. *Exceptional Children, 74,* 194–214.

Meadan, H., & Monda-Amaya, L. (2008).Collaboration to promote social competence for students with mild disabilities in the general classroom: A structure for providing social support. *Intervention in School and Clinic, 43*(3), 158–167.

Meadan, H., Shelden, D., Appel, K., & DeGrazia, R. L. (2010). Developing a long-term vision: A road map for students' futures. *Teaching Exceptional Children, 43*(2), 8–14.

Mechling, L. D., Gast, D. L., & Krupa, K. (2007). Impact of SMART Board technology: An investigation of sight word reading and observational learning. *Journal of Autism and Developmental Disorders, 37,* 1869–1882.

Mechling, L. C., Gast, D. L., & Seid, N. H. (2009). Using a personal digital assistant to increase independent task completion by students with autism spectrum disorder. *Journal of Autism and Developmental Disorders, 39,* 1420–1434.

Mechling, L. C., Gast, D. L., & Thompson, K. L. (2008–2009). Comparison of the effects of SMART board technology and flash card instruction on sight word recognition and observational learning. *Journal of Special Education Technology, 23*(1), 34–46.

Mellard, D., McKnight, M., & Jordan, J. (2010). RTI tier structures and instructional intensity. *Learning Disabilities Research & Practice, 25*(4), 217–225.

Meltzer, L. (2007). Executive function difficulties and learning disabilities: Understandings and misunderstandings. In L. Meltzer (Ed.), *Executive function in education: From theory to practice* (pp. 77–105). New York: Guilford.

Mercer, C. & Pullen, P. (2009). *Students with learning disabilities* (7th ed.). Upper Saddle River, NJ: Merrill/Pearson Education.

Miller, S., & Hudson, P. (2007). Using evidence-based practices to build mathematics competence related to conceptual, procedural, and declarative knowledge. *Learning Disabilities Research & Practice, 22*(1), 47–57.

Milner, H. R., & Ford, D.Y. (2005). Racial experiences influence as teachers: Implications for gifted education curriculum development and implementation. *Roeper Review, 28*(1), 30–36.

Miner, C. A., & Bates, P. E. (1997). The effect of person-centered planning activities on the IEP/transition planning process. *Education and Training in Mental Retardation and Developmental Disabilities, 32,* 105–112.

Mitchell, R. E. (2005). *Can you tell me how many deaf people there are in the United States?* Gallaudet Research Institute. Retrieved February 6, 2011, from http://research.gallaudet.edu/Demographics/deaf-US.php

Montague, M. (2007). Self-regulation and mathematics instruction. *Learning Disabilities Research and Practice, 22*(1), 75–83.

Montague, M. (2008). Self-regulation strategies to improve mathematical problem solving for students with learning disabilities. *Learning Disability Quarterly, 31,* 37–44.

Montague, M., Enders, C., Dietz, S., Dixon, J., & Cavendish, W. M. (2008). A longitudinal study of depressive symptomology and self-concept in adolescents. *The Journal of Special Education, 42*(2), 67–78.

Montague, M., Warger, C., & Morgan, T. (2000). Solve it! Strategy instruction to improve mathematical problem solving. *Learning Disabilities Research and Practice, 15*(2), 110–116.

Montgomery, D. J., Karlan, G. R., & Coutinho, M. (2001). The effectiveness of word processor spell checker programs to produce target words for misspellings generated by students with learning disabilities. *Journal of Special Education Technology, 16*(2), 27–41.

Montgomery, D. J., & Marks, L. J. (2006). Using technology to build independence in writing for students with disabilities. *Preventing School Failure, 50*(3), 33–38.

Morgan, J. J. (2010). Social networking web sites: Teaching appropriate social competence to students with emotional and behavioral disorders. *Intervention in School and Clinic, 45*(3), 147–157.

Morrissey, K. L., Bohanon, H., & Fenning, P. (2010). Teaching and acknowledging expected behaviors in an urban high school. *Teaching Exceptional Children, 42*(5), 27–35.

Moses, H. (1990, June 22). *The Americans with Disabilities Act of 1990—Summary: American Rehabilitation*. Retrieved January 6, 2012, from http://findarticles.com/p/articles/mi_m0842/is_n2_v16/ai_9373654/

MTA (Multimodal Treatment Study of Children with ADHD) Cooperative Group. (2004). National Institute of Mental Health multimodal treatment study of ADHD follow-up: 24-month outcomes of treatment strategies for attention-deficit/hyperactivity disorder. *Pediatrics, 113,* 754–761.

Munk, D. D. & Bursuck, W. D. (2004). Personalized grading plans: A systematic approach to making the grades of included students more accurate and meaningful. *Focus on Exceptional Children, 36*(9), 1–11.

Murawski, W., & Hughes, C. (2009). Response to intervention, collaboration, and co-teaching: A logical combination for successful systemic change. *Intervention in School and Clinic, 53,* 267–277.

Murdick, N., Gartin, B., & Crabtree, T. (2002). *Special education law*. Upper Saddle River, NJ: Merrill/Pearson Education.

National Center on Accessible Instructional Materials at CAST. (2011). *What is the National Instructional Materials Accessibility Standard (NIMAS)?* Retrieved March 2, 2011, from http://aim.cast.org/learn/policy/federal/what_is_nimas

National Center for Education Statistics. (2005). *NAEP 2004 trends in academic progress. Three decades of student performance in reading and mathematics: Findings in brief*. Retrieved January 6, 2012, from http://nces.ed.gov/pubsearch/pubsinfo.asp?pubid=2005464

National Center for Education Statistics. (2007). *Digest of Education Statistics, Table 124*. Retrieved January 6, 2012, from http://nces.ed.gov/pubsearch/pubsinfo.asp?pubid=2008022

National Center for Education Statistics. (2009). *Digest of Education Statistics: 2009*. Retrieved January 7, 2012, from http://nces.ed.gov/pubsearch/pubsinfo.asp?pubid=2010013

National Center for Education Statistics. (2010). *Condition of education 2010*. Washington, DC: U.S. Department of Education, Institution of Education Sciences. Retrieved January 25, 2011, from http://nces.ed.gov/programs/coe/

National Center for Hearing Assessment and Management. (n.d.). *Universal newborn hearing screening fact sheet*. Retrieved February 5, 2011, from http://www.infanthearing.org/resources/fact.pdf

National Consortium on Deaf-Blindness. (2007). *Children who are deaf-blind*. Retrieved February 6, 2011, from http://nationaldb.org/documents/products/population.pdf

National Consortium on Deaf-Blindness. (2010). *The 2009 national child count of children and youth who are deaf-blind*. Retrieved on February 5, 2011, from http://nationaldb.org/documents/products/population.pdf

National Council on Disability. (2008). *The No Child Left Behind Act and the Individuals with Disabilities Education Act: A progress report*. Washington, DC: National Council on Disability.

National Dissemination Center for Children with Disabilities (NICHCY). (2004). *Visual impairments: NICHCY Disability Fact Sheet No. 13*. Retrieved February 5, 2011, from http://www.nichcy.org/InformationResources/Documents/NICHCY%20PUBS/fs13.pdf

National Institute of Child Health and Human Development. (2000). Report of the National Reading Panel. *Teaching children to read: An evidence-based assessment of the scientific research literature on reading and its implications for reading instruction (NIH Publication No. 00-4769)*. Washington, DC: U.S. Government Printing Office.

National Institutes of Health (NIH). (2011). *Diabetes type 1*. Retrieved April 12, 2011, from http://www.nlm.nih.gov/medlineplus/diabetestype1.html

National Institutes of Health (NIH). (2011). *Transverse myelitis fact sheet*. National Institutes of Health, retrieved June 6, 2011, from www.ninds.nih.gov/disorders/transversemyelitis/detail_transversemyelitis.htm

National Reading Panel. (2000). *Teaching children to read: An evidence-based assessment of the scientific research literature on reading and its implications for reading instruction*. Washington, DC: National Institute of Child Health and Human Development.

National Research Council. (2001). *Educating children with autism*. Washington, DC: National Academy Press.

National Council for Accreditation of Teacher Education (NCATE) (2006). *NCATE Unit Standards: Glossary*. Retrieved January 6, 2012, from http://www.ncate.org/Standards/NCATEUnitStandards/tabid/123/Default.aspx

Nelson, J. R. (1996). Designing schools to meet the needs of students who exhibit disruptive behavior. *Journal of Emotional and Behavioral Disorders, 4*(3), 147–161.

Neubert, D. A., Moon, S., & Grigal, M. (2004). Activities of students with significant disabilities receiving services in postsecondary settings. *Education and Training in Developmental Disabilities, 39,* 16–25.

Newcomer, P. L., Barenbaum, E., & Pearson, N. (1995). Depression and anxiety in children and adolescents with learning disabilities, conduct disorders, and no disability. *Journal of Emotional and Behavioral Disorders, 3*(1), 27–39.

Nieto, S., & Bode, P. (2008). *Affirming diversity: The sociopolitical context of multicultural education* (5th ed.). Boston: Allyn & Bacon.

Nirje, B. (1972). The right to self-determination. In W. Wolfensberger (Ed.), *Normalization* (pp. 177–193). Ontario, Canada: National Institute on Mental Retardation.

Nix, S. J. (2008). Out of the hallway, into the classroom. *Principal Leadership, 8,* 28–31.

No Child Left Behind Act. (2001). 20 U.S.C. 6301 et seq.

North Carolina State Board of Education. (2007). *North Carolina extended content standards*. Retrieved January 6, 2012, from http://www.ncpublicschools.org/curriculum/ncecs

Nungesser, N. R., & Watkins, R. V. (2005). Preschool teachers' perceptions and reactions to challenging classroom behavior: Implications for speech-language pathologists. *Language, Speech, and Hearing Services in Schools, 36,* 139–151.

Ochs, E., Kremer-Sadlik, T., Solomon, O., & Sirota, K. G. (2001). Inclusion as social practice: Views of children with autism. *Social Development, 10*(3), 399–419.

Oetzel, J. G., & Ting-Toomey, S. (Eds.). (2006). *The SAGE handbook of conflict communication: Integrating theory, research, and practice*. Thousand Oaks, CA: Sage.

Olive, E. C. (2004). Practical tools for positive behavior facilitation. *Reclaiming Child Youth, 13*(1), 43–47.

Olley, G. J. (2005). Curriculum and classroom structure. In F. R. Volkmar, R. Paul, A. Klin, & D. Cohen (Eds.), *Hand-*

book of autism and pervasive developmental disorders: Vol. 2. Assessment, interventions, and policy (4th ed., pp. 863–881). Hoboken, NJ: Wiley.

Olson, L. (2005). AYP rules miss many in special education: More students left out of accountability ratings. *Education Week, 25*(4), 1, 24–25.

Oluwole, J. O. (2009). A principal's dilemma: Full inclusion or student's best interests? *Journal of Cases in Educational Leadership, 12*(1), 12–25.

O'Reilly, M., Sigafoos, J., Lancioni, G., Edrisinha, C., & Andrews, A. (2005). An examination of the effects of a classroom activity schedule on levels of self-injury and engagement for a child with severe autism. *Journal of Autism and Developmental Disorders, 35*(3), 305–311.

Orsak, C. (2011). Language characteristics and communication of individuals with autism. In K. M. McCoy (Ed.), *Autism from the teacher's perspective: Strategies for classroom instruction* (pp. 41–62). Denver: Love.

Osher, D., Morrison, G., & Bailey, W. (2003). Exploring the relationship between student mobility and dropout among students with emotional and behavioral disorder. *Journal of Negro Education, 72,* 79–96.

Owens, R. E., Metz, D. E., & Farinella, K. A. (2011). *Introduction to communication disorders: A life span evidence-based perspective* (4th ed.). Upper Saddle River, NJ: Pearson Education.

Owens, R. E., Metz, D. E., & Haas, A. (2003). *Introduction to communication disorders: A life span perspective* (2nd ed.). Boston: Allyn & Bacon.

Paine, S. C., Radicci, J., Rosellini, L. C., Deutchman, L., & Darch, C. B. (1983). *Structuring your classroom for academic success.* Champaign, IL: Research Press.

Parette, H. P. (1997). Assistive technology devices and services. *Education and Training in Mental Retardation and Developmental Disabilities, 32,* 267–280.

Parette, H. P., Hourcade, J. J., & Blum, C. (2011). Using animation in Microsoft PowerPoint to enhance engagement and learning in young learners with developmental delays. *Teaching Exceptional Children, 43*(4), 58–67.

Parette, H. P., Hourcade, J. J., & VanBiervliet, A. (1993). Selection of appropriate technology for children with disabilities. *Teaching Exceptional Children, 25*(3), 18–22.

Parette, H. P., & Peterson-Karlan, G. R. (2007). Facilitating student achievement with assistive technology. *Education and Training in Developmental Disabilities, 42,* 387–397.

Parette, P., & McMahan, G. A. (2002). What should we expect of assistive technology? Being sensitive to family goals. *Teaching Exceptional Children, 35*(1), 56–61.

Park, K. L. (2007). Facilitating effective team-based functional behavior assessments in typical school settings. *Beyond Behavior, 17*(1), 21–31.

Patall, E., Cooper, H., & Robinson, J. (2008). Parent involvement in homework: A research synthesis. *Review of Educational Research, 78,* 1039–1101.

Patrick, H., Turner, J., Meyer, D. K., & Midgley, C. (2003). How teachers establish psychological environments during the first days of school: Associations with avoidance in mathematics. *Teachers College Record, 105*(8), 1521–1558.

Patterson, G. R., Reid, J. B., Jones, R. R., & Conger, R. E. (1975). *A social learning approach to family intervention: Vol. 1. Families with aggressive children.* Eugene, OR: Castalia.

Paul, R. (2005). Assessing communication in autism spectrum disorders. In F. R. Volkmar, R. Paul, A. Klin, & D. Cohen (Eds.), *Handbook of autism and pervasive developmental disorders: Vol. 2. Assessment, interventions, and policy* (4th ed., pp. 799–816). Hoboken, NJ: Wiley.

Peck, C., Staub, D., Galucci, C., & Schwartz, I. (2004). Parent perception of the impacts of inclusion on their nondisabled child. *Research & Practice for Persons with Severe Disabilities, 29*(2), 135–143.

Pellegrino, L. (2007). Cerebral palsy. In M. L. Batshaw, L. Pellegrino, & N. J. Roizen (Eds.), *Children with disabilities* (6th ed., pp. 387–408). Baltimore: Brookes.

Peña, E. D., & Davis, B. L. (2000). Language disorders in infants, toddlers, and preschoolers. In R. B. Gillam, T. P. Marquardt, & F. N. Martin (Eds.), *Communication sciences and disorders: From science to clinical practice* (pp. 409–436). San Diego: Singular.

Petry, K., & Maes, B. (2007). Description of the support needs of people with profound multiple disabilities using the 2002 AAMR system: An overview of literature. *Education and Training in Developmental Disabilities, 42,* 130–143.

Pierce, C. D., Reid, R., & Epstein, M. H. (2004). Teacher mediated interventions for children with EBD and their academic outcomes. *Remedial and Special Education, 25*(3), 175–188.

Piers, E., & Harris, D. (1984). *The Piers-Harris children's self-concept scale.* Nashville, TN: Counselor Recordings and Tests.

Pivik, J., McComas, J., & Laflamme, M. (2002). Barriers and facilitators to inclusive education. *Exceptional Children, 69*(1), 97–107.

PLATO Learning. (2008). *PLATO achieve Now on PSP (Mathematics).* Retrieved January 6, 2012, from http://support.plato.com/

Ploessl, D., Rock, M., Schoenfeld, N., & Blanks, B. (2010). On the same page: Practical techniques to enhance co-teaching interactions. *Intervention in School and Clinic, 45,* 158–168.

Pohlmann, B. (1999–2011). *Strategies to implement technologies in a classroom.* Retrieved June 5, 2011, from http://www.ehow.com/way_5984431_strategies-implement-technology-classroom.html

Polsgrove, L., & Smith, A. W. (2004). Informed practice in teaching self-control to children with emotional and behavioral disorders. In R. B. Rutherford, Jr., M. M. Quinn, & A. R. Mathur (Eds.), *Handbook of research in emotional and behavioral disorders* (pp. 399–425). New York: Guilford.

Porte, L. (2001). Cut and paste 101: New strategies for note taking and review. *Teaching Exceptional Children, 34*(2), 14–20.

Pottie, C., & Sumarah, J. (2004). Friendships between persons with and without developmental disabilities. *Mental Retardation, 42,* 55–66.

Pressley, M. (2002). *Reading instruction that works: The case for balanced teaching* (2nd ed.). New York: Guilford.

Pullen, P. C., Lane, H. B., & Monaghan, M. C. (2004). Effects of a volunteer tutoring model on the literacy development of struggling first grade students. *Reading Research and Instruction, 43*(4), 21–40.

Putnam J. (1998). *Cooperative learning and strategies for inclusion (2nd ed.).* Baltimore: Brookes.

Rashotte, C., MacPhee, K., & Torgesen, J. (2001). The effectiveness of a group reading instruction program with poor readers in multiple grades. *Learning Disability Quarterly, 24*(2), 119–134.

Rea, P., McLaughlin, V., & Walther-Thomas, C. (2002). Outcomes for students with learning disabilities in inclusive and pullout programs. *Exceptional Children, 68*(2), 203–222.

Reed, V. A., & Spicer, L. (2003). The relative importance of selected communication skills for adolescents' interactions with their teachers: High school teachers' opinions.

*Language, Speech, and Hearing Services in Schools, 34,* 343–357.

Reichle, J. (2011). Evaluating assistive technology in the education of persons with severe disabilities. *Journal of Behavioral Education, 20,* 77–85.

Reid, R., & Ortiz-Lienemann, T. (2006). *Strategy instruction for students with learning disabilities.* New York: Guilford.

Reiff, M. (2004). *ADHD: A complete and authoritative guide.* Elk Grove Village, IL: American Academy of Pediatrics.

Renaissance Learning. (n.d.). *Accelerated reader best classroom practices.* Madison, WI: Author.

Reschly, D. (2005). Learning disabilities identification: Primary intervention, secondary intervention, and then what? *Journal of Learning Disabilities, 38*(6), 510–515.

Reschly, D., & Hosp, J. (2004). State SLD identification policies and practices. *Learning Disabilities Research and Practice, 27*(4), 197–213.

Reutzel, R. (2003). Organizing effective literacy instruction: Grouping strategies and instructional routines. In L. M. Morrow, L. B. Gambrell, & M. Pressley (Eds.), *Best practices in literacy instruction* (2nd ed., pp. 241–267). New York: Guilford.

Reynhout, G., & Carter, M. (2011). Evaluation of the efficacy of Social Stories using three single subject metrics. *Research in Autism Spectrum Disorders, 5,* 885–900.

Reynolds, M., Wang, M., & Walberg, H. (1987). The necessary restructuring of special education. *Exceptional Children, 53*(5), 391–398.

Rhode, G., Jensen, W. R., & Reavis, H. K. (1993). *The tough kid book: Practical classroom management strategies.* Longmont, CO: Sopris West.

Rice, E. H., & Yen, C. (2010). Examining gender and the academic achievement of students with emotional disturbance. *Education and Treatment of Children, 33*(4), 601–621.

Richards, H., Brown, A., & Forde, T. (2006). *Addressing diversity in schools: Culturally responsive pedagogy.* Tempe, AZ: National Center for Culturally Responsive Educational Systems, Arizona State University.

Riffel, L. A., Wehmeyer, M. L., Turnbull, A. P., Lattimore, J., Davies, D., Stock, S., & Fisher, S. (2005). Promoting independent performance of transition-related tasks using a palmtop PC-based self-directed visual and auditory prompting system. *Journal of Special Education Technology, 20*(2), 5–14.

Riggs, C. (2005). To teachers: What paraeducators want you to know. *Teaching Exceptional Children, 36*(5), 8–12.

Ritchey, K. (2011). The first "R": Evidence-based reading instruction for students with learning disabilities. *Theory into Practice, 50*(1), 28–34.

Ritzman, M. J., & Sanger, D. (2007). Principals' opinions on the role of speech–language pathologists serving students with communication disorders involved in violence. *Language, Speech, and Hearing Services in Schools, 38,* 365–377.

Rivers, J., & Sanders, W. (2002). Teacher quality and equity in educational opportunity: Findings and policy implications. In L. Izumi & W. Evers (Eds.), *Teacher quality* (pp. 13–23). Stanford, CA: Hoover Institution Press.

Rivken, S., Hanushek, E., & Kain, J. (2005). Teachers, schools, and academic achievement. *Econometrica, 73*(2), 417–458.

Robins D., Fein D., Barton M., & Green J. (2001). The modified checklist for autism in toddlers. *Journal of Autism and Developmental Disorders, 31*(2), 131–144.

Rodriguez, E., & Bellanca, J. (2007). *What is it about me you can't teach? An instructional guide for the urban educator.* Thousand Oaks, CA: Corwin.

Rogan, J. (2000). Learning strategies: Recipes for success. *Beyond Behavior, 10*(1), 18–22.

Rojewski, J. W., & Schell, J. W. (1994). Cognitive apprenticeship for learners with special needs: An alternative framework for teaching and learning. *Remedial and Special Education, 15,* 234–243.

Rorschach, H. (1932). *Psychodiagnostic: Methodik und Ergebnisse eines Wahrnehmungs-diagnostischen Experiments* (2nd ed.). Bern, Switzerland: Huber.

Rose, D., & Meyer, A. (2002). *Teaching every student in the digital age.* Alexandria, VA: Association for Supervision and Curriculum Development.

Rosenberg, M. (2007, September). *Double Check: Application of culturally responsive behavior management principles.* Paper presented at the initial training for PBIS Plus, Baltimore.

Rosenberg, M. S., Boyer, K. L, Sindelar, P. T., & Misra, S. (2007). Alternative route programs to certification in special education: Program infrastructure, instructional delivery, and participant characteristics. *Exceptional Children, 73,* 224–241.

Rosenberg, M. S., & Jackman, L. A. (2003). Development, implementation, and sustainability of comprehensive school-wide behavior management systems. *Intervention in School and Clinic, 39*(1), 10–21.

Rosenberg, M. S., O'Shea, L., & O'Shea, D. J. (2006). *Student teacher to master teacher: A practical guide for educating students with special needs* (4th ed.). Upper Saddle River, NJ: Merrill/Pearson Education.

Rosenberg, M. S., Sindelar, P. T., & Hardman, M. T. (2004). Preparing highly qualified teachers for students with emotional and behavioral disorders: The Impact of NCLB and IDEA. *Behavioral Disorders, 29,* 266–278.

Rosenberg, M. S., Westling, D. L., & McLeskey, J. (2008). *Special education for today's teachers: An introduction.* Upper Saddle River, NJ: Merrill/Pearson Education.

Rosenberg, M. S., Westling, D. L., & McLeskey, J. (2011). *Special education for today's teachers* (2nd ed.). Upper Saddle River, NJ: Merrill/Pearson Education.

Rosenberg, M. S., Wilson, R. J., Maheady, L., & Sindelar, P. T. (2004). *Educating students with behavior disorders* (3rd ed.). Boston: Allyn & Bacon.

Rosenfeld, J. S. (2005). Section 504 and IDEA: Basic similarities and differences. *Learning Disabilities OnLine.* Retrieved January 7, 2012, from http://www.wrightslaw.com/advoc/articles/504_IDEA_Rosenfeld.html

Rosenshine, B., & Meister, C. (1992). The use of scaffolds for teaching higher-level cognitive strategies. *Educational Leadership, 49*(7), 26–33.

Rosenshine, B., & Stevens, R. (1986). Teaching functions. In M. C. Wittrock (Ed.), *Handbook of research on teaching* (3rd ed., pp. 376–391). New York: Macmillan.

Ross, D., Bondy, E., Gallingane, C., & Hambacher, E. (2008). Promoting academic engagement through insistence: Being a warm demander. *Childhood Education, 84*(3), 142–146.

Ross, D., Kamman, M., & Coady, M. (2011). Accepting responsibility for the learning of all students: What does it mean? In M. Rosenberg, D. Westling, & J. McLeskey (Eds.), *Special education for today's teachers: An introduction* (2nd ed., pp. 50–77). Upper Saddle River, NJ: Merrill/Pearson Education.

Rotheram-Fuller, E., Kasari, C., Chamberlain, B., & Locke, J. (2010). Social involvement of children with autism spectrum disorders in elementary classrooms. *The Journal of Child Psychology and Psychiatry, 51,* 1227–1234.

Rutter, M. (1978). Diagnosis and definition. In M. Rutter & E. Schopler (Eds.), *Autism: A reappraisal of concepts and treatment* (pp. 1–26). New York: Plenum.

Ryan, A., Halsey H., & Matthews, W. (2003). Using functional assessment to promote desirable student behavior in schools. *Teaching Exceptional Children, 35,* 8–15.

Ryan, J., Katsiyannis, A., & Hughes, E. (2011). Medication treatment for attention deficit hyperactivity disorder. *Theory into Practice, 50,* 52–60.

Ryan, J. B., Hughes, E. M., Katsiyannis, A., McDaniel, M., & Sprinkle, C. (2011). Research-based educational practices for students with autism spectrum disorders. *Teaching Exceptional Children, 43*(3), 56.

Ryndak, D. L., Morrison, A. P., & Sommerstein, L. (1999). Literacy before and after inclusion in general education settings: A case study. *Journal of the Association for Persons with Severe Handicaps, 24,* 5–22.

Sabornie, E. J., & deBettencourt, L. U. (2009). *Teaching students with mild and high-incidence disabilities at the secondary level.* Upper Saddle River, NJ: Merrill/Pearson Education.

Saenz, L., Fuchs, L., & Fuchs, D. (2005). Peer-assisted learning strategies for English language learners with learning disabilities. *Exceptional Children, 71*(3), 231–247.

Safran, J. S. (2002). Supporting students with Asperger's syndrome in general education. *Teaching Exceptional Children, 34,* 60–66.

Safran, S. P. (2008). Why youngsters with autistic spectrum disorders remain underrepresented in special education. *Remedial and Special Education, 29,* 90–95.

Sailers, E. (2010). *iPhone, iPad, and iPod touch apps for (special) education.* Retrieved May 27, 2011, from http://www.scribd.com/doc/24470331/iPhone-iPad-and-iPod-touch-Apps-for-Special-Education

Salend, S. J. (2006). Explaining your inclusion program to families. *Teaching Exceptional Children, 38*(4), 6–11.

Salend, S. J., & Gajria, M. (1995). Increasing homework completion rates of students with mild disabilities. *Remedial and Special Education, 16,* 271–278.

Salend, S., & Duhaney, L. (1999). The impact of inclusion on students with and without disabilities and their educators. *Remedial and Special Education, 20*(2), 114–126.

Salend, S., & Duhaney, L. (2005). Understanding and addressing disproportionate representation of students of color in special education. *Intervention in School and Clinic, 40*(4), 213–221.

Salend, S., & Garrick Duhaney, L. (2007). Research related to inclusion and program effectiveness. In J. McLeskey (Ed.), *Reflections on inclusion: Classic articles than shaped our thinking* (pp. 127–159). Arlington, VA: Council for Exceptional Children.

Sandlund, M., McDonough, S., & Häger-Ross, C. (2009). Interactive computer play in rehabilitation of children with sensorimotor disorders: A systemic review. *Developmental Medicine & Child Neurology, 51,* 173–179.

Sanger, D., Maag, J. W., & Shapera, N. R. (1994). Language problems among students with emotional and behavioral disorders. *Intervention in School and Clinic, 30,* 103–108.

Sanger, D., Moore-Brown, B., & Alt, E. (2000). Advancing the discussion on communication and violence. *Communication Disorders Quarterly, 22,* 43–48.

Sanger, D., Spilker, A., Williams, N., & Belau, D. (2007). Opinions of female juvenile delinquents on communication, learning and violence. *Journal of Correctional Education, 58,* 69–92.

Sansoti, F. J., Powell-Smith, K. A., & Kincaid, D. (2004). A research synthesis of Social Story interventions for children with autism spectrum disorders. *Focus on Autism and Other Developmental Disabilities, 19*(4),194–204.

Santos, M. (2002). From mystery to mainstream: Today's school-based speech-language pathologist. *Educational Horizons, 80,* 93–96.

Scheffler, R., Hinshaw, S., Modrek, S., & Levine, P. (2007). The global market for ADHD medications. *Health Affairs, 26*(2), 450–457.

Scheurich, J. J., & Skla, L. L. (2003). *Leadership for equity and excellence.* Thousand Oaks, CA: Corwin.

Schifter, L. (2011). High school graduation rates for students with disabilities: How long does it take? *Exceptional Children, 77*(4), 409–422.

Schirmer, B. R. (2001a). *Psychological, social, and educational dimensions of deafness.* Boston: Allyn & Bacon.

Schirmer, B. R. (2001b). Using research to improve literacy practice and practice to improve literacy research. *Journal of Deaf Studies and Deaf Education, 6*(2), 83–91.

Schoenfeld, N. A., & Mathur, S. R. (2009). Effects of cognitive-behavioral intervention on the school performance of students with emotional or behavioral disorders and anxiety. *Behavioral Disorders, 34*(4), 184–195.

Scholastic, Inc. (2006). *Compendium of READ 180 research.* Retrieved January 6, 2012, from http://teacher.scholastic.com/products/read180/research/pdfs/READ180_Compendium_6_26_06.pdf

Schonberg, R. L., & Tifft, C. J. (2007). In M. L. Batshaw, L. Pellegrino, & N. J. Roizen (Eds.), *Children with disabilities* (6th ed., pp. 83–96). Baltimore: Brookes.

Schrepferman, L. M., Eby, J., Snyder, J., & Stropes, J. (2006). Early affiliation and social engagement with peers: Prospective risk and protective factors for childhood depressive disorders. *Journal of Emotional and Behavioral Disorders, 14,* 50–60.

Schumm, J. (1999). *Adapting reading and math materials for the inclusive classroom.* Reston, VA: Council for Exceptional Children.

Scott, G. S., & Compton, L. (2007). A new trick for the trade: A strategy for keeping an agenda book for secondary students. *Intervention in School and Clinic, 42*(5), 280–284.

Scott, T. M., Alter, P. J., Rosenberg, M. S., & Borgmeier, C. (2010). Decision-making in secondary and tertiary interventions of school-wide systems of positive behavior support. *Education and Treatment of Children, 33*(4), 513–536.

Scott, T. M., & Kamps, D. M. (2007). The future of functional behavioral assessment in school settings. *Behavioral Disorders, 32*(3), 146–157.

Scruggs, T., & Mastropieri, M. (1990). The case for mnemonic instruction: From laboratory research to classroom applications. *Journal of Special Education, 24*(1), 7–32.

Scruggs, T., & Mastropieri, M. (1996). Teacher perceptions of mainstreaming/inclusion, 1958–1995: A research synthesis. *Exceptional Children, 63,* 59–74.

Scruggs, T., Mastropieri, M., Berkeley, S., & Graetz, J. (2010). Do special education interventions improve learning of secondary content? A meta-analysis. *Remedial and Special Education, 31*(6), 437–449.

Scruggs, T., Mastropieri, M., & McDuffie, K. (2007). Co-teaching in inclusive classrooms: A metasynthesis of qualitative research. *Exceptional Children, 73*(4), 392–416.

Shackelford, J. (2006). State and jurisdictional eligibility definitions for infants and toddlers with disabilities under IDEA. NECTAC Notes, Issue no. 21. Retrieved November 18, 2010, from http://www.nectac.org/~pdfs/pubs/nnotes21.pdf

Shah, N. (2011, March). Special education pupils find learning tool in iPad applications. *Education Week, 30*(22), 1, 16–17.

Shakeshaft, C., Mann, D., Becker, J., & Sweeney, K. (2002). Choosing the right technology. *School Administrator, 59*(1), 34–37.

Shapiro, D. A. (1999). *Stuttering intervention: A collaborative journey to fluency freedom.* Austin, TX: Pro-Ed.

Shapiro, D. A. (2011). *Stuttering intervention: A collaborative journey to fluency freedom* (2nd ed.). Austin, TX: Pro-Ed.

Shapiro, E. S., Miller, D. N., Sawka, K., Gardill, M. C., & Handler, M. W. (1999). Facilitating the inclusion of students with EBD into general education classrooms. *Journal of Emotional and Behavioral Disorders, 7*(2), 83–93.

Shea, V., & Mesibov, G. B. (2005). Adolescents and adults with autism. In F. R. Volkmar, R. Paul, A. Klin, & D. Cohen (Eds.), *Handbook of autism and pervasive developmental disorders: Vol. 1. Diagnosis, development, neurobiology, and behavior* (4th ed., pp. 288–311). Hoboken, NJ: Wiley.

Sheets, R. H. (2005). *Diversity pedagogy.* Boston: Pearson Education.

Shippen, M. E., Simpson, R. G., & Crites, S. A. (2003). A practical guide to functional behavioral assessment. *Teaching Exceptional Children, 35,* 36–44.

Siebelink, E. M., de Jong, M. D. T., Taal, E., & Roelvink, L. (2006). Sexuality and people with intellectual disabilities: Assessment of knowledge, attitudes, experiences, and needs. *Mental Retardation, 44,* 283–294.

Siegel, L. S. (2003). Basic cognitive processes and reading disabilities. In H. L. Swanson, K. R. Harris, & S. Graham (Eds.), *Handbook of learning disabilities* (pp. 158–181). New York: Guilford.

Silva, M., Munk, D. D., & Bursuck, W. D. (2005). Grading adaptations for students with disabilities. *Intervention in School and Clinic, 41*(2), 87–98.

Simonsen, B., Fairbanks, S., Briesch, A., Myers, D., & Sugai, G. (2008). Evidenced-based practices in classroom management: Considerations for research to practice. *Education and Treatment of Children, 31*(3), 351–380.

Siperstein, G. N., Glick, G. C., & Parker, R. C. (2009). Social inclusion of children with intellectual disabilities in a recreational setting. *Intellectual and Developmental Disabilities, 47,* 97–107.

Sitlington, P. L., & Nuebert, D. A. (2004). Preparing youths with emotional or behavioral disorders for transition to adult life: Can it be done within the standards-based reform movement? *Behavioral Disorders, 29*(3), 279–288.

Skiba, R., Horner, R., Chung, C., Rausch, M. K., May, S., & Tobin, T. (2008). *Race is not neutral: A national investigation of African American and Latino disproportionality in school discipline.* Paper presented at the American Educational Research Association annual meeting, New York.

Skiba, R., Poloni-Staudinger, L., Gallini, S., Simmons, A., & Feggins-Azziz, L. (2006). Disparate access: The disproportionality of African American students with disabilities across educational environments. *Exceptional Children, 72,* 411–424.

Skiba, R., Simmons, A., Ritter, S., Gibb, A., Rausch, M., Cuadrado, J., & Chung, C. (2008). Achieving equity in special education: History, status, and current challenges. *Exceptional Children, 74*(3), 264–288.

Skiba, R., Simmons, A., Ritter, S., Kohler, K., Henderson, M., & Wu, T. (2006). The context of minority disproportionality: Practitioner perspectives on special educator referral. *Teachers College Record, 108,* 1424–1459.

Skinner, D., Correa, V., Skinner, M., & Bailey, D. (2001). Role of religion in the lives of Latino families of young children with developmental delays. *American Journal on Mental Retardation, 106*(4), 297–313.

Slavin, R. (1990). *Cooperative learning: Theory, research, and practice.* Upper Saddle River, NJ: Pearson Education.

Slavin, R. (1999). Comprehensive approaches to cooperative learning. Theory into Practice, 38(2), 74–79.

Slavin, R. (2004). Built to last: Long-term maintenance of success for all. *Remedial and Special Education, 25*(1), 61–66.

Slavin, R., & Madden, N. (2006). Success for all: Summary of research on achievement outcomes. Baltimore: Johns Hopkins University, Center for Data-Driven Reform in Education.

Smith, B., Barkley, R., & Shapiro, C. (2006). Attention deficit/hyperactivity disorder. In E. Mash & R. Barkley (Eds.), *Treatment of childhood disorders* (3rd ed., pp. 65–136). New York: Guilford.

Smith, K., & Geller, C. (2004). Essential principles of effective mathematics instruction: Methods to reach all students. *Preventing School Failure, 48*(4), 22–29.

Smith, P. (2007). Have we made any progress? Including students with intellectual disabilities in regular education classrooms. *Intellectual and Developmental Disabilities, 45,* 297–309.

Smith, T. E. C. (2001). Section 504, the ADA, and public schools. *Remedial and Special Education, 22*(6), 335–343.

Smith-Myles, B., & Simpson, R. L. (2001). Effective practices for students with Asperger's syndrome. *Focus on Exceptional Children, 34,* 1–16.

Smithgall, C., Gladden, R., Howard, E., Goerge, R., Courtney, M. (2004). *Educational experiences of children in out-of-home care.* Chicago: Chapin Hall Center for Children at the University of Chicago.

Snell, M., & Janney, R. (2005). *Collaborative teaming.* Baltimore: Brookes.

Someki, F., & Burns, M. (2009). Methods for measuring student response to stimulant medication: A meta-analytic review. *Psychology in the Schools, 46,* 388–396.

Soodak, L. C., Erwin, E. J., Winton, P., Brotherson, M. J., Turnbull, A. P., Hanson, M. J., et al. (2002). Implementing inclusive early childhood education: A call for professional empowerment. *Topics in Early Childhood Special Education (TECSE), 22*(2), 91–102.

Sperling, R. A. (2006). Assessing reading materials for students who are learning disabled. *Intervention in School and Clinic, 41*(3), 138–143.

Spina Bifida Association. (2008). *Fact sheets.* Retrieved September 3, 2008, and April 12, 2011, from http://www.spinabifidaassociation.org/site/c.liKWL7PLLrF/b.2642343/k.8D2D/Fact_Sheets.htm

Sprague, J. R., & Walker, H. M. (2005). *Safe and healthy schools. Practical prevention strategies.* New York: Guilford.

Sprick, M., Howard, L., & Fidanque, A. (1998). *Read well.* Longmont, CO: Sopris West.

SRA/McGraw-Hill. (2005). *Open court reading.* Columbus, OH: Author.

Stainback, W., & Stainback, S. (1984). A rationale for the merger of special and regular education. *Exceptional Children, 51*(2), 102–111.

Staudt, D. H. (2009). Intensive word study and repeated reading improves reading skills for two students with learning disabilities. *Reading Teacher, 63,* 142–151.

Stecker, P. M., Lembke, E. S., & Foegen, A. (2008). Using progress-monitoring data to improve instructional decision making. *Preventing School Failure, 52*(2), 48–58.

Steele, M. M. (2007). Teaching social studies to high school students with learning problems. *The Social Studies, 98*(2), 59–63.

Steele, M. M. (2008). Teaching social studies to middle school students with learning problems. *Clearing House: A Journal of Educational Strategies, Issues, and Ideas, 81*(5), 197–200.

Stein, M., Kinder, D., Silbert, J., & Carnine, D. (2006). *Designing effective mathematics instruction: A direct instruction approach* (4th ed.). Upper Saddle River, NJ: Pearson Education.

Stenhoff, D., & Lignugaris/Kraft, B. (2007). A review of the effects of peer tutoring on students with mild disabilities in secondary settings. *Exceptional Children, 74*(1), 8–30.

Stone, W. L., Coonrod, E. E., & Ousley, O. Y. (2000). Brief report: Screening tool for autism in two-year-olds (STAT): Development and preliminary data. *Journal of Autism and Developmental Disorders, 30*(6), 607–612.

Stormont, M. (2007). *Fostering resilience in young children at risk for failure.* Upper Saddle River, NJ: Merrill/Pearson Education.

Storti, C. (1999). *Figuring foreigners out: A practical guide.* Yarmouth, ME: Intercultural Press.

Stronge, J. H. (2002). *Qualities of effective teachers.* Alexandria, VA: Association for Supervision and Curriculum Development.

Stuart, S. K., & Rinaldi, C. (2009). A collaborative planning framework for teachers implementing tiered instruction. *Teaching Exceptional Children, 42*(2), 52–57.

Stump, C. S., & Bigge, J. (2005). Curricular options for individuals with physical, health, or multiple disabilities. In S. J. Best, K. W. Heller, & J. L. Bigge (Eds.), *Teaching individuals with physical or multiple disabilities* (5th ed., pp. 278–318). Upper Saddle River, NJ: Merrill/Pearson Education.

Sugai, G., & Horner, R. (2009). Responsiveness-to-Intervention and school-wide positive behavior supports: Integration of multi-tiered system approaches. *Exceptionality, 17,* 223–237.

Sugai, G., & Lewis, T. J. (1996). Preferred and promising practices for social skills instruction. *Focus on Exceptional Children, 29*(4), 1–16.

Sundeen, T. (2007). So what's the big idea? Using graphic organizers to guide secondary students with learning and behavioral issues. *Beyond Behavior, 16*(3), 29–34.

Suritsky, S. K., & Hughes, C. A. (1996). Notetaking strategy instruction. In D. D. Deshler, E. S. Ellis, & B. K. Lenz (Eds.), *Teaching adolescents with learning disabilities* (pp. 267–312). Denver: Love.

Swain, K., Bertini, T. D., & Coffey, D. (2010). The effects of folding-in of basic mathematics facts for students with disabilities. *Learning Disabilities: A Multidisciplinary Journal, 16,* 23–29.

Sze, S. (2009). The effects of assistive technology on students with disabilities. *Journal of Educational Technology Systems, 37,* 419–429.

Taylor, R., Richards, S. B., & Brady, M. (2005). *Mental retardation: Historical perspectives, current practices, and future directions.* Boston: Pearson/Allyn & Bacon.

Terrill, M. C., Scruggs, T. E., & Mastropieri, M. A. (2004). SAT vocabulary for high school students with learning disabilities. *Intervention in School and Clinic, 39,* 288–294.

Texas School for the Blind and Visually Impaired. (2007). *Dos and don'ts for teaching social skills.* Retrieved August 28, 2008, from http://www.tsbvi.edu/Education/do-dont-social-skills.htm

Therrien, W. J., Hughes, C., Kapelski, C., & Mokhtari, K. (2009). Effectiveness of a test-taking strategy on achievement in essay tests for students with learning disabilities. *Journal of Learning Disabilities, 42*(1), 14–23.

Thorson, S. (1996). The missing link: Students discuss school discipline. *Focus on Exceptional Children, 29,* 1–12.

Thuppal, M., & Sobsey, D. (2004). Children with special health care needs. In F. P. Orelove, D. Sobsey, & R. K. Silberman (Eds.), *Educating children with multiple disabilities: A collaborative approach* (2nd ed., pp. 311–377). Baltimore: Brookes.

Thurlow, M. L., Elliott, J. L., & Ysseldyke, J. E. (2003). *Testing students with disabilities* (2nd ed.). Thousand Oaks, CA: Corwin.

Todis, B. (1996). Tools for the task? Perspectives on assistive technology in educational settings. *Journal of Special Education Technology, 13*(2), 49–61.

Tomlinson, C. A. (1999). *The differentiated classroom: Responding to the needs of all learners.* Alexandria, VA: Association for Supervision and Curriculum Development.

Tomlinson, C. A. (2001). *How to differentiate instruction in mixed-ability classrooms* (2nd ed.). Alexandria, VA: Association for Supervision and Curriculum Development.

Tomlinson, C. A. (2003). *Fulfilling the promise of the differentiated classroom: Strategies and tools for responsive teaching.* Alexandria, VA: Association for Supervision and Curriculum Development.

Tomlinson, C. A. (2005). Grading and differentiation: Paradox or good practice? *Theory into Practice, 44,* 262–269.

Tomlinson, C. A. (2005). *How to differentiate instruction in mixed-ability classrooms* (2nd ed.). Upper Saddle River, NJ: Merrill/Pearson Education.

Tomlinson, C. A., & Jarvis, J. (2006). Teaching beyond the book. *Educational Leadership, 64*(1), 16–21.

Toplis, R., & Hadwin, J. A. (2006). Using Social Stories to change problematic lunchtime behavior in school. *Educational Psychology in Practice, 22*(1), 53–67.

Torgesen, J. (2000). Individual differences in response to early interventions in reading: The lingering problem of treatment resisters. *Learning Disabilities Research & Practice, 15*(1), 55–64.

Torgesen, J. (2009). The response to intervention instructional model: Some outcomes from a large-scale implementation in reading first schools. *Child Development Perspectives, 3*(1), 38–40.

Townsend, B. (2000). The disproportionate discipline of African American learners: Reducing school suspensions and expulsions. *Exceptional Children, 66,* 381–391.

Traxler, C. B. (2000). The Stanford Achievement Test (9th ed.): National norming and performance for deaf and hard-of-hearing students. *Journal of Deaf Studies and Deaf Education, 5*(4), 337–348.

Trenholm, S., & Rose, T. (1981). The compliant communicator: Teacher perceptions of appropriate classroom behavior. *Western Journal of Speech Communication, 45*(1), 13–26.

Trumbull, E., Rothstein-Fisch, C., & Greenfield, P. M. (2000). *Bridging cultures in our schools: New approaches that work. Knowledge brief.* San Francisco: WestEd.

Turnbull, A., Zuna, N., Hong, J. Y., Ho, X., Kyzar, K., Obremski, S., Summers, J. A., Turnbull, R., & Stowe, M. (2010). Knowledge-to-Action guides: Preparing families to be partners in making educational decisions. *Teaching Exceptional Children, 42*(3), 42–53.

Turnbull, H. R. (1993). *Free appropriate public education: The law and children with disabilities* (4th ed.). Denver: Love.

Turnbull, H. R., Stowe, M. J., & Huerta, N. E. (2007). *Free appropriate public education: The law and children with disabilities* (7th ed.). Denver: Love.

Tyler, N., Yzquierdo, Z., Lopez-Reyna, N., & Flippin, S. S. (2004). The relationship between cultural diversity and the special education workforce: A critical overview. *Journal of Special Education, 38*(1), 22–38.

U.S. Census Bureau. (2008). *Population: Ancestry, language spoken at home.* Retrieved November 29, 2010, from www.census.gov/compendia/statab/cats/population/ancestry_language_spoken_at_home.html

U.S. Department of Education. (2005). Assistance to states for the education of children with disabilities. *Federal Register, 70*(118), 34 CFR, Parts 300, 301, Amend. 304, Sec. 300.8.

U.S. Department of Education. (2006). *Individuals with Disabilities Education Act data.* Retrieved December 11, 2007, from https://www.ideadata.org/index.html

U.S. Department of Education. (2007a). *Twenty-seventh annual report to congress on the implementation of the Individuals with Disabilities Education Act, Parts B and C.* Retrieved May 16, 2008, from http://www.ed.gov/about/reports/annual/osep/2005/parts-b-c/index.html

U.S. Department of Education. (2007b). Retrieved July 2, 2007, from http://www.ed.gov/about/offices/list/ocr/504faq.html

U.S. Department of Education. (2008). *No Child Left Behind provision gives schools new flexibility and ensures accountability for students with disabilities.* Retrieved November 10, 2008, from http://www.ed.gov/nclb/freedom/local/specedfactsheet.html

U.S. Department of Education. (2009). *Twenty-Eighth annual report to Congress on the implementation of the Individuals with Disabilities Education Act, 2006,* vol. 2, Washington, DC.

U.S. Department of Education. (2010). *Twenty-ninth annual report to Congress on the implementation of the Individuals with Disabilities Education Act, 2007.* Retrieved January 25, 2011, from http://www2.ed.gov/about/reports/annual/osep/index.html

U.S. Department of Education. (2011). *Individuals with Disabilities Education Improvement Act (IDEA) data: Data Accountability Center.* Retrieved January 10, 12, and 25, 2011, from www.ideadata.org

U.S. Department of Education. (n.d.). *History: 25 years of progress in educating children with disabilities through IDEA.* Retrieved January 7, 2012, from http://www2.ed.gov/policy/speced/leg/idea/history.html

U.S. Department of Education, Office for Civil Rights. (2005). *Questions and answers on disability discrimination under Section 504 and Title II.* Retrieved March 3, 2011, from http://www2.ed.gov/about/offices/list/ocr/qa-disability.html

U.S. Department of Health and Human Services. (2005). Mental health in the United States: Prevalence of diagnosis and medication treatment for attention-deficit/hyperactivity disorder—United States, 2003. *Morbidity and Mortality Weekly Report (MMWR), 54*(34), 842–847. Retrieved January 6, 2012, from http://www.cdc.gov/mmwr/preview/mmwrhtml/mm5434a2.htm

University of Kansas. (1999–2005). *An introduction to classwide peer tutoring.* Retrieved on July 30, 2008, from http://www.specialconnections.ku.edu

University of Sheffield. (2008). *Teaching students with visual impairments.* Retrieved August 28, 2008, from http://www.shef.ac.uk/disability/teaching/visual/5_teaching.html

Unsworth, L. (1984). Meeting individual needs through flexible within-class grouping of pupils. *The Reading Teacher, 38*(3), 289–304.

van Garderen, D., & Whittaker, C. (2006). Planning differentiated, multicultural instruction for secondary inclusive classrooms. *Teaching Exceptional Children, 38*(3), 12–20.

Van Laarhoven, T., Johnson, J. W., Van Laarhoven-Myers, T., Grider, K. L., & Grider, K. M. (2009). The effectiveness of using a video iPod as a prompting device in employment settings. *Journal of Behavioral Education, 18,* 119–141.

Van Tassel-Baska, J., & Stambaugh, T. (2005). Challenges and possibilities for serving gifted learners in the regular classroom. *Theory into Practice, 44*(3), 211–218.

Vannest, K. J., & Hagan-Burke, S. (2010). Teacher time use in special education. *Remedial and Special Education, 31*(2), 126–142.

Vannest, K. J., Reynolds, C. R., & Kamphaus, R. W. (2008). *BASC-2 intervention guide.* Minneapolis, MN: Pearson.

Vaughn, S., Bos, C., & Schumm, J. (2007). *Teaching students who are exceptional, diverse, and at risk in the general education classroom* (4th ed.). Boston: Allyn & Bacon.

Vaughn, S., Box, C., & Schumm, J. (2011). *Teaching students who are exceptional, diverse, and at risk in the general education classroom* (5th ed.). Boston: Pearson.

Vaughn, S., Cirino, P. T., Wanzek, J., Wexler, J., Fletcher, J. M., Denton, C. D., Barth, A., Romain, M., & Francis, D. J. (2010). Response to Intervention for middle school students with reading difficulties: Effects of a primary and secondary intervention. *School Psychology Review, 39,* 3–21.

Vaughn, S., Gersten, R., & Chard, D. (2000). The underlying message in LD intervention research: Findings from research syntheses. *Exceptional Children, 67*(1), 99–114.

Vaughn, S., Hughes, M., Moody, S., & Elbaum, B. (2001). Instructional grouping for reading for students with LD: Implications for practice. *Intervention in School and Clinic, 36*(3), 131–137.

Vaughn, S., & Linan-Thompson, S. (2007). *Research-based methods of reading instruction for English language learners, grades K–4.* Alexandria, VA: Association for Supervision and Curriculum Development.

Vaughn, S., Linan-Thompson, S., Kouzekanani, K., Bryant, D., Dickson, S., & Blozis, S. (2003). Reading instruction grouping for students with reading difficulties. *Remedial and Special Education, 24*(5), 301–315.

Vaughn, S., & Roberts, G. (2007). Secondary interventions in reading: Providing additional instruction for students at risk. *Teaching Exceptional Children, 39*(5), 40–46.

Vaughn, S., Wanzek, J., Linan-Thompson, S., & Murray, C. S. (2007). Monitoring response to supplemental services for students at risk for reading difficulties: High and low responders. In S. R. Jimerson, M. K. Burns, & A. M. VanDerHeyden (Eds.), *Handbook of response to intervention: The science and practice of assessment and intervention* (pp. 234–243). New York: Springer.

Vaughn, S., Wexler, J., Roberts, G., Barth, A., Cirino, P., Romain, M., Francis, D., Fletcher, J., & Denton, C. A. (2011). Effects of individualized and standardized interventions on middle school students with reading disabilities. *Exceptional Children, 77*(4), 391–407.

Vellutino, F., Scanlon, D., Small, S., & Fanuele, D. (2006). Response to intervention as a vehicle for distinguishing between children with and without reading disabilities. *Journal of Learning Disabilities, 39*(2), 157–169.

Viel-Ruma, K., Houchins, D. E., & Jolivette, K. (2010). Direct instruction in written expression: The effects on English speakers and English language learners with disabilities. *Learning Disabilities Research & Practice, 25,* 97–108.

Villa, R., Thousand, J., & Nevin, A. (2008). *A guide to co-teaching: Practical tips for facilitating student learning* (2nd ed.). Thousand Oaks, CA: Sage.

Vittetoe, J. O. (1997). Why first year teachers fail. *Phi Delta Kappan, 58*(5), 429.

Wade, E., Boon, R. T., & Spencer, V. G. (2010). Use of Kidspiration software to enhance the reading comprehension of story grammar components for elementary-age students with specific learning disabilities. *Learning Disabilities: A Contemporary Journal, 8*(2), 31–41.

Wadsworth, D. E. D., & Knight, D. (1999). Preparing the inclusion classroom for students with special physical and health needs. *Intervention in School and Clinic, 34*(3), 170–175.

Wagner, M. M., & Blackorby, J. (1996). Transition from high school to work or college: How special education students fare. *Special Education for Students with Disabilities, 6*(1), 103–120.

Wagner, M., Blackorby, J., Cameto, R., Hebbeler, K., & Newman, L. (1993). *The transition experiences of young people with disabilities: A summary of findings from the national longitudinal transition study of special education students.* Menlo Park, CA: SRI International.

Wagner, M. M., Kutash, K., Duchnowski. A. J., Epstein, M. H., & Sumi, W. C. (2005). The children and youth we serve: A national picture of the characteristics of students with emotional disturbances receiving special education. *Journal of Emotional and Behavioral Disorders, 13*(2), 79–96.

Wahl, M. (2003). *What is early success?* Tallahassee, FL: Florida Center for Reading Research. Retrieved January 7, 2012, from *www.fcrr.org/FCRRReports/PDF/EarlySuccessReport.pdf*

Waldron, N. (2007). Teacher attitudes toward inclusion. In J. McLeskey (Ed.), *Reflections on inclusion: Classic articles that shaped our thinking* (pp. 161–187). Arlington, VA: Council for Exceptional Children.

Waldron, N., & McLeskey, J. (1998). The impact of a full-time inclusive school program (ISP) on the academic achievement of students with mild and severe learning disabilities. *Exceptional Children, 64*(2), 395–405.

Waldron, N., & McLeskey, J. (2010). Establishing a collaborative school culture through comprehensive school reform. *Journal of Educational and Psychological Consultation, 20*(1), 58–74.

Waldron, N., McLeskey, J., & Pacchiano, D. (1999). Giving teachers a voice: Teachers' perspectives regarding elementary inclusive school programs (ISPs). *Teacher Education and Special Education, 22,* 141–153.

Walker, H., Colvin, G., & Ramsey, E. (1995). *Antisocial behavior in school: Strategies and best practices.* Pacific Grove, CA: Brooks/Cole.

Walker, H. M. (1995). *The acting-out child: Coping with classroom disruption.* Longmont, CO: Sopris West.

Walker, H. M., Horner, R. H., Sugai, G., Bullis, M., Sprague, J. R., Bricker, D., & Kaufman, M. J. (1996). Integrated approaches to preventing antisocial behavior patterns among school-age children and youth. *Journal of Emotional and Behavioral Disorders, 4,* 194–209.

Walker, H. M., & Severson, H. H. (1992). *Systematic screening for behavior disorder (SSBD): User's guide and technical manual* (2nd ed.). Longmont, CO: Sopris West.

Walker, H. M., Severson, H. H., & Feil, E. G. (1995). *The early screening project: A proven child-find process.* Longmont, CO: Sopris West.

Walker, H. M., & Walker, J. E. (1991). *Coping with noncompliance in the classroom: A positive approach for teachers.* Austin, TX: Pro-Ed.

Walker-Dalhouse, D., Risko, V., Eswothy, C., Grasley, E., Kaisler, G., McIlvain, D., & Stephen, M. (2009). Crossing boundaries and initiating conversations about RTI: Understanding and applying differentiated instruction. *The Reading Teacher, 63*(1), 84–87.

Wallace, J., Goodkind, S., Wallace, D., & Bachman, J. (2008). Racial, ethnic, and gender differences in school discipline among U.S. High school students: 1991–2005. *Negro Educational Review, 59,* 47–62.

Walther-Thomas, C., Korinek, L., McLaughlin, V., & Williams, B. (2000). *Collaboration for inclusive education.* Boston: Allyn & Bacon.

Wanzek, J., Dickson, S., Bursuck, W. D., & White, J. M. (2000). Teaching phonological awareness to students at risk for reading failure: An analysis of four instructional programs. *Learning Disabilities Research and Practice, 15*(4), 226–239.

Wanzek, J., Vaughn, S., Wexler, J., Swanson, E. A., Edmonds, M., & Kim, A. (2006). A synthesis of spelling and reading interventions and their effects on the spelling outcomes of students with LD. *Journal of Learning Disabilities, 39,* 528–543.

Ware, F. (2006). Warm demander pedagogy: Culturally responsive teaching that supports a culture of achievement for African American students. *Urban Education, 41*(4), 427–456.

Wehmeyer, M. L. (1992). Self-determination and the education of students with mental retardation. *Education and Training in Mental Retardation, 27,* 302–314.

Wehmeyer, M. L. (2006). Beyond access: Ensuring progress in the general education curriculum for students with severe disabilities. *Research and Practice for Persons with Severe Disabilities, 31,* 322–326.

Wehmeyer, M. L., & Agran, M. (2006). Promoting access to the general curriculum for students with significant cognitive disabilities. In D. M. Browder & F. Spooner (Eds.), *Teaching language arts, math, & science to students with significant cognitive disabilities* (pp. 15–37). Baltimore: Brookes.

Wehmeyer, M. L., Kelchner, K., & Richards, S. (1996). Essential characteristics of self-determined behavior of individuals with mental retardation. *American Journal on Mental Retardation, 100,* 632–642.

Wehmeyer, M. L., & Metzler, C. A. (1995). How self-determined are people with mental retardation? The national consumer survey. *Mental Retardation, 33,* 111–119.

Wehmeyer, M. L., Palmer, S., Smith, S., Parent, W., Davies, D., & Stock, S. (2006). Technology use by people with intellectual and developmental disabilities to support employment activities: A single-subject design meta analysis. *Journal of Vocational Rehabilitation, 24,* 81–86.

Wehmeyer, M. L., & Schwartz, M. (1997). Self-determination and positive adult outcomes: A follow-up study of youth with mental retardation or learning disabilities. *Exceptional Children, 63,* 245–255.

Weiner, J. (2004). Do peer relationships foster behavioral adjustment in children with learning disabilities? *Learning Disability Quarterly, 27*(1), 21–30.

Weinstein, C., Curran, M., & Tomlinson-Clarke, S. (2003). Culturally responsive classroom management: Awareness in action. *Theory into Practice, 42*(4), 269–276.

Weinstein, C., Tomlinson-Clarke, S., & Curran, M. (2004). Toward a conception of culturally responsive classroom management. *Journal of Teacher Education, 55*(1), 25–38.

Weinstein, R. (2002). *Reaching higher: The power of expectations in schooling.* Cambridge, MA: Harvard University Press.

Weinstein, S., & Gaillard, W. D. (2007). Epilepsy. In M. L. Batshaw, L. Pellegrino, & N. J. Roizen (Eds.), *Children with disabilities* (6th ed., pp. 439–460). Baltimore: Brookes.

Weintraub, F. J., & Abeson, A. (1976). New education policies for the handicapped: The quiet revolution. In F. J. Weintraub, A. Abeson, J. Ballard, & M. L. LaVor (Eds.), *Public policy and the education of exceptional children* (pp. 7–13). Reston, VA: The Council for Exceptional Children.

Weishaar, M. K., & Boyle, J. R. (1999). Note-taking strategies for students with disabilities. *The Clearing House, 72*(6), 392–395.

Wenar, C., & Kerig, P. (2006). *Developmental psychopathology: From infancy through adolescence.* Boston: McGraw-Hill.

Werts, M., Wolery, M., Snyder, E., & Caldwell, N. (1996). Teachers' perceptions of the supports critical to the success of inclusion programs. *Journal of the Association for Persons with Severe Handicaps, 21,* 9–21.

Wery, J. J., & Nietfeld, J. L. (2010). Supporting self-regulated learning with exceptional children. *Teaching Exceptional Children, 42*(4), 70–78.

Westling, D. L., & Fox, L. (2009). *Teaching students with severe disabilities* (4th ed.). Upper Saddle River, NJ: Merrill/Pearson Education.

Whitbread, K., Bruder, M., Fleming, G., & Park, H. (2007). Collaboration in special education: Parent–professional training. *Teaching Exceptional Children, 39*(4), 6–14.

White, R. (1996). Unified discipline. In B. Algozzine (Ed.), *Problem behavior management: An educator's resource service* (pp. 11:28–11:36). Gaithersburg, MD: Aspen.

Wiley, A. L., Siperstein, G. N., Forness, S. R., & Brigham, F. J. (2009). School context and the problem behavior and social skills of students with emotional disturbance. *Journal of Child and Family Studies, 19,* 451–461.

Will, M. (1986). Educating children with learning problems: A shared responsibility. *Exceptional Children, 52*(5), 411–415.

Willard-Holt, C. (1998). Academic and personality characteristics of gifted students with cerebral palsy: A multiple case study. *Exceptional Children, 65,* 37–50.

Williams, S. C. (2002) How speech-feedback and word-prediction software can help students write. *Teaching Exceptional Children, 34*(3), 72–78.

Williamson, P., McLeskey, J., Hoppey, D., & Rentz, T. (2006). Educating students with mental retardation in general education classrooms: An analysis on national and state trends. *Exceptional Children, 72*(3), 347–361.

Wilson, B. L., & Corbett, H. D. (2001). *Listening to urban kids.* Albany, NY: SUNY Press.

Wingerden, C., Emerson, C., & Ichikawa, D. (2002). *Improving special education for children with disabilities in foster care. Education Issue Brief. Casey Family Programs.* Retrieved May 17, 2008, from http://www.fosterclub.org/training/upload/fosterclub_219.pdf

Wisconsin Assistive Technology Initiative. (2004). *The WATI assessment package.* Retrieved December 22, 2007, from http://www.wati.org/products/pdf/wati%20assessment.pdf

Wolfensberger, W. (1972). *The principle of normalization in human services.* Toronto: National Institute on Mental Retardation.

Wolff, J. C., & Ollendick, T. H. (2006). The comorbidity of conduct problems and depression in childhood and adolescence. *Clinical Child and Family Psychology Review, 9,* 201–220.

Wolffe, K. (2006). Teaching social skills to adolescents and young adults with visual impairments. In S. Z. Sacks & K. E. Wolffe (Eds.), *Teaching social skills to students with visual impairments: From theory to practice* (pp. 405–440). New York: American Foundation for the Blind.

Wolgemuth, J. R., Cobb, R. B., & Alwell, M. (2008). The effects of mnemonic interventions on academic outcomes for youth with disabilities: A systematic review. *Learning Disabilities Research & Practice, 23*(1), 1–10.

Xin, J. F., & Sutman, F. X. (2011). Using the SMART Board in teaching Social Stories to students with autism. *Teaching Exceptional Children, 43*(4), 18–24.

Yeargin-Allsopp, M., Rice, C., Karapurkar, T., Doernberg, N., Boyle, C., & Murphy, C. (2003). Prevalence of autism in a U.S. metropolitan area. *Journal of the American Medical Association, 289*(1), 49–55.

Yell, M. (2009). Classroom and behavior management II: Responding to behavioral skills in instruction and generalization strategies. In M. L. Yell, N. B. Meadows, E. Drasgow, & J. G. Shriner (Eds.), *Evidence-based practices for educating students with emotional and behavioral disorders* (pp. 261–281). Upper Saddle River, NJ: Merrill/Pearson.

Yell, M., & Bradley, M. R. (2009). Schoolwide positive behavior support. In M. L. Yell, N. B. Meadows, E. Drasgow, & J. G. Shriner (Eds.), *Evidence-based practices for educating students with emotional and behavioral disorders* (pp. 217–234). Upper Saddle River, NJ: Merrill/Pearson.

Yell, M. L., & Drasgow, E. (2005). *No Child Left Behind: A guide for professionals.* Upper Saddle River, NJ: Pearson Education.

Yell, M. L., Meadows, N. B., Drasgow, E., & Shriner, J. G. (2009). *Evidence-based practices for educating students with emotional and behavioral disorders.* Upper Saddle River, NJ: Merrill/Pearson.

Yell, M. L., Rogers, D., & Rogers, E. L. (1998). The legal history of special education: What a long, strange trip it's been! *Remedial and Special Education, 19*(4), 219–228.

Yell, M. L., Shriner, J. G., & Katsiyannis, A. (2006). Individuals with Disabilities Education Improvement Act of 2004 and IDEA Regulations of 2006: Implications for educators, administrators, and teacher trainers. *Focus on Exceptional Children, 39,* 1–16.

Zigmond, N., Jenkins, J., Fuchs, D., Deno, S., & Fuchs, L. (1995a). When students fail to achieve satisfactorily: A reply to McLeskey and Waldron. *Phi Delta Kappan, 77*(5), 303–306.

Zigmond, N., Jenkins, J., Fuchs, L., Deno, S., Fuchs, D., Baker, J., Jenkins, L., & Couthino, M. (1995b). Special education in restructured schools: Findings from three multiyear studies. *Phi Delta Kappan, 76*(7), 531–540.

Zimmerman, B. J., & Dibenedetto, M. K. (2008). Mastery learning and assessment: Implications for students and teachers in an era of high-stakes testing. *Psychology in the Schools, 45*(3), 206–216.

Zirkel, P. (2009). What does the law say? New Section 504 student eligibility standards. *Teaching Exceptional Children, 41*(4), 68–71.

Zirkel, P., & Thomas, L. (2010). State laws for RTI: An updated snapshot. *Teaching Exceptional Children, 42*(3), 56–63.

# Name Index

Abbott, M., 263, 287
Abeson, A., 33
Achenbach, T. M., 101
Agar, G., 103
Agnello, B., 332
Agran, M., 332
Ahlgrim-Delzell, L., 417
Al-Khabbaz, Z., 19
Alaimo, D., 117, 119
Albert, L., 368, 388, 394
Alberto, P. A., 411
Alkin, M., 18, 284
Allbritten, D., 49
Allen, K. D., 414
Alter, P. J., 364, 365, 374, 393
Alwell, M., 329
Amanti, C., 250
Andersen, M. N., 414
Anderson, C. L., 414
Anderson, K. M., 414
Anderson-Inman, L., 323
Andrews, A., 120
Angel, L., 417
Angold, A., 73
Apichatabutra, C., 315
Appel, K., 34
Aronson, E., 307, 327
Arreaga-Mayer, C., 263
Arthur-Kelly, M., 18, 84
Ault, M. J., 414
Austin, J. L., 103
Ayres, K. M., 413, 414, 423

Baccani, S., 414
Bachman, J., 269
Baglieri, S., 246
Bahrami, B., 156, 183
Bailey, C., 259–260
Bailey, D., 61
Bailey, W. ., 105
Baird, G., 115
Bak, S., 18
Baker, D. L., 46
Baker, J. N., 149
Baker, S., 263, 264, 284, 294, 310, 315, 398
Baker, S. K., 46
Banda, D., 191
Banks, J., 242, 249, 253, 254
Banks, R. A., 332–333, 416, 417
Barenbaum, E., 105
Barkley, R., 73
Barnes, M., 57, 60, 61, 259
Barth, A., 323, 330, 347
Barton, M., 115, 119
Basham, J. D., 47
Bates, P. E., 227
Bausch, M. E., 412, 414, 423
Beard, L. A., 405, 407, 408, 409, 410
Beatty, R., 24
Behrmann, M. M., 414
Beirne-Smith, M., 87, 89, 91
Bell, V., 413, 423
Bellanca, J., 265, 266, 267
Belland, B. R., 355
Benner, G. J., 131
Bergstrom, M. K., 205
Berkeley, S., 327, 330
Best, S. J., 144, 145, 146, 148, 150, 404
Bigge, J. L., 144, 148, 404

Biklen, D., 12
Bitter, G. G., 404, 412
Blackhurst, A. E., 412, 423
Blackorby, J., 105
Blaney, N., 327
Blank, W., 105
Blanks, B., 165
Blum, C., 413
Bocian, K. M., 103
Bode, P., 247, 270
Boe, E. E., 49
Bohanon, H., 381
Bond, R., 286
Bondy, E., 250, 252, 253, 265
Boon, R. T., 413
Borgmeier, C., 364, 365, 374, 393
Borich, G., 265, 266, 267, 282, 283, 285, 299, 303, 326, 355
Borman, G., 313
Bos, C., 177, 324
Bouck, E. C., 413, 414, 417
Boutot, E., 18
Boutot, E. A., 398
Bowen, S. L., 414
Boyer, K. L., 49
Boykin, A. W., 259–260
Boyle, C., 115
Boyle, J. R., 330, 349, 350
Bradley, M. R., 365
Bradshaw, C., 273, 274, 275, 364, 365
Bradshaw, C. P., 368, 393
Brady, M., 87, 89
Bransford, J. D., 322
Breen, K., 374
Bricker, D., 35
Brickham, D., 19
Briesch, A., 365, 379
Brigham, F. J., 103
Brookshire, M. A., 374
Brophy, J., 284, 285, 287, 307, 308, 309, 326
Brotherson, M. J., 33
Browder, D. M., 332, 417
Brown, A., 259, 261
Brown, A. L., 322
Brown, C. C., 414
Brown, L., 19, 90
Bruce, C. D., 24
Bruder, M., 168, 191
Bruner, E., 263, 282–283
Brunet, J., 18
Bryan, A., 141
Bryan, T., 62
Bryant, D., 18
Buck, G., 163
Buckley, M., 241–242, 249
Bulgren, J., 323, 327, 329, 330, 337, 338
Bullis, M., 105
Burish, P., 311
Burke, J. D., 103
Burke, M. D., 341
Burke, R. V., 414
Burns, B. J., 107
Burns, M., 78
Burns, M. K., 47
Burstein, K., 62
Burstein, N., 18
Bursuck, W. D., 211, 213
Busse, R. T., 101

Buttery, D., 106–107
Buzhardt, J., 287
Byers, C., 195

Cabello, B., 18
Cameto, R., 105
Campbell, M. L., 413
Canevaro, A., 414
Cao, M., 166
Capizzi, A. M., 362, 379
Carey, D. M., 414
Carlson, E., 24
Carnine, D., 283
Carpenter, L. B., 405, 407, 408, 409, 410
Carr, E. G., 92
Carr, V. G., 368
Carter, E., 18, 19, 22, 170, 195, 196
Carter, E. W., 105
Carter, J., 373
Carter, M., 398
Cartledge, G. W., 259, 260, 265, 269, 270, 271, 276
Caruso, A., 121
Castagnera, E., 286
Castillo, S., 374
Caterino, L. C., 114, 115
Causton-Theoharis, J., 187, 188
Cavalier, A. R., 412, 414, 423
Cavendish, W. M., 105, 318
Chadsey, J., 18
Chalfant, J., 179
Chalk, J. C., 341
Chamberlain, S. P., 247
Chan, J., 398
Chapman, C., 328
Chapman, J., 310
Chard, D., 284, 294, 315
Charles, C. M., 364
Charman, T., 115
Charney, R., 253
Chau, M., 157, 243
Chawarska, K., 119
Chen, H., 341
Cheney, D., 48, 105, 389
Cherup, S., 414
Christenson, S. L., 389
Chronis, A., 79, 168, 191
Chun, E. J., 332–333, 416, 417
Chung, C., 103, 244
Chung, Y., 414
Cihak, D., 414
Cihak, D. F., 411
Cirino, P. T., 323, 330, 347
Clark, H. B., 105
Clark, N. M., 332, 353
Clarke, B., 294, 317
Clay, M., 286, 309
Cloninger, C. J., 227
Coady, M., 11, 365
Cobb, R. B., 329
Cochran-Smith, M., 242, 249, 253, 254
Cocking, R. R., 322
Codell, E., 261
Cole, C., 18, 328
Cole, R. W., 253
Coleman, T., 191
Coles, E., 79, 168, 191
Collins, P., 263, 264
Colvert, G., 341, 342

Colvin, G., 365, 366, 368
Compton, D. L., 48
Compton, L., 331
Conderman, G., 330, 348, 353
Conger, R. E., 103
Connor, D., 78
Conroy, M. A., 115
Cook, B., 163–164
Cook, K., 163
Cook, L., 157, 158, 161, 164, 165, 175, 177, 178, 188
Cook, L. H., 49
Cook, S., 163–164
Cooney, J., 136
Coonrod, E. E., 114, 115
Cooper, H., 168, 191, 326
Corbett, D., 253, 254
Corbett, H. D., 253, 254
Corbett, W. P., 105
Correa, V., 20, 162, 167, 168, 175, 177, 178, 191, 192
Cosbey, J. E., 414
Costello, J., 73
Cote, D., 326, 355, 356
Cothran, D. J., 361
Coulter, G., 310
Courtad, C. A., 341, 417
Coutinho, M., 414
Coutinho, M. J., 102
Cox, C. J., 393
Cox, D., 191
Coyne, M., 289
Crabtree, T., 33, 39, 45
Craddock, C., 18, 259, 286, 287
Craun, G., 120, 121, 362
Crawford, S., 121
Crismond, D. P., 412
Crites, S. A., 393
Crone, D. A., 205
Cuadrado, J., 103, 244
Cullinan, D., 101, 103
Culpepper, M., 263
Cumming, T., 373
Curran, M., 252, 269, 270
Curwin, R. L., 365, 367, 385
Cushing, L. S., 332, 353
Cutler, L., 290

D'Agostino, J., 285, 309
Daddario, R., 371
Dalston, R. M., 127
Daniels, L. E., 414
Darch, C. B., 362
Darling-Hammond, L., 242, 245, 249, 253, 254
Davies, D., 411
Davis, B. L., 128
Davis, S., 62, 63, 64, 155, 163. 160
Day, M., 192
Dean, S., 25
deBettencourt, L. U., 329
DeGrazia, R. L., 34
Delpit, L., 269
DeLuca-Strauss, T., 121
Dennis, R. E., 227
Deno, E., 31
Deno, S. L., 47, 212, 300
Denton, C., 57, 310
Denton, C. D., 323, 330, 347
Deschenes, C., 328

Deshler, D. D., 61, 329, 330, 331, 338
Dettmer, P., 158, 165, 175, 176
Deutchman, L., 362
Dexter, D. D., 47
Diamond, K. E., 150
Dibenedetto, M. K., 212
Dickson, S., 211
Dietz, S., 105, 318
Dion, E., 18
Dixon, J., 105, 318
Doabler, C., 315
Doernberg, N., 115
Dofka, C., 10, 12
Dookie, L., 24
Doolabh, A., 92
Doorlag, D., 247
Dore, R., 18
Doubt, L., 149
Douglas, K. H., 413, 423
Dowling, N., 313
Doyle, M., 20, 187, 188
Doyle, W., 363
Drasgow, E., 43, 360
Dreyer, L., 309–310
Duchnowski. A. J., 101, 105
Duckworth, S., 374
Duffy, H., 242, 249, 253, 254
Duhaney, L. M. G., 18, 34, 247, 284
Dukes, C., 323
Dunlap, G., 317
Dunlap, L., 317
Dunn, L. M., 31
DuPaul, G., 62, 73, 77
Dwyer, K., 365, 368
Dyck, N., 158, 165, 175, 176
Dye, M., 195
Dymond, S., 17
Dymond, S. K., 332–333, 416, 417

Ebeling, D., 328
Eber, L., 365, 374
Eby, J., 103
Edelman, S. W., 227
Edmonds, M., 347, 348, 412, 414, 423
Edrisinha, C., 120
Edyburn, D. L., 47, 325
Eggen, P., 11, 168, 282, 283, 284, 285,
    303, 305, 355, 356, 360
Ehri, L., 309–310
Elbaum, B., 285, 289, 310
Elf, N., 330, 348
Elliott, S. N., 101
Ellis, E. S., 322, 327, 338, 341, 342
Emmer, E., 252
Enders, C., 105, 318
Eng, V., 21–22, 53, 60, 280
Engelmann, S., 263, 282–283
Englert, C. S., 341, 417
Epstein, M. H., 101, 105, 131
Ergul, C., 62
Erkanli, A., 73
Ertmer, P. A., 355
Erwin, E. J., 33, 34
Escolar, D. M., 144
Esmonde, I., 24
Esquith, R., 261
Eswothy, C., 323
Evertson C., 252

Fabiano, G., 79, 168, 191
Fahrenkrog, C., 414
Fahsl, A., 317
Fairbanks, S., 48, 365, 379
Fantuzzo, J., 169, 312
Fanuele, D., 18, 313
Farinella, K. A., 128, 129, 131
Farmer, T. W., 47
Feifer, S., 60, 62
Feil, E. G., 101
Fein, D., 115, 119
Fenning, P., 381
Ferguson, D. L., 35–36
Ferretti, R. P., 412, 423
Fidanque, A., 263
Fien, H., 46
Filbert, M., 412, 423
Firth, C., 156, 183

Fisher, M., 84, 167, 187
Fisher, S., 411
Fitch, C. L., 144
Flanagan, S. M., 413, 414
Fleming, G., 168, 191
Fletcher, J., 46, 57, 60, 61, 259,
    289–290, 313
Fletcher, J. M., 323, 330, 347
Flippin, S. S., 49
Flojo, J., 284, 294
Flower, A., 48
Flugman, B., 309–310
Fombonne, E., 115
Foorman, B, 288, 299
Ford, D. Y., 269, 276, 365
Forde, T., 259, 261
Foreman, P., 18, 84
Forest, M., 227
Forness, S., 17
Forness, S. R., 99, 102, 103
Forni, P. M., 364
Foster, B., 119
Fox, L., 32, 90, 208, 304, 332, 415
Fox, N., 22
Francis, D., 57
Francis, D. J., 323, 330, 347
Freeman, S., 18, 284
French, N., 167
Friedlander, B., 291, 293, 315
Friend, M., 157, 158, 161, 164, 165,
    175, 177, 178, 188
Fuchs, D., 16, 17, 18, 33, 47, 48, 201,
    259, 263, 286, 287, 294, 299,
    311, 313, 314
Fuchs, L., 16, 17, 18, 33, 47, 48, 57, 60,
    61, 201, 259, 263, 286, 287, 294,
    299, 311, 313, 314, 317
Fulk, B., 312

Gable, R. A., 394 101
Gaffney, J. S., 326
Gage, N., 115
Gaillard, W. D., 145
Gajria, M., 331, 337, 347
Gallingane, C., 250, 252, 253, 265
Galucci, C., 18
García, S., 250, 254
Gardner, A., 290
Gardner, R., 269, 276
Garrick Duhaney, L., 18, 59
Gartin, B., 33, 39, 45
Gast, D. L., 411, 413
Gately, S. E., 330, 347
Gavin, K., 263
Gay, G., 23, 242, 250, 252, 254, 259,
    260, 265, 267, 269, 271, 273,
    274
Geary, D., 61
Gersten, R., 263, 264, 284, 294, 310,
    317
Giangreco, M. F., 20, 187, 188, 227
Gibb, A., 103, 244
Gillam, R. B., 127
Gilson, C. L., 332–333, 416, 417
Ginsberg, M. G., 242, 254
Ginsburg-Block, M., 169, 312
Givner, C. C., 361
Glaeser, B. C., 105
Glazewski, K. D., 355
Glew, M., 163, 179
Glick, G. C., 84
Gnagy, E., 79, 168, 191
Goldman, S. K., 107
Goldstein, A. P., 373
Gongola, L. C., 371
Gonzalez, N., 250
Good, T., 284, 285, 287, 307, 308,
    309, 326
Goodkind, S., 269
Gorman, J.A., 330
Graden, J., 47
Graetz, J., 164
Graham, S., 266, 290, 291, 292, 293,
    315, 316, 341
Grasley, E., 323
Green, J., 115, 119
Greenfield, P. M., 248

Greenwood, C., 263, 287
Gregory, A., 269
Gresham, F. M., 46, 47, 57, 103
Grider, K. L., 414
Grider, K. M., 414
Griffin, H. C., 144
Griffin, L. W., 144
Grinker, R. R., 115
Gross, A., 309–310
Grossen, B., 310
Grover, L., 25, 279, 280
Guardino, D., 48
Gudykunst, W. B., 247
Gun Han, K., 18
Guth, C., 195
Guzel-Ozmen, R., 342

Haager, D., 284
Haas, A., 127
Hadwin, J. A., 398
Hagan-Burke, S., 341, 363
Häger-Ross, C., 148
Hairrell, A., 347, 348
Hall, S., 195
Hall, T. E., 412, 423
Hallahan, D, 10
Hallal, L., 63, 64, 155, 160, 163,
    196–197
Halsey H., 393
Hambacher, E., 250, 252, 253, 265
Hamlett, C., 18, 259, 286, 287
Hammer, J., 5–6, 199
Hampton, E. O., 137
Han, I., 166
Handleman, J. S., 116
Handler, M. W., 98
Hang, Q., 165
Hanley, G. P., 92
Hanner, S., 283
Hanson, M. J., 33
Hanushek, E., 280
Hardman, M. T., 49
Harlacher, J., 289
Harriott, W., 252
Harris, D., 101
Harris, K., 266, 291, 292, 293, 315, 316
Harris, S. L., 116
Harry, B., 192
Hartshorne, N., 136
Hasselbring, T. S., 412, 423
Hawken, L., 389
Hawken, L. S., 48, 205, 368
Haydt, L., 293–294
Hayes, L., 286, 310
Hebbeler, K., 105
Heflin, L., 117, 119
Heller, K. W., 146
Hendrickson, J. M., 394 101
Herrick, C. L., 118
Hershfeldt, P., 273, 274, 275, 364, 365,
    368, 393
Hetzroni, O. E., 412, 414, 423
Heutsche, A., 417
Hibbard, K., 355
Hill, S., 106–107, 321–322, 329,
    374–375
Hilton, A., 201
Hilvitz, P. B., 393
Hinshaw, S., 77
Hitchcock, C., 47, 325
Hoard, M., 61
Hollenbeck, K., 18, 259, 286, 287
Holler, R., 73, 74
Hollins, E. R., 254
Hong, E., 331
Hong, S-Y., 150
Hoover, J. J., 46
Hoover, N., 286, 309
Hoppey, D., 13, 33, 35, 57, 59, 60
Horner, R. H., 92, 368
Horney, M. A., 323
Horvath, B., 328
Hosp, J., 56
Hourcade, J. J., 413
Howard, L., 263
Howard, M. R., 414
Howland, J., 412

Huckaby, M., 7–8, 36, 49
Hudson, P., 294
Huerta, N. E., 33, 37
Huff, S., 54, 63, 64, 83–84, 88–89, 93,
    279, 280, 281
Hughes, C., 18, 22, 170, 183, 195,
    196, 331
Hughes, C. A., 47, 331, 345, 349, 412,
    423
Hughes, E., 73, 78
Hughes, E. M., 114
Hughes, M., 289
Humphry, R., 414
Hurley-Chamberlain, D., 164, 165
Huskins, J., 53, 159
Hutinger, P., 414
Hyman, S., 114, 115
Idol, L., 18

Irvine, J. J., 242, 249
Israel, M., 47
Itoi, M., 331, 349
Iversen, S., 310
Iverson, V. S., 227
Iwata, B. A., 92
Izzo, M. V., 413, 423

Jackman, L. A., 365, 371
Jackson, R., 47, 325
Janney, R., 160
Jarvis, J., 206
Jayanthi, M., 284, 294
Jensen, W. R., 386
Jerman, P. L., 219
Jimerson, S. R., 47
Jitendra, A., 293–294
Jitendra, A. K., 337, 347
Jocks-Meier, B. S., 341
Johanson, J., 414
Johns, B., 61, 62, 63, 300
Johns, B. H., 368
Johnson, D., 290
Johnson, G., 283
Johnson, G. O., 31
Johnson, J., 76
Johnson, J. W., 414
Johnston, L. J., 405, 407, 408, 409, 410
Johnston, S., 414
Jonassen, D. H., 412
Jones, H., 20, 162, 167, 168, 175, 177,
    178, 191, 192
Jones, L., 368
Jones, R. R., 103
Jones, T., 255
Jones, V., 368
Jordan, J., 57, 289, 299
Joseph, L. M., 331, 349
Justice, L. M., 127, 128, 129, 130, 131

Kagan, S., 308
Kain, J., 280
Kaisler, G., 323
Kalyanpur, M., 192
Kamman, M., 11, 365
Kamphaus, R. W., 373
Kamps, D., 106, 263, 374
Kamps, D. M., 101, 371
Kampwirth, T., 160, 161, 175
Kanner, L. ., 114
Kapelski, C., 331
Karapurkar, T., 115
Karlan, G. R., 414
Katsiyanis, A., 114
Katsiyannis, A., 48, 73, 78
Kauchak, D., 11, 168, 282, 283, 284,
    285, 303, 305, 355, 356, 360
Kaufenberg, J., 411
Kauffman, J., 10, 33, 43
Kavale, K., 17
Kavale, K. A., 99, 106
Kea, C. D, 365
Keating, T., 310
Keeler, G., 73
Kelley, K. R., 414
Kelley, M., 118
Kennedy, A., 144
Kennedy, C. H., 103, 332, 353

Kerig, P., 77
Kern, L., 103
Kessler, K., 90, 411
Ketterlin-Geller, L., 315
Kim, A., 412, 414, 423
Kim, S. H., 87, 89, 91
Kim, Y. Y., 247
Kincaid, D., 398
King, B. H., 119
King, B. S., 18, 84
King, K., 312
King-Sears, M. E., 47, 325, 328, 329, 345, 346
Kissam, J., 323, 327, 337
Klein, C., 414
Klin, A., 115
Klingner, J., 284
Knackendoffel, A., 158, 165, 175, 176
Knight, D., 213
Knight, V., 332
Knopf, J. H., 246
Knox-Quinn, C., 323
Kochhar-Bryant, C., 161, 168, 172, 178, 191
Koenig, L., 364
Konrad, M., 331, 349
Korinek, L., 161, 162, 177
Kourea, L., 259, 260, 265, 269, 270, 271
Kovaleski, J., 163, 179
Kramer, C., 374
Kraun, G., 119
Kremer-Sadlik, T., 116
Kulinna, P. H., 361
Kung, S., 166
Kutash, K., 101, 105
Kvavik, R. B., 402

Laflamme, M., 18, 19
Lamar-Dukes, P., 323
Lancioni, G., 120
Lancioni, G. E., 414
Landers, E., 13, 33, 57, 59, 60
Landrum, T. J., 101, 104
Lane, H., 286, 309, 310
Lane, H. B., 310
Lane, K., 163, 179
Lane, K. L., 103, 105, 361
Lang, R. B., 398
Langone, J., 413, 423
Larsen, L., 291, 292
Latham, P., 156, 183
Lathrop, M., 48
Lattimore, J., 411
Law, M., 155
Leaf, P., 273, 274, 275, 364, 365
Lee, A., 332
Lee, H., 24
Lee, H. J., 119
Lee, S., 18
Lee, S. H., 35
Legacy, J. M., 404, 412
Lehr, C. A., 389
Lenz, B. K., 327, 338
Lenz, K., 61, 323, 327, 337
Lenz, K. ., 329, 338
Lerner, J., 61, 62, 63, 300
Levin, B., 355
Levine, P., 77
Lewis, R., 247
Lewis, T. J., 365, 373
Lignugaris/Kraft, B., 286, 311, 312
Linan-Thompson, S., 47, 48, 263, 264
Lindsay, G., 18
Linn, A., 118
Lipkewich, A., 290
Little, A., 163, 179
Little, J., 374
Little, M., 47
Little, T D., 35
Loeber, R., 103
London, T. H., 374
Long, A., 324–326
Longstaff, J., 263
Loveland, K. A., 119
Loveland, T., 22
Luckner, J. L., 136

Ludwig, T., 324
Lusthaus, E., 227
Lynass, L., 389
Lyon, R., 57, 60, 61, 259
Lysaght, K., 330

Maag, J., 105
Maas, E., 127
MacArthur, C. A., 412, 414, 423
MacArthur, S., 293, 315
MacLean, W., 19
MacMillan, D. L., 103
MacPhee, K., 18
Madden, N., 307
Madj, M., 18
Maes, B., 90
Maheady, L., 103, 114, 118, 120
Mahoney, J. M., 114, 115
Mainzer, R., 49
Major, A., 76
Marcellino, R., 86
Mariage, T. V., 341
Markford, Rick, 6–7
Marks, L. J., 436
Marquis, J. G., 92
Marra, R. M., 412
Marshak, L., 330, 346
Marshall, L. H., 219
Martin, J. E., 219
Martin, N. M., 341
Martin, S., 252
Martinez, R. S., 46
Martins, M. P., 116
Martinussen, R., 76
Marzano, R., 286, 307
Mason, L., 266, 291, 293, 315, 316
Mason, L. H., 293, 315, 341
Mastropieri, M. A., 22, 48, 164, 165, 327, 330, 331, 345, 346
Mathes, P., 310
Mathur, S. R., 104, 106
Matthews, W., 393
Matuszny, R., 191
Maxson, L. M., 219
Mazurenko, R. ., 290
McArrell, B., 413, 423
McAtee, M. L., 92
McColl, M. A., 149
McComas, J., 18, 19
McConnell, M. E., 393
McCord, B. E., 92
McCoy, K. M., 119
McDaniel, M., 114
McDonald, M., 242, 249, 253, 254
McDonnell, J., 168
McDonough, S., 148
McDuffie, K., 164, 165
McDuffie-Landrum, K., 163–164
McGinnis, E., 373
McIlvain, D., 323
McKnight, M., 57, 289, 299
McLaughlin, D. M., 92
McLaughlin, V., 18, 161, 162, 177
McLeskey, J., 4, 5, 11, 13, 16, 17, 18, 19, 22, 31, 33, 35, 49, 57, 59, 60, 137, 138, 157, 161, 163, 166, 168, 172, 184, 282, 284, 285, 325
McMahon, A., 401–402, 411, 426
McMaster, K., 166, 287, 311
McPartland, J., 115
Meadan, H., 19, 34
Meade, C., 413, 423
Meadows, N. B., 360
Mechling, L. C., 411, 413
Mellard, D., 57, 289, 299
Melrath, D., 141
Meltzer, L., 76
Mendler, A. N., 365, 367, 385
Mercer, C., 60, 62
Mercer, C. D., 345, 346
Metz, D. E., 127, 128, 129, 131
Meyer, A., 15–16, 47, 325
Meyer, D. K., 252
Meyer, L. H., 84
Midgley, C., 252
Mielenz, C., 389

Mikulski, B., 86
Miller, D. N., 98
Miller, K., 61, 160, 199
Miller, S., 294
Mims, P. J., 417
Miner, C. A., 227
Misra, S., 49
Modrek, S., 77
Mokhtari, K., 331
Moll, L., 242, 249, 253, 254
Moll, L. C., 250
Monaghan, M. C., 310
Monda-Amaya, L., 19
Montague, M., 105, 266, 317, 318
Montgomery, D. J., 414, 436
Moody, S., 285, 289, 310
Mooney, J. F., 328, 329
Morgan, T., 317
Morphy, P., 284, 294
Morrison, A. P., 18, 84
Morrison, G., 105
Morrissey, K. L., 381
Morsink, C., 20, 162, 167, 168, 175, 177, 178, 191, 192
Moses, H., 44
Mostert, M. P., 106
Mount, B., 227
Moxley, K. D., 341
Muir, S. G., 136
Munk, D. D., 213
Murawski, W., 183
Murdick, N., 33, 39, 45
Murphy, C., 115
Murphy, J., 285, 309
Murray, C. S., 47, 48
Mustillo, S., 73
Myers, D., 365, 379

Nellis, L. M., 46
Nelson, J. R., 131, 365, 366
Newcomer, P. L., 105
Newman, L., 105
Nietfeld, J. L., 323
Nieto, S., 247, 270
Nirje, B., 12, 31
Niswander, V., 332–333, 416, 417
Nix, S. J., 363
Noguera, P., 269
Nuebert, D. A., 105
Nungesser, N. R., 131

O'Mullane, A., 141
O'Brien, J. C., 341
O'Connor, B., 79, 168, 191
O'Reilly, M., 120
O'Reilly, M. F., 398, 414
O'Shea, D. J., 107, 207, 326, 362, 364, 368, 372, 373, 374, 379, 380, 393
O'Shea, L., 107, 207, 326, 362, 364, 368, 372, 373, 374, 379, 380, 393
Obama, B., 86
Ochs, E., 116
Oetzel, J. G., 247
Okey, S., 374
Okolo, C. M., 341, 412, 417, 423
Oliva, D., 414
Ollendick, T. H., 105
Olley, G. J., 120
Olsen, K., 156, 183
Oluwole, J. O., 102
Orsak, C., 117
Ortiz, A., 250, 254
Ortiz-Lienemann, T., 347
Osher, D., 105, 365, 368
Oshita, L., 163–164
Oswald, D. P., 102
Ousley, O. Y., 115
Owens, R. E., 127, 128, 129, 131

Pacchiano, D., 18
Paine, S. C., 362
Palmer, S., 411
Parent, W., 411
Parette, H. P., 413, 414, 434
Park, H., 168, 191

Park, K. L., 368, 393
Parker, R. C., 84
Pascoe, S., 18, 84
Patall, E., 168, 191
Patrick, H., 252
Patterson, G. R., 103
Patterson, J., 251
Patton, J. M., 87, 89, 91
Patton, J. R., 46
Paul, R., 118
Pearson, N., 105
Peck, C., 18
Pedersen, T., 353
Pelham, W., 79, 168, 191
Pell, K., 273, 274, 275, 364, 365
Pellegrino, L., 144, 148
Peña, E. D., 128
Peterson-Karlan, G. R., 414
Petry, K., 90
Pickering, D., 286, 307
Pierce, N., 398
Piers, E., 101
Pierson, M., 163, 179
Pierson, M. R., 105, 361
Pivik, J., 18, 19
Pleasants, S., 167, 187
Ploessl, D., 165
Pohill, D., 119, 120, 362
Pohlmann, B., 424
Pollock, J., 286, 307
Polloway, E., 163
Polsgrove, L., 106, 373
Porte, L., 331
Poth, R., 47
Powell-Smith, K. A., 398
Powers, K., 160, 161, 175
Pratt, M., 53, 63, 141, 148, 155, 199, 279, 425–426
Prendergast, K. A. ., 46
Presley, J., 195
Pressley, M., 288
Pruess, J., 323–324
Pullen, P., 60, 62, 286, 310
Pullen, P. C., 310
Putnam J., 326
Pysh, M. ., 179

Quinn, B. S., 414

Rabran, K., 165
Radicci, J., 362
Ramsey, E., 365, 366, 368
Rashotte, C., 18
Rausch, M., 103, 244
Rawlinson, D., 374
Rawlinson, R., 374
Rea, P., 18
Reavis, H. K., 386
Reed, P., 404
Reed, V. A., 137
Rees, G., 156, 183
Regualos, R., 361
Reichle, J., 414
Reid, J. B., 103
Reid, R., 76, 347
Reiff, M., 71, 73, 77
Reilly, M., 414
Rentz, T., 33, 35
Renzaglia, A., 332–333, 416, 417
Reschly, D., 56, 58
Rescorla, L., 101
Reutzel, R., 284, 289
Reynhout, G., 398
Reynolds, C. R., 373
Reynolds, M., 32
Rhode, G., 386
Rice, C., 115
Rice, E. H., 105
Richards, H., 259, 261
Richards, S. B., 87, 89
Richert, A., 242, 249, 253, 254
Riffel, L. A., 411
Riggs, C., 188, 189
Rinaldi, C., 201
Risko, V., 323
Ritchey, K., 56, 289
Ritter, S., 103, 244

Rivers, J., 280
Rivken, S., 280
Roberts, G., 299, 313, 314
Robertson, E., 163, 179
Robin, D. A., 127
Robins, D., 115, 119
Robinson, J., 168, 191
Rock, M., 165
Rock, T., 355
Rodriguez, E., 265, 266, 267
Roepstorff, A., 156, 183
Rogan, J., 327
Rogers, D., 30
Rogers, E. L., 30
Rohrbeck, C., 169, 312
Romain, M., 323, 330, 347
Rorschach, H., 101
Rose, D., 47, 325
Rose, J., 374
Rose, T., 361
Rosellini, L. C., 362
Rosenberg, M. S., 11, 49, 103, 107, 114, 118, 120, 137, 138, 168, 207, 273, 274, 275, 326, 362, 364, 365, 368, 371, 372, 373, 374, 379, 380, 393
Rosenfeld, J. S., 44
Rosenshine, B., 282, 283
Rosenstein, A., 332–333, 416, 417
Ross, D., 11, 250, 252, 253, 265, 365
Ross, J., 24
Rothstein-Fisch, C., 248
Ruby, M., 289
Ruggles, B., 310
Ruhl, K. L., 331
Rupley, W. H., 347, 348
Russell, D., 17
Rutter, M., 117, 118
Ryan, A., 393
Ryan, J., 73, 78
Ryan, J. B., 114
Ryan, J. B., 114
Ryan, K. A., 92
Ryndak, D. L., 18, 84

Sabornie, E. J., 103, 329
Sacks, G., 337, 347
Saenz, L., 263
Safran, J. S., 118
Safran, S. P., 115
Sailers, E., 411
Sale, P., 414
Salend, S. J., 18, 34, 59, 247, 284, 331
Salmento, M., 293–294
Sanders, W., 280
Sandlund, M., 148
Sanford, A., 289
Sansoti, F. J., 398
Santos, M., 137
Sas, J. C., 331
Sas, M., 331
Sawka, K., 98
Scanlon, D., 18, 313
Scarcella, R., 263, 264
Schatschneider, C., 18, 259, 286, 287
Scheffler, R., 77
Schifter, L., 105
Schirmer, B. R., 136
Schneck, C., 313
Schoenfeld, N., 165
Schoenfeld, N. A., 104
Schonberg, R. L., 145
Schrepferman, L. M., 103
Schroll, K., 24
Schumaker, J., 331
Schumaker, J. B., 329, 330
Schumann, J., 48
Schumm, J., 177, 324
Schwartz, I., 18
Schwartz, I. S., 137
Scott, G. S., 331
Scott, L., 68, 71, 74, 75, 79–80, 280
Scott, T., 365, 374
Scott, T. M., 101, 364, 365, 371, 374, 393

Scruggs, T. E., 22, 48, 164, 165, 327, 330, 345, 346
Sears, S., 18
Sebald, A. M., 136
Sechrest, R., 273, 274, 275, 364, 365
Seid, N. H., 411
Severson, H. H., 101
Shackelford, J., 86
Shah, N., 411
Shamberger, C., 164, 165
Shanahan, T., 263, 264
Shankland, R. K., 341
Shapiro, C., 73
Shapiro, E. S., 98
Sharma, J. M., 101
Sheets, R. H., 259, 260
Shelden, D., 34
Shippen, M. E., 393
Shiraga, B., 90
Shrieber, B., 412, 414, 423
Shriner, J. G., 48, 360
Shukla, S., 103
Siegel, L. S., 62
Sigafoos, J., 120
Sikes, J., 327
Silva, M., 213
Simmons, A., 103, 244
Simmons, D., 347, 348
Simonsen, B., 365, 379
Simpson, R. G., 393
Simpson, R. L., 114, 119
Sinclair, M. F., 389
Sindelar, P. T., 49, 103, 114, 118, 120, 345, 346
Singh, N. N., 414
Siperstein, G. N., 84, 103
Sirota, K. G., 116
Sisco, L., 19
Sitlington, P. L., 105
Skiba, R., 103, 244, 269
Slavin, R., 307, 308, 326, 327
Small, S., 18, 313
Smith, A. W., 106, 373
Smith, B., 73
Smith, C., 365, 374, 414
Smith, C. E., 92
Smith, P., 88
Smith, S., 411
Smith, T. E. C., 45
Smith-Myles, B., 114, 118, 119
Smith-Rex, S., 374
Smith-Thomas, A., 163
Snapp, M., 327
Snell, M., 160
Snyder, J., 103
So, T. H., 22
Sobsey, D., 146
Solomon, O., 116
Someki, F., 78
Sommerstein, L., 18, 84
Sood, S., 337, 347
Soodak, L. C., 33, 34
Soukup, J. H., 35
Spagna, M., 18
Sparling, J. W., 414
Spencer, V. G., 413
Sperling, R. A., 211
Spicer, L., 137
Spooner, F., 149, 332, 417
Sprague, J., 328
Sprague, J. R., 360
Sprick, M., 263
Sprinkle, C., 114
Stage, S. A., 389
Stainback, S., 32
Stainback, W., 32
Staub, D., 18
Steele, M. M., 330
Steely, D., 283
Stenhoff, D., 286, 311, 312
Stephan, C., 327
Stephen, M., 323
Stevens, R., 282, 283
Stock, S., 411

Stone, W. L., 114, 115
Stoneburner, R., 414
Stormont, M., 249
Stowe, M. J., 33, 37
Strichter, J., 115
Stronge, J. H., 23–24
Stropes, J. ., 103
Stuart, S. K., 201
Sugai, G., 48, 365, 373, 374, 379
Sumi, W. C., 101, 105
Suritsky, S. K., 331, 349
Suter, J., 20
Sutman, F. X., 413
Swanson, E., 347, 348
Swanson, E. A., 412, 414, 423
Swanson, K., 22
Sweda, J., 345

Tapia, Y., 287
Taylor, M., 125–126
Taylor, R., 87, 89
Taymans, J., 323, 327, 337
Templeton, T., 48
Terrill, M. C., 346
Terry, B., 263
Tesi Rocha, A. C., 144
Thampi, K., 157, 243
Therrien, W. J., 331
Thomas, C., 20, 162, 167, 168, 175, 177, 178, 191, 192
Thomas, L., 58
Thompson, K. L., 413
Thorson, S., 364
Thuppal, M., 146
Thurston, L., 158, 165, 175, 176
Tifft, C. J., 145
Ting-Toomey, S., 247
Todis, B., 414
Tomlinson, C. A., 24, 206, 213
Tomlinson-Clarke, S., 269, 270
Toplis, R., 398
Torgesen, J., 11, 18, 47, 259, 287, 288, 313
Tosi, L. L., 144
Towbin, K. E., 114, 115
Traxler, C. B., 136
Trela, K., 149
Trenholm, S., 361
Trumbull, E., 248
Tunali-Kotoski, B., 119
Tunmer, W., 310
Turnbull, A. P., 33, 411
Turnbull, H. R., 30
Turner, J., 252
Tyler, K., 260
Tyler, N. C., 49

Unizycki, R. M., 374
Unsworth, L., 285
Utley, C., 263

Vadasy, P., 187, 188
Van Acker, R., 394 101
van Garderen, D., 253
Van Harssel, C., 120, 121
Van Laarhoven, T., 414
Van Laarhoven-Myers, T., 414
Vandercook, T., York, J., & Forest, M. ., 227
Vannest, K. J., 363, 373
Vaughn, S., 46, 47, 48, 57, 177, 285, 289–290, 299, 310, 313, 314, 323, 324, 330, 347, 348, 412, 414, 423
Vellutino, F., 18, 57, 313
Vincent, C. G., 48
Vittetoe, J. O., 360
Volkmar, F. R., 115, 119

Wade, E., 413
Wadsworth, D. E. D., 213
Wagner, M., 105
Wagner, M. M., 101, 105
Wagner, S., 18

Waiton, C., 263
Wakeman, S., 149
Walberg, H., 32
Waldron, N., 4, 5, 16, 17, 18, 19, 22, 59, 157, 161, 163, 166, 172, 282, 284, 285, 325
Walker, H., 365, 366, 368
Walker, H. M., 22, 101, 360, 361
Walker, N., 289
Walker-Dalhouse, D., 323
Wallace, D., 269
Wallace, J., 269
Walls, E., 25, 68, 111–112, 279–280, 359–360
Walther-Thomas, C., 18, 161, 162, 177
Wang, M., 32
Wanzek, J., 47, 48, 211, 323, 330, 347, 412, 414, 423
Ware, F., 251
Warger, C., 317
Washington, B.T., 196
Watkins, R. V. ., 131
Watson, S., 324–325
Waugh, M., 389
Wehmeyer, M. L., 35, 332, 411
Weiner, J., 62
Weinstein, C., 252, 269, 270
Weinstein, S., 145
Weintraub, F. J., 33
Weishaar, M. K., 350
Wenar, C., 77
Wery, J. J., 323
Westling, D. L., 11, 32, 90, 137, 138, 168, 208, 304, 332, 415
Wexler, J., 323, 330, 347, 412, 414, 423
Wheeler, S., 324–326
Whitbread, K., 168, 191
White, J. M., 211
White, P. J., 398
White, R., 366
Whitney, D. W., 137
Whittaker, C., 253
Wilcoxen, A., 18
Wiley, A. L., 103
Will, M., 32, 59
Williams, B., 161, 162, 177, 253, 254
Williams, S., 97–98, 102, 106–107
Williams, S. C., 414
Williamson, P., 13, 33, 35, 57, 59, 60
Wills, H., 263
Wilson, B., 253, 254
Wilson, B. L., 253, 254
Wilson, R. J., 103, 114, 118, 120
Winston, M., 47
Winton, P., 33
Wolfensberger, W., 31
Wolff, J. C., 105
Wolgemuth, J. R., 329
Woodruff, A. L., 414
Wright, V., 157, 243

Xin, J. F., 413

Yeargin-Allsopp, M., 115
Yell, M., 365
Yell, M. L., 30, 43, 48, 360
Yen, C., 105
Yoo, S., 18
York, J., 227
Young, J., 136
Ysseldyke, J., 22
Yurick, A., 413, 423

Zeichner, K., 242, 249, 253, 254
Ziegler, D., 49
Zimmerman, B. J., 212
Zipoli, R., 289
Zirkel, P., 58, 72, 73, 74, 203
Zwernik, K., 227

# Subject Index

AAC. *See* augmentative or alternative communication (AAC) device
AAIDD. *See* American Association on Intellectual and Developmental Disabilities
ABA. *See* applied behavior analysis
ability grouping
    flexible, 210
    ineffectiveness, 284–285
absence seizures, 145
academic achievement, attitude toward, 245, 259–260
academic characteristics
    autism spectrum disorders (ASD), students with, 119–120
    communication disorders, students with, 130–131
    emotional and behavioral difficulties (EBD), students with, 105
    health impairments, students with, 148–149
    intellectual disabilities, students with, 89–90
    learning disabilities, students with, 60–61
    multiple disabilities, students with, 148–149
    physical disabilities, students with, 148–149
    sensory impairments, students with, 135–137
academic English, 263
academic failure, disruption and, 363–364
academic problems, students with ADHD, 70, 77
academic progress, using CBM to measure, 233–235
Academy of Reading by School Specialty, 405
accessibility, classroom, 150–151
Access to Math, 410
accommodation approach, co-teaching, 165
accommodations, 7
    autism spectrum disorders, students with, 121
    to general curriculum, 207
    test taking, 353
    universal design for learning (UDL), 325
accountability
    collaboration, 158
    cooperative learning groups, 286
achievement, increased demands for, 157
Achieve Now Mathematics by PLATO Learning, 405, 429–430
acoustical amplification system, 44
ADA. *See* Americans with Disabilities Act
adaptive grading plan, 237–238
Adderall, 78
adequate yearly progress (AYP), 43
ADHD. *See* attention-deficit/hyperactivity disorder (ADHD)
administrative support, 164
advance organizers, 62
African American students, 11, 157

call-response pattern of interaction, 269
disability, prevalence of, 244
diverse curriculum, 254
emotional and behavioral disabilities (EBD), students with, 102
graduation rate, 244, 245
poverty rates, 243
teachers, 246
aggression, 103
    behaviors, 92
    communication disorders, students with, 131
    crisis situations, 367–368, 371
agitation, signs of, 387
Alaska, 87
Alaska Native students
    disability, prevalence of, 244
    graduation rate, 244, 245
    teachers, 246
alphabetics, 290
alternate assessments, 48–49
alternative grouping strategies, 284
alternative routes to certification, 49
American Academy of Pediatrics, 71–72
American Association on Intellectual and Developmental Disabilities (AAIDD), 84–86
American Foundation for the Blind, 134
American Psychological Association (APA), 70, 73, 77
    intellectual disabilities, 86
American Speech-Language-Hearing Association, 130, 132
Americans with Disabilities Act (ADA), 39, 44–45, 203
amphetamines, 78
amplification system, 44
amputations, 144
animals, 215
ANSWER strategy, 353–354
antisocial behavior, 103
anxiety, 104
    autism spectrum disorders, students with, 121
Apple Computer, 411
applied behavior analysis (ABA), 205
Arizona, 157, 245
Arkansas, 58, 87
arrangement, furniture, 213
articulation disorders, 127
artificial hands or legs, 145
art therapists, 21
ASD. *See* autism spectrum disorders (ASD), students with
Asian students, 157
    disability, prevalence of, 244
    teachers, 246
Asperger's disorder, 112, 113, 114
    ritualistic behavior, 119
    social use of language, 119
assessment, 10. *See also* test taking
    alternate, 48–49
    comprehensive plan, quality of, 370–371
    direct instruction, 304
    IEP, 202

severe disabilities, redesigning content for students with, 333
speech-language pathologists (SLPs), 130
    teaching guided by, 253–254
    UDL principles, 417
asset-oriented approach, 250–251
assignment management, 331
assistive technology (AT), 210, 231, 403, 404–405
    augmentative and alternative communication devices, 408–410, 439–440
    daily living devices, 412
    decision-making process for selecting, 433–434
    devices, 148, 151
    inclusion, facilitating, 414
    math support, 408, 410, 429–430, 437–438
    motorized wheelchairs, 441–442
    personal support, 410–411
    reading support, 405–407, 427–428
    secondary content areas, 329
    spelling support, 408
    teaching students to use, 414–415
    writing support, 409, 435–436
asthma, 145, 149, 150, 151
    live creatures, 215
AT. *See* assistive technology
ataxic CP, 144
attention, 372
    strategies to boost, 300
    teaching students with autism spectrum disorders, 121
attentional problems, 62
attention-deficit/hyperactivity disorder (ADHD)
    academic difficulties, 77
    behaviors, 74–76
    combined, 71
    definition, 69–71
    executive functions and working memory, 76
    identification, 71–73
    inclusion, benefits of, 67–68
    medication to address symptoms, 77–79
    prevalence, 73
    service delivery, 73–74
    social and behavior difficulties, 76–77
    students with learning disabilities, 55, 62
    symptoms for identifying, 69
    teachers' tips, 79–80
attention-seeking behavior, 394
augmentative or alternative communication (AAC) device, 404
authentic relationships, 106, 364
autism-specific screening, 115–116
autism spectrum disorders (ASD), students with
    age of onset, 119
    communication skills, 117–118, 129
    definitions, 9, 113–114
    identification, 114–115

inclusion, 111–112
intelligence and academic characteristics, 119–120
percentage of time in general education classroom, 34
prevalence, 115
repetitive, stereotypical, and ritualistic behaviors, 119
self-injurious behavior, 120
service delivery, 115–116
social reciprocity, limitations in, 118–119
teachers' tips, 120–121
technology, 411
autistic disorder, 113, 114
"Autistic Disturbances of Affective Content" (Kanner), 114
autoimmune disease, 145–146
avoidance approach, co-teaching, 165
avoidance-of-failure behavior, 394
AYP. *See* adequate yearly progress

background knowledge and skills for writing instruction, 315
backgrounds. *See* culturally and linguistically diverse backgrounds
basic skills instruction, 209, 229–230
beginning instruction
    mathematics, 293–294
    reading, 288–289, 313–314
    writing, 290–291
behavioral and social characteristics
    communication disorders, students with, 131
    health impairments, students with, 149–150
    multiple disabilities, students with, 149–150
    physical disabilities, students with, 149–150
    sensory impairments, students with, 137
    students with learning disabilities, 62–63
behavioral contracts, 391–392
behavioral deficits, 361
behavioral supports, 367
behavior difficulties. *See also* emotional and behavioral difficulties (EBD), students with
    ADHD, students with, 70, 76–77
    communication disorders, students with, 131
    confrontations, defusing, 387–388
    consequences, 367
    crisis situations, 367–368
    cultural diversity, 247
    dangerous behavior, 387–388
    goals of misbehavior, 394
    intellectual disabilities, students with, 92
    medication, 78
    motorized wheelchairs, 442
    what to expect, 361
behavior education programs, 389–390
behavior intervention plan (BIP), 92, 203, 205, 371, 393–395

behavior intervention plan (BIP) (continued)
    self-management, self-control, and independence, 373–374
    social skills, direct teaching of, 373
    target behaviors, strengthening and reducing, 371–373
behavior rating scales, 101
beliefs, reflecting on your own, 249
best effort, 36
biases, recognizing cultural, 269
Big:Calc, 410
BIP. *See* behavior intervention plan (BIP)
blindness. *See also* sensory impairments, students with
    concepts, learning, 136–137
    definition, 9, 132–133
body language
    care, demonstrating, 364
    crisis situations, 368, 388
body part, absence of, 144
bone tuberculosis, 144
boys
    ADHD prevalence, 73
    emotional and behavioral disabilities (EBD), students with, 100, 101
brain abnormalities, 70
brain injury
    attention-deficit hyperactivity disorder, 70
    cerebral palsy, 144
bribery, rewards versus, 386
*Brown v. Board of Education*, 33
buddy program, 168–170, 195–197
building-based support teams, 158
bullies
    externalized behavior problems, 103
    targets, 62
burns, 144

calculators, 410, 437–438
California
    culturally and linguistically diverse backgrounds, students from, 157, 243, 245
    intellectual disabilities, students with, 87
California Standards Test, 245
Cali's Geo Tools, 429
cancer, 150
care, demonstrating
    classroom management, 364–365
    culturally and linguistically diverse backgrounds, 250–253, 270, 273–274
Carl D. Perkins Vocational and Technology Education Act, 39
CAST. *See* Center for Applied Special Technology (CAST)
CAST eReader, 407
causes
    of autism spectrum disorders (ASD), 113
    of communication disorders, 129
    of health impairments, 143
    of intellectual disabilities, 85
    of multiple disabilities, 143
    of physical disabilities, 143
    of sensory impairments, 133
CBMs. *See* curriculum-based measurements (CBMs)
Center for Applied Special Technology (CAST), 209, 231, 416
central auditory processing disorder, 132
cerebral palsy, 86, 144
certification, alternate routes to, 49
Charleston County School District, 427–428
chats, co-teach, 184–185
check-in systems, 389–390
Checklist for Autism in Toddlers (CHAT), 115
check-out systems, 389–390
Child Find services, 134
childhood disintegrative disorder, 113

Choosing Options and Accommodations for Children (COACH), 227
chromosomal anomalies, 86
citizen of the week, 247
civility, 364
civil rights movement, 33
classroom management, 359–360
    arranging for inclusion, 150–151, 213, 215
    behavior, expectations of, 361
    behavioral contracts, 391–392
    behavior intervention plans, 371–374
    check-in systems, 389–390
    check-out systems, 389–390
    classroom organization, 362–363
    climate of care and respect, 364–365
    confrontations and dangerous behavior, 387–388
    connect systems, 389–390
    consequences, developing and delivering, 385–386
    culturally and linguistically diverse backgrounds, 269–271, 273–276
    effective instruction, 363–364
    functional behavioral assessment, 368–371
    function-based thinking, 393–395
    plan, 184
    rules and procedures, 379–381
    social skills, direct teaching of, 397–398
    surface management techniques, 383–384
    targeted interventions, 368
    tired management, 365
    universal inclusive practices and supports, 365–368
    warm demanders, 252–253
    wraparound supports, 374–375
class-wide peer tutoring (CWPT), 229, 263
CLD. *See* culturally and linguistically diverse backgrounds
closed captions, 325
clubfoot, 144
COACH. *See* Choosing Options and Accommodations for Children (COACH)
code, crisis, 368
co-existing conditions, 72
cognitive characteristics
    intellectual disabilities, students with, 90–91
    students with learning disabilities, 62
cognitive strategy instruction, mathematics, 317–318
Cognitive Tutor Algebra by Carnegie Learning, 405
collaboration, 7, 10, 172
    collaborative consultation, 166–168
    collaborative teams, 163
    communication skills strategy, 177–178
    co-teaching, 163–166, 165
    defined, 157–159
    dispositions, 159–161
    families, 191–193
    inclusion, 155–156
    intellectual disabilities, teaching students with, 93
    key components strategy, 175–176
    paraeducators, working with, 187–189
    peer assistance, 168–170, 195–197
    planning, 183–185
    roles, 162–168
    secondary content areas, 324–325
    skills, 162
    strategy fact sheet, 172–173
    teacher assistance teams, 179–181
    teachers of students with learning disabilities, 61

collaborative consultation, 166–168
collaborative teams, 163
collectivist cultures, 248
Colorado, 58, 87, 88
committee, inclusive practices, 5–6
communication devices, 408–410, 439–440
communication disorders, students with
    academic characteristics, 130–131
    definitions, 127–128
    identification, 128–129
    inclusion, 125–126
    prevalence, 129
    service delivery, 130
    social and behavioral characteristics, 131
    teachers' tips, 137–138
communication skills
    augmentative/alternative communication devices, 439–440
    autism spectrum disorders (ASD), students with, 117–118
    collaboration and teaming, 173, 177–178
    cultural dimension, 248
    with families, 191–192
    with paraeducators, 187–189
communication technology, 124
community, 107
    of learners, 260
    respectful, creating, 252
compatibility, co-teaching partners, 164
competitive approach, co-teaching, 165
completion, insisting on, 254
comprehension, 288, 290
    secondary content areas, 347
Comprehensive Behavior Management Plan, 366, 369
compromise approach, co-teaching, 165
Concerta, 78
concomitant impairments, 146
conductive hearing loss, 132
conduct problems. *See* behavior difficulties
confidence, teachers', 93
confidentiality, 41, 219
configuration of the hearing loss, 132
conflict. *See* crisis situations
conflict, team teaching, 162
confrontations, defusing, 387–388
congenital anomaly, 144
congenital hip dislocations, 145
Connecticut, 58, 87
connections, establishing, 246–247
connect systems, 389–390
consequences, 367, 373
    assessing, 370
    delivering consistently, 385–386
    developing, 385
consultant, 158
contagious diseases, 45
content disorders, 128
continuum of services, 14
contracts, behavioral, 391–392
cooperative learning, 10
    activities, 211
    common characteristics of groups, 286
    core academic areas, 307–308
    mixed-ability grouping, 285
    secondary content areas, 326–327
coordinating resources, 363
core academic areas, instruction in, 209, 279–280, 279–281
    cooperative learning, 307–308
    direct instruction, 303–305
    grouping students, 284–285
    inclusive classrooms, 281–282
    individual tutoring, 285–286
    mathematics instruction, 293–294, 317–318
    peer-assisted strategies, 311–312
    peer tutoring, 286–287

planning using UDL principles, 231–232
reading instruction, 287–290, 309–310, 313–314
research-based, 299–301
teacher behaviors, 282–283
writing instruction, 290–293, 315–316
Corrective Reading, 290
correctives, 283
co-teaching, 10
    collaboration and teaching, 158, 163–166
course credit for peer buddy programs, 195
Co:Writer, 409
crisis situations, 367–368, 371
culturally and linguistically diverse backgrounds, 157
    academic achievement and, 245
    assistive technology (AT) devices, 433
    care, demonstrating, 250–253
    classroom management, 269–271, 273–276
    connections, establishing, 246–247
    curriculum, diverse, 254–255
    English-Language Learners (ELLs), teaching reading to, 263–264
    expectations, maintaining high, 253–254
    including students from diverse, 11
    instructional practices, highly effective, 265–267
    norms, examples of, 247–249
    responsiveness, 241–242
    responsive practices, 364–365
    special education and, 243–245
    strategy fact sheet, 257–258
    teachers' role, 249
    teaching, culturally responsive, 259–261
    what to expect, 243–245
current practices, 34–36
curriculum, 10, 200. *See also* core academic areas, instruction in; secondary content areas
    diverse, 254–255, 274
    focusing on, 207–208
    instructional needs, identifying, 225
    modifications, 208
    secondary content areas, understanding, 324
curriculum-based measurements (CBMs), 212–213, 233–235, 300
    reading progress, 313–314
curvature of the spine (scoliosis), 145
CWPT. *See* class-wide peer tutoring (CWPT)
cystic fibrosis, 146

daily instruction planning, 208–211
daily lessons, 184
daily living devices, 412
dangerous behavior, responding to, 387–388
dangerous weapons, 41
data collection and analysis, 130
day schools, 15, 31
dB. *See* decibels (dB)
deaf-blindness
    classification, 126
    definition, 9, 131, 133
    percentage of time in general education classroom, 34
deafness, 9, 132
decibels (dB), 132
decision making
    assistive technology (AT), selecting, 433–434
    collaboration, 158
decision rules, 368
deductive reasoning, 331
DEFENDS writing strategy, 327

defiant behavior, 361
deinstitutionalization, 31
Delaware, 58
demographic divide, 246
demographics
    attention-deficit hyperactivity
        disorder, students with, 70
    autism spectrum disorders, students
        with, 113
    communication disorders, students
        with, 129
    emotional and behavioral disabilities
        (EBD), students with, 100
    intellectual disabilities, students with,
        85, 87
    physical disabilities, health
        impairments, and multiple
        disabilities, students with, 143
    sensory impairments, students with,
        133
    student diversity, 243–245
    students with learning disabilities, 55
demonstration, 326
depression, 99, 103, 105
design, building, 325
Destination Reading Series by Riverdeep,
    405
developmental aphasia, 54
developmental delay
    definition, 9
    percentage of time in general
        education classroom, 34
developmental milestones, 86
devices. See assistive technology (AT);
    educational technology (ET)
Dexedrine, 78
DI. See direct instruction (DI)
Diagnostic and Statistical Manual of
    Mental Disorders (DSM-IV-TR)
    attention-deficit hyperactivity
        disorder, 69, 70, 71–72
    autism spectrum disorders, 115
differentiated instruction, 24
    core content areas, 299
    planning, 205–215, 223–224
    students with learning disabilities, 63
difficulty adaptation, 328
digital books, 209
digital textbooks, 47
diplegia, 144
direct instruction (DI), 10, 210
    core academic skills, 303–305
    defined, 282
    secondary content areas, 325–326
disciplinary removals, 103
discipline. See classroom management
discouraged students, behavior
    problems with, 394
disposition
    collaboration and teaching, 159–161
    teachers, 23
disruptions
    ADHD, students with, 77
    communication disorders, students
        with, 131
distractible behaviors, 387
distributed practice, 294
double-check cultural responsive
    approach to classroom
    management, 273–274
Down syndrome, 86
draft, writing a, 291
Draft:Builder, 409
drill-and-practice software, 403–404
drop-out rates
    emotional and behavioral disabilities
        (EBD), students with, 105
    by ethnic group, 244, 245
drugs, 41
DSM-IV-TR. See Diagnostic and
    Statistical Manual of Mental
    Disorders
dual diagnosis, ADHD, 74
Duchenne muscular dystrophy, 144

due process, 37
dyskinetic CP, 144
dyslexia, 54

EAHCA. See Education for all
    Handicapped Children act of
    1975 (EAHCA)
early intervention services, funding for,
    41–42
Early Screening Profile (ESP), 101
Earobics, 290
EBD. See emotional and behavioral
    difficulties (EBD), students with
e-books, 405
echolalia, 118
edible reinforcer, 372
editing drafts, 291
Edmark Reading Program, 406
educational assistants. See paraeducators
educational technology (ET), 403
    drill-and-practice software, 403–404
    evaluating, 431–432
    inclusion, facilitating, 412–413
    integrated learning systems, 404
    interactive whiteboards (Smart
        Boards), 403, 425–426
    reading and math programs, 404
    teaching students to use, 413,
        423–424
    word processing software, 435–436
Education for all Handicapped Children
    act of 1975 (EAHCA), 13, 30,
    37, 39
    parent advocacy, 33
    serious emotional disturbance
        (SED), 99
educative technology, 210, 231
effective instruction, 363–364
efficacy, 47–48
ELLs. See English-Language Learners
    (ELLs)
emergent collaboration, 158
emotional and behavioral difficulties
    (EBD), students with
    definition, 99–100
    externalizing behavior problems, 103
    identification, 100–101
    inclusion, benefits of, 97–98, 104
    intelligence and academic
        characteristics, 105
    internalizing behavior problems,
        103–105
    prevalence, 101–102
    service delivery, 102–103
    social behavior, 105–106
    student's view of inclusion, 104
    teachers' tips, 106–107
emotional disturbance
    definition, 9
    percentage of time in general
        education classroom, 34
emotions, 387
empathy, 177
"end the r word" movement, 86
engineered instructional practices, 323
English, standard, 242
English-Language Learners (ELLs), 157
    demographics, 243, 244
    reading, teaching to, 263–264
enhancements, secondary content areas,
    327–329
enthusiasm, 24
environment, 362
epidemiologists, 87–88
epilepsy, 145
    behavioral disorder case associated
        with, 104
    peer reactions to, 150
equal protection, 37
ERASE strategy, 393
ESP. See Early Screening Profile (ESP)
eternal children, 12
e-texts, 412
ethnic groups, 242

ethnocentrism, 269
evaluation
    collaborative relationship, 175
    educational assistance technology,
        431–432
evidence-based practices, 24, 46
exclusion clause, 56
execution phase, RTI, 201
executive functions, 76
expectations
    for appropriate behavior, 107
    assessing, 370
    for behavior, 379
    culturally and linguistically diverse
        backgrounds, students from,
        253–254
    establishing clear, 269–270
    for paraeducators, 189
    for peer buddies, 195
    for severe disabilities, students with,
        332–333
    students with learning disabilities, 64
    writing, 292
expertise, collaboration, 158
explicit instruction, 288, 294
expository writing, 341–343
expulsions, 41
externalizing behavior problems, 100,
    103
extra help, 64
eye contact, 121
EZ Keys, 409

face-to-face interaction, cooperative
    learning groups, 286
facilitator, 227
fairness, 23
families
    collaboration and teaming, 167–168,
        173, 191–193
    influences, ADHD, 70
FAPE. See free and appropriate public
    education (FAPE)
FBA. See functional behavioral
    assessment (FBA)
feedback
    appropriate behaviors, 372
    daily progress form, sample, 390
    early reading, 289
    effective instruction, 283
    mathematics problem solving, 317
    RTI models, 201
    writing, 435
feelings, students with autism spectrum
    disorder, 120–121
figurative language, 118–119
flexibility
    ability grouping, 210
    autism spectrum disorders, students
        with, 121
    collaboration, 159–160
    designing instruction, 231
    No Child Left Behind (NCLB) act
        (2001), 43
Florida
    culturally and linguistically diverse
        backgrounds, students from,
        157, 243, 245
    Next Generation Sunshine State
        Standards, 200, 300, 304
fluency, 288, 290
fluency disorders, 127
formal English, 263
formative assessment, 223, 231–232
form disorders, 128
forms, sample
    daily progress feedback, 390
    referrals to teacher assistance teams
        (TATs), 179
    Section 504 referral, 204
    strategic note-taking activity, 350
foster care, 244
fractures, 144
frame of reference, 161

free and appropriate public education
    (FAPE), 30, 38
    civil rights movement, 33
    legal principles, 37
frustration tantrum, 394
full inclusion, 16, 33
full-time special education classroom,
    14–15
functional-based thinking, 393–395
functional behavioral assessment (FBA),
    92, 101, 205, 368, 371
functional behavior assessment (FBA),
    393–395
functional inclusion, 31
functional language, 118
functionally excluded, 30
function-based thinking, 368
funding for early intervention services,
    41–42
funds of knowledge, 250
furniture arrangement and spacing,
    213

Gallaudet Research Institute, 134
GDL. See guided discovery learning
    (GDL)
gender
    ADHD prevalence, 73
    emotional and behavioral disabilities
        (EBD), students with, 100
general curriculum. See curriculum
general education classroom, 14
general education teachers, 19–20
generalization
    intellectual disabilities, students
        with, 91
    mnemonic strategies, 345
    planning for, 229
generalized anxiety, 104
general outcome measures, 212
genetic inheritance, 86
Georgia, 58
    culturally and linguistically diverse
        backgrounds, students from,
        157, 243, 245
    intellectual disabilities, students
        with, 87
gifted and talented students, 11
Gilpin Manor Elementary School
    (GMES), 4, 5–6, 15–16
    assistive technology, inclusion and,
        401–402, 411
    collaboration needed for inclusive
        classrooms, 155–156,
        159–160
    communication disorders and
        sensory impairments, students
        with, 125–126
    effective instruction for core
        curriculum, 279–280
    intellectual disabilities, including
        students with, 83–84
    multiple disabilities, inclusion for
        student with, 141–142
    planning for inclusion, 199–200
girls, 73
GMES. See Gilpin Manor Elementary
    School (GMES)
goals
    collaborators sharing, 158, 183
    cooperative learning groups, 286
    emotional and behavioral disabilities
        (EBD), students with, 107
    IEP, 202
    instructional needs, identifying, 225
    of misbehavior, 394
    nonacademic, identifying, 208
    secondary content, redesigned, 328
grading adaptations, 213, 214
grading plan, personalized, 237–238
graduation rates, by ethnic group, 244,
    245
grammar support, 407–408
grand mal seizure, 145

graph, curriculum-based measure progress, 234
graphic organizers, 294, 329
grouping students, 284–285
GTCalc Scientific Calculator, 410
guided discovery learning (GDL), 326
guided notes, 325
guided practice, 326
   direct instruction, 303
   effective instruction, 283
Gus! Word Prediction, 409

Hawaii, 157, 243, 245
head banging, 150
health impairments, students with
   academic characteristics, 148–149
   attention-deficit/hyperactivity disorder (ADHD), 71
   definitions, 9, 145–146
   identification, 146–147
   percentage of time in general education classroom, 34
   prevalence, 147
   service delivery, 147
   social and behavioral characteristics, 149–150
   teachers' tips, 150–151
healthiness of classroom, 151
hearing impairments, students with
   definition, 9, 131, 132
   percentage of time in general education classroom, 34
hearing loss. See sensory impairments, students with
help, extra, 64
helpfulness, 364
hemiplegia, 144
hereditary influences, ADHD, 70
Heritage High School, 7–8
   autism spectrum disorders, students with, 117–118, 119
   classroom organization, 362
   cultural responsiveness, 241–242, 245
   emotional and behavioral difficulties (EBD), students with, 97–98, 102–103, 104, 106–107
   principal's view of inclusion, 36
   secondary content, teaching, 321–322, 323–324, 326–327
   wraparound behavioral supports, 374
heterogeneous grouping, 286
high frequency words, 288
high-level questions and material, 266
highly qualified professionals, 49
high-probability behaviors, 372
Hispanic students, 11, 157
   disability, prevalence of, 244
   graduation rate, 244, 245
   poverty rate, 243
   teachers, 246
historic figures, multicultural, 254
HIV/AIDS, 150
homebound, 15
homelessness, 244
home-school collaboration, 173, 191–193
homework, 283
Homework Wiz Plus and Speaking Homework Wiz, 406, 408
hospital, 15
"hot" words, reacting to, 177
human touch, 106
hyperactive behavior, 69, 70, 75

Idaho, 58
IDEA. See Individuals with Disabiltiies Education Improvement Act (IDEA)
identification
   ADHD, students with, 71–73
   attention-deficit/hyperactivity disorder (ADHD), 69

autism spectrum disorders (ASD), students with, 113, 114–115
communication disorders, students with, 128–129
emotional and behavioral difficulties (EBD), students with, 100–101
health impairments, students with, 143, 146–147
intellectual disabilities, students with, 85, 86–87
learning disabilities, students with, 55, 56–58
multiple disabilities, students with, 143, 146–147
multi-tiered response to intervention (RTI) frameworks, 46–47
physical disabilities, students with, 143, 146–147
sensory impairments, students with, 133, 134
struggling readers, 309
students requiring Section 504 plan, 221
IEP. See individualized education program (IEP)
IFSP. See individualized family service plan (IFSP)
immediacy, 363
impulsive behavior, 69, 70, 75
inappropriate behaviors or feelings, 99
inattentive behavior, 69, 70, 74–75
incidental learning, 90
inclusion
   alternative assessments, 48–49
   assistive technology (AT), 414
   assumptions, 32
   autism spectrum disorders (ASD), students with, 111–112, 117
   civil rights, 33
   classroom management practices and supports, 365–368
   collaboration and teaching, 155–156
   current practices, 34–36
   defined, 4
   effective instruction in core academic areas, 281–282
   effective programs, 15–17
   effective schools, examples of, 5–8
   emotional and behavioral difficulties (EBD), students with, 97–98, 103
   evolution, 31–36
   gifted and talented students, 11
   history, 30–31
   intellectual abilities, students with, 83–84
   least restrictive environment, concept of, 13–15
   legal foundations, 37–45
   multiple disabilities, students with, 141–142, 148
   multi-tiered response to intervention (RTI) frameworks, 45–48
   normalization concept, 12–13
   parent advocacy, 33–34
   parents' view, 3–4, 29
   planning for, 199–200
   principal's view, 36
   research, 17–19
   from segregation to, 31–33
   staff development, 49
   students at risk for difficulties in school, 10–11
   students from diverse cultural and linguistic backgrounds, 11
   students with attention-deficit/hyperactivity disorder (ADHD), 67–68
   students with disabilities and special education, 8–10
   students with learning disabilities, 53–54
   teaching practices, 19–25
independence, 373

independent practice, 326
   direct instruction, 303
   effective instruction, 283
Indiana, 87
individualist cultures, 247
individualized education program (IEP), 38, 39–40, 201–203
   contributing to, 219–220
   devices, considering, 414, 433
   health impairments, multiple disabilities, and physical disabilities, 142, 146
   instructional needs, identifying, 225
individualized family service plan (IFSP), 146, 168
Individuals with Disabiltiies Education Improvement Act (IDEA), 13, 39
   ADHD, students with, 71
   assistive technology services, 415
   autism spectrum disorders, 114
   blindness and visual disabilities, 132–133
   categories and definitions, 9
   confidentiality and access to information, 41
   deafness and hearing impairment, 132
   devices, considering, 414
   funding for early intevention services, 41–42
   health impairment, students with, 142
   individualized education program (IEP), 39–40
   intellectual disabilities, students with, 84
   learning disability, defined, 54
   least restrictive environment, 39
   legal principles, 37–38
   multiple disabilities, students with, 142, 146
   nondiscriminatory identification, assessment, and evaluation, 38
   other health impairment, 145
   procedural safeguards, 41
   services to infants, toddlers, and preschoolers, 41
   suspensions and expulsions, 41
individual tutoring, 285–286
infants
   intellectual disabilities, identifying those with, 86
   sensory impairments, serving those with, 134
   services to, 41
inflicting bodily injury, 41
information, access to, 41
input adaptation, secondary content, 328
instruction
   effective, 363–364
   highly effective practices, culturally and linguistically diverse backgrounds, 265–267
   materials, selecting, 209–210
   secondary content, redesigned, 328
   supplemental, 207–208
   time, valuing, 362–363
instructional assistants, 167
instructional delivery, 333
instructional needs, 225–226
instructional pace, 260
instructional support teams, 163
insulin, 145–146
insulin-dependent diabetes, 145–146, 222
integrated learning systems, 404
integrating challenging issues, team teaching, 162
intellectual disabilities, students with
   academic characteristics, 89–90
   cognitive characteristics, 90–91
   definition, 9, 84–86
   identification, 86–87

inclusion, 83–84, 88–89
   multiple disabilities, students with, 149
   percentage of time in general education classroom, 34
   prevalance, 87–88
   sensory impairments, students with, 136
   service delivery, 88
   social and behavioral characteristics, 91–92
   teachers' tips, 92–93
intelligence
   autism spectrum disorders (ASD), students with, 119–120
   emotional and behavioral difficulties (EBD), students with, 105
IntelliTools Reading: Balanced Literacy, 406
intensity, 10
interactive planning during instruction, 211–212
interactive whiteboards (Smart Boards), 403, 425–426
interdependence, cooperative learning groups, 286
internalizing behavior problems, 103–105
intervention
   delivery methods, 47
   home-school collaboration, 192
   integrating with general education practices and core content, 299
   multi-tiered response to intervention (RTI) frameworks, 46
   plans, 393–395
   speech-language pathologists (SLPs), 130
   targeted, 368
   writing instruction, 292
intervention assistance teams, 163
introduction, 303
Iowa, 58, 87, 88
iPads, 411
iPass by iLearn, 405
iPod, 124, 411
IQ
   autism spectrum disorders, students with, 119
   emotional and behavioral disabilities (EBD), students with, 105
   gifted and talented students, 11
   intellectual disabilities, students with, 84, 85, 87
   severe disabilities, content area instruction for students with, 331–332

Jigsaw method, 211, 307–308, 326–327
juvenile arthritis, 145
juvenile diabetes, 145–146, 222

Kentucky, 58, 87, 88
Key Skills for Reading: Letters and Words, 406
Kidspiration©, 413
Kurzweil 3000, 406

Ladders to Literacy, 290
language, 11
   autism spectrum disorders, students with, 119
   intellectual disabilities, students with, 90
language disorders, 127
Language Master 6000 SF, 408
Latino students, 11
laws, public education, 30
Leap Track Reading Pro, 405
learned helplessness, 63
learning about culture and difference, 249
learning differences, secondary content areas, 323–324

learning disabilities, students with
  academic characteristics, 60–61
  cognitive characteristics, 62
  definition, 54–56
  health impairments associated with, 149
  identification, 56–58
  inclusion, benefits of, 53–54
  percentage of time in general education classroom, 34
  prevalence, 58–59
  service delivery, 59–60
  social and motivational characteristics, 62–63
  spina bifida, 148
  staffing needs, 61
  teachers' tips, 63–64
Learning Disabilities Act of 1969, 59
learning disability, 9
least restrictive environment, concept, 5–6, 13–15, 38, 39
  legal foundations, 37
legal blindness, 132
legal foundations
  civil rights rulings, 33
  inclusion, 37–45
lesson organizers, 337–339
lessons, co-teachers' reviews, 164
Let's Go Read, 406
letter recognition, 288
lighting, 213
limb deficiencies, 145
limitations, understanding students', 93
Lindamood Phonemic Sequencing Program (LIPS), 290
linguistically diverse backgrounds. *See* culturally and linguistically diverse backgrounds
LINKS strategy, 349
LIPS. *See* Lindamood Phonemic Sequencing Program (LIPS)
listening skills, collaboration, 177
literacy skills, 136
literature, diverse curriculum, 254–255
litigation, 37–38
Local control, 43
loneliness, 103
loudness, 127
Louisiana, 58, 157, 243, 245
"low-status" students, 265
low vision, 132
lunchtime behaviors, teaching appropriate, 397–398

Maine, 87
mainstream culture, helping families move to, 192
mainstreaming, 31, 32
Making Action Plans (MAPs), 227
management style, cultural dimension, 248
MAPs. *See* Making Action Plans (MAPs)
Maryland, 58, 157, 243, 245
master plan for instruction, 184
materials
  secondary content, redesigned, 328
  severe disabilities, redesigning content for students with, 333
  UDL principles, 416
materials storage, 215
mathematics, 404
  assistive technology (AT), 408, 410, 429–430, 437–438
  concept diagram, 330
  Florida standards excerpt, 304
  students with learning disabilities, 61
mathematics instruction, 293–294
  beginning, 293–294
  cognitive strategy instruction, 317–318
  struggling, 294
Math Gallery, 429
MathPad (IntelliTools), 410

M-CHAT. *See* Modified Checklist for Autism in Toddlers (M-CHAT)
mediation, 41
medication
  attention-deficit hyperactivity disorder, 70, 72–73, 77–79
  emotional and behavioral disabilities (EBD), students with, 100
  health impairments, students with, 149, 151
member, absence of bodily, 144
memory problems, 62, 345–346
mentally retarded, 86
mental retardation, 86
metacognition, 323
metacognitive deficits, 62
methylphenidate (Ritalin or Concerta), 78
Microsoft PowerPoint, 413
mild-to-moderate disabilities, 8–9
Minnesota, 58
mission statement, 366, 370
Mississippi, 597
Missouri, 597
mixed-ability grouping, 285
mixed CP, 144
mixed hearing loss, 132
Modified Checklist for Autism in Toddlers (M-CHAT), 115
monitoring, 10
  culturally responsive teaching, 259
  progress in basic skills instruction, 229
  progress in core curriculum, 300
monthly review, 283
motivation
  secondary content, teaching, 322
  students with learning disabilities, 62–63
motorized wheelchairs, 441–442
motor speech disorders, 127
multidimensionality, 363
multiple disabilities, students with, 143–144, 146
  academic characteristics, 148–149
  definition, 9
  identification, 146–147
  inclusion, 141–142, 148
  percentage of time in general education classroom, 34
  prevalence, 147
  service delivery, 147
  social and behavioral characteristics, 149–150
  teachers' tips, 150–151
multi-tiered response to intervention (RTI) frameworks, 45–48
  efficacy, 47–48
  evidence-based practices, 46
  intervention delivery methods, 47
  prevention and intervention tiers, 46
  screening, identification, and process monitoring, 46–47
  universal design for learning, 47
muscular dystrophy, 144
musculoskeletal conditions, 145
music therapists, 21
myelomeningocele, 145

names, using with paraeducators, 189
narrative essays, 341–343
National Assessment of Educational Progress (NCES), 245
National Center for Educational Statistics, 246
National Center for Hearing Assessment and Management (NCHAM), 134
National Center on Accessible Instructional Materials, 210
National Center on Student Progress Monitoring, 233
National Consortium on Deaf-Blindness, 134
National Council for Accreditation in Teacher Education (NCATE), 159

National Dissemination Center for Children with Disabilities [NICHCY], 132
National Instructional Materials accessibility Standard (NIMAS), 210
Native American students, 157
  disability, prevalence of, 244
  graduation rate, 244, 245
  poverty rate, 243
  teachers, 246
native culture, helping move to mainstream, 192
NCATE. *See* National Council for Accreditation in Teacher Education (NCATE)
NCES. *See* National Assessment of Educational Progress (NCES)
NCHAM. *See* National Center for Hearing assessment and Management (NCHAM)
NCLB. *See* No Child Left Behind (NCLB) act (2001)
Nebraska, 87, 88
needs
  assistive technology devices, 433
  autism spectrum disorder, students communicating, 120–121
negative, nonverbal messages, 177
negative reinforcement, 120, 370, 372
neurological issues, 127
Nevada
  culturally and linguistically diverse backgrounds, students from, 157, 243, 245
  intellectual disabilities, students with, 88
New Hampshire, 87, 88
New Jersey, 87
New Mexico
  culturally and linguistically diverse backgrounds, students from, 157, 243, 245
  intellectual disabilities, students with, 87
New York, 87
Next Generation Sunshine State Standards
  math, 304
  reading, 300
NIMAS. *See* National Instructional Materials accessibility Standard (NIMAS)
No Child Left Behind (NCLB) act (2001), 42
  basic skills required, 281
  flexibility and local control, 43
  highly qualified teachers, 43
  parents, expanded options for, 43
  research, debate about, 17–18
  results, accountability for, 42–43
  teaching methods based on scientific research, 43
noise control, 213–214
nonacademic goals, identifying, 208
noncompliance, 92, 103
nondiscriminatory assessment, 38
non-Hispanic whites, 243
nonverbal communication, 177–178
normalization concept, 12–13, 31
norms, cultural, 247–249
North Carolina
  intellectual disabilities, students with, 87
  Standard Course of Study, 200
North Dakota, 88
note taking, 330–331, 349–351

objective instruments, 101
objectives, identifying nonacademic, 208
observational learning, 90
obsessive-compulsive disorder (OCD), 104
occupational therapists (OTs), 21, 146

OCD. *See* obsessive-compulsive disorder (OCD)
Ohio, 87
Oklahoma, 58
organization
  classroom, 362
  severe disabilities, redesigning content for students with, 333
  unit and lesson organizers, 337–339
organizers, lesson, 337–339
orientation
  ADHD, students with, in classroom, 74
  paraeducators to school, 187
  peer tutoring, 311
orthopedic conditions, 145
orthopedic impairments, students with
  definition, 9
  percentage of time in general education classroom, 34
osteogenesis imperfecta, 145
OT. *See* occupational therapists (OTs)
outcomes
  ADHD, students with, 70
  autism spectrum disorders (ASD), students with, 113
  communication disorders, students with, 129
  curriculum-based measurements (CBMs), 233
  health impairments, students with, 143
  intellectual disabilities, students with, 85
  learning disabilities, students with, 55
  multiple disabilities, students with, 143
  physical disabilities, students with, 143
  of sensory impairments, 133
output adaptation, 328

pace, instructional, 260
Pacific Islander students, 157, 244
paired instruction, 263
PALS. *See* Peer-Assisted Learning Strategies (PALS)
pancreas, 145–146
paraeducators, 20–21, 167
  collaboration and teaming, 173, 187–189
paragraph shrinking, 311
paraprofessionals. *See* paraeducators
parents
  advocacy, 33–34
  autism spectrum disorders, students with, 121
  expanded options under No Child Left Behind (NCLB) act (2001), 43
  home-school collaboration, 173, 191–192
  participation, 38
parents' view
  deaf-blind, child who was, 136
  inclusion, 3–4, 29
Parent Training and Information Centers, 39
parity, collaboration and, 158, 175
partially sighted, 132
participation
  collaboration, 158
  multiple ways of, 211
  secondary content, redesigned, 328
  UDL principles, 416
partner reading, 311
partnerships, collaborative, 172
part-time special education classroom, 14
PCL. *See* problem-centered learning (PCL)
PCP. *See* person-centered planning (PCP)
PDA. *See* personal digital assistants (PDAs)

PDD-NOS. *See* pervasive developmental disorder—not otherwise specified (PDD-NOS)
PECS. *See* Picture Exchange Communication System (PECS)
peer assistance. *See also* peer tutoring
 collaboration and teaming, 168–170, 173, 195–197
 English-Language Learners (ELLs), 263
Peer-Assisted Learning Strategies (PALS), 290, 311–312
peer buddy program, 169–170, 173
peer relationships, 103, 117
peers' views
 intellectual disabilities, including students with, 92
 multiple disabilities, including students with, 148
peer tutoring, 10, 31, 210
 class-wide, 229
 core-curriculum content, 284, 286–287
penalties, formal system of, 373
Pennsylvania, 58, 163
people-first language, 13
performance feedback, 372
personal digital assistants (PDAs), 410–411
Personal Futures Planning, 227
personality-oriented methods, 101
personal support, assistive technology (AT), 410–411
personal teaching efficacy, 24
person-centered planning (PCP), 208, 227–228
pervasive developmental disabilities (PDDs). *See* autism spectrum disorders (ASD)
pervasive developmental disorder—not otherwise specified (PDD-NOS), 113
petit mal seizures, 145
phonatory qualities, 127
phoneme
 matching, 288
 replacement of, 127
phonemic awareness, 19
phonics, 288, 290
phonological awareness, 288, 290
phonological disorders, 127
phonological processing, 56, 263
physical aggression, 103
physical barriers, 45
physical classroom environment, 362
physical disabilities, students with
 academic characteristics, 148–149
 definitions, 144–145
 identification, 146–147
 prevalence, 147
 service delivery, 147
 social and behavioral characteristics, 149–150
 teachers' tips, 150–151
physical restraint, 368
physical therapists (PTs), 21, 146
physical therapy, 20
physical violence, 387
Picture Exchange Communication System (PECS), 124
Picture It, 406
picture walks, 330
Piers-Harris Self-Concept Scale, 101
pitch, 127
P.K.'s Math Studio, 429
P.K.'s Place, 429
placement settings, 59
planning. *See also* individualized education program (IEP); response to intervention (RTI) frameworks; Section 504 Plans
 academic content instruction using UDL principles, 231–232
 basic skills instruction, 229–230

behavior intervention plan (BIP), 92, 203, 205
co-teaching, 164
daily instruction, 208–211
for differentiated instruction, 205–215
emotional and behavioral disabilities (EBD), students with, 107
identifying instructional needs, 225–226
for inclusion, 199–200
interactive during instruction, 211–212
needs, identifying students', 207–208
person-centered to support inclusion, 227–228
strategy fact sheet, 217–218
strengths, knowing students and their, 206–207
plants, 215
PLATO Algebra 1, 405
PLATO Elementary Language Arts, 405
PLATO Learning, 429–430
PlayStation® Portable (PSP) system, 429–430
Pocket Compass, 411
poliomyelitis, 144
Portable Calculator with Talking Multiplication Table, 410
positive behavior supports, 205
positive reinforcement, 120, 370, 385
positive viewpoint, 206
poverty, 10–11
 attention-deficit hyperactivity disorder, 70
 demographics, 243–244
 emotional and behavioral disabilities (EBD), students with, 101
 intellectual disabilities, 85
 school success, 245
POW (Pick my idea; Organize my notes; Write and say more), 315
power behavior, 394
PowerPoint (Microsoft), 413
pragmatic disorders, 128
pragmatics, 119
praise, 80, 372
prediction relay, 311
prenatal causes, 86
preschoolers, services to, 41
 communications disorders, 130
 sensory impairments, 134
presentation
 alternative modes, 211
 direct instruction, 303
 effective instruction, 283
 UDL principles, 231
prevalence
 ADHD, students with, 73
 autism spectrum disorders (ASD), students with, 115
 communication disorders, students with, 129
 emotional and behavioral difficulties (EBD), students with, 101–102
 health impairments, students with, 147
 intellectual disabilities, students with, 87–88
 learning disabilities, students with, 58–59
 multiple disabilities, students with, 147
 physical disabilities, students with, 147
 sensory impairments, students with, 134
prevention
 multi-tiered response to intervention (RTI) frameworks, 46
 speech-language pathologists (SLPs), 130

prewriting, 291, 341
principal's view of inclusion, 36
problem-centered learning (PCL), 326, 355–356
problem-solving approach, teaching guided by, 253–254
procedural safeguards, 38, 41
procedures
 assessing, 370
 classroom, 252–253, 367
 developing and maintaining, 379–381
process monitoring, multi-tiered response to intervention (RTI) frameworks, 46–47
professional demeanor, 107
professional development, 64, 175, 184
professional referrals, 103
progress, monitoring students', 212–213, 233, 423
projective measures, 101
Proloquo2Go, 124, 411
prompts, mathematics problem solving, 317
prosthetic devices, 145
proximity, cultural dimension, 248
pseudohypertrophy, 144
PSP (PlayStation® Portable) system, 429–430
psychological processing, 56
PTs. *See* physical therapists (PTs)
publicness, 363
publishing, 291
punishment, 372, 373
purpose, statement of, 366
purposeful pedagogy, 241
put-downs, 388

The Quaddle Family Mysteries®, 429
quadriplegia, 144
quality, insisting on, 254
Quicktionary II, 408
Quicktionary II, Reading Pen II, 407

READ 180—Next Generation by Scholastic, 405, 413, 427–428
reading
 assistive technology (AT), 405–407, 427–428
 beginning, 288–289, 313–314
 educational assistance technology, 404
 Florida standards excerpt, 304
 instruction, 287–290
 Reading Recovery, 309–310
 secondary content areas, 329–330, 347–348
 struggling students, 289–290
 students with learning disabilities, 60–61
Reading First program, 48
Reading Intervention for Early Success, 290
Reading Mastery, 282–283
Reading Recovery, 286, 309–310
recognition, individual, 247
Recordings for the Blind and Dyslexic, 407
recreational therapists, 21
recruiting peer buddies, 195
referrals, 104
 teacher assistance teams (TATs), 179
reflection, cooperative learning groups, 286
regular education initiative (REI), 32
Rehabilitation Act of 1973, Section 504, 44–45, 203
REI. *See* regular education initiative (REI)
related services professionals, 20
relationships
 attention-seeking behavior, 394
 authentic teacher-student, 106, 364
repetition, immediate, 118

repetitive movements, 150
repetitive ritualistic behaviors, 119
replacement behaviors, 101
reprimand, 373
research
 inclusion, 17–19
 No Child Left Behind (NCLB) act (2001), 17–18
 teaching methods based on, 43, 299–301
residential schools, 15
resources
 collaboration, 158
 coordinating, 363
respect, 23
 classroom management, 364–365
 culturally diverse backgrounds, 265–266
 interactions between team teachers, 161
 paraeducators, 189
 parents' perspective, 191
responding, alternative modes, 211
response accommodations for test taking, 353
response cost, 373
response to intervention (RTI)
 frameworks, 7, 45–48
 beginning reading, 313–314
 efficacy, 47–48
 evidence-based practices, 46
 intellectual disabilities, identification of, 87
 intervention delivery methods, 47
 plans, 200–201
 prevention and intervention tiers, 46
 screening, identification, and process monitoring, 46–47
 seamless tiers of instruction, 281–282
 severe discrepancy approach versus, 57
 students with learning disabilities, 58
 universal design for learning, 47
responsibilities
 co-teaching, 183
 paraeducators, 189
responsiveness, culturally and linguistically diverse backgrounds, 241–242
restraint, physical, 368
results, accountability, 42–43
Rett disorder, 113
revenge behavior, 394
review, 303
 effective instruction, 283
 expository writing in content-area classes, 341
 Section 504 plan, 221
revising a draft, 291
Rhode Island, 88
rhyme recognition, 288
Ritalin, 78
ritualistic behaviors, 119
roles
 collaboration and teaching, 162–168, 175, 183
 individualized education programs (IEPs), 219
room-clear, signaling, 387
Rosa's Law, 86
routines
 classroom, 252–253
 secondary content areas, 329
 students with autism spectrum disorders, 119, 120–121
RTI. *See* response to intervention (RTI) frameworks
rules
 assessing, 370
 classroom, 252–253, 367
 developing and maintaining, 379–381

sarcasm, 388
satisfactory interpersonal relationships, 99
Scandinavia, 12–13
scheduling
  paraeducators, 187
  peer tutoring, 311
  team teaching and collaboration, 160
  test taking accommodations, 353
Scholastic, 405
school guidance counselors, 21
school psychologists, 20, 21
School-to-Work Opportunities Act, 39
school-wide assistance teams, 163
school-within-a-school (SWAS) approach, 98, 103
SCOS. See standard course of study (SCOS)
screening
  autism spectrum disorders, students with, 114–115
  emotional and behavioral disabilities (EBD), students with, 100–101
  multi-tiered response to intervention (RTI) frameworks, 46–47
  students for peer buddies, 195
Screening Tool for Autism in Two-Year-Olds (STAT), 115
ScreenReader, 407
seatwork, 283
secondary content areas
  challenges, 321–322
  content enhancements, 327–329
  content survival strategies, 329–331
  cooperative learning, 326–327
  direct instruction (DI), 325–326
  expository writing, 341–343
  guided discovery learning (GDL), 326
  learning differences, 323–324
  learning strategies, 327
  mnemonic strategies, 345–346
  note taking, 330–331, 349–351
  problem-centered learning (PCL), 355–356
  reading, 329–330, 347–348
  severe disabilities, students with, 331–333
  test taking, 331, 353–354
  understanding curriculum, 324
  unit and lesson organizers, 337–339
  universal design for learning (UDL), 325
  working collaboratively, 324–325
The Secret of Googol, 429
Section 504 Plans, 203
  ADHD, students with, 72
  classroom accessibility, 150–151
  health impairments, students with, 142
  language from the Rehabilitation Act of 1973, 44–45
  multiple disabilities, students with, 142
  physical disabilities, students with, 142
  procedures for developing, 221–222
SED. See serious emotional disturbance (SED)
segregation, 31–33
seizure
  absence, 145
  behavioral disorder case associated with, 104
  peer reactions to, 150
self, concept of, 248
self-assessment, double-check, 275
self-check system, 385
self-control, 106, 373
self-determined, 12
self-esteem, 149
self-injurious behavior (SIB), 92, 150
  autism spectrum disorders (ASD), students with, 120

self-management, 103–104, 373–374
self-questioning, 294
self-regulated strategy development (SRSD), 293
  instruction, 341
  writing instruction, 315–316
self-regulation, 266
semantic disorders, 128
sensorineural hearing loss, 132
sensory impairments, students with
  academic characteristics, 135–137
  definitions, 131–133
  identification, 134
  inclusion, 125–126
  prevalence, 134
  service delivery, 134–135
  social and behavioral characteristics, 137
  teachers' tips, 137–138
separate day schools, 15, 31
separate residential schools, 15
separation anxiety, 104
serious emotional disturbance (SED), 99
service delivery
  ADHD, students with, 73–74
  autism spectrum disorders (ASD), students with, 115–116
  communication disorders, students with, 130
  emotional and behavioral difficulties (EBD), students with, 102–103
  health impairments, students with, 147
  intellectual disabilities, students with, 88
  learning disabilities, students with, 59–60
  multiple disabilities, students with, 147
  physical disabilities, students with, 147
  sensory impairments, students with, 134–135
service-learning requirements, 195
setting accommodations, for test taking, 353
severe disabilities, students with, 331–333
severe discrepancy approach, 56–57
show and tell, 425
SIB. See self-injurious behavior (SIB)
siblings, disabled, 101
sickle-cell disease, 145
significant behavioral excesses, 361
significant disabilities, 9–10
simultaneity, 363
size adaptation, 328
skills
  basic skills instruction planning, 209
  collaboration and teaching, 162, 172
  grouping based on, 284–285
  home-school collaboration, 192
  synthesis, 90
Skillstreaming series, 373
SLPs. See speech-language pathologists (SLPs)
Smart Boards, 403, 413, 425–426
social and behavioral characteristics
  communication disorders, students with, 131
  health impairments, students with, 149–150
  multiple disabilities, students with, 149–150
  physical disabilities, students with, 149–150
  sensory impairments, students with, 137
  students with learning disabilities, 62–63
social anxiety, 104
social interactions, 91
social problems, 62–63
  ADHD, students with, 76–77

social reciprocity, limitations, 118–119
social skills, 19
  instruction, 105–106, 373, 397–398
  RTI programs, 48
social status, 19
social stories, 397–398
social withdrawal, 103
social workers, 20, 21
SOLs. See Standards of Learning Tests (SOLs)
SoothSayer Word Prediction, 407
South Carolina, 87
spacing, furniture, 213
spastic CP, 144
Speaking Spelling Ace, Spelling Ace with Thesaurus, Speaking Spelling and Handwriting Ace, 408
special education
  and culturally and linguistically diverse backgrounds, 243–245
  inclusion, 8–10
  Tier-3 reading intervention, 314
special-education teachers, 20, 48
specific language impairment (SLI), 131
speech disorders, 127
speech-language pathologists (SLPs), 20, 21, 125, 127, 129
  responsibilities, range of, 130
speech or language impairment
  definition, 9
  percentage of time in general education classroom, 34
speech synthesis devices, 409
spelling support, assistive technology (AT), 407–408, 435
SpellRead, 290
spina bifida, 145, 148
SRSD. See self-regulated strategy development (SRSD)
SSBD. See Systematic Screening for Behavior Disorders (SSBD)
SSPs. See Student Success Plans (SSPs)
staff development, 49
standard course of study (SCOS), 200
standard English, 242
Standards of Learning Tests (SOLs), 321
STAT. See Screening Tool for Autism in Two-Year-Olds (STAT)
statement of purpose, 366
states. See also individual states listed by name
  curriculum mastery requirements, 157
  intellectual disabilities, students with, 87
  prevalance of students with learning disabilities, 58–59
  standard courses of study, 200
  standards for delay in developmental milestones, 86
STEP (student transition employability program), 411
stereotyped behaviors, 93
stereotypical behaviors, student with autism spectrum disorders, 119
stereotypies, 150
stimulant medications, 78
strategies, redirection, 80
strengths
  co-teaching, 172, 183
  understanding students', 93, 206–207
stress, 107
structure, 10
struggling students
  mathematics instruction, 294
  reading, 289–290, 309–310
  writing instruction, 291–293
student assistance teams, 163
student responses, 309
students at risk for difficulties in school, 10–11
Student Success Plans (SSPs), 199

students' views
  autism spectrum disorders, students with, 117–118
  meaning of inclusion, 88–89
  peer support program, benefits of, 169
student teams-achievement divisions (STAD), 327
stuttering, 127
substitute curriculum, 328
success, collectivist cultures, 248
summative assessment, 232
supervision of paraeducators, 188, 189
supplemental instruction, 207–208
support level adaptation, 328
Supreme Court of Illinois, 30
surface management, 367, 383–384
suspensions, 41
SWAS. See school-within-a-school (SWAS) approach
Swedish Association for Retarded Children, 12
SWEET (Student Work Experience Enabling transition) Shop, 8
syllables segmenting and blending, 288
symptoms. See identification
Systematic Screening for Behavior Disorders (SSBD), 101
system of care. See wraparound interventions

Talking Pocket Calculator, 410
Talking Texas Instruments Scientific Calculator, 410
tantrums, 394
targeted interventions, 365, 368
teacher aides. See paraeducators
teacher assistance teams (TATs), 163
  collaboration and teaming, 173, 179–180, 179–181
  response to intervention (RTI) models, 201
teachers
  behaviors in delivering instruction in core academic areas, 282–283
  culturally and linguistically diverse backgrounds, 249
  culturally responsive, 259–261
  high versus low tolerance for behavioral difficulties, 101
  in Jigsaw method, 307
  NCLB legislation, 43, 49
  professional development, 64, 175, 184
teacher's aides, 167
teachers' tips
  ADHD, students with, 79–80
  autism spectrum disorders (ASD), students with, 120–121
  communication disorders and sensory impairments, students with, 137–138
  emotional and behavioral difficulties (EBD), students with, 106–107
  health impairments, students with, 150–151
  intellectual disabilities, including students with, 92–93
  learning disabilities, students with, 63–64
  multiple disabilities, students with, 150–151
  physical disabilities, students with, 150–151
teacher support teams, 163
teachers' views
  ADHD, students with, 75
  learning disabilities, students with, 61
  warm demander, role of, 251
teaching routine, 329
teaming, 172
  collaborative consultation, 166–168
  collaborative teams, 163

teaming (*continued*)
 communication skills strategy, 177–178
 co-teaching, 163–166
 defined, 157–159
 dispositions, 159–161
 families, 191–193
 inclusion, 155–156
 inclusion and, 155–156
 key components strategy, 175–176
 paraeducators, working with, 187–189
 peer assistance, 168–170, 195–197
 planning, 183–185
 roles, 162–168
 skills, 162
 strategy fact sheet, 172–173
 teacher assistance teams, 179–180, 179–181
team members. *See also* collaboration
 IEP, 40
 person-centered plans, 227
technology, 47. *See also* assistive technology (AT); educational technology
 behavior management devices, 374
 communication systems, 124
 inclusion, facilitating, 401
 students with learning disabilities, 63
 writing, 292–293
temperature, classroom, 215
temper tantrums, 394
territoriality, 161
test taking
 secondary content areas, 331, 353–354
 Smart Board to prepare for, 425
Texas
 culturally and linguistically diverse backgrounds, students from, 157, 243, 245
 intellectual disabilities, students with, 87, 88
textbooks
 reading, 347
 secondary content, teaching, 322, 329
TextHelp Read and Write Gold, 407
text-to-voice applications, 412
thesaurus, 435
think-aloud strategies, 294, 347–348
thinking, functional-based, 393–395
thinking about thinking, 323

Tier-1 instruction, 281–282
 reading, 289, 313
Tier-2 instruction, 282
 reading, 289, 313–314
Tier-3 intervention, 314
tiered management, 365
time
 cultural dimension, 248
 instructional, valuing, 362–363
 for key academic content, 299
 secondary content, redesigned, 328
Timeless Jade Trade, 429
Timeless Math, 429
time management, 331
time-out, 44, 373
TM. *See* Transverse Myelitis (TM)
toddlers
 autism spectrum disorders, identifying those with, 119
 communication disorders, identifying students with, 128
 intellectual disabilities, identifying those with, 86
 sensory impairments, serving those with, 134
 services to, 41
tokens, 372
tonic-clonic seizure, 145
totally blind, 132
*The Tough Kid Book*, 386
Transverse Myelitis (TM), 3
traumatic brain injury
 definition, 9
 percentage of time in general education classroom, 34
TREE (Topic sentence—tell what you believe; Reasons—three or more, Why do I believe this? Will my readers believe this? etc.; Ending—Wrap it up right; Examine—Do I have all my parts?), 315
trust, collaboration and, 160–161, 364
tutoring
 individual, 285–286
 struggling readers, 309
Type-1 diabetes, 145–146, 222
typical students, 246–247
typing, speech synthesis devices for, 409

unemployed parents, 101, 105
unit and lesson organizers, 337–339

universal design for learning (UDL)
 academic content instruction, 231–232, 333
 effectiveness, example of, 416–417
 inclusive practices and supports, 365–368
 multi-tiered response to intervention (RTI) frameworks, 47
 planning academic content instruction, 209, 211
 principles and guidelines, 415–416
 secondary content areas, 325
universal inclusive practices and supports, 365
universal newborn hearing screening program, 134
unpredictability, 363
usage disorders, 128
U.S. Census Bureau, 11
U.S. Department of Education, 99
Utah, 87, 88

ventilation, classroom, 215
verbal aggression, 103
verbal communication skills, 177
verbal intervention techniques, 368
verbalizations, 368
verbal tantrums, 394
Vermont, 88
Virtual History Museum, 417
virtual manipulatives, 413
visual accessibility, 215
visual acuity, 132
visual aids, 280
visual disabilities, 132–133
visual field, 132
visual impairments, students with, 132–133
 definition, 9, 131
 percentage of time in general education classroom, 34
 teaching tips, 138
visual maps, 347
vocabulary, 288
 English-Language Learners (ELLs), 263
 secondary content area instruction, 347
vocal tone, 364
vocational education, 105
voice disorders, 127
voice-output devices, 409

walks, picture, 330
warm demander, 251–253
Washington D.C., 87, 88
Washington state, 87
Waterford Early Reading Program, 405
weaknesses
 collaboration, 172
 teaching to student strengths, 206
weekly review, 283
West Hernando Middle School (WHMS), 6–7
 autism spectrum disorders (ASD), students with, 111–112
 collaboration needed for inclusive classrooms, 155–156, 159–160, 163, 177, 196–197
 effective instruction for core curriculum, 279–280
 tiered classroom management system, 359–360
West Virginia, 87
wheelchairs, motorized, 441–442
WINGS behavior standards, 359–360
Wisconsin Supreme Court, 30
word prediction, 435
word prediction software, 407–408
word processing software, 407–408
 teaching writing, 435–436
WordQ Writing Aid Software, 409
WordSmith, 407
work experience, 105
working memory, 62, 76
workshops, professional development, 175
wraparound interventions, 365
 behavioral supports, 374–375
 emotional and behavioral disabilities (EBD), students with, 107
Write:Outloud, 409
writing instruction, 61, 290–293
 assistive technology (AT), 409, 435–436
 beginning, 290–291
 expository for secondary content areas, 341–343
 secondary content area learning strategy, 327
 self-regulated strategy development, 315–316
 struggling students, 291–293
WYNN 3.1 Freedom Scientific's Learning Systems Group, 406
zero reject, 37

# Photo Credits